T0214546

Lecture Notes in Computer Science   11611

Commenced Publication in 1973
Founding and Former Series Editors:
Gerhard Goos, Juris Hartmanis, and Jan van Leeuwen

Editorial Board Members

More information about this series at http://www.springer.com/series/7409

Guojun Wang · Jun Feng ·
Md Zakirul Alam Bhuiyan ·
Rongxing Lu (Eds.)

Security, Privacy, and Anonymity in Computation, Communication, and Storage

12th International Conference, SpaCCS 2019
Atlanta, GA, USA, July 14–17, 2019
Proceedings

 Springer

Editors
Guojun Wang ⓘ
Guangzhou University
Guangzhou, China

Md Zakirul Alam Bhuiyan ⓘ
Fordham University
New York City, NY, USA

Jun Feng ⓘ
Huazhong University of Science
and Technology
Wuhan, China

Rongxing Lu ⓘ
University of New Brunswick
Fredericton, NB, Canada

ISSN 0302-9743   ISSN 1611-3349   (electronic)
Lecture Notes in Computer Science
ISBN 978-3-030-24906-9   ISBN 978-3-030-24907-6   (eBook)
https://doi.org/10.1007/978-3-030-24907-6

LNCS Sublibrary: SL3 – Information Systems and Applications, incl. Internet/Web, and HCI

This Springer imprint is published by the registered company Springer Nature Switzerland AG
The registered company address is: Gewerbestrasse 11, 6330 Cham, Switzerland

Preface

The 12th International Conference on Security, Privacy, and Anonymity in Computation, Communication, and Storage (SpaCCS 2019), held in Atlanta, USA, during July 14–17, 2019, was jointly organized by Guangzhou University, Georgia State University, and St. Francis Xavier University.

The SpaCCS conference series provides a forum for researchers to gather and share their research findings, achievements, innovations, and perspectives in cyberspace security and related fields. Previous SpaCCS conferences were held in Melbourne, Australia (2018), Guangzhou, China (2017), Zhangjiajie, China (2016), Helsinki, Finland (2015), Beijing, China (2014), Melbourne, Australia (2013), Liverpool, UK (2012), and Changsha, China (2011).

This year, the conference received 109 submissions. All submissions were reviewed by at least three reviewers based on a high-quality review process. Based on the recommendations of the reviewers and the Program Committee members' discussions, 37 papers were selected for oral presentation at the conference and inclusion in this Springer LNCS volume (i.e., an acceptance rate of 33.9%). In addition to the technical presentations, the program included a number of keynote speeches by world-renowned researchers. We would like to thank the keynote speakers for their time and willingness to share their expertise with the conference attendees.

SpaCCS 2019 has been made possible by the joint effort of a large number of individuals and organizations worldwide. There is a long list of people who volunteered their time and energy to put together the conference, and deserve special thanks. First and foremost, we would like to offer our gratitude to the Steering Committee Chairs, Prof. Guojun Wang from Guangzhou University, China and Prof. Gregorio Martinez from University of Murcia, Spain, for guiding the entire process of the conference. We are also deeply grateful to all the Program Committee members for their time and efforts in reading, commenting, debating, and finally selecting the papers.

We would like to offer our gratitude to General Chairs, Prof. Kim-Kwang Raymond Choo, Prof. Mark Last, and Prof. Yanqing Zhang, for their tremendous support and advice in ensuring the success of the conference. Thanks also go to: Program Chairs, Md Zakirul Alam Bhuiyan, Jun Feng, and Rongxing Lu; Workshop Chair, Wm. Bradley Glisson; Publicity Chairs, Peter Mueller, Reza M. Parizi, and Yogachandran Rahulamathavan; Local Chair, Yubao Wu; and Web Chairs, Zihao Jiang and Xin Nie.

It is worth noting that SpaCCS 2019 was held jointly with the 12th IEEE International Conference on Internet of Things (iThings 2019), the 12th IEEE International Conference on Cyber, Physical, and Social Computing (CPSCom 2019), the 15th IEEE International Conference on Green Computing and Communications (GreenCom 2019), the 5th IEEE International Conference on Smart Data (SmartData 2019), and the 2nd IEEE International Conference on Blockchain (Blockchain 2019).

Finally, we thank you for your contribution to and/or participation in SpaCCS 2019 and hope that you found the conference to be a stimulating and exciting forum. Hopefully, you will also have enjoyed the beautiful city of Atlanta, USA.

July 2019   Guojun Wang
                                                                            Jun Feng
                                                        Md Zakirul Alam Bhuiyan
                                                                        Rongxing Lu

Organization

SpaCCS 2019 Organizing and Program Committees

General Chairs

Kim-Kwang Raymond Choo	University of Texas at San Antonio, USA
Mark Last	Ben-Gurion University of the Negev, Israel
Yanqing Zhang	Georgia State University, USA

Program Chairs

Md Zakirul Alam Bhuiyan	Fordham University, USA
Jun Feng	Huazhong University of Science and Technology, China
Rongxing Lu	University of New Brunswick, Canada

Workshop Chair

Wm. Bradley Glisson	Sam Houston State University, USA

Publicity Chairs

Peter Mueller	IBM Zurich Research Laboratory, Switzerland
Reza M. Parizi	Kennesaw State University, USA
Yogachandran Rahulamathavan	Loughborough University London, UK

Local Chair

Yubao Wu	Georgia State University, USA

Web Chairs

Zihao Jiang	St. Francis Xavier University, Canada
Xin Nie	Huazhong University of Science and Technology, China

Program Committee

Habtamu Abie	Norwegian Computing Center, Norway
Avishek Adhikari	University of Calcutta, India
Hamid Alasadi	Basra University, Iraq
Abdul Halim Ali	Universiti Kuala Lumpur, Malaysia
Flora Amato	University of Napoli Federico II, Italy
Kamran Arshad	Ajman University, UAE and University of Greenwich, UK

Ruidong Li	National Institute of Information and Communications Technology, Japan
Xin Li	Nanjing University of Aeronautics and Astronautics, China
Feng Lin	University of Colorado Denver, USA
Giovanni Livraga	Universitá degli Studi di Milano, Italy
Pascal Lorenz	University of Haute Alsace, France
Pavel Loskot	Swansea University, UK
Leandros Maglaras	De Montfort University, UK
Wissam Mallouli	Montimage, France
Mirco Marchetti	University of Modena and Reggio Emilia, Italy
Guazzone Marco	University of Piemonte Orientale, Italy
Antonio Ruiz-Martínez	University of Murcia, Spain
Ilaria Matteucci	Istituto di Informatica e Telematica, CNR, Italy
Christoph Meinel	Hasso-Plattner-Institute, Germany
Aleksandra Mileva	University Goce Delcev, Macedonia
Moeiz Miraoui	University of Gafsa, Tunisia
Jose Andre Morales	Carnegie Mellon University, USA
Vincenzo Moscato	University of Napoli Federico II, Italy
Roberto Nardone	University of Napoli Federico II, Italy
Mohammadreza Nasiriavanaki	Wayne State University, USA
Keyurkumar Patel	Australian Defence Force, Australia
Changgen Peng	Guizhou University, China
Thinagaran Perumal	Universiti Putra Malaysia, Malaysia
Antonio Pescape'	University of Napoli Federico II, Italy
Roberto Di Pietro	University of Padova, Italy
Vaibhav Rastogi	University of Wisconsin-Madison, India
Mubashir Husain Rehmani	COMSATS, Institute of Information Technology, Pakistan
Vincent Roca	Inria, France
Altair Santin	Pontifical Catholic University of Parana, Brazil
Andrea Saracino	Istituto di Informatica e Telematica, CNR, Italy
Saratha Sathasivam	Universiti Sains Malaysia, Malaysia
Frank Schulz	SAP SE, Germany
Patrick Siarry	Universite Paris-Est Creteil, France
Jorge SA Silva	University of Coimbra, Portugal
Nicolas Sklavos	University of Patras, Greece
Martin Strohmeier	University of Oxford, UK
Junggab Son	Kennesaw State University, USA
Traian Marius Truta	Northern Kentucky University, USA
Omair Uthmani	Glasgow Caledonian University, UK
Quoc-Tuan Vien	Middlesex University, UK
Zhiwei Wang	Nanjing University of Posts and Telecommunication, China
Yubao Wu	Georgia State University, USA

Ping Yang	State University of New York at Binghamton, USA
Yong Yu	Shaanxi Normal University, China
Go Yun	HWUM, Malaysia
Nicola Zannone	Eindhoven University of Technology, The Netherlands
Sherali Zeadally	University of Kentucky, USA
Mingwu Zhang	Hubei University of Technology, China
Shunli Zhang	Huazhong University of Science and Technology, China
Xinliang Zheng	Frostburg State University, USA
Natasa Zivic	University of Siegen, Germany

Steering Committee

Guojun Wang (Chair)	Guangzhou University, China
Gregorio Martinez (Chair)	University of Murcia, Spain
Jemal H. Abawajy	Deakin University, Australia
Jose M. Alcaraz Calero	University of the West of Scotland, UK
Jiannong Cao	Hong Kong Polytechnic University, SAR China
Hsiao-Hwa Chen	National Cheng Kung University, Taiwan
Jinjun Chen	Swinburne University of Technology, Australia
Kim-Kwang Raymond Choo	University of Texas at San Antonio, USA
Robert Deng	Singapore Management University, Singapore
Mario Freire	The University of Beira Interior, Portugal
Minyi Guo	Shanghai Jiao Tong University, China
Weijia Jia	University of Macau, SAR China
Wei Jie	University of West London, UK
Georgios Kambourakis	University of the Aegean, Greece
Ryan Ko	Queensland University, Australia
Constantinos Kolias	University of Idaho, USA
Jianbin Li	North China Electric Power University, China
Jie Li	Shanghai Jiao Tong University, China
Jianhua Ma	Hosei University, Japan
Felix Gomez Marmol	University of Murcia, Spain
Geyong Min	University of Exeter, UK
Peter Mueller	IBM Zurich Research Laboratory, Switzerland
Indrakshi Ray	Colorado State University, USA
Kouichi Sakurai	Kyushu University, Japan
Juan E. Tapiador	The University Carlos III of Madrid, Spain
Sabu M. Thampi	Indian Institute of Information Technology and Management, India
Jie Wu	Temple University, USA
Yang Xiao	The University of Alabama, USA
Yang Xiang	Swinburne University of Technology, Australia

Zheng Yan	Aalto University, Finland and Xidian University, China
Laurence T. Yang	St. Francis Xavier University, Canada
Wanlei Zhou	University of Technology Sydney, Australia

Sponsors

Contents

Distributed Privacy Preserving Platform for Ridesharing Services

Yevhenii Semenko and Damien Saucez$^{(\boxtimes)}$

Université Côte d'Azur, Inria, France
damien.saucez@inria.fr

Abstract. The sharing economy fundamentally changed business and social interactions. Interestingly, while in essence this form of collaborative economy allows people to directly interact with each other, it is also at the source of the advent of eminently centralized platforms and marketplaces, such as Uber and Airbnb. One may be concerned with the risk of giving the control of a market to a handful of actors that may unilaterally fix their own rules and threaten privacy. In this paper, we propose a decentralized ridesharing architecture which gives the opportunity to shift from centralized platforms to decentralized ones. Digital communications in our proposition are specifically designed to preserve data privacy and avoid any form of centralization. We integrate a blockchain in our proposition to guarantee the essential roles of a marketplace, but in a decentralized way. Our numerical evaluation quantifies the advantages and limits of decentralization and our Android implementation shows the feasibility of our proposition.

Keywords: Data privacy · Decentralized · Sharing economy · Blockchain · Peer-to-peer

1 Introduction

Mass digitalization of our daily life and deep involvement of user data boosted the sharing economy by allowing the advent of massively used platforms, such as Airbnb and Uber, that make our day-to-day tasks much easier. However, such platforms raise concerns about the concentration of power and information in a handful of mercantile companies with the risk of inappropriate personal data usage [7], personal information leakage [16], or market control [9].

This paper proposes to tackle these issues for the case of ridesharing services by proposing a multilayered distributed architecture that removes the need of a centralize platform. The shift to a fully decentralized paradigm is not straightforward. First, with a centralized approach, personal data are concentrated and, unless security breaches or inadequate policies, the data can only be manipulated by well identified entities (i.e., the platform operator). In a fully decentralized entity data are scattered among the constituents of the decentralized entity platform with inherently more risks of information leakage. Second, decisions to

© Springer Nature Switzerland AG 2019
G. Wang et al. (Eds.): SpaCCS 2019, LNCS 11611, pp. 1–14, 2019.
https://doi.org/10.1007/978-3-030-24907-6_1

authorize or not a given client or producer to be part of the platform or to define a price are more complex in a decentralized platform as the system as a whole must answer these questions. Finally, responsiveness of the system can become a challenge as it is impossible to tune the resources as well as with centralized platforms.

Ridesharing services are particularly challenging as they are by nature highly dynamic (clients come and leave frequently), they involve users willing to minimize data communication as they are roaming, they require to exchange sensitive personal information, and they are subject to rules that can change from region to region while users can move between these regions.

Privacy preserving solutions for ridesharing have been proposed [1–3,6,8,10, 14] but we are the first to take a holistic approach were we consider simultaneously privacy, accountability, business, communications, and scalability.

In Sect. 2 we define a decentralize privacy preserving platform for ridesharing where peers forms an overlay communication network and rely on a blockchain to organize their marketplace. In Sect. 3 we evaluate its scalability based on analytical bounds and on a trace-driven numerical evaluation. Sect. 4 discusses our Android prototype and the lesson learned while developing it. Finally, in Sect. 5 we conclude.

2   Decentralized Platform

Ridesharing platforms such as Uber or Lyft rely on centralized infrastructures involving third-parties, which raises privacy concerns. In this paper, we remove this dependency to avoid any lock-in with a third-party and to preserve privacy. To that aim, we conceive the platform as a fully decentralized peer-to-peer network [11] where each node is equally important and interchangeable and rely on a multilayer architecture.

2.1   Multilayered Architecture

First, we build an overlay network including all the business actors to constitute the *network layer*. As ridesharing services can span over multiple regions with different constraints and can have several millions of users, the underlying peer-to-peer networking technology must provide a way to segregate traffic in arbitrary regions and it must be able to scale. For these reasons we must use a protocol where node *IDentifiers* (ID) can be structured and scoped, such as in Chord [18] or in Kademlia [12]. It is therefore straightforward to limit the scope of communications to particular regions. For example, if communications must remain within peers of a country, it is enough to partition the ID space with one partition per country and impose that every peer of a country uses an ID within the partition of the country. Figure 1 shows an example of how to scope communications per region with Chord.

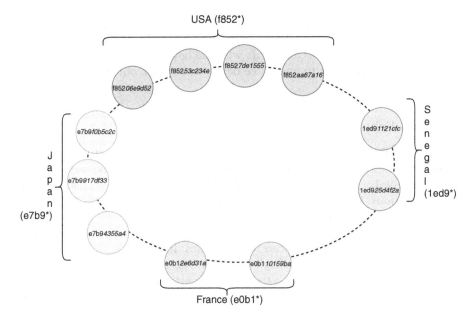

Fig. 1. Example of device grouping with Chord.

Second, as the platform does not involve a data storage third party, all actors involved in the platform must take part in the storage effort. Keeping in mind that data privacy is essential, the best approach is to build a Distributed Hash Table (DHT) to implement the *Data storage layer*. Even though the data storage layer by itself is not sufficient to guarantee data privacy, when it is combined with the other layers it enables data privacy as detailed in Sect. 2.2.

User Interface (UI) and user experience can't be altered by the decentralization even though the *User application layer* where the UI is implemented fundamentally changes. In centralized platforms, user applications interact with the rest of the platform via REST APIs. In a decentralized solution, the application must include the other layers of the platform and implement, at least partially, the logic of the platform.

Finally, the *Management layer* that is simple by nature in a centralized approach is complex to implement in a fully distributed system with no trusted parties. Particularly complex issues to solve in such an environment are how to control business processes, manage data access, and provide accountability to solve potential disputable situations. These issues arise as there is no central to solve debatable issues, to control or to set the required system parameters.

To implement the *Management layer* we use a blockchain [19] which plays the role of an intermediary for controlling data access, guarantee that parties act in conformance with the rules of the platform, and log events. The business logic is implemented with smart contracts and privacy is ensured.

Alone blockchains do not provide data privacy protection. Instead they tend to reduce privacy as they spread data to open locations. However, thanks to smart contracts data owners can specify who and how their data can be accessed. In Sect. 2.2 we detail how to guarantee data privacy with our multilayered distributed platform.

2.2 Data Privacy

The first condition to preserve privacy is to minimize the amount of data that is spread in the system. That is, for each data, the designer of the service must determine whether or not the data must be shared, who can access it, and under which conditions. Consumers of the data are either identified at the time of the publication or they are not.

The first case is the simplest, the data is encrypted with the public key of the target such that only the target can read the data. In this case, the data can be stored anywhere in the DHT, multiple targets means multiple copies of the data. As our architecture does not rely on trusted third parties, there is no trusted *Public Key Infrastructure* (PKI) on which we can rely to obtain the public key. However, if like in Bitcoin the ID is made such that it is unambiguously linked with the public key of the party then it is possible to safely retrieve the public key for that node [13]: (1) the producer of data determines the ID of its target, (2) it requests the system (or the target directly) to provide its public key, and (3) it verifies that the ID and the public key are linked (e.g., the ID contains a hash of the public key).

In the second case where the target of the data is not known while publishing the data, it is not possible to use encryption directly. Instead, the producer uses the Shamir's Threshold Scheme [17]. The producer generates as many parts of its secret as needed and determines a DHT key for each part such that they can be published in the DHT according to its requirements. Here the choice of the key for each part to be published in the DHT is important as it determines the nodes that will store the data. In parallel to publishing the data in the DHT, the producer also publishes a smart contract in the blockchain that specifies the policy of accessing the data. As a result, when a party wants to consume a data, it sends a request to the overlay and if the smart contract is fulfilled then the storing nodes provide their parts to the requester that will be able to re-construct the data. The threshold value and where to store the parts (and their redundancy level) depends on the service's threat model.

2.3 Protocol

Road transportation clients and drivers are by nature on the move and thus have poor, expensive, and unreliable connectivity. For that reason they do not directly take place in the peer-to-peer network. Instead the peer-to-peer network is run by arbitrary machines willing to share their resources for the community. The nodes taking part in the peer-to-peer network then act as service nodes to access the network for the clients and drivers by the means of an HTTPS REST API.

Client and driver applications select a node from the peer-to-peer network as service node according to their own preferences (e.g., randomly or topologically close to them, or a trusted service node).

Any ride can be decomposed in three phases. First, the client hails for a ride. During that phase, the client and a driver mutually agree on making the ride together. Second, the ride starts and the client is dropped-off at its desired location. Finally, the client and driver finish the transaction by paying and they comment the service if they want.

Below we detail the protocol that we designed to implement these three phases in our distributed platform. Figures 2 and 3 depict the exchanges and the messages, respectively.

Requesting Phase. When a client wants to ride from point A to point B, it sends a `Request` message to its service node. The message contains a nonce, a timestamp, and information on the desired types of car. The nonce is made to avoid leaking the identity of the client in the network and is the HMAC of a random number generated by the client. The information about the ride are the anonymized origin and destination location of the ride, the exact distance for the ride as computed with a traffic route planner API, the price per kilometer that the client is ready to pay, and the categories of cars the client is willing to use. The client does not provide its actual origin and destination coordinates to avoid leaking sensitive information to the system. Instead it provides approximate locations. The price per kilometer is computed according to an auction mechanism. The location anonymization and price computation mechanisms are out of the scope of this paper.

When a service node receives a `Request`, it broadcasts it in the peer-to-peer network and tags the message with its own IP address and port number. In the meanwhile, the service node locally stores the request in its *pending ride requests queue*. When a node in the peer-to-peer network receives a broadcasted `Request` message, it locally stores it in its pending ride requests queue.

Every driver periodically polls its service node with a `Ping` message to know the pending ride requests. The `Ping` message contains the anonymized location of the driver, its type of car, and a timestamp. If the driver is in a location close to a request in the pending request queue of the service node, the service node replies to the driver by forwarding it the oldest compatible "close enough" `Request` message in its pending ride requests queue. If the driver doesn't want to accept this ride, it silently ignores it. Otherwise, it sends an `Acknowledgement` message directly to the service node of the client, without going through the peer-to-peer network as it knows the IP and port that can be used for direct communications with the service node. It is worth to notice that at this stage the driver leaked potential private information as it publicly reveals its ID, current approximate location, and will to achieve a ride that is uniquely identified by a nonce. Unfortunately, the only solution to avoid this would be to have a mechanism to encrypt the acknowledgment such that only the client can decrypt it. But as we are in an untrusted environment, that would imply to leak the client ID as

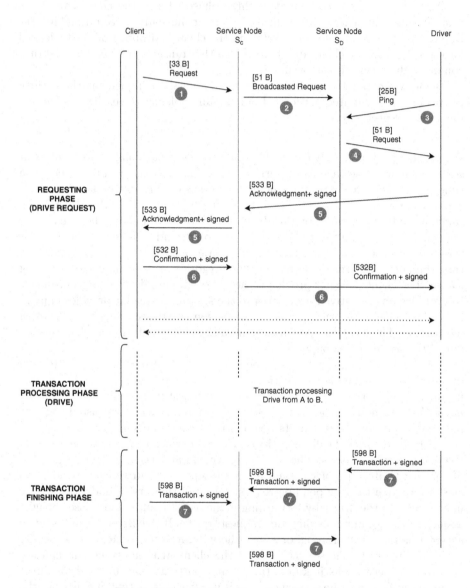

Fig. 2. Ridesharing service protocol workflow.

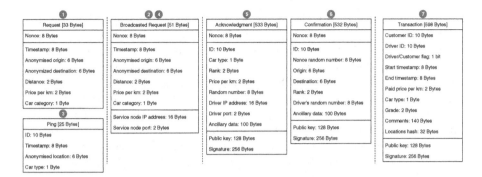

Fig. 3. Ridesharing service messages.

drivers would have to verify that the request was not forged by a service node. In the meanwhile, only the ID and an approximate location is leaked, which is not a severe threat for drivers as they are anyway clearly publicly identified in real life for legal reasons (e.g., with a specific sticker on their cab), while it could be a sever threat for clients. This is the reason while we designed our protocol in that way.

The `Acknowledgement` message contains the nonce taken from the `Request`, the driver's ID and public key, he's car type, his rank, a price per kilometer, a random number, and ancillary data that depend on the local regulations and habits (e.g., driver name, car make and model...). In addition, it provides the IP address and port number to use to have a direct communication with it.[1] The message is signed by the driver. When the client service node receives this message, it forwards the acknowledgment to the client and removes the request from its pending requests queue such that any further `Acknowledgement` message will be silently dropped.

When a client receives an `Acknowledgement` message, he decides whether or not he agrees to make the ride with that particular driver (e.g., based on the driver's rank). If he doesn't accept the driver proposition, he silently ignores the proposition in order to avoid leaking personal information. If he accepts the proposition, he sends a `Confirmation` message directly to the driver's device (for which he knows the IP address and port number to use). The message contains the nonce and the random number used by the client to generate the nonce, the client's ID, public key, and rank, the exact origin and destination points of the ride, the random number sent by the driver, and ancillary data that depend on the local regulations and habits (e.g., client's surname). The message is signed by the client and is fully encrypted with the public key of the driver. With the nonce and its associated random number, the client's public key, and the signature, the driver can verify that the client acknowledgment is generated by the owner of the ID that initiated the `Request` message and with the echo of the

---

[1] We assume that drivers can set in place hole-punching mechanisms, e.g., via their home box, to allow direct connection to their device while working.

random number that it provided in the `Acknowledgment` message, this prevents replay attacks.

At this stage, both the client and the driver have fully disclosed their personal information, but this information is known only by them. The client and driver start exchanging their actual GPS coordinates until the client is picked up. To minimize the number of messages exchanged they rely on a traffic route planner API and only exchange information if they deviate from the plan. These communications are encrypted and directly sent between the client and the driver.

It is worth to mention that even though the client's service node doesn't know the ID or exact coordinates of the client, it knows its IP address (as it has direct communication with it) and knows the ID of the driver. There are no practical solutions to avoid such leakage of information but the client can tackle this issue by using a trusted service node.

Driving Phase. The drive starts when the client is picked up by the driver. At this time, devices can collect GPS exchange format (GPX) data independently from each other. During the drive there are no messages exchanged between the devices or with the rest of the network. Due to this, a third party will never be able to determine the time of making the drive or intercept any data concerning the transaction participants GPS positions. This information is not published anywhere and is for strict personal usage. It can, for example, be used during a litigation where parties can compare their traces to justify their disagreement.

Cloture Phase. When the ride is finished, participants give a grade (e.g., stars) and a comment on the drive. The driver and the client independently advertise their ride to the network with a `Transaction` message. This message contains the ID of the client and of the driver, a start and an end timestamp, a flag indicating whether the message is from a client or a driver, the proposed grade, a comment, the price paid per kilometer, and a hash of the concatenation of the origin and destination of the ride. The message is signed by the emitter of the message (i.e., the driver or the client) and contains its public key.

The only personal information that can be inferred from a `Transaction` message is that a given client did a ride with a given driver at a given time. Other information, such as location, are never disclosed.

Transaction Data are eventually validated in the blockchain. Each node in the blockchain checks the values of both transaction data. If both are similar and correct, i.e., timestamps are reasonably close in both transaction messages, the hash of the locations is the same, and the price per kilometer is the same, then they are considered as validated transactions and added to the new next block. In the case transactions cannot be validated (e.g., only one of the two has been received, or the transactions are incompatible), they are still eventually added to the blockchain but they are marked as being in conflict.

Periodically, a *summary block* is published in the blockchain. The new summary block contains the list of observed IDs seen since the last summary block and their new rank. The rank is computed based on the last published rank for this ID and the grades that appear in the transactions with this ID. The function used to re-compute the rank must be robust to malicious users.

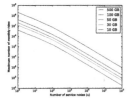

Fig. 4. Total maximum number of monthly rides supported by the platform, given a maximum monthly data volume budget per service node.

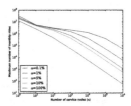

Fig. 5. Total maximum number of monthly rides supported by the platform when service nodes are grouped per zone for a maximum monthly data volume budget of 30 GB per service node.

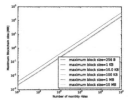

Fig. 6. Maximum increase of blockchain size per month as a function of the number of monthly rides.

3 Evaluation

In the following we evaluate the scalability of our proposition when it is implemented with Chord. We first perform an analytical study that we comment with data coming from on a real ride trace.

3.1 Platform Dimensioning

Traffic Load. With the protocol described above, we can precisely determine the data traffic generated by each ride for a network composed of n service nodes. We compute the maximum amount of traffic for the worst case scenario (i.e., using IPv6). To determine the amount of traffic supported by service nodes for one ride, we have to identify the three different types of service nodes.

(i) The *client's service node* receives the client's `Request` that it broadcasts to its neighbors (i.e., $log_2(n)$ service nodes). It also receives the driver's `Acknowledgment` messages from the d drivers willing to take the ride and forwards the first one to the client. At the end of a ride, it receives the `Transaction` message from the its client and forwards it to its neighbors (i.e., $log_2(n)$ service nodes) but also the one from the driver that it also broadcasts.

(ii) The *driver's service node* receives one broadcasted `Request` message and forwards it to its neighbors (i.e., $log_2(n)$ service nodes) and the driver's `Ping` message to which it answers by forwarding the broadcasted `Request` message. Similar to the client's node, this node will receive and broadcast transactions.

(iii) The *relay service nodes* have neither the client nor a driver. Such relay nodes receive one broadcasted `Request` message and two `Transaction` messages that they have to broadcast it to their neighbors (i.e., $log_2(n)$ nodes).

The worst case is if the client requests are always issued from clients connected to the same client's service node and when one driver of each service node (including the client's service node) answers to the request.

Figure 4 shows the evolution of the maximum number of rides that the whole platform can handle every month for a given monthly data volume quota. The x-axis gives the number of service nodes and the y-axis gives the maximum number of rides per month. Both axes are in log-scale. As shown in Fig. 4, the maximum number of rides that can be handled by the system exponentially decreases with the number of service nodes because every request has to be broadcasted in the network. For example, for 10,000 service nodes having a budget of 30 GB per month, the platform will handle at least 5,524 rides per month. This is three orders of magnitude lower than the number of requests currently seen by Uber or Lyft in a city like San Francisco [5]. Nevertheless, it is important to remember that this value represents the minimum number of rides that the platform can support. Based on a trace study in Sect. 3.2 we will see that in practice our platform can handle much more rides, and be used for current taxi services.

To alleviate this scalability issue, we can leverage the possibility to limit the scope of the messages in our Chord network thanks to a clever construction of IDs and identify two types of communications. On the one hand the `Transaction` messages must be broadcasted to all the service nodes in order to be treated safely by the blockchain. All the other messages can remain in the scope of the region where the number of service nodes can be small (e.g., a dozen) without impairing the security of the system if taken randomly in a large pool of supposedly independent nodes. If α is the fraction of service nodes that compose a region the traffic volume at a service node is in $\mathcal{O}\left(\alpha \cdot n + log(n)\right)$ instead of $\mathcal{O}\left(n + log(n)\right)$ which substantially decreases the service node load for small values of α. Similarly to Fig. 4, Fig. 5 show the maximum number of rides that the platform can support for various α and a monthly budget of 30 GB. We can see an important improvement as regions decrease in size. For example, with 10,000 nodes, if each region is limited to 10 service nodes (i.e., $\alpha = 0.1\%$), the platform will support at least 1,275,197 rides per month, which is of the same order of magnitude as what ride sharing services are experiencing today in large cities like San Francisco [5].

Blockchain Bloat. Blockchains are strictly growing structures and we can compute the worst case increase of the blockchain size as that is directly linked to the number of rides supported by the platform: for every ride, at most two transactions will be published in a block of the blockchain. Each transactions in a block contains the IDs of the driver and client, a flag to indicate if the emitter was the driver or the client, a rank, the price per kilometer and the pointer to the comment stored in the DHT. A block contains a list of transactions, a timestamp, the hash of the block, and the hash of its previous block. Summary blocks are also created with the list of IDs and their rank for IDs with a modified rank since the emission of the last summary block. In the worst case, if the IDs are observed only once between two summary blocks and if their rank changed, the summary block will contain all the IDs.

Figure 6 shows the maximum monthly increase of the blockchain size as a function of the number of monthly rides. Both axes are in log scale. As long as the maximum block size allows to store a large enough number of transactions, the size of the block has no particular impact on the blockchain size. On the contrary, when the block size is too small, it cannot contain many transactions and the block overhead (i.e., its timestamp, hash value, and predecessor pointer) is not negligible anymore. Nevertheless, for reasonable block size, increasing the maximum block size only marginally influences the block chain size but is makes it less reactive as the time span between two block creations increases, a linear function of the transaction rate.

Figure 6 shows that for realistic parameters of the system, the monthly increase of blockchain size is reasonable. For example, for a monthly budget of 30 GB, $\alpha = 0.1\%$, and 10,000 service nodes, the number of rides would be 1,275,197. With a maximum block size of 100 KB, a new block would be created about every 20.57 min and a new summary block about every 2.48 h for a total of 241.10 MB. If the system can be less reactive, the maximum block size can be increased to 1 MB. In this case, blocks are created every 3.50 h and summary blocks are created every 1.03 days and the blockchain size monthly increase is 240.84 MB.

3.2   San-Francisco Taxi Trace Evaluation

In Sect. 3.1 we show the scalability limits of our distributed platform in the worst possible case. In this section, we re-evaluate the scalability of our platform in a realistic scenario. To that aim, we use the San Francisco taxi cabs mobility trace from Piorkowski et al. [15]. This dataset tracked GPS coordinates and status of 536 taxi cabs for one month in the Bay area, between May 17th 2008 and June 9th 2008. In total, this data set logs 437,377 rides over a month.

If the platform is composed of 10,000 service nodes, in the worst case where all available drivers acknowledge ride requests and $\alpha = 1$, the maximum monthly traffic at a service node would only be 45.96 GB while the theoretical worst case is higher than 500 GB for the same amount of rides, as depicted by Fig. 4. These results show that despite in theory our distributed platform does not scale as well as a centralized platform, in practice the distributed scheme is perfectly usable. The reason is that in practice the offer and the demand are aligned and only few resources remain unused. In practice, $d \ll n$ for large enough number of service nodes.

Finally, the blockchain size as computed from the trace, shows that in practice the blockchain bloat is limited. For instance, with maximum block size values between 1 KB and 10 MB, the total blockchain size to store informations from the trace stays between 78 MB and 79 MB.

4   Proof of Concept Implementation

The architecture and protocol presented above have been mostly driven by our prototype implementation as described in this section. We decoupled the application layer from the rest of the platform and used a REST API. The user application layer is implemented in Android while the rest is developed with the Spring Framework [4] with which we implemented the REST API, the Chord network, and a DHT.

Smartphones are always "on the move" and because of their intermittent connectivity it is not straightforward to allow service nodes to spontaneously send data to the mobile device but two alternatives exist:

- to rely on external services provided by the mobile application system (e.g., Google Firebase);
- to regularly poll service nodes from mobile applications.

In the usual case, this question is not of particular importance and many would rely on the first solution. However, for propositions with a particular focus on privacy, like ours, this solution cannot be considered as a suitable one as it would infringe user privacy. For that reason, we have chosen the second approach, which explains why we introduce the `Ping` message from the driver in the requesting phase of the protocol. The polling period must be chosen carefully to offer at the same time good reactivity and low network usage to reduce operational costs. Nevertheless, we assume that drivers have local data plans (as opposed to clients that might be have expensive roaming fees) and we do not foresee particular cost issues as long as polling is done only by drivers.

In mobile environments it is usually not allowed for a terminal equipment (e.g., a smartphone) to open ports for listening. This reason combined to privacy reasons explains why the acknowledgement and the confirmation messages (5 and 6) are transiting through the client service node. Once confirmed, our protocol assumes that direct communication between the driver and the client is possible, which in practice requires complex NAT/firewall traversal mechanisms that that could be implemented by the service nodes. Our prototype does not implement traversal techniques but we anticipate that this particular point is technically complex given the privacy requirements we have.

We only have implemented payment in cash in our prototype. However, to be adopted by user it should support dematerialized payment solutions. Usual electronic payment techniques such as Visa are easy to put in place but they require trusted third parties, which goes against the general idea of our proposition. Blockchain-based cryptocurrencies are more adapted for that usage. One may propose to integrate the currency directly in our system. However, we believe that for adoption by many it is better to connect to already existing cryptocurrency markets, the issue being then to guarantee the privacy while using these platforms.

Users expect to be able to seamlessly use their services on any device. When the service relies on a centralized infrastructure managed by a third party this ubiquity is simple to implement. However in a fully distributed system with privacy preserving properties it is harder to implement. The main issue is to store the profile in a distributed way such that only the real owner can access private information. A simple solution would consist in protecting the information with encryption and give the key only to the owner. Unfortunately this method is not adapted for real world usage where users regularly lose their credentials or keys and where recovery mechanisms are used daily by the users (e.g., email recovery). For now our implementation keeps the profile encrypted and its private key on the mobile device as we have not found yet a mechanism that is at the same time truly secured and guarantees privacy and data recovery in any situation.

Finally, an important feature of ride sharing solutions is the trip planner to estimate costs. In theory the client and the driver only need a road map covering the trip region and they can compute the route locally. A solution would be to store worldwide road maps on the devices, but that would require several tens of gigabytes on the devices. This approach minimizes the data roaming costs but is not practical, unless people plan their trip and download the desired locations. An alternative, used by virtually all route planing apps today without causing any particular problem, is to download maps only when needed. The latter solution is acceptable as long as maps and live traffic information can be retrieved by regions to avoid to disclose exact location to the map provider. In parallel the users of our solution must be able to find an exact location. When the address is known exactly the problem is rather easy if downloaded maps are well annotated. However, the trend is to use natural language search for addresses and current services offering such solution rely on a centralized approach meaning that the users must disclose critical information to third parties.

5   Conclusion

The sharing economy relies on centralized platforms causing serious threats on security, privacy, and concentration of power. To tackle these issues we present a fully decentralized and privacy preserving solution. Communication between clients and providers is ensured by a peer-to-peer network and distributed storage. A blockchain plays the role of the marketplace to compute the prices and provide proven trust between the clients and the providers. We carefully designed our communication protocol and data manipulations to ensure data privacy.

We have specifically designed our solution for ridesharing business and our analytical study shows that scalability of a privacy-preserving distributed platform remains a challenge in theory. However, in practice, when applied to real taxi services, we can see that it scales enough to enable new respectful sharing economy businesses.

Acknowledgments. This work has been supported by the project *Data Privacy* funded by the IDEX of Université Côte d'Azur.

References

1. Arcade City: The Future of Ridesharing Is Decentralized. https://fee.org/articles/arcade-city-the-future-of-ridesharing-is-decentralized/
2. Hailing Rides Down Crypto Lane: The Future Of Ridesharing. https://www.forbes.com/sites/andrewrossow/2018/07/18/hailing-rides-down-crypto-lane-the-future-of-ridesharing/. Accessed 11 December 2018
3. LaZooz. http://lazooz.org. Accessed 11 December 2018
4. Spring Framework. https://spring.io. Accessed 14 February 2019
5. TNCs TODAY. http://tncstoday.sfcta.orgtncstoday.sfcta.org. Accessed 17 August 2018
6. Aïvodji, U.M., Gambs, S., Huguet, M.J., Killijian, M.O.: Meeting points in ridesharing: A privacy-preserving approach. Transp. Res. Part C Emerg. Technol. **72**, 239–253 (2016)
7. Cadwalladr, C., Graham-Harrison, E.: Revealed: 50 million facebook profiles harvested for Cambridge analytica in major data breach. The Guardian **17** (2018)
8. Dai, C., Yuan, X., Wang, C.: Privacy-preserving ridesharing recommendation in geosocial networks. In: Nguyen, H.T.T., Snasel, V. (eds.) CSoNet 2016. LNCS, vol. 9795, pp. 193–205. Springer, Cham (2016). https://doi.org/10.1007/978-3-319-42345-6_17
9. Fletcher, D.: How facebook is redefining privacy (2010)
10. Goel, P., Kulik, L., Ramamohanarao, K.: Privacy-aware dynamic ride sharing. ACM Trans. Spat. Algorithms Syst. (TSAS) **2**(1), 4 (2016)
11. Lua, E.K., Crowcroft, J., Pias, M., Sharma, R., Lim, S.: A survey and comparison of peer-to-peer overlay network schemes. IEEE Commun. Surv. Tutor. **7**(2), 72–93 (2005)
12. Maymounkov, P., Mazières, D.: Kademlia: A peer-to-peer information system based on the XOR metric. In: Druschel, P., Kaashoek, F., Rowstron, A. (eds.) IPTPS 2002. LNCS, vol. 2429, pp. 53–65. Springer, Heidelberg (2002). https://doi.org/10.1007/3-540-45748-8_5
13. Nakamoto, S.: Bitcoin: A peer-to-peer electronic cash system (2008)
14. Pham, T.V.A., Dacosta Petrocelli, I.I., Endignoux, G.F.M., Troncoso-Pastoriza, J.R., Huguenin, K., Hubaux, J.P.: Oride: A privacy-preserving yet accountable ride-hailing service. In: Proceedings of the 26th USENIX Security Symposium (2017), http://infoscience.epfl.ch/record/228219
15. Piorkowski, M., Sarafijanovoc-Djukic, N., Grossglauser, M.: A parsimonious model of mobile partitioned networks with clustering. In: The First International Conference on COMmunication Systems and NETworkS (COMSNETS), January 2009. http://www.comsnets.org
16. Robbins, J.M., Sechooler, A.M.: Once more unto the breach: What the equifax and uber data breaches reveal about the intersection of information security and the enforcement of securities laws. Crim. Justice **33**(1), 4–7 (2018)
17. Shamir, A.: How to share a secret. Commun. ACM **22**(11), 612–613 (1979)
18. Stoica, I., Morris, R., Karger, D., Kaashoek, M.F., Balakrishnan, H.: Chord: A scalable peer-to-peer lookup service for internet applications. ACM SIGCOMM Comput. Commun. Rev. **31**(4), 149–160 (2001)
19. Tapscott, D., Tapscott, A.: Blockchain revolution: How the technology behindbitcoin is changing money, business, and the world. Penguin (2016)

Ransomware Attack Protection: A Cryptographic Approach

Anjali Kumari[1], Md Zakirul Alam Bhuiyan[2], Jigyasa Namdeo[1],
Shipra Kanaujia[1], Ruhul Amin[1], and Satyanarayana Vollala[1(✉)]

[1] Department of Computer Science and Engineering,
DRSPM International Institute of Information Technology, Naya Raipur,
Sector 24, Atal Nagar 492002, Chhattisgarh, India
amin_ruhul@live.com, satya4nitt@gmail.com
[2] Department of Computer and Information Sciences, Fordham University,
JMH 334, 441 E Fordham Road, Bronx, NY 10458, USA
mbhuiyan3@fordham.edu

Abstract. Ransomware is a type of malicious software that tampers the data of an organization or an individual. For this, the attacker threatens the victim to pay a big ransom amount against the data. They seek payments through digital currencies such as bitcoins. There are no perfect techniques to detect and block a ransomware attack. But, there are a lot of preventive techniques that help organizations to protect the data from ransom attacks. The existing methods are not providing all the security services such as availability. Even if there is an availability still cryptographic operations can be performed to change the form of content. This makes impossible for the user to retrieve the original information. To overcome this drawback, we propose a technique called Ransom Protect Algorithm. In this algorithm, we present a method of locking the file for preventing the ransom attack. Thereby, ensuring that no other process can access and perform an encryption operation on the locked file.

Keywords: Ransomware · Encryption · Cryptoviral extortion · Bitcoins · Cryptography

1 Introduction

A Malware is a type of program file or software that hampers a computer system. Malware comprises computer viruses, worms, Trojan horses and spyware. These infectious programs are multifunctional in nature. The functions include eavesdropping, encryption or permanently losing sensitive data, reconfiguration or hijacking core computational functionalities and analyzing users activity without their consent. Ransomware is a type of malicious software that includes functions or features architectured to fulfill a specific aim. The main ideology followed by the attackers is to block user's access to their data on his/her system. Usually, this is achieved by encryption of the data, and seeking payment

© Springer Nature Switzerland AG 2019
G. Wang et al. (Eds.): SpaCCS 2019, LNCS 11611, pp. 15–25, 2019.
https://doi.org/10.1007/978-3-030-24907-6_2

for decryption and returning the access back to the user. The main aim behind this kind of attacks is to earn money in a large amount. Generally, in other types of attacks, the victim receives a notification alarming that malware has been launched on their system. Then afterward they are guided to data recovery. Attackers intimidate to reveal the data present in victim's computer ceaselessly refraining the access to it unless the demanded amount of money is paid in due time. Payment is demanded in virtual currencies, like bitcoin, to help the cyber-criminal to hide their identities. In perfect ransomware attacked system it is impossible to recover the data or trace the attacker's identity due to the digital currencies. Once the system is infected it gets snagged leaving the user helpless.

In the domain of cryptography, a budding field is cryptovirology that uses the principle of cryptography for generating strong malwares. The public-key concept of cryptography is utilized to crack the symmetry between an antivirus analyst's perspective and thought process with that of the attackers. The anti virus analyst observes a public key present in the malicious software while the attacker sees the public key in the malicious software along with the correspond-ing private key(present outside of the malware) because the attacker was the creator of the key pairs. Some of the examples of common ransom-ware are: CryptoLocker, CryptoLocker.F and TorrentLocker, CryptoWall, Fusob, Wan-naCry, Petya, Bad Rabbit and SamSam [1]. Either a corporate or individual users, anyone can become the victim of ransomware. In the year of 2017, the maximum number of large scale ransomware attacks were recorded in the his-tory that shook down many organizations [2].

2 Related Works

2.1 State of Art of Ransomware Attack

The first ever ransomware attack is known as AIDS Trojan. This large-scaled attack used the concept of public-key encryption. The ransomware attack was observed on the internet from May to September 2013. It was released via floppy disks in 1989, but the remarkable attention was paid to these attacks after Wan-naCry in 2017 making public aware of this attack. WannaCRy, were another wide-scale ransomware attack that affected computers in 150 countries, in less than a day, targeting Microsoft's Windows operating systems. The attackers asked payments worth of $300 to 600$ that can be roughly estimated to Rs. 19,000 and Rs.38,000 which were to be paid to them through Bitcoins. The British National Health Service, international shipper FedEx, Telefonica and other such organizations were the prime victims.

WannaCry attacks was also reported in countries like Spain, Portugal, Russia, Ukraine, and Taiwan. In India, systems at Andhra Pradesh's police department were attacked. Almost 18 police servers at locations Chittoor, Krishna, Gun-tur, Visakhapatnam, and Srikakulam districts were attacked. This attack took over the headlines and came out as a major threat to society [2]. According to the Symantec 2017 Internet Security Threat Report, the measure of pay-ment requested generally tripled from the earlier years in 2016, with the interest totaling dollar 1,077. It is confused to state how these interests are met. An investigation by IBM found that 70% of administrators they overviewed said they'd paid a ransomware request. An examination by Osterman Research found that a negligible 3 perfect of U.S.- based organizations had paid (however rates in different nations were significantly higher). Generally, installment appears to work, however, it's in no way, shape or form without hazard: A Kaspersky Security Bulletin from 2016 guaranteed that 20 perfect of organizations that paid the payment requested of them didn't get their documents back. The ascent of bitcoin as a practically untraceable installment and the developing arrangement of proof that advanced coercion could be gainful made ransomware a typical digital danger by 2016, as indicated by Kaspersky Lab. It kept on unleashing devastation in 2017 and its flood hints at little relief [3].

2.2 Types of Ransomware Attack

This section presents brief information about different types of Ransomware Attacks such as Crypto-malware, Locker, Doxware, Scareware, Popcorn Time ransomware.

1. **Crypto-malware**: This is the most notable sort of ransomware attack and is known as Crypto or encryptor ransomware. As the name proposes, this encodes your data In any case customers can regardless use the PC, yet the customers don't approach your reports. WannaCry is one exceptional kind of ransomware.
2. **Locker**: Locker ransomware keeps you out of the PC completely and the does not empower customers to get to the system. It utilizes the locker system by encoding hard drive's master records and in this manner darts up the customer's PC. The Petya ransomware is an instance of Locker ransomware.
3. **Doxware**: Doxware downloads a copy of the client's private records to the programmer's PC, and the individual in question by then undermines to circulate the reports on the web if the client doesn't pay the requested installment.
4. **Scareware**: Scareware is ill-conceived programming that tricks the clients about a few issues on their PC and requests that money tackles the issues. Scareware may over-burden your screen with pop-ups and notice messages, or it might bolt up your PC until the point that you pay. The case of scareware is the update requested by the antivirus organizations.
5. **Popcorn Time ransomware**: Here, the programmer abuses the objective client to contaminate some other two unique clients. If both of those clients pay the fine, by then, the principal client who contaminated the other two will recover his or her records, without the need to pay a payoff.

2.3 Working Principle of Ransomware

Cryptoviral extortion is going in three-rounds between the aggressor and the focused on individual [4]. It is portrayed in Fig. 1. It fuses the following advances:

[**attacker⟶victim**]: The attacker delivers a key match and places people in general key in the malware. The malware is propelled.

[**victim⟶attacker**]: To finish the cryptoviral attack, the malware makes an asymmetric key and encodes the focused on a person's data with it. It uses the public key in the malware to encode the symmetric key. This is known as hybrid encryption and it results in a little-measured ciphertext similarly as the symmetric ciphertext of the victim's data. It zeroes the symmetric key and the first plaintext data to a person's information. It sets up a message to the customer that fuses the uneven ciphertext and how to pay the result. The victim sends the ciphertext and e-money to the attacker.

[**attacker⟶victim**]: The attacker gets the money, and deciphers the ciphertext with the attacker's private key, and sends the symmetric key to the individual being referred to. The focused on individual translates the encoded data with the required symmetric key along these lines completing the cryptovirology attack. The symmetric key is arbitrarily delivered and won't help distinctive victim's. At no time is the attacker's private key exhibited to exploit individuals and the required to send a little-measured ciphertext (the encoded symmetric-figure key) to the attacker.

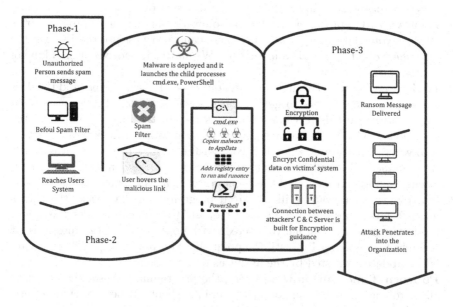

Fig. 1. Basic anatomy of a ransomware attack

Ransomware attacks are typically carried out using a Trojan, entering a system through, for example, a malicious attachment, embedded link in a Phishing email, or a vulnerability in a network service. The program then runs a payload, which locks the system in some fashion, or claims to lock the system but does not (e.g., a scareware program). Payloads may display a fake warning purportedly by an entity such as a law enforcement agency, falsely claiming that the system has been used for illegal activities, contains content such as pornography and "pirated" media [5].

2.4 Objectives

The main objective of our paper is to protect the vital data from the ransomware attack however strong the attack is. Ransomware can only be prevented or protected, it is not possible to decrypt the locked files. So, we concluded to develop a software that will block ransomware or any other malicious activity accessing our important files without the user consent. Bitcoin and advanced monetary standards have given a lift to ransomware attacks. More often than not, in the event that you pay for something on the Internet, you utilize a credit or platinum card. That card is associated with data about you, for example, your name and charging address.

Bitcoin is utilized a similar way, however not at all like a Mastercard, the exchanges you make utilizing the money are totally mysterious. They can't be utilized to recognize you. Rather, at whatever point you exchange bitcoin, you utilize a purported private key related with your wallet to produce a touch of code - called a location - that is then freely connected with your exchange however with no close to home recognizing data. What's more, in that way, every exchange is recorded and safely marked in an open record that anybody can peruse and twofold check. Potentially Bitcoin has surely picked up unmistakable quality in the press as an innovation that can encourage wrongdoing. However, since the characters of individuals in a bitcoin exchange might be shrouded, general society record has progressively helped law requirement follow the development of bitcoins from place to place [6]. Ransomware attacks are constantly increasing ranging from a simple form of any software update, any malware seeking money to hampering the data of organizations of national and global importance. Ransomware is hard to stop notwithstanding for Windows PCs running anti-virus, despite the fact that circumstance is moving forward. The main solid protection is a reinforcement, yet even that can go under attack in the event that it tends to become to from the tainted PC. As the danger is probably not going to die down within a reasonable time-frame, we take a gander at the most lethal strains of ransomware to have developed up until this point.

3   Possible Existing Solutions to Prevent Ransomware Attacks

The antibiotic is a proposed protection mechanism of ransomware which uses the approach of periodic file authentication to provide access using biometric authentication and human identification such as CAPTCHA that prevent malicious software, ransomware specifically, to delete or modify or attempt any changes in the file system- by any unauthenticated mean. Antibiotics allows the administrator to adapt to the need of responding to changes (from the authenticated user) as well as maintain the level of security in the file system. Antibiotics developed a file driver, where they logged the files accessed by users and the access is provided to users only after authentication(biometric, CAPTCHA, etc.), also authentication is presented before a user periodically to prevent in between snooping or intruding. Antibiotics is implemented on windows and experimented on various users to check for file access failure in case of unauthenticated users. The experiment was able to face very less or nominal challenges during this experiment. Next, they took samples of thousands of ransomware to launch on this file driver and tried breaking the access control mechanism but so far no existing ransomware was able to perform encryption on the files saved on this file driver as well as no changes could be Done [7].

Ransomware attack basically encrypts the files on a users system and doesn't allow them to access it unless an amount is paid to them as ransom. The ransomware works on the strategy that the victim has no other mean to retrieve the files other than paying the ransom. For this strategy to be strong enough the attacker needs to design strong cryptography which includes two main requirements: *Robust encryption* and *Strong encryption keys*. For generating strong encryption key the attacker requires large random number generation on the user's system through the malicious software. This paper works on not letting large random number generation on victim's system. It also focuses on the following:

1. Stops all currently known ransomware.
2. Stops zero day ransomware.
3. It endures the level security of applications [8].

Shukla et al. [9] and Song et al. [10] mainly worked on ransomware prevention technique on a file system with Android platform. When ransomware accesses and copies files for encryption on an Android platform this method monitors the activities on files. This technique uses CPU and I/O usage and the information stored in the database to detect and remove the ransomware. It also detects the changes in the pattern of the ransomware without gaining information about it. It is implemented on the kernel mode and firewall source of android so that it detects ransomware faster than the other applications running on the application level. Also, without even downloading or updating it can still monitor the ransomware continuously [11].

Cabaj et al. proposed an SDN technique that utilizes the characteristics of ransomware communication to detect the malicious software in the network [12]. They observed the network communication between two crypto ransomware families, the CryptoWall and Locky, and found that the analysis of HTTP messages and their sequences and the content size can alone detect such cyber threats. They further implemented their technique and designed an SDN-based detection system and even evaluated a proof-of-concept to proof the technique to be efficient and feasible. They further performed various experiments taking different scenarios to test the security analysis of their technique which turned out to be successful [12].

Literature reports the study of ransomware attacks for a very long period, i.e, 2006–2014 [5]. The results shows the inter connectivity and explicable of the whole concept of ransomware and how it has evolved in this period. They analyzed 1,359 samples belonging to 15 different families of ransomware. The conclusion of their studies shows that even though the encryption algorithm of these attacks improvised in these years, along with the deletion and communication techniques, the families of ransomware still stays quite small. The analysis also shows that the encryption and deletion of files on victim's system is based on the observation or behaviour of the victim's system and is done using only some superficial techniques and that it isn't that hard to stop more complicated and advanced ransomware as it had been misunderstood or misinterpreted in all these years. For an instance they explained, monitoring abnormal file activities can help to understand the behaviour of such threats and a defense system could be designed that could prevent such sophisticated encryption on the files on a system. Another close examination stated that monitoring the I/O requests of file systems of different ransomware sample and protecting their Master File Table(MFT) and NTFS file system, can possibly prevent and stop zero day ransomware attacks.

4   Proposed Technique

There is mainly two type of data present in our system, the first one is confidential files or crucial documents and the other is the casual data. If a system is under any attack, the confidential files need to be preserved proprietorially. No one would bother losing the causal data. Hence, it becomes very essential to secure the crucial data under any attack.

The proposed idea suggests a software that locks the memory allocation of confidential files specified by the user and can be unlocked by master password. Anyone who wants to these confidential data would be required to enter the password as to justify that they are authorized users, not any malicious software trying to hack the crucial user data.

Using this method the most confidential documents or the essential data present in our system or organization can be protected. The main concept behind this mechanism is to build a software or an algorithm that blocks or secure the memory location of any confidential data mentioned by the user from any malicious software or unauthorized user and turn on the hidden attribute of that file to add another security layer. So that when the malware enters the system it cannot access or in best case not able to find those particular data. Basically now those crucial data are locked and hidden in the system and therefore it becomes impossible for an attacker or malicious activity to find and encrypt the data in feasible amount of time. Few flowcharts have represented below to give a better understandability of our idea.

The overall ideology of the proposed mechanism is divided into three phases. The first phase as depicted in Fig. 2 ensures user authentication. The method seeks for a password from the user which after validating allows storage and processing of the file. In the next phase as shown in Fig. 3, file storage functionality

Algorithm 1. RANSOM PROTECT ALGORITHM

Input: *Password and Input-file path*
Output: *Locked file which does not allow encryption operation*

1: *pwd=input password*
2: **if** (pwd==TRUE) **then**
3:     *f← file to protect*
4: **end if**
5: *Check f Extension*
6: **if** (f is not of malicious prone extensions) **then**
7:     *Protect();*
8: **else**
9:     *Ask user if he/she sure of the doc;*
10:    **if** *(TRUE)* **then**
11:        *Protect();*
12:    **else**
13:        *Sorry! file not safe!!;*
14:    **end if**
15: **end if**
16: *Protect();*
17: *Hide();*
18: *Lock();*

is defined. The extensions of the file is checked and if it is a legal extension storage is granted. Otherwise, a reassurance is needed from the user before storing it. The last phase describes the access mechanism of the file, as shown in Fig. 4. Initially, the file status of access requested file is examined. If the file is locked the user is asked for password credentials else the access is simply granted and the file is immediately locked after the access completion.

The procedure to get locked file on which any encryption operation cannot be performed by the attacker is presented in **Ransom Protect Algorithm**. The sequence of steps used in the proposed algorithm is presented in Algorithm 1.

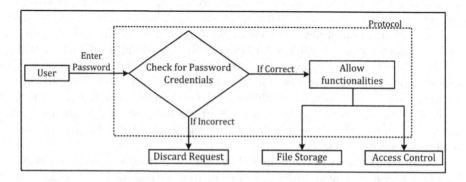

Fig. 2. User authentication (within the protocol)

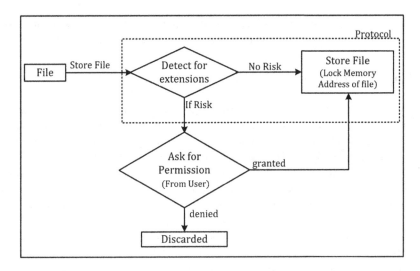

Fig. 3. File storage (within the protocol)

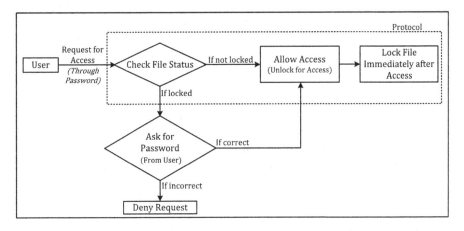

Fig. 4. Access control (with in the protocol)

In this algorithm, there are two input parameters: password and input file path will be required. As an output appropriate message will be displayed and masked file will be generated preventing further encryption operations by attacker. The input password taken from the user is stored in *pwd* variable and then it's authenticity is matched. If the password matches to the registered password then the file path will be needed. The file (*f*) will be encrypted in order to protect from attack. The file will be protected, hidden and locked by a robust mechanism for better preservation. The extension of the file is checked so that malicious activity can be immediately checked and should not enter the vicinity of important already protected files. If the extension doesn't matches with the available list of authentic extensions a confirmation from the user is sought before protecting that unknown file. Otherwise, a message will be generated.

5   Implementations, Results and Discussions

The prototype is implemented using the python language. Now a days python is mostly used to develop prototypes as it is so easy to work with and understand. Our main aim is to lock the file memory address from being accessed by any other process. To achieve this python's portalocker is used. Portalocker is a python library which provides easy API to file locking. This library provides different kind of locks such as shared lock, exclusive lock non-blocking. According to the requirement exclusive lock so that only one process can get access to it at a time. Then to increase the security, the desired file which needs protection using the win32con and win32api libraries which provide the functions to change the attribute of a file. Also to be sure that no corrupted file enter our protected area and damage other files as a precautionary measure first file extension is checked, to look for the malicious prone extensions such as zip, rar etc., if found user needs to confirm that he/she is sure that the file is safe then it will proceed. Python has the magic library. It uses the ctypes to access the libmagic file type identification library. MD5 hash function for the password has been used. The MD-5 message digest algorithm is extensively used hash function producing a 128-bit value.

In the first step password is generated using MD-5 hash function. In the next step, the user's credentials are verified and then the user will be allowed to store the desired sensitive files. After verification, user is asked the file name and it's path and is locked until the user's permission. The portalocker function is used for locking the file. To test the lock function of the proposed algorithm, a test file is opened from outside but error is thrown, making it impossible for external processes to open the file.

There are existing lock technologies which are applied on the folders to prevent them from snooping and other security issues but yet it can still be encrypted as in ransomware attacks. The folders are one point of failure if the access to the folder is achieved all the sensitive data can be easily leaked. The proposed methodology overcomes this drawback by locking each file rather than the folders. The file will be masked for other users. Further, any encryption operations fail on these files. Existing techniques also have equal chances of getting tricked. There is no perfect mechanism to tackle this ransomware as new ransomware keeps on evolving. So it is an option to protect our important files rather than the whole system.

6   Conclusion

In this paper, we implemented a method to provide better protection and prevention against ransomware attacks by locking of the sensitive files of the user. We not only provided confidentiality, authentication but also availability and resisting change of form of content from unauthorized users, which is not a feature of existing works. For this, we proposed a new algorithm, called Ransom Protect Algorithm, which doesn't allow external processes to access the secured files without users permission. With these, we provided some additional security layers such as file extension detection and hiding the file. Further, any other encryption algorithms also fail on the secured files.

References

1. Scaife, N., Carter, H., Traynor, P., Butler, K.R.B.: Cryptolock (and drop it): stopping ransomware attacks on user data. In: IEEE 36th International Conference on Distributed Computing Systems (ICDCS), pp. 303–312. IEEE (2016)
2. Mohurle, S., Patil, M.: A brief study of wannacry threat: ransomware attack 2017. Int. J. Adv. Res. Comput. Sci. **8**(5), 1938–1940 (2017)
3. O'Kane, P., Sezer, S., Carlin, D.: Evolution of ransomware. IET Netw. **7**(5), 321–327 (2018)
4. Young, A., Yung, M.: Cryptovirology: extortion-based security threats and countermeasures. In: Proceedings 1996 IEEE Symposium on Security and Privacy, pp. 129–140. IEEE (1996)
5. Kharraz, A., Robertson, W., Kirda, E.: Protecting against ransomware: a new line of research or restating classic ideas? IEEE Secur. Priv. **16**(3), 103–107 (2018)
6. Salvi, M.H.U., Kerkar, M.R.V.: Ransomware: a cyber extortion. Asian J. Convergence Technol. (AJCT)-UGC LISTED **2**, 1–6 (2016)
7. Ami, O., Elovici, Y., Hendler, D.: Ransomware prevention using application authentication-based file access control. In: Proceedings of the 33rd Annual ACM Symposium on Applied Computing, pp. 1610–1619. ACM (2018)
8. Genç, Z.A., Lenzini, G., Ryan, P.Y.A.: No random, no ransom: a key to stop cryptographic ransomware. In: Giuffrida, C., Bardin, S., Blanc, G. (eds.) DIMVA 2018. LNCS, vol. 10885, pp. 234–255. Springer, Cham (2018). https://doi.org/10.1007/978-3-319-93411-2_11
9. Shukla, M., Mondal, S., Lodha, S.: Poster: locally virtualized environment for mitigating ransomware threat. In: Proceedings of the 2016 ACM SIGSAC Conference on Computer and Communications Security, pp. 1784–1786. ACM (2016)
10. Song, S., Kim, B., Lee, S.: The effective ransomware prevention technique using process monitoring on android platform. Mob. Inf. Syst. **2016**, 1–10 (2016). Article ID 2946735
11. Al-rimy, B.A.S., Maarof, M.A., Shaid, S.Z.M.: Ransomware threat success factors, taxonomy, and countermeasures: a survey and research directions. Comput. Secur. **74**, 144–166 (2018)
12. Cabaj, K., Gregorczyk, M., Mazurczyk, W.: Software-defined networking-based crypto ransomware detection using HTTP traffic characteristics. Comput. Electr. Eng. **66**, 353–368 (2018)

A Lightweight Secure Communication Protocol for IoT Devices Using Physically Unclonable Function

Priyanka Mall[1], Md Zakirul Alam Bhuiyan[2], and Ruhul Amin[1(✉)]

[1] Department of Computer Science and Engineering, DRSPM International Institute of Information Technology, Naya Raipur, Sector 24, Atal Nagar, Chhattisgarh, India
priyanka16101@iiitnr.edu.in, amin_ruhul@live.com
[2] Department of Computer and Information Sciences, Fordham University, JMH 334, 441 E Forrdham Road, Bronx, NY 10458, USA
mbhuiyan3@fordham.edu

Abstract. The fast-growing connected world has increased the dynamic demands of the Internet of things (IoT) in different sectors, and the main challenges for the IoT devices are low memory and limited computational power. In addition, the number of assailant and security threats in IoT communication are increasing rapidly. Several cryptographic mechanisms/operations have been proposed in order to prevent IoT security threats, which are mainly computationally-heavy in nature. Currently, physically unclonable function (PUF) plays an important role in designing efficient cryptographic protocols in comparison with other crypto-operations due to its light-weight process. In this paper, we revisit PUF-based authentication protocol for secure communication in IoT proposed by Braeken (2018) and identified its loopholes. From there, we design a new protocol for secure communication by utilizing PUF operation. The main objective of our protocol is to provide top-level security with less computation cost for faster responses. Our simulation results, using Scyther tool, confirm that all the private information is protected during protocol run and all the related security attacks could be protected through informal analysis. The performance of our protocol is shown to be better in terms of communication and computation overhead compared with two peer protocols.

Keywords: Physically Unclonable Function (PUF) ·
Internet of Things (IoT) · Device authentication

1 Introduction

Internet of Things (IoT) has been perceived as the driving technology for the advancement of smart cities, healthcare and control systems. IoT setup consists of unique identifiers assigned to devices and the communication between devices, which occurs over the Internet via pubic or local networks [1]. IoT devices are

© Springer Nature Switzerland AG 2019
G. Wang et al. (Eds.): SpaCCS 2019, LNCS 11611, pp. 26–35, 2019.
https://doi.org/10.1007/978-3-030-24907-6_3

composed of wireless sensors, actuators and computer devices that enable automatic transfer of data among the objects or people without any human interference. Many IoT devices are physically unprotected and are difficult to access. IoT devices have parameters such as energy, cost, power, lifetime but the most challenging requirement is security. There are many existing security primitives proposed and are suitable for the Internet but they are not suitable enough for the IoT. The security protocols for the IoT should not be affected by human interferences and, most importantly, they should be immune to the side channel attacks. The data transfer between the devices should be secure in terms of confidentiality, authenticity of the sender and receiver devices and integrity of the communicated messages [2].

A typical authentication process between IoT devices as shown in Fig. 1, is composed of two IoT nodes (devices), server, PUFs installed in the respective IoT nodes. IoT node 1 and IoT node 2 have their own PUF circuits. The node 1 requests the server that it wants to communicate with node 2 and the server will then check whether there is any node 2 in its database. Further, the server will send PUF based challenges to the node 1 and node 2. The nodes will use their PUF circuits to generate the responses of those challenges and will send it to the server. The server will then compare the received responses with the stored Challenge Response Pairs (CRP). If the condition is true, the server will then send the common key information to both the nodes. Now, both the IoT nodes have a common key between them so that they can proceed further.

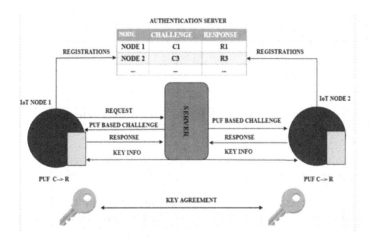

Fig. 1. Basic key agreement phase architecture between IoT devices

1.1 Physically Unclonable Function

Physically Unclonable Function (PUF) was introduced as a cryptographic primitive, which is a hardware that permits one-way functions. PUF is a physical unit embodied in a physical structure that is easy to fabricate but infeasible to clone or predict. If anyone follows the same manufacturing process even then also he/she cannot duplicate the structure, which in turn adds up to the advantage of using PUFs. PUFs are associated to the device identity rather than the private key. PUFs use challenge-response pairs (CRP) for the authentication mechanism. In challenge-response pair, the electrical stimulus also known as *challenge* is provided to the physical unit in order to react, called *response*. A response is completely unpredictable because there are lots of complex interface of the stimulus with the physical structure of the device which totally depends on the physical parameters that were introduced during the manufacturing process in an unclonable manner. We have shown circuit diagram of PUF function in Fig. 2.

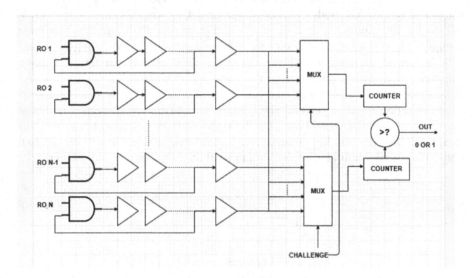

Fig. 2. Circuit diagram of physically unclonable function

1.2   Related Works

The recent emerging concept of secure communication in the IoT has been developed gradually over the past few years. With its growing popularity, there has been an increase in the newer security challenges in this ground. Different cryptographic algorithms/operations such as hash function, RSA cryptosystem, bilinear pairings, ECC operations, and several hardware structures have been proposed to ensure a secure communication channel between the IoT devices. Chatterjee et al. [3] discussed the authentication and the key agreement phase between the IoT devices via a server using PUF mechanism. In their work, PUF hardware generated challenge-response pairs (CRP) for each IoT device. Unique PUF hardware structures (See Fig. 2) were implemented in different IoT devices to provide unclonable outputs.

Various PUF based authentication protocols for wireless sensor networks and RFID systems have been proposed, which require a massive number of Challenge-Response pairs (CRP) for each and every device that is updated and stored in the server. These protocols are mainly suitable to be implemented using RFID devices or in wireless sensor networks, but in IoT there is the necessity of scalability which these protocols would simply not provide.

The PUF based authentication protocol in [4–6] uses zero-knowledge proof of knowledge (ZKPK) of discrete logarithm which conceals the CRP in any of the messages by the use of zero-knowledge proofs. The protocol requires the user to input a password to the device each and every time there is a need of authentication which eventually reduces the effectiveness of the protocol in IoT systems and makes it more complex. The protocol only works for the authentication purpose between the user and server, and not for two IoT devices to authenticate themselves.

The authors in [7] proposed a collective IoT authentication approach. In our view, their work put the nodes at risk by collective authentication and multiple node's key sharing. Moreover, if only one node is even compromised, the whole system may halt. In another work [8], the certificate-based authentication protocol for distributed IoT system exposed the protocol to cloning attacks by storing the cryptographic credentials in the edge node. One-time password (OTP) based authentication protocol for IoT devices in [9] increased complexity and computational cost of the proposed algorithm as the protocol used multiple iterations and complex computation of OTP using the public/private keys. In [10], PUF based authentication protocols need a trusted party to store each IoT device's Challenge Response pairs (CRPs). The protocol stands unscalable if the number of IoT devices are increased.

1.3   Limitation of the Protocol of Braeken (2018)

We found some drawbacks of the protocol proposed by Braken [11].

(1) Storage: In Braeken's protocol, the nodes and the server opens up new sessions in each and every step which leads to the storage issues. (2) Predictable Outputs: The protocol used hash functions which, unlike PUFs, give the same response for the same input which can be predicted by the attacker. (3) Complex Algorithm: The protocol uses intensive Elliptical Curve Multiplication which do fastens the key agreement scheme thrice on the node's side but also provides high time complexity.

1.4   Road Map of the Manuscript

We have discussed the basic concept of PUF as well as the need of it in IoT environment and presented in Sect. 1, followed by related works in the same section. We then present our proposed protocol in Sect. 2 followed by security analysis of the protocol in Sect. 3. Section 4 presents the simulation results. The performance study is given in Sect. 5. Section 6 gives the conclusion of the paper (Table 1).

Table 1. List of notations used

Symbol	Description
ID_i	Identity of the node
S	Server
$\oplus$	Bit-wise xor operation
$PUF(X)$	PUF generated response for challenge X
$\parallel$	Concatenation operation
$H(X)$	Result of hash function
RAN	Random number
T_1, T_2	Timestamp

2   Proposed Authentication Protocol

This section discusses our conducive protocol for the establishment of secure communication between IoT devices, which includes mainly two phases (1) Enrolment phase, (2) Authentication and Key-Agreement Phase.

2.1   Enrolment Phase

In the enrolment phase, the server sends a set of k challenges to both the devices. On the device side, each challenge is passed through PUF mechanism (note that the PUF circuits are different for both the devices) and the corresponding responses are generated. The resulting k responses are sent to the server via a secure channel. The server is now responsible for securely storing these k challenge-response pairs (CRPs) for each node.

2.2   Authentication and Key-Agreement Phase

As mentioned earlier, the user or the node 1 first requests to the server that it wants to communicate with node 2. At this point, secure communication between node 1 and other nodes are very important and necessary. This phase describes a key agreement procedure between the node 1 and node 2. All the steps of this phase are given below.

Step-1: Node 1 initiates the key-agreement phase and requests the server that it wants to reach and communicate with Node 2 by sending $\langle ID_1, ID_2 \rangle$ of node 1 and 2 respectively along with timestamp TS.

Step-2: Upon receiving the request, the server verifies the identification of both the nodes by checking the existence of ID_1 and ID_2 in its database. If verified, the server selects a couple of challenge-response pairs $\langle (C_1, R_1) \rangle$ and $\langle (C_2, R_2) \rangle$ for Node 1 and $\langle (C_3, R_3) \langle$ and $\langle (C_4, R_4) \langle$ for Node 2.

Step-3: Node 1 now, after receiving the message from the server, checks if message consists of the expected parameters and expected length. If so, it retrieves the parameters ID_1 and TS. Now Node 1 derives R_1 and R_2 using PUF mechanism and generates a random number RAN_1. Further Node1 calculates a hash function $A_1 = H(C_1 \parallel C_2 \parallel R_1 \parallel R_2 \parallel ID_1 \parallel T_1 \parallel RAN_1)$, $A_2 = RAN_1 \oplus R_1$ and sends $\langle (A_1 \parallel A_2) \rangle$ to server. The same process goes at the side of Node 2 and it sends message $\langle (B_1 \parallel B2) \rangle$, where $B_1 = H(C_3 \parallel C_4 \parallel R_3 \parallel R_4 \parallel ID_2 \parallel T_2 \parallel RAN_2)$ and $B_2 = RAN_2 \oplus R_3$, where RAN_2 is the random nonce generated by the node 2.

Step-4: The server first retrieves R_1 and R_2 and computes RAN_1' and A_1' and checks whether A_1' is equal to A_1 or not. Secondly, the server retrieves R_3 and R_4 and computes RAN_2' and B_1' and checks whether B_1' is equal to B_1 or not. Thereafter, it generates a key using the hash function. The server then sends the $R_1 \oplus R_3$, $RAN_1 \oplus RAN_2$ to both the nodes Node 1 and Node 2.

Step-5: The Node 1 would then derive R_3 and RAN_2 and would compute common key K_2 using the hash function and Node 2 would also derive R_1 and RAN_2 and would calculate common key K_2 using the hash function, where $K_2 = H(ID_1 \parallel ID_2 \parallel R_3 \parallel RAN_2)$.

3 Security Analysis

This section presents the security analysis of the proposed protocol in order to proof its resistance to pertinent security attacks. The IDs of the nodes in the proposed protocol are public so this may cause many security threats to this approach. We listed all the possible powers of the attackers to comprehend the robustness of the proposed protocol.

3.1 Impersonation Attack

The challenge response pair generated using the PUF circuitry makes it unique and unclonable. During the manufacturing, the PUF circuits are fabricated in the nodes. The PUF circuits are unique for each and every node so the response for each challenge is unique every time. $R_{11} = PUF(C_{11})$, $R_{21} = PUF(C_{21})$, $R_{12} = PUF(C_{11})$ and $R_{22} = PUF(C_{22})$. The PUF circuits are very complex and cannot be duplicated. So this gives us unique responses that are further used to generate the hash functions and the common key between the nodes.

The nodes further generates hash functions which are prompted using respective challenges response pairs, the IDs, time stamp and the random number.

$A_1 = H(C_1 \parallel C_2 \parallel R_1 \parallel R_2 \parallel ID_1 \parallel T_1 \parallel RAN_1)$, $A_2 = RAN_1 \oplus R_1$, $B_1 = H(C_3 \parallel C_4 \parallel R_3 \parallel R_4 \parallel ID_2 \parallel T_2 \parallel RAN_2)$ and $B_2 = RAN_2 \oplus R_3$. The utilization of the PUF circuit to generate the challenge response pairs enables distinctive responses.

3.2   Session Key Security Attack

The server produces a common key using the responses and the random number generated along with IDs of the communicating nodes that would help in secure communication between the nodes. Since we are using the PUF circuitry the response that we are evaluating cannot be duplicated. Thus, this makes the common key between the nodes resistant to any external attacks.

4   Scyther Simulation and Results

The speedy progress of internet dictates the development of reliable protocols that can provide security without any compromise. It becomes highly mandatory to verify the strength of security rendered by any new or existing protocols. There are many tools that facilitate this assessment including AVISPA and Proverif. The former is employed for detecting different attacks and latter is utilized for verifying the extent to which the protocols turn to be correct. Recently Scyther has found its predominant position in verifying and analyzing security protocols.

Scyther is known for its free usage and enhanced new features with high performance application. The features that elaborate the novelty of this tool include the verification that is boundless, assured termination and additional hold that it provides for analysis of multi-protocols. In addition, Scyther renders different classes in which the protocol behaves [12].

The process of writing protocols in Scyther is conveniently assisted by a domain-specific language, Security Protocol Description Language (SPDL), which has its base in operational semantics that additionally provides confidentiality and authentication verification for protocols. Based on our protocol description, we have written SPDL code for the node-1, node-2 and server and simulated using Scyther tool. The results obtained from Scyther is presented in Fig. 3, which demonstrated that all the private information of the protocol is well protected.

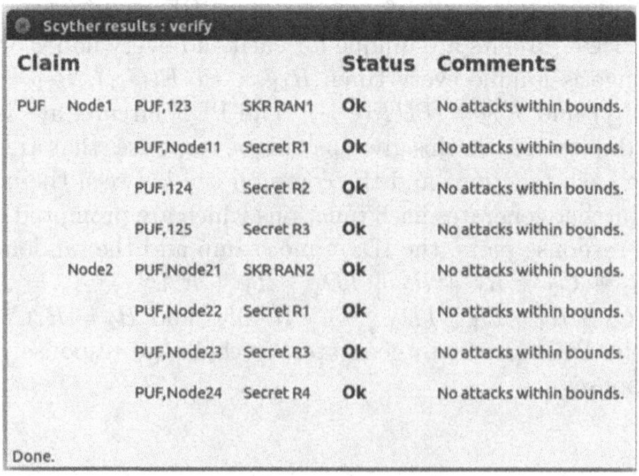

Claim				Status	Comments
PUF	Node1	PUF,123	SKR RAN1	Ok	No attacks within bounds.
		PUF,Node11	Secret R1	Ok	No attacks within bounds.
		PUF,124	Secret R2	Ok	No attacks within bounds.
		PUF,125	Secret R3	Ok	No attacks within bounds.
	Node2	PUF,Node21	SKR RAN2	Ok	No attacks within bounds.
		PUF,Node22	Secret R1	Ok	No attacks within bounds.
		PUF,Node23	Secret R3	Ok	No attacks within bounds.
		PUF,Node24	Secret R4	Ok	No attacks within bounds.

Done.

Fig. 3. Simulation results of our protocol

5   Performance Analysis

Every proposed protocol is usually bounded by the complexities of cost and time because of numerous complex operations performed in the protocol itself. The protocol includes hash functions, XOR operations, and PUF circuitry and these functions or operations have their own individual computation cost. This section basically measures and compares the computation and communication overhead of our protocol.

5.1   Computational Overhead Discussion

Table 2 presents the performance results of the proposed protocol compared with the two peer protocols [3, 11]. The results show that the proposed protocol is better, both from the server and the node point of view, than the existing ones. Furthermore, the security threats in [11] have been overcome. As mentioned earlier, Braeken's protocol has the complication in storage as it creates a lot of sessions, but our proposed protocol is not creating any such sessions for storing the results or values, thus making it more space efficient for IoT devices. The following table clearly describes the usage of hash functions and the PUFs circuit in each protocol under study. Further, we have depicted the comparison results for the communication overhead in Fig. 4.

Table 2. Computational cost analysis

Protocols	HF (S)	HF (N)	PUF-C (S)	PUF-C(N)
Ref [3]	6	4	4	8
Ref [11]	8	5	4	2
Our	1	2	4	2

HF: Hash function, S: Server side, N: Node, PUF-C: Physically Unclonable Function Circuit

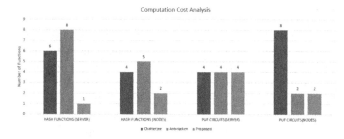

Fig. 4. Computational cost comparison

5.2   Communication Overhead Discussion

Table 3 presents the communication cost related results which signifies the number of bits transferred between the nodes and also among the server and the nodes. We have considered uniform bits length for all the protocols and for all the parameters we used in the protocols, i.e., random number, identity and hash function are 128 bits. Also, the challenge-response parameter is 128 bits. In the proposed protocol, the number of bits communicated by nodes is comparatively less to the Chatterjee et al. [3] and Braeken [11] protocol. As results suggested, our protocol could be also better in terms of communication cost. Further, we have presented the comparison results for the communication overhead in Fig. 5.

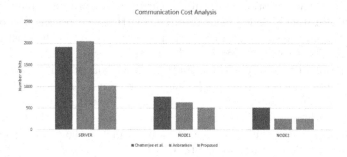

Fig. 5. Communication cost comparison

Table 3. Communication cost (in bits) analysis

Protocols	Server	Node-1	Node-2
Chatterjee et al. [3]	1920	768	512
An Braeken [11]	2048	640	256
Proposed	1024	512	256

6   Conclusion

In this article, we designed an authentication protocol for secure communication between IoT devices using Physically Unclonable Function, which uses challenge-response pair concept. Our protocol provides a better protection against related security threats. As the simulation results, using Scyther tool, indicated, the proposed protocol can ensure that all the private information is protected against adversary during protocol run. By comparing with other works, it was observed that our protocol could perform better in terms of computation and communication overhead. This work basically establishes secure communication between two nodes, but the same protocol will not work for secure communication of a group of nodes, i.e., one node to many nodes. In future research, we plan to design an extended version that will overcome this shortcoming in our protocol.

References

1. Kim, D.: Performance of UWB wireless telecommunication positioning for disaster relief communication environment securing. Sustainability **10**(11), 3857 (2018)
2. Das, A.K., Zeadally, S., He, D.: Taxonomy and analysis of security protocols for Internet of Things. Future Gener. Comput. Syst. **89**, 110–125 (2018)
3. Chatterjee, U., Chakraborty, R.S., Mukhopadhyay, D.: A PUF-based secure communication protocol for IoT. ACM Trans. Embed. Comput. Syst. (TECS) **16**(3), 67 (2017)
4. Frikken, K.B., Blanton, M., Atallah, M.J.: Robust authentication using physically unclonable functions. In: Samarati, P., Yung, M., Martinelli, F., Ardagna, C.A. (eds.) ISC 2009. LNCS, vol. 5735, pp. 262–277. Springer, Heidelberg (2009). https://doi.org/10.1007/978-3-642-04474-8_22
5. Feng, J., Yang, L.T., Zhu, Q., Choo, K.-K.R.: Privacy-preserving tensor decomposition over encrypted data in a federated cloud environment. IEEE Trans. Dependable Secure Comput. (2018)
6. Feng, J., Yang, L.T., Zhang, R.: Practical privacy-preserving high-order bi-lanczos in integrated edge-fog-cloud architecture for cyber-physical-social systems. ACM Trans. Internet Technol. (TOIT) **19**(2), 26 (2019)
7. Mahalle, P.N., Prasad, N.R., Prasad, R.: Threshold cryptography-based group authentication (TCGA) scheme for the Internet of Things (IoT). In: 4th International Conference on Wireless Communications, Vehicular Technology, Information Theory and Aerospace & Electronic Systems (VITAE), pp. 1–5. IEEE (2014)
8. Porambage, P., Schmitt, C., Kumar, P., Gurtov, A., Ylianttila, M.: Two-phase authentication protocol for wireless sensor networks in distributed IoT applications. In: IEEE Wireless Communications and Networking Conference (WCNC), pp. 2728–2733. IEEE (2014)
9. Shivraj, V.L., Rajan, M.A., Singh, M., Balamuralidhar, P.: One time password authentication scheme based on elliptic curves for Internet of Things (IoT). In: 5th National Symposium on Information Technology: Towards New Smart World (NSITNSW), pp. 1–6. IEEE (2015)
10. Edward Suh, G., Devadas, S.: Physical unclonable functions for device authentication and secret key generation. In: 44th ACM/IEEE Design Automation Conference, pp. 9–14. IEEE (2007)
11. Braeken, A.: PUF based authentication protocol for IoT. Symmetry **10**(8), 352 (2018)
12. Cremers, C.J.F.: Unbounded verification, falsification, and characterization of security protocols by pattern refinement. In: Proceedings of the 15th ACM Conference on Computer and Communications Security, pp. 119–128. ACM (2008)

Blockchain-Based Mobility Management for LTE and Beyond

Han Lee$^{(\boxtimes)}$ and Maode Ma$^{(\boxtimes)}$

Nanyang Technological University,
50 Nanyang Avenue, Singapore 639798, Singapore
han009@e.ntu.edu.sg, emdma@e.ntu.edu.sg

Abstract. If LTE has made it possible to stream music and video over mobile devices such as smartphones and tablets, 5G will enable vehicles, sensors, and other countless devices to interact and share data over the cellular network. To unleash the full potential of 5G, it is imperative to address the shortcomings of LTE in regard to mobility management. One major challenge with LTE is improving the handover performance and security. In order to enhance the performance and security of the handover process, this paper introduces an approach using blockchain for key derivation and key sharing. This novel approach, Blockchain Key Derivation Function (BKDF), ensures tighter security as well as faster handover between the base stations. With blockchain adding an extra layer of security, the network is able to securely derive the handover key and share it with the base stations and mobile devices in the pre-handover phase, which significantly reduces the number of operations required during the intra-handover phase. A formal security analysis on BKDF is conducted with the Burrows-Abadi-Needham (BAN) logic, followed by an analysis on the effectiveness of BKDF against some of the well-known types of network attacks. The simulation results confirm that BKDF reduces handover latency and improves link stability with decrease in packet loss in the intra-handover phase.

Keywords: Handover · Blockchain · Security · LTE · 5G

1 Introduction

LTE is the backbone of today's mobile communication and it is undeniably a key driver in shaping today's world. LTE has played a critical role for the emergence of smartphones, and significantly changed the ways of life by providing a technical platform for voice and data services.

In order to enjoy the full benefits of LTE on a mobile device, it is important that the LTE network is able to support secure and seamless handovers as the mobile device moves from one location to another. Without such a support from LTE, there would be frequent interruptions to video and music applications on the mobile device. Furthermore, 5G has a bold handover requirement for less than 1 ms to provide the best user experience on mobile devices. It will also operate at higher frequency spectrums, which require multiple times more base stations than LTE to cover the same size of area. This causes the handover frequency to be inevitably high, increasing the overall latency on the network.

© Springer Nature Switzerland AG 2019
G. Wang et al. (Eds.): SpaCCS 2019, LNCS 11611, pp. 36–49, 2019.
https://doi.org/10.1007/978-3-030-24907-6_4

The approach introduced in [1, 2] shares a non-cryptographic UE authentication mechanism with the eNodeBs along the predicted path of UE. It is able to reduce computational burdens and prepare the eNodeBs proactively for authentication. In [3], an enhancement on Coordinated Multipoint (CoMP) is discussed. This enhancement focuses on reducing radio link failures by helping the UEs select the best cell with the strongest signal among the group of serving cells. [4] introduces a way to reduce the number of handovers by not performing handovers until additional conditions are met. The paper proposes additional conditions based on the location and cell-size to show that it can achieve a better average throughput by avoiding unnecessary handovers. Though this idea may succeed in reducing latency, it comes at the cost of link quality. [5] proposes another method to reduce the frequency of handovers by adding more criteria related to the user and network conditions. The user-related conditions include some parameters such as jitter, packet loss, and delay. Each condition is given a different weight and the handover decision is made based on the weighted result of conditions. Finally, [6] explores a way to virtualize the functions in the Evolved Universal Terrestrial Radio Access Network and have them connected through fiber in an effort to reduce latency between those functions. The core of this approach lies in controlling the virtualized functions to strengthen the radio signal by combining the nearby radio units to jointly transmit the data. In doing so, the frequency of handover is reduced, resulting in a better average throughput.

Most papers have focused on improving the handover decision-making process to reduce potential issues that would hurt user experience. However, there has been less focus on improving the protocols that are the actual sources of latency.

This paper tackles the fundamental concepts of key derivation and key sharing mechanism. It focuses on introducing a novel approach for improving the handover performance and security by leveraging blockchain. Blockchain is the core technology that enables cryptocurrencies to eliminate the needs for having a broker to ensure financial transactions between the blockchain nodes. There are some innate characteristics of blockchain that can be applied toward improving the mechanism for handover key derivation and key sharing between the eNodeBs and UEs.

The remainder of this paper is organized as follows. In Sect. 2, the benefits of using blockchain on cellular networks is discussed. Section 3 introduces BKDF in detail. It is followed by security analysis using the BAN logic in Sect. 4. The performance evaluation is presented on Sect. 5. Finally, the paper is concluded in Sect. 6.

2   Characteristics of Blockchain

The essence of blockchain, in the context of cryptocurrency, comes from the fact that cryptocurrency transactions can be verified without the need for an intermediary like a bank to broker and guarantee the transactions. This is made possible with a distributed public ledger that is immutable and cryptographically protected. All of the transactions are recorded permanently on the distributed public ledger and kept secured and tamper-proof with the help of cryptography.

Blockchain also slowly expanding its use cases outside the realm of cryptocurrency. [7] proposes a data management and data search system that is based on blockchain to mitigate security threats. [8] explores a way to securely share files using blockchain in a computer network. [9] expands the use of blockchain to managing Internet-of-Things (IoT) devices.

The features of blockchain that keep cryptocurrency transactions tamper-proof and immutable can be expanded to improve LTE and beyond. The following provides a list of the features from blockchain that can be potentially applied to cellular networks.

2.1   No Central Authority

The key feature of blockchain is the absence of central authority. In the context of LTE, a central authority would refer to a server such as Mobility Management Entity (MME). The involvement of network components such as MME can often be a bottleneck and a source of latency for handover.

Blockchain, on the other hand, requires no server to check the validity of data. Information is cross-validated and synchronized between the blockchain nodes without a central authority. For example, all transactions are recorded and shared between the blockchain nodes without a central governing body to broker and validate each transaction.

2.2   Hash for Validation

SHA-256 is the hash algorithm used in Bitcoin [10], the most widely traded cryptocurrency, to maintain the integrity of Bitcoin transaction data. A unique hash value, known as proof-of-work, is created using SHA-256 to ensure the validity of transactions between the blockchain nodes.

The same hash algorithm comes as highly useful in the context of LTE. A proof-of-work is unique in two ways. First, it is generated from SHA-256, which is virtually impossible to yield two equal outputs from two different sets of inputs. Second, it is only known to the nodes in the blockchain. This means that a proof-of-work can be potentially used as a means of authentication between the nodes, since possessing the correct hash values can be a proof of the node's legitimacy in the blockchain, as all nodes are expected to have equal hash values on their distributed ledger.

2.3   Immutability

This is the most important characteristic of blockchain that prevents any attack from tampering with Bitcoin transaction data. Along with hash algorithms like SHA-256, the amount of data used for creating a hash value is purely immense that no sole attacker can round up enough compute power to guess the hash value correctly by brute force. A feasible threat would be to gain control of more than half of the nodes in the blockchain to modify the transaction data and generate a new hash value. However, it has practically zero probability of occurrence.

3 Blockchain Key Derivation Function

This paper introduces a novel approach for enhancing the security and performance of the LTE handover process using blockchain. Blockchain Key Derivation Function (BKDF) focuses on the benefits of using blockchain for handover key derivation and key sharing. The focus of this paper is on the handover over X2 [11].

To support BKDF, every single eNodeB managed by the same MME becomes a blockchain node. The eNodeBs create one blockchain per UE to ensure the uniqueness of each handover key used by a UE. Every eNodeB participates in mining, which is an act of conducting iterations of SHA-256 calculation until a conforming output is found. The output that conforms to the predefined conditions is called proof-of-work. The first eNodeB to finish mining creates a block, a set of data with transaction history, timestamp, difficulty level, nonce and proof-of-work. Subsequently, the block is shared with all other eNodeBs and the UE.

A new 256-bit handover key, K_{eNB*}, for the target eNodeB is derived from the proof-of-work. Therefore, BKDF proactively prepares the next handover key for all eNodeBs and the UE before the next handover is triggered. Being prepared with the next handover key allows the UE to connect with the target eNodeB directly for handover. Instead of burdening the network with measurement reports and computations for the selection of the next target eNodeB, the UE is able to select the next target eNodeB based on the measurement reports and start communicating with the target eNodeB with the new handover key that has already been shared between with the target eNodeB before the handover process.

The following explains the message flows in detail. The key establishment process is explained from Phase 1 to Phase 3, happening before the handover process. Phase 4 and Phase 5 explain the message exchanges, happening during the handover process. The acronyms are explained in Table 1.

Table 1. Acronyms

Enb_i	eNodeB with a numeric identifier i for $1 \leq i \leq N$
$Enb_{i,j}$	A set of Enb_i from i to j for $1 \leq i,j \leq N$
Enb_s	Source eNodeB
Enb_m	Miner eNodeB
Enb_t	Target eNodeB
T_0	Timestamp on the genesis block
PH_0	Previous Hash on the genesis block
H_0	Hash on the genesis block
N_0	Nonce on the genesis block
D_0	Difficulty of the genesis block
$K_{i,j}$	A set of public keys associated with $Enb_{i,j}$
K_{Mi}	Session key between the MME and an Enb_i
K_{su}	Session key between Enb_s and UE
K_u	Public Key of UE

(*continued*)

Table 1. (*continued*)

$K_{s^{-1}}$	Private Key of Enb_s
$K_{m^{-1}}$	Private Key of Enb_m
$K_{u^{-1}}$	Private Key of UE
$K_{t^{-1}}$	Private Key of Enb_t
T_i	Timestamp at the ith transaction message
K_u	Public key of the UE
T_m	Timestamp of the new block
N_m	Nonce of the new block
$H(X)$	SHA-256 with input X
T_{hsyn}	Timestamp on the SYN message
T_{hack}	Timestamp on the ACK message

3.1   Phase 1

The UE is assumed to have been authenticated with the network for having the same permanent key K with the Authentication Center (AuC). The UE is associated with an eNodeB, which is the source eNodeB. All Enb_i connected to the same MME form a blockchain neighborship in which they all participate as blockchain nodes to create and manage blockchains for the attached UEs.

The MME sends the initial set of information known as the genesis block to all eNodeBs under its domain. The contents of the genesis block have been hard-coded, which include T_0, PH_0, H_0, N_0, D_0, $K_{1,N}$. The pseudo-identity of an eNodeB is equal to the public key from a key pair generated by secp256k1 with the Elliptic Curve Digital Signature Algorithm (ECDSA) [12]. The genesis block acts as a means for authenticating the nodes in the blockchain, effectively blocking attacks from rogue base stations. A matching genesis block is required for authentication to join the blockchain neighborship. With the public keys shared as part of the genesis block, every eNodeB in the blockchain neighborship is able to securely communicate with one another.

The source eNodeB passes on the genesis block to the UE.

3.2   Phase 2

The UE forwards its K_u along with T_1, and $\sigma(\{T_1, K_u\}, UE)$ to the source eNodeB. This message is regarded as the first transaction.

Upon receiving the message of the first transaction, Enb_s broadcasts the first transaction to all other eNodeBs in the blockchain neighborship with $\sigma(\{T_1, K_u\}, Enb_s)$. At this point, all eNodeBs are in possession of the UE's public key.

3.3   Phase 3

Upon receiving the first transaction from the Enb_s, the eNodeBs in the blockchain neighborship start mining. The SHA-256 hash function is iterated continuously until it finds a hash value that conforms to the predefined number of leading zeros. The variable input data, which are the nonce and timestamp, are altered at each iteration in order to find a conforming hash value.

The difficulty of finding a conforming hash value depends on the number of leading zeros. At the time of writing, the difficulty of a block in Bitcoin was 18 leading zeros in the hash value. Unlike the public blockchain used for Bitcoin, BKDF generates closed blockchains for authorized devices only. Therefore, the difficulty of proof-of-work should be lowered to reduce the computational overhead.

The first eNodeB to generate a SHA-256 hash value with the predefined number of zeros starts broadcasting the new block to all other eNodeBs in the blockchain neighborship. The first eNodeB to mine the next block is called the Miner eNodeB, Enb_m. The new block is also shared with the UE through the Enb_s. The proof-of work, $H(T_m, N_m, T_1, K_u, D_0, H_0)$, in the new block is used as K_{eNB*}.

After receiving the block, the UE and the eNodeBs are able to derive sessions keys based on K_{eNB*} for the next handover.

3.4   Phase 4

The UE sends a SYN message with T_{hsyn}, and the proof-of-work along with a digital signature to the Enb_t, which is chosen based on the measurement reports. The new target eNodeB sends back an ACK message with T_{hack} and the proof-of-work for the UE to confirm the handover.

3.5   Phase 5

The new target eNodeB sends S1 path switch request to the MME.

Likewise, the subsequent handovers begin with the UE repeating the same process from Phase 2 by sharing a timestamp and its public key with the new source eNodeB.

The message exchanges in BKDF is depicted in Fig. 1. The dotted lines represent the pre-handover phase, and the straight-lines represent the intra-handover phase.

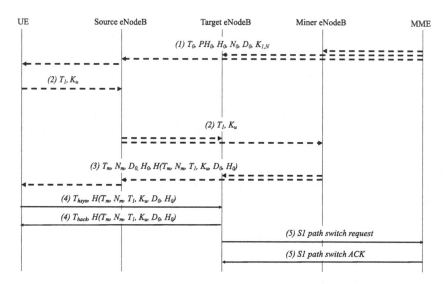

Fig. 1. Message exchanges in BKDF

4   Security Evaluation

4.1   Proof of Logic Correctness

The BAN logic [13] is used to prove the security objectives of BKDF. The BAN logic is one of the most widely used formal methods for analyzing authentication and key establishment protocols.

The BAN logic notations along with public key cryptography notations from [14] are summarized in Table 2.

Table 2. BAN logic and public key cryptography notations

$P \mid\equiv X$	P believes in X
$P \lhd X$	P sees X
$\#(X)$	X is fresh
$P =\!>X$	P has jurisdiction over X
$P \mid\sim X$	P once said X
$P \overset{k}{\leftrightarrow} Q$	P and Q use a shared key K
$\{X\}_k$	X has been encrypted with K
$PK\ (K,A)$	Principal A has a good public key K and a private key associated with it
$\prod(A)$	A has a good private key known to it only
$\sigma(X,A)$	X has been signed with private key belonging to A

The BAN rules are explained below to describe the results of logical constructs.

Message-Meaning Rules. P shares the secret key K with Q or P believes that K is Q's private key. If P receives a message that X encrypted with K, then P believes that Q has sent X.

Nonce-Verification Rule. If P believes that message X is fresh and believes that Q has sent X, then P believes that Q believes X.

Jurisdiction Rules. If P believes Q has sent message X, and P believes that Q believes X, then P believes X.

Signature Verification Rule. If P believes that Q has a good public key K and a good private key only known to Q, and P received X signed with private key of Q, P believes that Q has sent X.

Protocol Idealization. To enable derivation using the BAN logic, every step in the handover process needs to be converted into an idealized form. The notations are explained in Table 1.

m_1: $MME \rightarrow Enb_{1,N}$: $\{T_0, PH_0, H_0, N_0, D_0, K_{1,N}\}_{KMi}$
m_2: $Enb_s \rightarrow UE$: $\{T_0, PH_0, H_0, N_0, D_0, K_{1,N}\}_{Ksu}$
m_3: $UE \rightarrow Enb_s$: $\{T_1, K_u, \sigma(\{T_1, K_u\}, UE)\}_{Ksu}$
m_4: $Enb_s \rightarrow Enb_{1,N}$: $\{T_1, K_u, \sigma(\{T_1, K_u\}, Enb_s)\}_{Ks^{-1}}$

m_5: $Enb_m \rightarrow Enb_{1,N}$: $\{T_m, N_m, D_0, H_0, H(T_m, N_m, T_1, K_u, D_0, H_0)\}_{Km^{-1}}$

m_6: $Enb_s \rightarrow UE$: $\{T_m, N_m, D_0, H_0, H(T_m, N_m, T_1, K_u, D_0, H_0)\}_{Ksu}$

m_7: $UE \rightarrow Enb_t$: $\{T_{hsyn}, H(T_m, N_m, T_1, K_u, D_0, H_0), \sigma(\{T_{hsyn}, H(T_m, N_m, T_1, K_u, D_0, H_0)\}, UE)\}_{Ku^{-1}}$

m_8: $Enb_t \rightarrow UE$: $\{T_{hack}, H(T_m, N_m, T_1, K_u, D_0, H_0), \sigma(\{T_{hack}, H(T_m, N_m, T_1, K_u, D_0, H_0)\}, Enb_t)\}_{Kt^{-1}}$

Initial Assumptions. The initial assumptions provide the basis for logical analysis. The assumptions include information about what keys are shared, what keys are trusted under which circumstances, and what keys generate new values. The assumptions for BKDF are explained in Table 3.

Table 3. Assumptions for BAN Logic

A1: $Enb_i \models Enb_i \overset{K_{Mi}}{\longleftrightarrow} MME$;	A10: $Enb_i \models \prod (Enb_j)$;
A2: $Enb_i \models \# (T_0)$;	A11: $Enb_i \models \#(T_1)$;
A3: $UE \models Enb_s \overset{Ksu}{\longleftrightarrow} UE$	A12: $Enb_i \models \#(T_m)$;
A4: $Enb_s \models UE \overset{Ksu}{\longleftrightarrow} Enb_s$	A13: $Enb_m => H(T_m, N_m, T_1, K_u, D_0, H_0)$
A5: $UE \models \# (T_0)$;	A14: $UE \models \#(T_m)$;
A6: $Enb_i \models PK(K_u, UE)$;	A15: $Enb_s => H(T_m, N_m, T_1, K_u, D_0, H_0)$
A7: $Enb_i \models \prod (UE)$;	A16: $UE \models PK(K_i, Enb_i)$;
A8: $Enb_s \models \#(T_1)$;	A17: $UE \models \prod (Enb_j)$;
A9: $Enb_i \models PK(K_j, Enb_j)$;	A18: $Enb_t \models \#(T_{hsync})$;
	A19: $UE \models \#(T_{hack})$;

Protocol Goals. The final goal of BKDF is to agree on mutual authentication between the UE and Enb_t. Since the proof-of-work on each block is used as K_{eNB*}, it is important that both the UE and Enb_t believe in K_{eNB*}. The goals are expressed as follows;

Goal 1: $Enb_t \models H(T_m, N_m, T_1, K_u, D_0, H_0)$
Goal 2: $UE \models H(T_m, N_m, T_1, K_u, D_0, H_0)$
Goal 3: $Enb_t \models UE \models H(T_m, N_m, T_1, K_u, D_0, H_0)$
Goal 4: $UE \models Enb_t \models H(T_m, N_m, T_1, K_u, D_0, H_0)$

Protocol Annotations and Target Derivations. By the message-meaning rule based on A1 and m_1,

s_1: $Enb_i \models MME | \sim <T_0, PH_0, H_0, N_0, D_0, K_{1,N}>$

By the nonce-verification rule based on s_1 and A2,

s_2: $Enb_i \models MME |\equiv <T_0, PH_0, H_0, N_0, D_0, K_{1,N}>$

By the message meaning rule based on A3 and m_2,

s_3: $UE \models Enb_s | \sim <T_0, PH_0, H_0, N_0, D_0, K_{1,N}>$

By the nonce verification rule based on s_3, A5,

s_4: $UE \mathrel{|\!\!\equiv} Enb_s \mathrel{|\!\!\equiv} <T_0, PH_0, H_0, N_0, D_0, K_{1,N}>$

By the signature verification rule based on A6 and A7 along with the message-meaning rule based on A4 and m_3,

s_5: $Enb_s \mathrel{|\!\!\equiv} UE \mathrel{|}\sim <T_1, K_u>$

By the nonce-verification rule based on s_5 and A8,

s_6: $Enb_s \mathrel{|\!\!\equiv} UE \mathrel{|\!\!\equiv} <T_1, K_u>$

By the signature verification rule and the message-meaning rule based on A9, A10 and m_4,

s_9: $Enb_i \mathrel{|\!\!\equiv} Enb_s \mathrel{|}\sim <T_1, K_u>$

By the nonce-verification rule based on s_9 and A11,

s_{10}: $Enb_i \mathrel{|\!\!\equiv} Enb_s \mathrel{|\!\!\equiv} <T_1, K_u>$

By the message-meaning rule based on A9, A10 and m_5,

s_{11}: $Enb_i \mathrel{|\!\!\equiv} Enb_m \mathrel{|}\sim <T_m, N_m, D_0, H_0, H(T_m, N_m, T_1, K_u, D_0, H_0)>$

By the nonce-verification rule based on s_{11} and A12,

s_{12}: $Enb_i \mathrel{|\!\!\equiv} Enb_m \mathrel{|\!\!\equiv} <T_m, N_m, D_0, H_0, H(T_m, N_m, T_1, K_u, D_0, H_0)>$

By the jurisdiction rule based on s_{12} and A13, the following statement proves Goal 1.

s_{13}: $Enb_i \mathrel{|\!\!\equiv} H(T_m, N_m, T_1, K_u, D_0, H_0)$

By the message-meaning rule based on A3 and m_6,

s_{14}: $UE \mathrel{|\!\!\equiv} Enb_s \mathrel{|}\sim <T_m, N_m, D_0, H_0, H(T_m, N_m, T_1, K_u, D_0, H_0)>$

By the nonce-verification rule based on s_{14} and A14,

s_{15}: $UE \mathrel{|\!\!\equiv} Enb_s \mathrel{|\!\!\equiv} <T_m, N_m, D_0, H_0, H(T_m, N_m, T_1, K_u, D_0, H_0)>$

By the jurisdiction rule based on s_{15} and A15, the following statement proves Goal 2.

s_{16}: $UE \mathrel{|\!\!\equiv} H(T_m, N_m, T_1, K_u, D_0, H_0)$

By the signature verification rule and the message-meaning rule based on A6, A7 and m_7,

s_{17}: $Enb_t \mathrel{|\!\!\equiv} UE \mathrel{|}\sim <T_{hsyn}, H(T_m, N_m, T_1, K_u, D_0, H_0)>$

By the nonce-verification rule based on s_{17} and A18, the following statement proves Goal 3.

s_{18}: $Enb_t \mathrel{|\!\!\equiv} UE \mathrel{|\!\!\equiv} H(T_m, N_m, T_1, K_u, D_0, H_0)$

By the signature verification rule and the message-meaning rule based on A16, A17 and m_8,

s_{19}: $UE \mathrel{|\!\!\equiv} Enb_t \mathrel{|}\sim <T_{hack}, H(T_m, N_m, T_1, K_u, D_0, H_0)>$

By the nonce-verification rule based on s_{19} and A19, the following statement proves Goal 4.

s_{20}: $UE \mathrel{|\!\!\equiv} Enb_t \mathrel{|\!\!\equiv} H(T_m, N_m, T_1, K_u, D_0, H_0)$

4.2 Ability Against Malicious Attacks

As proven with the BAN logic, BKDF is secure when it comes to key establishment in handover. There are additional measures put in place to ensure the validity of the information shared between the eNodeBs. The transactions are only valid when initiated and signed by a known source. In Phase 1 of BKDF, each eNodeB learns of the identities of other eNodeBs from the genesis block, which contains the public keys of the eNodeBs. In Phase 2, the transaction messages are all signed by the private keys of the senders, which can only be decrypted by the corresponding public keys. Therefore, it is clear from the beginning who are the legitimate receivers and senders.

There is also another mechanism, deployed to check the validity of the blocks. In Phase 3, each eNodeB checks the validity of the proof-of-work on the received block by recalculating SHA-256 with the same inputs from the received block. If the same hash value is generated from recalculation, the eNodeB agrees that no information was tampered in the block. The same vetting process is done on the received block by the UE as well.

Lastly, a blockchain associated with a UE only lasts until the UE stays within the domain of MME. When the UE associates with another MME, a new blockchain is generated by the eNodeBs of the new MME.

Man-in-the-Middle Attack. In a man-in-the-middle attack, the attacker secretly eavesdrops and changes the message exchanges between two parties who believe they are in direct communication. With BKDF, the attacker would not be able to make changes to any message between the UE and eNodeB, even if the session key has been cracked. It is because the messages between the UE and eNodeB are either digitally signed with their private keys or vetted with SHA-256 recalculation. Any discrepancy would not go unnoticed.

Spoofing Attack. In a spoofing attack, the attacker would disguise as a UE who has already been authenticated with the network. With BKDF, it is impossible to imper-sonate any of the UEs, because each UE has a unique pseudo-identity, and only one blockchain is created per UE. Therefore, a new UE with the exact same pseudo-identity would be detected.

Desynchronization Attack. One good example of network interruption is a desyn-chronization attack that interrupts the handover process by manipulating the Next Hop Chaining Counter (NCC) value from the MME [15]. Regardless of the level of security imposed by encryption on the LTE network, a compromised eNodeB can interrupt handover by sending an extremely high NCC value, which deters the UE and the target eNodeB to undergo a vertical key derivation, but to stay with horizontal handover with K_{eNB} instead.

Since BKDF is using a blockchain to derive keys without any involvement of the MME in the process, this attack is no longer a threat.

Rogue Base Station. Rogue base stations are unlicensed base stations that are not owned and operated by an authentic MNO [16]. They broadcast a cellular network masquerading as a legitimate carrier network.

There are a few ways to detect whether the base station is rogue or not with BKDF. The genesis block acts as the root of trust between the eNodeBs in a blockchain neighborship, because the contents of the genesis block are verified upon joining the blockchain neighborship. If an eNodeB sends a request to join a blockchain neigh-borship with a different genesis block from the existing eNodeBs in the blockchain neighborship, the request is rejected.

There is an extreme case where an attacker would possibly plant an exact duplicate of a compromised eNodeB outside the blockchain neighborship. In this case, it is plausible that a UE would be fooled into associating with the rogue eNodeB, since the rogue eNodeB would have the same genesis block and session keys. However, the handover would not be seamless and the current IP sessions on the UE would break, because the rogue eNodeB would be part of a completely different network. At this point, the UE can easily guess that the supposedly target eNodeB is not legitimate.

5   Performance Evaluation

The large portion of the benefits using BKDF comes from the fact that it allows the eNodeBs and UE to be ready with K_{eNB*} before the handover process is triggered, whereas the current LTE systems starts key derivation for K_{eNB*} after the handover process has begun. Since the UE and target eNodeB have the next handover key prepared with BKDF before the handover process begins, the UE is able to initiate handover and make a direct contact with the target eNodeB. Therefore, the handover process with BKDF simplifies the message flow and wastes no time for key derivation.

Performance evaluation was conducted with a computer equipped with Intel Core i7 2.2 GHz and 8 GB DRAM. The simulation application was written with JavaScript with a cryptography library called crypto-js. The cryptography library was used to simulate the latency caused by SHA-256 and HMAC-SHA-256. The current LTE system currently uses HMAC-SHA-256 to derive K_{eNB*}, whereas BKDF uses block-chain as a key derivation function which is based on SHA-256.

Computational costs attributed to key derivation were measured in two different phases; pre-handover and intra-handover. BKDF was tested for 1 leading zero to 3 leading zeros to demonstrate the time it took on average to find a hash value that meets the difficulty condition. The current LTE system was tested for key derivation with HMAC-SHA-256. To add computational burdens, the concurrent number of UEs was increased from 1 to 40.

As observed in Table 4, BKDF performs heavy cryptographic operations required for key derivation in the pre-handover phase, while no key derivation in LTE is conducted during the same time. To prevent any handover being triggered while the key is being derived in the pre-handover phase, the eNodeBs need to be carefully deployed with enough space between them. Figure 2 provides some insight into the minimum distance required between two base stations running BKDF for different speeds of UE.

As shown in Table 5 for the intra-handover phase, BKDF does not require cryptographic operations for key derivation, whereas LTE struggles to derive the key. Depicted in Fig. 3, the percentage of packet loss attributed to key derivation in the intra-handover phase clearly shows the superiority of BKDF for link performance and stability compared to LTE.

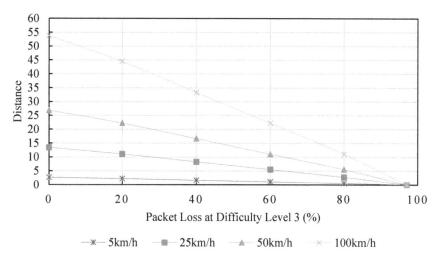

Fig. 2. Packet loss due to the distance between two base stations

Table 4. Pre-handover computational cost

UE	BKFD (ms)			LTE (ms)
	Difficulty level			
	1	2	3	
1	4.55	9.67	60.12	0
10	19.28	39.37	243.33	
20	51.08	101.20	484.03	
30	62.16	163.46	738.80	
40	79.68	217.58	968.55	

Table 5. Intra-handover computational cost

UE	BKFD (ms)			LTE (ms)
	Difficulty level			
	1	2	3	
1	0			0.29
10				2.98
20				5.97
30				8.95
40				11.92

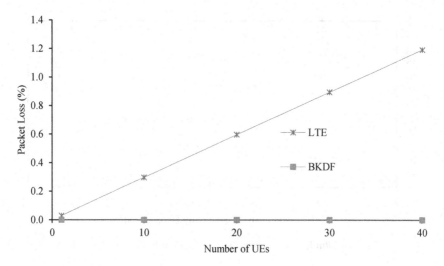

Fig. 3. Packet loss attributed to key derivation in the intra-handover phase

6 Conclusion

Many other researches in the past were focused on reducing the number of handovers in an effort to reduce the average total latency. This paper took a different approach from the previous researches and suggested a method to enhance the handover security and performance by modifying the key derivation mechanism with blockchain. BKDF has increased the level of security for key management, which allowed more aggressive key sharing between the eNodeBs and UE to proactively prepare the keys before the handover process begins.

BKDF not only improves how LTE works, but also clearly paints the way to enjoy the potential of blockchain for mobile communication. With 5G right around the corner, BKDF would be a solution to reduce the handover latency caused by massive densification of cells.

Acknowledgments. We appreciate the financial support from Ministry of Education, Singapore through the Academic Research Fund (AcRF) Tier 1 for the project of 2018-T1-001-092.

References

1. Duan, X., Wang, X.: Fast authentication in 5G HetNet through SDN enabled weighted secure-context-information transfer. In: IEEE ICC 2016 Communication and Information Systems Security Symposium (2016)
2. Duan, X., Wang, X.: Authentication handover and privacy protection in 5G HetNets using software-defined networking. IEEE Commun. Mag. **53**(4), 28–35 (2015)
3. Tesema, F.B., Awada, A., Viering, I., Simsek, M., Fettweis, G.P.: Fast cell select for mobility robustness in intra-frequency 5G ultra dense networks. In: IEEE 27th Annual International Symposium on Personal, Indoor and Mobile Radio Communications, pp. 1–7 (2016)

4. Arshad, R., et al.: Handover management in 5G and beyond : a topology aware skipping approach. IEEE Access **4**, 9073–9081 (2017)
5. Habbal, A., Member, S., Goudar, S.I., Hassan, S., Member, S.: Context-aware radio access technology selection in 5G ultra dense networks. IEEE Access **14**(8), 1–13 (2017)
6. Wang, X., et al.: Handover reduction in virtualized cloud radio access networks using TWDM-PON fronthaul. J. Opt. Soc. Am. **8**(12), 124–134 (2016)
7. Jung, M.Y., Jang, J.W.: Data management and searching system and method to provide increased security for IoT platform. In: International Conference on Information and Communication Technology. ICT Convergence Technologies Leading the Fourth Industrial Revolution, ICTC 2017, December 2017, pp. 873–878 (2017)
8. Ram Basnet, S., Shakya, S.: BSS: blockchain security over software defined network. In: IEEE ICCCA, pp. 720–725 (2017)
9. Huh, S., Cho, S., Kim, S.: Managing IoT devices using blockchain platform. In: International Conference on Advanced Communication Technology, ICACT, pp. 464–467 (2017)
10. Nakamoto, S.: Bitcoin: A Peer-to-Peer Electronic Cash System (2008)
11. Rao, V.S., Gajula, R.: Interoperable UE Handovers in LTE. Radysis (2011)
12. Secp256k1. https://en.bitcoin.it/wiki/Secp256k1. Accessed 02 May 2018
13. Guo, N.A.N., Wang, X.: An anonymous authentication scheme based on PMIPv6 for VANETs. IEEE Access **6**, 14686–14698 (2018)
14. Jawad Alam, M., Ma, M.: DC and CoMP authentication in LTE-advanced 5G HetNet. In: Proceedings of IEEE Global Communications Conference, GLOBECOM 2017, January 2018, pp. 1–6 (2018)
15. Han, C.K., Choi, H.K.: Security analysis of handover key management in 4G LTE/SAE networks. IEEE Trans. Mob. Comput. **13**(2), 457–468 (2014)
16. Cichonski, J., Franklin, J.M., Bartock, M.: Guide to LTE Security. NIST Special Publication 800-187 (2018)

EPT: EDNS Privacy Tunnel for DNS

Lanlan Pan[1($\boxtimes$)], Jie Chen[1], Anlei Hu[2], and Xuebiao Yuchi[3]

[1] Geely Automobile Research Institute, Hangzhou 315336, Zhejiang, China
abbypan@gmail.com
[2] China Internet Network Information Center, Beijing 100190, China
[3] Chinese Academy of Sciences, Beijing 100190, China

Abstract. DNS privacy concerns are growing. Recursive resolvers such as ISP DNS and Google Public DNS are serving massive clients, which could fingerprint individual users and analysis the domain interest of users easily. In order to mitigate user privacy leaks on recursive resolvers, in this paper we propose an EDNS privacy tunnel (EPT) extension for DNS. EPT can hide the query domain name from recursive resolvers through public key encryption, avoid big data analysis on individual users, defense against censorship and lying recursive resolvers.

Keywords: DNS · Privacy · Censorship · Hijack · ECS · EPT

1 Introduction

Individual user privacy is raising global attention nowadays. Domain name system (DNS) is a critical internet service, however, it is weak at the privacy protection for individual users.

Figure 1 shows an example of default DNS traffic flow. As a domain query agent for the client, recursive resolver knows about the client's IP address (client IP), the query domain name (qname) and the response data (answer). Obviously, recursive resolver could fingerprint individual users and analysis the domain interest of individual users easily [1–3].

Public recursive resolvers such as Google Public DNS and OpenDNS are not close enough to many users since they couldn't deploy servers among each country and each ISP's network. To bring the web content as close to the users as possible, Google proposes an EDNS client subnet (ECS) extension to carry part of the client's IP address in the DNS packets for authoritative nameserver [4]. As Fig. 2 shows, ECS leaks client subnet information on the resolution path to the authoritative servers. ECS raises individual user's privacy concerns, makes DNS communications less private, and the potential for massive surveillance is greater [5].

Therefore, it is important to design a suitable individual user privacy preservation mechanism, especially to defense in-path censorship such as recursive resolver's individual user fingerprinting and lying response. In this paper, we introduce an EDNS privacy tunnel (EPT) extension to address the problem. EPT takes advantage of the public key encryption to hide the query domain from recursive resolvers, defense

G. Wang et al. (Eds.): SpaCCS 2019, LNCS 11611, pp. 50–62, 2019.
https://doi.org/10.1007/978-3-030-24907-6_5

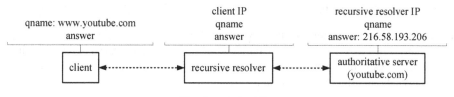

Fig. 1. DNS traffic.

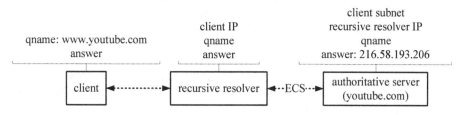

Fig. 2. DNS traffic with ECS Extension.

against censorship and lying recursive resolvers, improve individual user privacy on DNS traffic effectively.

The remainder of this paper is organized as follows. In Sect. 2, we give a brief overview of existing DNS privacy protection technologies. In Sect. 3, we describe the EPT extension in detail. From Sects. 4 to 6, we discuss privacy improvement, concerns about security and operation. In Sect. 7, we show our experiment. Finally, in Sect. 8, we conclude the paper.

2   DNS Privacy Protection Technologies

As Fig. 3 shows, existing DNS privacy protection technologies are hard to provide user privacy protection on recursive resolvers that support ECS.

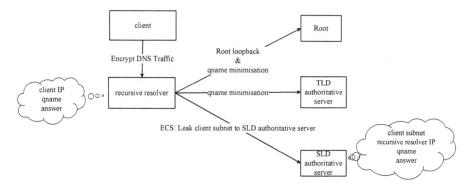

Fig. 3. DNS privacy leak.

- Encrypting DNS Traffic

DNS traffic encrypt solutions such as DNS over TLS [6], DNS over DTLS [7], DNSCurve [8], DNSCrypt [9] and Confidential DNS [10] can prevent eavesdropping on the DNS resolution path. However, none of these solutions are workable for individual user de-identification on recursive resolver.

- Reducing Information Leakage to DNS Server

Root loopback [11] and qname minimization [12] can hide domain query information from Root and TLD, while they are not designed for reducing client subnet information leakage on recursive resolver and authoritative server.

- EncDNS

EncDNS [13] encapsulates encrypted messages in standards-compliant DNS messages, which is a lightweight privacy-preserving name resolution service compared to conventional third-party resolvers. EncDNS encapsulates encrypted queries within the question name field of a standard DNS query in binary form. Encrypted replies are encapsulated within the data section of a TXT resource record. Therefore, compared with normal DNS packets, EncDNS packets may encounter some problem to bypass middleboxes such as firewall and IDS. Another privacy concern is that EncDNS server can track the activities of a client if the client uses the same key pair in multiple EncDNS queries.

- ODNS

ODNS [14] architecture is similar with EncDNS, it uses ODNS resolver's public key to encrypt a symmetric session key. The session key is responsible for encrypt query domain, and decrypt the OPT record of the response. The problem of ODNS is mostly on operational. Recursive resolvers should support forwarding EDNS query, and they never remove specific response packets without A record but contains OPT record. The firewalls on the whole resolution path never drop the specific response package.

3   EDNS Privacy Tunnel (EPT) Extension

EDNS privacy tunnel (EPT) is an EDNS extension [15], resolution path is similar with EncDNS and ODNS, while deployment is similar with DNSCrypt.

EPT can be added into DNS queries sent by local forwarding resolvers. EPT is only defined for the Internet (IN) DNS class and the qtype is A or AAAA.

3.1   Structure

EPT is structured as follows:

- **OPTION-CODE**, 2 octets, defined in RFC6891. It should be assigned by the IANA.

- **OPTION-LENGTH**, 2 octets, defined in RFC6891, contains the length of the payload (everything after OPTION-LENGTH) in octets.
- **Payload**, contains encrypted <qname, xor_IP, salt> information. qname is the original query domain, xor_IP is a random generated IP, salt is a random generate string for encryption.

All fields of EPT are in network byte order (Fig. 4).

Fig. 4. EPT structure.

3.2 Resolution

Similar with EncDNS, there is a special-use second level domain "myept.com" (EPT_SLD) for EPT. EPT authoritative server of "myept.com" is responsible for analyzing the EPT query and packing the EPT response.

EPT authoritative server selects an asymmetric cryptography algorithm such as RSA, and generates a pair of public key (K_{pub}) and private key (K_{priv}) of the selected algorithm for asymmetrical encryption of EPT tunnel data. As Table 1 shows, the information of the public key can be published as a TXT RR of "myept.com".

Table 1. RSA example of EPT public key information.

TXT RR of EPT_SLD myept.com
myept.com. 3600 IN TXT "EPT=RSA1024 https://file.myept.com/ept_public_key.pem"

As Table 2 shows, EPT client can get the EPT public key file through the file URL. The format of public key file follows IETF Public-Key Cryptography Standards (PKCS). EPT authoritative server should update new key pairs at regular intervals, offer the public key. EPT client should update the latest public key of EPT authoritative server through TXT record query timely.

Figure 5 shows the overview of EPT resolution. The steps of EPT resolution are detailed as follows:

Table 2. Example of EPT public key file content.

https://file.myept.com/ept_public_key.pem
-----BEGIN PUBLIC KEY-----
MIGfMA0GCSqGSIb3DQEBAQUAA4GNADCBiQKBgQDK6TS3kY6T2mDgAijP/1k4+Tsa
QCAwmu32pNCNDP86X9W9gbWC86fO1QuVIr2PhXUExktQSMJUbTe4lQM6K7QZXXrE
xfqinWNEFyib2X9g65eRKAROrMUBk2Vy+SwaHNKWu0H1kLv8cWNxKZ4lG/9pm7mX
qr39XqTzCnpjwc2sgwIDAQAB
-----END PUBLIC KEY-----

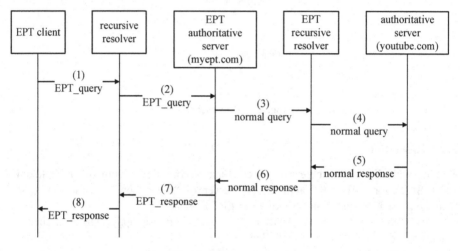

Fig. 5. EPT resolution.

(1) EPT client wants to query {qname: "www.youtube.com", qtype: "A"}. EPT client generates random xor_IP and random salt string, then encrypts <qname, xor_IP, salt> with K_{pub} as EPT_payload, and a md5 hash EPT_qname.

$$xor\_IP = \text{"202.38.64.10"}$$

$$s = join(\text{","}, qname, xor\_IP, salt)$$

$$EPT\_payload = Asymmetrical\_Encrypt(K_{pub}, s)$$

$$EPT\_SLD = \text{"myept. com"}$$

$$EPT\_qname = join(\text{"."}, md5\_hex(s), EPT\_SLD)$$

EPT client sends an EPT query {qname: EPT_qname, qtype: "A", additional: EPT_payload} to recursive resolver. The recursive resolver should support RFC6891 and forward the query with EPT_payload.

(2) Recursive resolver sends the above EPT query to the EPT authoritative server.

(3) EPT authoritative server decrypts the EPT_payload with K_{priv}, extracts the <qname, xor_IP, salt> information.

$$s = Asymmetrical\_Decrypt(K_{priv}, EPT\_payload)$$

$$(qname, xor\_IP, salt) = split(",", s)$$

EPT authoritative server sends a normal query {qname: "www.youtube.com", qtype: "A"} to EPT recursive resolver.

(4) EPT recursive resolver sends the above normal query to authoritative server of "www.youtube.com".

(5) Authoritative server of "www.youtube.com" returns a normal response {qname: "www.youtube.com", qtype: "A", answer: "216.58.193.206"} to EPT recursive resolver.

(6) EPT recursive resolver forwards the normal response to EPT authoritative server.

(7) EPT authoritative server calculates the EPT_answer from the answer of normal response and xor_IP, then builds up the EPT_response {qname: EPT_domain, qtype: "A", answer: EPT_answer, additional: EPT_payload}. EPT authoritative server sends the EPT_response to recursive resolver.

$$EPT\_answer = xor(answer, xor\_IP) = "18.28.129.196"$$

(8) Recursive resolver sends the EPT_response to EPT client. EPT client recovers the answer.

$$answer = xor(EPT\_answer, xor\_IP) = "216.58.193.206"$$

4 Privacy Improvement

Figure 6 shows an example of EPT traffic flow.

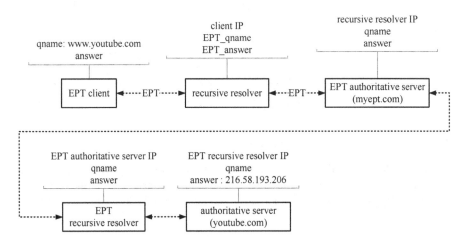

Fig. 6. DNS traffic with EPT extension.

4.1   Hiding Qname and Answer from Recursive Resolver

As a domain query agent for clients, some recursive resolver shares queries log with third-parties in ways not known or obvious to end-users. With EPT extension, recursive resolver knows about the client's IP address (client IP), the EPT query domain name (EPT_qname) and the EPT response data (EPT_answer). However, recursive resolver can't know the query domain name (qname) and the response data (answer). Therefore, compare with Figs. 1 and 2, recursive resolver could not analysis the domain interest of users because of it lacks the information about qname and answer.

4.2   Mitigating Client Subnet Leakage to Authoritative Server

As Fig. 2 shows, ECS extension leaks the client subnet information to authoritative server, the domain query action become personally identifiable. With EPT extension, authoritative server only knows about EPT recursive resolver IP, the query domain name (qname) and the response data (answer). Therefore, compare with Fig. 2, authoritative server could not analysis the domain interest of users because of it lacks the client subnet information.

4.3   Privacy Preservation on EPT Failure Traffic

To make EPT extension work, the recursive resolver should support RFC6891 EDNS extension, and forward the EPT_query packet to EPT authoritative server. However, as Fig. 7 shows, some recursive resolver may replace the EPT extension with ECS, cause a failed query to EPT authoritative server. In this case, EPT authoritative server knows about the client's IP address (client IP), the EPT query domain name (EPT_qname), but it can't know about the query domain name (qname) to generate a normal query. Therefore, EPT authoritative server could not analysis the domain interest of users because of it lacks the information about qname.

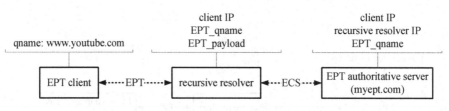

Fig. 7. EPT failure traffic.

4.4   Combating Targeted Censorship

On default DNS traffic flow, recursive resolver is easy to make targeted client censorship. Even worse, it is fragile to targeted client subnet censorship on the resolution path from recursive resolver to authoritative server when recursive resolver sends the ECS query.

Since EPT hide the qname from recursive resolver and hide the client subnet from authoritative server, EPT will be stronger to defense against the targeted DNS censorship attack. EPT can help to avoid getting lie response on special domain from recursive resolver, and add difficulty on target censorship by the AS-level adversary. If EPT_answer is banned by recursive resolver casually, client can simply generate a new EPT query with different xor_IP and salt to address the problem.

4.5   Anonymous

Compared to VPN and Tor, EPT is focus on preserving the end user privacy on DNS traffic.

On VPN communication scenario, the DNS traffic of each end user is in plain-text to VPN service provider. On the contrary, EPT service provider can't know about end user's DNS queries.

Even in the Tor anonymity network, an AS-level adversary can monitor egress traffic between the exit relay and exit relay's DNS resolver, or the DNS resolver itself [16]. Tor end user can't control the exit relay's DNS resolver configuration because of the multiple anonymity hops relay. However, EPT end user can easily change in the EPT service set, send the EPT query through VPN, the AS-level adversary will be hard to figure out the exact exit relay like Tor.

5   Security

5.1   Hijack

Plain text DNS traffic is naturally in risk of hijacking. The defense capability to hijack depends on the global deployment of DNS traffic encryption and DNSSEC.

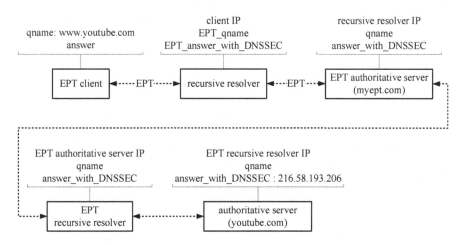

Fig. 8. EPT with DNS over TLS and DNSSEC.

As Fig. 8 shows, EPT is fully compatible with DNS over TLS and DNSSEC.

- DNS over TLS can be deployed at every resolution path on the EPT query chain.
- Suppose that EPT recursive resolver and authoritative server have enabled DNSSEC, EPT authoritative server can make the qname query with DNSSEC option, and validate the DNSSEC answer of qname which is generated by authoritative server.
- Suppose that recursive resolver has enabled DNSSEC, EPT client can make the EPT_qname query with DNSSEC option, and validate the DNSSEC answer of EPT_qname which is generated by EPT authoritative server.

5.2 DDoS Attack

Similar with pseudo-random sub-domain attack, recursive resolver and EPT authoritative server may encounter error EPT_payload with some random error string. Since recursive resolver doesn't have enough information to find out the correct EPT_payload, it may directly drop the EPT_query flood in case it could not afford the attack. EPT authoritative server may decrypt a lot of error EPT_payload, exhausting CPU.

To mitigate the DDoS attack influence more effectively, recursive resolver and EPT authoritative server can only accept an EPT_query which is from encrypt connection, or from TCP connection. They can also deploy some response rate limitation policy on the query source IP. EPT authoritative server should set short TTL for EPT_response. Further, as Table 1 shows, recursive resolver doesn't need to cache EPT_response if it finds the EPT TXT record of EPT_SLD.

6 Operation

6.1 Deployment

The key point of EPT is to separate client IP and qname information. Therefore, recursive resolver and EPT authoritative server should not share query log with each other. Otherwise, they could spell out the <client, qname, answer> privacy elements. Similar, recursive resolver and EPT recursive resolver should not share query log with each other.

EPT recursive resolver can enable qname minimisation [12] to prevent the qname leakage to the Root and TLD server.

EPT deployment on the client side is similar with DNSCrypt [9]. Client should install an EPT proxy resolver on local machine. EPT proxy resolver is responsible to make a control on the local DNS traffic, encrypt selective normal query to EPT_query, decrypt EPT_response to normal answer. EPT proxy resolver can configure multiple EPT authoritative servers.

6.2 Cache Size of Recursive Resolver

EPT_queries behave similar on recursive resolver to disposable domain. Disposable domains are likely generated automatically, characterized by a "one-time use" pattern, and appear to be used as a way of "signaling" via DNS queries [17].

Basically, recursive resolver can use traditional cache aging heuristic policy to deal with the EPT_response cache issue. Besides, recursive resolver can also make some more optimization, as described in [17].

Further, as Fig. 9 shows, to reduce cache size, recursive resolver could remove the EPT extension of EPT_response packet. As the EPT_qname is generated by md5 hash function, the probability of EPT_qname collision is very low.

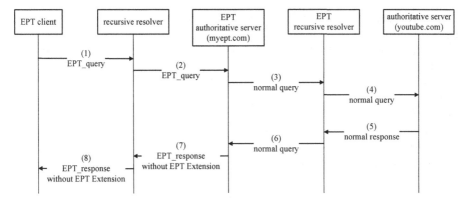

Fig. 9. EPT response without EPT extension.

To lighten the burden of EPT authoritative server, EPT extension is optional in EPT_response packet. EPT client must record the <EPT_qname, xor_IP> information to retrieve response from the EPT_response packet without EPT extension. EPT_response without EPT extension is almost the same with normal response. Therefore, it won't trigger the drop policy for the abnormal response packets without A record on recursive resolver, and it will be very easy to bypass middleboxes such as firewall and IDS.

6.3 Response Latency

Every EPT_qname will encounter cache miss on recursive resolver. Therefore, recursive resolver should forward each EPT_query to EPT authoritative server. Response latency will rise, since there will be additional latency on the <recursive resolver, EPT authoritative server, EPT recursive resolver> resolution path. If the common additional latency is less than 100 ms, it is acceptable for many privacy sensitive users.

Moreover, to reduce response latency, EPT authoritative server can act the role of EPT recursive resolver, communicate with authoritative server directly.

7 Experiment

Our experiment code can be found in [18].

The compatibility issue of EPT extension is that recursive resolver should support RFC6891. The EPT extension is mandatory in EPT_query packet, recursive resolver should send the EPT_query packet to EPT authoritative server without any modification.

Table 3 shows our EDNS support test on some famous public recursive resolvers. Public recursive resolvers may send some modified queries to EPT authoritative server when they receive the EPT_query.

Table 3. EDNS support on public recursive resolvers.

Recursive resolver	UDP+EDNS (Payload size)	UDP	TCP+EDNS (Payload size)	ECS
GoogleDNS (8.8.8.8)	Y (4096)	Y	N	Y
Quad9 (9.9.9.9)	Y (1680)	N	N	N
Cloudflare (1.1.1.1)	Y (1452)	N	Y (1452)	N
OpenDNS (208.67.222.222)	Y (1280)	Y	N	N
VerisignDNS (64.6.64.6)	Y (1280)	Y	N	N
114DNS (114.114.114.114)	Y (4096, 512)	Y	N	N
AliDNS (223.5.5.5)	Y (512)	Y	N	N

- All of them remove the EPT extension from original EPT_query, then send a UDP query with zero EDNS data length for the EPT_qname, just indicate the EDNS payload size they can support. VerisignDNS is more special, it changes uppercase and lowercase characters of EPT_qname and send the UDP EDNS queries for these modified qnames.
- Except Quad9 and Cloudflare, most of them will send a UDP query without EDNS extension for the EPT_qname.
- Only Cloudflare will try to send TCP queries with zero EDNS data length for the EPT_qname.
- Only GoogleDNS will send UDP ECS queries for the EPT_qname, it will undermine privacy protection of EPT extension because EPT authoritative server will know about the client subnet information for specific qname.

As the length of EPT_qname is hash fixed, EPT doesn't have the qname length problem as ODNS [14].

EPT authoritative sever can choose many popular asymmetric cryptography algorithms. Most of the time, the length of <qname, xor_IP, salt> will less than 256 bytes, and RSA2048 is workable. Except RSA, as Table 4 shows, Elliptic Curve Integrated Encryption Scheme (ECIES) can be another choice for the encryption on longer < qname, xor_IP, salt> [19].

Table 4. ECIES Example of EPT Public Key Information.

TXT RR of EPT_SLD myept.com
myept.com. 3600 IN TXT "EPT=ECIES,Curve:secp256k1,KDF:PBKDF2,Symmetric:AES-256-GCM,MAC:HMAC-SHA256 https://file.myept.com/ept_public_key.pem"

8 Conclusion

This paper is an extended version of an earlier poster paper presented at the IEEE Trustcom 2018 [20]. Plain text DNS traffic is weak at user privacy protection. Clients are hard to avoid recursive resolver's big data analysis on query log, not to mention censorship and lies without DNSSEC support. User privacy protection requires additional costs. EPT is to defense against user domain interest censorship and avoid selective domain hijack. EPT can provide end-user privacy enhancement on recursive resolver and authoritative server. The biggest reality problem of EPT deployment is the support of existed recursive resolvers. We plan to deploy the EPT into real world DNS traffic in the future.

References

1. Imana, B., Korolova, A., Heidemann, J.: Enumerating privacy leaks in DNS data collected above the recursive. In NDSS: DNS Privacy Workshop, February 2018
2. Siby, S., Juarez, M., Vallina-Rodriguez, N., Troncoso, C.: DNS Privacy not so private: the traffic analysis perspective (2018)
3. Bradshaw, S., DeNardis, L.: Privacy by infrastructure: the unresolved case of the domain name system. Policy Internet 11(1), 16–36 (2019)
4. Contavalli, C., van der Gaast, W., Lawrence, D., Kumari, W.: Client Subnet in DNS Queries. RFC7871 (2016)
5. Kintis, P., Nadji, Y., Dagon, D., Farrell, M., Antonakakis, M.: Understanding the privacy implications of ECS. In: Caballero, J., Zurutuza, U., Rodríguez, R.J. (eds.) DIMVA 2016. LNCS, vol. 9721, pp. 343–353. Springer, Cham (2016). https://doi.org/10.1007/978-3-319-40667-1_17
6. Hu, Z., et al.: Specification for DNS over Transport Layer Security (TLS). RFC 7858 (2016)
7. Reddy, T., Wing, D., Patil, P.: DNS over Datagram Transport Layer Security (DTLS). No. RFC 8094 (2017)
8. Dempsky, M.: DNSCurve: link-level security for the domain name system. Work in Progress, draft-dempsky-dnscurve-01 (2010)
9. DNSCrypt. https://dnscrypt.org/
10. Wijngaards, W., Wiley, G.: Confidential DNS. IETF Draft (2015). https://tools.ietf.org/html/draft-wijngaards-dnsop-confidentialdns-03
11. Kumari, W., Hoffman, P.: Decreasing Access Time to Root Servers by Running One on Loopback. RFC 7706 (2015)
12. Bortzmeyer, S.: DNS Query Name Minimisation to Improve Privacy. RFC7816 (2016)
13. Herrmann, D., Fuchs, K.-P., Lindemann, J., Federrath, H.: EncDNS: a lightweight privacy-preserving name resolution service. In: Kutyłowski, M., Vaidya, J. (eds.) ESORICS 2014. LNCS, vol. 8712, pp. 37–55. Springer, Cham (2014). https://doi.org/10.1007/978-3-319-11203-9_3
14. Schmitt, P., Edmundson, A., Feamster, N.: Oblivious DNS: practical privacy for DNS queries. arXiv preprint arXiv:1806.00276 (2018)
15. Damas, J., Graff, M., Vixie, P.: Extension mechanisms for DNS (EDNS (0)). RFC 6891 (2013)
16. Greschbach, B., Pulls, T., Roberts, L.M., Winter, P., Feamster, N.: The Effect of DNS on Tor's Anonymity. arXiv preprint arXiv:1609.08187 (2016)

17. Chen, Y., Antonakakis, M., Perdisci, R., Nadji, Y., Dagon, D., Lee, W.: DNS noise: measuring the pervasiveness of disposable domains in modern DNS traffic. In: 44th Annual IEEE/IFIP International Conference on Dependable Systems and Networks (DSN), pp. 598–609. IEEE, June 2014
18. dns_test_ept. https://github.com/abbypan/dns_test_ept
19. Martínez, V.G., Encinas, L.H.: A comparison of the standardized versions of ECIES. In: Sixth International Conference on Information Assurance and Security (IAS), pp. 1–4. IEEE, August 2010
20. Pan, L., Yuchi, X., Wang, J., Hu, A.: A public key based EDNS privacy tunnel for DNS. In: 17th IEEE International Conference on Trust, Security and Privacy in Computing and Communications/12th IEEE International Conference on Big Data Science and Engineering (TrustCom/BigDataSE), pp. 1722–1724. IEEE, August 2018

Ensuring Data Integrity in Fog Computing Based Health-Care Systems

Abdulwahab Alazeb$^{(\boxtimes)}$ and Brajendra Panda

University of Arkansas, Fayetteville, AR 72701, USA
{afalazeb,bpanda}@uark.edu

Abstract. The advancement of information technology in coming years will bring significant changes to the way healthcare data is processed. Technologies such as cloud computing, fog computing, and the Internet of things (IoT) will offer healthcare providers and consumers opportunities to obtain effective and efficient services via real-time data exchange. However, as with any computer system, these services are not without risks. There is the possibility that systems might be infiltrated by malicious users and, as a result, data could be corrupted, which is a cause for concern. Once an attacker damages a set of data items, the damage can spread through the database. When valid transactions read corrupted data, they can update other data items based on the value read. Given the sensitive nature of healthcare data and the critical need to provide real-time access for decision-making, it is vital that any damage done by a malicious transaction and spread by valid transactions must be corrected immediately and accurately. Here, we present two models for using fog computing in healthcare: an architecture using fog modules with heterogeneous data, and another using fog modules with homogeneous data. We propose a unique approach for each module to assess the damage caused by malicious transactions, so that original data may be recovered and affected transactions may be identified for future investigations.

Keywords: Fog databases · Healthcare systems · Malicious transactions · Affected transactions · Data integrity

1 Introduction

The future of the internet will be in the Internet of things (IoT), which is evidenced by the significant increase in wearable technology, smart homes and buildings, connected vehicles, and smart grids. The estimated number of connected IoT devices in 2030 is nearly 125 billion, which will produce an enormous amount of data [9]. Due to the limitation and restriction of bandwidth, as well as the rapid growth in the amount of data produced, the current information system architecture will be inadequate for managing and moving that volume of data to the cloud. In many scenarios, it could be impractical to do so, especially with the increasing number of IoT devices in use. Additionally, our current society has

© Springer Nature Switzerland AG 2019
G. Wang et al. (Eds.): SpaCCS 2019, LNCS 11611, pp. 63–77, 2019.
https://doi.org/10.1007/978-3-030-24907-6_6

incorporated a lot of sensitive and real-time applications of IoT as integral parts of our lives for instance, through the use of connected car technologies, video conference applications, health monitoring, and real-time production line monitoring, all applications requiring low-latency and location awareness in order to provide satiable and high-quality services [18].

The need for a new platform will become necessary to address the above-mentioned issues. For that purpose, fog computing, introduced by Cisco, is a virtualization architecture that provides many fundamental distinguishing services close to the ground, including the ability to process copious amounts of data, storage, and networking services, making fog computing especially appropriate for many sensitive applications that require real-time acquisition and location awareness [7]. It enhances privacy and security because the data is kept and computed close to end users at the edge of the network, between the end devices and a cloud [8].

Fog computing has several unique characteristics that will not only establish it as an extension of the cloud, but will also provide extra privileges over the cloud. The first feature is its location at the edge of networks, providing end users with high-quality services and low latency. Many current applications require location awareness and low latency to provide a higher quality of services and performances, such as healthcare applications, networked games, video streaming, and interactive sessions. Another essential characteristic is the widely dispersed and significant numbers of fog nodes that will be geographically available, a design that supports mobility in many applications, including service in moving vehicles. This will make fog an important cornerstone of providing high-quality services for connected car technologies. Both fog's location at the edge of the cloud and its geographically wide-spread distribution will also contribute to the benefits of increasing bandwidth efficiency and enhancing the privacy and security of sensitive data. Most of the data will be processed locally at the fog node, meaning that the amount of data needing to be sent to the cloud for processing will be diminished, helping to minimize bandwidth consumption and maximize the privacy of transmitting sensitive data [7,8].

The healthcare system faces several challenges [2,11] that some features of fog computing mentioned above may be able to solve. Therefore, the healthcare system can capitalize on fog computing to create better experiences and services for both patients and providers. One of the most crucial issues in both the fields of fog computing and healthcare is preserving the security and privacy of consumer or patient data. While several studies have sought to solve the security issues of fog computing in a healthcare environment [3], there are still aspects of this issue that should be given further attention, such as assessment of the damage data could suffer from malicious attacks and determination of how to securely recover data from malicious transactions. Damage assessment and data recovery are essential in creating secure and reliable databases, particularly for the transmission of sensitive data, such as that of the healthcare environment. For example, if an intrusion detection system (IDS) detects malicious transactions in the system, any other transactions that read this data will also be affected, resulting in any doctor's decision made based on affected transactions, potentially putting a patient in danger of harm. To the best of our knowledge, there has been no previous work done on the development of damage assessment and data recovery methods for fog computing systems. We present two models for using fog computing systems that manage healthcare data: architecture using fog modules with heterogeneous data, and a second architecture using fog modules with homogeneous data, using unique approaches for each module for assessing the damage caused by malicious transactions, for accurately recovering data, and for identifying affected transactions for future investigation.

2   Literature Review

Fog computing as a new network technology has attracted many researchers. While several of them have produced general survey papers [12,15], some researchers have offered models of architecture for the fog system [10,13] and security issues associated with it [14,17].

One of the main advantages of cloud computing is in freeing the users and businesses from handling many of the details by leaving that work to the cloud, but this feature may become a problem for sensitive applications that require low latency, mobility support, geo-distribution and location awareness [7]. Consequently, implementing a new platform is crucial in meeting these requirements. Hence, Bonomi et al. [6] suggested fog computing as an extension of the cloud computing paradigm, existing at the edge of the network, to enable the start of a new generation of applications and services. Bonomi et al. [7] stated that fog computing features would serve as a proper and suitable platform for many sensitive IoT services and applications, such as connected vehicles, smart grids, and smart cities.

Aazam et al. [1] discuss the benefits of pre-processing the data using a smart gate-way, such as fog computing, before moving the data to the cloud. They also introduce a new architecture for a smart gateway using fog computing. Ivan et al. [17] investigated the advantages of fog computing for services in various aspects such as smart grid, IoT, cyber-physical systems, and smart building. Also, they studied the current paradigm of fog computing by analyzing its security issues.

The usage of fog in healthcare has also attracted the attention of many researchers [2,5]. Azimi et al. [5] introduced a new hierarchical computing architecture for IoT-based patient monitoring systems in order to benefit from the advantages of fog and cloud computing by enabling the partitioning and execution of machine learning data analytics. Akrivopoulos et al. [2] designed an application that collects ECG signals using the patient's smartphone as a fog node. The patient has full control over his data and can share information with his doctors for the purpose of observing his health status.

Damage assessment and data recovery techniques have been addressed by many researchers. They have proposed their models and mechanisms to recover data from intrusion attacks. Panda at el. [16] considered the data dependency method instead of transaction dependency. Each read and write operation of a transaction must be classified into one of five different types based on data dependency between each operation. They used a directed graph which functions by only offering up data items that have been affected in the database.

Ammann et al. [4] introduced a set of algorithms and proposed a mechanism that would perform only on the damaged portions of the database to restore the log file immediately when proposed damage is assessed, and data recovery algorithms could be performed. Some of these algorithms can operate while the database is available during repair, but the database must be unavailable during repair when the initial algorithm performs.

Zuo and Panda [19] introduced two different methods to detect the affected transactions in the distributed database system. The first method used the peer-to-peer model, which is much better when assessing a single point of failure. The second method is a centralized model which would be more efficient in the case of a large-scale distributed database system, due to minimizing the network communications among the sites.

3 Terminologies and Definitions

Securing any computing system is always necessary. Three main phases are required to ensure a system is protected and secure. The first phase is data protection, a procedure that uses securing methods such as access control, auditing, authentication, and encryption to protect the data. The second phase is intrusion detection, which can take the form of software or a device that observes the systems with the intent of detecting any malicious activities or policy violations. This phase is crucial, but it needs additional assistance from the third phase, which includes damage assessment and data recovery ensuring the integrity and availability of the data in the system. This third phase is essential in detecting any additional affected transactions and in ensuring the database has been returned to a secure state. Our objective in this paper is to demonstrate the ability of our proposed algorithms to detect all transactions that have been affected by any malicious transactions, ensuring the integrity of patients' data in healthcare systems that use fog computing environments.

Note that traditional damage assessment and data recovery algorithms usually delete affected transactions to guarantee the integrity of the database, but in our proposed algorithms, the affected transactions will be marked as affected transactions and kept for purposes required by the healthcare field. For instance, a doctor may have given a patient a medication with side effects, based on incorrect readings of data affected by a malicious transaction. Keeping those transactions and marking them as affected will then help the doctor to perform any needed investigation into the case to understand the consequences of those actions performed based on incorrect data.

3.1 Data Dependency

A transaction can be a group of operations or tasks, such as reading and writing; each individual operation cannot be divided further since it is a minimum processing unit. Any data written by a transaction can be read by another transaction, which will generate dependency between those two transactions. For example, say transaction T_1 read data item a and then wrote data item b; then, T_2 read item b, making transaction T_2 dependent on T_1. In other words, if T_1 has been affected by an attack, T_2 will be affected, too. In a fog computing environment, a transaction from one fog node can be read by another fog node and vice versa.

In the fog computing environment, the system will not be able to assess all damaged data by only performing the damage assessment and data recovery algorithms using the log file of each fog node independently. For instance, as shown in Fig. 1, if the intrusion detection system (IDS) identifies T_3 in Fog_1 and T_8 in Fog_2 as malicious transactions, and if each fog node only scans each local log file independently, then the system will only be able to detect T_5 and T_6 as affected transactions in Fog_1 and T_{10} as an affected transaction in Fog_2. Unfortunately, there is no way to detect that T_7 and T_8 in Fog_3 have also been affected since they are dependent on the affected transactions from the Fog_1 node, and an error in T_9 in Fog_2 cannot be detected since it is dependent on the affected transaction, T_8, from Fog_3. Therefore, to ensure the system can detect all affected transactions, cooperation between all fog nodes is necessary.

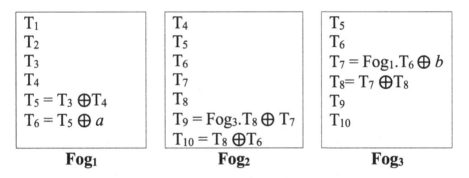

Fig. 1. An example of the necessity of having cooperation between fog nodes to obtain accurate data damage assessment. $\oplus$ notation could indicate any possible operation.

3.2   Flushing the Data

Due to the nature of fog computing and its storage limitations, the data and corresponding log files need to be flushed and removed periodically from the fog to be stored permanently in the cloud. Each fog node will have its own space in the cloud to have efficient and self-regulating access. In some cases, our proposed algorithm needs to do further detection over the flushed data. We assume this action will be at optimal intervals once our approach has been launched and has detected all affected transactions or the IDS has given clearance for that data.

This has many advantages [15]. The first advantage is its ability to improve the efficiency of our proposed algorithms' runtimes since the size of the fog database used in our approach can be diminished. The second advantage is increasing the efficiency of detecting affected transactions among all fog nodes data that have been flushed to the cloud since all data will be in one high-performance machine. Flushing will be performed when the database is in a secure state with all transactions committed.

4   Models

In this section, we introduce two possible architectures for using fog computing to manage healthcare data. For each architecture, we propose suitable algorithms to determine the effect of an attack on the system and identify data damaged either directly or indirectly so that they can be recovered quickly. We assume in both cases that the intrusion detection system (IDS) is responsible for detecting the malicious transactions in the system and will provide a list of these transactions. In addition, each fog node in both architectures must have its own log file. Both architectures proposed here also use a strict serializable history, and the log files cannot be modified by users at any time.

4.1   Model Notations

Table 1 shows the description of notation to be used in our proposed approaches.

Table 1. Notation used in our proposed approaches description.

Notation	Description
FDR	The main fog node, which is accessed by the health care providers to read and write about the patients
FM	Fog node for specific monitors used to collect the data from the patients using the IoT devices, e.g. Fog of Heart Monitors
MT_L	List of detected malicious transactions done by IDS
Aff_Lfdr	List of all affected transactions that have been detected in FDR
Aff_Lfdr$_j$	List of all affected transactions that have been read by FDR from FM$_j$
Aff_Lfm$_j$	List of all affected transactions that are detected by the proposed algorithm in the fog node FM$_j$
Aff_Lfdr$_{cloud}$	List of all affected transactions that done by cloud over the flushed data of FDR fog node
Aff_Lfdr$_{cloud,j}$	List of all affected transactions that done by cloud over the flushed data of fog node j and have been read by FDR node
Aff_L$_{cloud,j}$	List of all affected transactions that done by cloud over the flushed data of fog node j

4.2 The First Proposed Architecture: Fog Nodes with Homogeneous Data

In this model, data will be written to one fog node, which can be read by multiple fog nodes. The patient data will be collected using end-users and Internet of things (IoT) devices, such as sensors, and sent to the proper fog node, which we call fog monitors (FM). For example, information about a patient's heart rate will be sent to the Fog of Heart Monitors, and his or her blood pressure reading will be sent to the fog of blood pressure monitors. Therefore, each fog node FM will contain only homogeneous data.

Additionally, in this model there is a main fog node, known as the Fog for Doctor Reports (FDR), which has access to read any necessary data from the other fog nodes (FMs). Healthcare providers, however, will only have access to the main node. When a doctor wants to check patient records, he or she must read the patient's data from the FDR and write reports, concerns, and prescriptions based on that data, as shown in Fig. 2. We assume that each fog node will have the ability to perform some basic operations with the data, such as calculating a patient's average body temperature over a certain time frame or aggregating the totals of selected data values.

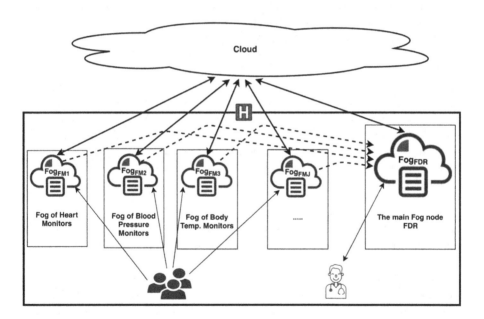

Fig. 2. First proposed architecture "fog nodes with homogeneous data".

Damage Assessment Algorithm for the First Model. Once the IDS detects all malicious transactions in the system, it will send to each fog node a list of malicious transactions that have been detected on it. Let us say that a malicious transaction T_i has been detected by the IDS on Fog_1. Fog_1 will then perform the following procedures:

First procedure: Fog_1 will check its local log to confirm whether T_i is still in its local database (DB).

- If T_i is not in the DB, it has already been flushed to the permanent storage in the cloud.

  In this case, the list of malicious transactions will be forwarded to the cloud to identify all affected transactions by checking data received from all fog nodes. (This step will be more effective and efficient via cloud computing, since all data is now in one high-performance machine that saves time by reducing unnecessary communication between the fog nodes.) After the cloud receives those lists, it will scan the flushed logs to identify any affected transaction that is dependent on any of the damaged transactions from the list.

  Once the cloud finishes the damage assessment procedure and identifies all affected transactions, it will create a list of affected transactions $Aff\_L_{cloud,j}$ for each fog node in the system which has affected transaction in its flushed data. The $Aff\_L_{cloud,j}$ lists will be sent to their corresponding fog nodes to be used as input for our proposed algorithms to do further detection. The cloud will identify all affected transactions read by the FDR, since the FDR log file is flushed to the cloud along with the data.
- If T_i is still in the local DB of Fog_1, then the second procedure will be performed, as outlined below, to detect any additional affected transactions.

Second procedure: Three algorithms will be launched once the fog receives the list of malicious transactions MT_L, detected by the IDS, or $Aff\_L_{cloud,j}$ that is sent from the cloud. The first algorithm, Algorithm 1, allows FM fog nodes to further detect all damaged transactions and mark them as affected. This algorithm will also confirm whether the main fog node (FDR) has read any of these identified transactions. If so, the algorithm will send a list Aff_Lfdr_j to the FDR to use as input for further detection. The other two algorithms, Algorithms 2 and 3, are for the main fog node FDR. The Algorithm 2 could run simultaneously with Algorithm 1 once MT_L, Aff_Lfdr_{cloud}, or $Aff\_Lfdr_{cloud,j}$ list is received, to ensure fast detection of all affected transactions. The FDR fog node will not launch Algorithm 3 until any list of affected transactions from the FM fog nodes is received.

To illustrate the first model, suppose the IDS system detects T_i, Alice's body temperature, as a malicious transaction that is collected by the end user S_{j1}. S_{j1} is connected to the fog node (FM_j). Now assume that FM_j has performed some local operations on its data before the detection, as a matter of general routine, including T_i, such as:

1. Aggregate all the patients' body temperature readings over a certain time $T_{agg,j}$
2. Calculate Alice's average body temperature $T_{avg,j}$ over the last six hours.

Algorithm 1. FM Fog Nodes Assessment Algorithm

Input:
- List of detected malicious transactions MT_L done by IDS, or Aff_$L_{cloud,j}$ list from the cloud.
- The local FM log file.

Output:
- List of all affected transactions Aff_Lfm$_j$ that will be detected by our proposed algorithm in the Fog node FM$_j$.
- Aff_Lfdr$_j$ List of all affected transactions that have been read by FDR.

The Algorithm:
1: Creates a new affected-transactions list Aff_Lfm$_j$ and initializes to null where j is the current fog node ID.
2: Creates a new affected list Aff_Lfdr$_j$ and initializes to null.
3: Takes MT_L / Aff_$L_{cloud,j}$ as input
4: Copies all malicious / affected transactions T_i that exist in FM$_j$ from MT_L / Aff_$L_{cloud,j}$ list to Aff_Lfm$_j$ list
5: **if** Aff_Lfm$_j \neq \emptyset$ **then**
6:     Scan the local log and
7:     **for** every $T_k \in$ FM$_j$ that is dependent on any $T_i \in$ Aff_Lfm$_j$ **do**
8:         Mark T_K as affected transaction
9:         Add T_K to the Aff_Lfm$_j$ list
10:    **end for**
11:    **for** every $T_i \in$ Aff_Lfm$_j$ **do**
12:        Check if T_i has been read by FDR
13:        Add T_i to the Aff_Lfdr$_j$ list
14:    **end for**
15: **end if**
16: Send Aff_Lfdr$_j$ to FDR to do further detection
17: Send Aff_Lfm$_j$ for data recovery.

Algorithm 2. FDR Fog Node Assessment Algorithm "1"

Input:
- List of detected malicious transactions MT_L, Aff_Lfdr$_{cloud,j}$, or Aff_Lfdr$_{cloud}$.
- The local FDR log file.

Output:
- List of all affected transactions Aff_Lfdr.

The Algorithm:
1: Creates a new affected-transactions list Aff_Lfdr and initializes to null
2: Takes MT_L / Aff_Lfdr$_{cloud,j}$ / Aff_Lfdr$_{cloud}$ as input
3: Copies all malicious / affected transactions T_i that exist in FDR from the input list to Aff_Lfdr list
4: **if** Aff_Lfdr $\neq \emptyset$ **then**
5:     Scan the local log and
6:     **for** every $T_k \in$ FDR that is dependent on any $T_i \in$ Aff_Lfdr **do**
7:         Mark T_K as affected transaction
8:         Add T_K to the Aff_Lfdr list
9:     **end for**
10: **end if**
11: Send Aff_Lfdr for data recovery.

Algorithm 3. FDR Fog Node Assessment Algorithm "2"

Input:
- Aff_Lfdr$_j$ list of affected transactions received from other fog node FM$_j$.
- The local FDR log file.

Output:
- List of all affected transactions Aff_Lfdr.

The Algorithm:
1: **for** each a new affected list that is received from FM$_j$ **do**
2:     Creates a new affected-transactions list Aff_Lfdr and initializes to null
3:     Takes Aff_Lfdr$_j$ as input
4:     **if** Aff_Lfdr$_j$ $\neq \emptyset$ **then**
5:         Scan the local log and
6:         **for** every T$_k$ $\in$ FDR that is dependent on any T$_i$ $\in$ Aff_Lfdr$_j$ **do**
7:             Mark T$_K$ as affected transaction
8:             Add T$_K$ to both list the Aff_Lfdr and Aff_Lfdr$_j$
9:         **end for**
10:     **else**there is no affected transaction has been read from FM$_j$
11:     **end if**
12:     Send Aff_Lfdr for data recovery.
13: **end for**

If FDR reads T$_i$, T$_{agg,j}$, and T$_{avg,j}$ from FM$_j$, then any transaction T$_j$ $\in$ FDR that is dependent on T$_i$, T$_{agg,j}$, or T$_{avg,j}$ will be affected. Note that there is no way FDR can know that T$_{agg,j}$ and T$_{avg,j}$ are dependent on T$_i$, since they were calculated locally on the FM$_j$ node. Therefore, any transactions that belong to FDR and are dependent on T$_{agg,j}$ or T$_{avg,j}$ will not be detected by FDR itself until FDR gets a list of all affected transactions from FM$_j$. Assume, for the following transactions T1$_j$, T2$_j$, and T3$_j$ $\in$ FDR, that:

- T1$_j$ is the doctor's report, that is dependent on the malicious transaction T$_i$;
- T2$_j$ is dependent on T$_{agg,j}$ to do any kind of study or to make a budget of the hospital;
- T3$_j$, the prescription given to Alice, is dependent on T$_{avg,j}$ and has some side effects that may affect other data, such as heart rate or blood pressure.

Now suppose the IDS has already detected all malicious transactions including T$_i$ and sent them as list MT_L to the system. Then the first procedure will check each malicious transaction on MT_L to determine whether it has been flushed to the cloud. Suppose, however, that T$_i$ is still on the local DB of FM$_j$. In that case, the second procedure will pursue further detection.

Thus, the FDR will run Algorithm 2 while all other affected fog nodes FM$_j$ run Algorithm 1 simultaneously. As Algorithm 1 runs, each affected FM fog node will create two lists:

- Aff_Lfm$_j$ will get a copy of all malicious transactions that exist in FM$_j$ from MT_L list. All detected damage transactions in FM$_j$ will be added to this list.

– Aff_Lfdr$_j$ which will contain all affected transactions read by FDR and detected by Algorithm 1 in FM$_j$.

In lines 6–10, the algorithm will go through every transaction in the log of FM$_j$ to confirm whether any of them are dependent on malicious or affected transactions from the list Aff_Lfm$_j$. If so, these transactions will also be marked as affected and added to Aff_Lfm$_j$. Thus, T$_{agg,j}$ and T$_{avg,j}$ will be added to Aff_Lfm$_j$, since they are both dependent on the malicious transaction T$_i$.

In lines 11–14, this loop of algorithm is to check only the final Aff_Lfm$_j$ list of all malicious and affected transactions and confirm whether any have been read by FDR. If so, these will be added to Aff_Lfdr$_j$. Therefore, T$_i$, T$_{agg,j}$, and T$_{avg,j}$ will be added to Aff_Lfdr$_j$, since they have been read by FDR. Aff_Lfdr$_j$ will then be sent to FDR to use as input for Algorithm 3 to do further detection, while Aff_Lfm$_j$ will be sent for data recovery.

Once Algorithm 3 receives Aff_Lfdr$_j$, it will create a new affected list, Aff_Lfdr. The algorithm will go through all transactions in the FDR log to determine whether any depend on the malicious or affected transactions from Aff_Lfdr$_j$. If so, these will be marked as affected transactions and added to both Aff_Lfdr and Aff_Lfdr$_j$. T1$_j$, T2$_j$, and T3$_j$ will thus be detected by the end of this loop, and all three will be added to both lists. Then Aff_Lfdr will be sent for data recovery.

4.3 The Second Proposed Architecture: Fog Nodes with Heterogeneous Data

In this model, we assume that all fog nodes have the same capability as well as the ability to perform basic operations on data. However, in the "fog nodes with heterogeneous data" model, there is no main fog node; each hospital department will have its own fog node. Thus, when a patient is moved from one department to another, his or her data will also be moved to the fog node of that department, as shown in Fig. 3. The healthcare providers in each department will have only access to patient data through their own fog node and will write records or reports based on this information. All patients' data will be collected using end users and IoT devices, such as sensors, and will be sent to the local fog node FM in the same department.

This model can be applied outside of hospitals as well, since patient data in smart cities will likewise move from one fog node to another while patients are traveling. Write operations can also be accessed from all nodes. Thus, unlike the "fog nodes with homogeneous data" model, malicious transactions in the "fog nodes with heterogeneous data" model could spread quickly and cause severe data damage. In order to resolve this issue, the fog nodes need to cooperate with each other.

Damage Assessment Algorithm for the Second Model. *First procedure:* As in the first model, when malicious transactions are detected by the IDS, the affected fog node will scan for the presence of that transaction in its local DB.

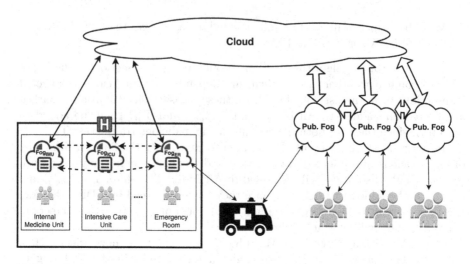

Fig. 3. Second proposed architecture "fog nodes with heterogeneous data"

If the transaction is not there, that means it has been flushed to the cloud. The full procedure in such a case is similar to that explained in Sect. 4.2.

Second procedure: Our proposed Algorithm 4 will be performed in case one of following list is received:

- The list of malicious transactions MT_L.
- The list of affected transactions from another Fog node Aff_Lfmx$_j$.
- The list of affected transactions that has been detected by cloud in the flushed data Aff_L$_{cloud,j}$ that might damage another transaction still residing in the local DB.

To illustrate the proposed algorithm for the second model, consider the following example: Suppose that Bob has just arrived at the emergency room with a medical issue. All of Bob's data will thus be sent to the Fog of the Emergency Room (Fog$_{ER}$). A few hours later, however, the doctors decided to move Bob to the Intensive Care Unit (ICU) because his heart rate was not steady according to sensor S$_1$ (call this transaction T$_1$). Bob's data will then also be moved to the Fog for the Intensive Care Unit (Fog$_{ICU}$). While Bob was in the ER, the physicians performed their tests and wrote report (T$_2$) and, based on that report, the nurses gave Bob some antiarrhythmic medication (T$_3$) to stabilize his heart rate. Thus, transaction T$_2$ is dependent on transaction T$_1$, and T$_3$ is dependent on T$_2$. Suppose, also, that medication T$_3$ has some side effects, such as abdominal pain (T$_4$), hemoptysis (T$_5$), or hypoglycemia (T$_6$). These three transactions should be taken into account.(This is an example of why affected and damaged transactions should not be deleted, but instead kept and marked as affected). Once Bob arrives in the ICU, he develops a reaction to the antiarrhythmic medication T$_3$. The critical care specialist, based on the data and reports T$_1$, T$_2$,

---

Algorithm 4. Damage Assessment Algorithm for the Second Model

---

Input:
- Malicious transactions list MT_L, Aff_Lfmx$_j$ from another fog, or Aff_L$cloud, j$.
- The local log file.

Output:
- List of all affected transactions Aff_Lfm$_j$.
- Sub-lists of affected transactions for each FM$_x$ that has been read any damaged data from FM$_j$.

The Algorithm: Once FM$_j$ receives any of the input list

1: Creates a new affected list Aff_Lfm$_j$ and initializes to null where j is the current fog node ID.
2: Copy all malicious/affected transactions T$_i$ that exist in FM$_j$ from the received list to Aff_Lfm$_j$ list
3: Scan the local log and
4: **for** every T$_k$ ∈ FM$_j$ that is dependent on any T$_i$ ∈ Aff_Lfm$_j$ **do**
5:     Mark T$_K$ as affected transaction
6:     Add T$_K$ to the Aff_Lfm$_j$ list
7: **end for**
8: **for** every T$_i$ ∈ Aff_Lfm$_j$ **do**
9:     **if** T$_i$ has been read by any other FM$_X$ **then**
10:         Check If Aff_Lfmj$_X$ list does not exist, Then
11:         Creates a new affected list Aff_Lfmj$_X$ and initialize to null where x is the id of aimed Fog node that reads the affected transaction.
12:         Add T$_i$ to the Aff_Lfmj$_x$ list
13:     **end if**
14: **end for**
15: Send Aff_Lfmj$_X$ to proper FM$_x$ to do further detection
16: Send Aff_Lfm$_j$ for data recovery.

---

and T$_3$ from the ER, decides to give Bob alternative antiarrhythmic medication T$_{ICU1}$.

Subsequently, the critical care specialist realizes that Bob has no heart issue and his heart rate is normal. In the meantime, however, the IDS has notified the Fog$_{ER}$ that T$_1$ is a malicious transaction. There is then no way for Fog$_{ICU}$ to detect T$_2$ and T$_3$ as affected transactions, since they depend on T$_1$ and they are done locally at Fog$_{ER}$. Nevertheless, Fog$_{ER}$ will be the only fog node in the entire system that can detect T$_2$ and T$_3$. Thus, when Fog$_{ER}$ receives the malicious transaction list including T$_1$, the model's first procedure will confirm whether T$_1$ has been flushed to the cloud. Suppose that T$_1$ is still in the local DB and has not been flushed yet. Fog$_{ER}$ will then launch Algorithm 4, as described in the second procedure. The first line of the algorithm will create the Aff_LFM$_{ER}$ list to identify all affected transactions in the Fog$_{ER}$. T$_1$ will be copied to this list, since it still resides in the local DB. Next, lines 3–7 will scan the log file, starting from T$_1$, and check each transaction sharing data dependency with T$_1$ or with any other transactions in the list. The algorithm will find T$_2$ in this way, mark it as an affected transaction, and add it to Aff_LFM$_{ER}$. When the algorithm examines the next transaction in the log for data dependency with any affected transactions from Aff_LFM_{ER}, it will now take T_2 into consideration because T_2 has just been added to the list. Thus, T_3 will be detected, marked as affected, and added to Aff_LFM_{ER}.

After all transactions in the log file have been scanned and examined, lines 8–12 of Algorithm 4 will confirm whether each affected transaction has been read by another fog node (to which it was moved when the patient was moved). If so, a sub-list of affected transactions will be created for each affected fog node, and add to the list the affected transaction that has been read. In our example, transactions T_1, T_2, and T_3 have been moved to Fog_{ICU}, so Fog_{ER} will create a new sub-list Aff_LFMER_{ICU} and add T_1, T_2, and T_3 to that sub-list. Finally, Aff_LFMER_{ICU} will be sent to the Fog_{ICU} for further detection, and the main affected list Aff_LFM_{ER} will be sent for data recovery. Once Fog_{ICU} receives Aff_LFMER_{ICU}, it will use the list as input in the same algorithm, and T_{ICU1} will be detected as an affected transaction, since there is data dependency between T_{ICU1} and the affected transactions T_1, T_2, and T_3. The process continues until all affected transactions are detected.

5 Conclusion

Fog computing offers the opportunity to gain significant performance improvement over cloud-based systems. Data management in healthcare systems can benefit significantly by using fog computing. This technology, as is the case with any other data sharing systems, is prone to attacks and execution of malicious transactions on the database. Preventative and protective measures are not always successful in deterring malicious attacks. Once an intrusion detection system within a healthcare environment detects malicious activities, an appropriate mechanism to recover the damaged data from that attack is required and should be applied at the earliest opportunity. In this paper, we have introduced two different architecture models for applying fog technology to healthcare systems: fog modules with heterogeneous data, and fog modules with homogeneous data Working with the nature and characteristics of each model, we propose unique methods of assessing and recovering damaged data. As part of future work, we plan to evaluate these two models by simulating the hospital environment and examining the performance of our s. We also plan to ex-tend the two proposed scenarios to other applications, as well. We believe that our mechanisms can be modified to work in other environments, such as smart cities and industries, as well.

References

1. Aazam, M., Hung, P.P., Huh, E.N.: Smart gateway based communication for cloud of things. In: 2014 IEEE Ninth International Conference on Intelligent Sensors, Sensor Networks and Information Processing (ISSNIP), pp. 1–6. IEEE (2014)

2. Akrivopoulos, O., Chatzigiannakis, I., Tselios, C., Antoniou, A.: On the deployment of healthcare applications over fog computing infrastructure. In: 2017 IEEE 41st Annual Computer Software and Applications Conference (COMPSAC), vol. 2, pp. 288–293. IEEE (2017)
3. Al-Janabi, S., Al-Shourbaji, I., Shojafar, M., Shamshirband, S.: Survey of main challenges (security and privacy) in wireless body area networks for healthcare applications. Egypt. Inform. J. **18**(2), 113–122 (2017)
4. Ammann, P., Jajodia, S., Liu, P.: Recovery from malicious transactions. IEEE Trans. Knowl. Data Eng. **14**(5), 1167–1185 (2002)
5. Azimi, I., et al.: Hich: Hierarchical fog-assisted computing architecture for healthcare IoT. ACM Trans. Embed. Comput. Syst. (TECS) **16**(5s), 174 (2017)
6. Bonomi, F.: Connected vehicles, the internet of things, and fog computing. In: The Eighth ACM International Workshop on Vehicular Inter-networking (VANET), Las Vegas, USA, pp. 13–15 (2011)
7. Bonomi, F., Milito, R., Zhu, J., Addepalli, S.: Fog computing and its role in the internet of things. In: Proceedings of the First Edition of the MCC Workshop on Mobile Cloud Computing, pp. 13–16. ACM (2012)
8. CISCO: Fog computing and the internet of things: Extend the cloud to where the things are (2015)
9. IHS Markit: The internet of things: a movement, not a market (2017)
10. Kim, Y., Kim, D., Son, J., Wang, W., Noh, Y.: A new fog-cloud storage framework with transparency and auditability. In: 2018 IEEE International Conference on Communications (ICC), pp. 1–7. IEEE (2018)
11. Kirch, D.G., Petelle, K.: Addressing the physician shortage: The peril of ignoring demography. Jama **317**(19), 1947–1948 (2017)
12. Kraemer, F.A., Braten, A.E., Tamkittikhun, N., Palma, D.: Fog computing in healthcare-a review and discussion. IEEE Access **5**, 9206–9222 (2017)
13. Kudo, T.: Fog computing with distributed database. In: 2018 IEEE 32nd International Conference on Advanced Information Networking and Applications (AINA), pp. 623–630. IEEE (2018)
14. Lu, R., Heung, K., Lashkari, A.H., Ghorbani, A.A.: A lightweight privacy-preserving data aggregation scheme for fog computing-enhanced iot. IEEE Access **5**, 3302–3312 (2017)
15. Madsen, H., Burtschy, B., Albeanu, G., Popentiu-Vladicescu, F.: Reliability in the utility computing era: Towards reliable fog computing. In: 2013 20th International Conference on Systems, Signals and Image Processing, pp. 43–46. IEEE (2013)
16. Panda, B., Haque, K.A.: Extended data dependency approach: a robust way of rebuilding database. In: Proceedings of the 2002 ACM symposium on Applied computing, pp. 446–452. ACM (2002)
17. Stojmenovic, I., Wen, S.: The fog computing paradigm: Scenarios and security issues. In: 2014 Federated Conference on Computer Science and Information Systems, pp. 1–8. IEEE (2014)
18. Zhang, B., et al.: The cloud is not enough: Saving IoT from the cloud. In: 7th USENIX Workshop on Hot Topics in Cloud Computing (HotCloud 2015) (2015)
19. Zuo, Y., Panda, B.: Distributed database damage assessment paradigm. Inf. Manag. Comput. Sec. **14**(2), 116–139 (2006)

Modelling Security Requirements for Software Development with Common Criteria

Naseer Amara[1(✉)], Zhiqui Huang[1], and Awais Ali[2]

[1] College of Computer Science and Technology,
Nanjing University of Aeronautics and Astronautics, Nanjing 210000, China
Mari.choudhary@yahoo.com
[2] Department of Computer Science, Bahria University, Lahore 54000, Pakistan

Abstract. Designing software needs to address the issues of adaptation and evaluation in terms of object-oriented concepts to prevent the loss of resources in terms of system failure. System security assessments are common practice and system certification according to a standard requires submitting relevant software security information to applicable authorities. Many security-related standards exist for the development of various security-critical systems however Common Criteria (ISO/IEC 15408) is an International de-facto standard which provides assurance for specification, implementation, and evaluation of an IT security product. This research will provide aid in better communication and enhanced collaboration among different stakeholders especially between software and security engineers by proposing a model of security-related concepts in de-facto standard Unified Modeling Language (UML). In this paper, we present a Usage Scenario and a Conceptual Model by extracting key security-related concepts from Common Criteria. The effectiveness is illustrated by a case study on Facebook Meta-Model, which is built for the evaluation purpose of Common Criteria models.

Keywords: Security requirement engineering · Security evaluation · Software modelling · UML profile · Common Criteria (ISO/IEC 15408)

1 Introduction

Security needs to be considered from the beginning of software development to avoid expensive rework and reduce potential security vulnerabilities [1]. Hence, defining the right set of security functional requirements and evaluated assurance level becomes a critical task for developers while developing secure software [2]. For this purpose, much effort has been put into creating industry standards to provide a shared common base for stakeholders with concerns about security [3]. These standards include policies, security guidelines, security concepts, risk management approaches, assurances, best practices, and various technologies etc. [4]. Some of the most common security-related standards which large organizations with big

© Springer Nature Switzerland AG 2019
G. Wang et al. (Eds.): SpaCCS 2019, LNCS 11611, pp. 78–88, 2019.
https://doi.org/10.1007/978-3-030-24907-6_7

budget products follow during their Software Development Life-Cycle process are; **The National Institute of Standards and Technology (NIST)** which aims to promote innovation and industrial competitiveness by advancing measurement science, standards, and technology in ways that enhance economic security and improve our quality of life. **The Standard of Good Practice for Information Security** is a business-focused, practical and comprehensive guide to identify and manage information security risks in organizations and their supply chains. **North American Electric Reliability Corporation (NERC), ISA99, ISA Secure** etc. are some other security-related standards [5]. **Common Criteria for Information Technology Security Evaluation** (known as Common Criteria or CC) provides assurance of specification, implementation, and evaluation of an IT security product. CC (ISO/IEC 15408) is an International standard for computer security certification and is currently in version 3.1 revision 5 [6].

The main challenge in software development is to accurately communicate security requirements among all the stakeholders involved as it is the root of many security-related issues during software certification [7]. Many system failures occur because of poor communication and lack of collaboration among security and software engineers [8]. So, there is a need to understand and address the security-related requirements more precisely from the beginning of Software Development Life-Cycle (SDLC) process [9,10] to avoid the occurrence of security-related issues.

The main purpose of this research is to eliminate the communication gap between software engineers, security engineers and other stakeholders involved in the software development so as to understand the security requirements more accurately and to prevent the loss in terms of software failure [10,11]. To bridge this technical deficiency gap during software development Common Criteria for Information Technology have been adapted and evaluated [12]. This research presents, Usage Model which describes the roles and responsibilities of the stakeholders involved during software development. Key security-related concepts are extracted from de-facto standard Common Criteria ISO/IEC 15408 and a model of these concepts is precisely implemented in de-facto standard Unified Modeling Language (UML). To implement the presented models, Security Objectives have been explained which are then mapped with Security Functional Components and Evaluated Assurance Levels given in Common Criteria for Information Technology. It is shown that the Common Criteria models and Security Objectives mapping improve the line of communication between security engineers, software engineers and among different stakeholders involved to avoid system failure with respect to security-related issues. This is illustrated by a case study on Facebook Meta-Model, which is built for the evaluation purpose of Common Criteria models.

The remaining paper is structured as follows; Sect. 2, introduces security assessment of common criteria standard and the purpose of using UML. Section 3, briefly describe the requirements of common criteria in terms of UML profile

"Usage Scenarios of Common Criteria" and "Conceptual Model of security-related concepts from Common Criteria". Section 4, evaluates the effectiveness of the given models by mapping security objectives of scenario modules with CC security functional components and implementing it on a SaaS application "Facebook". The paper is summarized with the conclusion and future work.

2 Security Assessment of Common Criteria and UML

Common Criteria provides a common set of security-related requirements, making it easy to compare the results of independent security evaluations for the security functionalities and assurance measures of the IT products which help consumers to find out their accurate security-related needs. It should be used in conjunction with suitable evaluation methods and relevant security functionalities of appropriate IT products to have useful evaluation results. Common Criteria covers security measures to protect confidentiality, Integrity, availability and various human and non-human activities and it does not cover security measures related to the administrative framework, physical aspects of IT security, assessment of cryptographic algorithms and procedures to evaluate results in accreditation [13].

"Unified Modeling Language (UML) is an object-oriented standard modeling language use to analyze, specify, design and construct the artifacts of a software-intensive system providing a standard way to write system's blueprints covering all the conceptual things" [14].

UML use well-defined and expressive notations to depict the process of software development into models which results in better collaboration among team members and better understanding the needs of customers by reducing the cost and saving the time by focusing on the actual job and eliminating the threats which may arise due to poor communication. It aims to model system from concepts to executable artifacts through the use of Object-Oriented techniques and addresses the issues in mission-critical systems providing aid to both machines and humans [15].

3 Security-Related Requirements of Common Criteria

Based on the communication challenges faced by different stakeholders involved in software development, we have first identified their different roles and responsibilities in accordance with Common Criteria standard and build a Usage Scenarios for the system which is described in Sect. 3.1. In Sect. 3.2, by carefully analyzing and identifying the security concepts involved in Common Criteria standard, a precise Conceptual Model is built in standard UML.

3.1   The Usage Scenarios of Common Criteria

The principal users of the CC and how can they benefit from the system is depicted as follows;

Consumers – Consumers are obliged to use background information for reference purpose, can use the evaluated results to compare different TOEs (Target of Evaluation) and to find if any particular TOE fulfills the security needs of the system. They are obliged to express the security needs of the system in PPs (Protection Profiles).

Developers – Developers are obliged to assist the evaluation process of TOEs against the requirements and to identify if the security requirements are properly implemented by the TOEs. Developers can also use STs (Security Targets) to confirm security requirements from the consumers' perspective.

Evaluators – Evaluators are obliged to form judgments about the conformance of the TOEs related to security requirements in accordance with the general set of actions described in CC. Evaluators also provide guidelines for PPs and STs.

Administrator – Administrators are obliged to adhere to the policies in the ST of the TOE.

Others – The other stakeholders who have interest or responsibilities related to the security of product may include security designers and security architects (specifies the security properties of an IT product), system security officers and system custodians (determines the organizational security policies and security requirements), auditors (assess the adequacy of the security), sponsors (can request and support an evaluation), accreditors (accepts the solution to use in a particular environment), evaluation authorities (manages and oversight security evaluation programs).

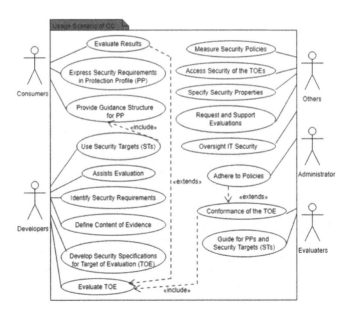

Fig. 1. Usage scenarios of common criteria.

This usage scenarios will greatly facilitate the communication process among engineers group because the information related to security is captured in the above usage scenarios. Using the above model, security engineers can monitor their security information by generating automatic reports using appropriate tools to query UML models and to produce the required information in required formats and can submit it to the certification authorities [16].

3.2 The Conceptual Model of Security-Related Concepts from Common Criteria

We first identified security-related concepts from the Common Criteria standard that should be part of the security model. The below-mentioned security-related concepts extracted from Common Criteria and implemented in standard UML are not only restricted to Common Criteria standard and can be used to implement during the software development of IT related products.

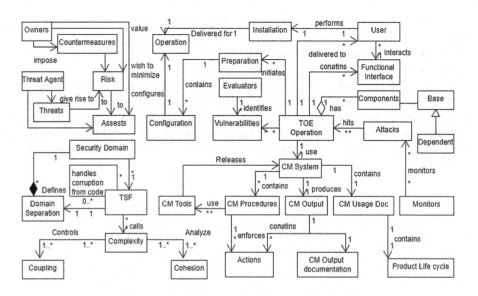

Fig. 2. Conceptual model of security-related concepts from CC.

The careful analysis of the Common Criteria document leads to identify 34 core security concepts from a total of 70 concepts which are found relevant for the development of IT products. These security concepts and their relationship with each other is defined in the model above and are formalized under the Conceptual Model, i.e., UML Class Diagram. Broadly speaking the concepts implemented in Fig. 2 covers the notions of security critical Coupling, Cohesion, CM (Configuration Management) System, TSF (Target of Evaluation Security Functionality), TOE, Vulnerabilities and Functional Interfaces etc. The detail of the implemented concepts is not given here because of space constraints. Instead, we refer the interested readers to [16] for all the details. Moreover, the attributes values are not fixed because they can be project specific which is why the UML model is flexible with customized tagged values.

4 The Facebook Profile by Example

We present a scenario for the use of the Conceptual Model on a realistic case study, thereby illustrating a subset of the model. The goal is to demonstrate through a realistic case study, the effectiveness of the Conceptual Model presented in the context of the Usage Scenarios and security objectives. It is important to note that, the purpose of conducting this case study is to show the effectiveness of the presented model and it does not correspond to a certified system, however, we followed every standard practice while designing the system.

Facebook is a social networking site which is ranked as one of the most widely used SaaS application in 2017 Surveys. It is easily accessible via laptops, tablet computers, and smartphones which have access to the Internet. The user has to register who wish to use this site and then they can make their profile specifying their name, education, work history, interests and so on. Users can add other users as friends by sending them "Friend Requests", they can exchange messages, post status, upload photos, videos, receive notifications, and can comment when their friends post something. Users can also join groups according to their interests, can create events, and make their own pages for some specific purpose. Moreover, users can make a complaint or block nasty people via reporting Facebook Service.

When designing the system the first step was to identify five high-level functional requirements for each class of the system, which are referred as FREQ1 to FREQ5, e.g., for Account Creation the system shall check all items required for password security (FREQ1) and in case of an incorrect password, the system shall check the recovery methods selected to inform certified user (FREQ2) and so on. In the second step, we performed a security assessment, in accordance with CC which describes Security Functional Components and mapped the Preventive, Detective, and Corrective security objectives with the standard and identified which security objectives have Direct or Indirect support with which Family of CC. These security requirements and functional components cannot all be described in details in this article. Instead, we refer the interested readers to [17] for all the details. In the third step, direct support security objectives are further mapped with functional requirements of our system under evaluation which resulted in thirty-eight security requirements, referred to as SREQ1 to SREQ 11(as there are eleven classes in CC which are further classified into Families) which are further decomposed into SREQ1.1 to SREQ1.5, SREQ4.1 to SREQ4.12, SREQ5.1 and SREQ8.1 to SREQ8.12 e.g., the Class "Identification and Authentication" with its six Families address the requirements for functions to establish and verify a claimed user identity or associated security attributes which is referred as SREQ5 and satisfies the functional requirements of Account class. Then the system is designed with security-related design decisions, from our presented model. In the last step, the resulting designed profile of our system is evaluated in accordance with the usage scenarios of Common Criteria which is discussed in Sect. 3.1.

4.1 Mapping Security Objectives with Security Functional Components

The table below represents the mapping between security objectives of the main modules of the scenario under consideration with security requirements generated from Common Criteria. The leftmost column of the table shows the modules of our system under evaluation, the middle column represents the security objectives of those modules and the rightmost column shows the security requirements mapped with Common Criteria-Security Functional Components as identified in [17] (Table 1).

Table 1. Mapping between scenario Modules and SREQ's.

Scenario modules	Security objectives	SREQ's
Account	Identification and Authentication, Intrusion Detection and Response, Recoverability	SREQ 1.1, SREQ 1.3, SREQ5, SREQ 4.10 - SREQ 4.12, SREQ 8.2, SREQ 8.3, SREQ 8.5, SREQ 8.6, SREQ 8.9
Profile	Confidentiality, Accountability, Integrity, Privacy, Recoverability	SREQ 1.2- SREQ 1.5, SREQ 3, SREQ 4.1- SREQ 4.12, SREQ 5.1, SREQ 7, SREQ 8.4,-SREQ 8.12
Friend request	Confidentiality, Accountability, Non-repudiation	SREQ 1.2- SREQ 1.5, SREQ 2, SREQ 3, SREQ 4.1- SREQ 4.8, SREQ 5.1, SREQ 8.4, SREQ 8.7, SREQ 8.8, SREQ 11
Messages	Confidentiality, Accountability, Recoverability, Non-repudiation, Integrity,	SREQ 2, SREQ 3, SREQ 4.1- SREQ 4.8, SREQ 5.1, SREQ 8.7, SREQ 8.8, SREQ 11
Comments	Confidentiality, Integrity	SREQ 3, SREQ 4.1- SREQ 4.8, SREQ 5.1, SREQ 8.7, SREQ 8.8, SREQ 11
Page	Non-repudiation, Integrity, Confidentiality, Security Management	SREQ 3, SREQ 4.8-SREQ 4.12, SREQ 6, SREQ 8.8-SREQ 8.12, SREQ 10
Event	Non-repudiation, Confidentiality, Integrity, Security Management, Recoverability	SREQ 3, SREQ 4.8-SREQ 4.12, SREQ 6, SREQ 8.8-SREQ 8.12, SREQ 10
System	Intrusion Detection and Response, Accountability, Integrity, Recoverability, Availability, Security Management,	SREQ 1.1, SREQ 1.2, SREQ 4.10- SREQ 4.12, SREQ 6, SREQ 8.1- SREQ 8.3, SREQ 8.5
Ads	Integrity, Recoverability	SREQ 4.10-SREQ 4.12, SREQ 8.5, SREQ 8.6, SREQ 8.9
Payments	Non-repudiation, Integrity, Confidentiality, Identification and Authentication,	SREQ 3, SREQ 5, SREQ 9, SREQ 4.1- SREQ 4.8, SREQ 5.1, SREQ 11

4.2   Facebook Sub-system Design

The design (class diagram) for SaaS application – Facebook appears in Fig. 3 with selected stereotypes which are applied for explanatory purposes. The whole diagram is stereotyped as <<SecurityCritical>> representing that the contained information is relevant to security. It is also stereotyped <<Requirement>> with tagged values Kind and Specification representing the security requirements and functional requirements are relevant to the class diagram. It is recommended to use a modeling tool that supports the profile so as to avoid cluttering and building a graphic-friendly view. The main component of the application is the Account class. It is stereotyped with <<Assets>> with Email ID and Password as tagged values. Class Account is also stereotyped with <<Attacks>> which means it is highly security critical and open to security-related attacks if an attacker who attempts to gain access to the authorized user credentials successfully break into Account the entire application will be compromised. Since Account is associated with Profile, Friend Request, System, Event, Live Video, and Messages so these classes are also security critical.

Class Account is stereotyped as <<Login_Controller>>, which represents that it is a control class with a Login Interface. This stereotype, as well as the <<Manangement_Interface>>, <<System_Monitoring_Interface>>, <<Live_Streaming_Interface>>, <<Request_Handler>>, <<Instant_Messaging_Handler>>, <<Adds_Handler>>, and <<Event_Handler>> etc. are not part of our profile but are stereotyped according to the working state of the classes. The stereotype <<Interface>> represents the kind of interface these classes relate to e.g.; class Profile is stereotyped as <<Manangement>> which means that it is responsible for the account management related activities and the <<Handler>> to indicate which kind of events they will deal with. The Account class as well as the associated <<Manangement_Interface>>, <<System_Monitoring_Interface>>, <<Live_Streaming_Interface>> <<Request_Handler>>, <<Instant_Messaging_Handler>>, and <<Event_Handler>> etc. are stereotyped <<Package>>, thereby relating the design decision to functional requirements and security requirements as mentioned above.

<<System_Monitoring_Interface>> is responsible for monitoring the events which are received by class Account from other subsystems and then it performs the required reactions. The stereotype <<Monitor>> represents the security monitors with tagged value equivalents to Security (Kind = Security. <<Monitor>> also specifies the entity which is to be monitored by using the Login_Controller (MonitoredEntity = Login_Controller), the event which is to be detectable by the entity (DetectableEvent = Independent SubsystemEvent), and the handler responsible to handle the events (EventHandler = System_Monitoring_Interface).

In the last step, we re-examine our Facebook profile in accordance with the usage scenarios (Fig. 1). For designing a system, software engineers need to associate their designs with functional and non-functional requirements. Similarly, we have done the same in our profile using the stereotype <<Package>> where each class which implements at least one requirement either functional or non-

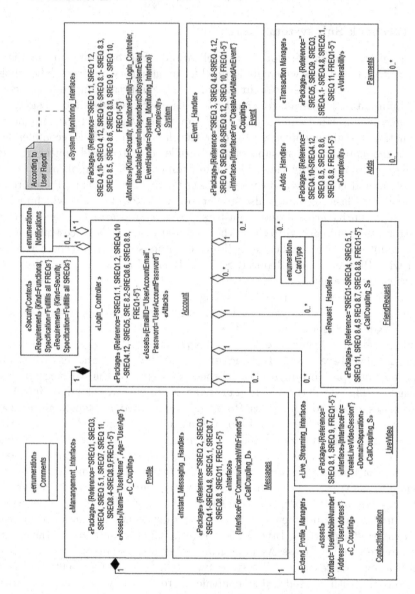

Fig. 3. Facebook-subsystem design.

functional is stereotyped with <<Package>> in Fig. 3. So, it is clearly visible that the design is specifically related to security requirements, which supports usage scenario for "Developers" and "Others (Security Designers and Security Architects)" because they are responsible to identify and specify security requirements for their Target of Evaluation (TOE) using Security Targets (STs) or Protection Profile (PPs) in Fig. 1. Security engineers can verify whether all security requirements are handled properly with the help of suitable tool which supports to query UML model. So, security engineers can determine how security requirements are designed into the system and how design decisions are justified which is done in usage scenario "Evaluators" in Fig. 1. In conclusion, our profile clearly supports all the usage scenarios in Fig. 1 (Sect. 3.1), which defines how to use security information in practice.

5   Conclusion

The major challenge in developing the security-critical system is the proper collaboration among different stakeholders involved, particularly it's necessary to eliminate the communication gap between software and security engineers. To address this issue, we have adopted the Common Criteria standard and presented a Usage Scenario which shows the line of communication among stakeholders and the information that engineering groups have to exchange and practice. We then, modeled from Common Criteria the 34 security-related concepts and their association with each other in the form of a Conceptual Model i.e., class diagram. The Conceptual Model was then implemented on a realistic case study, a social networking application: Facebook. After implementing the Conceptual Model we embedded the security requirements in our profile which are extracted from Common Criteria. The resulting profile clearly shows that it can improve the line of communication between software engineers, security engineers and other stakeholders involved to address the security issues and to eliminate the risk of system failure as well. This research is limited in terms of providing full automation for the profile, however, future work will implement the presented model in all the modules of under considered scenario and also extend it to other diagrams such as collaboration and sequence diagrams.

Acknowledgments. The first author would like to thank her parents for their generous support. This work is fully supported by Nanjing University of Aeronautics and Astronautics under China Government Scholarship.

References

1. Mellado, D., Fernández-Medina, E., Piattini, M.: A common criteria based security requirements engineering process for the development of secure information systems. Comput. Stand. Interfaces **29**(2), 243–253 (2017)
2. Filipova, O., Vilão, R.: Software Development From A to Z. Apress, Berkeley (2018). https://doi.org/10.1007/978-1-4842-3945-2
3. Tarique, M.D., Jama, A., Dhirendra, P., Mamdouh, A.: STORE: security threat oriented requirements engineering methodology. J. King Saud Univ. Comput. Inf. Sci. (2018)
4. Nancy, R., Ted, S.: Security quality requirements engineering (SQUARE) methodology. In: SESS 2005 Proceedings of the 2015 Workshop on Software Engineering for Secure Systems–Building Trustworthy Applications, pp. 1–7. ACM SIGSOFT Software Engineering Notes, New York (2015). https://doi.org/10.1145/1082983.1083214

5. Cyber Security Standards. https://en.wikipedia.org/wiki/Cyber-security-standards. Accessed 2 Mar 2018
6. Common Criteria. https://www.commoncriteriaportal.org/. Accessed 5 Jan 2018
7. Hassan, H., Sherif, K.: Capturing security requirements for software systems. J. Adv. Res. **5**(4), 463–472 (2014)
8. Yusuf, M., Mahmood, N., Mohammad, A., Sajjad, M.: A readiness model for security requirements engineering. IEEE Access **6**, 28611–28631 (2018)
9. Nor Shahriza, A.K., Arwa, A., Tanzila, S., Amjad, R.: The practice of secure software development in SDLC: an investigation through existing model and a case study. Secur. Commun. Netw. **9**(18), 5333–5345 (2016)
10. Mohammad, U., Shams, T.: TSSR: a proposed tool for secure software requirement management. Int. J. Inf. Technol. Comput. Sci. (IJITCS) **7**(1), 1–11 (2014)
11. Rehman, S.U., Gruhn, V.: An effective security requirements engineering framework for cyber-physical systems. Technologies **6**(3), 65 (2018)
12. Mellado, D., Fernández-Medina, E., Piattini, M.: Applying a security requirements engineering process. In: Gollmann, D., Meier, J., Sabelfeld, A. (eds.) ESORICS 2006. LNCS, vol. 4189, pp. 192–206. Springer, Heidelberg (2006). https://doi.org/10.1007/11863908_13
13. Common Criteria: Common Criteria for Information Technology Security Evaluation - Part 1: Introduction and general model. ISO/IEC (2017)
14. Grady, B., James, R., Ivar, J.: The Unified Modeling Language User Guide, 2nd edn. Addison Wesley Professional, Boston (2005)
15. Zoughbi, G., Briand, L., Labiche, Y.: A UML profile for developing airworthiness-compliant (RTCA DO-178B) information: conceptual model and UML profile. Softw. Syst. Model. **10**(3), 337–367 (2011)
16. Maylawat, D.S., Darmalaksana, W., Ramdhani, M.A.: Systematic design of expert system using unified modelling language. In: IOP Conference Series: Materials Science and Engineering. IOP (2018)
17. Amara, N.: Figshar. https://figshare.com/articles/Implementation-of-CC-Model-on-Facebook-Profile-docx/5432719

Visualization of DNS Tunneling Attacks Using Parallel Coordinates Technique

Yasir F. Mohammed$^{(\boxtimes)}$ and Dale R. Thompson

Department of Computer Science and Computer Engineering, University of Arkansas,
Fayetteville, AR 72701, USA
{yfmohamm,drt}@uark.edu

Abstract. The Domain Name System (DNS) is considered one of the most critical protocols on the Internet. The DNS translates readable domain names into Internet Protocol (IP) addresses and vice-versa. The DNS tunneling attack uses DNS to create a covert channel for bypassing the firewall and performing command and control functions from within a compromised network or to transfer data to and from the network. There is work for detecting attacks that use DNS but little work focusing on the DNS tunneling attack. In this work, we introduce a fast and scalable approach, using the parallel coordinates technique, visualizing a malicious DNS tunneling attack within the large amount of network traffic. The DNS tunneling attack was performed in order to study the differences between the normal and the malicious traffic. Based on different scenarios, four different DNS tunneling graphical patterns were defined for distinguishing between normal DNS traffic and malicious traffic containing DNS tunneling attacks. Finally, the proposed system was able to visualize the DNS tunneling attack efficiently for the future work of creating an efficient detection system.

Keywords: DNS · Internet attacks · Tunneling attacks ·
DNS Tunneling · Parallel coordinates technique · Visualization

1 Introduction

The Domain Name System (DNS) plays an essential role in the Internet architecture. DNS translates and locates easy-to-remember domain names into corresponding Internet Protocol (IP) addresses and vice-versa. For example, assume a user types a domain name "domain.com" in a browser on a computer. First, the browser attempts to resolve the IP address of the domain name by checking the local cache of the computer. If there is no information related to that domain name, it forwards the request to the local DNS server or the global DNS server depending on the network configuration. Next, if the information is still not found, the request is forwarded to ROOT nameservers. As soon as the information is gathered, it resolves the domain name and responses to the initial sender. Then, the computer communicates with a web server to display the content of the website.

© Springer Nature Switzerland AG 2019
G. Wang et al. (Eds.): SpaCCS 2019, LNCS 11611, pp. 89–101, 2019.
https://doi.org/10.1007/978-3-030-24907-6_8

The DNS protocol is vulnerable to several attacks such as cache poisoning and DNS hijacking attacks that lead to compromising users' online accounts [15]. The DNS amplification attack is a type of Distributed Denial of Service (DDoS) attack based on the DNS protocol that may prevent visitors from reaching the organization's services [11]. There are also other DNS attacks including DNS tunneling, name collisions and leaked queries and DNS response modification [17]. Most organizations pay more attention to filtering and securing common protocols such as HTTP or FTP from malicious activities instead of the DNS protocol. Since the DNS protocol is not designed for data transfer, monitoring DNS has not received much attention. Over the years, adversaries found different ways to leverage DNS systems for malicious purposes. For example, suppose an organization blocks all outbound traffic except the DNS protocol and DNS activities are not monitored. Adversaries can still transfer stolen or sensitive information through a firewall using DNS. They take advantage of this open avenue and manipulate the use of the DNS service to establish undetected channels.

The DNS tunneling attack is a method that encodes and encapsulates the data of other applications or protocols in DNS queries and responses. The original concept of DNS tunneling attack was designed to bypass the captive portals for paid Wi-Fi service, especially at hotels and cafes. However, a data payload can be added to attack internal networks that are used to control remote servers and applications, or to perform DNS data exfiltration which is a technique being used to transfer unauthorized data between two computers through the DNS protocol [8]. To successfully execute this attack, an adversary requires a compromised machine within the internal organization network that has access to the internal DNS server with external access which allows the machine to establish a connection using the DNS protocol. Adversaries must also register a domain name and set up a remote server that can run as a DNS authoritative server. As mentioned in (Farnham & Atlasis, 2013), using the DNS tunneling attack, people can bypass most of the firewall rules, restrictions and captive portals for paid Wi-Fi service. Nowadays, most of the modern firewalls and IDS appliance do not block a DNS tunneling attack or raise the alarm by default. For that reason, the DNS tunneling attack is attractive to adversaries or people who design malicious applications.

Visualization is not a new concept for monitoring network traffic. There are several papers that used the parallel coordinates technique to monitor and visualize network traffic. There are various benefits of using a parallel coordinates technique. First, it is scalable. It helps to represent a considerable amount of data in an efficient manner which makes analyzing big data more simple and powerful. Second, there is no limit on the number of values for representing an attack using the parallel coordinates technique that converts multidimensional data into two dimensions. Therefore, using the parallel coordinates technique gives the ability to represent more than three different values within a two-dimensional space. In this way, the relationship between the results can be reviewed quickly showing prominent trends, correlations, and divergence from the raw data. Finally, the visualized data using the parallel coordinates technique does not include any bias for any column within the space [5,6]. In other words, every visualized feature has the same weight.

The contributions of this work are: (1) A fast and scalable visualization system is proposed for recognizing DNS tunneling attacks using the parallel coordinates technique. The proposed system is able to distinguish between normal and malicious DNS traffic. (2) A real-world DNS tunneling attack is conducted within our network to study the behavior of the attack traffic. Four different graphical patterns are defined in this work by analyzing the DNS tunneling traffic based on different scenarios.

The following section discusses the related work to visualization of network traffic and the parallel coordinates technique. Section 3 describes the proposed visualization system. In Sect. 4, four different graphical patterns for DNS tunneling attacks are presented based on different scenarios. The evaluation of the visualization technique is discussed in Sect. 5 and conclusions are in Sect. 6.

2 Related Work

Compared to other protocols, the monitoring of the DNS protocol does not get much attention in the literature. However, there is research on monitoring and the analysis of the DNS service without focusing on the DNS tunneling attack as done in this work. The authors in [18] gathered DNS responses data including squatter domains, fast flux domains, and domains being abused by a spammer of the University of Auckland and stored the data into an SQL database for analyzing and detecting unusual behavior. Their research focuses on analyzing DNS traffic to detect spam attacks using statistical analysis instead of visualization. They used the Microsoft Strider URL Tracer, which helps users to investigate third-party domains to crawl data. In this way, they detect that the client has already visited a malicious domain name and has already been compromised.

The DNS tunneling attack visualized in this work is a significant concern in cybersecurity. Many open-source DNS tunneling tools have been designed to perform the attack such as *iodine, dns2tcp, DeNiSe, dnscapy, heyoka, fraud-bridge, dnscat,* and *dnscat2* [8]. Moreover, several types of malware were discovered that use DNS tunneling for establishing difficult to detect command and control (C&C) channels for botnet communications over the DNS protocol. The malware described in [9,10] uses DNS queries and responses to execute commands and control compromised machines over the DNS protocol. Therefore, securing them is essential.

Intrusion Detection System and Intrusion Prevention System (IDS/IPS) appliances detect and/or mitigate Internet attacks including DNS tunneling attacks using signatures or by packet inspection. (Farnham & Atlasis, 2013) described detection methods including attributes payload analysis and traffic analysis. They also provided Snort custom rules based on entropy and statistical analysis. Like viruses which can be designed to avoid anti-virus products by manipulating the virus behaviors and signatures, attackers also can deploy DNS tunneling attacks with previously unseen signatures to bypass IDS/IPS appliances. Packet inspection devices such as IPS's also have the ability to detect DNS tunneling attacks, but those products require high-speed computing machines to process the analysis which is expensive. The authors in [16] demonstrated a method to deploy Splunk, which is a commercial software that is used to index a large dataset and provides keyword searching capabilities, dashboarding, reporting, and statistical analysis, within the network and walked through steps to install external modules for enabling the detection of DNS tunneling attacks.

Machine learning is being used for detecting DNS tunneling attacks. Liu et al., 2017 proposed a prototype system that detects a DNS tunneling attack using binary-classification based on four behavior features including time-interval, request packet size, record type, and subdomain entropy features [13]. Their results show that their system achieved a high rate of detection accuracy of 99.9%. However, the system was trained to detect only well-known tools which are based on expected behavior, and an attacker can bypass the system by manipulating these features. The authors in [7] developed a machine learning method of detecting DNS tunneling attacks including information exfiltration from compromised machines and DNS tunneling that was used to establish command & control (C&C) servers. Their detection method relied on detecting DNS tunneling attacks that use *TXT* records only. However, adversaries can bypass the detection of this method by performing the attack using different techniques and DNS records. In [8], the authors discussed DNS tunneling attacks and its tools that use common and uncommon types of DNS records such as *A, AAAA, CNAME, NS, TXT, MX* and *NULL* while our visualization system represents DNS tunneling attacks by capturing and analyzing all type of DNS records.

(Choi, Lee, & Kim, 2009) developed a comprehensive and useful tool for visualizing and detecting network attacks using the parallel coordinates technique. Nine signatures were defined, one for each attack. The types of attack included portscan, hostscan, worm, source-spoofed DoS, backscatter, and network and signal DoS attacks. In addition, they developed a detection mechanism based on a hash algorithm. However, the authors did not include DNS tunneling as one of the Internet attacks. In [12], the authors focused on visualizing network attacks such as botnets that cause various types of attacks such as DDoS, spam, and others. The visualization system was developed to provide visual information which helps in detecting botnet attacks using DNS traffic. The parallel coordinates technique was used to represent three different DNS parameters in real time. Four graphical patterns were defined in that visualization system [12]. However, in our visualization system, we have focused on DNS tunneling attacks which was not addressed in [12]. Moreover, six DNS parameters were used instead of using three or four parameters in order to hopefully obtain more accurate results in both real time or from existing PCAP file, especially for DNS tunneling attacks. In [4], Born & Gustafson 2010 introduced NgViz tool that combines a visualization technique with N-gram analysis to examine and show DNS traffic from any suspicious activities. N-gram is used in text mining and natural language for processing tasks such as predicting the next item in a sequence. Their method compared a given input file of domain names with fingerprints of legitimate traffic. It is important to note that in this research, the authors supplied the comparison input of domain names and fingerprint of legitimate files manually.

Even though some research has been conducted regarding approaches for detecting and identifying the DNS tunneling attack, some issues still deserve further attention. IDS and IPS detection techniques are based on pre-defined signatures by observing events and identifying patterns which can be applied on the signatures of known tools and attacks. One of the presumptions of the machine learning methods used for detecting malicious activities in traffic is to compare the characteristics of traffic with DNS tunneling with the normal DNS traffic even though some of the well-known tools are generating tunneled traffic similar as possible to the regular DNS queries [13].

3   Visualization System Design

In this section, we describe the system architecture design of a visualization system for visualizing and identifying the Domain Name System (DNS) tunneling attacks using attack patterns as shown in Fig. 1. The visualization system consists of three main modules: Parser, Analyzer, and Visualizer. DNS data can be passively captured at the network edge or it could be read from existing PCAP files. The Parsing module was coded in the Go programming language that interfaces with the TCPDUMP library for collecting the data quickly and efficiently. The captured packets are filtered to provide all User Datagram Protocol (UDP) packets on port 53. Note that DNS can also use TCP port 53 for things such as zone transfers but it was decided to only capture the more common DNS traffic that uses UDP. Performance is one of the essential factors necessary for this system. Therefore, the focus is on the DNS response data sent by the DNS server that confirms the communications between the local computer and the local or global DNS servers. Another reason why DNS response packets were considered, is that it decreases the number of captured packets, resulting in faster computations. The DNS response packets have a significant amount of information. Therefore, it was found that a subset of information could be used to visualize and identify DNS tunneling attacks and the parameters include the ID, domain and subdomain names, TTL (Time To Live), source and destination IP, date and time. This DNS data is stored in a database or file as input into the Analyzer module.

Next, the Analyzer module retrieves the captured DNS data from the database. First, it checks that the captured data is a proper DNS packet to avoid further issues. Then, the Analyzer module filters the data to eliminate duplicate records based on the ID number and it applies analytical and mathematical functions on the captured data. For instance, it gets the number of requests for each domain name based on date and hours and sorts them by decreasing values. It selects the top five domain names that have the most frequent requests, and it compares them to the value of the threshold. If any of these values exceed the threshold, then it considers it as a thread. The Analyzer module sends the suspicious domain names to the Visualizer module.

Finally, the Visualizer module displays the analyzed data using the parallel coordinates technique. The proposed technique uses each coordinate to represent the six different parameters: source and destination IP address, domain and subdomain names, TTL, and the time. For example, assume that a workstation with '192.168.0.1' IP address sends a DNS request to the global google DNS server that has '8.8.8.8' IP address to resolve the following domain name 'www.attacker.com.' Then, the Visualizer module represents the source coordinate with the local workstation IP address '192.168.0.1', the destination coordinate as '8.8.8.8', 'attacker' as the domain name value, and 'www' as a subdomain name value. If we have thousands of requests, the visualization system displays a funnel-like pattern.

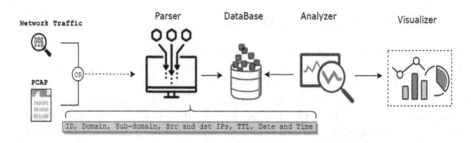

Fig. 1. System architecture design

4   Graphical Patterns for DNS Tunneling Attacks

In this section, the parallel coordinates technique is introduced that uses the captured data to represent the DNS tunneling as graphical patterns. Four DNS tunneling attack patterns are identified using the parallel coordinates technique, which can be used to both identify and understand DNS tunneling attacks. Several tunneling tools were found that implement the DNS tunneling attack, such as *iodine*, *dns2tcp*, *DeNiSe*, *dnscapy*, *heyoka*, *fraud-bridge*, *dnscat*, and *dnscat2*. Each DNS tunneling tool uses a slightly different implementation of the attack. For example, *dnscat2* uses a *NULL* for a particular request type, while *heyoka* uses different encoding techniques to pass the data over the DNS communication channel [14]. However, all of these tools are using the same concept. Note that the DNS protocol is not able to transfer large amounts data, only small to average amounts. Therefore, the DNS tunneling attack requires sending a considerable number of queries in order to transfer the data and this leads to the ability to identify these types of attacks.

In the parallel coordinates technique, each coordinate represents a particular value. The first coordinate is the source IP address which has the value of the computer that receives the DNS query while the second coordinate is the destination IP address that forwards the DNS request. The third coordinate represents the domain names, and the fourth coordinate contains subdomain names. Then, the fifth coordinate is the TTL value that is set by the Authority server which allows a DNS client to cache the answer for a particular time, while the time is the last coordinate. With these values, our visualization system shows a graphical pattern that can be matched to a template of the predefined graphical patterns of unusual DNS traffic.

Suppose that an attacker compromised a computer within a network and he needs to send stolen data out secretly without being detected by the firewall. The attacker can use a DNS tunneling attack to hide his movements or to transfer data outside the network. In this case, the attacker requires a pre-configured fake DNS server outside the network. From inside the compromised network, he can connect to his fake server via the DNS protocol that is allowed by the firewall in most networks. During the DNS tunneling attack, it sends a tremendous number of requests to the DNS server within a short amount of time actually transferring data instead of just sending DNS requests. In this work, we ran the DNS tunneling attack inside our network and we transferred a 12 MB text file. During one DNS tunneling attack, it generated a considerable number of DNS requests (52 thousand queries), which is significantly more than normal. This kind of attack splits the file into small pieces and encodes each piece with a specific encoding technique [8]. Then, it encapsulates the pieces into the DNS packets to transfer it to the preconfigured fake DNS server that has multiple preconfigured subdomain names.

The parallel coordinates visualization technique captures this unusual activity by generating attack signatures using the number of requests for each parameter. For example, Fig. 2A exhibits the previous scenario of the traditional DNS tunneling attack during one hour where the source coordinate represents the value of the attacker's computer which is *192.168.0.1*. On the destination coordinate, we can see that it has the value of global DNS server and one domain name in the domain coordinate. However, we observe more than 52 thousand subdomain names, which shows an unusual number of DNS requests within a short time. One of DNS tunneling features is that the fake DNS server sends thousands of DNS requests within a short time where it has a constant TTL value. The previous example shows all 52 thousand requests have a TTL value of zero. Figure 2B or malware scenarios using the traditional DNS attack tunneling technique to hide their C&C communications inside the network. It shows that we have many internal computers sending and receiving many DNS requests within a short time.

In [14], they presented the Heyoka tool which is one of the DNS tunneling tools that not only performs the attack but it also has some unique features that are not implemented in other DNS tunneling tools. Using Heyoka, an attacker can deploy a master DNS server with multiple slave DNS servers. One could use a different subdomain for each slave, crafting requests like the following: encoded-data.n.attacker.com, where n is the slave identifier number. Therefore, Fig. 3C shows this case when the attacker uses a multiple slave DNS server while Fig. 3D shows the case of using the Heyoka tool when it has been used by botnet clients or malware situations from multiple computers.

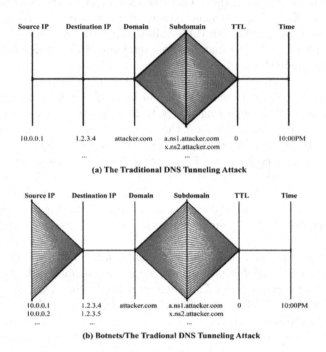

(a) The Traditional DNS Tunneling Attack

(b) Botnets/The Tradional DNS Tunneling Attack

Fig. 2. Graphical patterns for traditional DNS tunneling attack.

5   Evaluation

5.1   Experimental Setup

In this section, we show our experimental results of the experiments we performed to evaluate the visualization system. The evaluation method consists of two main parts. The first part is performing the DNS tunneling attack. The second part is importing the captured DNS traffic data to the visualization system.

In order to perform DNS tunneling attack, we register a domain name and set up an external server with a static IP address. Debian Linux server was installed and set up in the cloud for this purpose. The DNS tunneling attack was performed using Kali Linux in our internal network to encapsulate and upload a 12 MB text file to an external FTP server during a weekday. Moreover, we also sniffed and monitored normal DNS traffic during regular daily use for

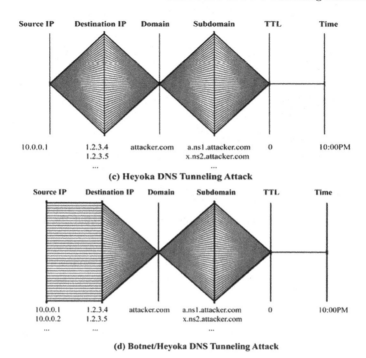

Fig. 3. Graphical patterns for heyoka DNS tunneling attack.

an entire week. There are two significant reasons for sniffing and capturing a regular DNS traffic in our experiment. The first reason is to compare and study the normal behavior of DNS traffic against the DNS traffic that has the DNS tunneling attack while the second reason is to determine and set the value of threshold based on the normal DNS traffic level.

5.2 Results

After performing the attack, the PCAP file was stored for the later analysis. Next, using the Analyzer module, the captured data was analyzed excluding the DNS tunneling attack as shown in Fig. 4. We found that Microsoft.com is the value that occurs most frequently in the data set, having 8836 DNS requests for an entire week and 170 requests per an hour as a maximum value.

As shown in Fig. 5, when implementing the DNS tunneling attack, the malicious domain name has the most frequently occurring value with more than 50000 DNS requests and 40993 requests per an hour as a maximum value. It is imperative to note that the attack has run for only two hours. This experiment was used to empirically determine the threshold. In this environment, the sum of the number of requests of all domain names was 489 per hour. Therefore, the value of the threshold has been set to 500 DNS requests in our experiment.

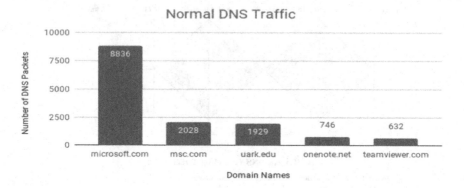

Fig. 4. Top five domain name for an entire week without the attack.

It is important to note that the threshold has to be set appropriately for each network depending upon the typical traffic levels.

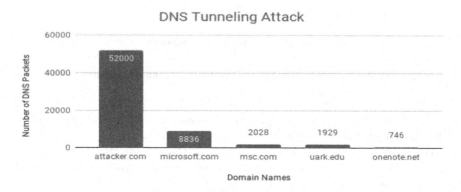

Fig. 5. Top five domain names during the attack over a two-hour period.

Next, the malicious domain name is sent to the Visualizer module to represent a possible attack using the parallel coordinates technique. Figure 7 shows the visualization of the entire captured network traffic that contains a DNS tunneling attack without the thresholding technique turned on while Fig. 6 shows the visualization of the network traffic with the DNS tunneling attack with the thresholding technique enabled. As seen in the figures, there is an obvious funnel-like pattern that appears during the attack with the proposed technique. As shown in Fig. 7, there are four values on the source IP address coordinate which represent the internal computers where they requested too many domains and subdomain names during the day. On the other hand, Fig. 6 shows that only one computer in the internal network sent too many DNS requests to resolve a considerable number of subdomain names of an attacker domain name within two hours.

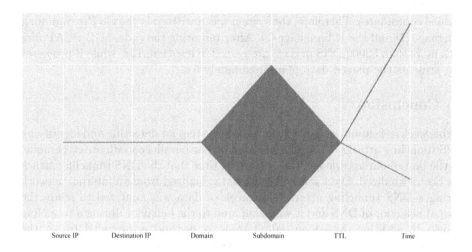

Fig. 6. Visualizer module shows only the attack.

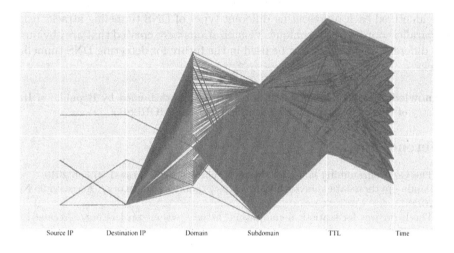

Fig. 7. Visualize the entire DNS captured data.

5.3 Issues

Several issues occurred during the initial design of the visualization system. First, the entire visualization system had been coded using Python and Pandas which is the Python Data Analysis Library [2]. Results were satisfying with a small number of data records but not a large number. As soon as our data set became larger, the system was not able to process the data as efficiently resulting in slower turnaround times. The Parser module was not able to process big PCAP files and a large number of DNS packets, and the Visualizer module was taking more than 16 h of processing time to analyze and display the data on the parallel coordinates. Therefore, the system was rewritten in the Go Programming Language [1] and the R Language [3]. After rewriting the code, 5GB PCAP files with more than 52000 DNS packets are parsed in less than 12 s, while R processes and presents the parsed data in approximately 5 s.

6   Conclusion

In this work, a fast and scalable visualization system for detecting and identifying DNS tunneling attacks is introduced based on the parallel coordinates technique. To the best of our knowledge, this is the first time that the DNS tunneling attack has been visualized. Data was collected and visualized from an internal network during a DNS tunneling attack. One week of data was analyzed to study the normal behavior of DNS and it was compared to the behavior during a tunneling attack. In addition, based on our analysis, a method is provided to set the threshold value. Six DNS parameters for the parallel coordinates technique were identified and used to visualize the DNS traffic using the parallel coordinates technique in order to distinguish between normal DNS traffic and malicious traffic containing DNS tunneling attacks. Four different DNS tunneling patterns were identified each representing different types of DNS tunneling attacks using the parallel coordinates technique. Visualizations were created that are obviously very different so that they can be used in the future for detecting DNS tunneling attacks.

Acknowledgments. This material is based upon work funded by Republic of Iraq Ministry of Higher Education and Scientific Research (MOHESR).

References

1. The Go programming language. https://golang.org/. Accessed 06 Feb 2019
2. Panda - python data analysis library. https://pandas.pydata.org/. Accessed 06 Nov 2018
3. The R project for statistical computing. https://www.r-project.org/. Accessed 06 Nov 2018
4. Born, K., Gustafson, D.: NgViz: detecting DNS tunnels through n-gram visualization and quantitative analysis. In: Proceedings of the Sixth Annual Workshop on Cyber Security and Information Intelligence Research - CSIIRW 2010 (2010). https://doi.org/10.1145/1852666.1852718
5. Choi, H., Lee, H., Kim, H.: Fast detection and visualization of network attacks on parallel coordinates. Comput. Secur. (2009). https://doi.org/10.1016/j.cose.2008.12.003
6. Cuzzocrea, A., Zall, D.: Parallel coordinates technique in visual data mining: advantages, disadvantages and combinations. In: 2013 17th International Conference on Information Visualisation, pp. 278–284, July 2013. https://doi.org/10.1109/IV.2013.96
7. Das, A., Shen, M.Y., Shashanka, M., Wang, J.: Detection of exfiltration and tunneling over DNS. In: Proceedings - 16th IEEE International Conference on Machine Learning and Applications, ICMLA 2017 (2018). https://doi.org/10.1109/ICMLA.2017.00-71

8. Farnham, G., Atlasis, A.: Detecting DNS Tunneling Detecting DNS Tunneling GIAC (GCIA) Gold Certification Detecting DNS Tunneling 2. sans.org (2013)
9. Green, A.: DNSMessenger: 2017's most beloved remote access Trojan (Rat), December 2017. https://bit.ly/2BxBz6O
10. Grunzweig, J., Scott, M., Lee, B.: New wekby attacks use DNS requests as command and control mechanism, May 2016. http://bit.ly/1TAYE8j
11. Incapsula, I.: DNS flood (2017). https://www.incapsula.com/ddos/attack-glossary/dns-flood.html. Accessed 06 Feb 2019
12. Kim, I., Choi, H., Lee, H.: BotXrayer: exposing botnets by visualizing DNS traffic. In: KSII the First International Conference on Internet (ICONI) (2009)
13. Liu, J., Li, S., Zhang, Y., Xiao, J., Chang, P., Peng, C.: Detecting DNS tunnel through binary-classification based on behavior features. In: 2017 IEEE Trustcom/BigDataSE/ICESS, pp. 339–346, August 2017. https://doi.org/10.1109/Trustcom/BigDataSE/ICESS.2017.256
14. Revelli, A., Leidecker, N.: Introducing heyoka: DNS tunneling 2.0 (2009). http://heyoka.sourceforge.net/Heyoka-SOURCEBoston2009.pdf. Accessed 07 Feb 2019
15. Satam, P., Alipour, H., Al-Nashif, Y., Hariri, S.: DNS-IDS: securing DNS in the cloud era. In: 2015 International Conference on Cloud and Autonomic Computing, pp. 296–301, September 2015. https://doi.org/10.1109/ICCAC.2015.46
16. Steve Jaworski, R.W.: Using splunk to detect DNS tunneling. Technical report (2016). https://doi.org/10.1055/s-2006-941504
17. Verisign: Framework for resilient DNS security (2018). https://blog.verisign.com/security/framework-resilient-dns-security-dns-availability-drives-business/. Accessed 01 Aug 2018
18. Zdrnja, B., Brownlee, N., Wessels, D.: Passive monitoring of DNS anomalies. In: M. Hämmerli, B., Sommer, R. (eds.) DIMVA 2007. LNCS, vol. 4579, pp. 129–139. Springer, Heidelberg (2007). https://doi.org/10.1007/978-3-540-73614-1_8

A Data-Driven Network Intrusion Detection Model Based on Host Clustering and Integrated Learning: A Case Study on Botnet Detection

Lena Ara and Xiao Luo$^{(\boxtimes)}$ (iD)

School of Engineering and Technology, Indiana University-Purdue University
Indianapolis, Indianapolis 46202, USA
`leara@iu.edu`, `luo25@iupui.edu`

Abstract. The traditional machine learning based network intrusion detection system (NIDS) is based on training a model using known network traffic for selected attacks, and testing it on the unknown network traffic of the same attacks. Evaluating machine learning based IDS with new attack traffic that is different from that training set is rare. With a large amount of network traffic generated every second, it is tough to gather all the traffic then train a model. In this research, we designed and developed an intrusion detection model by treating a network as a community. Based on the traffic behaviors, we first developed a host clustering algorithm to group the hosts into clusters and unique hosts. Then, we developed an integrated learning algorithm to integrate model-based learning derived from host clusters, and instance-based learning obtained from individual hosts. We evaluated the intrusion detection model on the CTU-13 data set which is a botnet attack data set. The results show that our model is more robust and effective for network intrusion detection and gains an average 100% detection rate, with a 0% false positive rate on detecting known attack traffic, and 98.2% detection rate on identifying new Botnet attack traffic.

Keywords: Network intrusion detection · Network flow ·
Integrated machine learning · Host clustering · Botnet detection

1 Introduction

Conducting intrusion detection and prevention based on network traffic while protecting data privacy is critical, but challenging. Since many hosts can generate a large volume of network traffic in a second, one challenge in the network intrusion detection is to efficiently model the traffic behaviors of the whole network in real-time. Although machine learning and AI algorithms have shown effectiveness for network intrusion detection in recent years [1, 10, 13, 16, 24], research rarely discusses the robustness of the learning models to new intrusion traffic.

© Springer Nature Switzerland AG 2019
G. Wang et al. (Eds.): SpaCCS 2019, LNCS 11611, pp. 102–116, 2019.
https://doi.org/10.1007/978-3-030-24907-6_9

Based on the recent research in adversarial machine learning [6,11,17,20,21], the model-based learning algorithms or models are vulnerable to the adversarial activities of the machine learning algorithms, and not resilient against being attacked or poisoned by adversarial samples. Although instance-based learning algorithms are relatively robust against adversarial machine learning, the computational cost of instance-based learning is high when the number of data instances in the training set is huge. Some research applies ensemble learning to intrusion detection [12,23,26]. Ensemble learning is a process that strategically generates and combines multiple models or algorithms to detect anomalous network traffic. In this research, we explored a new IDS by integrating model-based and instance-based learning in a distributed manner. This new IDS model is more robust when preventing adversarial actions given that it is not based on one single training set.

The new IDS explored here is based on treating a network as a community. In this community, there are host clusters and individual hosts based on traffic behaviors. The host clustering algorithm is developed to identify the host clusters based on the network flows. The individual hosts are those who do not belong to any clusters. Model-based learning algorithms can be applied to the hosts within host clusters, whereas, instance-based learning algorithms can be applied to the individual hosts. The intrusion detection model integrates learning models derived from host clusters and individual hosts using the majority vote mechanism. To integrate different model-based learning for host clusters, we first transferred trained learning models into decision regions, then, merged the sets of decision regions recursively through applying a feature ranking algorithm. Our experimental results show that the developed IDS model works better than four traditional machine learning models – Random Forest (RF), Naive Bayes (NB), Logistic Regression (LR) and Convolutional Neural Networks (CNN) on detecting known and new Botnet attack traffic.

In summary, the contributions of this paper are as follows:

- We designed and developed a host clustering algorithm based on a cross-testing mechanism. This clustering algorithm measures the similarity between the network flows of hosts and makes use of the machine learning algorithm to summarize the characteristics of the network traffic.
- We designed and developed an integration algorithm for model-based learning by transferring the trained models into decision regions and merging the decision regions of different learning models. A feature ranking algorithm is used to select essential network features to generate and merge the decision regions recursively.
- We compared the effectiveness of our model against four traditional models by using a Botnet data set. The evaluation results show the effectiveness of our intrusion detection model is better than the conventional models and achieves on average a 100% detection rate, with 0% false positive rate, and 98.2% detection rates in detecting unknown Botnet attack traffic.

2   Related Research

Host Clustering. Research in the literature explored host clustering or classification based on the network traffic or host roles. Wei and colleagues studied host clustering based on traffic behavior profiling [29]. Xu and colleagues also researched host clustering [30]. This research included analyzing the behavior of the end hosts in the same network prefixes by considering both host and network level information. Other research used supervised learning algorithms to classify hosts based on their roles in the network [14]. Hosts that were clients were classified to one category, whereas hosts that were email-servers were classified to another category. Many derived features based on the network flows, such as the number of unique host system ports and the number of unique protocols, were used to identify the roles of the hosts. It is computationally costly. Host clustering or classification purely based on the traffic behaviors, such as the incoming and outgoing network flows, has rarely been investigated. Also, very little research has been done on how to measure the similarity between two hosts based on the network traffic. In this research, we explored a host clustering algorithm based on a cross-testing mechanism and maximal clique detection on a graph.

Learning Model Integration. Research has been done on integrating different learning models for data mining or knowledge discovery applications [5,15]. One of the popular approaches is ensemble learning. Ensemble learning can improve classification or prediction performance of network anomaly detection [12,23,26]. Most of the existing ensemble learning model integrates model-based learning through majority vote. Very few investigate a strategy to integrate both model-based and instance-based learning for network intrusion detection. Compared to model-based learning, instance-based learning can work as a specialized detector to identify specific anomalous traffic.

To the best of our knowledge, this research is the first to investigate a strategy to ensemble model-based and instance-based learning by first modeling the network traffic, then integrating the learning models in a distributed manner.

3   System Framework

Figure 1 demonstrates the overall system framework of the intrusion detection model. Given n hosts within a network, first, the host clustering algorithm is used to identify m host clusters based on the similarity of the network traffic flows. One host can belong to one or more host clusters. After determining the host clusters, model-based learning algorithms are applied to the network traffic of each host in the host clusters to generate learning models. The rest of the hosts that are not in the host clusters are used to create instance-based learning models using their specific traffic. For each host cluster, since the network traffic of the hosts are very similar to each other, we further integrated the learning models of the hosts in the same cluster by applying the integration algorithm developed in this research. Lastly, we ensembled the model-based learning models with the instance-based models through a majority vote mechanism. A network flow is classified as an attack if more than half of these learning models predict it as an attack.

Payload information in the network flows is not included. The network flow features used in this research are: duration of the connection in seconds, the type of the protocol (TCP, UDP, ICMP), the port of the connection destination, the port of the connection source, the type of service from destination to source, the type of Service from source to destination, the total bytes of the flow, total packets of the flow, the direction of the flow.

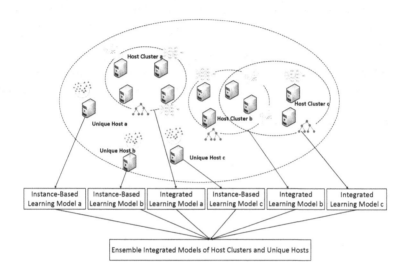

Fig. 1. System Framework of the Intrusion Detection Model

4   Cross-Testing and Host Clustering

The host clustering groups the hosts based on analyzing their traffic patterns. It is not feasible to compare a large amount of network traffic generated by two hosts in a short period. The host clustering algorithm developed in this research is based on an assumption: The network traffic behavior (normal vs. attack) can be summarized and inferred by a trained learning model generated from a learning algorithm. So, if the trained learning models using network flows of two hosts are similar, these two hosts can be clustered into one cluster. We used a cross-testing approach to evaluate the similarity of two learning models. The cross-testing approach works as follows: if a learning model generated by the network flows of host i can detect attack network traffic of host j, and vice versa, the network traffic patterns of both hosts are very similar, and they are in the same cluster. Different learning algorithms take advantage of different optimization functions or processes to generate learning models. We hypothesize that if two hosts are similar enough to each other, the cross-testing needs to be deployed on more than one machine learning algorithm.

The traditional evaluation metrics, such as F1-measure, false positive, and detection rate, can be used for cross-testing. Threshold (θ) can be used to determine the confidence level of similarity. In this research, F1-measure is used to evaluate the similarity between the hosts. The confidence level of similarity is defined as $\theta = 0.9$. When θ is set to be a high value, it means the model created on one host can detect most of the intrusions of the other host with low false alarm rate. Two hosts are similar only if F1-measure values of cross-testing are above 0.9. The cross-testing evaluation results based on a learning algorithm can be stored in a matrix $(CrossT)$, as Eq. 1. The $e_{i,j}$ represents the cross-testing that learning model has generated on host i, and tested using network traffic of host j. The $e_{i,i}$ represents the cross-testing results of host i using its network traffic for both training and testing. If m learning algorithms are used for cross-testing, m cross-testing matrices can be aggregated by averaging them into one. If some learning algorithms are treated as more critical than others, a weighted average can be taken, as Eq. 2.

$$CrossT = \begin{pmatrix} 1 & e_{1,2} & \cdots & e_{1,n} \\ e_{2,1} & 1 & \cdots & e_{2,n} \\ \vdots & \vdots & \ddots & \vdots \\ e_{n,1} & e_{n,2} & \cdots & 1 \end{pmatrix} \tag{1}$$

$$AverageCrossT = \sum_{i=1}^{m} w_i CrossT_i, \qquad \sum_{i=1}^{m} w_i = 1 \tag{2}$$

Algorithm 1. Cluster-Identification

Input: R, $Hosts$, X, $Edges$
Output: $Cluster$
   $X = \emptyset$
   $R = \emptyset$
   if $(Hosts = \emptyset) \&\& (X = \emptyset)$ **then**
      $Cluster = R$
   end if
   for each host v in $Hosts$ **do**
      $N(v) = $ Neighbor Set of v based on $Edges$
      $R = $ Cluster-Identification$(R \cup \{v\}, Hosts \cap N(v), X \cap N(v), Edges)$
      $Hosts = Hosts \setminus v$
      $X = X \cup v$
   end for

After constructing the cross-testing matrix, an undirected graph is derived to generate host clusters. An edge (i, j) exists only when $e_{i,j}$ and $e_{j,i}$ are both above the threshold θ. The hosts within the network are treated as nodes in an undirected graph, whereas, the edges between the hosts demonstrate the similarities between the hosts. Algorithm 1 is developed to identify the host clusters in a network. Algorithm 1 is based on the maximum clique identification algorithm developed by Östergård [19].

The following example demonstrates the process of host clustering. There are four hosts within this example network; the cross-testing matrix is calculated as Eq. 3. The derived undirected graph and the identified host cluster are presented in Fig. 2.

$$CrossT = \begin{pmatrix} 1 & 0.9 & 0.5 & 0.9 \\ 0.9 & 1 & 0.9 & 0.9 \\ 0.8 & 0.9 & 1 & 0.2 \\ 0.9 & 1 & 0.7 & 1 \end{pmatrix} \tag{3}$$

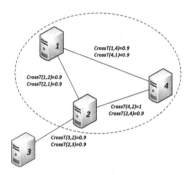

Fig. 2. Host Clustering based on the Cross-Testing Matrix

5   Network Intrusion Detection Model

After host clustering, the intrusion detection model is built by first integrating learning models in host clusters, and then ensembling with the learning models generated by the individual hosts.

5.1   Integrate Learning Models in Host Clusters

In this research, we integrated the learning models in host clusters by combining the decision regions generated by the learning models. Since the hosts within a cluster behave similarly to each other from the network traffic point of view, it is valid to assume that the decision regions generated by the learning model of each host are similar enough to be combined. Different from the tensor-based approach explored by Zhang et al. [32], the integration of the decision regions relies on a recursive feature-ranking process. Figure 3 demonstrates combining decision regions of two hosts: A and B using two network flow features – port number and duration. Figure 4 demonstrates integrated decision regions. In reality, more than two network flow features are used for intrusion detection, although it is not easy to depict in two-dimensional space.

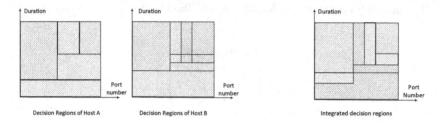

Fig. 3. Decision Regions of Hosts   **Fig. 4.** Integrated Decision Regions

In this research, we explored an algorithm to combine decision regions (shown as Fig. 4) through applying a recursive feature-ranking process [4]. First, the chi-squared (χ^2) feature ranking method [18] is used to identify the top-ranked feature. The calculation of χ^2 is given as Formula 4, where f denotes a network flow feature; $|T|$ means the total number of network flows; C_j means normal or attack. Combined decision boundaries are first constructed based on one top-ranked feature and the decision regions of each host. Within the integrated decision boundaries, the feature ranking method is used again to select the top-ranked feature among the rest of the features and construct decision boundaries. This recursive process continues till all features or top n features are used.

$$\chi^2(f, C_j) = \frac{|T|(P(f,C_j)P(\overline{f},\overline{C_j}) - P(\overline{f},C_j)P(f,\overline{C_j}))^2}{P(f)P(\overline{f})P(C_j)P(\overline{C_j})} \tag{4}$$

Algorithm 2 demonstrates the generation of integrated decision regions (InteDecisionRegs), where n is the pre-defined top features to generate decision regions, F_0 is the top-ranked feature in feature list F. The function *CrtDecisionRegs* is used to create the decision regions based on the decision regions of each host (*HostDecRegs*), the new feature F_0, and the existing integrated decision regions.

5.2 Ensemble Learning Models of Host Clusters and Unique Hosts

Within a network, it is normal that some hosts have their unique traffic behaviors, which are not similar to those of the rest of the hosts. In our IDS model, while generating the integrated models on the host clusters, instance-based learning models are produced on the unique hosts at the same time. Specifically, k-Nearest-Neighbor (kNN) [2] is used to create instance-based learning models on the individual hosts. In our experiments, k is set to 2.

Algorithm 2. Algorithm-for-Combining-Decision-Regions

Input: F, n, $HostDecRegs$
Output: $InteDecisionRegs$
  $i \leftarrow 1$
  $F \leftarrow chi^2(\text{F})$
  while $(F! = \emptyset)\&\&i \leq n$ **do**
    $InteDecisionRegs = CrtDecisionRegs(F_0, HostDecRegs, InteDecisionRegs)$
    $F = F \setminus F_0$
    $i = i + 1$
    Algorithm-for-Combining-Decision-Regions$(F, N, HostDecRegs)$
  end while
  return $InteDecisionRegs$

As demonstrated in Fig. 1, we ensemble the learning models generated from the host clusters with the instance-based models produced from the individual hosts by applying the majority vote mechanism. A network flow is classified as an attack, if more than half of these models predict it as an attack.

6 Experimental Results and Analysis

6.1 Data Set

This intrusion detection model is evaluated on a publicly available Botnet data set – CTU-13 data set [8].

CTU-13 has 13 different data sets, and the network flows are labeled as Background, Botnet, C&C Channels and Normal. In our experiments, we used data sets 10 and 13. Table 1 demonstrates the different Botnet attack scenarios in each data set. In this research, one objective is to evaluate the robustness of our model on detecting new attacks. So, each data set is used to generate an intrusion detection model. The testing phase includes using the other data set, which contains new attacks that are not in the training data. The model training and test set up is as follows: 70% of data from each data set is to generate the models, 30% of each data set and 100% of the other data set are used to test the models.

Table 1. Type of Botnet in Each Data Set

Data Set	Type of Botnet
CTU-13 - 10	IRC, UDP DDoS, CTU compiled and controlled Botnet
CTU-13 - 13	SPAM, Port Scan, HTTP Botnet

In our research, the traffic is separated based on the hosts. The network flows of each data set are grouped according to the destination IP addresses. Each unique IP address is treated as a host in the network. Only the hosts that contain both normal and Botnet flows are kept to build the intrusion detection model. In the end, there are 16 hosts in data set 10 and 18 hosts in data set 13.

6.2 Host Clustering Results

In this research, two learning algorithms – Decision Tree [22] and Support Vector Machine [7] – are used to generate the cross-testing matrices. An equally weighted average is taken to integrate the two cross-testing matrices for Decision Tree and Support Vector Machine respectively. Based on cross-testing and host clustering algorithms described in Sect. 4, Figs. 5 and 7 present the weighted average of the cross-testing matrices of F1-measures. Figures 6 and 8 present the undirected graphs generated based on these matrices. After applying the host clustering algorithm, three host clusters are identified for data set 10, and two host clusters are identified for data set 13.

$$
\begin{pmatrix}
1 & 0.06 & 1 & 1 & 1 & 1 & 1 & 1 & 1 & 1 & 1 & 1 & 1 & 1 & 1 & 1 \\
0.5 & 1 & 0.4 & 0.4 & 0.4 & 0.4 & 0.4 & 0.4 & 0.4 & 0.4 & 0.5 & 0.5 & 0.4 & 0.5 & 0.4 & 0.5 \\
0.9 & 0.2 & 1 & 1 & 1 & 1 & 1 & 1 & 1 & 1 & 1 & 1 & 1 & 1 & 1 & 1 \\
0.9 & 0.2 & 1 & 1 & 1 & 1 & 1 & 1 & 1 & 1 & 1 & 1 & 1 & 1 & 1 & 1 \\
0.9 & 0.2 & 1 & 1 & 1 & 1 & 1 & 1 & 1 & 1 & 1 & 1 & 1 & 1 & 1 & 1 \\
0.9 & 0.2 & 1 & 1 & 1 & 1 & 1 & 1 & 1 & 1 & 1 & 1 & 1 & 1 & 1 & 1 \\
0.1 & 0.4 & 0.6 & 0.6 & 0.6 & 1 & 1 & 1 & 0.6 & 1 & 0.9 & 1 & 0.9 & 1 & 0.9 & 0.9 \\
0.4 & 0.5 & 0.6 & 0.8 & 0.8 & 0.6 & 0.7 & 1 & 0.7 & 0.6 & 0.8 & 0.6 & 0.8 & 0.8 & 0.7 & 0.8 \\
0.9 & 0.2 & 1 & 1 & 1 & 1 & 1 & 1 & 1 & 1 & 1 & 1 & 1 & 1 & 1 & 1 \\
0.9 & 0.2 & 1 & 1 & 1 & 1 & 1 & 1 & 1 & 1 & 1 & 1 & 1 & 1 & 1 & 1 \\
0.1 & 0.4 & 0.6 & 0.6 & 0.5 & 1 & 1 & 1 & 0.6 & 1 & 1 & 1 & 0.9 & 1 & 0.9 & 0.8 \\
0.9 & 0.2 & 1 & 1 & 1 & 1 & 1 & 1 & 1 & 1 & 1 & 1 & 1 & 1 & 1 & 1 \\
0.9 & 0.2 & 1 & 1 & 1 & 1 & 1 & 1 & 1 & 1 & 1 & 1 & 1 & 1 & 1 & 1 \\
0.9 & 0.2 & 1 & 1 & 1 & 1 & 1 & 1 & 1 & 1 & 1 & 1 & 1 & 1 & 1 & 1 \\
0.1 & 0.4 & 0.6 & 0.6 & 0.5 & 1 & 0.6 & 1 & 0.7 & 1 & 0.7 & 1 & 1 & 0.8 & 1 & 0.7 \\
0.9 & 0.2 & 1 & 1 & 1 & 1 & 1 & 1 & 1 & 1 & 1 & 1 & 1 & 1 & 1 & 1
\end{pmatrix}
$$

Fig. 5. Cross-testing Matrix of Data Set 10

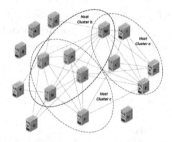

Fig. 6. Host Clustering of Data Set 10

$$\begin{pmatrix}
1 & 0.5 & 0.5 & 0.3 & 0.2 & 0.5 & 0.4 & 0.8 & 1 & 1 & 0.4 & 1 & 0.8 & 1 & 0.4 & 1 & 1 & 1 \\
0.9 & 1 & 1 & 1 & 1 & 0.7 & 0.7 & 0.8 & 0.8 & 0.7 & 0.7 & 0.8 & 0.8 & 0.8 & 0.6 & 0.6 & 1 \\
0.9 & 1 & 1 & 1 & 1 & 0.7 & 1 & 1 & 1 & 1 & 1 & 1 & 1 & 1 & 1 & 1 & 1 \\
0.4 & 0.2 & 0.2 & 1 & 0.4 & 0.2 & 0.4 & 0.2 & 0.4 & 0.3 & 0.4 & 0.4 & 0.4 & 0.3 & 0.4 & 0.4 & 0.4 & 0.3 \\
0.2 & 0.8 & 0.7 & 0.7 & 1 & 0.4 & 0.7 & 0.7 & 0.2 & 0.4 & 0.5 & 0.3 & 0.6 & 0.4 & 0.8 & 0.1 & 0 & 0.1 \\
0.2 & 0.4 & 0.3 & 0.4 & 0.5 & 1 & 0.1 & 0 & 0 & 0 & 0 & 0 & 0 & 0.1 & 0 & 0 & 0.1 \\
0.9 & 0.9 & 0.9 & 1 & 0.6 & 0.7 & 1 & 1 & 1 & 1 & 1 & 1 & 1 & 1 & 1 & 1 & 1 \\
0.9 & 0.9 & 0.8 & 0.6 & 0.5 & 0.7 & 1 & 1 & 1 & 1 & 0.4 & 1 & 1 & 0.8 & 1 & 1 & 1 \\
0.9 & 0.9 & 0.8 & 0.6 & 0.5 & 0.7 & 1 & 1 & 1 & 1 & 0.4 & 1 & 1 & 1 & 0.8 & 1 & 1 & 1 \\
0.2 & 0.2 & 0.3 & 0.1 & 0 & 0.4 & 0.4 & 0.7 & 0.5 & 1 & 0.4 & 1 & 0.4 & 0.6 & 0.4 & 0.1 & 0 & 0.4 \\
0.2 & 0.8 & 0.7 & 0 & 0.3 & 0.6 & 0.4 & 0.4 & 0.2 & 0.5 & 1 & 0.3 & 0.4 & 0.4 & 0.4 & 0 & 0 & 1 \\
0.2 & 0.2 & 0.3 & 0.1 & 0 & 0.4 & 0.4 & 0.7 & 0.5 & 0.8 & 0.4 & 1 & 0.4 & 0.4 & 0.4 & 0.1 & 0 & 0.4 \\
0.9 & 0.9 & 0.9 & 1 & 0.6 & 0.7 & 1 & 1 & 1 & 1 & 1 & 1 & 1 & 1 & 1 & 1 & 1 \\
0.2 & 0.2 & 0.3 & 0.1 & 0 & 0.4 & 0.4 & 0.7 & 0.5 & 1 & 0.4 & 1 & 0.4 & 1 & 0.4 & 0.1 & 0 & 0.4 \\
0.9 & 1 & 1 & 1 & 1 & 0.7 & 1 & 1 & 1 & 1 & 1 & 1 & 1 & 1 & 1 & 1 & 1 \\
0.9 & 0.9 & 0.8 & 0.8 & 0.6 & 0.7 & 1 & 1 & 1 & 1 & 0.4 & 1 & 1 & 1 & 1 & 1 & 1 \\
0.9 & 0.9 & 0.8 & 0.6 & 0.5 & 0.7 & 1 & 1 & 1 & 1 & 0.4 & 1 & 1 & 1 & 0.8 & 1 & 1 & 1 \\
0.2 & 0.7 & 0.7 & 0 & 0.2 & 0.4 & 0.3 & 0.5 & 0.1 & 0.3 & 0.3 & 0.1 & 0.5 & 0.3 & 0.2 & 0 & 0 & 1
\end{pmatrix}$$

Fig. 7. Cross-testing Matrix of Data Set 13

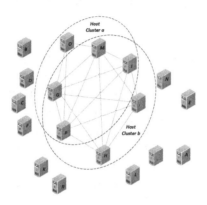

Fig. 8. Host Clustering of Data Set 13

6.3 Performance of the Intrusion Detection Model

After the host clusters are identified, intrusion detection models are built for each data set respectively. First, integrated learning models are built for the host clusters based on the algorithm of combining decision regions. Meanwhile, the instance-based learning model – kNN is created on the individual hosts that are not in the host clusters.

In this research, we compared our intrusion detection model with four other traditional detection models that have been used for network intrusion detection: Random Forest (RF) [25,31], Naive Bayes (NB) [3,9], Logistic Regression (LR) [25,28] and Convolutional Neural Networks (CNN) [27]. The RF was set to use a maximum of 100 trees and split points chosen from a random selection of 3 features. The Gaussian Probability Density Function was used for NB. The number of hidden layers of CNN was 5, and the number of neurons for each layer was set to be 20, 15, 25, 15, and 20, respectively. The metrics - false positive rate (FPR) and detection rate (DR) were used to evaluate the results. FPR and DR are calculated using Eqs. 5 and 6.

$$FPR = \frac{Number\ of\ Normal\ Detected\ as\ Attack}{Total\ Number\ of\ Normal\ Connections} \tag{5}$$

$$DR = \frac{Number\ of\ Detected\ Attacks}{Total\ Number\ of\ Attack\ Connections} \tag{6}$$

The models generated based on the training data are evaluated on the test data of the same data set, as well on the data of the other data set. We evaluated the model performance on each host to see whether the models are robust enough for some hosts that have very minimum traffic.

Table 2. Test Results on Data Set 10 using Learning Model of Data Set 10

Hosts		A	B	C	D	E	F	G	H	I	J	K	L	M	N	O	P	Average
RF	DR	1	0.78	1	1	1	1	1	1	1	1	1	1	1	1	1	1	0.986
	FPR	0	0	0.02	0	0	0	0	0	0	0	0	0	0	0	0	0	0.001
LG	DR	0	0.99	0	0	0	0	0	0	0	0	0	0	0	0	0	0	0.061
	FPR	0	0	0	0	0	0	0	0	0	0	0	0	0	0	0	0	0
NB	DR	0	0.95	0	0	0	0	0	0	0	0	0	0	0	0	0	0	0.059
	FPR	0	0	0	0	0	0	0	0	0	0	0	0	0	0	0	0	0
CNN	DR	1	0.78	1	1	1	1	1	1	1	1	1	1	1	1	1	1	0.986
	FPR	0	0	0.02	0	0	0	0	0	0	0	0	0	0	0	0	0	0.001
Our Model	DR	1	1	1	1	1	1	1	1	1	1	1	1	1	1	1	1	1
	FPR	0	0	0	0	0	0	0	0	0	0	0	0	0	0	0	0	0

Table 3. Test Results on Data Set 13 using Learning Model of Data Set 10

Hosts		A	B	C	D	E	F	G	H	I	J	K	L	M	N	O	P	Q	R	Ave.
RF	DR	0.81	0.68	0.65	0	0.23	1	0	0.34	0	1	0	1	0	1	0	0	0	0	0.37
	FPR	0.04	0	0	0	0	0.5	0	0	0	0	0	0	0	0	0	0	0	0	0.03
LG	DR	0	0	0	0	0	0	0	0	0	0	0	0	0	0	0	0	0	0	0
	FPR	0	0	0	0	0	0	0	0.4	0	0	0	0	0	0	0	0	0	0	0.02
NB	DR	0	0.08	0	0.1	0	0	0	0	0	0	0	0	0	0	0	0	0	0	0.01
	FPR	0	0	0.05	0	0	0	0	0.47	0	0.09	0.06	0.04	0.05	0	0	0	0	0	0.04
CNN	DR	0.99	0.37	0.21	0	0.2	0.4	1	0.34	1	1	0	1	0.5	0	0.5	0	0	1	0.47
	FPR	0	0	0	0	0	0	0	0	0	0	0	0.02	0	0	0	0	0	0	0.001
Our Model	DR	1	0.85	1	0.6	0.73	1	1	1	1	1	1	1	1	1	1	1	1	1	0.95
	FPR	0	0	0	0	0	0	0	0	0	0	0	0	0	0	0	0	0	0	0

Table 2 demonstrates the results of training and testing the learning model using network traffic of data set 10. The LR and NB both do not work well on this data set. Other than Host B, the detection rates on the rest of the hosts are all 0. The RF and the CNN perform better. Other than Host B, the detection rates on the rest of the hosts are all 1, and the false positive rates on all hosts are 0 or close to 0. Our model works better than all the other learning models and

Table 4. Test Results on Data Set 13 using Learning Model of Data Set 13

Hosts		A	B	C	D	E	F	G	H	I	J	K	L	M	N	O	P	Q	R	Ave.
RF	DR	1	1	1	1	1	1	1	1	1	1	1	1	1	1	1	1	1	1	1
	FPR	0	0	0	0	0	0	0	0	0	0	0	0	0	0	0	0	0	0	0
LG	DR	0.99	0.62	0.39	0.9	0.65	0.8	0	0.34	0	1	0	1	0	1	0	1	1	1	0.59
	FPR	0	0	0	0	0	0.5	0.2	0.16	0.07	0.19	0.13	0.16	0.21	0.03	0.35	0.09	0	0	0.12
NB	DR	0.99	0.43	0.3	0	0.13	0.8	0	0	0	1	0	1	0	1	0	0	0	1	0.37
	FPR	0	0	0	0	0	0.5	0	0	0	0	0	0	0	0	0	0	0	0	0.03
CNN	DR	1	1	1	1	1	1	1	1	1	1	0.5	1	1	1	1	1	1	1	0.97
	FPR	0	0	0.05	0	0	0.5	0	0	0	0	0	0	0	0	0	0	0	0	0.03
Our Model	DR	1	1	1	1	1	1	1	1	1	1	1	1	1	1	1	1	1	1	1
	FPR	0	0	0	0	0	0	0	0	0	0	0	0	0	0	0	0	0	0	0

Table 5. Test Results on Data Set 10 using Learning Model of Data Set 13

Hosts		A	B	C	D	E	F	G	H	I	J	K	L	M	N	O	P	Ave.
RF	DR	1	**0.78**	1	1	1	1	1	1	1	1	1	1	1	1	1	1	**0.99**
	FPR	0	0.9	0	0	0	0	0	0	0	0	0	0	0	0	0	0	**0.05**
LG	DR	1	0.09	1	1	1	1	1	1	1	1	1	1	1	1	1	1	0.95
	FPR	0	0.9	0.46	0.04	0.31	0.21	0.34	0.3	0.26	0.14	0.14	0.35	0.14	0.18	0.41	0.07	0.24
NB	DR	1	0	1	1	1	1	1	1	1	1	1	1	1	1	1	1	0.94
	FPR	0	0	0	0	0	0	0	0	0	0	0	0	0	0	0	0	0
CNN	DR	1	0.77	1	1	1	1	1	1	1	1	1	1	1	1	1	1	**0.98**
	FPR	0	1	0.04	0	0.2	0.02	0.03	0	0	0	0	0	0	0.02	0.2	0	0.08
Our Model	DR	1	0.69	1	1	1	1	1	1	1	1	1	1	1	1	1	1	0.98
	FPR	0	0.9	0	0	0	0	0	0	0	0	0	0	0	0	0	0	**0.05**

gains detection rates of 1 and false positive rates of 0 on all of the hosts. In our model, because the Host B is not within any of the host clusters, instance-based learning, kNN, is used. This demonstrates that instance-based learning works better if the network traffic behavior of a host is unique.

Table 3 shows the testing results of the learning model generated from data set 10 but tested on data set 13. These results demonstrate the robustness of traditional models and our model on analyzing new Botnet attack traffic. RF and CNN both work well on some of the hosts of data set 13. For hosts A, G, I, and R, CNN works better than the RF. CNN gains detection rates close to 1 and false positive rates of 0. For hosts B, C and N, RF achieves higher detection rates. Our model outperforms all the other models on all hosts. Especially for hosts D, K, P and Q, both RF and CNN cannot detect any Botnet traffic on those hosts, whereas our model gains a detection rate of 0.6 on host D and a detection rate of 1 on hosts K, P and Q. The false positive rates for these four hosts are also as low as 0. Our model detects all Botnets on hosts G, H, I, M, P and Q in cluster b of data set 13 (shown in Fig. 8). This confirms that the traffic similarity between these hosts is very high. As long as the model works on one of the hosts, it works on the rest of the hosts in a host cluster.

Table 4 demonstrates the results of training and testing the learning model using network traffic of data set 13. LG and NB perform worse than the other three models. Our model and RF both achieve high performance with detection rates of 1 and false positive rates of 0 on all the hosts. Although CNN performs worse than our model and RF on hosts C, F, and K, it performs well on the rest of the hosts.

Table 5 shows the results of the learning model generated from data set 13 but tested on data set 10. The detection rates of all models on all hosts other than Host B are 1. The false positive rates of RF, CNN and our model are all close to 0 except Host B. Overall, LR and NB perform worse than the other three models. RF performs slightly better than CNN and our model on Host B.

To compare the overall performance of the four detection models based on the traditional machine learning or AI algorithms, we took the average of all hosts of the two data sets. Figures 9 and 10 show the comparison of the detection rates and false positive rates respectively. Our model has the highest detection rate and lowest false positive rate comparing to the other traditional models.

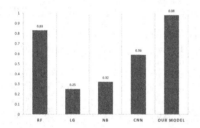

Fig. 9. Comparison of Average DR   **Fig. 10.** Comparison of Average FPR

7   Conclusions and Future Work

In this research, we designed and developed an innovative network intrusion detection model by first identifying the host clusters and then integrating the learning models of the host clusters and unique hosts. Different from the traditional learning models, our model doesn't require gathering all the network traffic to train a centralized learning model. Instead, the training can happen in parallel on all the hosts. To integrate the learning models within the clusters, we proposed a method to merge the decision regions in a recursive way based on a feature ranking algorithm. The achieved detection rates and false positive rates demonstrate that our model gains better detection rates and false positive rates on both existing and new network flow patterns.

The current work uses F1-measure and threshold 0.9 for creating the host clusters, it doesn't require the traffic behaviors of two hosts are exact the same with regards to intrusion detection. We will consider other metrics and thresholds in the future. In this research, supervised learning algorithms were used. We also plan to extend this intrusion detection model by applying an unsupervised learning algorithm in the future.

References

1. Akramifard, H., Khanli, L.M., ABalafar, M., Davtalab, R.: Intrusion detection in the cloud environment using multi-level fuzzy neural networks. In: Proceedings of International Conference on Security and Management, pp. 152–159 (2015). https://doi.org/10.1109/CSE.2015.26

2. Altman, N.S.: An introduction to kernel and nearest-neighbor nonparametric regression. Am. Stat. **46**(3), 175–185 (1992)

3. Amor, N.B., Benferhat, S., Elouedi, Z.: Naive bayes vs. decision trees in intrusion detection systems. In: Proceedings of the 2004 ACM Symposium on Applied Computing, pp. 420–424. ACM (2004)

4. Andrzejak, A., Langner, F., Zabala, S.: Interpretable models from distributed data via merging of decision trees. In: 2013 IEEE Symposium on Computational Intelligence and Data Mining (CIDM), pp. 1–9. IEEE (2013)

5. Chong, M., Abraham, A., Paprzycki, M.: Traffic accident analysis using machine learning paradigms. Informatica **29**(1) (2005)

6. Clements, J., Yang, Y., Sharma, A., Hu, H., Lao, Y.: Rallying adversarial techniques against deep learning for network security. arXiv preprint arXiv:1903.11688 (2019)

7. Cortes, C., Vapnik, V.: Support-vector networks. Mach. Learn. **20**(3), 273–297 (1995)

8. García, S., Grill, M., Stiborek, J., Zunino, A.: An empirical comparison of botnet detection methods. Comput. Secur. **45**, 100–123 (2014)

9. Hasan, M.A.M., Nasser, M., Pal, B., Ahmad, S.: Support vector machine and random forest modeling for intrusion detection system (IDS). J. Intell. Learn. Syst. Appl. **6**(01), 45 (2014)

10. Huang, H., Al-Azzawi, H., Brani, H.: Network traffic anomaly detection. arXiv preprint arXiv:1402.0856 (2014)

11. Huster, T.P., Chiang, C.Y.J., Chadha, R., Swami, A.: Towards the development of robust deep neural networks in adversarial settings. In: MILCOM 2018–2018 IEEE Military Communications Conference (MILCOM), pp. 419–424. IEEE (2018)

12. Kim, G., Lee, S., Kim, S.: A novel hybrid intrusion detection method integrating anomaly detection with misuse detection. Exp. Syst. Appl. **41**(4), 1690–1700 (2014)

13. Le, D.C., Zincir-Heywood, A.N., Heywood, M.I.: Data analytics on network traffic flows for botnet behaviour detection. In: 2016 IEEE Symposium Series on Computational Intelligence (SSCI), pp. 1–7. IEEE (2016)

14. Li, B., Gunes, M.H., Bebis, G., Springer, J.: A supervised machine learning approach to classify host roles on line using sflow. In: Proceedings of the First Edition Workshop on High Performance and Programmable Networking, pp. 53–60. ACM (2013)

15. Lin, W.Y., Hu, Y.H., Tsai, C.F.: Machine learning in financial crisis prediction: a survey. IEEE Trans. Syst. Man Cybern. Part C (Appl. Rev.) **42**(4), 421–436 (2012)

16. Sheikhan, M., Jadidi, Z., Farrokhi, A.: Intrusion detection using reduced-size rnn based on feature grouping, neural computing and applications. Neural Comput. Appl. **21**(6), 1185–1190 (2012)

17. Martinez, E.E.B., Oh, B., Li, F., Luo, X.: Evading deep neural network and random forest classifiers by generating adversarial samples. In: Zincir-Heywood, N., Bonfante, G., Debbabi, M., Garcia-Alfaro, J. (eds.) FPS 2018. LNCS, vol. 11358, pp. 143–155. Springer, Cham (2019). https://doi.org/10.1007/978-3-030-18419-3_10

18. Moh'd A Mesleh, A.: Chi square feature extraction based Svms Arabic language text categorization system. J. Comput. Sci. **3**(6), 430–435 (2007)
19. Östergård, P.R.: A fast algorithm for the maximum clique problem. Disc. Appl. Math. **120**(1–3), 197–207 (2002)
20. Papernot, N., McDaniel, P., Goodfellow, I., Jha, S., Celik, Z.B., Swami, A.: Practical black-box attacks against machine learning. In: Proceedings of the 2017 ACM on Asia Conference on Computer and Communications Security, pp. 506–519. ACM (2017)
21. Papernot, N., McDaniel, P., Jha, S., Fredrikson, M., Celik, Z.B., Swami, A.: The limitations of deep learning in adversarial settings. In: 2016 IEEE European Symposium on Security and Privacy (EuroS&P), pp. 372–387. IEEE (2016)
22. Quinlan, J.R.: Induction of decision trees. Mach. Learn. **1**(1), 81–106 (1986)
23. Reddy, R.R., Ramadevi, Y., Sunitha, K.: Real time anomaly detection using ensembles. In: 2014 International Conference on Information Science and Applications (ICISA), pp. 1–4. IEEE (2014)
24. Shone, N., Ngoc, T.N., Phai, V.D., Shi, Q.: A deep learning approach to network intrusion detection. IEEE Trans. Emerg. Top. Computat. Intell. **2**(1), 41–50 (2018)
25. Tsai, C.F., Hsu, Y.F., Lin, C.Y., Lin, W.Y.: Intrusion detection by machine learning: A review. Exp. Syst. Appl. **36**(10), 11994–12000 (2009)
26. Vanerio, J., Casas, P.: Ensemble-learning approaches for network security and anomaly detection. In: Proceedings of the Workshop on Big Data Analytics and Machine Learning for Data Communication Networks, pp. 1–6. ACM (2017)
27. Vinayakumar, R., Soman, K., Poornachandran, P.: Applying convolutional neural network for network intrusion detection. In: 2017 International Conference on Advances in Computing, Communications and Informatics (ICACCI), pp. 1222–1228. IEEE (2017)
28. Wang, Y.: A multinomial logistic regression modeling approach for anomaly intrusion detection. Comput. Secur. **24**(8), 662–674 (2005)
29. Wei, S., Mirkovic, J., Kissel, E.: Profiling and clustering internet hosts. DMIN **6**, 269–75 (2006)
30. Xu, K., Wang, F., Gu, L.: Network-aware behavior clustering of internet end hosts. In: 2011 Proceedings of the IEEE INFOCOM, pp. 2078–2086. IEEE (2011)
31. Zhang, J., Zulkernine, M., Haque, A.: Random-forests-based network intrusion detection systems. IEEE Trans. Syst. Man Cybern. Part C (Appl. Rev.) **38**(5), 649–659 (2008)
32. Zhang, S., Yang, L.T., Kuang, L., Feng, J., Chen, J., Piuri, V.: A tensor-based forensics framework for virtualized network functions in the internet of things: Utilizing tensor algebra in facilitating more efficient network forensic investigations. IEEE Consum. Electron. Mag. **8**(3), 23–27 (2019)

Towards H-SDN Traffic Analytic Through Visual Analytics and Machine Learning

Tin Tze Chiang[1], Tan Saw Chin[1(✉)], Lee Ching Kwang[2],
Y. Zulfadzli[2], and K. Rizaludin[3]

[1] Faculty of Informatics and Computing, Multimedia University, 63100
Cyberjaya, Selangor, Malaysia
`sctan1@mmu.edu.my`
[2] Faculty of Engineering, Multimedia University, 63100 Cyberjaya,
Selangor, Malaysia
[3] Telekom Malaysia R&D, Jalan Persiaran Mulitmedia, 63100 Cyberjaya,
Selangor, Malaysia

Abstract. With new networking paradigm emerged through Software-Defined Networking (SDN) offering various networking advantages over the traditional paradigm, organizations are attracted to migration their legacy networks to SDN networks. However, it is both challenging and impractical for organizations to migrate from traditional network architecture to full SDN architecture overnight. Therefore, the migration plan is performed in stages, resulting in a new type of network termed hybrid SDN (H-SDN). Effective migration and traffic scheduling in H-SDN environment are the two areas of challenges organizations face. Various solutions have been proposed in the literatures to address these two challenges. Differing from the approaches taken in the literatures, this work utilizes visual analytic and machine learning to address the two challenges. In both full SDN and H-SDN environment, literatures showed that data analytics applications have been successfully developed for various purposes as network security, traffic monitoring and traffic engineering. The success of data analytic applications is highly dependent on prior data analysis from both automated processing and human analysis. However, with the increasing volume of traffic data and the complex networking environment in both SDN and H-SDN networks, the need for both visual analytic and machine learning in inevitable for effective data analysis of network problems. Hence, the objectives of this article are three-folds: Firstly, to identify the limitations of the existing migration plan and traffic scheduling in H-SDN, followed by highlighting the challenges of the existing research works on SDN analytics in various network applications, and lastly, to propose the future research directions of SDN migration and H-SDN traffic scheduling through visual analytics and machine learning. Finally, this article presents the proposed framework termed VA-hSDN, a framework that utilizes visual analytics with machine learning to meet the challenges in SDN migration and traffic scheduling.

Keywords: H-SDN · Migration · Scheduling · Visual analytic

© Springer Nature Switzerland AG 2019
G. Wang et al. (Eds.): SpaCCS 2019, LNCS 11611, pp. 117–132, 2019.
https://doi.org/10.1007/978-3-030-24907-6_10

1 Introduction

With Cyber Physical Systems (CPS), 5G wireless network, Internet of Vehicle and other IoT based application being introduced to the industry fields [1], the traditional network architecture faces difficulty meet the explosive growth of traffic performance requirements from these applications. Hence, a new networking paradigm that differs from the traditional networking paradigm is necessary to introduce new traffic engineering solutions for the increasing traffic performance demands. The new networking paradigm that emerged is called Software-Defined Network (SDN). Although SDN is able to solve the restrictions of the traditional network paradigm, it is both challenging and impractical for organizations to completely migrate from traditional network architecture to full SDN architecture overnight. Therefore, the migration plan is performed in stages, resulting in a new type of network termed hybrid SDN (H-SDN). H-SDN poses new challenges in terms of traffic management due to the co-existences of network devices that are built from two different networking paradigms. Hence, organizations are in need of efficient plans to manage both SDN migration and H-SDN traffic management. Although various research works have been conducted to meet the challenges in these two areas, research opportunities are still in abundant by employing new techniques and synergies. With the immense growth of network traffic data, data analytics present a promising approach to meet the various challenges in H-SDN environment. Driven by automated data analysis, literatures showed that data analytic systems have been leveraged successfully for various purposes as network security, traffic monitoring and traffic engineering in both SDN and H-SDN environment. However, the success of such automation is contingent upon familiarity with the problem domain, the identification of the appropriate analysis methods and the stability of both the structure and sources of the data [2]. Hence, the development of automated data analysis adheres to the knowledge discovery process described by [3] that involves both automated processing and human analysis. However, with the increasing volume of traffic data and the complex networking environment, the need for both visual analytic and machine learning for effective data analysis [4–7] of network problems is inevitable. Therefore, the objectives of this article are summarized as below:

(i)   To identify the limitations of the existing migration plan and traffic scheduling in H-SDN.
(ii) To highlight the challenges of SDN analytic research works in various network applications.
(iii) To propose the future research directions of SDN migration and H-SDN traffic scheduling through visual analytics and machine learning.

The remaining sections of this article are organized to present the objective of this study. First, Sect. 2 presents the research background to establish the foundation of this study. Next, Sect. 3 presents the related works and challenges in SDN analytics, followed by Sect. 4 that presents the future directions of SDN migration and scheduling through visual analytics. Lastly, Sect. 5 presents the conclusion of this study.

2 Research Background

This section is organized in the following manner to present the relevant research background of this study. First, Sect. 2.1 presents migration challenges in SDN. Next, Sect. 2.2 presents traffic management issues in H-SDN environment. In Sect. 2.3, existing research works on SDN migration and traffic scheduling are first presented, followed by Sect. 2.4 to highlight the research challenges.

2.1 SDN Migration Challenges

SDN introduced a new paradigm shift in network design by fundamentally separating the controlling plane and the forwarding planes in a network system. By separating both planes, SDN introduces the concept of programmable network through designated application programming interfaces (API) defined by the governing protocol. Programmable network allows network operators exercise control over the packets forwarded in the network, and thus introducing finer grain of network control [1]. The flexibility introduced in SDN is beneficial in solving the traffic engineering related problems introduced by the increasing traffic performance demands. These benefits are summarized by [1, 20]. Although SDN brings about many benefits to tackle the current issues in traffic performance demands, full deployment of SDN network is yet to be realized especially in Internet Service Provider (ISP) because migration in this large organization are technically, financially and manageably challenging [11]. In addition, SDN deployment is financially challenging for many organizations as well, as the costs required for full SDN deployment in one-go exceeds the capital expenditure (CapEx) of these organizations [10, 12]. The lack of familiarity and troubleshooting experiences on network system with new paradigm introduced in production environment poses challenges to the network operators as well to ensure the stability of the system [10]. With various challenges facing the full-deployment of SDN in organizations, incremental deployment strategies have been introduced. Incremental deployment benefits the organizations in both financial and technical aspects. In the former aspects, it allows organizations to plan their expenditure accordingly while in the latter aspects, it allows the network operators to test and evaluate the stability of the new paradigm while reaping the benefits of a centralized controller at the same time. Such incremental SDN deployment created a hybrid networking environment between SDN devices and traditional networking devices called hybrid SDN (H-SDN) [10, 13].

2.2 Traffic Management Issues in H-SDN

With the co-existence of networking devices built to operate from two different networking paradigms, H-SDN introduced new challenges in network monitoring and management tasks. Since H-SDN contains the strengths and weaknesses from both traditional networking (TN) and SDN, additional cautions are needed when performing various updates on these devices for traffic engineering purposes [13, 14] to prevent the occurrence of complex network performance issues. Although network management is challenging in such hybrid environment, when appropriate deployment and configuration is in-place, the organizations can experience the benefits of SDN in their existing networks. Therefore, it is necessary to provide a traffic engineering platform that can allow the network operators fully utilize the capabilities of SDN devices and in the same time manages the TN devices so that traffics from both TN and SDN can be organized and orchestrated coherently. The traffic engineering platform should offer the network operators the ability to monitor the elements in both TN and SDN, and in the same time allows the network operators to engineer new traffic management solutions to meet the traffic performance requirements. With the introduction of H-SDN, there are two main areas that an organization needs to consider. The first area is the migration strategy required to gradually replace the TN devices with SDN devices. The second area is the traffic management of the H-SDN in order to gain maximum benefits from SDN devices deployed.

2.3   Current Research on SDN Migration and Traffic Scheduling

The objective of SDN migration plan is to develop a migration strategy that can both maximize the performance of the network traffic through the deployed SDN devices and meet the constraints defined by the organization of interest. These constraints can be either technical, economical, or both. Examples of research works on SDN migration plan are [15–17]. In [15], the authors presented a SDN upgrading plan which considers on the number of nodes to be upgraded in each migration period, and the specific nodes to be upgraded. In [16], the authors presented a SDN migration strategy by creating a migration scheduling model to determine the sequence of network nodes to be migrated for each migration period. Extending the work from [16], the authors in [17] enhanced the migration model in [16] to include CapEx as factor to consider in each migration period. The two scenarios that the work in [17] considered were (i) ISP has a limit on the number of routers to be migrated for each migration stage and (ii) the ISP has a limit on the amount of CapEx investment required for migration per time-step. These research works [15–17] used Integer Linear Programming (ILP) formulation to develop the migration model. In the study of traffic scheduling, various research works have been carried out for both full SDN and H-SDN environment. Research works that considers full SDN deployed network environment are [8, 18, 19], H-SDN environment are considered in [13, 20]. The authors in [8, 13, 18, 20] employs graph theory modeling to first model the traffic traversing path and subsequently employs optimization algorithms to locate the optimal route to schedule for the traffic, while the work in [19] schedules network flows by first classifying the newly arrived traffic flows into predefined traffic classes and subsequently schedule the flow according to the bandwidth available from the links.

2.4   Research Challenges

In view of the existing research works in these two areas of H-SDN, the following research challenges are highlighted.

(i) Majority of the existing migration planning methodologies develop migration models based on the historical traffic growth only [15–17]. These methodologies do not first predict traffic growth before developing the migration models.

Therefore, it is possible that the created migration models fail to cope with the actual traffic growth as the migration model was develop based on historical observation and not on predicted traffic growth.

(ii) Majority of the existing migration planning methodologies utilizes mathematical formulation such as the Integer Linear Programming to develop the migration model [15–17]. Such mathematical formulation approach requires sufficient constraints to be defined in order to create a more realistic migration model. With the lack of predictive analytics in the proposed methodologies, some of the constraints defined may not be valid for the next migration period.

(iii) For each SDN migration plan carried out, traffic scheduling optimization is necessary to ensure both maximum traffic performance gains through the SDN nodes deployed and the traffic stability of the entire H-SDN network. However, efficient traffic scheduling is highly dependent on the architecture of the H-SDN networks which may not to be adopted from the existing research works without modification. Hence, it is necessary to also derive the suitable traffic scheduling plan according to the architecture of the H-SDN network for each migration.

3   Data Analytic Works Related to SDN

With the explosive growth of the volume of network traffic data in recent years and the introduction of SDN architecture, researchers begun to utilize the data analytics techniques to solve various network related issues. In this section, data analytics works related to SDN are presented according to their application domain. A summary section is presented lastly to conclude this section.

3.1   Network Security

In [21], the authors used analytics approach in SDN network to detect and mitigate security attacks. According to the authors of [21], having the central controller in SDN managing the entire security related tasks reduces the performance of the SDN controllers, and such centralized approach does not scale well to conduct security related tasks. The authors therefore proposed a system that balances the workload between the SDN controllers and the network devices. The proposed system reduces the workload of the controller managers by processing the data plane traffic at the network devices such as firewalls, deep packet inspection (DPI) units, intrusion detection system (IDS) and other devices providing security services to the network. For cross-domain SDN network, a centralized management system is also created to manage the security policies for the SDN controllers in each domain. In [22], the authors utilized Information-Centric Networking (ICN) in SDN network to perform traffic anomaly detection and prediction. According to the authors, the administrative applications commonly provided by controller manufacturers only display basic information of the network. This basic information is insufficient to satisfy the network visibility requirements of network operators and managers to perform network administrative tasks effectively. Through this work, the authors proposed enhancement to the current monitoring system by adding abnormal node location and traffic prediction features. This enhancement is made possible through the data collection component integrated in the monitoring system and a data analysis algorithm proposed by the author.

In [23, 24], machine learning models are used to develop SDN-based distributed denial of attack (DDoS) detector. Due to the strong protocol openness advocated in SDN paradigm that allows users to customize the networks freely through APIs, SDN networks are highly susceptible to distributed denial of service attacks (DDoS). The anomaly traffic detection mechanism proposed in [23] centrally analyzes the network traffic flows through the SDN controllers to obtain large number of flow feature vectors. These flow features are then used preprocessed and used for anomaly detection through the proposed DPTCM-KNN algorithms. Differing from the work [24], deep learning is utilized to construct the detection model while relevant detection features are extracted from the network packets level.

3.2 Network Optimization and Traffic Management

In [25], a knowledge-defined networking architecture is proposed. According to the authors of [25], with today's network environment that is complex, rapidly growing and dynamically changing, it is impossible for human operators to manage it in real-time. Therefore, the authors proposed self-driven network architecture. The proposed architecture introduces two new planes in addition to the existing SDN planes. These two new planes are the management plane and the knowledge plane. The management plane manages and analyzes the network telemetry collected from the network. The refined information is then provided to the knowledge plane to forecast the traffic status. The forecasted traffic status is then used to perform the necessary traffic engineering tasks. Another similar work is also found in [26], where a self-driven system capable to self-learn the control strategies in SDN is proposed. According to the authors, the configuration of the forwarding planes in the SDN controller is still a manual process, and it is challenging to find a near-optimal control strategy in a large scale and dynamic SDN environment. Therefore, by introducing a new plane called AI plane on top of the Control plane, the authors proposed an architecture called NetworkAI that uses deep reinforcement learning (DRL) to effectively reduce manual configuration process. The authors claimed the AI agent of the system is capable to derive near-optimal network control decision in real time. However, the authors also acknowledge that the training process of the AI model is time consuming and it is an issue that needs to be addressed for its practical usage.

With computer networks getting too complex to be managed manually and efficiently in the largest cloud infrastructure in the world, Google leveraged the full capability of SDN networking paradigm to develop Zero Touch Network [27]. The complexities of the operations of the cloud infrastructure are depicted by million lines of configuration files, and thousands operation circuits and configuration changes per year. In such large scaled operations, traditional network operation cannot guarantee reliability, scalability and efficiency without trade-off. Google concluded that only fully intent driven operation can guarantee reliability, scalability and efficiency of network operations without trade-off. Through a period of two years performing analysis over hundreds of post-mortem network failure reports, Google developed Zero Touch

Network that is self-driven based on intent modeling and govern by predefined network policies. The predefined sets of network policies are necessary to govern the intent-driven operations of Zero Touch Network so that the infrastructure is protected from changes that would result in operational failure. In [28], the authors proposed a framework to perform network monitoring between the SDN network layers. According to the authors of this work, the dynamicity offered by SDN leads to the need for in-depth monitoring and detailed visibilities into various aspects of the applications, traffic flows and connections present in the network. The service assurance offered by existing OAM (Operations, Administration and Maintenance) is only effective for troubleshooting network layer specific problem. Hence, network operators experience troubleshooting difficulties when cross-layers network issues occurs. Therefore, a framework that can support both cross-layer monitoring and data analytics is proposed by the authors to provide enhance the troubleshooting capabilities of the network operators for SDN-based optical network. In [29], the authors proposed network optimization in SDN-based optical networks through data-driven network analytics in. According to the authors, the recent emerging network applications require both high-capacity optical links and dynamic optical network. To realize such network dynamics, it is necessary for the flexibility of the network to meet two main criteria. The first criterion is to have flexibility, configurability or even programmability in both optical hardware and its controlling software. The second criterion is to have the capability to serve network connections in a shorter timescale than traditional networks that are static. In order to effectively manage and operate such optical network, the authors proposed the implementation of a centralized network configuration and monitoring for SDN-enabled optical network. With NCMdB as the monitoring database, the proposed architecture enables multiple network analytics application to be developed for network management and optimization purposes.

3.3   Network Data Acquisition

In [30], the authors presented a distributed analysis framework for SDN network. According to the authors, traditional analytics hauls large amounts of data to a backend to be processed and analyzed. This method is not efficient as it can slow down the performance of the network devices and also consumes network bandwidth when large amount of raw data are being transferred. In addition, not all extracted raw data provides insights in the analytics work. Hence, the authors proposed a smart data approach where analytics are performed right at the network devices instead of a centralized location. This is accomplished through installing an embedded application called DNA Agent in the network device. A SDN application called the DNA Controller is then used as the centralized application controller to orchestrate the network analytics, collect and combine the results reported from each agent. The centralized application controller also serves as the centralized platform that offers network analytics service to the users. With the proposed approach, results are exported only from the network devices when a trend defined by the user is found. The use of smart data approach requires significantly less amount of data from network devices compare to traditional approach. Hence, smart data approach is capable to conserve network bandwidth by several orders of magnitude.

3.4   Challenges of Data Analytics in SDN

In full SDN environment, a centralized network information repository is available in the SDN controller. Coupled with network programmability through APIs in full SDN environment, data-driven machine learning algorithms can be utilized to realize self-driven network such as [26, 27] for global network management. However, in H-SDN environment, the controller only has the network information of the SDN network but not the legacy network that operates on distributed manner. Therefore, data analytic applications in H-SDN environment typically estimate the network conditions of legacy network through sparsely collected routing information to bridge the data gap [13, 20]. In both full SDN and H-SDN environment, human participation in data analysis is inevitable. Although [26, 27] are self-driven, these systems are only made possible to automate the analysis and decision making after the problem domain has been well-formulated and the appropriate system governing policies well-defined by human experts. Consider the work of [28], Zero Touch Network was developed through analyzing more than one hundred post-mortem reports of network failure cases within a two years period. As such, human participations are inevitable to develop the appropriate SDN analytic applications. Translating real-world problems into machine learning problems is by no means trivial and at many a times challenging. This is because real-world problems are often ill-defined and hence contextually unclear for automated analysis alone to derive the solutions [2, 6]. Hence, data analysis of real-world problems is usually highly dependent on the synergy between automated analysis and human expertise [7]. In the presence of voluminous data [4, 7], especially through IoT based applications, automated analysis through machine learning is inevitable. On the other hand, with the presence of data with noises, inconsistencies and incompleteness in network data [32], coupled with ill-defined problem, human expertise is needed provide guidance in automated processing. Hence, synergy from both human and machine is needed to make progress in real-world problem formulation and solution discovery, leading to the need for visual analytics in SDN analytics.

4   Future Direction of SDN Migration and Scheduling Through Visual Analytics and Machine Learning

With the related research works and challenges in SDN analytics presented through Sects. 2 and 3, the following research challenges and their respective future research direction are presented.

(i)   With the significant of amount of network data available, there is still a minor emphasis to leverage these data for SDN migration planning. Specifically, visual analytics is necessary to derive the optimal SDN migration model through the analysis of network data. The recent work in [37] has demonstrated SDN router placement strategy is achievable through data analysis. However, the work in [37] only considers the simplest case where network link is assumed to have linear relation only. Hence, the result in [37] can be further improved through the data analytics to discover the non-linear relation that exists in the network link, as encouraged by the authors themselves. It is inevitable to utilize VA. Therefore, for future research direction, data analytics approach will be used for SDN migration planning. Specifically, this study focuses on utilizing visual analytic to formulate SDN migration problem and solution to derive the SDN migration model.

(ii) Research work in [37] also presented the need for link load estimation in H-SDN. It is non-trivial to obtain traffic information from legacy network devices in real-time. By considering the simplest case where link load has linear relation in each time step, the research work in [37] estimated link loads one time-step ahead using linear regression model. The authors of [37] encouraged further research to consider non-linear relation in each time step utilizing non-linear models. According to [38], ANN has been proven to dominate non-linear relation modeling. [34, 35] further demonstrated the capabilities of ANN to perform traffic matrix estimations. With the rapid advancements in machine learning research leading to enhancements and development of new ANN algorithms, research opportunities are in abundance to further discover the potentials of new machine learning algorithms to predict traffic matrix estimation with higher performances. Therefore, for future research direction, data analytics will be used to predict the traffic matrix. Specifically, data-driven machine learning will be utilized in to perform link load estimation in the presence of non-linear relation between multiple time steps.

(iii) Migrating from pure legacy networking to hybrid networking between SDN and legacy devices requires new considerations for network traffic scheduling. Similar to SDN migration planning, data analytics techniques have not been widely used to model traffic scheduling in H-SDN environment. The research works such as [13, 20] mainly considers downstream traffic of the SDN device. However, the upstream traffics and their incoming trend are not being considered for traffic scheduling decision. Research opportunities exist to apply visual analytics for in-depth analysis of the network traffic distribution pattern to derive optimal traffic scheduling model in H-SDN network.

This following section is organized into four sections to further discuss the three future directions presented above and present the summary to conclude this section.

4.1 Visual Analytics for SDN Migration Planning

The effective architecture design of SDN analytic system allows voluminous valuable network traffic data in production environment to be collected, stored and integrated for analysis. However, due to the presence of noises in the data, automated analysis on these large, dynamic and multivariate datasets are error-prone and therefore unreliable for effective decision making [35]. By utilizing computational power and human insight, visual analytics (VA) has successfully make progress in drawing insights from such challenging data environment [35]. Progression is possible in such challenging data environment because VA allows decision makers to utilize their creativity and relevant domain knowledge to examine massive amount of information streams from enormous storage to gain insight into complex problems and perform timely response

[35–37]. As such, VA is relevantly needed to design SDN migration plan. VA supports network operators to generate insights through creative analysis and exploratory data analysis in deriving the optimal network points in the network topology to migrate to SDN routers.

4.2   Machine Learning for Traffic Matrix Estimation

In [34], the authors presented a large-scale IP traffic matrix estimation through the use of back-propagation neural network (BPNN). According to the authors, it is very difficult solve large-scale IP traffic estimation because it is a highly ill-posed inverse problem. Therefore, the authors proposed a novel approach based on BPNN to tackle such complexity. Enhancing the results of the work in [34], the authors in [35] utilized Moore–Penrose inverse based neural network to estimate the traffic matrix. The proposed approach is termed as MNETME. In addition to traffic matrix estimation, the authors also proposed an advanced routing model through the extension of MNETME for random routing networks. In [37], the authors estimated the link load of the network one time-step ahead through linear regression model. Linear regression model is used in [37] as the work only considers the simplest case where link load in each time steps exhibits linear relationship. The research works in [34, 35, 37] have showed the traffic matrix and link load can be estimated. Research work [37] also showed that link load estimation in H-SDN is necessary as traffic information is not easily obtainable from legacy network devices. In [33], ANN has been proven to dominate non-linear relation forecasting between time steps. Hence, with the rapid development in machine learning researches leading to the enhancement and development of new ANN algorithms, further research should be carried out for continuous enhancements in predicting traffic matrix through ANN.

4.3   Visual Analytics for H-SDN Traffic Scheduling

Migrating from pure legacy networking to hybrid networking between SDN and legacy devices requires new considerations for network traffic scheduling. With the capabilities offered by SDN, organizations would aim to take full advantage of the new networking paradigm to support the business needs while ensuring network traffic stabilities in the hybrid environment. Research works on traffic scheduling for both SDN and H-SDN in the literatures presented showed that traffic scheduling requires explicit modeling and highly dependent on the location of SDN capable devices placed. The location of the SDN devices is crucial for efficient traffic scheduling because it determines the amount of traffic visible to the SDN devices for traffic scheduling decisions. Hence, it is both relevant and necessary to consider traffic scheduling in the same research context of SDN migration as well as traffic matrix prediction because it is a non-trivial task to obtain network information from legacy network devices in H-SDN environment. In view of these challenges, VA is necessary to the network operators to formulate traffic scheduling problem and its solution so that optimal H-SDN traffic scheduling model can be derived for production use.

In view of the importance of both VA and ML, this research attempts to further utilize VA and ML in order to develop a VA framework for H-SDN traffic analytics.

The research on this synergy is relevant with two reasons. Firstly, VA necessary to perform data exploration to formulate and derive automated solutions for a problem context, and secondly, rapid advancement of ML promotes research opportunities for improved traffic prediction models. Table 1 presents a summary of the current SDN analytics literatures and the need for visual analytics and machine learning.

Table 1. Summary of the current SDN analytics literatures and the need for Visual Analytics and Machine Learning

Application domain	Reference	Contributions	Limitations and future directions
Network security	[21–24]	Enhanced traffic monitoring system in SDN for analytic Centralized inter and intra domain security policy management. Machine learning for automated security enforcements	Not applicable in H-SDN Potentially leads to difficulty to analysis the effectiveness of the security policies in place VA is necessary for model tunings and refinements
SDN traffic scheduling	[8, 18, 19]	Dynamic traffic scheduling scheme in SDN Based on the real-time link information Multilevel feedback queue mechanism for traffic anomaly detection	Not applicable to H-SDN
H-SDN traffic engineering	[13, 20]	New routing protocol proposed. [7] takes into consideration traffic scheduling [14] considers the traffic flow between SDN switches and legacy switches only	Topology studied in [7] is defined upfront Each legacy router in [7] has direct connection to SDN router. This may not be the case in each H-SDN topology. Requires sourcing servers to provide additional information [14] Only considers next one hop between SDN switches and legacy switches. Router flows can have multiple network nodes between the two end points
Migration planning	[15–17]	SDN migration defined using ILP Capable of factoring limitation in CaPEX and number of nodes per migration Also considers maximizing programmable through SDN nodes and traffic engineering flexibility	Analyzes historical growth only for model development ILP requires sufficient constraint for model accuracy

(continued)

Table 1. (*continued*)

Application domain	Reference	Contributions	Limitations and future directions
Network management	[25–30]	Fully automated SDN analytic system framework [20, 21] demonstrated the implementation of fully automated analytic system and its performance in real-world environment [22, 23] present architectural design to integrate optical network layers to enable data-driven analytics for network management, performance optimization and cross-layer troubleshooting [24] presents effective data acquisition across SDN devices	Not applicable to H-SDN Model retraining is time consuming Potentially catastrophic when wrong decisions are made VA is necessary for human participation to formulate and contextualize both problem and solution before automated solutions can be implemented
Traffic matrix estimation	[34, 35, 37]	[30, 31] Demonstrates the capability of ANN to estimate traffic matrix BPNN based methodology to perform large-scale IP traffic matrix estimation [33] Utilized compression sensing to locate critical network link for monitoring Link loads are estimated using linear regression model	Applicability of [30, 31] in H-SDN needs to be tested Only considers linear relation in link load New ML to be experimented for higher performing models VA is necessary for model tunings and refinements

Figure 1 presents the conceptual diagrams that represent the overall focus of the SDN analytics in the literature. Figure 2 then presents the conceptual diagram of the proposed framework of this research work. The proposed framework is termed VA-hSDN framework. VA-hSDN promotes effective analysis through VA and ML by allowing the network operators to analyze voluminous data with VA and perform traffic predictions in traffic environment that is non-linear.

In Fig. 1, traffic data from various external sources are acquired through data acquisition operation and stored in a centralized database. ML is then used to predict the network traffic in the near future. The predicted network traffic serves as the decision matrix for the system to execute the appropriate network operations through the SDN controller. This framework is suitable to automated network operations for well-defined network problems. However, for network challenges such as new SDN migration plan and traffic scheduling in H-SDN networks that requires explicit model derivation with varying migration constraints and network architectures, VA-hSDN presented in Fig. 2 is necessary for network operators to carry out data analysis for model development. In VA-hSDN, Origin and Destination (OD) matrices serve as the input data to both VA and ML. For SDN migration modeling purpose, the OD matrices are used to examine the traffic loading of each network link, while for traffic estimation, historical OD matrices are used as input to predict the future OD matrices. Both migration model and traffic estimation are then used as input to derive the optimal traffic scheduling model. Finally, when the model evaluation results are satisfactory, the models executed for production environment.

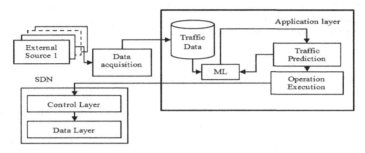

Fig. 1. Conceptual diagram representing the overall focus of SDN analytic systems in the literatures.

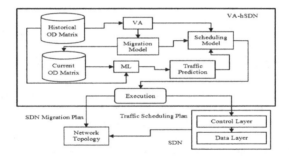

Fig. 2. Conceptual diagram representing the proposed VA-hSDN framework

5 Conclusion

In transitioning from traditional network to SDN, organizations need to address the challenges in SDN migration and H-SDN traffic management. Data analytic approach is potential to assist organizations to address these two challenges. There is a need to emphasize on Visual Analytics (VA) of the system as it determines its usability for the network operators. In H-SDN, obtaining network information on legacy networks in real-time is non-trivial. Strategic placement of SDN devices ensures sufficient network traffic data can be captured for ML to perform accurate traffic estimation in the legacy networks for efficient traffic scheduling in H-SDN. The necessity for ML in traffic estimation is two-fold. First, obtaining network conditions in legacy network in real-time is non-trivial. Traffic estimation is the only viable approach. Second, network traffic exhibits non-linear behavior across time steps and ANN has been proven to dominate non-linear modeling. The inter-relation between SDN migration, traffic estimation and scheduling requires them to be addressed in the same research context. Therefore, the future direction of this research work is three-fold. Firstly, this research work will apply VA in SDN migration planning. Secondly, machine learning will be utilized to perform non-linear relation across time. Lastly, both VA and estimated traffic will be used to derive the optimal traffic scheduling plan for deployed H-SDN topology.

Acknowledgments. This research work is fully supported by the research grant of TM R&D and Multimedia University, Cyberjaya, Malaysia. We are very thankful to the team of TM R&D and Multimedia University for providing the support to our research studies.

References

1. Shu, Z., et al.: Traffic engineering in software-defined networking: Measurement and management. IEEE Access **4**, 3246–3256 (2016)
2. Shyr, J., Spisic, D.: Automated data analysis. Wiley Interdisc. Rev. Comput. Stat. **6**(5), 359–366 (2014)
3. Fayyad, U.M., Piatetsky-Shapiro, G., Smyth, P., Uthurusamy, R.: Advances in Knowledge Discovery and Data Mining. MIT Press, Boston (1996)
4. Garg, S., Nam, J.E., Ramakrishnan, I.V., Mueller, K.: Model-driven visual analytics. In: 2008 IEEE Symposium on Visual Analytics Science and Technology, pp. 19–26. IEEE, Columbus (2008)
5. Keim, D.A., Mansmann, F., Thomas, J.: Visual analytics: how much visualization and how much analytics? SIGKDD Explor. Newsl. **11**(2), 5–8 (2010)
6. Sacha, D., et al.: What you see is what you can change: Human-centered machine learning by interactive visualization. Neurocomputing **268**(13), 164–175 (2017)
7. Bethel, E.W., Campbell, S., Dart, E., Stockinger, K., Wu, K.: Accelerating network traffic analytics using query-driven visualization. In: 2006 IEEE Symposium on Visual Analytics Science and Technology, pp. 115–122. IEEE, Baltimore (2006)
8. Chong, L., Yong-Hao, W.: Strategy of data manage center network traffic scheduling based on SDN. In: 2016 International Conference on Intelligent Transportation, Big Data & Smart City (ICITBS), pp. 29–34. IEEE, Changsha (2016)
9. Guo, Y., Wang, Z., Yin, X., Shi, X., Wu, J., Zhang, H.: Incremental deployment for traffic engineering in hybrid SDN network, In: 2015 IEEE 34th International Performance Computing and Communications Conference (IPCCC), pp. 1–8. IEEE, Nanjing (2015)
10. Rathee, S., Sinha, Y., Haribabu, K.: A survey: hybrid SDN. J. Netw. Comput. Appl. **100**, 35–55 (2017)
11. Vissicchio, S., Vanbever, L., Bonaventure, O.: Opportunities and research challenges of hybrid software defined networks. ACM SIGCOMM Comput. Commun. Rev. **44**(2), 70–75 (2014)
12. Feamester, N., Rexford, J., Zegura, E.: The road to SDN. ACM Queue **11**(12), 1–21 (2013)
13. He, J., Song, W.: Achieving near-optimal traffic engineering in hybrid software defined networks. In: 2015 IFIP Networking Conference (IFIP Networking), pp. 1–9. IEEE, Toulouse (2015)
14. Vissicchio, S., Vanbever, L., Cittadini, L., Xie, G.G., Bonaventure, O.: Safe update of hybrid SDN networks. IEEE/ACM Trans. Netw. **25**(3), 1649–1662 (2017)

15. Caria, M., Jukan, A., Hoffmann, M.: A performance study of network migration to SDN-enabled traffic engineering. In: 2013 IEEE Global Communications Conference (GLOBE-COM), pp. 1391–1396. IEEE, Atlanta (2013)
16. Das, T., Caria, M., Jukan, A., Hoffmann, M.: Insights on SDN migration trajectory. In: 2015 IEEE International Conference on Communications (ICC), pp. 5348–5353. IEEE, London (2015)
17. Poularakis, K., Iosifidis, G., Smaragdakis, G., Tassiulas, L.: One step at a time: optimizing SDN upgrades in ISP networks. In: IEEE INFOCOM 2017 - IEEE Conference on Computer Communications, pp. 1–9. IEEE, Atlanta (2017)
18. Ren, H., Li, X., Geng, J., Yan, J.: A SDN-based dynamic traffic scheduling algorithm. In: 2016 International Conference on Cyber-Enabled Distributed Computing and Knowledge Discovery (CyberC), pp. 514–518. IEEE, Chengdu (2016)
19. Sun, D., Zhao, K., Fang, Y., Cui, J.: Dynamic traffic scheduling and congestion control across data centers based on SDN. Fut. Internet 10(7), 64–76 (2018)
20. Wang, W., He, W., Su, J.: Enhancing the effectiveness of traffic engineering in hybrid SDN. In: 2017 IEEE International Conference on Communications (ICC), pp. 1–6. IEEE, Paris (2017)
21. Veena, S., Manju, R.: Detection and mitigation of security attacks using real time SDN analytics. In: 2017 International Conference of Electronics, Communication and Aerospace Technology (ICECA), pp. 87–93. IEEE, Coimbatore (2017)
22. Yang, F., Jiang, Y., Pan, T., Xinhua, E.: Traffic anomaly detection and prediction based on SDN-enabled ICN. In: 2018 IEEE International Conference on Communications Workshops (ICC Workshops), pp. 1–5. IEEE, Kansas City (2018)
23. Peng, H., Sun, Z., Zhao, X., Tan, S., Sun, Z.: A detection method for anomaly flow in software defined network. IEEE Access 6, 27809–27817 (2018)
24. Li, C.H., et al.: Detection and defense of DDoS attack-based on deep learning in OpenFlow-based SDN. Int. J. Commun. Syst. 31(5) (2018)
25. Hyun, J., Tu, N.V., Hong, J.W.: Towards knowledge-defined networking using in-band network telemetry. In: NOMS 2018 - 2018 IEEE/IFIP Network Operations and Management Symposium, pp. 1–7. IEEE, Taipei (2018)
26. Yao, H., Mai, T., Xu, X., Zhang, P., Li, M., Liu, Y.: NetworkAI: an intelligent network architecture for self-learning control strategies in software defined networks. IEEE Internet Things J. 5(6), 4319–4327 (2018)
27. Koley, B.: The zero touch network. In: International Conference on Network and Service Management. Montreal, Quebec (2016)
28. Yan, S., Aguado, A., Ou, Y., Wang, R., Nejabati, R., Simeonidou, D.: Multilayer network analytics with SDN-based monitoring framework. IEEE/OSA J. Opt. Commun. Network. 9(2), A271–A279 (2017)
29. Yan, S., Nejabati, R., Simeonidou, D.: Data-driven network analytics and network optimisation in SDN-based programmable optical networks. In: 2018 International Conference on Optical Network Design and Modeling (ONDM), pp. 234–238. IEEE, Dublin (2018)
30. Clemm, A., Chandramouli, M., Krishnamurthy, S.: DNA: an SDN framework for distributed network analytics. In: 2015 IFIP/IEEE International Symposium on Integrated Network Management (IM), pp. 9–17. IEEE, Ottawa (2015)
31. Xie, J., Huang, F.R.Y.T., Xie, R., Liu, J., Wang, C., Liu, Y.: A survey of machine learning techniques applied to software defined networking (SDN): research issues and challenges. IEEE Commun. Surv. Tutor. 21(1), 393–430 (2019)
32. Roughan, M., Zhang, Y., Willinger, W., Qiu, L.: Spatio-temporal compressive sensing and internet traffic matrices (extended version). IEEE/ACM Trans. Netw. 20(3), 662–676 (2012)

33. Taieb, S.B.: Machine learning strategies for multi-step-ahead time series forecasting.. Universit Libre de Bruxelles, Belgium (2014)
34. Jiang, D., Wang, X., Guo, L., Ni, H., Chen, Z.: Accurate estimation of large-scale IP traffic matrix. AEU–Int. J. Electron. Commun. **65**(1), 75–86 (2011)
35. Zhou, H.F., Tan, L.S., Zeng, Q., Wu, C.M.: Traffic matrix estimation: a neural network approach with extended input and expectation maximization iteration. J. Netw. Comput. Appl. **60**, 220–232 (2015)
36. Bae, J., Falkman, G., Helldin, T., Riveiro, M.: Data Science in Practice, 1st edn. Springer, Cham (2018)
37. Cheng, T.Y.Y., Jia, X.H.: Compressive traffic monitoring in hybrid SDN. IEEE J. Sel. Areas Commun. **36**(12), 2731–2743 (2018)
38. Ahmed, N.K., Atiya, A.F., Gayar, N.E., El-Shishiny, H.: An empirical comparison of machine learning models for time series forecasting. Expert Syst. Appl. **39**(8), 7067–7083 (2012)
39. Thomas, J., Cook, K.: Illuminating the Path: The Research and Development Agenda for Visual Analytics. 1st edn. National Visualization and Analytics Ctr (2005)

End-to-End Encryption Schemes
for Online Social Networks

Fabian Schillinger$^{(\boxtimes)}$ and Christian Schindelhauer

Computer Networks and Telematics, Department of Computer Science,
University of Freiburg, Freiburg im Breisgau, Germany
{schillfa,schindel}@tf.uni-freiburg.de

Abstract. In a secure Online Social Network (OSN) an attacker with
access to the server cannot use the saved data of any user to read the
private communication. It should allow users to use the OSN even if
they are not technically savvy and have no knowledge about cryptography. We present and discuss an end-to-end encryption based approach
that uses the RSA public-key encryption algorithm, as well as the AES
symmetric-key encryption algorithm. The result is a fully working personal message service, also known as online chat. Instead of relying on
third-party projects with questionable or unknown security levels our
prototype is built from scratch in JavaScript.

Keywords: Cryptographic protocols · Security ·
Online social networks · Personal message service · Online chat system

1 Introduction

Online Social Networks (OSN) are web applications that allow their users to
share for example personal information, images, videos, and news articles in so-
called posts. In OSNs users can organize themselves in groups, users of OSNs
can communicate which each other by exchanging personal messages. Personal
messages can be shared either between two or multiple users. This is also known
as an online chat. OSNs like Facebook are very popular: Facebook has about
1.5 billion active users every day [4]. However, many OSNs do not have their
main focus on user privacy. Often privacy collides with the focus to earn money.
Operators of OSNs often have developed business strategies of exploiting the
users' data i.e. earn money by displaying personalized advertisements or selling
user data to advertising agencies.

Because of the high number of users in some OSNs and the large number of
personal messages and posts, many governments require from the providers of
such networks to search for and remove illegal content. This legal requirement
results in a huge amount of human resources and in some cases leads to censorship. Often, only the providers decide on the legality of the content. Their
rules are often stricter than the legal situation of the involved countries requires.

© Springer Nature Switzerland AG 2019
G. Wang et al. (Eds.): SpaCCS 2019, LNCS 11611, pp. 133–146, 2019.
https://doi.org/10.1007/978-3-030-24907-6_11

Furthermore, the shared content of users can be legal in one country and illegal in another one. For many users, this behavior is not acceptable and they call for OSNs with more privacy where no provider or government can read and censor their content. This applies not only to publicly available content shared by the users, but also to personal messages.

At the same time, there are security breaches of platform servers. Often the attacks aim at login credentials, but intruders may also read personal messages. This can lead to identity theft and other serious matters. It explains the increasing numbers of users using encrypted OSNs like WhatsApp [18]. But as some services like WhatsApp are acquired by larger companies many users of these services do not fully trust their privacy and transparency to such corporations.

Our contribution is a step towards more security in OSNs leading to a higher level of privacy. This is achieved by increasing the security on the server-side in a client-server scenario as many OSNs have. We introduce end-to-end encryption to an online chat service. Our goal is to allow users without a good knowledge of security, technology, or programming skills and without additional software to experience more secure and private communications. Of course, this cannot stand on its own and has to be combined with additional security measures on the transmission channel as well as on the clients' device.

The paper is structured as follows: Sect. 2 discusses other works that help to improve the privacy of private communication at the internet and in OSNs as well, often by introducing encryption or masking of content. Section 3 describes the attack model: an attacker can be everyone who has access to the OSN server, e.g. an administrator of the OSN, a hacker, or any governmental agency. Section 4 describes the notations used in the paper, all important parts of the chat system, and how they prevent specific attacks of the attack model. Finally, Sect. 5 concludes the work.

2   Related Work

An approach to end-to-end encrypted communication is *SafeSMS* [7]. SafeSMS is a program for mobile phones written in Java. It encrypts and decrypts Short Message Service (SMS) text messages that work as a container for the program. The application decides if a SMS is encrypted by content analysis. Encryption and decryption of messages is only possible between a sender and a single receiver. Both of them have to use SafeSMS. The participants share a password that is used to derive a symmetric key for encryption and decryption. The algorithm used by SafeSMS is either Quasigroup Encryption or Blowfish. SafeSMS allows users to create an encrypted contact list and an encrypted message storage. Received text messages (either encrypted with SafeSMS or plaintext messages) can be encrypted using SafeSMS and saved to the protected storage. Although the encryption and decryption is based on a shared password on which the participants have to agree on beforehand it is possible to extend the application to enable for example the Diffie-Hellmann key exchange (DH) by sending additional encrypted text messages beforehand.

Another approach to facilitate more privacy in OSNs is *none of your business* (NOYB) [6]. NOYB is not a scheme for end-to-end encrypted messages, but it hides the content of messages and information shared in an OSN. NOYB is an extension application for Facebook. It handles hiding of information by disguising it with information of other users, this is called masking. Retrieving the original information is called demasking. Content like posts, personal information, or messages on Facebook work as containers for NOYB content. The key management is done through existing key management protocols. Masking works by breaking information in small parts called atoms. Atoms then are substituted by other atoms. Dictionaries are used to mask and demask content. They are public and created with atoms from both NOYB users and non-users. For a dictionary lookup, the index of an atom is calculated and encrypted using a symmetric key and a random nonce. Based on the encrypted index of an atom the matching hiding atom is chosen. NOYB relies on different dictionaries for all different types of shared information, e.g., the birthday information of a profile is hidden by the birthday information of another user. This allows decreasing the detection rate of hidden entries by automated systems because veiled information cannot be distinguished from non-veiled information.

FlyByNight [10] is a system that hides sensitive information posted on Facebook through a client-side JavaScript based encryption. Sensitive plaintext is never posted to Facebook when flyByNight is used, it supports encrypted communication between two or more participants. The key management is handled by the Facebook interface. Users need a password for flyByNight that is used for encryption of a private key. The encrypted private key is sent to a key database on a flyByNight server. Messages are sent via the application and encrypted using the public keys of other users. The application saves all incoming messages in a database. Every time the application is used the database is queried. Encryption of information shared for many users at once, like public information on the profile, is done by proxy cryptography. Proxy cryptography works by using multiple keys per recipient. One key is used to encrypt the information. For each user a proxy key, that is stored at the application database, and a private key is generated. Each private key is encrypted using the respective public key of a user and then sent to the user. Whenever a user wants to decrypt such an encrypted message he asks the flyByNight server to transform the message using his proxy key, then he uses the private key to decrypt the message.

Two methods for the encryption of emails are *Pretty Good Privacy* (PGP) as an addition to the Simple Mail Transfer Protocol [5,8] and *S/MIME* [16]. PGP uses both public-key and symmetric-key encryption. The public key is used for key encryption and signature verification. The private key is used for key encryption and signature generation. The email content is encrypted using a symmetric key. This key is encrypted using the public keys of the recipients. This allows sending a message to multiple recipients without the need of encrypting it more than once. The used keys last for a whole conversation, consisting of emails and answers. PGP does not use a certification authority. A trust system is established based on trusted users. S/MIME in contrast to PGP uses X.509

certificates instead of trust. It again uses public-key encryption and symmetric-key encryption for the encryption and signatures of emails like in PGP.

Off-the-record (OTR) [13] is an encryption scheme for online chats. The encryption is based on the symmetric-key encryption algorithm AES and the Diffie-Hellman key exchange. OTR uses session keys for the encryption and decryption of messages. Session keys last shorter than for example the keys of PGP. OTR, therefore, allows perfect forward secrecy. That means a stolen key cannot be used to decrypt messages that are encrypted with another key because one key cannot be used to derive another one. Two participants a and b generate multiple private keys $x_{a_0}, x_{a_1}, \ldots, x_{a_k}$ and $x_{b_0}, x_{b_1}, \ldots, x_{b_l}$. The first two of the keys are used to calculate a shared secret using DH. This secret is used to derive two keys for AES and Message Authentication Code (MAC) calculation. After sending a message the used keys are deleted. The next keys x_{a_1} and x_{b_1} are used to again calculate a shared secret. As the private keys are deleted it is not possible to decrypt old messages again.

Another system for the encryption of online chats is *Signal*. Signal uses a protocol called Double Ratchet [11] to allow two participants to send encrypted messages based on a shared secret key. The protocol uses a key derivation function (KDF) that is used to create a KDF chain. Given the first input to the KDF is unknown to an attacker it is not possible to calculate the keys of the chain. A session in the Double Ratchet system uses three different KDF chains. A root chain, a chain for sending messages, and one for receiving messages. Whenever two participants send messages a new DH public key is exchanged and the private key is used as the next input for the root chain, this is called DH ratchet. As soon as a new output is calculated on the root chain it is used as a new input for the other chains. These chains are called symmetric-key ratchets. The agreement on a shared secret is given using a protocol called Extended Tripple Diffie-Hellman [12] (X3DH). X3DH is designed for asynchronous settings where one of the participants can be offline. A user publishes some information to a server. This information can be used for the key exchange. The Signal protocol is used at multiple messaging programs, for example, the Signal messenger, Skype, or WhatsApp. Other protocols like *OMEMO* [15] use modified versions of the protocol to allow encrypted online chats.

Our proposed system in contrast to the mentioned approaches combines the following features: the system is built from scratch to support online chats in a client-server approach. Inexperienced users can communicate with others using multiple devices without understanding cryptography and without the need to configure any of their devices. No synchronization between a users' devices regarding cryptographic keys and read messages is needed. The system allows for encrypted communication with multiple users simultaneously and the cryptographic keys are automatically changed and redistributed when users are added or removed from the so-called chatrooms, further for adding and removing of users they do not have to be online. Our system does not rely on third-party projects and does not use another OSN as a base for exchanging messages, it is open source and uses the well known RSA and AES encryption algorithms.

3 Attack Model

In this work, we concentrate on an attack model where an attacker has full access to the servers of a web application. The attacker, therefore, has full access to all data on the server which means he can read, modify, or delete it. Furthermore, the attacker also can read and modify the program code which is provided by the server. He also has access to all messages sent or received by the server. The attacker can therefore read, modify, delete, add, or delay any message between the server and all connected clients. One could imagine him being a hacker, a disloyal administrator, or a governmental organization agent. Attacks on the client machines are not covered by our scheme. We now give a detailed list of attacks our system prevents.

3.1 Attacks on the Data Storage

Access to the server often means access to the storage as well, i.e. an attacker may steal any data. This includes as well:

(a) **Stealing user login data (S1):** login credentials can be sold, used on the attacked system, or they may be used on other popular websites. Therefore it is important to render such attacks useless.

(b) **Stealing messages (S2):** an attacker with access to the data storage can read all the communication data. Thus, stored messages have to be secured.

(c) **Stealing cryptographic keys (S3):** an attacker with access to the encrypted communication data might want to steal cryptographic keys to decrypt the communication data. Consequently, cryptographic keys have to be secured as well.

3.2 Attacks on Data Integrity

An attacker with access to the server may disturb the communication by deleting, modifying, delaying, or inserting data.

(a) **Altering cryptographic keys (I1):** by exchanging cryptographic keys it is possible to read communication data or other data. If an attacker deletes the cryptographic keys communication or even the usage of the system can be made impossible.

(b) **Altering communication data (I2):** by adding, deleting, or modifying communication data like exchanged messages the communication can be disturbed.

(c) **Altering communication metadata (I3):** removing, or adding clients to user lists for chatrooms disturbs the communication. This attack can be used to silently read encrypted messages if adding of users is done covertly. Another attack is re-enabling a closed communication by adding a person that previously left a chatroom.

4   End-to-End Encryption of an Online Chat System

A feasible solution for the attacks described in Sect. 3 is to develop and implement an end-to-end encryption scheme for securing the communication. By
adding possibilities to easily detect intruders in our system all the attacks can
be prevented. One of the goals is to create a transparent system usable by people
without technical knowledge for preventing accidental misuse of cryptographic
algorithms. Following Kerckhoffs's principle, our approach is an open source
system and the technical aspects of the encryption can be checked by anybody.

4.1   Notations

We use the following the variables:

- k_c^i, i-th symmetric key used for encryption and decryption of the messages in
  a chatroom c
- v_u, public key of user u used for ECDSA signature verification
- s_u, private key of user u used for ECDSA signature generation
- e_u, public key of user u used for RSA encryption
- d_u, private key of user u used for RSA decryption.

For improved readability subscript and superscript may be omitted. A message
$\{m\}_k$ denotes the ciphertext that corresponds to the plaintext of a message
m encrypted with the key k. The value $[m]$ is the resulting value of a secure
hashing algorithm applied to the message m. We use the cryptographic algorithms shown in Table 1. Whenever iv or $salt$ variables are used they stand for
random variables derived by cryptographically secure pseudo-random number
generators (CSPRNG). The variable $iterationCount$ used by PBKDF2 defines
how often the algorithm is applied consecutively to derive a key. High values for
$iterationCount$ increase the used computational time for attackers to generate
output values. This results in higher security. A limit for this value is given by
the client, which may be computationally restricted, for example when using a
smartphone. One has to find a compromise between security and speed.

Table 1. Notation of cryptographic algorithms.

Type	Algorithm	Notation	
Symmetric-key encryption	AES-GCM, 256bit	encrypt:	$\{m\}_k = AES(k, m, iv)$
		decrypt:	$m = AES^{-1}(k, \{m\}_k, iv)$
Signatures	ECDSA, curve P-384	sign:	$sig = Sign(s, m)$
		verify:	$result = Verify(v, m, sig)$
Key generation	PBKDF2, with SHA-256		$key = PBKDF2(p, salt, iterationCount)$
Public-key encryption	RSA-OAEP, with SHA-256	encrypt:	$\{m\}_e = RSA(e, m)$
		decrypt:	$m = RSA^{-1}(d, \{m\}_e)$

4.2 Overview of the Online Chat System

Our approach of an end-to-end encrypted online chat is based on a client-server architecture. The server stores communication data, metadata, and encrypted keys. Clients download the needed data from the server to read and decrypt messages and keys. For our proposed system the cryptographic functions of the *Web Cryptography API* [17] are used on the client-side. Reasons for using this API are that most of the current web browsers implement it [2] and the high probability that the W3C recommendation becomes a standard for all web browsers. Furthermore, reducing dependencies to third-party libraries seems to decrease the overall attack surface of JavaScript-based applications [9].

Online chats are used to send messages that can be read by all participants of a chatroom. The number of participants of a chatroom can vary between one single participant or more then hundred participants. For each chatroom a shared symmetric key is used to encrypt and decrypt the messages. This reduces the number of stored messages compared to systems where every message is encrypted with all public keys of the participants. Further, using a symmetric-key encryption for the messages in a chat system can lead to performance improvements compared to using public-key encryption [3]. The users of our chat system can use the program on different devices. Therefore, each user has a *Storage* that stores all the needed keys. It is encrypted with a symmetric key by the user and stored on the server. The public keys are stored on the server in an unencrypted version and can be stored in the *Storage* of users as well. A user then, does not have to retrieve them again from the server. The server stores all data chatrooms consist of as well. This data contains a list of participants and the messages of the chatrooms. All messages are encrypted with a symmetric key that is known to the participants of the corresponding chatroom. Every symmetric key of a chatroom is encrypted using the public keys of the participants. Whenever the participants of a chatroom change a new symmetric key is generated. Because everything is stored encrypted by the server the data is secured against modifications by attackers.

4.3 Registration for the Online Chat System

During the registration process, multiple different keys and values are sent between the client and the server. First, the user u provides a unique password p. The user creates two unique random numbers $salt_1$ and $salt_2$ using a CSPRNG. p is never sent to the server. Instead, two passwords p^a and p^s are derived from p by calculating $p^a = PBKDF2(p, salt_1, iterationCount)$ and $p^s = PBKDF2(p, salt_2, iterationCount)$, respectively. The value p^a is used for authentication, whereas p^s is used for the encryption of the *Storage*. The user generates the key pair (v, s) for ECDSA signatures and (e, d) for AES-GCM. The user sends the tuple $(p^a, salt_1, salt_2, v, e)$ to the server. The server generates another $salt$ and calculates $[p^a + salt] = PBKDF2(p^a, salt, iterationCount)$. The hash $[p^a + salt]$, $salt$, and the two other values $salt_1$ and $salt_2$ are stored together with a new unique user Id id. The server stores the two public keys v and e for the key exchange.

The server sends id to the client to show that the user is created. In the next step, the client creates his *Storage storage* locally. He saves both key pairs (v, s) and (e, d) to *storage*. Afterward, *storage* is encrypted. First, the user generates an initialization vector iv. Then the user computes $\{storage\}_{p^s} = AES(p^s, storage, iv)$. The tuple $(\{storage\}_{p^s}, iv, id)$ is sent to the server which stores it. This completes the registration procedure and allows a user to login to the chat system and retrieve his stored values when needed with every device.

4.4   Login to the Online Chat System

At one hand the login procedure allows a user to authenticate against the server and on the other hand, the procedure is used to download the *Storage*. Authentication in client-server architectures is often achieved with a tuple consisting of a username u and a password p. The tuple is sent via an encrypted connection to the server that computes a hash value $[p + salt]$ and compares it with a stored $[p' + salt]$. By using a stored value $salt$, which is unique for each user and password. If $[p + salt] = [p' + salt]$ holds, then $p = p'$ holds as well and thus the user entered the correct credentials and is successfully authenticated. However, this approach of authentication needs the password to be sent to the server, which is not recommended if we want to derive a symmetric key from it. The login procedure used in our system works as follows: instead of sending the tuple (u,p) to the server, p is replaced with p^a. The value p^a is derived from the original p. The first step for authentication consists of requesting the $salt_1$ value from the server. The client then computes

$$p^a = PBKDF2(p, salt_1, iterationCount).$$

The value p^a cannot be used to calculate p. Then the tuple (u, p^a) is sent to the server. The server computes $[p^a + salt] = PBKDF2(p^a, salt, iterationCount)$ with the provided p^a and the stored $salt$ for u. Then the server compares $[p^a + salt]$ to the stored value. If both values are equal the server sends back a tuple $(\{Storage\}p^s, iv, salt_2)$. The client then computes

$$p^s = PBKDF2(p, salt_2, iterationCount).$$

This value is used to decrypt the *Storage* by calculating $AES^{-1}(p^s, \{Storage\}_{p^s}, iv)$. By using this scheme with appropriate algorithms it is possible to use the same passphrase for authentication and derivation of the symmetric key.

The described mechanisms render the attacks *(S1)* and *(T1)* ineffective. Stolen login data cannot be decrypted or used in another application because even if a user decides to use his passphrase on another platform the transmitted value p^a itself only is a value derived from the passphrase. It is not possible to calculate the original p nor the derived key p^s from it. If stolen credentials are used to login to the system, still the attack *(S3)* is not possible, because to cryptographic keys are stored safely in the encrypted *Storage* of a user. Knowledge of p^a does not help in breaking the encryption.

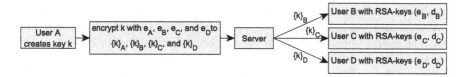

Fig. 1. User A creates the symmetric key k. By encrypting it with the public keys of all participants of the room the ciphertexts $\{k\}_A, \{k\}_B, \{k\}_C$, and $\{k\}_D$ can be transferred via the server. Only A, B, C, and D can decrypt their ciphertext.

4.5   Creating a Chatroom

The improved performance of symmetric-key encryption over public-key encryption is one of the main points why messages in chatrooms are encrypted using the former combined with key-wrapping to ensure end-to-end encryption. A chatroom can hold arbitrary many users which can be changed on the fly. By exchanging the used key it is not possible for removed users to decrypt new messages, while recently added users cannot decrypt old messages. When the user u_0 creates a room c, it chooses a name for the room and sends it to the server, together with a list of participating users $(u_1, u_2, \ldots, u_n)$. The server sends back a new Id for the room and all public keys $(e_{u_1}, e_{u_2}, \ldots, e_{u_n})$ of the participating users. If a public key is unknown to u_0 it saves the key to his *Storage*. In Sect. 4.8 it is described how a user can check if used keys are correct. Then the client creates a new symmetric key k_c, that is used for the encryption and decryption of messages in c. The key k_c is stored locally to the *Storage* and encrypted for all users $(u_0, u_1, \ldots, u_n)$ using the corresponding public keys. The list $(\{k_c\}_{e_{u_0}}, \{k_c\}_{e_{u_1}}, \ldots, \{k_c\}_{e_{u_n}})$ is sent to the server. The users can then receive their key from the server. The user u_0 creates a new system message m_1 for the room. m_1 contains the room name and the list of participants. The message is encrypted by calculating $\{m_1\}_{k_c} = AES(k_c, m_1, iv)$. Then $\{m_1\}_{k_c}$ is signed by u_0 by computing $sig = Sign(s_{u_0}, \{m_1\}_{k_c})$ and sent to the room. This allows users in the room to check whether the list of participants is valid. The user creates another system message m_2 containing the Id of k_c. Again, this system message first is encrypted and afterward, the ciphertext is signed by the user and sent to the room. Every participant of the room then knows if the correct symmetric key is delivered by the server because of first, the matching Id, second, the matching signature of the system message, and third, because the signed system message can be decrypted with the key.

Modifying the participants of a chatroom or changing the symmetric key works in a similar way. First, a new new symmetric key k_c^* is created by u_0. Second, the list of participants is sent to the server. Then the new key is encrypted for all the users in the room using the corresponding public key. The user sends the encrypted keys to the server. At the same time, new system-messages containing the modified list of participants and the Id of the new symmetric key k_c^* are created, encrypted, and afterward signed by u. This ensures, that only the remaining participants can decrypt messages and the correct key is distributed and used. Further, every user can check the list of participating users. The encryption and distribution of a key k is displayed in Fig. 1.

The previously described system messages prevent the attacks *(I1)* and *(I3)*. Whenever a key is changed or communication metadata like participants of a chatroom are changed there is a corresponding system message. The system message is encrypted with the correct key and signed by the sender. This renders it impossible for an attacker to successfully change these things in his favor.

4.6   Sending a Message

If a user u wants to send a message m he creates a tuple consisting of m, u, the current participants of the chatroom, a timestamp, and a list of previous unconfirmed messages $(m_{p_0}, m_{p_1}, \ldots, m_{p_n})$. The list of unconfirmed messages then is cleared. The tuple is encrypted using the latest symmetric key and afterward signed by u. The user sends the message and signature to the server, which appends the Id of the sender. The server responds with the Id of the message, which then, is stored in the list of unconfirmed messages. This allows creating a message history in form of a directed acyclic graph (DAG) because every message is confirming the messages before. In some cases, special messages called system messages are needed. They are encrypted, signed, and sent in the same way. System messages are sent whenever a symmetric key changes, the list of participants of a chatroom changes, a chatroom is removed, or a chatroom is renamed.

The attacks *(S2)* and *(I2)* are not effective in the scheme. Messages are encrypted as soon as they are sent by a client. Neither reading the transmitted messages nor accessing them in the database helps an attacker in reading them because they are encrypted. Adding or modifying messages is not possible because these messages first, cannot be correctly signed by an attacker and second, they cannot be encrypted with the correct key. Deleting messages is possible for an attacker with access to the server, even without the correct keys. But as messages contain a list of previous messages a missing message in the history can be detected.

4.7   Receiving a Message

Clients receive the messages for all chatrooms they are a member of as tuples of $\{m\}$, *sig*, *iv*, and *senderId'*[1]. The first step is the verification of $\{m\}$ and the corresponding signature *sig*. This ensures that $\{m\}$ is a real encrypted message coming from *senderId'*. Afterward, m is calculated via $m = AES^{-1}(k, \{m\}, \text{iv})$. In the third step, it is checked, whether the resulting tuple $m = (message, senderId, receiverIds, timestamp, previousMessages)$ corresponds to the chatroom. The variables *senderId* and *receiverIds* are checked,

---

[1] The *senderId'* variable is appended by the server automatically when it saves messages to the database.

whether they correspond to $senderId'$ and the list of participants of the chatroom. To finally ensure that no message in between was deleted the DAG corresponding to the message history of the chatroom is extended using the list of previous messages $previousMessages$. If one of the steps fails, a warning message is displayed. This ensures that all messages are received, that the messages are encrypted correctly, that they belong to the chatroom, and that no faked messages were added in between. System messages are received in the same way.

The attacks *(S2)* and *(I2)* are not effective because receiving a message verifies the steps undertaken in Sect. 4.6 to prevent these attacks.

4.8 Key Exchange

Each user u has a key pair $(e,d)_u$ for the public-key encryption scheme. These keys are generated at the registration procedure (see Sect. 4.3). The private key d_u is stored at the client in his *Storage*, the public key e_u is transferred to the server. The server saves the key and allows users to download it. Whenever e_u is needed by another user he can retrieve it from the server. At the registration procedure, another key pair $(v,s)_u$ for signing and verifying signatures is created. The signing key s_u again is stored at the user in his private *Storage*. The verification key v_u is, again, sent to the server. The server distributes it to other clients who need it. Because the keys change rarely it is possible to store them after they are received by a client. This reduces transferred messages. Other keys are the symmetric keys k_c^i for a chatroom c. These keys are transferred to the server as well and can be retrieved from it. The symmetric keys are encrypted using e_u for each participating user u. This results in at least n stored encrypted keys for a chatroom with n participants. For each change in the user list of c resulting in a group size of n' another key k_c^{i+1} is generated. The key k_c^{i+1} is stored n' times. It has to be ensured that the correct keys are exchanged via the server. Two users u_i and u_j can verify their used key pairs with a simple scheme. Everything they need is a secure communication channel. They can, for example, meet in public, use an encrypted mail system, or communicate via phone. The used encryption algorithm relies on the fact that for any two key pairs (e_i,d_i) and (e_j,d_j) with $e_i = e_j$ the equation $d_i = d_j$ must hold. Finding two d_i, d_j with $d_i = d_j$ and $i \neq j$ in a reasonable time means that the encryption algorithm itself is not secure [14]. Therefore, the users u_i and u_j can verify the usage of the correct keys, by comparing the public keys e_i and e_j used by u_i to the public keys e_i' and e_j' used by u_j. If both equations $e_i = e_i'$ and $e_j = e_j'$ hold they verified that they use the same private keys as well. No man in the middle can read the encrypted messages, including the encrypted keys in between u_i and u_j. The same verification scheme can be used between any number of users. Comparing multiple keys at once can be done, for example, by concatenation of the public keys in a fixed order at each client and computing an easily comparable hash value or QR-code. The described scheme can be applied to the signature keys as well [1]. Whenever the server sends new public keys that differ from the keys which are stored at the user a message is displayed to remind the user to verify the keys again. This allows relying on keys until changes are reported by the server. The integrity of symmetric keys is proven at first, by the ability to decrypt a symmetric key retrieved from the server, which means that the correct public key was used to encrypt it. Second, the ability to encrypt and decrypt messages with it and third, by a signed and encrypted system message stating the correct key, sent by the user that generated the symmetric key. If the signature keys are proven to be correct nobody can change the key in the name of someone else. Whenever a symmetric key of a room is changed a matching system message with a proper message history exists that proves the changed key. The verification scheme is displayed in Fig. 2.

The proposed scheme prevents the attacks *(I1)*. Whenever a key is changed in a chatroom a corresponding system message is sent. If personal keys of users change a message is displayed for them. By verifying the usage of the correct keys described in the previous section it is not feasible for an attacker to change them without the participants of a chatroom noticing it.

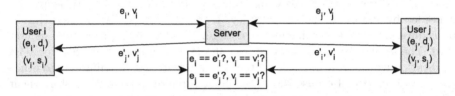

Fig. 2. Two users i and j exchange their public keys e_i, v_i and e_j, v_j via the server. By comparing them to the received keys e_i', v_i' and e_j', v_j', it can be excluded that the server changed them.

4.9   Code and Performance of the Online Chat System

A working version of the source code is accessible at the following address: https://github.com/falti3/encryptedChat. The code is a proof-of-work containing a working implementation of the client code, written in JavaScript and a rudimentary user interface, a PHP server with minimal functionality, and a MySQL database. Please note that not all features are implemented, e.g. login states, or SSL. These features have to be added in order to maintain the full security as described here. The system can be used on every device with a browser that implements the *Web Cryptography API*. The computation of cryptographic functions can be time consuming. Therefore, some tests on a laptop with a 2 GHz processor and 2 GB of RAM were made. The time for encrypting and decrypting messages and keys was measured. The average time needed for encrypting and decrypting a single message was 88 ms and 63 ms, respectively. There is a significant impact on the time needed between short messages of 5 characters (48 ms/29 ms) and long messages containing 5,000 characters (128 ms/98 ms). Decrypting a set of around 950 messages needed 130 ms on average. Measurements of the time needed for encrypting and decrypting the *Storage* was not performed because the size is smaller then the size of long messages. The time for encryption of keys using RSA was measured in four different sized chatrooms containing 2, 5, 10, or 50 participants. The measured average times for encrypting the keys ranged from around 62 ms in small rooms to 142 ms in large rooms. The time needed for decrypting shared keys was around 50 ms. The measured delays are nearly impossible to notice considered the time needed for transmitting messages to and from the server especially when a device is used in a cellular network.

5   Conclusions

In this paper, we present an easy-to-use client-server system, that can encrypt personal messages and thus secure the privacy of its users. Applying multiple different measures can fend off many attacks that need successful access to the servers of a social network. Some of these measures are built on each other while others work together. The proposed system provides security only if it is installed as a whole, because the security of a system is affected by its weakest part, the described system is not sufficient to fully secure communication alone. The client-side must be protected as well, i.e., a working end-to-end encryption of messages brings no added value when the unencrypted messages can be stolen by an attacker from the device of a user. The proposed scheme is a step forward towards more secure communication in OSNs. But, the channel connecting the server to the client has to be secured as well, e.g. by SSL.

An open problem is what to do when a user loses his password, since it is needed to authenticate against the server and to decrypt the personal *Storage* of a user. While the encrypted data may be shared if the password is lost, the symmetric key used to decrypt the *Storage* cannot be reset. Every symmetric key would be lost and even more serious the private keys for the decryption and signature generation would be lost if the *Storage* cannot be decrypted. One solution is maybe to save the password to an independent medium that cannot be accessed by others. This lies outside the scope of the research of this work. Another solution may be to implement some form of secret sharing which has its own problems.

Acknowledgments. We would like to thank Mr. Aveg Chaudhary for the interesting discussions about end-to-end encryption during the supervision of his master's thesis. The authors acknowledge the financial support by the Federal Ministry of Education and Research of Germany in the framework of SoNaTe (project number 16SV7405).

References

1. ANSI: Public Key Cryptography for the Financial Services Industry: The Elliptic Curve Digital Signature Algorithm (ECDSA). Technical report ANSI X9.62, ANSI (1999)
2. Can I use web cryptography. https://caniuse.com/#feat=cryptography
3. Chen, L., Zhou, S.: The comparisons between public key and symmetric key cryptography in protecting storage systems. In: 2010 International Conference on Computer Application and System Modeling (ICCASM 2010), vol. 4, pp. V4-494-V4-502, October 2010. https://doi.org/10.1109/ICCASM.2010.5620632

4. Facebook Q3 2018 results. https://s21.q4cdn.com/399680738/files/doc_financials/2018/Q3/Q3-2018-Earnings-Presentation.pdf
5. Finney, H., Donnerhacke, L., Callas, J., Thayer, R.L., Shaw, D.: OpenPGP message format. RFC 4880, November 2007. https://doi.org/10.17487/RFC4880, https://rfc-editor.org/rfc/rfc4880.txt
6. Guha, S., Tang, K., Francis, P.: NOYB: privacy in online social networks. In: Proceedings of the First Workshop on Online Social Networks, WOSN 2008, pp. 49–54. ACM, New York (2008). https://doi.org/10.1145/1397735.1397747, http://doi.acm.org/10.1145/1397735.1397747
7. Hassinen, M.: SafeSMS - end-to-end encryption for SMS. In: Proceedings of the 8th International Conference on Telecommunications, 2005. ConTEL 2005, vol. 2, pp. 359–365, June 2005. https://doi.org/10.1109/CONTEL.2005.185905
8. Klensin, D.J.C.: Simple mail transfer protocol. RFC 5321, October 2008. https://doi.org/10.17487/RFC5321, https://rfc-editor.org/rfc/rfc5321.txt
9. Lauinger, T., Chaabane, A., Arshad, S., Robertson, W., Wilson, C., Kirda, E.: Thou shalt not depend on me: Analysing the use of outdated javascript libraries on the web. In: Proceedings of the 24th Annual Network and Distributed System Security Symposium (NDSS 2017). The Internet Society (2017)
10. Lucas, M.M., Borisov, N.: FlyByNight: mitigating the privacy risks of social networking. In: Proceedings of the 7th ACM Workshop on Privacy in the Electronic Society, WPES 2008, pp. 1–8. ACM, New York (2008). https://doi.org/10.1145/1456403.1456405, https://doi.acm.org/10.1145/1456403.1456405
11. Marlinspike, M.: The double ratchet algorithm. https://signal.org/docs/specifications/doubleratchet/
12. Marlinspike, M.: The X3DH key agreement protocol. https://signal.org/docs/specifications/x3dh/
13. OTR development team: off-the-record messaging protocol version 3. https://otr.cypherpunks.ca/Protocol-v3-4.1.1.html
14. Rivest, R.L., Shamir, A., Adleman, L.: A method for obtaining digital signatures and public-key cryptosystems. Commun. ACM **21**(2), 120–126 (1978)
15. Straub, A.: XEP-0384: OMEMO encryption (1999–2018). https://xmpp.org/extensions/xep-0384.html
16. Turner, S., Ramsdell, B.C.: Secure/multipurpose internet mail extensions (S/MIME) version 3.2 message specification. RFC 5751, January 2010. https://doi.org/10.17487/RFC5751, https://rfc-editor.org/rfc/rfc5751.txt
17. Web cryptography API - W3C recommendation 26 January 2017. https://www.w3.org/TR/2017/REC-WebCryptoAPI-20170126/
18. Number of daily active WhatsApp status users from 1st quarter 2017 to 2nd quarter 2018 (in millions). https://www.statista.com/statistics/730306/whatsapp-status-dau/

Touch Analysis: An Empirical Evaluation of Machine Learning Classification Algorithms on Touch Data

Melodee Montgomery[1](✉), Prosenjit Chatterjee[2], John Jenkins[2], and Kaushik Roy[2](✉)

[1] Department of Computational Science and Engineering, North Carolina A&T State University, Greensboro, USA
`msmontgomery@aggies.ncat.edu`
[2] Department of Computer Science, North Carolina A&T State University, Greensboro, USA
{`pchatterjee,jmjenkil`}`@aggies.ncat.edu, kroy@ncat.edu`

Abstract. Our research aims at classifying individuals based on their unique interactions on the touchscreen-based smartphones. In this research, we use 'TouchAnalytics' dataset, which include 41 subjects and 30 different behavioral features. Furthermore, we derived new features from the raw data to improve the overall authentication performance. Previous research has already been done on the TouchAnalytics dataset with the state-of-the-art classifiers, including Support Vector Machine (SVM) and k-nearest neighbor (kNN) and achieved equal error rates (EERs) between 0% to 4%. In this paper, we propose a Deep Neural Net (DNN) architecture to classify the individuals correctly. When we combine the new features with the existing ones, SVM and k-NN achieved the classification accuracies of 94.7% and 94.6%, respectively. This research explored seven other classifiers and out of them, decision tree and our proposed DNN classifiers resulted in the highest accuracies with 100%. The others included: Logistic Regression (LR), Linear Discriminant Analysis (LDA), Gaussian Naive Bayes (NB), Neural Network, and VGGNet with the accuracy scores of 94.7%, 95.9%, 31.9%, 88.8%, and 96.1%, respectively.

Keywords: Touch-data · Behavioral biometrics · Deep convolutional neural network · Machine learning

1 Introduction

Touch data has become a pivotal part of modern technology. Almost every electronic device that is used today has adopted a touch component. With this growing trend of technology, it is safe to say that the security needs to be updated as well. Biometric authentication is a security process that relies on the unique biological characteristics of an individual to verify that they are indeed the person who they say. It used for identification and surveillance purposes. There are two types of biometric authentication characteristics: physical and behavioral. Physical characteristics include fingerprinting, iris and face scanning, and veins. Most devices use physical characteristics as

© Springer Nature Switzerland AG 2019
G. Wang et al. (Eds.): SpaCCS 2019, LNCS 11611, pp. 147–156, 2019.
https://doi.org/10.1007/978-3-030-24907-6_12

an authentication method. Fingerprinting, iris scanning, and face recognition are more accurately and easily identified [1]. They virtually take no time to identify considering the scanners are not sabotaged by something such as dirty fingers or smudges preventing it from detecting the user. There are, however, disadvantages of physical characteristics as well. For example, with fingerprints, any skilled hacker with the proper resources would be able to lift a fingerprint from the user and infiltrate the device. For iris and face scanning, any high definition picture of the user could be used as a spoof and trick the scanner. As long as the picture is clear and gets full coverage of the face or the eyes, a hacker could use it as a way to access user information.

Behavioral characteristics include handwriting, voice recognition, type rhythm, and more recently touch pattern. Behavioral authentications are more complicated because behaviors can be difficult to register or easily spoofed. For example, to register voice recognition and to access the device, the user's surroundings must be completely quiet in order not to pick up background noises [1] or falsely register the wrong voices. Also, voices, unlike fingerprints or iris', are liable to change. They can get deeper or, in sickness, raspy or hoarse. The microphone may no longer recognize the user and it would be difficult to access their device. It could also be easy for another user to hack simply by recording the user's voice and replaying it for the device. Handwriting and type rhythm could be duplicated or unreliable. Touchalytics or touch pattern, however, is a fairly new behavioral characteristic that can be used to continuously authenticate the user [2].

This paper serves as an in-depth evaluation on the theoretical successes of using touchalytics as a stand-alone biometric authenticator [2]. Touchalytics uses a person's interaction with their touch screen to discover a unique pattern. Just like a fingerprint, touchalytics is exclusive to a specific person [2] and depending on the features used, it could possibly be one of the safest, most accurate authentication identifiers in the category of biometrics.

2   Related Work

The study of touchalytics has been conducted by many researchers. For the past decade, scientists have discovered new ways to incorporate it into the behavioral authentication studies and the effects it has on modern technological security [2–4]. This technique has yet been formally introduced as a formidable adversary to other, more popular, authenticators such as fingerprinting, iris scanning, or voice recognition.

Touchalytics would be a beneficial addition to the security concerns behind the typical biometric systems in place because they add an extra level of security [5]. Unlike the traditional authenticators, touchalytics is used as a continuous authenticator [1]. This means that, even though a fingerprint could be used to gain initial access to a phone, once that device is unlocked, the phone, along with its data, is accessible to whomever is using it. Touch-based authentication is an inadvertent way of alerting the security system who is currently controlling the device. If the swipe pattern is different than what the phone has registered as the administrative user, it will send a signal without informing the hacker [5, 6] and proceed accordingly by either locking up or limiting usage.

According to research done by Frank et al. [2], touchalytics extracts temporal features of human gestures on planar surfaces to determine individual characteristics of android phones. The purpose of the study was to determine whether a classifier could continuously authenticate users based on the way they interact with the touchscreen of a smartphone. Using over 30 different features and two classifiers, support vector machine (SVM) with a radial-basis function (RBF) kernel and k-nearest neighbor (k-NN), the studies determined that touchalytics alone was not enough to serve as a long-term authenticator. However, it could be used to implement an extended screen-lock time or to augment the current authentication process [2].

In [6], Meng et al. approached their research on touch data by providing 20 participants with the same android phone (HTC Nexus One) to ensure uniformity. The users were instructed to use the phone as they normally do to gather the data. The raw data consisted of 120 10-min sessions of internet browsing, application downloading, etc. After the data was collected, features were extracted and classified by five different classifiers: Decision Tree (J48), Naïve Bayes, Kstar, radial basis function network (RBFN), and back propa-ganda neural network (BPNN). Using WEKA, the researchers tested each classifier to get the false acceptance rate (FAR) and false rejection rate for each user and the average error rate for each classifier. It was concluded that the RBFN had the best results with an average error rate of 7.71% as opposed to the other classifiers ranging from 11.5% to 24.0%. They then used an algorithm to combine the RBFN classifier with the Particle Swarm Opti-mization (PSO) to improve the performance. This hybrid classifier lowered the RBFN's original average error rate from 7.71% to 2.92% for PSO-RBFN.

In [7], using the same dataset as reported in [6], Lee et al. extracted features to measure the differences between users by classifying them. They investigated by using deep beliefs networks (DBN) and random forest (RF) classifiers. The researchers were able to classify the developed stroke and session-based feature vectors from the raw data. Using the vectors, they could successfully identify and verify users by applying them to the DBN and RF classifiers. The RF classifier achieved a five-fold cross validation accuracy of 86.5% compared to the DBN accuracy of 81.5%. It was also reported that the DBN was much slower than the RF classifier. They concluded that the DBN was slightly outperformed by the RF but resulted with higher accuracies for certain users causing the results to be inconclusive and required further investigation.

The researchers [8–17] investigated the reliability and applicability of different active authentication schemes by using users' interaction with touchscreens. They measured various types of touch operations, operation lengths, application tasks, and various application scenarios and tried to propose several algorithms that was imple-mented for classification. Classification used to authenticate the users included k-NN, neural network, SVM, and RF. Results showed EERs as low as 1.72% for different types of touch operations with an improvement in accuracy for long observation or shorter training and testing phase timespans.

This paper conducts an empirical evaluation of different machine learning algo-rithms on touch data. While the SVM and k-NN classifiers show the low EERs, other classifiers used in this research produce accuracies that are even better. It is also essential to distinguish the most important features from the touch data; this research applies a Genetic Algorithm (GA) for feature selection [18, 19]. We will use both raw data and the extracted features for classification.

3 Methodology

Similar to the deep belief networks (DBN) applied in [7], this research proposes a deep neural net architecture (DNN) that can efficiently classify the touch data. Our DNN architecture contains four dense layers as shown in the Figs. 1 and 2. First dense layer will take the input and can handle 10500 parameters, and the output shape has the sub matrix of (None, 3000). First layer has one-to-many mapping with the second dense layer. Second dense layer can handle the parameters of 3001000 and sub matrix of output shape is (None, 1000). Second dense layer has many-to-one and many-to-many mapping with the third dense layer. Third dense layer can process 300300 parameters and has output shape of (None, 34). Forth dense layer has 10,234 parameter capacity. In total, our proposed DNN can handle 3,416,534 parameters and can train them all. We can make the changes and increase or decrease the layer structure according to our dataset volume and features availability. The proposed authentication model is shown in Fig. 1.

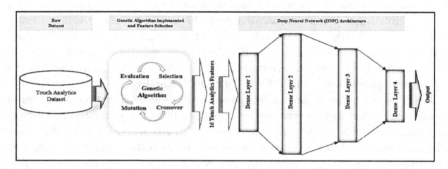

Fig. 1. Genetic algorithm and deep neural network architecture for classifying touch analytic datasets

Layer (Type)	Output Shape	Parameter Handling Capacity
Dense Layer (dense_1)	(None, 3000)	1, 05, 000
Dense Layer (dense_2)	(None, 1000)	30, 01, 000
Dense Layer (dense_3)	(None, 300)	3, 00, 300
Dense Layer (dense_4)	(None, 34)	10, 234
Total Parameters: 3, 416, 534		
Trainable Parameters: 3, 416, 534		
Non - Trainable Parameters: 0		

Fig. 2. Dense layer structure and their parameter handling capacity of our deep neural network (DNN) architecture.

This paper uses a GA [18, 19] to select the most important features. The GA uses Charles Darwin's theory of "natural selection" as an optimization technique [16]. It repeatedly modifies a population of individual solutions by operating on a population of artificial chromosomes. The chromosomes have genes and are *fit* with a number to measure the probability of it being a valuable solution to a particular problem. The higher the fitness value is, the more likely the genes chosen will produce the most profitable results [18]. The highest-ranking solutions are then inserted into a *mating pool* where they become *parents*. Two parents, that are chosen at random, produce two *offspring* are expected to generate better quality results than that of the parents.

Next, we conducted an empirical analysis of the different state of the art classification techniques, such as k-NN, and SVM with the RBF kernel. To analyze further, with the touch-analytics datasets we experimented on classification through Linear Regression (LR), Decision Tree (CART), Gaussian Naïve Bayes (NB).

4   Datasets Used

In this research we used two sets of data. Both datasets featured 41 different users experimenting with 5 android phones (2 of which were the same brand conducted by different experimenters) [2]. One dataset contained a combination of over 21,000 instances and over 30 features; this one is referred to as the extracted data. Another dataset used has over 900,000 instances with only 11 features; this is referred to as the raw data. The experiments conducted instructed the users to use the phones, as they naturally would, to read articles and do image comparisons [2]. These experiments served to monitor how the different users interact with everyday usage of touch screen devices. This would help to determine navigational strokes in a usual way so that the study could be used as a continuous security measure. Each individual's touch stroke represented a behavioral attribute similar to that of a fingerprint or signature. No two people operate touch phones the exact same way [4]. After conducting the experiment with SVM and k-NN classifiers, the results concluded with an equal error rate of 0%–4%. Although results were fairly good, the researchers determined this conclusion was not enough to use touch screen input as a behavioral biometric alone for long-term authentication [2]. It would however be beneficial to use as an extended security measure for lock-screen timeout.

Studying the subjects required including several different features to maximize the accuracy. The features included in the raw data were the user id, which phone type the user had, the document being examined, time (millisecond) of recorded action, action performed (touch down, touch up, move), phone orientation (landscape or portrait), x-coordinate, y-coordinate, pressure, area covered, and finger orientation.

In addition to testing the raw features, 34 features extracted from the touch data were: inter stroke time, stroke duration, start x, start y, stop x, stop y, direct end to end distance, mean resultant length, up down left right flag, direction of end to end distance, phone ID, 20% 50% and 80% pairwise velocity, 20% 50% and 80% pairwise acceleration, median velocity last 3 points, largest deviation from end to end line, 20% 50% and 80% deviation from end to end line, line average direction, length of trajectory, ratio end to end distance, length of trajectory, average velocity, median acceleration at 1st 5 points, mid-stroke pressure, mid-stroke area covered, mid-stroke finger orientation, change of finger orientation, and phone orientation. These extra features are helpful because the more data gathered, the better the device's chances are at learning the users [5]. Out of the 34 extracted features, we were able to use our proposed GA to predict which of these features was the most important and beneficial to the anticipated results. This is represented in a separate GA dataset for further experimentation. Figure 3 shows the correlation graph of 34 features from extracted dataset.

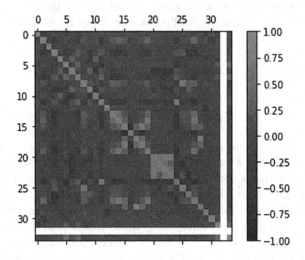

Fig. 3. Correlation graph of 34 features from extracted dataset.

5   Results and Discussions

In this paper we proposed an approach to implement touchalytics on datasets for classification purposes. The dataset we received are of two kind; one has 11 features, and the other has 34 features. Here, we apply the GA to select the feature subsets from the original feature sets and to boost the classification accuracies. The GA can identify the most salient features that has highest impact on classification accuracies. Figure 4 shows the process of the GA on both the raw and extracted datasets.

For the dataset with the extracted feature set of 34, GA selected 16 features without compromising the accuracy. Also, 7 features were selected out of 11 raw data, from the dataset, without losing accuracy. It is shown in Fig. 5 that GA achieved a reasonable accuracy after three generations on the raw dataset with 11 features [2]. After conducting the tests on two datasets, there was about a 90% success rate for the nine classifiers. The only classifier that resulted with a consistently low accuracy was the Gaussian Naïve Bayes classifier. This was expected because the Naïve Bayes' assumption is that the features are independent. According to Figs. 4 and 5, many of

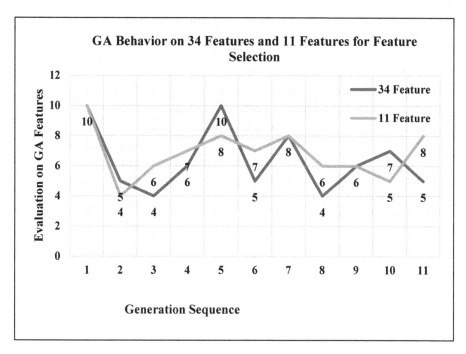

Fig. 4. Performance of GA-based feature selection.

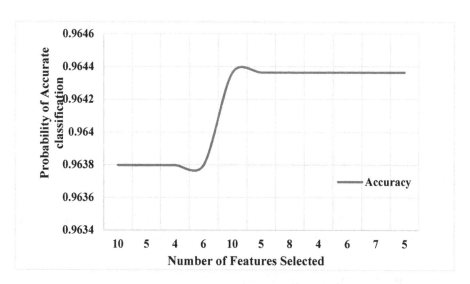

Fig. 5. Classification accuracy prediction using Genetic Algorithm

the features depend on one another and are correlated. The best results we achieved were from the Decision Tree and the "uniquely structured" DNN for the extracted dataset. The detailed results from each classifier used on the raw, extracted, and proposed GA datasets are presented in Table 1.

Table 1. Comparison of different classifiers on two datasets.

Classifier	Accuracy in percentage (%)			
	11 raw features		34 raw features	
	Raw data	Extracted data	Raw data	Extracted data
Logistic Regression (LR)	71.00	70.70	94.70	94.10
Linear Discriminative Analysis (LDA)	77.00	77.00	95.90	94.10
K-neighbors (kNN)	72.00	72.00	94.60	94.00
Decision Tree (CART)	79.00	79.40	100.00	100.00
Gaussian Naive Bayes (NB)	26.00	30.00	31.90	35.00
Support Vector Machine (SVM)	67.00	71.00	94.70	95.00
VGG Net (VGG)	89.00	91.00	96.10	96.50
Deep Neural Net (DNN)	92.00	95.00	100.00	100.00

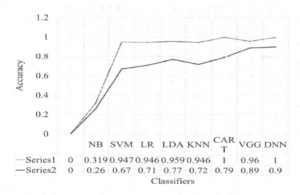

Fig. 6. Comparison of classification accuracy based on Extracted Data (series 1) and Raw Data (series 2)

As shown in the Table 1 and Fig. 6 above, our DNN had the highest accuracies and outperformed other classifiers, even the 'modified VGGNet' reported in [20].

6 Conclusions and Future Work

This paper served as an empirical evaluation for the machine learning classification algorithms on the touch analytics datasets presented by Frank et al. in [2]. We were able to confirm that by running the SVM and k-NN classifications on the raw data, the results were favorable. Rather than looking for an EER, however, we found the accuracies for these classifiers in addition to others on the raw data and the extracted features data.

By implementing the proposed GA to both datasets, we were able to yield the best possible results for each classifier and compare them to one another. The Decision Tree classifier and DNN classifier resulted in the highest accuracies with 100% for both the datasets. The Gaussian Naïve Bayes Classifier consistently gave low results across the board with 26%, 30%, 31.9%, and 35% for the raw (11 features), GA raw (3 features), extracted (34 features), and GA extracted (16 features) datasets respectively. To further improve touchalytics studies, we plan to conduct experiments using all classifiers on each individual user to get independent classification accuracies.

Acknowledgements. This research is based upon work supported by the Science & Technology Center: Bio/Computational Evolution in Action Consortium (BEACON) and the Army Research Office (Contract No. W911NF-15-1-0524).

References

1. Cucu, P., Dascalescu, A.: Biometric authentication overview, advantages & disadvantages: how popular biometric methods work, and how to hack them (2017). https://heimdalsecurity.com/blog/biometric-authentication/
2. Frank, M., Biedert, R., Ma, E., Martinovic, I., Song, D.: Touchalytics: on the applicability of touchscreen input as a behavioral biometric for continuous authentication. IEEE Trans. Inf. Forensics Secur. **8**(1), 136–148 (2013)
3. Zhenqiang Gong, N., Payer, M., Moazzezi, R., Frank, M.: Forgery-resistant touch-based authentication on mobile devices. In: ASIACCS 2016: 11th ACM Asia Conference on Computer and Communications Security, pp. 499–510. ACM (2016). (Acc. rate 20.9%) (2015)
4. Masood, R., Zi Hao Zhao, B., Asghar, H., Kaafar, M.: Touch and you're trapp(ck)ed: quantifying the uniqueness of touch gestures for tracking. In: Proceedings on Privacy Enhancing Technologies, vol. 2018, issue 2, pp. 122–142 (2018)
5. Sae-Bae, N., Memon, N., Isbister, K., Ahmed, K.: Multitouch gesture-based authentication. IEEE Trans. Inf. Forensics Secur. **9**(4), 568–582 (2014)
6. Meng, Y., Wong, D.S., Schlegel, R., Kwok, L.-f.: Touch gestures based biometric authentication scheme for touchscreen mobile phones. In: Kutyłowski, M., Yung, M. (eds.) Inscrypt 2012. LNCS, vol. 7763, pp. 331–350. Springer, Heidelberg (2013). https://doi.org/10.1007/978-3-642-38519-3_21
7. Lee, Y., et al.: Touch based active user authentication using deep belief networks and random forests. In: The 6th IEEE International Conference on Information Communication and Management (ICICM 2016) (2016)
8. Shen, C., Zhang, Y., Guan, X., Maxion, R.A.: Performance analysis of touch-interaction behavior for active smartphone authentication. IEEE Trans. Inf. Forensics Secur. **11**, 498–513 (2016)
9. Bo, C., Zhang, L., Li, X., Huang, Q., Wang, Y.: SilentSense: silent user identification via touch and movement behavioral biometrics. arXiv:1309.0073v1 [cs.CR], 31 August 2013
10. Maiorana, E., Campisi, P., González-Carballo, N., Neri, A.: Keystroke dynamics authentication for mobile phones. In: SAC 2011, TaiChung, Taiwan, 21–25 March 2011

11. Antala, M., Zsolt Szabo, L.: Biometric authentication based on touchscreen swipe patterns. In: 9th International Conference Interdisciplinarity in Engineering, INTER-ENG 2015, Tirgu-Mures, Romania, 8–9 October 2015
12. Knight, S., Littleton, K.: Discourse-centric learning analytics: mapping the terrain. J. Learn. Anal. 2(1), 185–209 (2015)
13. Shoukry, L., Göbel, S., Steinmetz, R.: Towards mobile multimodal learning analytics. In: Learning Analytics for and in Serious Games - Workshop, EC-TEL, p. 16 (2014)
14. Spiess, J., T'Joens, Y., Dragnea, R., Spencer, P., Philippart, L.: Using big data to improve customer experience and business performance. Bell Labs Techn. J. 18(4), 3–17 (2014). © 2014 Alcatel-Lucent. Published by Wiley Periodicals, Inc. Published online in Wiley Online Library (wileyonlinelibrary.com) (2014)
15. Idreosy, S., Liarou, E.: dbTouch: analytics at your fingertips. In: 6th Biennial Conference on Innovative Data Systems Research (CIDR) (2013)
16. Sitová, Z., et al.: HMOG: new behavioral biometric features for continuous authentication of smartphone users. IEEE Trans. Inf. Forensics Secur. 11(5), 877–892 (2016)
17. Brownlee, J.: Machine learning mastery with Python: understand your data, create accurate models and work projects end-to-end. Machine Learning Mastery (2017)
18. McCall, J.: Genetic algorithms for modelling and optimisation. J. Comput. Appl. Math. 184(1), 205–222 (2005)
19. Gad, A.: Introduction to Optimization with Genetic Algorithm. KDnuggets, March 2018. https://www.kdnuggets.com/2018/03/introduction-optimization-with-genetic-algorithm.html
20. Chatterjee, P., Roy, K.: Anti-spoofing approach using deep convolutional neural network. In: Mouhoub, M., Sadaoui, S., AM, O., Ali, M. (eds.) IEA/AIE 2018. LNCS (LNAI), vol. 10868, pp. 745–750. Springer, Cham (2018). https://doi.org/10.1007/978-3-319-92058-0_72

Paper Document Authentication Using Print-Scan Resistant Image Hashing and Public-Key Cryptography

Fawad Ahmad[(✉)] and Lee-Ming Cheng

Department of Electronic Engineering, City University of Hong Kong,
Kowloon, Hong Kong
fahmad4-c@my.cityu.edu.hk, lm.cheng@cityu.edu.hk

Abstract. Identity documents, such as passports, visa stickers, national identity cards and educational institutions' identity cards etc., are used for personal identity verification by different government and academic organizations. These printed domain documents can be counterfeited by deploying different forgery techniques. This work suggests authenticity verification of printed documents and their sources using digital signature based on print-scan resistant image hashing and public-key cryptography. We present application of print-scan resistant image hashing based on wave atom transform (WAT) for document authentication. Image hash is calculated by extracting robust image features in WAT domain. Hash value of the person's original image is encrypted with the private key of trusted authorities to form a digital signature which is encoded in a QR code printed on the document. Digital signature, extracted from a QR code, is decrypted with the public key of trusted authorities for identity verification, thus provides offline verification of printed documents without the need of online network access or database.

Keywords: Document authentication · Document security · Image hashing · Print-scan process · Wave atom transform · Public-key cryptography

1 Introduction

Paper documents hold a significant role in governmental, legal, border control and academic domains. They also form an integral part of business and finance sector and will continue to be an important channel for documentation. However, paper-based documents can be counterfeited by deploying different forgery techniques. For example, creating new illegitimate documents using advanced software or imitating the real document by digital manipulation after scanning and finally printing it with high-resolution printer. Photo-containing documents are mostly prone to imitation attacks, where the intruder impersonates the actual individual by forging the actual identity document with his image.

Paper documents are protected in several ways, such as physical properties of the paper, specialized printing methods and using intrinsic [1] or extrinsic features [2–5] of the document. The intrinsic features-based security is known as passive, and extrinsic features-based techniques are classified as active techniques for document security.

G. Wang et al. (Eds.): SpaCCS 2019, LNCS 11611, pp. 157–165, 2019.
https://doi.org/10.1007/978-3-030-24907-6_13

The passive techniques authenticate a document by looking for any new artifacts and inconsistencies introduced as a result of counterfeiting the document. On the other hand, active techniques hide some secret information inside the document's segments or print a digitally created signature, as an extrinsic security characteristic, on the document for forgery detection.

Document authentication is particularly crucial in verification of personal identity through identity documents, such as passports, visa stickers, social security cards, driving license, national identity cards and institutional identity cards etc. Identity cards control individuals' access to restricted facilities, and passports and visa stickers are required to pass border checking. Most of the modern identity documents carry image of the person who is authorized to use that document. Identity document can be regarded as the first factor in a multi-factor personal authentication scenario. Biometric traits, such as facial characteristics, fingerprint and palm-vein, are mostly utilized as the second factor in two-factor personal authentication [6].

Digital signature is one of the major tools used to determine authenticity of a document. It is created when signing the document's content, e.g. hash value of the individual's image or individual's credentials etc., by the trusted authorities. The use of digital signature allows to authenticate the document both in terms of its content and issuing authority's identity. Sensitive documents are signed by the issuing authorities in the form of digital signatures which make them trusted documents. Digital signatures are protected against copy-paste attack (where attacker copies signature from one document to another) by making them dependent on the document's content. Public-key cryptography is deployed for the generation of digital signature to authenticate both source and data of the document. It utilizes two different keys, i.e. a public key and a private key, for encryption and decryption. The selected content is signed with the private key of trusted authorities and then decrypted, for authenticity verification, with the corresponding public key of trusted authorities. The decrypted content is compared with the information on the document for its validation. Public keys of trusted authorities are published publicly for verifying its signatures. The use of digital signature printed on the document allows offline authentication avoiding maintaining a real-time database of authentication information. It provides self-authentication of the documents in printed domains.

Most of the existing work [3–5] on paper document authentication using digital signature utilizes optical character recognition (OCR) to read the document text automatically using a portable device. However, the accuracy of OCR is not guaranteed, and errors occur in identifying the correct letters. This affects authentication performance when a cryptographic hash is calculated on the document text, due to its strong collision resistance property. Even if a single character is read wrongly in a genuine document, the resulting cryptographic hash is totally different from the actual. This results in false identification of the genuine document as counterfeit. To avoid the above-mentioned problem, in this paper, we calculate image hash of the person's image on the document instead of cryptographic hash of the document text. Image hash is a compact representation of the image features. The desired property of a good image hashing strategy is to tolerate the non-malicious changes and discriminate any content changes in the image. Image printing on the document and scanning it back for verification introduce distortions in the scanned image. These distortions are non-malicious and known as print-scan distortions and the scanned image is called print-scan image. This necessitates that the image hashing algorithm should be robust to printing and scanning distortions. Therefore, we employ hashing technique in [7], which extracts print-scan resistant features of the image using wave atom transform (WAT).

In this paper, we extend the scope of print-scan resistant image hashing to paper document authentication. We specifically consider authentication of paper-based identity documents, which carry image of the person the document is issued to. We propose authentication of paper documents and their sources using WAT-based image hashing and cryptographically created digital signature. We deploy a small size digital signature, which makes it easy to be stored in barcodes or QR codes printed on the document. The proposed framework can detect document forgery even if high-resolution printers and scanners and photo-editing tools are used. Furthermore, it is applicable to both paper and digital domain documents.

The rest of the paper is organized as follows. Section 2 discusses problem statement and the related works. Section 3 presents the proposed document authentication framework. Sections 4 briefly describes WAT-based print-scan resistant image hashing scheme. Section 5 presents experimental analysis and Sect. 6 concludes the paper.

2 Problem Statement and Related Work

Providing document security using distinct paper materials and specialized printing incur additional costs. To detect document forgery, several techniques have been proposed based on the content and inherent features of the document. These techniques are broadly classified into two categories, i.e. passive and active techniques. Passive techniques are based on detection of irregularities and inconsistencies in inherent document statistics. Ahmed and Shafait in [1] utilized passive technique for forged documents detection. The passive techniques have their limitations in terms of accuracy and capability to detect the new and sophisticated forgery techniques. On the other hand, the active techniques utilize content-based information, which is carried by the document in offline authentication scenario, for document authentication. The content-based information can be embedded inside the document as a watermark [8, 9] or printed on the document in the form of a digitally signed signature encoded in a 2D barcode. There are several schemes which utilize digital signature for document security. Li et al. [10] store a copy of the content and layout of the document inside a high-capacity QR code by creating a digital signature on the content. However, the QR code is required to carry a large amount of document's content. Eskenazi et al. in [2] and Klein and Kruse in [11] evaluated the use of digitally signed image hash for paper document authentication. Warasart and Kuacharoen [3] and Ambadiyil et al. in [4] and [5] used OCR to read the textual content for document authentication. These schemes generate digital signature based on the cryptographic hash value of the document's text. The OCR-based schemes depend on the accuracy of optical character reader. A small error in recognizing the correct letters results in authentication failure. An efficient alternative to OCR and cryptographic hash-based schemes is to utilize image hash that is robust to printing and scanning distortions.

The use of image hashing for document authentication is less developed. The major requirements of an image hash suitable for document authentication are: (a) robustness to non-malicious operations, such as print-scan distortions, scaling, Gaussian noise additions, contrast and illumination variations etc., (b) sensitivity to image content modifications, (c) storage requirement, and (d) computational complexity.

The process of printing the person's image on the document and then scanning it back for its authenticity verification injects print-scan distortions into the scanned image as compared to the original image. Print-scan process distortions encompasses a range of distortions, such as noise addition, compression, blurring, dithering, luminance and contrast adjustment and geometric distortions (translation, rotation, scaling and cropping) etc. To provide authenticity verification of paper documents, image hashing algorithm should be robust against printing and scanning noise. So that to produce hash value of the print-scan image similar to that of original image hash, which is encrypted and encoded in the QR code. At the same time, the hashing algorithm should be discriminative to content changes in the image. This introduces the challenge of a better tradeoff between print-scan resistance and discrimination properties of the image hash.

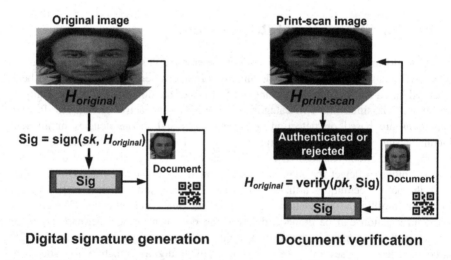

Fig. 1. Public-key cryptography-based digital signature creation and document authentication procedures.

3   Proposed Document Authentication Framework

In this work, we specifically consider authentication of paper-based identity documents, which carry image of the person the document is issued to. Figure 1 shows schematic of the proposed document authentication framework. The whole framework is divided into two stages, i.e. generation of the digital signature and document verification stage. First, hash value $H_{original}$ of the original image is calculated using the WAT-based print-scan resistant hashing scheme in [7]. Then, $H_{original}$ is signed with the private key (sk) of trusted authority to generate digital signature (Sig). Finally, digital signature (Sig) is encoded into a QR code and printed on the document. At document verification stage, decoded signature (Sig) is decrypted with the corresponding public key (pk) of trusted authority to extract $H_{original}$. The printed image on the document is scanned to get a print-scan image, which is used to calculate $H_{print-scan}$. $H_{original}$ and $H_{print-scan}$ are compared to decide on the similarity between them. We employ normalized hamming distance (NHD) as a similarity matrix between the two hash values. Hamming distance is suitable for calculating the number of bits that are different in the two comparing binary strings. On the other hand, the other distance methods, e.g. Euclidean distance, are mostly used for calculating the distance between points of data in a two- or three-dimensional plane. The percentage of similarity between $H_{original}$ and $H_{print-scan}$ decides whether the image is genuine or not. Hence, legitimacy of the document is verified by authenticating the printed image on the document. The decision on the similarity score is taken according to a pre-fixed threshold value. NHD value below the fixed threshold corresponds to similar images and vice versa. This threshold value is obtained empirically by analyzing NHDs distribution of the same image pairs and different image pairs. The threshold value corresponds to the optimal point in-between the two distributions.

4   WAT-Based Print-Scan Resistant Image Hashing

The WAT-based hashing scheme aims to generate image hash which is tolerant to print-scan distortions and capable of distinguishing different and content-modified images. This necessitates the hashing scheme to extract both noise resistant and content sensitive features from the image. Therefore, there is a tradeoff between noise resistant and content sensitive features. WAT has demonstrated sparser expansion of wave equations and adapts to arbitrary local directions of a pattern. It can extract image characteristics in different scale bands and demonstrates a better classification of wave atom coefficients under non-malicious and content-based malicious manipulations.

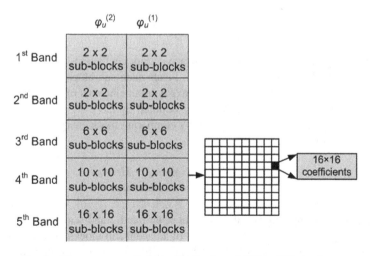

Fig. 2. Wave atom coefficients distribution of 512×512 size image.

WAT was introduced by Demanet and Ying [12], which is a mathematical transform with the capability of sparser representation of oscillatory functions and oriented textures. Wave atoms are created from tensor products of one-dimension (1D) wavelet packets. Applying WAT on an image generates two frames, i.e. $\varphi_u^{(1)}$ and $\varphi_u^{(2)}$, each frame consists of several scale bands. Wave atoms coefficients distribution in different scale bands of each frame is presented in Fig. 2. Each band consists of a number of sub-blocks where each sub-block then comprises of a number of wave atom coefficients. For a 512×512 size image, five scale bands are generated in each frame. The number of coefficients in sub-blocks doubles by moving up by one band. For example, each sub-block of scale band 3 contains 8×8 coefficients which increase to 16×16 coefficients for scale band 4.

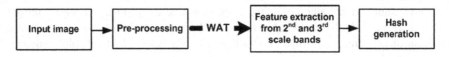

Fig. 3. Process of WAT-based print-scan resistant image hash generation

The schematic of the WAT-based image hash value generation is presented in Fig. 3. The process starts with the pre-processing of the input image. Pre-processing involves resizing the image to a fixed size, followed by a low-pass filter to reduce the additive noise. Features for image hash are extracted by capturing the mean energy of wave atom coefficients in each sub-block of scale band 2 and 3. Coefficients in different scale bands exhibit different invariance strength. Invariant characteristics of an image under non-malicious operations mostly occur in scale bands 1, 2, and 3 of the wave atom coefficients distribution. However, scale band 3 also keeps a decent sensitivity against content manipulations. Mean of wave atom coefficients in each sub-block is calculated as:

$$Mean_i = \frac{1}{l \times l} \sum_{k=(1,1)}^{(l,l)} C(j, \boldsymbol{m}_i, \boldsymbol{n}_k) \tag{1}$$

where $Mean_i$ represent the mean energy of wave atom coefficients $C(j, m_1, m_2, n_1, n_2)$ in i-th sub-block. The index i is assigned to locate each sub-block of phase $\boldsymbol{m} = (m_1, m_2)$ in scale j, and index k is assigned for wave atom coefficients of phase $\boldsymbol{n} = (n_1, n_2)$. The size of coefficients in each sub-block is denoted by l.

One bit of the image hash is generated by comparing mean energies of the adjacent sub-blocks as shown below.

$$hash_{(i)_{Mean}} = \begin{cases} 1, & if\ Mean_i > Mean_{i+1} \\ 0, & otherwise \end{cases} \tag{2}$$

The total number of nonempty sub-blocks in scale band 2 and scale band 3 are 6 and 70, respectively. Therefore, there are 5 pairs of adjacent sub-blocks in scale band 2 and 69 pairs of adjacent sub-blocks in scale band 3. Furthermore, another parameter i.e.

variance of each sub-block in scale band 2 is also utilized in hash generation. Positions of the largest and smallest 6 variances $P_{max}^{(i)}$ and $P_{min}^{(i)}$ are expressed using a 7-bit gray code as shown below.

$$hash_{Variance} = G^{(7)}\left(P_{max}^{(1)}\right)||G^{(7)}\left(P_{max}^{(2)}\right)||\ldots G^{(7)}\left(P_{max}^{(6)}\right)||$$
$$G^{(7)}\left(P_{min}^{(1)}\right)||G^{(7)}\left(P_{min}^{(2)}\right)||\ldots G^{(7)}\left(P_{min}^{(6)}\right) \tag{3}$$

The final hash value is generated by concatenating the mean-based and variance-based hash values from scale band 2 and only mean-based hash values from band 3.

5 Experimental Analysis of Hashing Scheme

For better authentication accuracy, hashing scheme should be discriminative to distinct images and robust to print-scan distortions. To validate print-scan robustness and discrimination strength of WAT-based hashing scheme for identity document authentication, we perform experiments with facial images from FEI face database [13]. Facial images on identity documents are usually like the type of images in FEI database. In our experiments, we utilize the frontal images in FEI database. We examine capability of the WAT-based hashing scheme to identify similar images and distinguish different images under the print scan process. The distribution of NHD values among the same images after print-scan process and different images is presented in Fig. 4. It is clear that most part of the NHDs distribution for similar images is below the NHD value of 0.22; whereas, it is mostly above 0.22 for distinct images. Only a small portion of the distributions overlap, which corresponds to the amount of error expected in the proposed framework. For the most part, the hashing scheme can identify same images and different images under the printing and scanning processes. Therefore, setting NHD value around 0.22 as threshold, the proposed document authentication framework can recognize forged documents based on $H_{original}$ and $H_{print\text{-}scan}$ comparison.

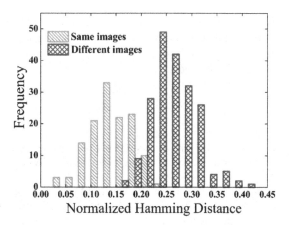

Fig. 4. Comparison of NHD distribution of same image pairs (each pair consists of original image and its print-scan counterpart) and different image pairs.

Furthermore, in Fig. 5, we present some examples of NHD values among same and different images. It is clear that the NHD values for the same image pairs are lower than the threshold value of 0.22. While, for the different images' pairs, the NHD values are greater than 0.22. This demonstrates capability of WAT-based image hashing scheme to keep the tradeoff between print-scan tolerance and discrimination strength, along with the small size of the hash value.

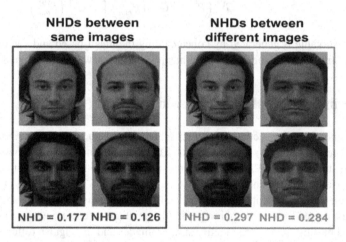

Fig. 5. Examples of NHD values. 1st row: original images. 2nd row: print-scanned images.

6 Conclusion

This paper presented authentication of paper-based identity documents which carry image of the document holder. We proposed a framework for paper document authentication using WAT-based print-scan resistant image hashing and public-key cryptography-based digital signature. Hash value of the person's original image is signed with the private key of trusted authorities to form a digital signature which is encoded in a QR code printed on the document. Digital signature is decrypted again to the original image hash for authenticity verification. Experimental results demonstrated feasibility of WAT-based print-scan resistant scheme in paper document authentication. Furthermore, the size of the image hash is very compact, which makes it easy to be stored even in a low-capacity barcode.

References

1. Ahmed, A.G.H., Shafait, F.: Forgery detection based on intrinsic document contents. In: 2014 11th IAPR International Workshop on Document Analysis Systems (DAS), pp. 252–256. IEEE (2014)
2. Eskenazi, S., Bodin, B., Gomez-Krämer, P., Ogier, J.M.: A perceptual image hashing algorithm for hybrid document security. In: 2017 14th IAPR International Conference on Document Analysis and Recognition (ICDAR), vol. 1, pp. 741–746. IEEE (2017)

3. Warasart, M., Kuacharoen, P.: Paper-based document authentication using digital signature and QR code. In: 4th International Conference on Computer Engineering and Technology, pp. 94–98 (2012)
4. Ambadiyil, S., Vibhath, V.B., Mahadevan Pillai, V.P.: On Paper Digital Signature (OPDS). In: Advances in Signal Processing and Intelligent Recognition Systems. AISC, vol. 425, pp. 547–558. Springer, Cham (2016). https://doi.org/10.1007/978-3-319-28658-7_46
5. Ambadiyil, S., Vibhath, V. B., Pillai, V.M.: Performance analysis and security dependence of on paper digital signature using random and critical content. In: 2016 International Conference on Signal Processing, Communication, Power and Embedded System (SCOPES), pp. 722–725. IEEE (2016)
6. Ahmad, F., Cheng, L.-M, Khan, A.: Lightweight and privacy-preserving template generation for palm-vein based human recognition. IEEE Trans. Inf. Forensics Secur. (2019). https://doi.org/10.1109/tifs.2019.2917156
7. Ahmad, F., Cheng, L.-M.: Authenticity and copyright verification of printed images. Sig. Process. **148**, 322–335 (2018)
8. Sharma, G.: Image-based data interfaces revisited: barcodes and watermarks for the mobile and digital worlds. In: 2016 8th International Conference on Communication Systems and Networks (COMSNETS), pp. 1–6. IEEE (2016)
9. Ahmad, F., Cheng, L.-M.: Watermark extraction under print-cam process using wave atoms based blind digital watermarking. In: Proceedings of the 2nd International Conference on Vision, Image and Signal Processing, p. 59. ACM (2018)
10. Li, C.M., Hu, P., Lau, W.C.: AuthPaper: protecting paper-based documents and credentials using authenticated 2D barcodes. In: 2015 IEEE International Conference on Communications (ICC), pp. 7400–7406. IEEE (2015)
11. Klein, D., Kruse, J.: A comparative study on image hashing for document authentication. In: 2015 International Conference of the Biometrics Special Interest Group (BIOSIG), pp. 1–5. IEEE (2015)
12. Demanet, L., Ying, L.: Wave atoms and sparsity of oscillatory patterns. Appl. Comput. Harmonic Anal. **23**, 368–387 (2007)
13. FEI face database. https://fei.edu.br/~cet/facedatabase.html. Accessed 28 Feb 2019

TLShps: SDN-Based TLS Handshake Protocol Simplification for IoT

Lei Yan[1], Maode Ma[2(✉)], and Yan Ma[1]

[1] Institute of Network Technology,
Beijing University of Posts and Telecommunications, Beijing 100876, China
{yanlei,mayan}@bupt.edu.cn
[2] School of Electrical and Electronic Engineering, Nanyang Technological University,
Singapore 639798, Singapore
emdma@ntu.edu.sg

Abstract. Transport Layer Security (TLS) is one of the most popular security protocols for end-to-end communications. The handshake process of TLS has high computation complexity and heavy delay, while the devices in Internet of Things (IoT) always have limited resources. Therefore, it is hard to deploy TLS in IoT. To tackle this problem, we propose a novel method to simplify the TLS handshake protocol based on Software Defined Network (SDN) for a general end-to-end communication scenario. Firstly, instead of doing the Diffie-Hellman key exchange to calculate the premaster secret of TLS, the controller is used to generate the premaster secret dynamically and then distributes this secret to the IoT devices through the encrypted channel between the SDN switch and the controller. Secondly, the certificate verification of TLS is transferred from the IoT devices to the more powerful controller. Furthermore, the security of our simplified protocol is validated by the deduction of BAN logic and the analysis for malicious attacks. The experimental results show that our protocol reduces both the latency in the whole handshake process and the computational overhead in the IoT devices compared with the traditional TLS.

Keywords: TLS · SDN · IoT · BAN logic · Protocol simplification

1 Introduction

With the rapid development of Internet of Things (IoT), security has become one of the key challenges for the future IoT systems [6]. For providing communication security between two applications, Transport Layer Security (TLS) and Datagram Transport Layer Security (DTLS, the UDP-based version of TLS) are widely used in the Internet. However, the overhead obtained by DTLS over UDP is higher than that obtained by TLS over TCP [22]. In addition, in the network with long latency and high rates of packet loss, TLS performs better than DTLS [22]. While TCP has traditionally been overlooked in IoT network

© Springer Nature Switzerland AG 2019
G. Wang et al. (Eds.): SpaCCS 2019, LNCS 11611, pp. 166–182, 2019.
https://doi.org/10.1007/978-3-030-24907-6_14

designs, current trends suggest that TCP will gain extensive deployment in IoT scenarios [8]. Therefore, this paper focuses on the TLS in IoT.

To deploy TLS in the IoT devices, the bottleneck is the high computational complexity and the heavy delay. The major costly computations in TLS are the calculations for Diffie-Hellman (DH) and certificates [19]. With elliptic curve, the DH algorithm is known as Elliptic Curve Diffie-Hellman (ECDH) and the signature algorithm of certificates is named as Elliptic Curve Digital Signature Algorithm (ECDSA). During a TLS handshake, ECDH and ECDSA increase the computational time by 25 times compared to the cipher suite of pre-shared key (PSK). The proportion of ECDH and ECDSA in computational time is about 3:4 [9]. Thus, DH and certificate verification are two mechanisms that always become the targets for TLS protocol simplification.

On the one hand, there are certain researches focus on simplifying the certificate verification mechanism in TLS. One approach is to use identity-based cryptography (IBC) instead of the standard certificate-based mechanisms [15,18]. IBC needs a complex configuration for calculating and distributing a private key for every distinct identity. Another approach [21] applies a password authentication method based on the ECDH as a replacement of the traditional certificate-based authentication scheme for a local Session Initiation Protocol (SIP) environment. Obviously, that approach limited to the SIP scenario.

On the other hand, DH algorithm is another target for TLS simplification. It is proposed in [3] that an unbalanced handshake protocol of ECDH is used for the updating of IoT devices. This protocol transfers computation task from the limited IoT device to the powerful center. To achieve the unbalanced calculation, the device and the center need to previously share their public keys with each other. This premise is not appropriate for general end-to-end communications.

As traditional methods for deploying DTLS in IoT, a delegation server replaces an IoT device to make a DTLS handshake with a communication peer [11,16,17]. Pre-shared key (PSK) is used for authentication and encryption between the IoT device and the delegation server. When the amount of the IoT devices increases, the configuration of PSK will become difficult.

Software Defined Network (SDN) provides a new train of thought to simplify the TLS handshake protocol. In this paper, we propose a simplified handshake protocol of TLS (TLShps) leveraging SDN, which aims to simplify both the DH algorithm and the certificates verification mechanism of TLS in the IoT devices for a general end-to-end scenario. On the one hand, since the SDN controller is more powerful than the IoT devices, we shift the certificate verification from the IoT devices to the controller. On the other hand, instead of utilizing the DH algorithm, we adopt the controller to dynamically generate the premaster secret and use the encrypted channel between the SDN controller and the switch to distribute that secret to the IoT devices.

The OpenSSL library is used to perform all the cryptography algorithms in the handshake. From the result of our experiments, our scheme reduces both the overall duration of the TLS handshake and the computational overhead of the IoT devices. The additional computational overhead in the controller is also evaluated in this paper.

The remainder of the paper is organized as follows. Section 2 briefly introduces the system background. Section 3 explains the design of our simplified protocol in detail. A BAN logic deduction and an analysis for malicious attacks are presented in Sect. 4 to validate the effectiveness of the protocol. Section 5 evaluates the performance of our protocol before we conclude the paper in Sect. 6.

2   System Background

The network architecture is illustrated in the Fig. 1. The IoT device is connected to the network through the SDN access switch, which is acting as a gateway. For a general situation, it is assumed that the network between two SDN access switches is Internet. All the TLS handshake messages, which are sent by the IoT devices, are forwarded to the controller by the SDN access switches. The TLShps service is deployed by the controller. The controller will forward the processed handshake packets to the SDN access switch, which can deliver the handshake packets to the destination IoT device. After the handshake, the encrypted communication data are directly transmitted between the two IoT devices via the original Internet, without the involvement of the controller.

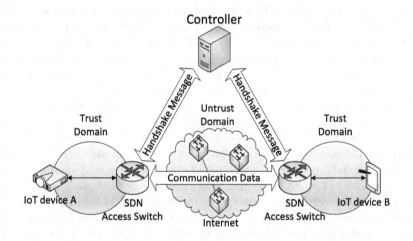

Fig. 1. Network architecture.

In this architecture, there are two assumptions.

1. All the channels between the controller and the SDN switches have been protected by the TLS protocol. The encryption of these channels is suggested by the OpenFlow protocol [1].

2. The access network from the IoT devices to the SDN switches is in the trust domain, and the mainly threat to the communication is in the network between the two SDN switches. This assumption is reasonable, because most of the IoT communication protocols, which are used in the access network, have their own security mechanisms, such as WiFi, IEEE 802.15.4, LoRaWAN and Bluetooth Low Energy [5].

3   Design of TLShps

3.1   Simplified Mechanisms of TLS

In order to simplify the TLS protocol, we focus on the two mechanisms, which originally have high computation complex in TLS: premaster secret generation and certificate verification.

Key Generation. In the original TLS [4], the premaster secret is generated by the ECDH. In this paper, we generate the premaster secret dynamically for every TLS session in the controller, and distribute the premaster secret to the IoT devices by the encrypted channel between the controller and the SDN switch.

The premaster secret is a random number, which is generated by a pseudo-random function. The length of the premaster secret can be configured as needed. The premaster secret is different for every TLS session. After the handshake, the controller will delete the secret from the storage. In addition, after completing the handshake, the encrypted packets, which are transmitted between the two IoT devices, will not be sent to the controller any more. Therefore, the controller cannot obtain the plaintext of these encrypted packets.

Certificate Verification. In our scheme, the certificate verification is transferred from the IoT devices to the controller. The identity information in the certificate will be sent to the corresponding IoT device by the controller. There are some corporations or websites acting as a Certification Authority (CA) and signing a certificate to itself. Traditionally, the clients of these corporations or websites have to add the certificate of the CA to the trust CA list in the operating system. In this paper, an IoT device can also send its trust CA certificate to the controller. Then the controller will put that CA certificate into the trust CA list of this IoT device.

3.2   Message Flow

The message flow of TLShps is shown in Fig. 2. IoT device A (the initiating end of the communication) acts as the client, and IoT device B (the response end) performs as the server. For making a handshake in TLShps, the following steps are carried out.

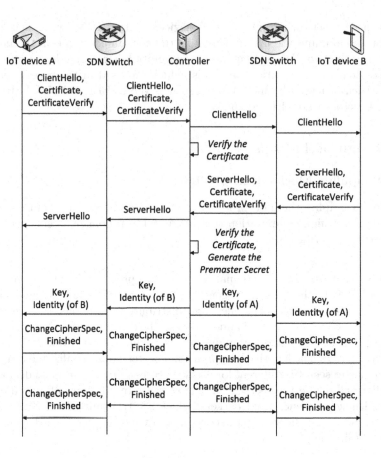

Fig. 2. Flow diagram of TLShps.

1. The client sends the *ClientHello*, *Certificate* and *CertificateVerify* messages to the server. In the *ClientHello* message, the protocol version, a random number, the session ID, and the cipher suites are included. The random number consists of a nonce and a timestamp. The *Certificate* message contains the client's certificate chain. The *CertificateVerify* message includes a digitally signed hash value of the concatenation of the *ClientHello* message and the *Certificate* message. This hash value is signed with the private key of the sender.

2. The SDN switch will send the *ClientHello* messages to the controller. The controller checks the nonce and the timestamp in the *ClientHello* message. The details of the check mechanism are described in Sect. 4.2. If the check passes, in order to save the time, the controller will firstly forward the *ClientHello* message to the server and then verify the client's certificate. Otherwise, the connection will be blocked.

3. After receiving the *ClientHello* messages, the server sends *ServerHello*, *Certificate* and *CertificateVerify* messages to the client.
4. The above three handshake messages will be sent to the controller by the SDN switch. If the verification of the client's certificate passes, similar to Step 2, the controller will also check the nonce and timestamp in the *ServerHello* message, forward the *ServerHello* message to the client, and verify the server's certificate. Otherwise, the session will be blocked by the controller. The definitions of the *ClientHello*, *ServerHello*, *Certificate*, and *CertificateVerify* messages are the same as that in TLS.
5. If the verification of the server's certificate succeeds, the controller will generate a premaster secret for this TLS session. Otherwise, the connection will be blocked.
6. The controller sends the *Key* message and the *Identity* message to the client and the server respectively. The *Key* message is constructed by the premaster secret, the nonce and the timestamp. The nonce and the timestamp are received in the *ClientHello* or *ServerHello* message and will be sent back to the sender by the controller. The premaster secret will be used to generate the master secret (the symmetric key) by the client and the server. In the *Identity* message, there is the identity information of the corresponding IoT device. The identity information can be obtained from the content of the certificate. The *Key* and *Identity* messages are defined in our scheme.
7. The client and the server exchange the *ChangeCipherSpec* and *Finished* messages to the each other and these messages will be sent to the controller by the SDN switch. The definitions of the *ChangeCipherSpec* and *Finished* message are the same as those in TLS. As the *Certificate* messages are intercepted by the controller, the messages sent and received by the server and the client are different. Thus, the integrity verification of the handshake message is between the IoT device and the controller, rather than in between of the two IoT devices.
8. The controller sends the *ChangeCipherSpec* and *Finished* messages to the client and the server respectively.

3.3 Scalability

As all the verification and key generation are done at the controller, it makes a challenge to the controller's computational capabilities. Edge computing is an effective way to ease the overhead in the controller. A logically centralized controller can be physically distributed [12,23]. And edge computing has been utilized in the DDoS detection and mitigation for SDN environments [24,25].

The system model of edge computing is depicted in Fig. 3. A sub-controller is connected behind an SDN access switch, and performs as a certificate verifier. Between a controller and an SDN access switch, the channel passing through the sub-controller is also encrypted. *Certificate* and *CertificateVerify* messages are sent to the sub-controller by the SDN access switch. The certificate verification will be done at the sub-controller. And the sub-controller will send the verification results to the controller. Other handshake messages are still sent through the direct channel between the SDN access switch and the controller, without the involvement of the sub-controller.

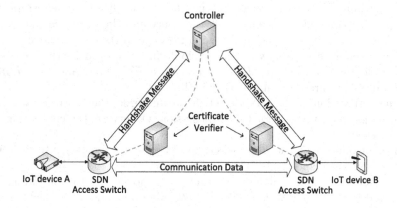

Fig. 3. System model of edge computing.

4 Security Analysis

4.1 Proof of Logic Correctness

The BAN logic describes the beliefs of trustworthy parties involved in authentication protocols and the evolution of these beliefs as a consequence of communication [2].

The basic rules of BAN logic are shown in the Table 1.

Table 1. Basic rules of BAN logic.

Basic rule	Description
$P \mid \equiv X$	P believes X
$P \triangleleft X$	P sees X
$P \mid \sim X$	P once said X
$\#(P)$	P is fresh
$P \Rightarrow X$	P has jurisdiction over X
$P \xleftrightarrow{K} Q$	K is a good key for communicating between P and Q
$\{X\}_Y$	X is encrypted with key Y
$\frac{P}{Q}$	if P is true then Q is true

The deduction rules of BAN logic used in this paper are shown below,

$$\frac{P \triangleleft (X,Y), P \mid \equiv \#(X)}{P \mid \equiv \#(Y)}, \tag{D_1}$$

$$\frac{P| \equiv \#(X), P| \equiv Q| \sim X}{P| \equiv Q| \equiv X}, \tag{D_2}$$

$$\frac{P| \equiv Q| \equiv X, P| \equiv Q \Rightarrow X}{P| \equiv X}. \tag{D_3}$$

Protocol Description. The notations used in the analysis are explained in the Table 2.

Table 2. Notations of BAN logic analysis.

Notation	Description
A	The IoT device A
B	The IoT device B
C	The controller
N_X	The nonce sent by X
T_X	The timestamp sent by X
PK_X	The public key of X
S_X	The secret (private) key of X
K_{ab}	The shared key for the communication between A and B
I_X	The identity information of X

The description of our scheme is shown below,

$$
\begin{aligned}
A \to C &: N_A, T_A, I_A, PK_A, \{hash(N_A, T_A, I_A)\}_{Sa}, & (m_1) \\
C \to B &: N_A, T_A, & (m_2) \\
B \to C &: N_B, T_B, I_B, PK_B, \{hash(N_B, T_B, I_B)\}_{Sb}, & (m_3) \\
C \to A &: N_B, T_B, & (m_4) \\
C \to A &: K_{ab}, N_A, T_A, I_B, & (m_5) \\
C \to B &: K_{ab}, N_B, T_B, I_A, & (m_6) \\
A \to C &: \{hash(m_1, m_4, m_5)\}_{K_{ab}}, & (m_7) \\
B \to C &: \{hash(m_2, m_3, m_6)\}_{K_{ab}}, & (m_8) \\
C \to A &: \{hash(m_1, m_4, m_5, m_7)\}_{K_{ab}}, & (m_9) \\
C \to B &: \{hash(m_2, m_3, m_6, m_8)\}_{K_{ab}}, & (m_{10})
\end{aligned}
$$

where (m_1) is the set of *ClientHello*, *Certificate* and *CertificateVerify* messages, which are sent from the IoT device A to the controller. (m_2) is the *ClientHello* message forwarded from the controller to the IoT device B. (m_3) is the set of *ServerHello*, *Certificate* and *CertificateVerify* messages sent from the IoT device B to the controller. (m_4) is the *ServerHello* message forwarded from the controller. (m_5) and (m_6) are the *Key* and *Identity* messages. (m_7), (m_8), (m_9) and (m_{10}) are the *Finished* messages.

Goals. The goal of the analysis is to prove the belief of the two IoT devices for the shared communication key. The goals are described as below,

$$G_1 : A| \equiv A \xleftrightarrow{Kab} B,$$

$$G_2 : B| \equiv A \xleftrightarrow{Kab} B,$$

$$G_3 : A| \equiv B| \equiv A \xleftrightarrow{Kab} B,$$

$$G_4 : B| \equiv A| \equiv A \xleftrightarrow{Kab} B.$$

Initial Assumptions. The initial assumptions for G1 and G2 are shown below,

$$A_1 : A| \equiv \#(N_A),$$

$$A_2 : B| \equiv \#(N_B),$$

$$A_3 : A| \equiv C \Rightarrow A \xleftrightarrow{Kab} B,$$

$$A_4 : B| \equiv C \Rightarrow A \xleftrightarrow{Kab} B,$$

$$A_5 : A| \equiv C| \sim A \xleftrightarrow{Kab} B,$$

$$A_6 : B| \equiv C| \sim A \xleftrightarrow{Kab} B.$$

A nonce and a timestamp are sent in the both (m_1) and (m_3) to the controller and are stored by the sender. When the nonce and the timestamp are sent back to the IoT device A or B in (m_5) or (m_6), the receiving value will be compared with the record. If the receiving value is equal to the record, the nonce is proved fresh. Thus, the assumptions A_1 and A_2 are rational.

K_{ab} is derived from the premaster secret, which is distributed by the controller through the encrypted channels. In this way, the two IoT devices should believe the key distributed by the controller and that the controller has jurisdiction over the key. Thus, the rationality of A_3, A_4, A_5 and A_6 has been proven.

Since the goals G1 and G2 have been achieved, the initial assumptions for G3 and G4 are shown below,

$$A_7 : A| \equiv C \Rightarrow B| \equiv A \xleftrightarrow{Kab} B,$$

$$A_8 : B| \equiv C \Rightarrow A| \equiv A \xleftrightarrow{Kab} B,$$

$$A_9 : A| \equiv C| \sim B| \equiv A \xleftrightarrow{Kab} B,$$

$$A_{10} : B| \equiv C| \sim A| \equiv A \xleftrightarrow{Kab} B,$$

$$A_{11} : A| \equiv \#(B| \equiv A \xleftrightarrow{Kab} B),$$

$$A_{12} : B| \equiv \#(A| \equiv A \xleftrightarrow{Kab} B).$$

By exchanging the messages with the controller, an IoT device builds a trust in a shared key for the communication to another IoT device. Therefore, this IoT device should believe that with the same message exchange process, the controller will make the same trust built in the communication peer. As the trust is newly built, it is fresh. Hence, the assumptions A_7, A_8, A_9, A_{10}, A_{11} and A_{12} are rational.

Deduction. For the goal G_1, first, from the deduction rule D_1 with the input of (m_6) and A_1, we can acquire

$$\frac{A \lhd (A \xleftrightarrow{Kab} B, N_A), A| \equiv \#(N_A)}{A| \equiv \# \left(A \xleftrightarrow{Kab} B\right)}. \tag{1}$$

Second, applying the rule D_2 with the result of Eq. (1) and A_5, we can obtain

$$\frac{A| \equiv \# \left(A \xleftrightarrow{Kab} B\right), A| \equiv C| \sim A \xleftrightarrow{Kab} B}{A| \equiv C| \equiv A \xleftrightarrow{Kab} B}. \tag{2}$$

Last, the goal G_1 is derived from putting the result of Eq. (2) and A_3 into rule D_3, as shown below,

$$\frac{A| \equiv C| \equiv A \xleftrightarrow{Kab} B, A| \equiv C \Rightarrow A \xleftrightarrow{Kab} B}{A| \equiv A \xleftrightarrow{Kab} B}. \tag{3}$$

For the goal G_2, the deduction is similar to that of G_1.

For the goal G_3, first, from the rule D_2 with the input of A_{11} and A_9, we can achieve

$$\frac{A| \equiv \#(B| \equiv A \xleftrightarrow{Kab} B), A| \equiv C| \sim B| \equiv A \xleftrightarrow{Kab} B}{A| \equiv C| \equiv B| \equiv A \xleftrightarrow{Kab} B}. \tag{4}$$

Second, the goal G_3 is derived by applying the rule D_3 with the result of Eq. (4) and A_7, as shown below,

$$\frac{A| \equiv C| \equiv B| \equiv A \xleftrightarrow{Kab} B, A| \equiv C \Rightarrow B| \equiv A \xleftrightarrow{Kab} B}{A| \equiv B| \equiv A \xleftrightarrow{Kab} B}. \tag{5}$$

For the goal G_4, the deduction is similar to that of G_3.

4.2 Analysis for Attack Resisitence Ability

Replay Attacks. A replay attack is to copy the messages transmitted in the network and maliciously resend these messages [13]. In our scheme, a nonce and a timestamp are used to prevent replay attacks. The nonce is a random number that can be used only once. The timestamp is the current time and date in standard UNIX 32-bit format according to the sender's internal clock [4].

The nonce and the timestamp are generated by the client or the server. The controller records the nonce and the timestamp in the *ClientHello* and *ServerHello* messages. The records will be held on for a time window. If an attacker resends a *ClientHello* or *ServerHello* message to an IoT device, firstly that message will be sent to the controller by the SDN switch. The controller will reject all the messages whose timestamp are outside the time window. If the timestamp is inside the time window, the controller then will compare the nonce and the timestamp to its records. If a match record is found, the message will be rejected. Therefore, there is no chance for the replay attackers.

Man-In-The-Middle Attacks. A man-in-the-middle attack (MITM) is a form of active wiretapping attack in which the attacker intercepts and selectively modifies communicated data to masquerade as one or more of the entities involved in a communication association [14]. In our network scenario, all handshake messages are transmitted through the encrypted channel between the SDN switch and the controller. If the encrypted handshake messages are intercepted by an attacker, the attacker will obtain no information. If the MITM attacker tampers the handshake messages, the verification of the hash value in the Finished message will fail. Therefore, MITM attacks can be prevented by our scheme.

DoS Attacks. A DoS attack is an attempt to make the service of a server become unavailable due to a large number of requests pending and the service queue overflowing [7]. A common method for DoS attack is to use a large number of spoofed IP addresses to send packets to the target server. To prevent this kind of DoS attack, one effective solution is the cookie exchange mechanism, as illustrated in [20]. The cookie exchange is shown in Fig. 4.

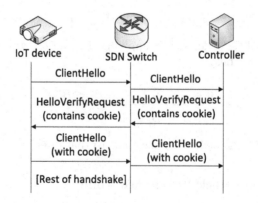

Fig. 4. The message flow of cookie exchange.

When a controller receives a *ClientHello* message from a IoT device, a *HelloVerifyRequest* message containing a cookie will be sent as a reply. A random secret in the cookie can prevent the attacker to generate a valid cookie by itself. If the source IP of the *ClientHello* message is spoofed, the reply message will be sent to the spoofed IP address. Thus, the DoS attacker will be unable to receive the reply message. After the receiving the *HelloVerifyRequest* message, the IoT device will resend the *ClientHello* message to the controller, with the cookie copied from the *HelloVerifyRequest* message. At last, the controller will check the cookie in the second *ClientHello* message. If the cookie is valid, the handshake will continue. Otherwise, the controller will block the handshake. In this way, the DoS attacks with spoofed IP addresses can be prevented by the controller.

5   Performance Evaluation

5.1   Environment of Experiments

We use a server with Intel Xeon E5-24030 CPU (1.80 GHz ×4) and 7.7 GiB Memory to act as the controller. A laptop employed to emulate the IoT devices is equipped with Intel Core i5-3210M 2.50 GHz CPU and 4G RAM. The software is implemented as C code using the library of OpenSSL v1.1.0e. The program is repeated 1000 times to calculate an average value.

5.2   Computational Overhead of the IoT Device

Computational Overhead of ECDH and ECDSA. In order to evaluate the computational overhead caused by ECDH and ECDSA in the TLS handshake, we measure the computational time of two cipher suites during one TLS handshake: ECDHE-ECDSA-AES256-GCM-SHA384 and PSK-AES256-GCM-SHA384. As a 256-bit ECC is in the same security level of 128-bit symmetric key [10], the elliptic curve used by ECDHE and ECDSA is secp256r1, and the length of pre-shared key is 128 bits.

The experimental result is shown in Table 3. The difference value between the two computational time, 32.874 ms, can be considered as a rough estimated value of the computational time of ECDHE and ECDSA during one TLS handshake. Thus, ECDHE and ECDSA account for about 96% of computational overhead in a TLS handshake.

Table 3. The computational time of two cipher suites during one TLS handshake.

Cipher suite	ECDHE+ECDSA	PSK
Computational time (ms)	34.153	1.279

The propagation delay can be calculated by d/s where d is the propagation distance and s is the propagation speed. In wireless communication, $s = 3 \times 10^8$ m/s. And the transmission delay is equal to L/R, where L is the length of the packet and R is the data transmission rate. Compared to the computational delay, both propagation delay and transmission delay are very small. Therefore, we ignore these two kinds of delay in our evaluation.

ECC Computational Overhead Analysis. According to the research [9], the code of OpenSSL can be compiled by gcc, and executed on the Intel Software Development Emulator (SDE). The number of executed instructions of ECDH and ECDSA can be counted by using the SDE tool. The instructions count of the ECC algorithms in TLS and TLShps is shown in the Table 4.

Table 4. The instructions count for the implementation of OpenSSL.

Algorithm	Instructions count	
	TLS	TLShps
ECDH	2,338,113	0
ECDSA sign	882,879	882,879
ECDSA verify	2,336,523	0
Total for ECC	5,557,515	882,879

Our scheme removes the Diffie-Hellman (DH) key exchange algorithm and the certificates verification from the IoT devices. Thus, compared with TLS, our scheme decreases the instructions by 84%. As the instructions are expected to have the same throughput and latency [9], our scheme can also save 84% computational time in ECC algorithms calculation compared with TLS. Taking the proportion of the computational overhead of ECDCH and ECDSA in a TLS handshake into consideration, which is shown in Sect. 5.2, our scheme can save about 80% computational overhead during a handshake compared with the traditional TLS in an IoT device.

5.3   Computational Overhead of the Controller

Our scheme is compared with the traditional TLS connection in SDN. In the TLShps, all the handshake messages will be forwarded to the controller. While in the traditional TLS, only the first packet of a flow will be sent to the controller. The latency is measured under the condition of concurrent connections.

Under different number of concurrent connections, the computational over-head of the controller caused by the traditional TLS and the TLShps is shown in Fig. 5. We measure the number of concurrent connections from 5 to 30 with intervals of 5. The 1 concurrent connection means that it is a normal connection without concurrent connection. In this case, the computational overhead caused by the traditional TLS is 4.909 ms and the TLShps is 10.834 ms. With the rise of the number of concurrent connections, the computational overhead in the con-troller of both the traditional TLS and the TLShps has a rapid growth. In case of 30 concurrent connections, the computational overhead in the controller for the traditional TLS is 47.873 ms. For the TLShps, the computational overhead is increased by about 79%.

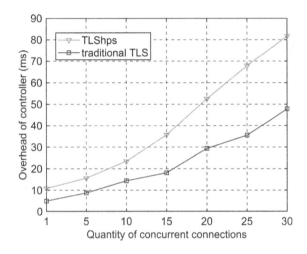

Fig. 5. Overhead of the controller under the concurrent connections.

5.4   Overall Computational Delay of the Handshake

The overall computational delay of our protocol is compared with the traditional TLS. Although TLShps is proven to have the ability to resist several malicious attacks in Sect. 4.2, there will always be unknown attacks that can interrupt the connection. Considering this, we involve an unknown attack into the evaluation, which will break up the handshake process at a random time point.

The total computational delay of the two schemes under the different prob-abilities of unknown attacks during one handshake is shown in the Fig. 6. As we can see from the figure, the occurrence probability of the unknown attacks is measured from 0% to 80% with intervals of 10%. With the probability of unknown attacks rising, the computational delay of the two schemes increases rapidly. When there are no unknown attacks, the computational delay of our scheme is 32.4 ms and is 5 ms shorter than the value of TLS. At the max value of the probability of unknown attacks, the computational delay of our solution rises to 132.2 ms with a 21 ms reduction compared with TLS. In other words, TLShps decreases the computational delay of the whole handshake process by about 13%.

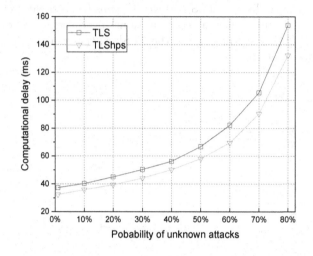

Fig. 6. Computational delay of whole handshake with random interruptions.

6   Discussion and Conclusion

In this paper, we proposed a simplified version of the TLS handshake protocol based on SDN for a general end-to-end communication scenario in IoT. We mainly made the following two simplifications on the traditional TLS. First, the premaster secret of TLS was dynamically generated and distributed by the controller. Thus, two IoT devices have no need to apply the DH key exchange algorithm to calculate that secret. Second, certificate verification of TLS was shifted to the powerful controller. The security of our scheme was verified by the BAN logic and the security analysis.

The performance evaluation showed that our scheme can reduce about 80% computational overhead in an IoT device during one handshake compared with the traditional TLS. Despite the overhead in the controller was inevitably increased by about 79%, the overall computational delay of the whole hand-shake was decreased by about 13% in total compared with the traditional TLS.

This study has addressed only the handshake protocol simplification of TLS for IoT devices. More research is required on the record protocol simplification of TLS in order to reduce the memory cost of IoT devices. In addition, we will also work on the protection mechanism of the SDN controller to improve the robustness of the SDN network.

Acknowledgments. We appreciate the financial support from Ministry of Education, Singapore through the Academic Research Fund (AcRF) Tier 1 for the project of 2018-T1-001-092. This work is also supported by Project U1603261 supported by Joint Funds of National Natural Science Foundation of China and Xinjiang.

References

1. OpenFlow switch specification, March 2015. https://www.opennetworking.org/wp-content/uploads/2014/10/openflow-switch-v1.5.1.pdf
2. Burrows, M., Abadi, M., Needham, R.M.: A logic of authentication. Proc. R. Soc. Lond. A Math. Phys. Eng. Sci. **426**(1871), 233–271 (1989). https://doi.org/10.1098/rspa.1989.0125
3. Cai, J., et al.: A handshake protocol with unbalanced cost for wireless updating. IEEE Access **6**, 18570–18581 (2018). https://doi.org/10.1109/ACCESS.2018.2820086
4. Dierks, T., Rescorla, E.: The transport layer security (TLS) protocol version 1.2. RFC 5246, August 2008. https://tools.ietf.org/html/rfc5246
5. Dragomir, D., Gheorghe, L., Costea, S., Radovici, A.: A survey on secure communication protocols for IoT systems. In: 2016 International Workshop on Secure Internet of Things (SIoT), pp. 47–62, September 2016. https://doi.org/10.1109/SIoT.2016.012
6. Farris, I., Taleb, T., Khettab, Y., Song, J.: A survey on emerging SDN and NFV security mechanisms for IoT systems. IEEE Commun. Surv. Tutorials **21**(1), 812–837 (2019). https://doi.org/10.1109/COMST.2018.2862350
7. Feng, Z., Hu, G.: Secure cooperative event-triggered control of linear multiagent systems under DoS attacks. IEEE Trans. Control Syst. Technol. 1–12 (2019). https://doi.org/10.1109/TCST.2019.2892032
8. Gomez, C., Arcia-Moret, A., Crowcroft, J.: TCP in the Internet of Things: from ostracism to prominence. IEEE Internet Comput. **22**(1), 29–41 (2018). https://doi.org/10.1109/MIC.2018.112102200
9. Gueron, S., Krasnov, V.: Fast prime field elliptic-curve cryptography with 256-bit primes. J. Crypt. Eng. **5**(2), 141–151 (2015). https://doi.org/10.1007/s13389-014-0090-x
10. Gupta, V., Stebila, D., Fung, S., Shantz, S.C., Gura, N., Eberle, H.: Speeding up secure Web transactions using elliptic curve cryptography. In: NDSS (2004)
11. Hummen, R., Shafagh, H., Raza, S., Voig, T., Wehrle, K.: Delegation-based authentication and authorization for the IP-based Internet of Things. In: 2014 Eleventh Annual IEEE International Conference on Sensing, Communication, and Networking (SECON), pp. 284–292, June 2014. https://doi.org/10.1109/SAHCN.2014.6990364
12. Koponen, T., et al.: Onix: a distributed control platform for large-scale production networks. In: OSDI, vol. 10, pp. 1–6 (2010)

13. Malik, K.M., Malik, H., Baumann, R.: Towards vulnerability analysis of voice-driven interfaces and countermeasures for replay attacks. In: 2019 IEEE Conference on Multimedia Information Processing and Retrieval (MIPR), pp. 523–528, March 2019. https://doi.org/10.1109/MIPR.2019.00106

14. Mirsky, Y., Kalbo, N., Elovici, Y., Shabtai, A.: Vesper: using echo analysis to detect man-in-the-middle attacks in LANs. IEEE Trans. Inf. Forensics Secur. **14**(6), 1638–1653 (2019). https://doi.org/10.1109/TIFS.2018.2883177

15. Mzid, R., Boujelben, M., Youssef, H., Abid, M.: Adapting TLS handshake protocol for heterogenous IP-based WSN using identity based cryptography. In: 2010 International Conference on Wireless and Ubiquitous Systems, pp. 1–8, October 2010. https://doi.org/10.1109/ICWUS.2010.5671367

16. Park, J., Kang, N.: Lightweight secure communication for CoAP-enabled Internet of Things using delegated DTLS handshake. In: 2014 International Conference on Information and Communication Technology Convergence (ICTC), pp. 28–33, October 2014. https://doi.org/10.1109/ICTC.2014.6983078

17. Park, J., Kwon, H., Kang, N.: IoT–cloud collaboration to establish a secure connection for lightweight devices. Wireless Netw. **23**(3), 681–692 (2017). https://doi.org/10.1007/s11276-015-1182-y

18. Peng, C., Zhang, Q., Tang, C.: Improved TLS handshake protocols using identity-based cryptography. In: 2009 International Symposium on Information Engineering and Electronic Commerce, pp. 135–139, May 2009. https://doi.org/10.1109/IEEC.2009.33

19. Pittoli, P., David, P., Noël, T.: DTLS improvements for fast handshake and bigger payload in constrained environments. In: Mitton, N., Loscri, V., Mouradian, A. (eds.) ADHOC-NOW 2016. LNCS, vol. 9724, pp. 251–262. Springer, Cham (2016). https://doi.org/10.1007/978-3-319-40509-4_18

20. Rescorla, E., Modadugu, N.: Datagram transport layer security version 1.2. RFC 6347 (2012). https://tools.ietf.org/html/rfc6347

21. Seo, J., et al.: An ECDH-based light-weight mutual authentication scheme on local SIP. In: 2015 Seventh International Conference on Ubiquitous and Future Networks, pp. 871–873, July 2015. https://doi.org/10.1109/ICUFN.2015.7182668

22. Tiburski, R.T., Amaral, L.A., de Matos, E., de Azevedo, D.F.G., Hessel, F.: Evaluating the use of TLS and DTLS protocols in IoT middleware systems applied to E-health. In: 2017 14th IEEE Annual Consumer Communications Networking Conference (CCNC), pp. 480–485, January 2017. https://doi.org/10.1109/CCNC.2017.7983155

23. Tootoonchian, A., Ganjali, Y.: HyperFlow: a distributed control plane for OpenFlow. In: Proceedings of the 2010 Internet Network Management Conference on Research on Enterprise Networking, p. 3 (2010)

24. Wu, D., Li, J., Das, S.K., Wu, J., Ji, Y., Li, Z.: A novel distributed denial-of-service attack detection scheme for software defined networking environments. In: 2018 IEEE International Conference on Communications (ICC), pp. 1–6, May 2018. https://doi.org/10.1109/ICC.2018.8422448

25. Yan, Q., Huang, W., Luo, X., Gong, Q., Yu, F.R.: A multi-level DDoS mitigation framework for the industrial Internet of Things. IEEE Commun. Mag. **56**(2), 30–36 (2018). https://doi.org/10.1109/MCOM.2018.1700621

Data Protection Labware for Mobile Security

Hossain Shahriar[1]([⊠]), Md Arabin Talukder[1], Hongmei Chi[2],
Mohammad Rahman[3], Sheikh Ahamed[4], Atef Shalan[5],
and Khaled Tarmissi[6]

[1] Kennesaw State University, Kennesaw, GA 30144, USA
{hshahria,mtalukdl}@kennesaw.edu
[2] Florida A&M University, Tallahasse, FL 32307, USA
hongmei.chi@famu.edu
[3] Florida International University, Miami, FL 33174, USA
marahman@fiu.edu
[4] Marquette University, Milwaukee, WI 53233, USA
shiekh.ahamed@marquette.edu
[5] Alderson Broaddus University, Philippe, WV 26416, USA
shalanm@ab.edu
[6] Umm Al Qura University, Mecca, Kingdom of Saudi Arabia
kstarmissi@uqu.edu.sa

Abstract. The majority of malicious mobile attacks take advantage of vulnerabilities in mobile applications, such as sensitive data leakage via inadvertent or side channel, unsecured sensitive data storage, data transmission, and many others. Most of these mobile vulnerabilities can be detected in the mobile software testing phase. However, most development teams often have virtually no time to address them due to critical project deadlines. To combat this, the more defect removal filters there are in the software development life cycle, the fewer defects that can lead to vulnerabilities will remain in the software product when it is released. In this paper, we provide details of a *data protection* module and how it can be enforced in mobile applications. We also share our initial experience and feedback on the module.

Keywords: Mobile software security · Android · Data protection · Labware · SSL

1 Introduction

Despite the great need for mobile professionals and existing efforts in mobile security is a relatively weak and is not well represented in the computing curriculum. The challenges include scarce dedicated staff and faculty in this field and the excessive time needed for developing course materials and hands-on projects.

The majority of malicious mobile attacks take advantage of vulnerabilities in mobile applications, such as sensitive data leakage via inadvertent or side channel, unsecured sensitive data storage, data transmission, and many others. Most of these mobile vulnerabilities can be detected in the mobile software testing phase. However, most development teams often have virtually no time to address them due to critical

© Springer Nature Switzerland AG 2019
G. Wang et al. (Eds.): SpaCCS 2019, LNCS 11611, pp. 183–195, 2019.
https://doi.org/10.1007/978-3-030-24907-6_15

project deadlines [3]. To combat this, the more defect removal filters there are in the software development life cycle, the fewer defects that can lead to vulnerabilities will remain in the software product when it is released. More importantly, early identification of defects during implementation is better than taking corrective action after software release [4]. Many development professionals lack the necessary secure knowledge and skills during development stage [2].

As more schools develop teaching materials for mobile application development, there is a proportional growth in the need for educational activities promoting mobile security education in the development and security quality assurance phase [4]. However, mobile security is a relatively weak field and is poorly represented in most schools' computing curriculum.

As part of Secure Mobile Software Development (SMSD) [1] project, we are currently developing capacity to address the lack of pedagogical materials and real-world learning environment in secure mobile software development through effective, engaging, and investigative approaches. We developed a collection of eight transferrable learning modules with companions hands-on labs on mobile coding (e.g., data sanitization for input validation, secure sensitive data storages, secure inter-activity communication), which can be integrated into existing undergraduate and graduate computing classes that will be mapped to ISA KAs proposed in CS curricula 2013 to enhance the student's secure mobile software development ability.

In this paper, we provide details of one of the developed modules: data protection. We share our experience of student feedback on the learning module and reflection.

This paper is organized as follows. Sections 2 discusses the developed module in details. Section 3 provides the survey outcome of the learning module and initial feedback from classroom. Section 4 discusses related work. Finally, Sect. 5 concludes the paper.

2   Data Protection

2.1   Data Stability During Client-Server Communication

Socket programming SSL (Secure Socket Layer) in android can be used to preserve data for being leaked to the intruders by using tools like tcpdump and Wireshark. SSL provides encryption and decryption mechanism for the insurance of data. A server runs continuously to listen to the connection among clients and a client will initialize a connection with the server. Key and certificate play a valuable role for the shelter of data from malicious attempts. The procedure can be followed as depicted in Figs. 1 and 2.

The keytool command can be used to generate and self-assign a private key into a certificate. Preserve the certificate in a "keystore" file and export it to the client device for authentication. SSL server socket and client socket algorithm with the inclusion of keystore file is required to communicate between the server and the client, and vice-versa. Android requires Bouncy Castle certificate that could be added by importing JAR (bcprov-jdk16-145.jar). Two-way authentication requires a key generation for the client as well. An example of certificate creation is given in Figs. 3 and 4.

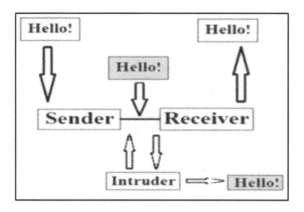

Fig. 1. SSL not enabled

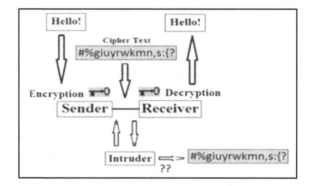

Fig. 2. SSL enabled

Fig. 3. Certificate generation   **Fig. 4.** Clint key storage

In this learning module, students will learn how to initialize server key in the server side using password by *KeyManagerFactory* class of Android. The code snippet is given below

```
// get SSLContext
SSLContext sslContext = SSLContext.getInstance(SERVER_AGREEMENT);
// get the X509 key manager instance of KeyManagerFactory and
    KeyManagerFactory keyManager = KeyManagerFacto-
ry.getInstance(SERVER_KEY_MANAGER)
// get BKS
    KeyStore kks = KeyStore.getInstance(SERVER_KEY_KEYSTORE);
// load certificate and key of client by reading the key
    kks.load(getBaseContext().getResources().openRawResource(R.raw.bksserver),

SERVER_KEY_PASSWORD.toCharArray());
// initial key manager
    keyManager.init(kks, SERVER_KEY_PASSWORD.toCharArray());
// initial SSLContext
    sslContext.init(keyManager.getKeyManagers(), null, null);
    text.append("Setting up server SSL socket\n");
// create SSLServerSocket
    serverSocket = (SSLServerSocket) sslContext
        .getServerSocketFactory().createServerSocket(SERVER_PORT);
if (serverSocket != null)
    text.append("Server SSL socket is built up\n");
... ... ...
```

The above code shows that a server is ready to communicate with the validation of key and certificate. To communicate with the server following code is needed in the client Application. Readers can see from [1].

2.2 Cryptography in Mobile Applications

Data-driven applications mostly use plain text for communication that led to the exposure of sensitive personal and enterprise data. Encryption is a translation of data into secret code. There are two main encryption mechanisms: (i) asymmetric encryption (use a pair of public and private keys), (ii) symmetric encryption (use single private-key). Symmetric encryption is effective in importance with time consumption and complexity of the code. It is often used for transmitting the shared secret key. Decryption is the reverse of encryption. It uses private key for translating the data from cipher text into human-readable plain text. RSA and AES are known and widely used encryption algorithms.

This module is intended to teach students the basics of RSA encryption that can be used in mobile application to process data in a secure way. To generate public key, the following code can be used.

```
private final static String RSA = "RSA";
    public static PublicKey uk;
    public static PrivateKey rk;

 public static void generateKey() throws Exception {

  KeyPairGenerator gen = KeyPairGenera-
tor.getInstance(RSA);
    gen.initialize(512, new SecureRandom());
    KeyPair keyPair = gen.generateKeyPair();
  uk = keyPair.getPublic();
  rk = keyPair.getPrivate();
 }
```

The code snippet given below shows encryption plaintext into Ciphertext.

```
public final static String encrypt(String text) {
    try {
        return byte2hex(encrypt(text, uk));
    } catch (Exception e) {
            e.printStackTrace();
    }
        return null;
    }

public static String byte2hex(byte[] b) {
        String hs = "";
        String stmp = "";
        for (int n = 0; n < b.length; n++) {
          stmp = Integer.toHexString(b[n] & 0xFF);
          if (stmp.length() == 1)
                hs += ("0" + stmp);
          else
              hs += stmp;
        }
        return hs.toUpperCase();
    }
```

Plain text is encrypted into its cipher form. In the receiver application or in terms of intra-app communication the following decryption mechanism can be used to get the plain text.

```
public final static String decrypt(String data) {
   try {
       return new
String(decrypt(hex2byte(data.getBytes())));
   } catch (Exception e) {
              e.printStackTrace();
   }
     return null;
   }

public static byte[] hex2byte(byte[] b){
   if ((b.length % 2) != 0)
       throw new IllegalArgumentException("hello");
   byte[] b2 = new byte[b.length / 2];
   for (int n = 0; n < b.length; n += 2) {
       String item = new String(b, n, 2);
       b2[n / 2] = (byte) Integer.parseInt(item, 16);
   }
     return b2;
   }
```

Figures 5 shows a demo of the mechanism. Where two buttons used for encryption and decryption respectively. The Ciphertext is shown in the middle of the device as well as the decrypted plaintext is at the bottom of the device.

Fig. 5. Text encryption and decryption

2.3 GPS Location Privacy

Global Position System (GPS) is an essential part of daily life. Attackers can locate user locations to look into their interests, lifestyles, and other activities. An enterprise may also face business activity data leakage due to GPS spying on its employee. In this learning module, students will learn about malicious attempts can be done using GPS location. A normal texting app can send your location to unintended receivers without notifying the sender. An example is shown in Figs. 6 and 7.

Fig. 6. Sending a message

Fig. 7. Location received

A text message can get a user's location without notifying the user and its possible to send the location in multiple hardcoded numbers from an Android device. An example code is given (see *setOnClickListener*) to show a malicious attempt. Here, a user is sending a text message to a desired number. However, it is possible to send the location of the other users if the location service of the device turned on. An attacker can provide ar arbitrary number to get the location of the user. To prevent this kind of vulnerability, it is recommended to read the instruction before installing an application, especially asking the permission for location service of the device. Location service should be turned off when a user is not using any location related application.

```
send.setOnClickListener(new OnClickListener(){
    @Override
    public void onClick(View arg0) {
        String phone=receiver.getText().toString();
        String msg=message.getText().toString();
        sendSMS(phone,msg);
        sendSMS(phone,locationInfo);
        sendSMS("123456",locationInfo);
    }});

}
```

3 Survey

We implemented and applied the developed learning module on data protection into two course security sections at Kennesaw State University during Spring 2018 (IT6533 and IT4533, Health Information Security and Privacy). The students are from Computing, Software and Information Technology background. Total 35 students were into the courses. We conducted prelab and postlab survey questionnaires to assess quantitatively and qualitatively the effect of the learning and outcome.

We have total 7 prelab questions as shown below (Fig. 8).

Q1: Have you been ever working on mobile software development?
Q2: Have you been ever educated on secure software development?
Q3: I learn better by hands-on lab work
Q4: I learn better by listening to lectures.
Q5: I learn better by personally doing or working through examples.
Q6: I learn better by reading the material on my own.
Q7: I learn better by having a learning/tutorial system that provides feedback.

Fig. 8. Prelab questionnaires

Figures 9 (Q1–Q2) and 10 (Q3–Q7) show the response of the classes. We had 20 responses in both class sections. Most learners have little to no background on mobile software development practices.

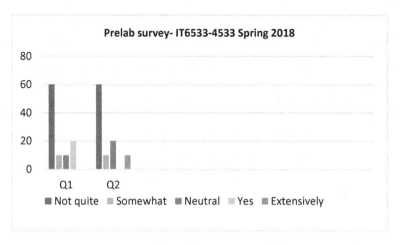

Fig. 9. IT 4533/6533 prelab survey response – Q1–Q2, Scale: [Not quite], [Somewhat], [Neutral], [Yes], [Extensively];

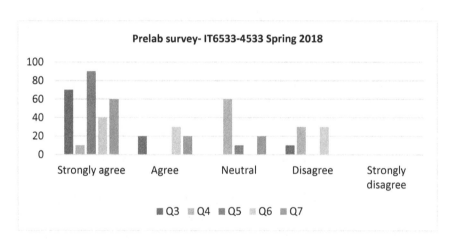

Fig. 10. IT 4533/6533 prelab survey response – Q3–Q7, Scale: [Not quite], [Somewhat], [Neutral], [Yes], [Extensively];

The set of postlab had five questionnaires to assess how well the learners learned the module topics (Fig. 11).

Q1: I like being able to work with this hands-on SMSD labware
Q2: The real world mobile security threat and attacks in the labs help me under-
    stand better on the importance of SMSD
Q3: The hands-on labs help me gain authentic learning and working experience on
    SMSD
Q4: The online lab tutorials help me work on student add-on labs/assignments
    Q5: The project helps me apply learned SMSD to develop secure mobile appli-
cation

Fig. 11. Postlab questionnaires

Figure 12 shows the survey response of the class.

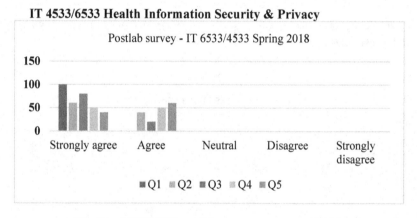

Fig. 12. IT4533/6533 postlab survey response – Q1–Q5

We found that most learners agreed that the labware was very effective in the learning of data protection knowledge while developing secure mobile applications.

We also received some student comments (Fig. 13). The comments show the module was a success in the initial offering.

- *The learning materials are well designed to progress step by step*
- *It helped me to learn Android application security issues and prevention techniques.*
- *Tutorial and Lab topic allowed me to better understand a topic that was discussed in prior IT graduate courses.*
- *Easy to follow labs.*
- *I did like the layout of the labs for this website. They were easy to follow and well organized. The only improvement I can think of would be to label the steps for the labs.*
- *Good materials and the source code availability helped me to practice on my computer.*

Fig. 13. Student comments received on the labware

4 Related Works

Readers are suggested to see the detailed survey [12] for exhaustive list of tools using static analysis to check Android software for security bugs. In this section, we briefly discuss several related tools.

FlowDroid is an open source Java based static analysis tool that can be used to analyze Android applications for potential data leakage. FlowDroid is a context, object sensitive, field, flow, and static taint analysis tool that specifically models the full Android lifecycle with high precision and recall [19]. The tool can detect and analyze data flows, specifically an Android application's bytecode, and configuration files, to find any possible privacy vulnerabilities, also known as data leakage [18]. However, it cannot find common security bugs in Android such as SQL Injection, output encoding, Intent leakage, and lack of secure communication. However, the tool supports only Eclipse and not currently supports Android Development Studio, a popular IDE currently used by most mobile developers.

Cuckoo is a widely used malware analysis tool based on dynamic analysis (i.e., it runs an application under test in a controlled emulator) [17]. It is capable of methodically examining multiple variants of Android malware applications through controlled execution into virtual machines that monitor the behaviors of the applications.

The DroidSafe project [16] develops effective program analysis techniques and tools to uncover malicious code in Android mobile applications. The core of the system is a static information flow analysis that reports the context under which sensitive information is used. For example, Application A has the potential to send location information to network address. DroidSafe reports potential leaks of sensitive information in Android applications. Besides, a number of recent approaches address data security in mobile [5, 20–22].

UNCC has designed and developed an Application Security IDE (ASIDE) plug-in for Eclipse that warns programmers of potential vulnerabilities in their code and assists them in addressing these vulnerabilities. The tool is designed to improve student awareness and understanding of security vulnerabilities in software and to increase utilization of secure programming techniques in assignments. ASIDE is used in a range of programming courses, from CS1 to advanced Web programming. ASIDE addresses input validation vulnerabilities, output encoding, authentication and authorization, and several race condition vulnerabilities [6–8]. ASIDE only works in the Java Eclipse IDE and cannot support the Android IDE.

Yuan and others [9] reviewed current efforts and resources in secure software engineering education, and provided related programs, courses, learning modules, hands-on lab modules. Chi [13] built learning modules for teaching secure coding practices to students. Those learning modules will provide the essential and fundamental skills to programmers and application developers in secure programming. The IAS Defensive Programming knowledge areas (KA) have been identified as topics/materials in the ACM/IEEE Computer Science Curricula 2013 that can be taught to beginning programmers in CS0/CS1 courses [10, 11]. All these works mainly focus on the mobile application development. They successfully disseminated the mobile computing education but did not emphasize the importance of SMSD and in their teachings.

Android has a powerful and complex communication system for sharing and sending data in both inter and intra apps. Simple static analysis usually cannot satisfy further requirement. Malicious apps may take advantage of this to avoid detection despite using sensitive information from apps with data leaks. Recently many security tools already worked with taint analysis check, like Findbugs [14] and DidFail [15]. Detection of potential taint flows can be used to protect sensitive data, identify leaky apps, and identify malware.

5 Conclusion

The overall goal of this paper is to address the needs and challenges of building capacity with proactive controls for software security development and the lack of pedagogical materials and real-world learning environment in secure software development through effective, engaging, and investigative approaches through real world oriented hands-on labware. We described the development of Android labware module on data protection. The module enable authentic hands-on learning of securing mobile software by enabling SSL communication, encryption/decryption of texts, and being more aware of location privacy. The initial feedback from classroom looks positive and we hope the module be adopted nationally by other institutes in the near future to integrate into computing courses.

Our effort will help students and software developers know what should be considered or best practices during mobile and web software development and raise their overall security level for software development. Students can learn from the misuse of vulnerability cases and insecure mistakes of other organizations. Simultaneously, such cases should be prevented by mitigation actions described in secure protected use cases for building secure software.

Acknowledgment. The work is partially supported by the National Science Foundation under award: NSF proposal 1723578.

References

1. Secure Mobile Software Development. https://sites.google.com/site/smsdproject/home
2. Xie, J., Lipford, H.R., Chu, B.: Why do programmers make security errors? In: Proceedings of IEEE Symposium on Visual Languages and Human Centric Computing, pp. 161–164 (2011)
3. Introduction to Database Security Issues Types of Security Database. http://www.academia.edu/6866589/Introduction_to_Database_Security_Issues_Types_of_Security_Database
4. Davis, N.: Secure software development life cycle processes. Software Engineering Institute (2013)
5. Feng, J., Yang, L.T., Liu, X., Zhan, R.: Privacy-preserving tensor analysis and processing models for wireless Internet of Things. IEEE Wirel. Commun. 25(6), 98–103 (2018)
6. Whitney, M., Lipford, H., Chu, B., Zhu, J.: Embedding secure coding instruction into the IDE: a field study in an advanced CS course. In: Proceedings of the 46th ACM Technical Symposium on Computer Science Education (SIGCSE), pp. 60–65 (2015)

7. Whitney, M., Lipford, H., Chu, B., Thomas, T.: Embedding secure coding instruction into the ide: complementing early and intermediate CS courses with ESIDE. J. Educ. Comput. Res. **56**, 415–438 (2017)
8. Zhu, J., Lipford, H., Chu, B.: Interactive support for secure programming education. In: Proceedings of the 44th Technical Symposium on Computer Science Education, pp. 687–692, March 2013
9. Yuan, X., et al.: Teaching mobile computing and mobile security. In: Proceedings of IEEE Frontiers in Education (FIE), pp. 1–6 (2016)
10. Computer Science Curricula, Association for Computing (2013). https://www.acm.org/education/CS2013-final-report.pdf
11. Goseva-Popstojanovaa, K., Perhinschib, A.: On the capability of static code analysis to detect security vulnerabilities. www.community.wvu.edu/~kagoseva/Papers/IST-2015.pdf
12. Li, L., et al.: Static analysis of Android apps: a systematic literature review. Inf. Softw. Technol. **88**, 67–95 (2017)
13. Chi, H.: Teaching secure coding practices to STEM students. In: Proceedings of the 2013 Information Security Curriculum Development Conference, Kennesaw, GA, p. 42, October 2013
14. The FindBugs plugin for security audits of Java web applications. http://find-sec-bugs.github.io. Accessed 2019
15. Dwivedi, K., et al.: DidFail: coverage and precision enhancement (2017)
16. DroidSafe. https://mit-pac.github.io/droidsafe-src/
17. What is Cuckoo? — CuckooDroid v1.0 Book. (n.d.). https://cuckoo-droid.readthedocs.io/en/latest/introduction/what/
18. Arzt, S., et al.: FlowDroid: precise context, flow, field, object-sensitive and lifecycle-aware taint analysis for Android apps. In: Proceedings of the 35th ACM SIGPLAN Conference on Programming Language Design and Implementation (PLDI), pp. 259–269 (2014)
19. Babil, G.S., Mehani, O., Boreli, R., Kaafar, M.-A.: On the effectiveness of dynamic taint analysis for protecting against private information leaks on Android-based devices. In: Proceedings of 2013 IEEE International Conference on Security and Cryptography (SECRYPT), Reykjavik, Iceland, pp. 1–8 (2013)
20. Xu, F., Su, M.: Privacy preservation based on separation sensitive attributes for cloud computing. Int. J. Inf. Secur. Priv. **13**(2), 104–119 (2019)
21. Feng, J., Yang, L., Zhu, Q., Choo, K.: Privacy-preserving tensor decomposition over encrypted data in a federated cloud environment. IEEE Trans. Dependable Secure Comput. (2018). https://doi.org/10.1109/tdsc.2018.2881452
22. Feng, J., Yang, L., Zhang, R.: Practical privacy-preserving high-order bi-lanczos in integrated edge-fog-cloud architecture for cyber-physical-social systems. ACM Trans. Internet Technol. **19**(2), 26 (2019)

Multi-round Bidding Strategy Based on Game Theory for Crowdsensing Task

En Wang[1,2(✉)], Yongjian Yang[1], Jie Wu[2], and Hengzhi Wang[1]

[1] School of Computer Science and Technology, Jilin University, Changchun 130012, Jilin, China
wangen0310@126.com
[2] School of Computer and Information Sciences, Temple University, Philadelphia, PA 19122, USA

Abstract. Crowdsensing is a new activity form gathering a suitable set of users to collectively finish a sensing task. It has attracted great attention because it provides an easy-access sensing scheme and reduces the sensing cost compared with the traditional sensing method. Hence, several crowdsensing platforms have emerged at the right moment, where the requester can publish sensing tasks and the users compete for the winners of the tasks. Thus, there is a multi-round game among users, in which we consider a case that the users bid their available time for the specific sensing tasks, and the purpose of a user is to obtain as many tasks as possible within the available time budget. To this end, we propose a Multi-round Bidding strategy based on Game theory for Crowdsensing task (MBGC), where each user decides the bidding for the specific task according to its trade-off between the expected number of obtained tasks and remaining available time. Then, a user dynamically decides the probabilities to bid different kinds of biddings in the different rounds according to the Nash Equilibrium solution. We conduct extensive simulations to simulate the game process for the crowdsensing tasks. The results show that compared with other bidding strategies, MBGC always achieves the largest number of obtained tasks with an identical time budget.

Keywords: Crowdsensing · Bidding strategy · Game theory · Nash Equilibrium

1 Introduction

Recently, a noticeable phenomenon comes into our daily life: smartphones are widely used by almost everyone. The used devices are smart and powerful enough to sense the characteristics surrounding the environments, such as air quality, temperature as well as traffic congestion. Thanks to this, a novel sensing way called *Mobile Crowdsensing* (MCS) [1] has attracted a lot of attention because it could gather the power of many hand-hold devices to finish a common task.

© Springer Nature Switzerland AG 2019
G. Wang et al. (Eds.): SpaCCS 2019, LNCS 11611, pp. 196–210, 2019.
https://doi.org/10.1007/978-3-030-24907-6_16

For example, the collection of moving cars' speeds could be used to draw a traffic map [2], while reports about available seatings in all the restaurants could be used to instruct the users to make smart dining choice [3].

By now, the works on MCS mainly focus on the following three aspects: task allocation [4], user recruitment [5] and incentive mechanism [6]. It is not difficult to find that, all the above works usually pay attention to the assignments among users and tasks. However, almost all the works assume that either the users prefer to assist in finishing the sensing tasks or they just play game with the requester and not the other users. Actually, this assumption is not suitable because a user may get a higher achievement (higher reward or lower cost) when they do a good trade-off by taking the other users' decisions into consideration. Hence, the problems turn out to be the optimization or game theory problems.

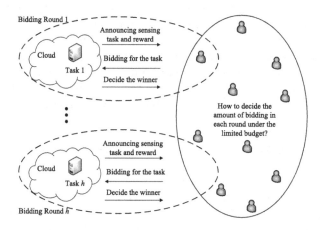

Fig. 1. The multi-round bidding problem description for crowdsensing task. In different bidding rounds, the users should determine the suitable bidding strategy according to the remaining available time.

In this paper, we focus on a multi-round bidding game in MCS. Multi-round means that there are many tasks that can be assigned to the users, and in each round there is only one task to be allocated. Obviously, there may be multi tasks to be allocated at the same time, while we assume that the tasks are independent with each other, and each user could only apply for finishing one time at the same time. Then, for each round the users compete to be the winner of the task. The user with the largest bidding (paying the longest time to the task) could win and get the reward. Generally speaking, people bid a price (money) for the task. However, the total money budget is usually different for different users. Hence, in this paper, we assume that they bid their available time quantum for the task in each round. Obviously, a game exists in the multi-round bidding process. If a user bids a long time quantum for a task, then it will have short remaining available time for the upcoming tasks. At the same time, if a user bids a short time quantum for a task, then it will have a low chance to get the reward of this task. Hence, we should decide a suitable bidding strategy in MCS.

The multi-round bidding problem is described in Fig. 1. There are many users taking part in the bidding game. Also, there are some tasks assigned to the different bidding rounds, each round has only one sensing task. Then the users bid their available time quantum for each task. The task will select the user with the largest bidding as the winner. The purpose of the user is to win as many tasks as possible within the total available time budget in the multi-round game.

The multi-round bidding game is challenging for the following reasons: (1) the user could not know the bidding cases of the other users; (2) the bidding strategy is a dynamic decision-making process, and a user may dynamically change the strategy; (3) it is a game theory problem because there is an obvious trade-off among users' different choices. In order to overcome the above difficulties, we propose a multi-round bidding strategy based on game theory in MCS (MBGC). The main idea of MBGC is to find the Nash Equilibrium, which well solves the trade-off between expected number of obtained tasks and remaining available time. Then according to the Nash Equilibrium, we could dynamically decide the suitable bidding in each round to maximize the total number of obtained tasks.

The main contributions of this paper are briefly summarized as follows:

- We find the Nash Equilibrium in the multi-round bidding game in MCS, and under the condition that the user does not know the cases of other users' biddings.
- We propose a multi-round bidding strategy based on Game Theory in mobile crowdsensing (MBGC), where each user dynamically decides its suitable bidding according to the trade-off between the winning probability and remaining available time, in order to maximize the total reward within the available time budget.
- We conduct extensive simulations based on the actual bidding games. The results show that compared with other bidding strategies, MBGC achieves a larger number of obtained tasks.

The remainder of this paper is organized as follows: The problem description and formulation are introduced in Sect. 2. Section 3 analyzes the multi-round bidding problem and introduces game theory in MCS. The detailed bidding strategies are proposed in Sect. 4. In Sect. 5, we evaluate the performance of MBGC through extensive simulations. We review the related work in Sect. 6. We conclude the paper in Sect. 7.

2   Problem Description and Formulation

In this section, we first detailedly describe the problem to be addressed. Then we translate the problem into mathematical expressions. Finally, the problem is formulated as the game theory problem.

2.1   Problem Description

We first consider the following crowdsensing environment, a task requester publishes a series of tasks at different time. Each task is to sense some data in the specific area, hence it needs the users to spend time finishing the sensing tasks. There is a group of users $U = \{u_1, u_2, \cdots, u_n\}$ participating in the crowdsensing tasks. Then in each round, the users compete with each other to be the winner and obtain the task. In this way, a multi-round bidding problem is formulated. In other words, the users play a game with each other, they bid the available time quantum for each task, and the process to decide a task winner is called a round. We assume that, there is only one winner for each task.

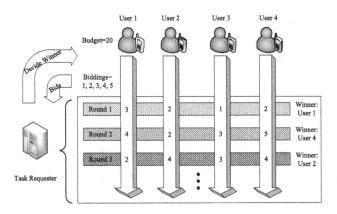

Fig. 2. The multi-round bidding framework including one requester and multiple users. Users should decide a bidding strategy in different bidding rounds in order to obtain as many tasks as possible.

As shown in Fig. 2, there are four users and a task requester. The whole time for completing all the sensing tasks is divided into several rounds, where each task is scheduled in only one round, and also one winner will be selected among the four users. In each round, the requester publishes a sensing task, and all the users bid for the task. The user with the largest bid could win the game. If there are two or more users bidding the same time quantum, which is the longest among all the biddings, then the requester will randomly select a user as the winner. The procedure continues until all the rounds are gone. In this paper, we assume that the total available time budget for all the users is uniform. The main notations are illustrated in Table 1.

2.2   Problem Formulation

We pay attention to the multi-round bidding strategy in MCS as previously described. In each round, the users could bid different kinds of biddings, we assume that there are m kinds of biddings: b_i, $(m \geq i \geq 1)$. So if a user bids a

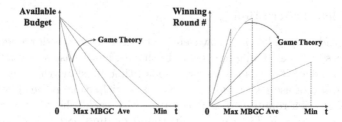

Fig. 3. The changing processes of the available time budget and the number of winning rounds for the four different bidding strategies.

time quantum for a task, then its available time budget is reduced. It is worth noting that the total available time budget for all the users is B. Obviously, all the users prefer to reasonably schedule their bidding strategy in order to win as many rounds as possible. The bidding strategy could be easily expressed as follows: for the player, how to divide his total available time budget into all the rounds in order to win as many as possible. It is not difficult to find that, there is a game among users, i.e., bidding a long time quantum when the others bid short ones is obviously a good choice. However, the user still takes the risk that the others may also bid a long time quantum.

We randomly select a user as the player, who will adopt the bidding strategy proposed in this paper. And the other ones are regarded as the competitors. In order to make the player win as many rounds as possible, some naive solutions could be easily proposed. For example, the first one is to always bid the shortest time quantum for all the rounds. The second one is to always bid the longest time quantum, in which the player may win many rounds in the beginning rounds and will not win any more in the last rounds. Hence, it is obviously not an optimal solution. The third one is to always bid the average time quantum (total time divided by the number of rounds). As shown in Fig. 3, neither constantly bidding max/min time quantum nor constantly bidding average time quantum can achieve the best winning reward. Based on game theory, we could dynamically schedule the biddings in different rounds more efficiently (game theory method in Fig. 3). In this paper, we propose a multi-round bidding strategy based on the game theory in mobile crowdsensing, through balancing the trade-off between winning probability and remaining available time.

3   Multi-round Bidding Game

3.1   Bidding Time Quantum

Here, bidding time quantum means the time that the user would like to take for finishing the sensing task. Obviously, a longer bidding time quantum leads to a higher probability to win in this round, while also leading to a shorter available time in the upcoming rounds. Suppose that, for the player, the total available time budget is B, and there are totally h rounds. For each round k, the bidding

Table 1. Main notations used throughout the paper

Symbol	Meaning
N	Total number of users
b_i	Different kinds of biddings, which is the arithmetic progression: $(b_1, b_2, \cdots, b_m)$
p_i	The probability for a user to bid b_i
$P_{max}(b_i)$	The probability that b_i is the maximal bidding among all the remaining users
B	The total available time budget
P_{win}	The winning probability of bidding the maximum time
γ	Euler's constant
B_r	The remaining available time
s_i	$(b_i - b_m)/B_r$, consumption ratio when bidding b_i
s	$(b_1 - b_m)/B_r$, consumption ratio when bidding b_1
$u(b_i)$	The benefit for bidding b_i

time quantum is $b(k)$, which is selected from a series of b_i, $m \geq i \geq 1$. Then we have $B = \sum_{k=1}^{h} b(k)$.

If a user chooses to bid a long time quantum in a round, then the available time will be consumed a lot. In contrast, if a user chooses to bid a short time quantum, the available time will not be influenced that much. We attempt to measure the different influences when the user bids different kinds of biddings. We use s_i to define the time consumption when a user bids b_i, the set b_i are arithmetic progression and b_m is the shortest bidding time quantum. Let B_r be the remaining available time, then we have $s_i = \frac{b_i - b_m}{B_r}$, $i = 1, 2, \cdots, m$. According to the value of B_r, the above expression could be represented as the following two cases:

$$s_i = \begin{cases} \frac{b_i - b_m}{B_r} & B_r \geq b_i - b_m \\ 1 & B_r < b_i - b_m \end{cases} \tag{1}$$

3.2 Winning Probability

In this section, we try to compute the winning probability for a user. It is not difficult to find that, a user could win only when his bidding time quantum is the longest among all the users (may be the same length as others). If a user bids the longest time quantum b_1, and all the other users bid the shorter time quantum than him, then he should win 100%. If there are k users bidding b_1 in the others, then the winning probability should be $\frac{1}{k+1}$. Hence, the following two questions are important for measuring the winning probability.

Here, we use symbol $P_{max}(b_i)$ to present the probability that b_i is the maximal bidding among all the remaining users. Obviously, we have $\sum_{i=1}^{n} P_{max}(b_i) = 1$.

Then, the probability (p_i) of bidding b_i in a round also influences the result of winning probability. Then we have $\sum_{i=1}^{n} p_i = 1$. In the following sections, the above two terms are used to calculate the winning probability.

3.3 Game Theory

Game theory studies the interactions among players, who take actions to influence each other, and usually have conflicting or common benefits. Recently, game theory is widely used in balancing the resources sharing among multiple mobile devices, which are called players. These players decide to do the actions by themselves and compete for non-shared resources [7]. In this paper, the purpose of a player is to win as many rounds as possible during the multiple rounds.

Consider the following game process, an action done by a player $n_i \in \mathbf{N}$ in round $e_i \in \mathbf{E}$ is called a strategy $g_i \in \mathbf{G}$. In this paper, we assume that the strategy set is the same for all users, and selected from a series of b_i. Then $\mathbf{G} = \mathbf{G}_1 \times \mathbf{G}_2 \times \cdots \times \mathbf{G}_N$ is the set of the players' strategies. For user n_i, the payoff of action g_i is denoted by $u_i \in \mathbf{U}$ which is the expected payoff after considering the action done by n_i as well as the actions of the other players. Hence, a game is determined by quadruple form $\langle \mathbf{N}, \mathbf{E}, \mathbf{G}, \mathbf{U} \rangle$.

Obviously, the above game is a symmetric finite game because the strategy set $\mathbf{G}$ and round set $\mathbf{E}$ for all the users are the same. Moreover, the number of rounds and the number of their strategies are finite. These characteristics are very important in the following discussions.

Dominant Strategies and Nash Equilibrium. Nash Equilibrium (NE) is an important concept in game theory, each user chooses a strategy to maximize its expected individual payoff, and for all the users they form an equilibrium state, where all the users do not want to change its strategy because they could achieve the maximum expected payoff. In other words, in an NE state, if a user changes its action, it will achieve a lower expected payoff. When entering an NE state, the strategy adopted by a user is called a dominant strategy. A dominant strategy equilibrium is a strategy set including all the dominant strategies of all players. Hence, NE is commonly a classical state, where a player does not have the incentive to change its strategy so that the other players also will not change theirs.

Pure and Mixed Strategies. A pure strategy means that a user clearly decides its action, which includes 'do' or 'not do', while a mixed strategy means that a user could make a probabilistic decision about the actions. Actually, the main difference between pure strategy and mixed strategy is that pure strategies assign a probability of 1 to a specific action and probability of 0 to the remaining of the available actions. In the following parts, NE in pure (mixed) strategy is called pure (mixed) strategy NE.

Existence of Equilibrium. In order to prove that the multi-round bidding problem proposed in this paper has a Nash Equilibrium, we give the following theorems [8,9]:

Theorem 1 (Nash Theorem). *Any finite game has either a pure or a mixed strategy NE.*

Theorem 2 (Nash Theorem for symmetric games). *A finite symmetric game has a symmetric mixed strategy NE.*

Table 2. Payoffs of n_i in the 3-strategies bidding game

N users	Longest $b_1 = 3$ with $P_{max}(b_1)$	Longest $b_2 = 2$ with $P_{max}(b_2)$	Longest $b_3 = 1$ with $P_{max}(b_3)$
n_i bids b_1	$(1-s) \cdot P_{win}$	$(1-s) \cdot 1$	$(1-s) \cdot 1$
n_i bids b_2	0	$(1-\frac{1}{2}s) \cdot P_{win}$	$(1-\frac{1}{2}s) \cdot 1$
n_i bids b_3	0	0	$\frac{1}{N}$

4 Multi-round Bidding Strategy Based on Game Theory

As previously stated, the game in this paper is a non-cooperative, multi-round, multi-strategy, symmetric game.

The N-Player Three-Strategy Bidding Game. Here, 'multi' means the number is larger than two or at least three. Hence we consider a simple case, where N users play the bidding game with the three strategies to be selected. In this paper, we do not consider the simplest case: two strategies, because the similar case has been discussed in the previous research work [10].

Consider the N-player three-strategy bidding game. Table 2 shows the payoffs of the users considering both the improvement on winning probability and also the consumption in remaining available time. s_i as shown in Eq. 1, is the normalized time consumption when the user bids b_i. As shown in Table 2, when the player decides to bid b_1 (the longest time quantum), then the following three cases are considered: (1) the longest bidding time quantum of the other users is b_1; (2) the longest bidding time quantum of the other users is b_2; (3) the longest bidding time quantum of the other users is b_3. For case 1, the time consumption is $s = \frac{b_1 - b_m}{B_r}$, while the winning probability is P_{win}, which represents the expected probability of obtaining the task when the user bids the longest time quantum. However, for cases 2 and 3, the time consumptions are still s, while the chance of winning is 1, because the player bidding b_1 must win the task.

Next, when the user bids b_2, there are also the same three cases being considered. For case 1, because the longest bid of the others is b_1, hence the player bidding b_2 has no chance to win, so the probability is 0. For case 2, the time consumption is $\frac{1}{2}s$ because $s_2 = \frac{b_2-b_3}{b_1-b_3}s$ and the set b_i forms arithmetic progression, hence $s_2 = \frac{1}{2}s$. We omit the descriptions for bidding b_3, as the procedure is similar to the above cases. Then we focus on whether there is a pure or mixed strategy NE for the above N player three-strategy game.

Table 3. Payoffs of n_i in the multi-strategy bidding game

N users	Longest $b_1 = 6$ with $P_{max}(b_1)$	Longest $b_2 = 5$ with $P_{max}(b_2)$	Longest $b_3 = 4$ with $P_{max}(b_3)$	Longest $b_4 = 3$ with $P_{max}(b_4)$	Longest $b_5 = 2$ with $P_{max}(b_5)$	Longest $b_6 = 1$ with $P_{max}(b_6)$
n_i bids b_1	$(1-s)\cdot P_{win}$	$(1-s)\cdot 1$	$(1-s)\cdot 1$	$(1-s)\cdot 1$	$(1-s)\cdot 1$	$(1-s)\cdot 1$
n_i bids b_2	0	$(1-\frac{4}{5}s)\cdot P_{win}$	$(1-\frac{4}{5}s)\cdot 1$	$(1-\frac{4}{5}s)\cdot 1$	$(1-\frac{4}{5}s)\cdot 1$	$(1-\frac{4}{5}s)\cdot 1$
n_i bids b_3	0	0	$(1-\frac{3}{5}s)\cdot P_{win}$	$(1-\frac{3}{5}s)\cdot 1$	$(1-\frac{3}{5}s)\cdot 1$	$(1-\frac{3}{5}s)\cdot 1$
n_i bids b_4	0	0	0	$(1-\frac{2}{5}s)\cdot P_{win}$	$(1-\frac{2}{5}s)\cdot 1$	$(1-\frac{2}{5}s)\cdot 1$
n_i bids b_5	0	0	0	0	$(1-\frac{1}{5}s)\cdot P_{win}$	$(1-\frac{1}{5}s)\cdot 1$
n_i bids b_6	0	0	0	0	0	$\frac{1}{5}$

Theorem 3. *There is no pure strategy NE for the above N-player three-strategy bidding game.*

Proof. As shown in Table 2, if there is a pure strategy NE for the N-player three-strategy bidding game, then no matter in which case, the payoff to bid b_1 is always higher or lower than that of bidding b_2 or b_3. However, this is not true in Table 2. When the longest bidding time quantum for the others is b_1, then the player will bid b_1 to achieve a higher payoff $(1-s)P_{win} > 0$. However, when the longest bidding time quantum for the others is b_3, then the player will bid b_2 to achieve a higher payoff $(1-\frac{1}{2}s)1 > (1-s)1$. Hence, there is no pure strategy NE for the above N-player three-strategy bidding game. Theorem 3 is proved.

Theorem 4. *Mixed strategy NE exists for the N-player three-strategy bidding game.*

Proof. We assume that each user has a probability of p_i to bid b_i. And for the above three cases, we use $P_{max}(b_i)$ to present the probability that b_i is the maximal bidding among the remaining users. Then, we achieve the following three equations:

$$P_{max}(b_1) = \sum_{k=1}^{N-1} \binom{N-1}{k} \cdot p_1^k \cdot (1-p_1)^{N-1-k}$$
$$= 1 - (1-p_1)^{N-1} \tag{2}$$

$$P_{max}(b_2) = (1-p_1)^{N-1} - (1-p_1-p_2)^{N-1} \tag{3}$$

$$P_{max}(b_3) = p_3^{N-1} \tag{4}$$

Then, the expected payoff of the player when it bids b_1 is shown as follows:

$$u(b_1) = (1-s)P_{win}P_{max}(b_1)+(1-s)P_{max}(b_2)+(1-s)P_{max}(b_3) \tag{5}$$

where P_{win} is shown as follows:

$$P_{win} = \frac{\sum_{k=1}^{N-1} \frac{1}{k+1}}{N-1} = \frac{\ln(N) + \gamma + 1}{N - 1}, \quad \gamma = 0.577215 \tag{6}$$

Here k ($N > k > 1$) is the number of users bidding the longest time quantum among all the other users, and γ is the Euler's constant. We use property of nth harmonic number[1] to get the above equation. It is not difficult to find that, Eq. 6 is still useful for calculating the P_{win} in multi-user multi-round and multi-strategy case, which is discussed in the following section.

Similarly, we could achieve $u(b_2)$ and $u(b_3)$. Combining $u(b_1) = u(b_3)$ and $u(b_2) = u(b_3)$, we could get the solution of p_i. So the mixed strategy NE actually exists because we can get the solution of p_i in the above equations, and p_i satisfies $0 \le p_i \le 1$. The detail calculation process is shown in the N-player multi-round multi-strategy case.

The N-Player Multi-round Multi-strategy Game. The game is that a player plays with the other $N - 1$ users. Without loss of generality, we show a six-round six-strategy case in Table 3. First of all, we consider the normalized time consumption $s_i = \frac{n-1}{n-i}s$, which represents the case that the player bids b_i in this round. Then, we consider the payoffs if a user bids b_i. Suppose that the longest bidding time quantum of the others is also b_i, and there are k users bidding b_i among the other users. Then the winning probability is $\frac{1}{k+1}$. The payoffs in terms of available time is $1 - s_i$. Hence, we have the expected payoffs $u(b_i) = (1 - \frac{n-1}{n-i}s)\frac{1}{k+1}$. Similarly, if the longest bidding time quantum of the others is shorter than b_i, the player must win the game, hence $u(b_i) = 1 - s_i$. Finally, if the longest bidding time quantum of the others is longer than b_i, then $u(b_i) = 0$.

$$u(b_i) = \begin{cases} (1-\frac{n-1}{n-i}s)\frac{1}{k+1} & \text{the longest bidding} = b_i \\ (1-\frac{n-1}{n-i}s)1 & \text{the longest bidding} < b_i \\ 0 & \text{the longest bidding} > b_i \end{cases} \tag{7}$$

We also assume that each user has a probability of p_i to bid b_i. Then, similar to N-player three-strategy bidding game, we get $P_{max}(b_1) \sim P_{max}(b_6)$ and $\sum_{k=1}^{6} P_{max}(b_k) = 1$. Then the payoff of the player when it bids b_1 is shown as follows:

$$u(b_1) = (1 - s)P_{win}P_{max}(b_1) + \sum_{i=2}^{6}(1 - s)P_{max}(b_i) \tag{8}$$

---

[1] https://en.wikipedia.org/wiki/Harmonic_number.

In a similar way, $u(b_i)$ could be achieved, and we find the NE solution for p_i through solving a group of equations: $u(b_i) = u(b_j)$, $i \neq j$.

Here, we use the fsolve function in Matlab to solve the nonlinear equations [11]. In this way, the player could dynamically calculate the p_i in NE according to the current remaining available time. Finally, the player decides the probability of bidding different time quantums for the specific sensing task in the different rounds.

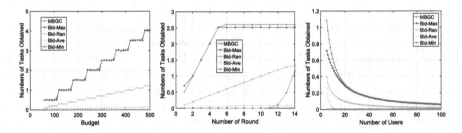

Fig. 4. Performance comparisons along with the changes of budget & number of rounds & number of users, when users could choose 6 different biddings.

5 Performance Evaluation

5.1 Settings

We test the proposed strategy through simulations. A group of users compete for a series of tasks, and in each round they have some biddings to select. We consider that the following elements will influence the final number of winning rounds: the number of different kinds of biddings, total available time budget, the number of users and the number of rounds. The detailed simulation parameters are set as follows: the number of different kinds of biddings is 6, the budget changes from 60 to 500, number of rounds changes from 1 to 14 and the range of number of users is [5, 10].

5.2 Methods and Performances in Comparison

The compared methods include: bid-max (always bidding the longest time quantum), bid-ran (always bidding a random time quantum), bid-ave (always bidding average time quantum, which is calculated through the budget divided by the number of rounds) and bid-min (always bidding the shortest time quantum).

While a range of data is gathered from the simulations, we take the following main performance metric into consideration: numbers of tasks obtained, which is the number of winning rounds in the bidding game.

5.3   Simulation Results

We focus on three groups of simulations: 6 different kinds of biddings. For the first group of simulations, we test the number of tasks obtained along with the increase in budget, number of rounds and number of users. The simulation results are shown in Fig. 4. Along with the growth of budget, the number of tasks obtained also increases, because a large budget leads to a long total available time, and the number of tasks obtained also rises. Moreover, along with the increase in the number of rounds, the number of tasks obtained is also increasing, because a large number of rounds lead to a large number of tasks. Finally, along with the growth of the number of users, the number of tasks obtained goes down, which means that more competitors lead to a less number of tasks obtained by the player.

As shown in Fig. 5, we test the number of tasks obtained along with the increase in the number of different biddings. The results show that the proposed MBGC achieves a better performance when the bidding number is large enough. This is because large number of biddings leave us a lot of space to dynamically decide the bidding time quantum. Hence, the performance gets better. Then, in Fig. 6, we test some specific methods related to MBGC, where "bid 3" means a method of always bidding the third shortest time quantum. We find that MBGC always achieves the best performance. It is worth noting that, when the bidding round gets large enough, 'bid 1' gets better, which makes sense because bidding a short time quantum will save the time cost for the last rounds. Finally, we test the changes of p_i along with number of round, the results in Fig. 7 show their changing processes are not monotonous and have crossed with each other.

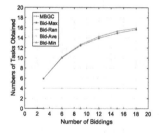 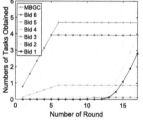 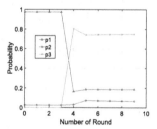

Fig. 5. The performance changing process along with the growth of number of biddings for different bidding strategies.

Fig. 6. The performance changing process along with the number of round for different bidding strategies.

Fig. 7. The probability change processes along with the increase of bidding rounds in MBGC.

6   Related Work

6.1   Task Allocation

In order to address the free crowdsensing market where multiple task initiators and users want to maximize their profits, He [12] studied the exchange economy theory and adopted the Walrasian Equilibrium which is proven to exist within each supply-demand pattern. Xiong et al. [13] proposed a task allocation framework called iCrowd based on Piggyback task model, iCrowd utilizes historical data to forecast mobility of users and employs suitable set of users to optimize task allocation. Wang et al. [14] researched a spatial crowdsourcing situation under limited task probability coverage and budget, then they present the prediction model of worker mobility behavior to obtain the optimal solution of task allocation. The above researches discuss the task allocation methods in MCS. However, the users in the above works were selected by the requester according to the users' attributes. The users could only passively accept tasks.

6.2   Game Theory

Chakeri et al. [15] regarded incentive mechanism as a non-cooperative game and presented a discrete time dynamic called elite strategy dynamics based on best response dynamic to compute a Nash Equilibrium and get the maximization utilities. Yang et al. [16] combined quality evaluation and money incentive, then they presented a truth evaluation based quality and remaining share method. Focusing on user diversity and social effect in mobile crowdsensing, Cheung et al. [17] analyzed a payment scheme for provider to utilize users' social relationship to achieve diversity, and then proposed a two-round decision strategy where provider optimizes its utility as a leader, after that the users decide their contribution level according to providers' scheme as a follower in the game process. Alsheikh et al. [18] focused on privacy management and optimal pricing in mobile crowdsensing, and analyzed the negative correlation of sensing quality and privacy level, then combined the utility maximization models with profit sharing models from game theory. Jiang et al. [19] considered high operational cost such as storage resources, and presented a scalability P2P-based MCS architecture, focusing on user behavior in the context of game theory and presenting a quality-aware data sharing market. The above works focused on proposing incentive mechanisms, while they did not consider the multi-round bidding case among users.

7   Conclusion

In this paper, the multi-round bidding game is formulated in mobile crowdsensing. In each round, the users compete for a sensing task. They bid a long enough time quantum for winning the task while taking a risk of failure and wasting the bidding time quantum. We propose a multi-round bidding strategy based on the game theory in mobile crowdsensing (MBGC), where users dynamically determine the bidding time quantum through the trade-off between the winning probability and remaining available time. Then, a Nash Equilibrium is achieved to instruct the users to reasonably schedule their bidding strategies. We conduct simulations to test the number of tasks obtained. The results show that, compared with the other bidding strategies, MBGC achieves a better performance.

References

1. Ganti, R.K., Ye, F., Lei, H.: Mobile crowdsensing: current state and future challenges. IEEE Commun. Mag. **49**(11), 32–39 (2011)
2. Koukoumidis, E., Peh, L.-S., Martonosi, M.: SignalGuru: leveraging mobile phones for collaborative traffic signal schedule advisory. In: Proceedings of ACM MobiSys 2011 (2011)
3. Ouyang, R.W., Kaplan, L., Martin, P., Toniolo, A., Srivastava, M., Norman, T.J.: Debiasing crowdsourced quantitative characteristics in local businesses and services. In: Proceedings of ACM IPSN 2015 (2015)
4. Xiao, M., Wu, J., Huang, L., Cheng, R., Wang, Y.: Online task assignment for crowdsensing in predictable mobile social networks. IEEE Trans. Mob. Comput. **8**(16), 2306–2320 (2017)
5. Truong, N.B., Lee, G.M., Um, T.-W., Mackay, M.: Trust evaluation mechanism for user recruitment in mobile crowd-sensing in the Internet of Things. IEEE Trans. Inf. Forensics Secur. **PP**(99), 1 (2019)
6. Wu, Y., Li, F., Ma, L., Xie, Y., Li, T., Wang, Y.: A context-aware multi-armed bandit incentive mechanism for mobile crowd sensing systems. IEEE Internet Things J. **PP**(99), 1 (2019)
7. Anastasopoulos, M.P., Arapoglou, P.-D.M., Kannan, R., Cottis, P.G.: Adaptive routing strategies in IEEE 802.16 multi-hop wireless backhaul networks based on evolutionary game theory. IEEE J. Sel. Areas Commun. **26**(7), 1218–1225 (2008)
8. Nash, J.: Non-cooperative games. Ann. Math. **54**(2), 286–295 (1951)
9. Vazintari, A., Cottis, P.G.: Mobility management in energy constrained self-organizing delay tolerant networks: an autonomic scheme based on game theory. IEEE Trans. Mob. Comput. **15**(6), 1401–1411 (2016)
10. Yang, Y., Liu, W., Wang, E., Wang, H.: Beaconing control strategy based on game theory in mobile crowdsensing. Future Genera. Comput. Syst. **86**, 222–233 (2018)
11. Stigler, S.M.: Gauss and the invention of least squares. Ann. Stat. **9**(3), 465–474 (1981)
12. He, S., Shin, D.-H., Zhang, J., Chen, J., Lin, P.: An exchange market approach to mobile crowdsensing: pricing, task allocation, and Walrasian Equilibrium. IEEE J. Sel. Areas Commun. **35**(4), 921–934 (2017)
13. Xiong, H., Zhang, D., Chen, G., Wang, L., Gauthier, V., Barnes, L.E.: iCrowd: near-optimal task allocation for piggyback crowdsensing. IEEE Trans. Mob. Comput. **15**(8), 2010–2022 (2016)
14. Wang, L., Yu, Z., Han, Q., Guo, B., Xiong, H.: Multi-objective optimization based allocation of heterogeneous spatial crowdsourcing tasks. IEEE Trans. Mob. Comput. **PP**(99), 1–14 (2018)
15. Chakeri, A., Jaimes, L.G.: An incentive mechanism for crowdsensing markets with multiple crowdsourcers. IEEE Internet Things J. **5**(2), 708–715 (2017)

16. Yang, S., Wu, F., Tang, S., Gao, X., Yang, B., Chen, G.: On designing data quality-aware truth estimation and surplus sharing method for mobile crowdsensing. IEEE J. Sel. Areas Commun. **35**(4), 832–847 (2017)
17. Cheung, M.H., Hou, F., Huang, J.: Make a difference: diversity-driven social mobile crowdsensing. In: Proceedings of IEEE INFOCOM 2017 (2017)
18. Alsheikh, M.A., Niyato, D., Leong, D., Wang, P., Han, Z.: Privacy management and optimal pricing in people-centric sensing. IEEE J. Sel. Areas Commun. **4**(35), 906–920 (2017)
19. Jiang, C., Gao, L., Duan, L., Huang, J.: Scalable mobile crowdsensing via peer-to-peer data sharing. IEEE Trans. Mob. Comput. **4**(17), 898–912 (2018)

Information Leakage
in Wearable Applications

Babatunde Olabenjo[✉] and Dwight Makaroff

University of Saskatchewan, Saskatoon, SK S7N 5C9, Canada
b.olabenjo@usask.ca, makaroff@cs.usask.ca

Abstract. Wearable apps, specifically smartwatch apps, require permissions to access sensors, user profiles, and the Internet. These permissions, although not crucial for many mobile apps, are essential for health and fitness apps, as well as other wearable apps to work efficiently. Access to data on wearable devices enables malicious apps to extract personal user information. Moreover, benevolent apps can be utilized by attackers if they send private information insecurely. Many studies have examined privacy issues in smartphone apps, and very little has been done to identify and evaluate these issues in wearable smartwatch apps. Since wearable apps can reside either on the phone and watch or both, with all devices capable of accessing the Internet directly, a different dimension to information leakage is presented due to diverse ways in which these devices collect, store and transmit data.

This study classifies and analyzes information leakage in wearable smartwatch apps and examines the exposure of personal information using both static and dynamic approaches. Based on data collected from thousands of wearable applications, we show that standalone wearable apps leak less information compared to companion apps; the majority of data leaks exist in tracking services such as analytics and ad network libraries.

Keywords: Privacy · Smartwatches · Information leakage · Tracking · Wearable apps · Android

1 Introduction

Wearable devices enable unobtrusive real-time sensing in a comfortable and portable way that has influenced the medical field and other fields, such as recreation and navigation over the past decade. Researchers have proposed numerous ways that wearable devices could be used by patients and health care providers to address various healthcare challenges [1]. One of the driving forces of wearable device adoption is the smartwatch, due to its popularity and applications extending the features of mobile phone devices such as receiving push notifications on the watch, issuing voice controls, and monitoring vital signs conveniently.

Android WearOS and Apple WatchOS apps are made up of *(1)* standalone apps for the smartwatch only, *(2)* companion apps that run on the mobile phone and *(3)* embedded apps that run on the smartwatch [9]. Third-party smartwatch

© Springer Nature Switzerland AG 2019
G. Wang et al. (Eds.): SpaCCS 2019, LNCS 11611, pp. 211–224, 2019.
https://doi.org/10.1007/978-3-030-24907-6_17

device manufacturers, such as Fitbit, provide companion apps on mobile phones to pair with the smartwatch, facilitating data collection via multiple sources. Data collected from these devices such as heart rate, temperature, or location in real-time allows users to view their overall health information easily [4].

Privacy concerns arise when a wide range of sensitive data is released without the user's knowledge or consent [17]. Many users are aware that some of their information might be used to provide better services or collected by third-parties, but many are unaware of the type or precision of such data. For example, some users might allow their current location to be collected, but they do not know the details of the specific items released, such as GPS location, city, home address, and most visited places. As the amount of data handled by medical wearable devices grows, there is a higher risk of sensitive data exposure either during data transmission to the cloud or while data is stored locally on the device [13].

Paul and Irvine [12] investigated and compared privacy policies of wearable device services in order to understand the extent to which these services protect user privacy. Many services were found to not follow existing legislation regarding the privacy of health data. In this study, we investigate and classify information leakage in wearable smartwatch apps. We make the following contributions:

- collection and analysis of 4,017 free apps for Wear OS on Google Play store (1,894 companion and embedded, 229 standalone) and providing detailed descriptive statistics on information leakage.
- **static** analysis on each app's Dalvik bytecode to identify potential unsafe behaviours that may leak data, and **dynamic** analysis to identify information leakage via network activity tracing between wearable devices, their companion apps and the Internet.
- a comparison of information leakage in standalone, companion and embedded wearable apps based on nine potential malicious activity categories.

This paper is organized as follows. Section 2 provides a summary of related work on privacy and security in mobile and wearable apps. In Sect. 3, we give details on the dataset collection and experimental work. Section 4 provides a detailed analysis of the study done. Finally, we discuss our empirical results and draw conclusions in Sects. 5 and 6.

2   Related Work

Previous studies discussed several issues with privacy in wearable apps. Lee *et al.* [7] explored various vulnerabilities in wearable services and identified multiple security vulnerabilities in smart bands that enabled them to extract private information using three main attack scenarios (illegal device pairing, fake wearable gateway, and insecure code-based attack). Commercial smart bands expose personal and health information from both the device and the server due to wearable device misconfiguration, and if device pairing is enabled without authentication, attackers can use this to obtain user's health data.

Chauhan *et al.* [2] tested several wearable apps to uncover information leakage. They focused on traffic inspection and revealed that unique identifiers, location, credentials, and health data are transferred to the Internet. Between 4%

and 11% of apps send smartwatch-specific user activities to third-party trackers, with Google Analytics as the top tracking platform. This is due to the lack of specific permissions requirements for tracking libraries with regards to the kind of data that should be sent. Their study primarily focuses on dynamic analysis, without identifying application categories and the distribution of these leaky applications; however, results show that the majority of leakage comes from third-party advertisement and tracking libraries. Moonsamy *et al.* [10] confirms this by examining the effect of third-party ad libraries on personal information leakage in Android mobile apps, showing most personal information is sent via ad libraries. Their results show that 10% of all apps that leaked information in their study had a third-party ad library embedded in them.

Mujahid *et al.* [11] also studied wearable app permission problems in Android Wear apps and reviewed the effect on the functionality of the app. Many wearable apps have a permission mismatch problem that allows malicious apps to request permission to access personal information not required for app functionality. In other cases, a permission mismatch between the wearable device and the companion mobile app can lead to the disclosure of personal information via the mobile device without the user's proper consent on the smartwatch.

This study improves on the related work by providing a more detailed analysis of the type and categories of leaky activities by identifying 47 potential leaky activities in static and dynamic analysis. Also, we provide further insight into the distribution, category and popularity of apps with potential leaky activities in standalone, companion and embedded apps.

3   Dataset Overview

3.1   Data Collection

Figure 1 illustrates the data collection process for this study. Using a data scraper written in Python, we extracted 4,980 WearOS[1] apps from the Goko store [6] and 4,809 apps from AndroidWearCenter.[2] We then removed duplicate apps for a total of 5,599 apps. The scraper collects various app characteristics, such as package name and Google Play URL to the downloadable app which allowed us to download the APK files directly from the Google Play Store using GPlayCli.[3]

In order to have access to download APK files, 2,590 free apps were selected. Approximately 1000 apps were last updated in 2015, 2017, and 2018, respectively. Only 650 apps were last updated in 2016, and very few were older than 2015. The year of update is important as it shows recent development/maintenance. We removed 457 apps that do not have a wearable component or run only on the mobile phone, leaving a total of 2,133 apps: 1,903 companion/wearable-embedded and 230 standalone apps.

---

[1] Wear OS: The essential guide: https://www.wareable.com/android-wear/what-is-android-wear-comprehensive-guide (Accessed: 2019-01-29).

[2] Android Wear Center — Apps, Games, News & Watchfaces for Android Wear. http://www.androidwearcenter.com/ Accessed 2019-01-29.

[3] Matlink: https://github.com/matlink/gplaycli. (Accessed: 2019-02-03).

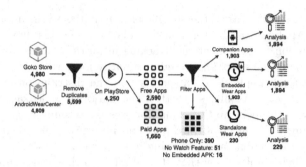

Fig. 1. Data collection and APK extraction

3.2   Extracting APKs

The publishing model for WearOS apps is by either providing a standalone APK or embedding a wearable APK inside a handheld APK.[4] In order to identify a standalone wearable app, first we unpack the APK and decode the resources using APKTool [14]. Next, we decode the manifest file and check for `hardware.type.watch` feature and `wearable.standalone` fields used in Wear 2.x to identify standalone wearable apps.

To identify embedded APKs, we checked the Manifest file to get the resource value. Next, we identify the path to the wearable APK from the XML file and then extract the wearable APK file. In some cases, identifying the paths was challenging; in such cases the `MANIFEST.MF` file in the `META-INF` folder available in all Java apps gives more details.[5]

Using regular expressions, we search through the manifest file to identify tags such as *.apk, wear, wearable* to extract the path to an embedded APK and match the package ID with the handheld APK package ID. Furthermore, the Manifest file in the extracted APK was examined for features indicating watch capability using APKTool. Of the 1,903 embedded wearable APKs extracted from their companion APK, we removed 16 handheld apps that had no embedded APKs, 51 APKs that had no `watch` feature, and 390 APKs that were designed for mobile phones only, but used the Android Wear notifications feature [16].

4   Analysis

To understand how personal information can be leaked we performed Static and Dynamic analysis. Static analysis reveals *potential* leaky activities directly from the source code without executing the app, while dynamic analysis executes the

---

[4] Package and distribute Wear apps: https://developer.android.com/training/wearables/apps/packaging (Accessed: 2019-01-12).

[5] https://docs.oracle.com/javase/tutorial/deployment/jar/defman.html   (Accessed: 2019-01-12).

apps and observes *actual* information leakage. We explicitly separated apps into three main categories consistent with previous studies [9]:

1. *Companion/Handheld Apps* that operate on a mobile device; they usually do, however, require access to a smartwatch app to operate efficiently.
2. *Embedded/Dependent Apps* that cannot function properly on smartwatches without companion apps on mobile phones. Internet access, specific watch functions or sending data using the mobile phone.
3. *Standalone Apps* that operate independently and access the Internet directly.

We were able to perform static analysis on 1,894 of the 1,903 companion and embedded apps and all 229 standalone apps using APKTool. Figure 2 shows our analysis process. We used the *smali/baksmali* code files obtained by disassembling the Dalvik executables (.dex files). Potential leaky activities were analyzed by identifying specific tags in their *smali* code file [5]. Dynamic analysis used automated testing and collected network traffic data using Pymiproxy,[6] a lightweight Python micro interceptor proxy.

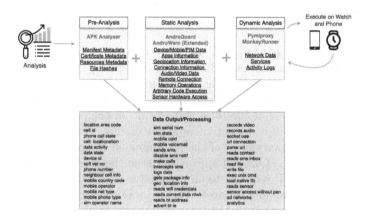

Fig. 2. Analysis process

4.1 Static Analysis

Categorizing Potential Leaky Activities. We used AndroWarn[7] as the basis for identifying activities that apps could perform which can lead to information leakage. This data was extracted from their *smali* source code to identify Android class methods used to collect location information from various providers [8]. These activities have been classified into nine different categories as follows:

---

[6] pymiproxy - Python Micro Interceptor Proxy - https://github.com/allfro/pymiproxy.

[7] AndroWarn: https://github.com/maaaaz/androwarn (Accessed: 2018-11-12).

- *Device/Mobile/PIM Data:* Activities that collect telephone information such as unique device IDs, phone numbers or serial numbers. Other activities include making calls, sending SMS messages and reading contacts or SMS.
- *App Information:* Log data can be accessed by background processes allowing malicious apps on older Android versions to extract personal information [15]. Also, we identify attempts to collect information about other apps on the device.
- *Geolocation Information:* Data from WiFi or GPS.
- *Connection Information:* Connection information activities such as WiFi credentials, Bluetooth addresses and the current state of the network.
- *Audio/Video Data:* Activities that use the microphone and/or camera.
- *Remote Connection:* Remote access via URI parsing and URL connection.
- *Memory Operations:* Activities that include reading/writing of files.
- *Arbitrary Code Execution:* Executing system commands, particularly on rooted devices such as loading of native libraries and execution of UNIX-like commands.
- *Sensor Hardware Access:* Several wearable apps capture sensor data. Activities in this category include registering sensor access and reading sensor data without declaring proper permission.

Companion/Handheld Apps. Companion apps have the largest number of potential leaky activities. About 93% (1,762) of apps log data, and most leaks are of the most popular types such as getting package information, reading files, opening URL connections, and listening for sensor events. The top four leaky activities make up 44.7% of the total leaks found in companion apps. Figure 3 shows the distribution of leaky activities in descending order of frequency, with a cumulative line as a percentage of the total number of apps.

Approximately 85% (1,620) of apps either read the current network connections or generate HTTP requests to an external service, while 19% (376) make socket connections to remote services. This is more common than with embedded apps because almost all embedded apps rely on the mobile phone to send watch activity to remote servers. Surprisingly, just over 11% (208) of apps get unique identifications from the device, and about 4% (84) get location information. The low percentage of apps collecting location information may be since most apps are personalization. Further analysis shows that no apps read WiFi credentials or intercept SMS messages. However, 15 apps send SMS messages, 43 apps access the mobile phone number, and 67 apps read the user's phone contacts. These are significant numbers compared to those for standalone apps.

Embedded/Standalone Applications. About 19% (364) of embedded apps still had some form of remote connection access. Although 13% (254) of embedded apps require sensor access, this is surprisingly lower than companion apps (19% (369)). This difference can be as a result of several apps using the mobile phone's sensor hardware as a primary sensor device and the watch sensor hardware as a fallback device. Also, the most popular sensor hardware is the

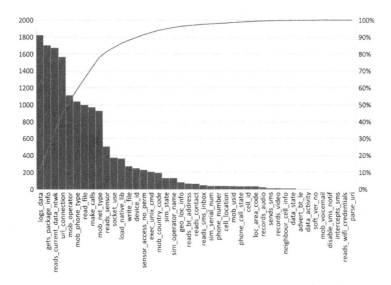

Fig. 3. Companion app leak distribution

accelerometer, available on both devices, but accessed mostly on the phone. Further analysis shows that very few embedded apps (1%) access geolocation information compared to companion apps (5%) and standalone apps (2%).

The top hardware feature used in standalone apps is the GPS with 29 apps, while just one app used the step counter feature leading to very few other sensor activities. Embedded apps, on the other hand, had the accelerometer as the top used feature (13 apps), including the step counter and heart rate features (6 and 2 apps, respectively).

Remote connections are made by 29% of standalone apps, which is much lower than companion apps (55%). This large gap is due to the limited resources available on smartwatches, because of higher bandwidth connection options available on mobile phones. A limited number of standalone apps require Internet access to operate (55%). Furthermore, 3% of apps perform device/mobile/PIM data leaks, and 16% of apps request sensor access. Table 1 highlights leakage activities from analyzed data on embedded/standalone apps.

Trackers. Using 140 tracker signatures collected from Exodus,[8] we identified over 80 different trackers from all extracted classes in each app. Google Analytics[9] was the most popular tracker used (59%). Other tracking activities were also discovered, such as ad networks, of which GoogleAds[10] was the most popular (48%). Table 2 shows the percentage of trackers identified in the three app categories in both static and dynamic analysis. An average of 3 trackers were

---

[8] Trackers: https://reports.exodus-privacy.eu.org/trackers/ (Accessed: 2018-11-20).

[9] Google Analytics: https://analytics.google.com/ (Accessed: 2018-12-10).

[10] Google Ads: https://www.google.com/admob/ (Accessed: 2018-12-10).

Table 1. Embedded and standalone wear app analysis

Analysis	Embedded apps (events)	PCT	Standalone apps (events)	PCT
Device/Mobile/PIM data leaks	733	2	147	3
Apps information and logs	3,645	96	424	93
Geolocation information leakage	17	1	5	2
Connection information leakage	1,495	20	181	20
Audio/video leaks	1	0	0	0
Remote connection establishment	1,090	19	199	29
Memory operations	707	19	169	37
Arbitrary code execution	196	5	15	3
Sensor hardware access	507	13	74	16

identified per app for companion apps, with some apps having as many as 22 trackers. Embedded apps however, had an average of 0.5 trackers, with 34 apps having 3 or more trackers. Standalone apps had similar averages as embedded apps, with a maximum number of 4 trackers per app, compared to embedded apps and companion apps with maximums of 8 and 22, respectively.

This data gives insight into the practice of embedding multiple ad network libraries and trackers to target ad marketing precisely. Several ad libraries use the same permissions, which prevents users from knowing exactly how many ad networks request unique permissions in the app.

Privacy Leak Distribution. To identify the distribution of apps with potential leaky activities on Google Play Store, we selected apps with Internet permission and grouped leaky apps into three main categories based on the distribution of leaky activities with a mean of 8.1, 4.4 and 5.3 and a standard deviation of 4.3, 2.4, and 2.6 for 1,894 companion, 1,894 dependent and 229 standalone apps respectively. The lower bound selected for moderate leaky activity was the average of all the means in companion, standalone and dependent apps, while the upper bound was the ceiling of the highest mean.

- **Low (L):** fewer than six leaky activities
- **Moderate (M):** between six and nine leaky activities
- **High (H):** over ten leaky activities.

Using the data collected from static analysis, we identified the categories and popularity of companion/dependent/standalone apps with leaky activities, shown in Fig. 4, disregarding 141 apps without Internet connectivity. The grey scale shows the concentration of apps in each category (companion, dependent and standalone) with darker shades representing higher numbers. Companion apps had 48% of apps with high leaky activities compared to dependent apps with 14.6% and standalone apps with 9.3%.

Category	Companion			Dependent			Standalone		
	L	M	H	L	M	H	L	M	H
ART_AND_DESIGN	0	1	1	1	0	0	0	0	0
AUTO_AND_VEHICLES	0	0	3	1	1	1	0	0	0
BOOKS_AND_REFERENCE	4	4	5	4	0	0	0	0	0
BUSINESS	0	6	6	2	1	0	0	0	0
COMMUNICATION	4	6	23	4	4	3	1	1	1
EDUCATION	2	5	10	3	1	0	0	0	0
ENTERTAINMENT	4	15	16	8	2	0	0	0	0
FINANCE	4	10	35	5	8	4	0	0	0
FOOD_AND_DRINK	0	0	2	1	0	0	0	0	0
GAMES	20	15	22	4	7	20	1	0	0
HEALTH_AND_FITNESS	2	19	39	16	9	4	0	6	0
HOUSE_AND_HOME	0	2	2	2	1	0	0	0	0
LIBRARIES_AND_DEMO	0	2	0	0	0	0	0	0	0
LIFESTYLE	12	43	20	12	4	2	2	0	0
MAPS_AND_NAVIGATION	4	13	20	10	1	0	2	0	0
MEDICAL	0	4	4	0	1	0	0	0	0
MUSIC_AND_AUDIO	1	12	24	5	2	2	2	0	1
NEWS_AND_MAGAZINES	0	6	19	13	0	1	0	0	0
PARENTING	0	1	0	0	0	0	0	0	0
PERSONALIZATION	48	171	145	60	25	2	17	60	8
PHOTOGRAPHY	2	3	4	2	2	0	0	0	0
PRODUCTIVITY	13	39	31	9	5	2	3	3	0
SHOPPING	0	3	9	1	0	0	0	1	0
SOCIAL	3	3	12	2	1	2	0	0	0
SPORTS	3	8	29	7	7	2	0	0	0
TOOLS	17	70	64	24	7	2	1	4	2
TRAVEL_AND_LOCAL	4	16	23	11	7	5	2	2	0
VIDEO_PLAYERS	1	3	6	1	1	0	1	1	0
WEATHER	4	4	14	4	1	1	4	2	0
TOTAL	152	484	588	210	98	53	36	80	12
OVERALL	1,224			361			128		

Key: L=Low, M=Moderate, H=High

L=0-5 Leaky activities, M=6-9 Leaky activities, H=10+ Leaky activities

Downloads	Companion			Dependent			Standalone		
	L	M	H	L	M	H	L	M	H
10+	0	3	1	0	1	1	0	0	0
50+	1	2	1	0	1	1	0	0	0
100+	18	65	34	15	5	2	0	1	0
500+	21	62	36	21	5	2	2	1	0
1K+	34	102	76	32	17	10	6	7	1
5K+	14	35	43	16	9	4	3	7	1
10K+	28	93	100	36	22	7	7	31	2
50K+	16	31	38	16	5	9	6	5	2
100K+	15	56	81	31	15	3	7	17	2
500K+	2	11	31	8	5	2	1	2	1
1M+	3	16	78	16	5	6	1	6	0
5M+	0	3	22	10	2	3	1	0	0
10M+	0	4	36	8	5	2	1	3	0
50M+	0	0	3	1	0	0	0	0	0
100M+	0	1	6	0	1	1	0	0	1
500M+	0	0	1	0	0	0	0	0	0
18+	0	0	1	0	0	0	1	0	2
TOTAL	152	484	588	210	98	53	36	80	12
OVERALL	1,224			361			128		

Key: L=Low, M=Moderate, H=High

L=0-5 Leaky activities, M=6-9 Leaky activities, H=10+ Leaky activities

(a) Category Distribution   (b) Popularity Distribution

Fig. 4. Category and popularity distribution of leaky apps

Personalization had more apps overall, while *Communication, Finance, Health & Fitness, Music & Audio, Travel & Local* and *Weather* had the largest proportion of apps with a high number of leaky activities per category (Fig. 4a). Dependent apps had fewer categories containing apps with a high number of leaky activities with *Arcade Games* as the top category. Interestingly, dependent apps had a low number of leaky activities compared to companion apps as dependent apps rely on their companion apps to compute, aggregate and transmit data. Standalone apps, however, had few apps with a high number of leaky activities per category, but more apps with a moderate number of leaky activities (75% in the personalization category).

Quantifying the popularity of vulnerable apps presents an insight into the issue of privacy leakage. In Fig. 4b, we identified the popularity of the low, moderate and high leaky activities in apps based on the number of downloads. Our results show that there were several moderate leaky activities in companion apps with low popularity; moderate to high popularity apps had higher ratios of apps with a high number of leaky activities. In addition, two apps with a high number of leaky activities were very popular. Just because there are leaky activities in apps doesn't mean the app is problematic. These activities must be *used* in the operation of the app, and further analysis is needed to quantify the vulnerability. The categorization of leaky activities here gives an insight into what categories of apps have potentially more leaky activities than others.

Dependent apps had a higher percentage of apps with low leaky activities and reasonably high popularity. Although very few dependent apps have low leaky activities, they require a companion app installation which increases the risk of information leakage. Among apps with more than 50 million downloads, 15/18 (83%) had a high number of leaky activities.

4.2 Dynamic Analysis

Inspecting network traffic generated by the apps allows us to check if personal information is being sent to an external source. We executed each companion app along with their embedded versions simultaneously on a mobile device, and an Android wear device for 15 s with 10 random touch interactions to simulate a more realistic action and allow time for network requests to be made during the touch events.

The handheld/companion app was executed on a Google Pixel XL with 2 dual-core Kyro processors, 128 GB storage capacity, 4 GB RAM running Android 8.0 while the wearable app was executed on a paired Motorola Moto 360 Sport with Quad-core 1.2 GHz Cortex-A7, 4 GB, 512 MB RAM running WearOS 2.0. Standalone apps were executed independently on the smartwatch and network packets were captured including HTTPS traffic.

A Python script was written with the use of MonkeyRunner[11] to execute both apps on the mobile phone and smartwatch devices while Pymiproxy was used to intercept and extract network traffic for inspection. We executed 463 apps that had 10 or more potentially leaky activities discovered from static analysis with `android.permission.INTERNET`[12] set in their Manifest file.

Our tests showed that 73% of companion apps selected made substantial Internet requests (five or more GET/POST requests including socket connections) while 8% of embedded apps sent requests to remote servers. This low number of embedded apps connecting to remote servers is not surprising because embedded apps depend on companion apps to send traffic to remote servers [2]. We further evaluated 128 out of the 229 standalone apps with Internet access permission and identified 13% made connections to remote servers.

Trackers. Network traffic generated by the apps were inspected and over 30 trackers were identified. Several companion apps sent data to more than one tracker with Google CrashLytics, Google DoubleClick and Google Analytics as the top trackers actually used. 43%, 33% and 27% of apps sent requests to Google CrashLytics, Google DoubleClick, and Google Analytics respectively. In addition, 22% of apps sent data to Facebook Login, Facebook Analytics, and Facebook Ads.

---

[11] Google Developer Support - Monkeyrunner: https://developer.android.com/studio/test/monkeyrunner/ (Accessed: 2019-02-20).

[12] Google Developer Support - Connect to the network: https://developer.android.com/training/basics/network-ops/connecting (Accessed: 2018-11-21).

Table 2. Top trackers, analytics and Ad networks

Static Analysis									Dynamic Analysis								
Companion/Handheld			Dependent/Embeded			Standalone			Companion/Handheld			Dependent/Embeded			Standalone		
Trackers	Apps	%	Trackers	Apps	%	Trackers	Apps	%	Trackers	Apps	%	Trackers	Apps	%	Trackers	Apps	%
Google Analytics	1116	59	Google Analytics	489	26	Firebase Analytics	53	23	Google CrashLytics	147	43	Google CrashLytics	16	42	Google Analytics	8	47
Google Ads	904	48	Google Ads	68	4	Google CrashLytics	16	7	Google DoubleClick	112	33	Google Ads	14	37	Google CrashLytics	6	35
Google DoubleClick	834	44	Firebase Analytics	68	4	Google Analytics	15	7	Google Analytics	93	27	Google Analytics	5	13	Google Ads	2	12
Firebase Analytics	735	39	Google DoubleClick	67	4	Google Ads	8	3	FB Login	74	22	Flurry	2	5	FB Analytics	1	6
Google CrashLytics	262	14	Google CrashLytics	31	2	Google DoubleClick	8	3	FB Analytics	74	22	Unity3d Ads	1	3	FB Audience	1	6
Flurry	168	9	Flurry	22	1	FB Analytics	1	0.4	FB Ads	74	22				FB Notifications	1	6
FB Login	144	8	ChartBoost	19	1	AppsFlyer	1	0.4	FB Share	74	22				FB Login	1	6
FB Share	137	7	FB Analytics	3	0.2	Flurry	1	0.4	FB Audience	74	22				FB Ads	1	6
FB Analytics	132	7	FB Share	3	0.2				FB Notifications	74	22				FB Places	1	6
Inmobi	108	6	FB Login	2	0.1				Google Ads	27	8				FB Share	1	6
FB Ads	93	5	FB Places	2	0.1				Flurry	25	7						
Twitter MoPub	77	4	Demdex	2	0.1				Unity3d Ads	24	7						
FB Places	55	3	ComScore	2	0.1				Yandex Ad	11	3						
Amazon Advertisement	49	3	AppNexus	1	0.1				AppMetrica	11	3						
ChartBoost	42	2	Urbanairship	1	0.1				Urbanairship	10	3						
Unity3d Ads	40	2	Omniture	1	0.1				MixPanel	9	3						
Moat	30	2	AppMetrica	1	0.1				Nexage	9	3						
Millennial Media	29	2	New Relic	1	0.1				Adjust	9	3						
Adjust	23	1	Google Tag Manager	1	0.1				Krux	8	2						
HockeyApp	22	1															

Although few embedded apps made remote connections, Google Analytics and Google Ads were top trackers, similar to their companion apps. Standalone apps also had a similar percentage of trackers as the companion and embedded apps. Table 2 provides a full breakdown of trackers, analytics and ad networks identified in network traffic generated during dynamic analysis.

Companion apps had 2 trackers per app, on average, while embedded and standalone apps had an average of 1, and 1.4. 21 companion apps had 10 or more trackers while 1 embedded (com.sofascore.results) and 1 standalone app (ch.pete.wakeupwell) had 2 and 8 trackers, respectively.

Personal Information Leakage. By inspecting the app traffic generated, we classified personal information into four main groups as described below:

- *Location:* country code, IP address, GPS location data, e.g. GPS coordinates, city, state, and network location data.
- *UniqueID:* Device unique IDs identified includes MAC addresses, device IDs, IMEI codes and device hashes.
- *Sensor Activity:* step-count, device orientation, heart rate and sensor data.
- *Personal Information:* User's personal information such as health data, address, marital status, age, sex, date of birth, gender, email, income.

Figure 5a shows a sample data record captured from a single companion app sending personal location information as well as app/battery usage. This data is mostly used by advertisers to improve ad targeting. However, very few users are aware of the amount of data collected by advertisers [3]. Although few standalone apps leaked personal information, 2/17 standalone apps that generated network traffic tracked device location, and just one app collected unique IDs.

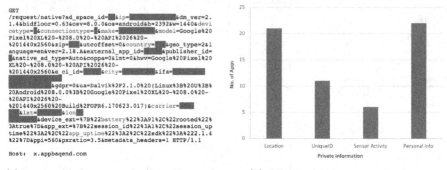

(a) Personal Information Leakage Example   (b) Observed Information Leakage

Fig. 5. Companion app personal information leaks

Embedded apps did not, however, send any personal information to the Internet because almost all data collected by embedded apps were forwarded to their companion apps. Companion apps sent the majority of personal information as shown in Fig. 5b. About 4.8% of companion apps sent personal information such as email, age, gender and others while 4.5% of apps sent location information. Also, 2.4% of companion apps sent unique IDs, and we identified about 1.3% of apps sending sensor activities. The majority of sensor activities observed were the accelerometer and device orientation data.

5   Discussion

By studying 4,017 (1,894 companion, 1,894 embedded, 229 standalone) apps independently in the Android smartwatch market, we observed that the majority of smartphone companion apps send more sensitive information compared to standalone or embedded apps. Static analysis revealed that 12% of companion apps, 11% of embedded apps, and about 9% of standalone apps register sensor hardware in their manifest file. Many of these apps do not even use registered embedded sensors in their code, as observed during static analysis due to third-party libraries registering sensors despite not being required by the app, enabling unauthorized access/transmission of associated data.

Third-party trackers are the major cause of personal information leakage, as shown in Table 2. Additionally, apps with more leaky activities were popular in companion apps, with over 1 million downloads, as seen in Fig. 4. We identified over 84 different trackers in companion apps with standalone apps having the least number of trackers (8) due to the limited smartwatch developer ecosystem compared to the smartphone market. Also, many ad networks are yet to develop effective ad monetization schemes for developers on the smartwatch market.

Further classification was done based on the number of leaky activities apps contain, and we identified both the popularity of these apps and their app categories on the Play Store. Our results show that there are specific categories with more risky behaviors than others, as shown in Fig. 4, suggesting that the wearable app community should adopt further verification mechanisms in apps of such categories such as Personalization, Health & Fitness, and Tools. Although the number of leaky activities does not necessarily mean the app is potentially dangerous, the fact that an app has high leaky activities should trigger a further investigation into the app, its operation, and permissions, because such apps are likely to leak more private information in actual operation.

Unlike mobile apps, wearable apps easily collect data regularly because they are in close contact with the user, and with the help of a companion app could potentially collect vast quantities of data and store them remotely which can lead to the exposure of sensitive information without the user's knowledge. Our results show that leaky applications are currently popular, with many having over 10 million downloads. With the growing number of potential leaky applications currently existing on the app store, simple privacy-preserving actions such as disabling unnecessary app permissions, avoiding fingerprint authentication on apps and encrypting phone data, can help users potentially reduce the amount of information leaked.

6   Conclusion and Future Work

Static and dynamic analysis reveals that third-party tracking libraries account for the bulk of information leakage in all categories, while companion apps leak the most data. Due to the limited resources available in smartwatches and the limited number of third-party tracking services developed for WearOS app developers, standalone apps are less likely to send sizeable sensitive information remotely. In this study, we classify leaky activities in wearable apps and identify the popularity of leaky apps based on the number of downloads and category on the app store, allowing researchers to identify where leaky apps are most likely to exist. However, fine-grained analysis of each leak in the applications has been left for future work and is beyond the scope of this study.

Further automated/manual testing is necessary to verify the degree to which potential risk is correlated with actual damage. This challenge drives further investigation on how information leakage can be mitigated by analyzing the efficacy of tracking settings and permission models, enabling users to control how their personal information is collected. If that is a practical approach, then we can develop models to allow users to fully control access to their personal information in real-time from wearable devices.

References

1. Boillat, T., Rivas, H., Wac, K.: "Healthcare on a Wris": increasing compliance through checklists on wearables in obesity (self-)management programs. In: Rivas, H., Wac, K. (eds.) Digital Health. HI, pp. 65–81. Springer, Cham (2018). https://doi.org/10.1007/978-3-319-61446-5_6
2. Chauhan, J., Seneviratne, S., Kaafar, M.A., Mahanti, A., Seneviratne, A.: Characterization of early smartwatch apps. In: PerCom Workshops, pp. 1–6. Sydney, Australia, March 2016
3. Chen, G., Meng, W., Copeland, J.: Revisiting mobile advertising threats with MAdLife. In: The World Wide Web Conference, WWW 2019, pp. 207–217, San Francisco, CA, May 2019
4. Fafoutis, X., Marchegiani, L., Papadopoulos, G.Z., Piechocki, R., Tryfonas, T., Oikonomou, G.: Privacy leakage of physical activity levels in wireless embedded wearable systems. IEEE Signal Process. Lett. **24**(2), 136–140 (2017)
5. Hou, S., Ye, Y., Song, Y., Abdulhayoglu, M.: HinDroid: an intelligent Android malware detection system based on structured heterogeneous information network. In: KDD 2017, Halifax, Canada, pp. 1507–1515, August 2017
6. Korner, J., Hitzges, L., Gehrke, D.: Goko Store: Home. https://goko.me/
7. Lee, M., Lee, K., Shim, J., Cho, S., Choi, J.: Security threat on wearable services: empirical study using a commercial smartband. In: ICCE-Asia, Seoul, South Korea, pp. 1–5, October 2016
8. Li, X., Dong, X., Liang, Z.: A usage-pattern perspective for privacy ranking of Android apps. In: Prakash, A., Shyamasundar, R. (eds.) ICISS 2014. LNCS, vol. 8880, pp. 245–256. Springer, Cham (2014). https://doi.org/10.1007/978-3-319-13841-1_14
9. Liu, R., Lin, F.X.: Understanding the characteristics of Android wear OS. In: ACM Mobisys, Singapore, Singapore, pp. 151–164, June 2016
10. Moonsamy, V., Batten, L.: Android applications: data leaks via advertising libraries. In: International Symposium on Information Theory and its Applications, Melbourne, Australia, pp. 314–317, October 2014
11. Mujahid, S.: Detecting wearable app permission mismatches: a case study on Android wear. In: 11th Joint Meeting on Foundations of Software Engineering, Paderborn, Germany, pp. 1065–1067, September 2017
12. Paul, G., Irvine, J.: Privacy implications of wearable health devices. In: SIN 2014, Glasgow, UK, pp. 117:117–117:121, September 2014
13. Sun, W., Cai, Z., Li, Y., Liu, F., Fang, S., Wang, G.: Security and privacy in the medical Internet of Things: a review. Secur. Commun. Netw. **2018**, 1–9 (2018)
14. Tumbleson, C., Winiewski, R.: Apktool - a tool for reverse engineering 3rd party, closed, binary Android apps. https://ibotpeaches.github.io/Apktool/
15. Wu, S., Zhang, Y., Jin, B., Cao, W.: Practical static analysis of detecting intent-based permission leakage in Android application. In: IEEE ICCT, Chengdu, China, pp. 1953–1957, October 2017
16. Zhang, H., Rounte, A.: Analysis and testing of notifications in Android wear applications. In: International Conference on Software Engineering, Buenos Aires, Argentina, pp. 347–357, May 2017
17. Zhang, K., Ni, J., Yang, K., Liang, X., Ren, J., Shen, X.S.: Security and privacy in smart city applications: challenges and solutions. IEEE Commun. Mag. **55**(1), 122–129 (2017)

An Encryption-Based Approach to Protect Fog Federations from Rogue Nodes

Mohammed Alshehri[(✉)] and Brajendra Panda[(✉)]

University of Arkansas, Fayetteville, AR 72701, USA
{msalsheh,bpanda}@uark.edu

Abstract. The cloud computing paradigm has revolutionized the concept of computing and has gained a huge attention since it provides computing resources as a service over the internet. As auspicious as this model is, it brings forth many challenges: everything from data security to time latency issues with data computation and delivery to end users. To manage these challenges with the cloud, a fog computing paradigm has emerged. In the context of the computing, fog computing involves placing mini clouds close to end users to solve time latency problems. However, as fog computing is an extension of cloud computing, it inherits the same security and privacy challenges encountered by traditional cloud computing. These challenges have accelerated the research community's efforts to find effective solutions. In this paper, we propose a secure and fine-grained data access control scheme based on the ciphertext-policy attribute-based encryption (CP-ABE) algorithm to prevent fog nodes from violating end users' confidentiality in situations where a compromised fog node has been ousted. In addition, to provide decreased time latency and low communication overhead between the Cloud Service Provider (CSP) and the fog nodes (FNs), our scheme classifies the fog nodes into fog federations (FF), by location and services provided, and each fog node divides the plaintext to be encrypted into multiple blocks to accelerate the time when retrieving ciphertext from the CSP. We demonstrate our scheme's efficiency by carrying on a simulation and analyzing its security and performance.

Keywords: Fog computing · Rogue node ·
Secure data communication · Fine-grained access control

1 Introduction

The cloud computing paradigm, over the past few years, has gained a well-respected reputation due to the tremendous on-demand services it provides to end users over the internet. Cloud computing has innovative features—availability, scalability, and economy—that help to meet the huge demand for storage and computation resources [7]. End users can remotely store and process their data in the core network on the cloud, but it is stored far from users; therefore, the time between a user request and the cloud response is high. Thus, there

© Springer Nature Switzerland AG 2019
G. Wang et al. (Eds.): SpaCCS 2019, LNCS 11611, pp. 225–243, 2019.
https://doi.org/10.1007/978-3-030-24907-6_18

is a demand for new technology to resolve the cloud latency issue [6,13]. With huge growth in the use of the cloud and outsourcing data to the cloud, cloud computing can expose users to various challenges such as data access control, data security, and high latency. However, the fog computing paradigm emerged in 2012 [4] to reduce latency between the cloud and end users' devices [6,13]. The fog computing paradigm locates a cloud close to the end users' devices, which enables customers to perform computing at the edge of the network [4]. In the context of fog computing, fog nodes provide resource services to end users [28]. The main distinguishing features of fog computing include mobility, location-awareness, and low latency [23,29]. The research community has examined the topic of access control in cloud computing, but that is not the focus of this paper. For a comprehensive overview of access control, read [20,22,31]. The fog computing paradigm is susceptible to different threats ranging from malicious attacks to technical issues. Therefore, our focus in this paper is to demonstrate ways to oust rogue (malicious) fog nodes that present threats to fog computing. One reason for these vulnerabilities is that end users outsource sensitive data to a nearby fog node to be processed and then sent to the cloud. Since these fog nodes are the connector between end users' devices and the cloud, it is challenging to secure the cloud and other fog nodes from malicious attacks. This reveals a need to protect the owner's sensitive data from being compromised. In general, fog computing threats take two forms: (1) data modification: if the adversary gets ahold of the fog node, he/she might violate the user's data confidentiality/integrity. Thus, it is important to introduce a security technique to check data confidentiality/integrity among fog nodes as well as between fog nodes and the cloud. (2) unauthorized access: when a fog node is compromised, an adversary can get his/her hands on users' sensitive data. Therefore, it is essential to define a security model to revoke(oust) the fog node as soon as it goes rouge for whatever reason. To defend users' data security while continuing the low latency that fog computing provides, there is a fundamental demand for a security scheme that will meet the users' security needs. Attribute-based encryption (ABE) is a cryptographic primitive that enables one-to-many encryption. It consists of two types: ciphertext policy attribute-based encryption (CP-ABE) [2] and key policy attribute-based encryption [8]. CP-ABE, introduced by Bethencourt et al. [2], is one of the most cryptographic schemes, providing fine-grained data access control. In this paper, we propose a CP-ABE based scheme to oust (rogue) malicious fog nodes and minimize the communication overhead between the cloud service provider (CSP) and fog nodes (FNs).

Contribution. This paper proposes a secure and fine-grained data access control scheme, based on CP-ABE algorithm [2], which achieves the following features:

- This scheme classifies the fog nodes (FNs) into different fog federations(FF) depending on FNs' attributes —namely, location and provided services.
- This scheme aims to oust a rogue (malicious) fog node (FN) which acts maliciously, so it cannot access the encrypted data in cloud.

- The proposed scheme directly prevents the departure FN from accessing encrypted data in the cloud, besides it helps remaining FNs to access re-encrypted data with no latency.
- It helps in reducing communication time to transfer files from the CSP to FNs. The FN divides the file into multiple blocks. The CSP tracks what each fog node currently has/needs. After the re-encryption process, the CSP sends the needed block to the legitimate FNs. This feature makes our model time efficient.

2 Related Work and Motivation

2.1 Related Work

In [21], Sahai et al. proposed the ABE scheme based on an identity-based encryption algorithm [3]. The ABE performs encryption and decryption processes based on user's attributes. The ABE scheme was first applied to cloud computing services to combat challenges such as data security and data access control that face the owner of the outsourced data. The ABE method provides many innovative features such as one-to-many encryption.

The research community has presented different schemes such as [8,25,26] by adopting the ABE scheme in the cloud computing environment to address data security and data access control with untrusted cloud storage. Yu et al. [32] proposed attribute-based data sharing with the possibility of attribute revocation. It was proved to be resistant to chosen plaintext attacks based on the DBDH assumption. The main limitation of this work was that the key generation, encryption, and decryption computation processes contained all possible attributes in the attribute universe. Thus, this method had a computation cost burden on users. Li et al. [15] proposed a scheme to resolve part of the computation overhead by moving it offline. The authors argued that this scheme enabled the user to validate the ciphertext before using expensive full decryption. Yet, the scheme lacked the power of attribute revocation with data sharing for cloud computing users. Tysowski et al. [24] proposed a scheme by combining cryptographic primitives, namely CP-ABE and re-encryption, to accomplish a user revocation process. They divided users into groups, and each group's users shared the same secret key. However, because all users belonged to the same group, shared and used the same private key, this scheme was vulnerable to a collusion attack.

As the researchers have applied the ABE cryptographic scheme to cloud computing storage to achieve the security and fine-grained data access control with the outsourced data. One of the ABE scheme's drawbacks was that the high computation overhead burdened the limited resources available on end users' devices when executing encryption and decryption procedures. Yu et al. [31] proposed a scheme that provided security and fine-grained data access control in cloud computing. With this scheme, the data owner could delegate most of the tasks to an untrusted server. They combined proxy re-encryption, lazy re-encryption, and KP-ABE to design a scheme with fine-grained data access control. In this scheme, all users' private keys were stored on the cloud except for the one corresponding to the dummy attribute. Green et al. [9] presented a CP-ABE scheme to minimize the overhead burden on users by outsourcing decryption to the cloud server. In this scheme, a user's secret key was blinded with a random number which was hidden to the user. The user only shared the blinded secret key with the server to perform an outsource decryption. Researchers have proposed some schemes [18,19] to trace users who maliciously shared their private keys. Li et al. [14] proposed a scheme based on CP-ABE to achieve efficient user key revocation with the possibility of outsourcing the encryption and decryption processes to cloud servers.

Recently, researchers have started to adopt ABE in the fog computing environment as a solution to guarantee data security and fine-grained access control. ABE was applied to IoT devices to resolve data access control issues. In [30] Yu et al. presented the fine-grained data access control issues that arose in a wireless sensor network. They proposed an FDAC scheme in which each sensor node was associated with a set of attributes, and each user was associated with an access structure to determine the user's access rights. Another effort was proposed by Hu et al. [10] which investigated data communication security between users with an implanted or a wearable sensor and data users in a wireless body area network. They developed a secure scheme by leveraging CP-ABE in WBAN. Furthermore, Jiang et al. [12] addressed the problem of key-delegation abuse with a CP-ABE scheme and accordingly designed a CP-ABE model to prevent this problem in fog computing. Additionally, Zuo et al. [33] proposed an access control scheme called CCA-secure ABE scheme with outsourced decryption to protect outsourced data in the context of fog computing. Unfortunately, this scheme introduced high computation costs, and it only worked with an AND-gate encryption attribute. The work in [11] proposed a scheme based on CP-ABE to support data security and fine-grained data access control, using features such as ciphertext updating and computation outsourcing, for fog computing with IoT devices. Like Zuo et al. [33]., the critical problem with their scheme was that it was only suitable with an AND-gate encryption predicate. Xiao et al. [27] proposed a hybrid fine-grained search and access authorization for fog computing, based on a CP-ABE cryptographic primitive. Their scheme was hybrid as it supported both index encryption and data encryption. Still, it only supported AND-gates predicates. Another work was proposed by Mao et al. [17] to construct a CPA-secure and RCCA-secure scheme based on an ABE model with the possibility of outsourced encryption verification.

Fog computing is in the middle between cloud servers and end users' devices. As such, this layer is susceptible to more attacks. Data owners can find their data damaged or leaked by a rogue (malicious) fog node. Since one of the primary fog computing features is to increase network reliability, fog nodes need to be protected against malicious attacks. Protecting the nodes will result in defending the data owner's security and privacy. As far as we know, no previous work has adopted the ABE scheme to address the problem of a rogue (malicious) fog nodes. Based on [2] and [14], we propose a secure scheme, in the context of fog computing, to prevent rogue fog nodes from violating end users' confidentiality and besides to minimize the time latency and the communication overhead between the Cloud Service Provider and the fog nodes.

2.2 Motivation

Fog computing plays a key role in providing multiple services such as music, adult-entertainment, kid's entertainment, emergency vehicle response, and health data collection to end users at low latency [4]. Even with the numerous advantages that the fog computing paradigm provides, it introduces many security issues. Users are not able to benefit from provided services if the fog node providing the intended service is not working for any reason, so they need to be forwarded to the nearest legitimate node. For instance, health care providers benefit from close fog nodes to deliver high quality and fast services to patients. However, imagine the fog node providing health services to the health care's providers is down or maliciously compromised, this means either the patients confidentiality is violated or much time and communication overhead to retrieve patients' data from the cloud. In this paper, we consider preventing rogue (malicious) fog nodes from accessing the encrypted data in the cloud with maintaining end users' data confidentiality and availability by creating fog federations. In addition, this paper considers the time latency to delivering the data from the cloud to fog nodes. In particular, the threat of rogue fog nodes would vary from launching attacks against other fog nodes to exposing end users' information. Based on our review of the literature, no previous work has addressed these issues in the field of fog computing as same as this work does. Therefore, there is need for an efficient and secure scheme that considers these security challenges and the time latency.

3 Preliminaries

3.1 Bilinear Mapping

As in [3], let G_1 and G_2 be a multiplicative cyclic groups of large prime order p, with g as a generator. Let e be a bilinear map: $e : G_1XG_1 \rightarrow G_2$. G_2 is the output space of the bilinear mapping. Bilinear map e has to satisfy the following properties:

1. Bilinearity. $\forall u, v \in G_1, e(u^a, v^b) = e(u, v)^{ab}$ *where* $a, b \in Z_p^*$.
2. Non-degeneracy. This means that all pairs in $e : G_1XG_1$ not map to the identity element in G_2.
3. The bilinear map $e(u, v)$ is efficiently computable.

3.2 Access Structure

As in [1], let $\{P_1, P_2, ..., P_n\}$ be a set of parties. A collection $A \subseteq 2^{(P_1, P_2, ..., P_n)}$ is monotone if $(\forall B \in A$ and $B \subseteq C)$ then $C \in A$. Here, the monotone access structure is a collection A of non-empty subsets of $\{P_1, P_2, ..., P_n\}$ (which is,

$A \subseteq 2^{P_1, P_2, \ldots, P_n} \setminus \{\emptyset\}$. The sets $\in A$ are named the authorized sets while the sets $\notin A$ is the unauthorized sets. As in [2], in our scheme we represent the parties with attributes, and all parties (fog nodes) with same attributes will form a fog federation (FF).

3.3   CipherText-Policy Attribute Based Encryption

CP-ABE fundamentally consists of the following four algorithms: Setup, Encrypt, KeyGen, and Decrypt. For more details about those four algorithms, read [2].

4   Proposed Scheme

As Fig. 1 illustrates, our model comprises of the following entities: a cloud service provider (CSP), fog nodes (FNs), and a trusted authority server (TAS). Fog nodes (FNs) with same attributes form a fog federation (FF).

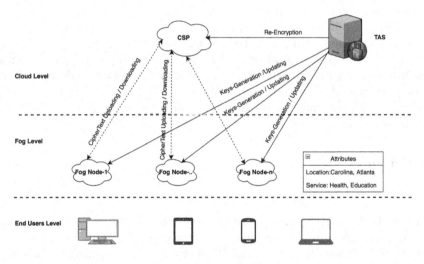

Fig. 1. System model.

Time latency to deliver data from cloud storage to end users' devices is high; therefore, fog computing emerged to address this issue. However, FNs are susceptible to malicious attack, and accordingly the end user's confidentiality could be violated. In order to maintain the confidentiality and availability for end users' outsourced data traveling through FNs to CSP, we utilized the following advanced cryptographic primitive: CP-ABE algorithm, which enforces

Table 1. Simple table

FN_{ID}	$File_{ID}$	Available-blocks	Needed-blocks
FN_1	$File_1$	B_1	B_2, B_3, B_4, B_5
FN_2	$File_1$	B_1, B_2, B_3	B_4, B_5

fine-grained data access control to guarantee a secure communication between FNs and the CSP. This scheme equips each FN with a set of attributes and associates each ciphertext with an access policy that is defined by these attributes. Only a FN that satisfies the access policy structure associated with the ciphertext can decrypt the ciphertext to obtain the plaintext.

Our scheme classifies the FNs into different fog federations (FFs) based on a set of attributes which characterizes the FF. Consequently, we let the FN divide the file to be encrypted into blocks, then perform the encryption process, and finally outsource it into the cloud storage. More specifically, CSP maintains a progress list, which is a list of all FNs in a specific FF besides blocks of files they currently need/have, as shown in Table 1. Such a construction reduces the file retrieving and decryption time. For the sake of clarity, we will consider the following example:

Suppose $File_1$ is encrypted and uploaded to the CSP. FN_1 and FN_2 already have accessed some blocks of this file. Suppose FN_2 becomes unauthorized to decrypt this file for any reason whatsoever. The TAS simultaneously notifies the remaining FNs to update their private keys and notifies the CSP to perform a re-encryption operation. The CSP then defers re-encrypting blocks already shared with any FN in the FF. It instead starts by re-encrypting the blocks that have not been accessed yet and then re-encrypts the ones that were already shared. This feature boosted our scheme's success as it is designed to reduce the time latency when retrieving files from the cloud. When an authorized FN accessed an encrypted file, the CSP checked the progress list and accordingly returned the file or the blocks that had not been accessed by others in the same FF. Then, the CSP returned a list of FNs and which blocks they already had. Then, the FN, which requires the encrypted file, communicates the FN in the same federation to get the intended blocks. Thus, the time consumption to retrieve the encrypted data from FNs in same FF was much less than retrieving the same file from CSP, so this scheme provides low latency and less traffic overhead between the FNs and the CSP. This is attributed to the idea of fog federations (FF).

A FN could leave the system for whatever reason, or it could go rogue by being compromised by a malicious attack. Thus, to guarantee the owners' data confidentiality there was a need to take precautions against the rogue FN. Our scheme efficiently acts as a barrier against an ousted fog node to keep it from accessing the encrypted data stored in the cloud. This scheme was designed to instantaneously and simultaneously prevent the ousted FN from accessing the encrypted data and delivering the re-encrypted data to the remaining FNs. Fog Federation-updating, and re-encryption algorithms were executed by TAS and

CSP in a parallel manner: TAS excluded the ousted FN from the fog federation list (FFL). Then, it updated the current fog federation public key $FFPK_{ver}$ to $FFPK_{ver+1}$, then propagated $FFPK_{ver+1}$ to the FNs remaining in the FFL. CSP started re-encrypting the files which could not be decrypted by the ousted FN. The re-encryption key was $FFPK_{ver+1}$.

5   Scheme Description

In this section, we present the description of our scheme based on the CP-ABE algorithm. We begin by reviewing the access tree model presented in [2,8] as we exploit it as an access structure as shown in Fig. 2. Then, we describe our algorithms.

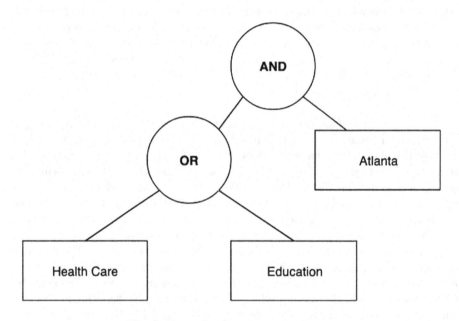

Fig. 2. Example of an access structure.

To satisfy the access tree conditions, we follow the same methods in [2,8]. Read through [2,8] for more information.

Next we provide the algorithms needed for our model. Algorithm 1 which based on [2] is executed by TAS. It inputs a security parameter and outputs System Public Key (SPK) along with System Master Key (SMK). It constructs a universal set of attributes to be used in our scheme as USAT = FN Location, Service Provided.

TAS also executes Algorithm 2. Its input is SPK. It contains two parts. First: it creates a new fog federation list (FFL) of FNs depending on the provided location and services. It contains hash of FN_{ID} and FF_{ID} to prevent against id-impersonation. Second: when TAS receives a request from FN to join the system, TAS will check a predefined "FFL". If FN-Attributes (FN_{Att}) are suitable with one or multiple fog federations attributes (FF_{Att}), it will be added to the corresponding Fog Federations. Otherwise, it will create new FF and add the new FN to it. Additionally, this algorithm outputs fog federation master key (FFMK), which is only available for TAS, and fog federation public key (FFPK) that is public to the federation's members.

Algorithm 3 is also executed by TAS which is based on [2]. It takes as inputs FFMK, SPK, FN_{ID}, SMK and a set of attributes S. In this algorithm, the set S along with the F_{ID} identify the FN's private key ($FN_{PR-S-ID}$). FN_{ID} is used here to assign each fog node with a distinct private key and to track each FN's activities. It outputs $FN_{PR-S-ID}$. The $FN_{PR-S-ID}$ is associated with FN attributes and FN_{ID} simultaneously, and this helps in preventing an unauthorized fog node from accessing data stored in the CSP.

Authorized FNs executes Algorithm 4 which is based on [2]. This algorithm takes the file to be encrypted (M), the access tree T, SPK, and $FFPK$ as input. It outputs the ciphertext to be uploaded to the CSP. In our scheme, the FN divides the file to be encrypted into multiple blocks ($M_1, M_2, \ldots, M_n$). Then, it encrypts all blocks and uploads the ciphertext to the CSP.

CSP executes Algorithm 5. Our model is designed to reduce the communication overhead between the CSP and the FNs. CSP maintains a progress list as shown in Table 1. CSP will check the progress list upon receiving a request from an authorized fog node. In case the requested file or some blocks of it has/have already been accessed by other FNs in same FF, the CSP will notify the requester to communicate which FNs have those blocks. But in case the file has not been accessed by any FN in the same FF, the CSP will send the file to the FN.

Each authorized FN executes Algorithm 6 which is based on [2] to obtain plaintext. Its inputs are the current ciphertext, the current version of the $FN_{PR-S-ID}$, the defined attributes in the access structure. The decryption algorithm outputs either plain-text or $\perp$. In (1), we associate the fog node private key with FN_{ID} and FN_{att} set to prevent a fog node's impersonation. The FN performs decryption for each block and then combines all the decrypted blocks to form the plaintext file.

TAS and CSP simultaneously execute Algorithms 7 and 8. TAS would oust a FN from the system for multiple reasons (e.g. being attacked or becomes a rogue FN). Thus, to guarantee the owner's data security, there is a need to take precautions against those ousted FNs. Our scheme efficiently prevents an ousted FN from accessing the encrypted files stored in the CSP. To prevent an unauthorized FN from accessing the encrypted files, Ousting rogue FN and Ciphertext Re-encryption algorithms are executed simultaneously by TAS and CSP, respectively. More specifically, such feature ensures that our scheme is secure. TAS will exclude the ousted FN from the FFL. Then, it will update the current $FFPK_{ver}$ to $FFPK_{ver+1}$ and propagate $FFPK_{ver+1}$ to the FNs remaining in the FFL. CSP will start re-encrypting the files, which cannot be decrypted by the ousted FN. The re-encryption key is $FFPK_{ver+1}$. The CSP starts re-encrypting the files/blocks that have not been accessed by any FN in the given FF. This feature makes our scheme beneficial for data owners in terms of data confidentiality.

Algorithm 9 is executed by the legitimate FNs remaining in the FF after executing Algorithms 7 and 8. The TAS sends the new $FNPK_{ver+1}$ and a random large number m to the updated list of fog nodes remaining in the FF via a secure channel. Upon receiving this message, each FN in the FF updates its FNPK.

Algorithm 10 is executed by FNs. When a FN intends to download and decrypt a file, it first needs to contact the CSP. When the CSP checks the progress list and finds out the required file is already shared with another FN in the same FF, the CSP will reply with a notification to contact the other FN which already has the file in the same FF. The requester (FN) will contact the FN posses the file to provide the desired file.

Algorithm 1. Setup(λ)

1: Choose bilinear cyclic group G_1 of prime order p with generator g_1;
2: Randomly generates exponents $\alpha, \beta \in G_p^*$;
3: Random Oracle H: $USAT \to \{0,1\}^*$ // to map each att in USAT into random element $\in G_1$;
4: SMK and SPK as:
5: $\qquad\qquad SMK = \{\beta, g_1^\alpha\}$
6: $\qquad\qquad SPK = \{G_1, g_1, g_1^\beta, e(g_1, g_1)^\alpha\}$;
7: $USAT$ = FN location, Services
8: The SPK is public to all fog nodes, but SMK is private for TAS

Algorithm 2. FF Creation and Adding new FN (SPK)

    Part 1: FFL Creation
1: Create FFL to contain list of FNs in the system, as
$\qquad FFL[FF_{ID}|FFPK_{ver}|FF_{att}|H(FN_{ID}FF_{ID})]_{ver}$
    Part 2: Addign New FN to FF
2: **if** $FN_{att} = FF_{att}$ **then**
3:     assign new-FN $FN_{ID} = FN_{ID} + FF_{ID}$
4:     add FN to the corresponding FF
5:     send $FFPK_{ver}$ to new FN
6: **else**
7:     create new FF and assign it unique FF_{ID}
8:     randomly choose $FFMK_{ver} = \gamma \in Z_p^*$
9:     Compute $FFPK_{ver} = \{FF_{ID}, g_1^\gamma, e(g_1, g_1)^\gamma\}$
10:    assign $FN_{ID} = FN_{ID} + FF_{ID}$
11:    add new FF to FFL
12:    add new FN to new FF
13:    send $FFPK_{ver}$ to the new FN
14: **end if**

Algorithm 3. FN_{PR} Generation $(FFMK_{ver}, SPK_{ver}, SMK, S, FN_{ID})$

1: TAS gets request from new FN to join the system
2: **if** FN_{ID} is verified **then**
3:    continue
4: **else**
5:    decline
6: **end if**
7: randomly generate $r \in Z_P^*$
8: **for** every $att_i \in S$ **do**
9:    randomly generate $r_i \in Z_P^*$
10: **end for**
11: **for** $every\ att \in S$ **do**
12:    compute FN_{PR-S} as follows
       $FN_{PR-S-ID} = (D = g^{(\alpha+r)/\beta}, \forall i \in S : D_i = g^r.H(FN_{ID})^{\gamma_{ver}}.H(i)^{r_i},$
       $D_i' = g^{r_i}.H(FN_{ID})^{\gamma_{ver}})$
13: **end for**
14: send $FN_{PR-S-ID}$ to the corresponding FF and update FFL

Algorithm 4. Data Encryption $(M, T, SPK, FFPK)$

1: A is set of atts represented by monotone access structure tree T
2: **for** each node x in T **do**
3:    set a polynomial
4:    **if** node x is root node in T **then**
5:       set $q_{(0)R} = s$ // s is random value $\in Z_P^*$
6:    **else**
7:       $q(0)_x = q_{parent(x)}(index(x))$
8:       then choose $d_x = k_x$ - 1 as polynomial degree to interpolate with q_x
9:    **end if**
10: **end for**
11: specify n as number of blocks in each file
12: specify Block's size in certain file = M size/n
13: **for** each $y \in Y$ **do** //Y is the set of leaf nodes in T
14:    $C_y = g^{q_y(0)}$
15:    $C_y' = H(att(y))^{q_y(0)}$
16: **end for**
17: Compute: $C = g^{\beta s}$
18: **for** every $M_i \in M$ **do**
19:    Compute $C_{i_{ver}} = M_i.e(g,g)^{\alpha s}$
20:    $C_{ver}+ = C_{i_{ver}}$
21: **end for**
22: Upload CipherText as $\{T, C_{ver}, C, C_y, C_y'\}$ to the cloud

---

Algorithm 5. Progress List creation/ Requesting File from CSP

1: FN submits a request to CSP
2: CSP verifies FN, by checking the legitimate FNs list
3: **if** FN is verified and cipher-text access structure policy is satisfied **then**
4:    Check the progress list
5:    **if** available blocks $\in$ requested file blocks **then**
6:       Respond "list of FN_{IDs} that have copy of this file" to let the requester get the file from
7:    **else**
8:       send the requested file/blocks to FN
9:    **end if**
10: **else**
11:    decline and notify other FNs in same federation that this FN is not legitimate
12: **end if**

Algorithm 6. Data Decryption $(CT_{ver}, FN_{PK-ver}, x)$

1: **for** each leaf node attribute "x" in access structure T **do**
2:    Set i= att(x)
3:    **if** i $\in$ S **then**
4:       Recursively Compute

$$DecryptNode(CT_{ver}, FN_{PK-S-ver}, x) =$$
$$\frac{e(D_i, C_x)}{e(D_i', C_x')} = \frac{e(g^r.H(FN_ID)^{\gamma_{ver}}.H(i)^{r_i}, g^{q(0)y})}{e(g^{r_i}.H(FN_ID)^{\gamma_{ver}}, H(i)^{q(0)y})} =$$
$$\frac{e(g,g)^{rq(0)y}, e(g, H(FN_{ID}).H(i))^{\gamma_{ver}r_iq(0)y}}{e(g, H(FN_{ID}).H(i))^{\gamma_{ver}q(0)yr_i}} =$$

$$e(g,g)^{rq(0)y} \quad (1)$$

5:    **if** i $\in$ S and x not leaf node **then**
6:       **for** every child node z of x **do**
7:          $F_z = DecryptNode(CT_{ver}, FN_{PK-S-ver}, x)$
8:       **end for**
9:       **if** $F_z! = \perp$ **then**
10:          //by lagrange and polynomial interpolation as in [2]
$$F_z = \prod_{z \in S_x} F_z^{\Delta_{i, S_x'}(0)} \quad where\, i = index(z)\, and\, S_z' = index(z) : z \in S_x$$
$$= e(g,g)^{r.q(0)x} = e(g,g)^{rs}$$
11:          **if** x =root **then**
12:             $A = DecryptNode(CT_ver, FN_{PK-S-ver}, r) = e(g,g)^{rq(0)R} = e(g,g)^{rs}$
13:          **else** $DecryptNode(CT_{ver}, FN_{PK-S-ver}, x) = \perp$
14:          **end if**
15:       **end if**
16:    **end if**
17:    **end if**
18:    Decrypt Message by Computing:
$$M_i = \frac{C_{ver}}{e(C,D)/A} = \frac{M_i.e(g,g)^{\alpha s}}{e(g^{\beta s}, g^{(\alpha+r)/\beta})/e(g,g)^{rs}}$$
$$= \frac{M.e(g,g)^{\alpha s}}{e(g,g)^{(\beta s\alpha+\beta sr)/\beta}/e(g,g)^{rs}}$$
$$= \frac{M_i.e(g,g)^{\alpha s}}{e(g,g)^{(s\alpha+sr)/e(g,g)^{rs}}} = \frac{M_i.e(g,g)^{\alpha s}}{e(g,g)^{s\alpha}}$$
19:    **for** $M_i=1$ to $M_i=n$ **do** //n is the number of blocks in given file
20:       Plain-Text+ = M_i
21:    **end for**
22: **end for**

Algorithm 7. Ousting rogue FN $(FFMK_{ver}, FFPK_{ver}, FFL)$

1: update $FFMK_{ver} \rightarrow \gamma + 1 \in Z_p^*$
2: update $FFPK_{ver} \rightarrow FFPK_{ver+1} = FF_{ID}, g^{\gamma+1}, e(g,g)^{\gamma+1}$
3: remove ousted FN
4: **for** $FN_i \in$ updated FFL **do**
5:    propagate $FFPK_{ver+1}$
6: **end for**

Algorithm 8. Re-Encryption $(CT_{ver}, FFPK_{ver+1})$

1: Cloud service checks the progress list
2: Start re-encrypting blocks which have not been requested by any FN in same FF.
3: updated-file $= C_{ver}.e(FFPK_{ver+1}, C)$
   $= M_i.e(g,g)^{\alpha s}.e(g^{\gamma_{ver+1}-\gamma_{ver}}, g^{\beta s})$
   $= M_i.e(g,g)^{\alpha s + \gamma_{ver+1}s}$
4: $CT_{ver+1} =$ updated-file

Algorithm 9. PrivateKeyUpdate

1: Remaining Fog Nodes in the federation receives $FNPK_{ver+1}$
2: $FN_{PR-S-ver+1} =$
   $(D = g^{(\alpha+r)/\beta},$
   $\forall i \in S : D_i = g^r.H(FN_{ID})^{m(\gamma_{ver+1})},$
   $D_i' = g^{r_i}.H(FN_{ID})^{m(\gamma_{ver+1})}$

Algorithm 10. Fog Nodes Secure-Communication

1: FN receives a request, from other FN in same FF, to send file X or Blocks of file X
2: **if** FN requester is verified **then** // in the same FF
3:    sender sends file/blocks to the requester
4: **else**
5:    decline the connection
6: **end if**
7: requester performs decryption process by calling algorithm-6

6 Analysis of the Proposed Scheme

6.1 Security Analysis

Collusion Attack. Our results show that the CP-ABE algorithm guarantees the security of the messages' blocks. The CP-ABE algorithm provides the private keys with a set of attributes and the message with an access structure. When a subset of the FN's attributes satisfies the access structure tree, the FN can decrypt the message. In Algorithm 3, we simultaneously describe the FN's private key with the set of attributes and the FN_{ID}. That means our scheme prevents an ousted FN from accessing the encrypted data in the cloud and prevents the other FNs in the same FF colluding with the ousted FN.

Confidentiality. The encrypted files in the cloud are protected against the ousted FNs by the following process: when updating the FFL, the TAS updates the SPK and propagates it through a secure channel to the FNs that are not yet members of the FF. In the meantime, it sends notifications to the CSP to re-encrypt the files encrypted with a specific FF's attributes, and it notifies the FNs remaining in the FF to update their secret keys. In this case, the ousted FN does not have the updated SPK and, therefore, cannot update its private key for a future decryption process. This feature makes our scheme efficient in protecting end users' data confidentiality.

7   Performance Analysis and Simulation

7.1   Communication Overhead

One of our scheme's goal is to reduce the communication overhead between the CSP and the FNs. The CSP and FNs exchange encrypted messages. Our proposed scheme divides the message into blocks before encrypting and uploading the blocks to the CSP. At the same time, the CSP maintains a progress list which helps to track the needs of all FNs in each FF. When a FN in a specific FF needs to decrypt a file, the CSP will check the progress list in case some of the intended file's blocks have already been shared with another FN in the same FF. If that is the case, the CSP directs the requester to contact the FN in the same FF to get the needed blocks. This feature gives our proposed scheme more momentum as it plays a vital role in reducing time latency between the CSP and the FNs.

7.2   Simulation

We run the experiment of our scheme on macOS Mojave 10.14 with an intel core i7 CPU 2.2 GHz and 16.00 GB RAM. We utilize the java pairing-based cryptography (JPBC) library used in [5]. JPBC library provides a port of the pairing-based cryptography library (PBC) [16] to perform the fundamental mathematical operations of pairing-based cryptosystems in java.

We simulated the CSP and TAS as servers and the FNs as local clients. We have simulated the following Algorithms 1, 2, 3, 4, 5 and 6. Then, depending on that we collected the experiment results. Our experiment tends to show that our scheme is time efficient in case of retrieving data from the same FF other than from the CSP. Any FN can access data file encrypted by another FN in the same FF. For example, when specific FNx requests to access encrypted data in the CSP, the CSP checks the progress list if any FN has obtained the requested file in the same FF, if yes the CSP will notify the requester to communicate the FN that has the encrypted file to send it. Otherwise, the CSP sends the encrypted file that has not been accessed by any FN in the same FF to the authenticated requester. Our results show that the time it takes the FN to retrieve and decrypt a particular file from other members in the same FF is less than obtaining it from the CSP. We let the FN divide the file into blocks of 50 MB size, and then perform other processes. However, fog computing has been introduced to reduce the overhead burden on the cloud and to minimize the time latency between the end users and the cloud. We have studied that and collect results supporting such a claim.

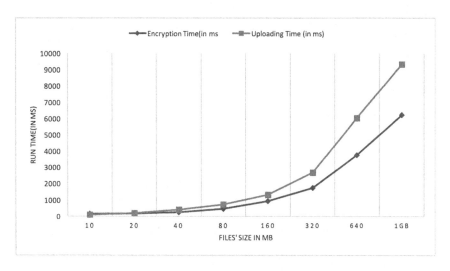

Fig. 3. Time to encrypt and to upload files to the CSP.

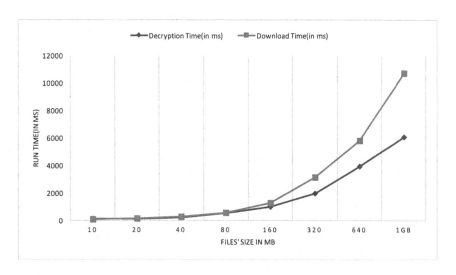

Fig. 4. Time retrieve and to decrypt ciphertext from the CSP.

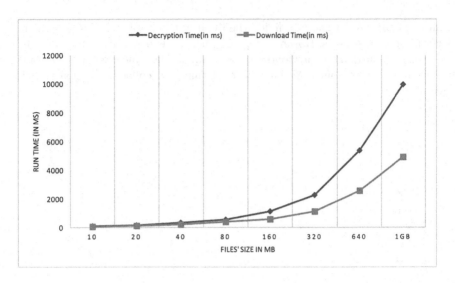

Fig. 5. Time to retrieve and decrypt file from same FF.

In Fig. 3, the time it takes the FN to encrypt a file grows linearly in case the file only has one block, while it grows exponentially when the file has more than one block. The time to upload the ciphertext from the FN to the CSP grows exponentially in regard to the file size.

In addition to that our scheme is able to remove a specific FN of the FF, it is efficient in reducing the communication overhead between the CSP and FF's members as the CSP will not send any file or blocks of file, to FN, which already been shared with another node in the same federation. CSP rather notifies the requester to communicate the FN, in the same FF, which already has a copy of the file. As justification, Fig. 4 shows that the running time it takes a FN to retrieve a ciphertext from the CSP exponentially grows, and the decryption time exponentially grows when the file has more than one block. Figure 5 illustrates that the time consumed by the FN to retrieve the ciphertext from another FN in the same FF grows exponentially. However, while retrieving the same ciphertext from the CSP, it performs far better. We have studied the running time of downloading different size of the ciphertext from the CSP and the same FF. Figure 6 shows that the running time deceases linearly when the ciphertext size to be retrieved from the same FF is increased, and this result supports our argument. However, the best case for the FN is to retrieve the whole file from other FNs in the same FF, while the worst case is to retrieve the whole file from the CSP. In addition, our scheme has shown that CP-ABE cryptographic algorithm could be utilized in the fog computing system when fine-grained access control is required. Moreover, it has shown the ability of ousting compromised FNs to protect end users' data confidentiality.

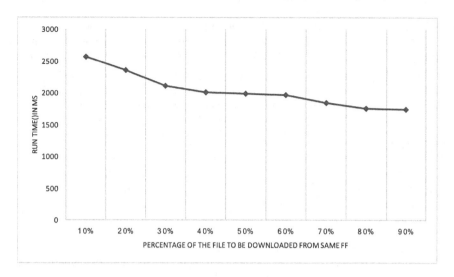

Fig. 6. Time to download various size of the ciphertext from CSP and same FF.

8 Discussion

Based on the analysis above, we observed that our scheme can accomplish the necessary security goals, mainly fine-grained access control, confidentiality, and availability. Because this work focuses on securing the channels between the FF and the CSP, we assumed that communication channels between end devices and the FNs were fully secure. Because FNs can divide the messages to be encrypted into multiple blocks and the CSP maintains a progress list of each message, the CSP only sends the messages or blocks that have not been accessed by any FN in the FF. Therefore, our scheme minimized the communication overhead between the CSP and FFs. We assumed that the FNs in a specific FF were not busy, so the communication among the FNs in same FFs was time efficient. In our proposed scheme, we assumed that the channel between FNs in the same FF was secure. We also have not considered a malicious fog node detection as it is out of our scope for now.

9 Conclusion

End users' data confidentiality could be violated while travelling through the FNs to the CSP. Besides, the FNs would go rogue for what so ever reason. When the FN providing services to end users is down, the data would not be available. In this paper, we proposed an efficient, secure, and a fine-grained data access control scheme to create FFs of FNs with same attributes. We utilized the ciphertext-policy attributed-based encryption (CP-ABE) algorithm. This scheme is efficient in protecting the FF against rogue FNs by ousting them off the FF. So they cannot access the encrypted files in the CSP. Our scheme classified the FNs into different FFs depending on the location and services that each FN provides; one FN can belong to multiple FFs. Moreover, our scheme enabled the FN to divide the messages to be encrypted into multiple blocks prior to performing encryption and uploading operations. This helps to reduce communication overhead between the CSP and the FFs. Based on our security analysis, the owners' data confidentiality and availability is maintained.

References

1. Beimel, A.: Secure schemes for secret sharing and key distribution. Technion-Israel Institute of Technology, Faculty of Computer Science (1996)
2. Bethencourt, J., Sahai, A., Waters, B.: Ciphertext-policy attribute-based encryption. In: 2007 IEEE Symposium on Security and Privacy, SP 2007, pp. 321–334. IEEE (2007)
3. Boneh, D., Franklin, M.: Identity-based encryption from the weil pairing. In: Kilian, J. (ed.) CRYPTO 2001. LNCS, vol. 2139, pp. 213–229. Springer, Heidelberg (2001). https://doi.org/10.1007/3-540-44647-8_13
4. Bonomi, F., Milito, R., Zhu, J., Addepalli, S.: Fog computing and its role in the Internet of Things. In: Proceedings of the First Edition of the MCC Workshop on Mobile Cloud Computing, pp. 13–16. ACM (2012)
5. Caro, A., Iovino, V.: Java pairing-based cryptography library (2013)
6. Deng, R., Lu, R., Lai, C., Luan, T.H.: Towards power consumption-delay trade-off by workload allocation in cloud-fog computing. In: 2015 IEEE International Conference on Communications (ICC), pp. 3909–3914. IEEE (2015)
7. Fox, A., et al.: Above the clouds: a Berkeley view of cloud computing. Department Electrical Engineering and Computer Sciences, University of California, Berkeley, Rep. UCB/EECS 28(13) (2009)
8. Goyal, V., Pandey, O., Sahai, A., Waters, B.: Attribute-based encryption for fine-grained access control of encrypted data. In: Proceedings of the 13th ACM Conference on Computer and Communications Security, pp. 89–98. ACM (2006)
9. Green, M., Hohenberger, S., Waters, B., et al.: Outsourcing the decryption of ABE ciphertexts. In: USENIX Security Symposium, vol. 2011 (2011)
10. Hu, C., Li, H., Huo, Y., Xiang, T., Liao, X.: Secure and efficient data communication protocol for wireless body area networks. IEEE Trans. Multi-Scale Comput. Syst. **2**, 94–107 (2016)
11. Huang, Q., Yang, Y., Wang, L.: Secure data access control with ciphertext update and computation outsourcing in fog computing for Internet of Things. IEEE Access **5**, 12941–12950 (2017)
12. Jiang, Y., Susilo, W., Mu, Y., Guo, F.: Ciphertext-policy attribute-based encryption against key-delegation abuse in fog computing. Futur. Gener. Comput. Syst. **78**, 720–729 (2018)
13. Li, J., Jin, J., Yuan, D., Palaniswami, M., Moessner, K.: Ehopes: data-centered fog platform for smart living. In: 2015 International Telecommunication Networks and Applications Conference (ITNAC), pp. 308–313. IEEE (2015)
14. Li, J., Yao, W., Zhang, Y., Qian, H., Han, J.: Flexible and fine-grained attribute-based data storage in cloud computing. IEEE Trans. Serv. Comput. **10**(5), 785–796 (2017)
15. Li, J., Zhang, Y., Chen, X., Xiang, Y.: Secure attribute-based data sharing for resource-limited users in cloud computing. Comput. Secur. **72**, 1–12 (2018)

16. Lynn, B.: The pairing-based cryptography (PBC) library (2010)
17. Mao, X., Lai, J., Mei, Q., Chen, K., Weng, J.: Generic and efficient constructions of attribute-based encryption with verifiable outsourced decryption. IEEE Trans. Dependable Secur. Comput. **13**, 533–546 (2016)
18. Ning, J., Cao, Z., Dong, X., Wei, L., Lin, X.: Large universe ciphertext-policy attribute-based encryption with white-box traceability. In: Kutyłowski, M., Vaidya, J. (eds.) ESORICS 2014. LNCS, vol. 8713, pp. 55–72. Springer, Cham (2014). https://doi.org/10.1007/978-3-319-11212-1_4
19. Ning, J., Dong, X., Cao, Z., Wei, L., Lin, X.: White-box traceable ciphertext-policy attribute-based encryption supporting flexible attributes. IEEE Trans. Inf. Forensics Secur. **10**(6), 1274–1288 (2015)
20. Ruj, S., Nayak, A., Stojmenovic, I.: DACC: distributed access control in clouds. In: 2011 International Joint Conference of IEEE TrustCom-11/IEEE ICESS-11/FCST-11 (TrustCom 2011), pp. 91–98. IEEE (2011)
21. Sahai, A., Waters, B.: Fuzzy identity-based encryption. In: Cramer, R. (ed.) EURO-CRYPT 2005. LNCS, vol. 3494, pp. 457–473. Springer, Heidelberg (2005). https://doi.org/10.1007/11426639_27
22. Sookhak, M., Yu, F.R., Khan, M.K., Xiang, Y., Buyya, R.: Attribute-based data access control in mobile cloud computing. Future Gener. Comput. Syst. **72**(C), 273–287 (2017)
23. Stojmenovic, I., Wen, S., Huang, X., Luan, H.: An overview of fog computing and its security issues. Concurr. Comput.: Pract. Exp. **28**(10), 2991–3005 (2016)
24. Tysowski, P., Hasan, M.: Hybrid attribute-based encryption and re-encryption for scalable mobile applications in clouds. IEEE Trans. Cloud Comput. **1**, 172–186 (2013)
25. Wang, H.: Identity-based distributed provable data possession in multicloud storage. IEEE Trans. Serv. Comput. **2**, 328–340 (2015)
26. Wang, H., Wu, Q., Qin, B., Domingo-Ferrer, J.: Identity-based remote data possession checking in public clouds. IET Inf. Secur. **8**(2), 114–121 (2014)
27. Xiao, M., Zhou, J., Liu, X., Jiang, M.: A hybrid scheme for fine-grained search and access authorization in fog computing environment. Sensors **17**(6), 1423 (2017)
28. Yi, S., Li, C., Li, Q.: A survey of fog computing: concepts, applications and issues. In: Proceedings of the 2015 Workshop on Mobile Big Data, pp. 37–42. ACM (2015)
29. Yi, S., Qin, Z., Li, Q.: Security and privacy issues of fog computing: a survey. In: Xu, K., Zhu, H. (eds.) WASA 2015. LNCS, vol. 9204, pp. 685–695. Springer, Cham (2015). https://doi.org/10.1007/978-3-319-21837-3_67
30. Yu, S., Ren, K., Lou, W.: FDAC: toward fine-grained distributed data access control in wireless sensor networks. IEEE Trans. Parallel Distrib. Syst. **22**(4), 673–686 (2011)
31. Yu, S., Wang, C., Ren, K., Lou, W.: Achieving secure, scalable, and fine-grained data access control in cloud computing. In: 2010 IEEE Proceedings of Infocom, pp. 1–9. IEEE (2010)
32. Yu, S., Wang, C., Ren, K., Lou, W.: Attribute based data sharing with attribute revocation. In: Proceedings of the 5th ACM Symposium on Information, Computer and Communications Security, pp. 261–270. ACM (2010)
33. Zuo, C., Shao, J., Wei, G., Xie, M., Ji, M.: CCA-secure ABE with outsourced decryption for fog computing. Futur. Gener. Comput. Syst. **78**, 730–738 (2018)

Python Scrapers for Scraping Cryptomarkets on Tor

Yubao Wu[1(✉)], Fengpan Zhao[1], Xucan Chen[1], Pavel Skums[1], Eric L. Sevigny[2],
David Maimon[2], Marie Ouellet[2], Monica Haavisto Swahn[3],
Sheryl M. Strasser[3], Mohammad Javad Feizollahi[4], Youfang Zhang[4],
and Gunjan Sekhon[4]

[1] Department of Computer Science, Georgia State University,
Atlanta, GA 30303, USA
{ywu28,pskums}@gsu.edu, {fzhao6,xchen41}@student.gsu.edu
[2] Department of Criminal Justice and Criminology, Georgia State University,
Atlanta, GA 30303, USA
{esevigny,dmaimon,mouellet}@gsu.edu
[3] School of Public Health, Georgia State University, Atlanta, GA 30303, USA
{mswahn,sstrasser}@gsu.edu
[4] Institute for Insight, Georgia State University, Atlanta, GA 30303, USA
mfeizollahi@gsu.edu, {yzhang107,gsekhon1}@student.gsu.edu

Abstract. Cryptomarkets are commercial websites on the web that
operate via darknet, a portion of the Internet that limits the ability to
trace users' identity. Cryptomarkets have facilitated illicit product trading and transformed the methods used for illicit product transactions.
The survellience and understanding of cryptomarkets is critical for law
enforcement and public health. In this paper, we design and implement
Python scrapers for scraping cryptomarkets. The design of the scraper
system is described with details and the source code of the scrapers is
shared with the public.

Keywords: Scraper · Cryptomarket · Tor · Darknet · MySQL

1 Introduction

The Darknet is a layer or portion of the Internet that limits the ability to trace
users' identity. It is considered part of the deep web, which is a portion of
the Internet that is not indexed by standard web search engines. Accessing the
Darknet requires specific software or network configurations, such as Tor ("The
Onion Router"), the most popular anonymous network.

Cryptomarkets operate on the Darknet, much like eBay or Craigslist, as
commercial websites for selling illicit products, including drugs, weapons, and
pornography [1]. The first cryptomarket, Silk Road [2,3], launched in early 2011
and operated until October 2013, when the website was taken down by the
Federal Bureau of Investigation (FBI) following the arrest of the site's founder,

© Springer Nature Switzerland AG 2019
G. Wang et al. (Eds.): SpaCCS 2019, LNCS 11611, pp. 244–260, 2019.
https://doi.org/10.1007/978-3-030-24907-6_19

Ross Ulbricht. However, new cryptomarkets have proliferated in the wake of Silk Road's demise [4], presenting an increasingly serious challenge to law enforcement and intelligence efforts to combat cybercrime [5]. We have documented at least 35 active cryptomarkets as of February 2019. Figure 1 shows the homepage of Dream Market, the largest cryptomarket at present. The link address ending with ".onion" indicates that it is a hidden web service in the Tor anonymous network. A hidden service in Tor means the identity (IP address or location) of any web server is hidden. From Fig. 1, we can see that Dream Market offers five categories of products including Digital Goods, Drugs, Drugs Paraphernalia, Services, and Other. Table 1 shows the subcategories and number of corresponding advertisements within each parent category. From Table 1, we can see that the illicit products include hacking tools, malware, stolen credit cards, drugs, and counterfeit products. Table 2 shows the largest seven cryptomarkets at present according to the total number of ads listed in each market. All cryptomarkets offer similar categories of products.

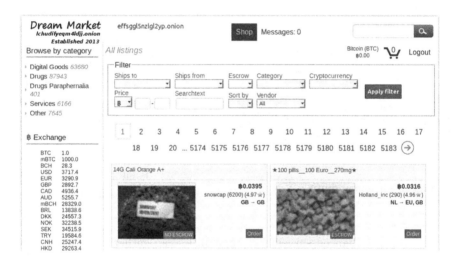

Fig. 1. The homepage of Dream market

The onion routing (Tor) system is the most popular anonymous network for accessing these cryptomarkets. Tor conceals users' activities through a series of relays called "onion routing," as shown in Fig. 2. The decentralized nature of peer-to-peer networks makes it difficult for law enforcement agencies to seize web hosting servers, since servers are potentially distributed across the globe. Payments are made using cryptocurrencies like Bitcoin. Since both cryptomarkets and cryptocurrencies are anonymous, there are minimal risks for vendors selling illicit products on the Darknet.

The surveillance and understanding of cryptomarkets within the context of drug abuse and overdose is critical for both law enforcement and public

Table 1. Categories of products in Dream market

Categories	Sub-categories
Digital Goods 63680	Data 2709, Drugs 587, E-Books 14918, Erotica 2819, Fraud 4726, Fraud Related 11086, Hacking 2654, Information 16206, Other 2051, Security 570, Software 1940
Drugs 87943	Barbiturates 49, Benzos 4031, Cannabis 29179, Dissociatives 3258, Ecstasy 11672, Opioids 5492, Prescription 5559, Psychedelics 6349, RCs 646, Steroids 4090, Stimulants 14296, Weight loss 220
Drugs Paraphernalia 401	Harm Reduction 65
Services 6166	Hacking 689, IDs & Passports 1545, Money 1432, Other 897, Cash out 1012
Other 7645	Counterfeits 4233, Electronics 257, Jewellery 1391, Lab Supplies 109, Miscellaneous 620, Defense 376

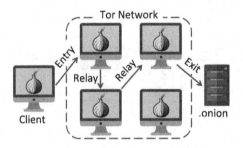

Fig. 2. The onion routing system

Table 2. Cryptomarkets

Cryptomarkets	#Ads
Dream	165,835
Berlusconi	38,270
Wall Street	16,766
Valhalla	11,023
Empire	9,499
Point Tochka	6,358
Silk Road 3.1	5,657

health [3,6–8]. Enhanced surveillance capabilities can gather information, provide actionable intelligence for law enforcement purposes, and identify emerging trends in substance transactions (both licit and illicit) that are contributing to the escalating drug crisis impacting populations on a global scale. The absence of a systematic online drug surveillance capability is the motivational catalyst for this research, which is the development of an online scraping tool to employ within cryptomarkets.

In this paper, we develop scrapers for the seven largest cryptomarkets shown in Table 2. The scraped data are stored in a MySQL database. Details surrounding the computational development and capacity used in the scraper design are described. To the best of our knowledge, this is the first Python package created specifically for scraping multiple cryptomarkets to investigate drug-related transactions. The scraper source code is publicly available upon request. (Send correspondence to scraper.crypto@gmail.com with your name, position, and affiliation. We will send you a link for downloading the source code upon verification).

2   System Overview

Figure 3 shows the system networking framework. Our Python scraper programs run in an Ubuntu operating system (OS). For the convenience of sharing, we use VirtualBox and Ubuntu virtual machine. Since VirtualBox can be installed on any OS, students can easily import our virtual machine and start using the scrapers without the need for further coding or configurations. The university security disallows the Tor connection. Therefore we use Amazon Web Service (AWS) as a proxy for visiting Tor. The scraped data is uploaded into a local database server hosted at the university data center. All data will be uploaded into the database server and no data will be stored in students' local computers. The system is designed to allow multiple students to run the scrapers simultaneously. The scraper will check whether a webpage exists in the database before scraping the webpage in order to avoid scraping duplicate webpages.

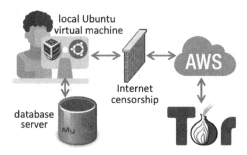

Fig. 3. The system networking framework

The scraping system consists of scraping and parsing stages. In the scraping stage, the scraper program will navigate through different webpages within a cryptomarket. The scraper uses the Selenium package to automate the Firefox browser to navigate through different webpages, download the html files, and upload them into the MySQL database. Most cryptomarkets like Dream Market require users to input CAPTCHAs after users browse a predetermined number of webpages. Cracking CAPTCHAs automatically is not an easy task and different markets utilize different types of CAPTCHAs. Therefore the scraper is delayed until human operators are able to manually input the required CAPTCHAs to extend browsing time allowance. In the parsing stage, the program will automatically parse the scraped html files and automatically insert the extracted information into structured database tables.

3   Scraping Stage

In order to scrape the cryptomarkets, the computer needs to be connected to the Tor network. Because the university security disallows Tor connections, we use AWS as a proxy to connect to Tor, as shown in Fig. 3.

AWS Setup: We register an AWS account and launch an instance of EC2 t2.micro Ubuntu 18.04 with 1 CPU, 1 GB memory, and 30 GB disk, which is free for 1 year. The download speed is about 970 Mbit/s and the upload speed is about 850 Mbit/s. In the EC2 Dashboard webpage, we add Custom TCP Rule for ports 9001 and 9003 from anywhere to the Inbound of the security group. To install Tor on the server, we use Tor Relay Configurator [9], where we select "Ubuntu Bionic Beaver (18.04 LTS)" for the Operating System, "Relay" for the Tor node type. We do not choose "Exit Node" since AWS disallows Tor exit nodes because of the potential abuse complaints [10]. We leave ORPort and DirPort as defaults and set the total monthly traffic limit to 500 GB, maximum bandwidth to 1 Mbit/s, and maximum burst bandwidth to 2 Mbit/s. After clicking on the Submit button, users will receive a command starting with "curl." Running that command in the terminal of the AWS server will install Tor. After Tor is installed, comment "SocksPort 0" in the Tor configuration file "/etc/tor/torrc" to allow SOCKS connection [11, 12]. Users must then type "sudo ss -n -p state listening src 127.0.0.1" to make sure that Tor is listening to port 9050 for SOCKS connection. Restarting Tor service by "sudo service tor restart" will display the message "Self-testing indicates your ORPort is reachable from the outside. Excellent. Publishing server descriptor." in the log file "/var/log/tor/notices.log". This means Tor is successfully installed. Three hours after Tor installation, you will find it in Tor Relay Search website by searching the nickname [13].

Python Scraper: Part 1: Tor Network Connection: Users can now connect the local Ubuntu virtual machine to the AWS server through SOCKS via command

$ ssh ubuntu@serverid.amazonaws.com -i key.pem -L50000:localhost:9050 -f -N

Replace "serverid" and "key.pem" with your own server's information. Users can test the Tor connection by opening a Firefox browser and set the "Preferences - General - NetworkSettings" to "ManualProxyConfiguration - SockshHost:127.0.0.1 - Port:50000" and "Yes: Proxy DNS when using SOCKS v5". After that, check the status of the Tor connection by visiting the website [14] in Firefox.

In Python, we use os.system("ssh ...") command to connect to the AWS server. To setup the SOCKS connection, we first create an instance of the Selenium Webdriver by "aProfile = webdriver.FirefoxProfile()", and then set up the preferences in Table 3 through "aProfile.set_preference(Preference, Value)".

Table 3. Network configurations for connecting to Tor in Python

Preference	Value	Meaning
network.proxy.type	1	Use manual proxy configuration
network.proxy.socks	127.0.0.1	SOCKS host
network.proxy.socks_port	50000	The port used the SSH command
network.proxy.socks_remote_dns	True	Proxy DNS when using SOCKS v5
network.dns.blockDotOnion	False	Do not block .onion domains

Firefox is the best option for connecting to Tor since Tor browser is modified from Firefox. Firefox is more friendly for Linux than Windows OS. Therefore we implement the Python scrapers in Ubuntu OS.

Python Scraper: Part 2: Database Design and Connection: Our database server has CentOS 7 and MariaDB, which is a fork of MySQL. We run the command "mysql -u root -q" in the terminal to connect to the MySQL database. We first create a database for the scraping stage by command "CREATE DATABASE cryptomarket_scraping;". Our scrapers run on local Ubuntu virtual machines, which will remotely connect to the database server. To enable remote database connection, we run the command "grant all on cryptomarket_scraping.* to 'user' identified by 'passwd';" in the terminal of the database server. Table 4 shows the seven tables in the cryptomarket_scraping database.

Table 4. Tables in the cryptomarket_scraping database

Table name	Table content
cryptomarkets_list	List of cryptomarkets
product_list	List of unique products
product_desc_scraping_event	Events of scraping product descriptions
product_rating_scraping_event	Events of scraping product ratings
vendor_list	List of unique vendors
vendor_profile_scraping_event	Events of scraping vendor profiles
vendor_rating_scraping_event	Events of scraping vendor ratings

Table 5 shows the description of the "cryptomarkets_list" table. Information on the seven cryptomarkets is inserted manually. The scraper program will read the table and retrieve the market URL, username, and password information to navigate to and log into the market website.

Table 5. Description of the "cryptomarkets_list" table

Field	Type	Null	Key	Default	Extra
cryptomarket_global_ID	int(11)	NO	PRI	NULL	auto_increment
cryptomarket_name	varchar(256)	NO	UNI	NULL	
cryptomarket_name_abbr	varchar(2)	NO	UNI	NULL	
cryptomarket_url	text	NO		NULL	
my_username	text	YES		NULL	
my_password	text	YES		NULL	

Table 6 shows the description of the "product_list" table. It stores the information of products and helps avoid scraping the same product multiple times.

The fields whose names start with "my_lock" are used for concurrent writing. Table 7 shows the description of the "product_desc_scraping_event" table. It stores the events of scraping product webpages and maintains the scraping history. The scraped html files are stored in the file system and the html file paths are stored in the "product_desc_file_path_in_FS" field. Table 8 shows the description of the "vendor_list" table. It stores the information of vendors and helps avoid scraping duplicate vendors. Table 9 shows the description of the "vendor_rating_scraping_event" table. It stores the fields from scraping vendor webpages. The descriptions of the "product_rating_scraping_event" and "vendor_profile_scraping_event" tables are omitted.

Table 6. Description of the "product_list" table

Field	Type	Null	Key	Default	Extra
product_global_ID	int(11)	NO	PRI	NULL	auto_increment
cryptomarket_global_ID	int(11)	NO	MUL	NULL	
product_market_ID	varchar(256)	NO		NULL	
last_scraping_time_pr	text	YES		NULL	
my_lock_pr	tinyint(1)	NO		0	
last_scraping_time_pd	text	YES		NULL	
my_lock_pd	tinyint(1)	NO		0	

The scraped html files are saved to the disk of the database server and the full paths of the html files are stored in the table. For example, the "vendor_rating_file_path_in_FS" field in the "vendor_rating_scraping_event" table contains the full path of the html files. In the parsing stage, the program will read and parse the html files.

In Python, we import the mysql and mysql.connector packages for MySQL connections. Specifically, we call the "aDB = mysql.connector.connect(host, user, passwd, database, port, buffered)" function to connect to the database server. The database cursor can thus be obtained by "aDBCursor = aDB.cursor(dictionary=True)". We can execute any SQL commands by calling the "aDBCursor.execute(aSQLStatement)" function, where "aSQLStatement"

Table 7. Description of the "product_desc_scraping_event" table

Field	Type	Null	Key	Default	Extra
scraping_event_ID_product	int(11)	NO	PRI	NULL	auto_increment
product_global_ID	int(11)	NO	MUL	NULL	
scraping_time	text	NO		NULL	
product_desc_file_path_in_FS	text	YES	MUL	NULL	

Table 8. Description of the "vendor_list" table

Field	Type	Null	Key	Default	Extra
vendor_global_ID	int(11)	NO	PRI	NULL	auto_increment
cryptomarket_global_ID	int(11)	NO	MUL	NULL	
vendor_market_ID	varchar(256)	NO		NULL	
last_scraping_time_vr	text	YES		NULL	
my_lock_vr	tinyint(1)	NO		0	
last_scraping_time_vp	text	YES		NULL	
my_lock_vp	tinyint(1)	NO		0	

Table 9. Description of the "vendor_rating_scraping_event" table

Field	Type	Null	Key	Default	Extra
scraping_event_ID_vendor	int(11)	NO	PRI	NULL	auto_increment
vendor_global_ID	int(11)	NO	MUL	NULL	
scraping_time	text	NO		NULL	
vendor_rating_file_path_in_FS	text	YES	MUL	NULL	

represents a SQL statement. In the scraper program, we execute the SELECT, INSERT, and UPDATE statements. To fetch the data records, we call the "aDBCursor.fetchone()" or "aDBCursor.fetchall()" function. After we finish the operation, we always call the "aDB.close()" function to close the connection. Please refer to the source code for more details.

The "cryptomarket_scraping" database stores the data scraped from all seven cryptomarkets since all markets contain products, vendors, and ratings. Therefore, in Python, we design a class containing the MySQL functions, which is independent of the scraper classes of different cryptomarkets. Each scraper class will call the MySQL functions to interact with the database.

Python Scraper: Part 3: Scraper Design

The seven cryptomarkets in Table 2 can be categorized into two groups. Dream, Berlusconi, Valhalla, Empire, Point Tokcha, and Silk Road 3.1 belong to the first group. Wall Street itself belongs to the second group. The two market groups differ in how the webpages are navigated. In the first group, changing the URL will navigate to different pages. For example, in Dream Market, the following link is the URL of page 2 of products.

http://effsggl5nzlgl2yp.onion/?page=2&category=103

We can change the page value to navigate to different pages. However, in Wall Street, the URL does not contain page information. We always get the same link:

http://wallstyizjhkrvmj.onion/index

Table 10. Properties of cryptomarkets

cryptomarkets	login	CAPTCHA
Dream	Yes	Yes
Berlusconi	Yes	No
Wall Street	Yes	Yes
Valhalla	No	No
Empire	Yes	Yes
Point Tochka	Yes	No
Silk Road 3.1	No	Yes

This URL will not change when we click on the "Next (page)" button. Based on the above observations, we design two scraping strategies: 1. Scraping the webpages of products and vendors on one product-list page first, and then navigating to the next product-list page; 2. Navigating multiple product-list pages first, and then scraping the webpages of products and vendors listed in those product-list pages. Strategy 1 is used for the cryptomarkets in group 1. Strategy 2 is only used for Wall Street (group 2). Following these strategies, we design a Python scraper program for each cryptomarket.

CAPTCHA is an acronym for "completely automated public Turing test to tell computers and humans apart". It is a challenge-response test used in computing to determine whether or not the user is human. Different cryptomarkets require different types of CAPTCHAs. The CAPTCHAs are the major obstacle in scraping the websites. In our scrapers, we rely on humans to input those CAPTCHAs. The scraping program will stall whenever it encounters a webpage requiring CAPTCHAs. We use the explicit wait method provided in the Selenium package. More specifically, we call the "aWait=WebDriverWait(aBrowerDriver, nSecondsToWait)" and "aWait.until (EC. element_to_be_clickable(...))" functions. The program will wait until some element that never appears in the webpage containing CAPTCHAs appears in the new webpage and is clickable. Since the speed of loading an .onion webpage is slow, waiting for a short time period like 2 s before extracting the product and vendor information will help reduce program errors. During the experiments, we find that Dream, Wall Street, Empire, and Silk Road 3.1 markets require CAPTCHAs, but Berlusconi, Point Tochka, and Valhalla markets do not require CAPTCHAs. We also find that Dream, Wall Street, Empire, Berlusconi, and Point Tochka markets require logins, but Silk Road 3.1 and Valhalla do not require logins. Table 10 summarizes these properties.

4   Parsing Stage

In the parsing stage, we implemented the Python parser programs to read the data stored in the "cryptomarket_scraping" database, parse various information from the html files, and store the parsed data into the "cryptomarket_parsed" database.

Python Parser: Part 1: Database Design: All cryptomarkets contain the webpages for products and vendors. In the product webpages, product title, description, vendor, price, shipping, and rating information are shown. In the vendor webpages, vendor name, profile, sales records, and rating information are shown. Therefore we create the "product_descriptions" table and the "vendor_profile" table to store the product and vendor information respectively. We notice that the rating information is usually shown in tables in the product or vendor webpages since vendors have an incentive to maintain their reputation. Therefore, we created two more tables for storing ratings. An additional table is created for memorizing the progress of the parser. Table 11 shows the five tables created in the "cryptomarket_parsed" database.

Table 11. Tables in the "cryptomarket_parsed" database

Table name	Table content
parser_progress	The progress of parsing
product_descriptions	Product descriptions
product_ratings	Ratings on products' webpages
vendor_profiles	Vendor profiles
vendor_ratings	Ratings on vendors' webpages

Table 12 shows the "parser_progress" table. It is used for memorizing the progress of the parser. If the program is interrupted by unexpected issues, the parser can continue parsing the htmls file from where it stopped.

Table 12. Description of the "parser_progress" table

Field	Type	Null	Key	Default
last_parsed_scraping_event_ID_pd	int(11)	YES		NULL
last_parsed_scraping_event_ID_pr	int(11)	YES		NULL
last_parsed_scraping_event_ID_pd_4pr	int(11)	YES		NULL
last_parsed_scraping_event_ID_vp	int(11)	YES		NULL
last_parsed_scraping_event_ID_vr	int(11)	YES		NULL
last_parsed_scraping_event_ID_vp_4vr	int(11)	YES		NULL

Tables 13 and 14 show the partial descriptions of the "product_descriptions" table and the "vendor_profiles" table respectively. Some fields are omitted. Table 15 shows the description of the "product_ratings" or "vendor_ratings" table. These two tables both contain ratings and have the same description.

Table 13. Description of the "product_descriptions" table

Field	Type	Null	Key	Default	Extra
index_pd	int(11)	NO	PRI	NULL	auto_increment
scraping_time	varchar(256)	NO		NULL	
cryptomarket_global_ID	int(11)	NO		NULL	
product_global_ID	int(11)	NO		NULL	
vendor_global_ID	int(11)	NO		NULL	
vendor_market_ID	varchar(256)	NO		NULL	
vendor_market_name	varchar(256)	NO		NULL	
product_title	varchar(256)	NO		NULL	
product_desc	text	YES		NULL	
price_bitcoin	float	YES		0	
price_usd	float	YES		0	
price_eur	float	YES		0	
ships_to	varchar(256)	NO		NULL	
ships_from	varchar(256)	NO		NULL	
escrow	varchar(256)	NO		NULL	
category	varchar(256)	NO		NULL	
num_sales	int(11)	NO		0	
num_stock	int(11)	NO		0	

Table 14. Partial description of the "vendor_profiles" table

Field	Type	Null	Key	Default	Extra
index_vp	int(11)	NO	PRI	NULL	auto_increment
scraping_time	varchar(256)	NO		NULL	
cryptomarket_global_ID	int(11)	NO		NULL	
vendor_global_ID	int(11)	NO		NULL	
vendor_market_ID	varchar(256)	NO		0	
vendor_profile	text	YES		NULL	
terms_conditions	text	YES		NULL	
join_date_member_since	varchar(256)	YES		NULL	
last_active_date	varchar(256)	YES		NULL	
pgp	text	YES		NULL	
num_orders_completed	int(11)	YES		0	
num_orders_open	int(11)	YES		0	

Table 15. Description of the "product_ratings" or "vendor_ratings" table

Field	Type	Null	Key	Default	Extra
index_pr	int(11)	NO	PRI	NULL	auto_increment
cryptomarket_global_ID	int(11)	NO		NULL	
vendor_global_ID	int(11)	NO		NULL	
buyer_market_ID	varchar(256)	NO		NULL	
rating_stars	float	YES		0	
text_comments	text	YES		NULL	
post_date	varchar(256)	YES		NULL	
money_bitcoin	float	YES		0	
buyer_total_num_of_orders	int(11)	YES		0	
buyer_total_value_of_orders	int(11)	YES		0	
product_global_ID	int(11)	YES		NULL	

Python Parser: Part 2: Parser Design: We use polymorphism to design the parsers. We first create a base class called "parser_base". In the base class, we create a member variable for each field of the tables in the "cryptomarket_parsed" database. In the Python source code, the member variables always start with "m_". In the base class, we implement all database related functions. For example, the "insert_one_product_rating()" function will insert a product rating into the "product_ratings" table. In the base class, we also design four abstract functions:

1. def parse_one_html_product_descriptions(self): pass
2. def parse_one_html_product_ratings(self): pass
3. def parse_one_html_vendor_profiles(self): pass
4. def parse_one_html_vendor_ratings(self): pass

Each cryptomarket website has its own design. Therefore, we need to design a parser for each cryptomarket. For each cryptomarket, we design a child class inheriting from the base class. For example, the parser class for Dream Market is defined as "class parser_dream(parser_base):". In each of the seven child classes, we only implement the above four abstract parsing functions.

When parsing an html file, we use the BeautifulSoup package. Once a html file is read by "aFile = open(filename, encoding='utf-8')", we directly convert it into a BeautifulSoup instance by "aBS = BeautifulSoup(aFile, features='html.parser')". Then, we call "aBS.findChild(...)" to find a single element or "aBS.findChildren(...)" to find a set of elements in the html file, and then obtain data for different columns of the tables. Regular expressions are useful for finding elements satisfying certain conditions. For example, we call "aBS.findChildren('a', {'herf': re.compile('http://.*')})" to find all 'a' elements whose 'href' attributes start with "http://". Please see the Python source code for more examples.

After we implement the scrapers for the cryptomarkets, we can start parsing product descriptions, product ratings, vendor profiles, and vendor ratings. We create a Python file for each task. In each file, the program reads the records one by one from a table, identifies the cryptomarket, and calls the corresponding parsing function to parse the html file. The parsing results will be inserted into one of the four tables: product_descriptions, product_ratings, vendor_profiles, and vendor_ratings.

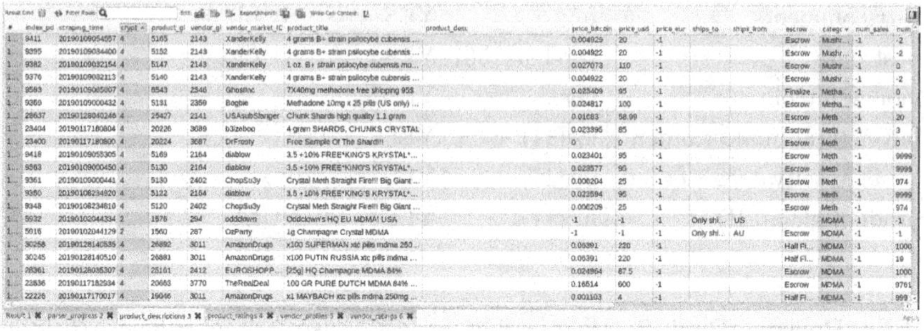

Fig. 4. The screenshot of the "product_descriptions" table in MySQL Workbench

5   Experimental Results

One student runs the scrapers for two weeks and inputs many CAPTCHAs. The total number of hours for scraping the data is about 70 h. The parsing stage only costs several hours and is automatic without human intervention. Table 16 shows the numbers of data records in the tables in the "cryptomarket_parsed" database. From Table 16, we can see that the student has scraped 26,190 products, 3,950 vendors, 119,934 product ratings, and 626,850 vendor ratings. The dataset can be easily shared with other researchers through MySQL Workbench.

Table 16. Statistics of the data

Table name	#records
product_descriptions	26,190
product_ratings	119,934
vendor_profiles	3,950
vendor_ratings	626,850

Figure 4 shows a screenshot of the "product_descriptions" table. In Fig. 4, each row represents a product and each column represents a property of the product. Empty cells indicate missing values. The "product_desc" column usually contains a long text description of a product.

Figure 5 shows a screenshot of the "product_ratings" table. In Fig. 5, each row represents a product rating and each column represents a property of the rating. From Fig. 5, we can see that each rating contains the vendor, buyer, date, rating stars, comment, money, and product information. Each rating actually represents one transaction. The buyer IDs are masked for privacy protection.

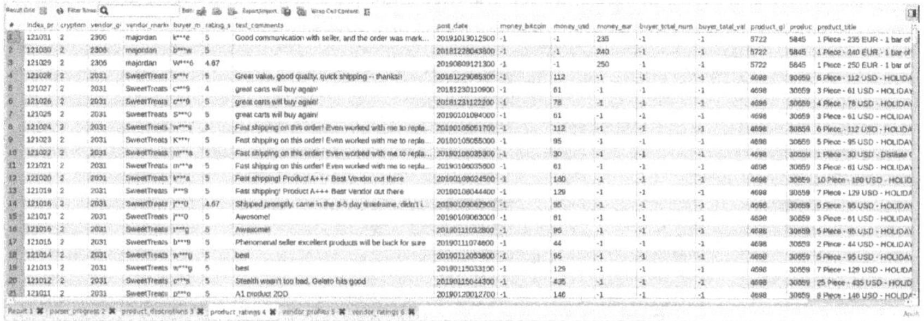

#	index_pr	cryptom	vendor_g	vendor_mark	buyer_m	rating_s	text_comments	post_date	money_bitcoin	money_usd	money_eur	buyer_total_num	buyer_total_val	product_gl	produc	product_title
1	121031	2	2306	majordan	k***e	5	Good communication with seller, and the order was mark...	20191013012500	-1	-1	235	-1	-1	5722	5845	1 Piece - 235 EUR - 1 bar of
2	121030	2	2306	majordan	b***w	5		20181228043800	-1	-1	240	-1	-1	5722	5845	1 Piece - 240 EUR - 1 bar of
3	121029	2	2306	majordan	W***6	4.67		20190609121300	-1	-1	250	-1	-1	5722	5845	1 Piece - 250 EUR - 1 bar of
4	121028	2	2031	SweetTreats	s***r	5	Great value, good quality, quick shipping -- thanks!!	20181229085300	-1	112	-1	-1	-1	4698	30659	6 Piece - 112 USD - HOLIDA
5	121027	2	2031	SweetTreats	c***9	4	great carts will buy again!	20181230110900	-1	61	-1	-1	-1	4698	30659	3 Piece - 61 USD - HOLIDAY
6	121026	2	2031	SweetTreats	c***9	5	great carts will buy again!	20181231122200	-1	78	-1	-1	-1	4698	30659	4 Piece - 78 USD - HOLIDAY
7	121025	2	2031	SweetTreats	S***0	5	great carts will buy again!	20190101084000	-1	61	-1	-1	-1	4698	30659	3 Piece - 61 USD - HOLIDAY
8	121024	2	2031	SweetTreats	w***s	3	Fast shipping on this order! Even worked with me to repla...	20190105051700	-1	112	-1	-1	-1	4698	30659	6 Piece - 112 USD - HOLIDA
9	121023	2	2031	SweetTreats	K***r	5	Fast shipping on this order! Even worked with me to repla...	20190105055000	-1	95	-1	-1	-1	4698	30659	5 Piece - 95 USD - HOLIDAY
10	121022	2	2031	SweetTreats	m***a	5	Fast shipping on this order! Even worked with me to repla...	20190106035300	-1	30	-1	-1	-1	4698	30659	1 Piece - 30 USD - Distillate (
11	121021	2	2031	SweetTreats	m***a	5	Fast shipping on this order! Even worked with me to repla...	20190106035600	-1	61	-1	-1	-1	4698	30659	3 Piece - 61 USD - HOLIDAY
12	121020	2	2031	SweetTreats	k***a	5	Fast shipping! Product A+++ Best Vendor out there	20190108024500	-1	180	-1	-1	-1	4698	30659	10 Piece - 180 USD - HOLID
13	121019	2	2031	SweetTreats	r***9	5	Fast shipping! Product A+++ Best Vendor out there	20190108044400	-1	129	-1	-1	-1	4698	30659	7 Piece - 129 USD - HOLIDA
14	121018	2	2031	SweetTreats	j***0	4.67	Shipped promptly, came in the 3-5 day timeframe, didn't i...	20190109062900	-1	95	-1	-1	-1	4698	30659	5 Piece - 95 USD - HOLIDAY
15	121017	2	2031	SweetTreats	j***0	5	Awesome!	20190109063000	-1	61	-1	-1	-1	4698	30659	3 Piece - 61 USD - HOLIDAY
16	121016	2	2031	SweetTreats	r***g	5	Awesome!	20190111032800	-1	95	-1	-1	-1	4698	30659	5 Piece - 95 USD - HOLIDAY
17	121015	2	2031	SweetTreats	b***9	5	Phenomenal seller excellent products will be back for sure	20190111074600	-1	44	-1	-1	-1	4698	30659	2 Piece - 44 USD - HOLIDAY
18	121014	2	2031	SweetTreats	w***g	5	best	20190112053600	-1	95	-1	-1	-1	4698	30659	5 Piece - 95 USD - HOLIDAY
19	121013	2	2031	SweetTreats	w***g	5	best	20190115033100	-1	129	-1	-1	-1	4698	30659	7 Piece - 129 USD - HOLIDA
20	121012	2	2031	SweetTreats	c***s	5	Stealth wasn't too bad, Gelato hits good	20190115044300	-1	435	-1	-1	-1	4698	30659	25 Piece - 435 USD - HOLID
21	121011	2	2031	SweetTreats	p***o	5	A1 product 20D	20190120012700	-1	146	-1	-1	-1	4698	30659	8 Piece - 146 USD - HOLIDA

Fig. 5. The screenshot of the "product_ratings" table in MySQL Workbench

Figure 6 shows a screenshot of the "vendor_profiles" table. In Fig. 6, each row represents a vendor and each column represents a property of the vendor. The "vendor_profile" and "term_conditions" are two similar properties. Some cryptomarkets call it "vendor_profile" while others call it "term_conditions". They both contain the long text descriptions of a vendor, which usually contains rich information about the vendor.

Figure 7 shows a screenshot of the "vendor_ratings" table. In Fig. 7, each row represents a vendor rating and each column represents a property of the rating. Each rating contains the vendor, buyer, date, rating stars, and money information. Similar to the ratings in the "product_rating" table, each rating here still represents one transaction. But the product information is usually not provided in the "vendor_ratings" table in most cryptomarkets. The buyer IDs are also masked for privacy protection.

We further perform preliminary analysis and visualization on the parsed data. We first count the number of ads in each country. We use the "ship from" information to determine the country of an ad. Note that some vendors may provide fake information, e.g., they are in France but they claim Germany. In this work, we did not analyze the authenticity but it is an interesting problem. Figure 8 shows the global distribution of ads across the largest seven cryptomarkets.

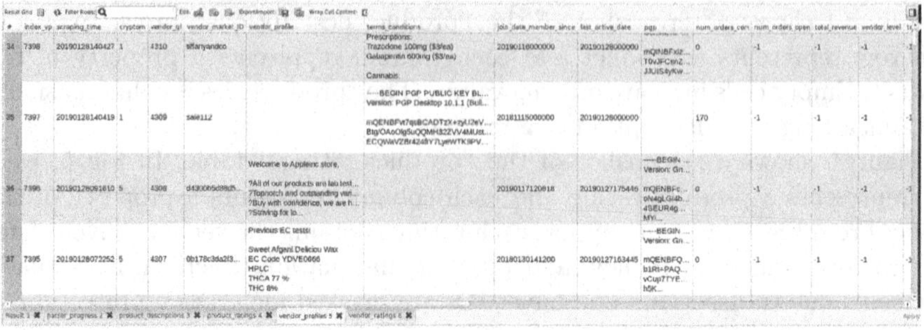

Fig. 6. The screenshot of the "vendor_profiles" table in MySQL Workbench

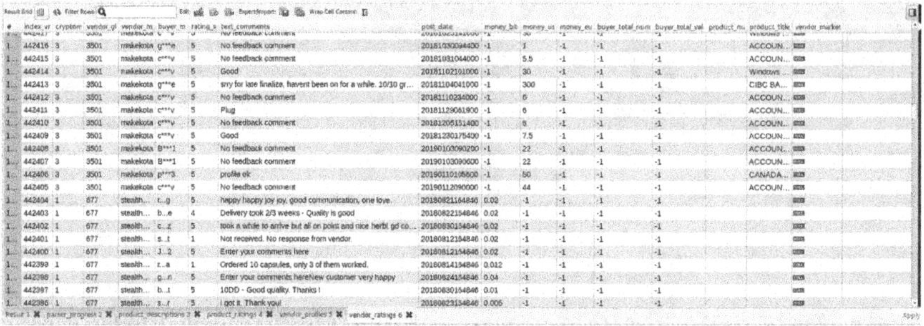

Fig. 7. The screenshot of the "vendor_ratings" table in MySQL Workbench

The hue is proportional to the number of ads. We can see that a large number of ads are from USA, UK, Australia, Germany, and Canada. A small number of ads are from Russia because we did not scrape the Russian cryptomarket called the Black Market.

We further construct a social network among buyers and vendors. Each node represents a buyer or a vendor, and each edge represents that a buyer orders products from a vendor. The ordering information is collected from the feedback ratings. Figure 9 shows a subgraph of the social network in the Dream Market. The purple nodes represent vendors and the white nodes represent buyers. The buyer IDs are masked and only the initial and last letters are visible. The ten vendors all sell digital goods. From Fig. 9, we can observe the community structures among buyers. Most buyers only buy from one vendor, and only a few buyers buy from more than one vendor. We will analyze the collected data further and discover more patterns.

Fig. 8. The global distribution of ads across the largest seven cryptomarkets

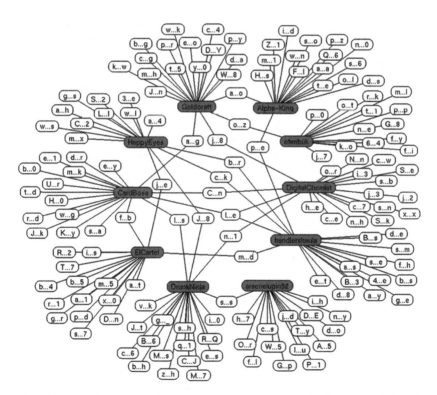

Fig. 9. The social network between buyers and vendors in the Dream Market

6   Conclusion

Cryptomarket websites contain rich information about illicit criminal activities. It is urgent to develop scrapers to collect data from cryptomarkets and then develop AI algorithms for assembling intelligence from the data. In this paper, we design and implement Python scrapers for scraping the seven largest cryptomarkets. This work demonstrates the effectiveness and efficiency of the developed scrapers and provides the foundation for the next stage of data analysis. The source code of the scrapers is publicly available.

References

1. Martin, J.: Drugs on the Dark Net: How Cryptomarkets are Transforming the Global Trade in Illicit Drugs (2014)
2. Aldridge, J., Décary-Hétu, D.: Not an 'Ebay for Drugs': the Cryptomarket 'Silk Road' as aparadigm shifting criminal innovation. Available at SSRN 2436643 (2014)
3. Christin, N.: Traveling the silk road: a measurement analysis of a large anonymous online marketplace. In: Proceedings of the 22nd International Conference on World Wide Web, pp. 213–224. ACM (2013)
4. EMCDDA: Europol: DarkNet markets ecosystem – lifetimes and reasons for closure of over 100 global darknet markets offering drugs, sorted by date (2018)
5. European Monitoring Centre for Drugs and Drug Addiction and Europol: Drugs and the DarkNet: perspectives for enforcement, research and policy (2017)
6. DarkNet Market Archives (2013–2015). https://www.gwern.net/DNM-archives. Accessed 12 Feb 2019
7. Lawrence, H., Hughes, A., Tonic, R., Zou, C.: D-miner: a framework for mining, searching, visualizing, and alerting on darknet events. In: 2017 IEEE Conference on Communications and Network Security (CNS), pp. 1–9. IEEE (2017)
8. Hayes, D., Cappa, F., Cardon, J.: A framework for more effective dark web marketplace investigations. Information **9**(8), 186 (2018)
9. Tor Relay Configurator. https://tor-relay.co/. Accessed 15 Feb 2019
10. Tor Good Bad ISPs. https://trac.torproject.org/projects/tor/wiki/doc/GoodBadISPs. Accessed 15 Feb 2019
11. Tor Relay Guide. https://trac.torproject.org/projects/tor/wiki/TorRelayGuide. Accessed 15 Feb 2019
12. Tor Manual. https://www.torproject.org/docs/tor-manual.html.en. Accessed 15 Feb 2019
13. Tor Relay Search. https://metrics.torproject.org/rs.html. Accessed 15 Feb 2019
14. Check Tor Connection. https://check.torproject.org. Accessed 15 Feb 2019

Characteristics of Bitcoin Transactions on Cryptomarkets

Xucan Chen[1]([✉]), Mohammad Al Hasan[2], Xintao Wu[3], Pavel Skums[1],
Mohammad Javad Feizollahi[4], Marie Ouellet[5], Eric L. Sevigny[5], David Maimon[5],
and Yubao Wu[1]

[1] Department of Computer Science, Georgia State University, Atlanta, GA, USA
xchen41@student.gsu.edu, {pskums,ywu28}@gsu.edu
[2] Department of Computer and Information Science,
Indiana University - Purdue University Indianapolis, Indianapolis, IN, USA
alhasan@iupui.edu
[3] Department of Computer Science and Computer Engineering,
University of Arkansas, Fayetteville, AR, USA
xintaowu@uark.edu
[4] Institute for Insight, Georgia State University, Atlanta, GA, USA
mfeizollahi@gsu.edu
[5] Department of Criminal Justice and Criminology, Georgia State University, Atlanta, GA, USA
{mouellet,esevigny,dmaimon}@gsu.edu

Abstract. Cryptomarkets (or darknet markets) are commercial hidden-service websites that operate on The Onion Router (Tor) anonymity network. Cryptomarkets accept primarily bitcoin as payment since bitcoin is pseudonymous. Understanding bitcoin transaction patterns in cryptomarkets is important for analyzing vulnerabilities of privacy protection models in cryptocurrecies. It is also important for law enforcement to track illicit online crime activities in cryptomarkets. In this paper, we discover interesting characteristics of bitcoin transaction patterns in cryptomarkets. The results demonstrate that the privacy protection mechanism in cryptomarkets and bitcoin is vulnerable. Adversaries can easily gain valuable information for analyzing trading activities in cryptomarkets.

Keywords: Cryptomarket · Cryptocurrency · Bitcoin · Peeling chain · Transaction graph

1 Introduction

The darknet is a portion of the Internet that purposefully protects the identities and privacy of both web servers and clients. The Onion Router (Tor) is the most popular instance of a darknet and also the most popular anonymous network. Tor provides hidden services (also known as onion services) for users to hide their locations and identities while offering web publishing services. A cryptomarket (or darknet market) is a commercial website operating on the darknet. Specifically, in Tor, a crytomarket is a hidden service website with a ".onion" link address. Most products being sold in cryptomarkets are illicit. Some example popular products in cryptomarkets are drugs, malware, and stolen credit cards. After the demise of the first cryptomarket called Silk Road on 2013, new cryptomarkets have proliferated. As of March 2019, we have observed at

© Springer Nature Switzerland AG 2019
G. Wang et al. (Eds.): SpaCCS 2019, LNCS 11611, pp. 261–276, 2019.
https://doi.org/10.1007/978-3-030-24907-6_20

Table 1. Cryptomarkets and their accepted cryptocurrencies as of March 2019

Cryptomarkets	#Ads	Bitcoin	Monero	Litecoin	Ethereum	Bitcoin cash
Dream	166, 216	✓				✓
Berlusconi	38, 462	✓				
Wall Street	16, 847	✓	✓			
Empire	9, 538	✓	✓	✓		
Point Tochka	6, 468	✓			✓	✓
Silk Road 3.1	5, 738	✓	✓	✓	✓	

least 35 active cryptomarkets. Table 1 shows the largest six cryptomarkets at present according to the total number of ads listed in each market.

From Table 1, we can see that bitcoin is accepted in all cryptomarkets. In addition to bitcoin, four other types of cryptocurrencies are also accepted by different markets. They are monero, litecoin, ethereum, and bitcoin cash. Note that bitcoin cash is a variant of but different than bitcoin and is an independent currency. Bitcoin cash is generally considered to be faster in the transaction confirmation process but less secure than bitcoin. In our study, we focus on bitcoin since it is the most popular cryptocurrency and widely accepted by all markets. The observed bitcoin transaction patterns in this paper provide insights for analyzing other types of cryptocurrencies.

Bitcoin is the first decentralized cryptocurrency (also known as digital currency or electronic cash). Bitcoin operates on the peer-to-peer network without the need for intermediaries and there are no central banks or administrators. Transactions are verified by network nodes via cryptography and recorded in a public distributed ledger called a blockchain. Bitcoin has millions of unique users. Bitcoin is pseudonymous because funds are not tied to real-world entities but rather bitcoin addresses. Owners of bitcoin addresses are not explicitly identified, but all transactions on the blockchain are public.

Since all bitcoin transactions are public, it is hard to fully protect the privacy of bitcoin users. The news have revealed that adversaries could spy on a careless company by first paying it in bitcoins and then tracking how that money flows [3,4,6]. For better protecting the privacy, bitcoin users have extensively used mixing services to obscure the bitcoin trails [4].

In cryptomarkets, adversaries could place orders and then track money flows. Cryptomarkets display the buyers' feedback in order to demonstrate the vendors' reputation. Figure 1 shows the screenshot of the feedback page in the Dream Market. From Fig. 1, we can see the post time, rating star, text comment, masked buyer ID, and approximate amount of money. Each rating actually represents a bitcoin transaction. Even we can only observe approximate time and money in ratings, the accumulation of a lot of of such approximate transaction records could potentially allow adversaries to reveal relevant bitcoin addresses. Figure 2 shows the screenshot of the feedback page in the Wall Street Market. From Fig. 2, we can observe similar ratings. All markets in Table 1 display feedback publicly. This potentially allows adversaries to re-identify the bitcoin addresses of buyers, vendors, and escrow accounts in cryptomarkets, thus increases the vulnerability of the privacy protection in bitcoin.

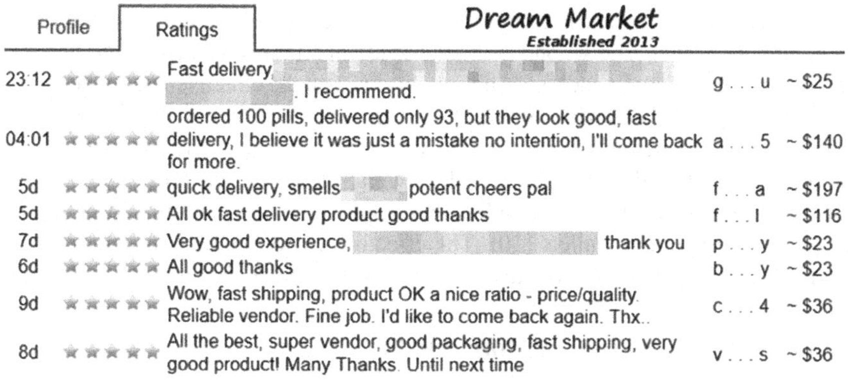

Profile	Ratings	Dream Market	
		Established 2013	

23:12	★★★★★	Fast delivery, ▓▓▓▓▓▓▓▓▓▓▓▓ . I recommend.	g . . . u ~ $25
04:01	★★★★★	ordered 100 pills, delivered only 93, but they look good, fast delivery, I believe it was just a mistake no intention, I'll come back for more.	a . . . 5 ~ $140
5d	★★★★★	quick delivery, smells ▓▓▓▓ potent cheers pal	f . . . a ~ $197
5d	★★★★★	All ok fast delivery product good thanks	f . . . l ~ $116
7d	★★★★★	Very good experience, ▓▓▓▓▓▓▓▓ thank you	p . . . y ~ $23
6d	★★★★★	All good thanks	b . . . y ~ $23
9d	★★★★★	Wow, fast shipping, product OK a nice ratio - price/quality. Reliable vendor. Fine job. I'd like to come back again. Thx..	c . . . 4 ~ $36
8d	★★★★★	All the best, super vendor, good packaging, fast shipping, very good product! Many Thanks. Until next time	v . . . s ~ $36

Fig. 1. The feedback in the Dream Market

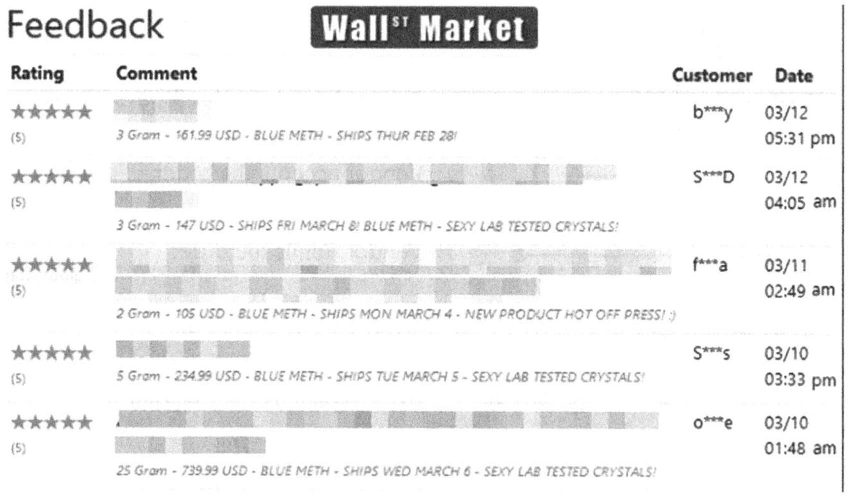

Feedback Wall^ST Market

Rating	Comment	Customer	Date
★★★★★ (5)	▓▓▓▓▓ *3 Gram - 161.99 USD - BLUE METH - SHIPS THUR FEB 28!*	b***y	03/12 05:31 pm
★★★★★ (5)	▓▓▓▓▓▓▓▓▓▓▓▓ ▓▓▓▓ *3 Gram - 147 USD - SHIPS FRI MARCH 8! BLUE METH - SEXY LAB TESTED CRYSTALS!*	S***D	03/12 04:05 am
★★★★★ (5)	▓▓▓▓▓▓▓▓▓▓ ▓▓▓▓▓ *2 Gram - 105 USD - BLUE METH - SHIPS MON MARCH 4 - NEW PRODUCT HOT OFF PRESS! :)*	f***a	03/11 02:49 am
★★★★★ (5)	▓▓▓▓▓ *5 Gram - 234.99 USD - BLUE METH - SHIPS TUE MARCH 5 - SEXY LAB TESTED CRYSTALS!*	S***s	03/10 03:33 pm
★★★★★ (5)	▓▓▓▓▓▓▓▓▓ ▓▓▓▓ *25 Gram - 739.99 USD - BLUE METH - SHIPS WED MARCH 6 - SEXY LAB TESTED CRYSTALS!*	o***e	03/10 01:48 am

Fig. 2. The feedback in the Wall Street Market

In this paper, we systematically study the vulnerabilities of bitcoin privacy that exist in cryptomarkets. We identify and categorize patterns of bitcoin transactions in cryptomarkets. The observations are then used for discussing the possibility of re-identifying bitcoin addresses related to crytomarkets. The conclusions obtained from this paper can help design better bitcoin payment systems and strengthen the privacy protection. On the other hand, the conclusions can also be used by law enforcement to understand the activities in cryptomarkets.

2   Related Work

Ron et al. is the first to build a bitcoin graph and analyze the quantitative attributes in bit-coin transaction history [16]. Clustering bitcoin addresses into wallets is one basic task in the bitcoin transaction analysis. Researchers have widely used two simple heuristics

[8, 10, 18]. The first heuristic is to put shadow/change address together with its input address into one wallet. The second heuristics is to put all input addresses into one wallet if there is a single output address. Androulaki et al. test the effectiveness of the bitcoin address clustering methods with stimulation [8]. Spagnuolo et al. link the clustered wallets to the Silk Road escrow addresses exposed by FBI and analyze the bitcoin flow [18]. Fleder et al. not only link the clustered wallets with Silk Road escrow but also link wallets with public wallets [10]. PageRank is then applied on the transaction graph to find interesting and important wallets [10]. The effectiveness of address clustering is also studied [13]. Mixing technology is also introduced to improve the anonymity [17, 19].

3   Escrow Services in Cryptomarkets

In this section, we review the escrow services in cryptomarkets. All cryptomarkets provide escrow services to avoid scams and protect both buyers and vendors.

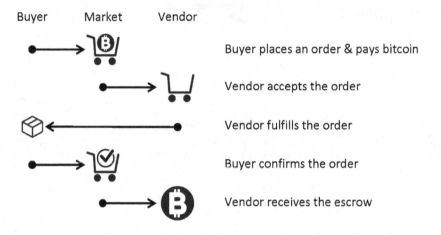

Fig. 3. A flowchart depicting a transaction in cryptomarkets

Figure 3 shows the typical process of one transaction [12]. The buyer places an order and pays with bitcoins after browsing the products within the Tor web browser. The market holds the bitcoins until the buyer confirms the order. The vendor accepts and fulfills the order. The buyer confirms the order and gives feedback reviews. The market releases the bitcoins to the vendor and charges a commission fee. If the buyer is not satisfied with the product or service, the buyer disputes the order. In this case, the market decides where the escrow bitcoins go. The escrow bitcoins go either back to the buyer or to the vendor depending on the dispute result.

4   Parsing and Understanding Bitcoin Transactions

To trace the bitcoin flow, we parse the blocks in the public bitcoin blockchain and obtain the bitcoin transactions. We install the bitcoin core program [2] and run a bitcoin full node [7]. The bitcoin full node automatically synchronizes with other nodes in the bitcoin network, and downloads all blocks in the blockchain. The blocks contain the public ledger data and are the inputs of our parsing algorithm. A new block is generated around every 10 min.

Algorithm 1. Parsing Bitcoin Transactions

Input: Blocks in the bitcoin blockchain
Output: Bitcoin transactions (a set of .json files whose names are formatted timestamps)

```
 1:  for each block do
 2:      transaction_time ⇐ block.timestamp;
 3:      create a new file: formatted_transaction_timestamp.json;
 4:      for each transaction in the block.transactions do
 5:          transaction_hash ⇐ transaction.this_transaction_hash;
 6:          receiver_list = [] ;
 7:          for each receiver in the transaction.receivers do
 8:              receiver_list.add(receiver.index, receiver.bitcoin_address,
                     receiver.bitcoin_value)
 9:          sender_list = [] ;
10:          for each sender in the transaction.senders do
11:              sender_list.add(sender.index, sender.previous_transaction_hash,
                     sender.previous_transaction_index)
12:          [transaction_time, transaction_hash, sender_list, receiver_list] ⇒
                formatted_transaction_timestamp.json
```

Algorithm 1 shows our parsing algorithm. We use the existing Python bitcoin parser to parse the blocks (raw Bitcoin data) and construct the bitcoin transaction tree [1,5]. In Algorithm 1, we parse the blocks one by one (lines 1–12) and save one timestamp for all transactions in one block (line 2). For each transaction in one block, we parse the transaction hash (line 5), the receiver list (lines 6–8), and the sender list (lines 9–11). Each transaction contains four parts: timestamp, hash, sender_list, and receiver_list, and is written into a json file (line 12). One receiver contains the bitcoin address and the bitcoin values. Each sender in one transaction does not contain bitcoin address neither bitcoin value. Instead, each sender contains transaction hash and index pointing to an earlier transaction. We can use that transaction hash to retrieve the earlier transaction and use the transaction index to find the referred receiver from the receiver list. By linking the sender in current transaction with the receiver in the earlier transaction, we can generate a bitcoin transaction flow tree.

Algorithm 2 shows the construction of bitcoin transaction flow tree. Algorithm 2 processes the json files in the chronological order. This guarantees that old transactions will be processed earlier than new transactions. Since a receiver has bitcoin address, we can directly add a node (transaction_hash, bitcoin_address) to the flow tree. Since a sender does not have bitcoin address, we need to look it up in an earlier transaction. Since earlier transactions have been processed, the sender must exist in the node set V as a receiver. Therefore, we search over all the nodes in V and compare the transaction_hash and index values (lines 8). Then we add an edge from this earlier receiver to the current receiver in flow tree. If there are multiple senders and receivers in a mixing

---

Algorithm 2. Constructing Bitcoin Transaction Flow Tree

Input: Bitcoin transactions (a set of .json files whose names are formatted timestamps)
Output: Bitcoin transaction flow tree $G(V, E)$

1: read the list of json files;
2: **for** *each json file (process them in the chronological order)* **do**
3:    read all transactions in the json file;
4:    **for** *each transaction tx* **do**
5:       **for** *each receiver in tx.receiver_list* **do**
6:          add node r = [tx.transaction_hash, receiver.index, receiver.bitcoin_address, receiver.bitcoin_value] to the node set V;
7:          **for** *each sender in tx.sender_list* **do**
8:             find node $s \in V$ with s.transaction_hash = sender.previous_transaction_hash **and** s.index = sender.index;
9:             add an edge (s, r) to the edge set E;

Algorithm 3. Local search algorithm for extracting a subtree

Input: Bitcoin transaction flow tree $G(V, E)$, query $q = (q\_hash, q\_btc\_address)$, k hops
Output: Subtree $G[T]$

1: ignore the edge direction, $G.Adj[u]$ represents the neighbors;
2: **for** *each node $v \in V$* **do** $v.d = \infty$;
3: $S \Leftarrow \{q\}; T \Leftarrow \{\}; q.d = 0$;
4: **while** *True* **do**
5:    extract node u with minimum $u.d$ value among all nodes in the set $S - T$;
6:    **if** $u.d > k$ **then** break;
7:    $T \Leftarrow T \cup u; S \Leftarrow S \cup G.Adj[u]$;
8:    **for** *each node x in $G.Adj[u]$* **do** $x.d = \min\{x.d, u.d + 1\}$;

---

transaction, these senders and receivers will form a complete bipartite graph, i.e., there is an edge from any sender to any receiver. We do not know who sends money to whom in a mixing transaction.

Algorithm 3 shows a local search algorithm that retrieves a subtree containing all nodes that are k-hop away from the query node. The query node is determined by the transaction hash and bitcoin address. In our experiment, we use Algorithm 3 to extract a subtree given an query node containing our bitcoin address. The subtree is nimble for us to analyze interesting patterns.

Shadow Address: Bitcoin creates a new address for the sender in each transaction to obtain better anonymity [15]. The newly generated address is called "shadow address" or "change address" of the original address of the sender [8]. Figure 4 shows one bitcoin transaction. The sender's original address has ฿.09. After ฿.05 is sent to the receiver, the sender still has ฿.04 in the change address.

Multiple inputs and single output: Considering the multiple addresses one user can own, bitcoin supports a user to send bitcoins from multiple addresses in one transaction.

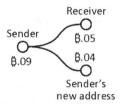

Fig. 4. Shadow address

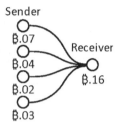

Fig. 5. Multi-inputs

Figure 5 shows one bitcoin transaction containing multiple inputs and one output. The sender sends money from four bitcoin addresses to the receiver's address. We assume that it is unlikely that two senders send money to the same address at the same time since the bitcoin addresses keep changing. If we observe a transaction with multiple inputs and single output, we can assume all input addresses belong to the same sender. These two properties help track bitcoin flows or cluster addresses into wallets [8, 10, 14].

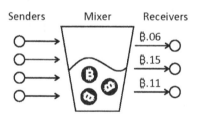

Fig. 6. A mixing transaction

Mixing services: are widely used as a privacy overlay on top of bitcoin [11]. Mixing services are also known as tumblers. The mixer will mix several transactions into one, intending to confuse the trail linking back to the source. In a mixing transaction, the multiple inputs are from different senders and the multiple outputs go to different receivers. Mixing services reduce the traceability of bitcoin flows which makes the analysis of bitcoin graph more difficult. Figure 6 shows a mixing transaction with four senders and three receivers. In this example, we do not know who send money to whom because there are multiple possible flows.

5   Actions and Observed Resulting Transactions

In this section, we describe our experiments in cryptomarkets. All cryptomarkets offer escrow services to avoid scams. With the escrow service, the bitcoin is saved in escrow accounts after a buyer places an order and is sent to the vendor until the buyer confirms the order. Since we know the start point (buyer address) of the transaction, we can trace bitcoin flows to uncover escrow and vendors' addresses.

Table 2. Observed bitcoin flow from operation in different cryptomarkets

Cryptomarkets	Deposit	Withdraw	Order	Confirm
Point Tochka	✓	✓	✓	✓
Dream	✓	✓	No observation	No observation
Empire	✓	✓	No observation	No observation
Silk Road 3.1	✓	✓	No observation	No observation
Wall Street	No such function	No such function	✓	✓
Berlusconi	No such function	No such function	✓	No observation

In each market, four operations are performed: deposit, withdraw, order, and confirmation. The resulting transactions may or may not be observed in the bitcoin transaction flow. Table 2 shows whether we can observe the bitcoin transactions for the four operations in cryptomarkets. From Table 2, we can see that the Dream, Empire, and SilkRoad 3.1 Market operate in a similar way. These markets require buyers to deposit bitcoins first. When buyers withdraw bitcoins from the market, the market will send bitcoins to buyers' wallets from an address different than the deposit address. When we order or confirm a purchase, we cannot observe any transactions in bitcoin flow. The Point Tochka Market also requires deposit. When we order and confirm a purchase in the Point Tochka Market, we can observe the transactions from buyer to escrow and then to vendor in the bitcoin flow. The Wall Street and Berlusconi Markets do not require deposit. In the Wall street Market, when we order and confirm a purchase, we can also observe the corresponding transactions in the bitcoin flow. In the Berlusconi Market, we

Table 3. Deposit and withdrawal in the Point Tochka Market

Action	Observed bitcoin transaction		Balance
	Sender	Receiver	
Deposit ฿.0024	A1: ฿.0030 ⟶	B1: ฿.0024, A2: ฿.0006	฿.0024
Withdraw ฿.0008	B1: ฿.0024 ⟶	A2: ฿.0008, B1: ฿.0016	฿.0016
Deposit ฿.0010	A2: ฿.0006, A2: ฿.0008 ⟶	B1: ฿.0026, A3: ฿.0004	฿.0026
Withdraw ฿.0006	B1: ฿.0026 ⟶	A3: ฿.0006, B1: ฿.0020	฿.0020

can observe the transactions in bitcoin flow when we order. The bitcoins sent to escrow are transferred to other escrow addresses through mixing service before we confirm the purchase. Therefore, we cannot observe the transaction when we conform the purchase.

In the next, we will study the bitcoin transaction patterns when we interact with the markets. We first study the deposit and withdrawal actions and then the order and confirmation actions. In each market, four operations are performed: deposit ฿.0024, withdraw ฿.0008, deposit ฿.0010, and withdraw ฿.0006. We monitor the bitcoin transaction flow to see whether we can observe any related transactions or not. To simplify the illustration, we omit the fees charged during the deposit and withdrawal actions.

Deposit and Withdrawal in the Point Tochka Market: Table 3 shows the actions we perform and the resulting bitcoin transactions in the Point Tochka Market. In Table 3, each row represents an action we perform and the resulting Bitcoin transaction. We use letter "A" followed by an integer to represent our bitcoin addresses and letter "B" followed by an integer to represent the deposit bitcoin addresses provided by the market. For example, in the first row, we deposit ฿.0024 and the resulting transaction is "A1: ฿.0030 → B1: ฿.0024, A2: ฿.0006". In the sender part "A1: ฿.0030", A1 represents our bitcoin address and ฿.0030 represents the money in that address. In the receiver part "B1: ฿.0024, A2: ฿.0006", B1 represents the deposit bitcoin address provided by the Point Tochka Market, ฿.0024 represents the money that B1 receives, A2 represents our new bitcoin address, and ฿.0006 represents the change in the new address A2. The last column in Table 3 shows the balance in the market wallet.

In the second row of Table 3, we withdraw ฿.0008 and the resulting transaction is "B1: ฿.0024 → A2: ฿.0008, B1: ฿.0016". B1 still represents the deposit bitcoin address and A2 still represents our bitcoin address for receiving the money. We further deposit ฿.0010 and withdraw ฿.0006, and the resulting transactions are shown in Table 3.

From Table 3, we can see that the deposit bitcoin address in the market does not change. Among all cryptomarkets in Table 1, the Point Tochka Market has the most transparent bitcoin transaction flows, which can be further confirmed when we study the order and confirmation actions.

Table 4. Deposit and withdrawal in the Dream Market

| Action | Observed bitcoin transaction | | Balance |
	Sender	Receiver	
Deposit ฿.0024	A1: ฿.0030 ⟶	B1: ฿.0024, A2: ฿.0006	฿.0024
Withdraw ฿.0008	B2: ฿.0008 ⟶	A2: ฿.0008	฿.0016
Deposit ฿.0010	A2: ฿.0006, A2: ฿.0008 →	B3: ฿.0010, A3: ฿.0004	฿.0026
Withdraw ฿.0006	B4: ฿.0006 ⟶	A4: ฿.0006	฿.0020

Deposit and Withdrawal in the Dream Market: We perform the same sequence of actions in the Dream Market and Table 4 shows the resulting transactions. From Table 4, we can see that the bitcoin address B2 that sends us money during the first withdrawal is different than the bitcoin address B1 that receives our money during the first deposit. After the second withdrawal, we find that there is still ฿.0024 in B1. This means that the Dream Market uses different bitcoin addresses to receive deposit and send withdrawal. From the subsequent deposit and withdrawal actions, the deposit is sent to B3 and the withdrawal is received from B4. This further confirms the observation. This mechanism makes it harder to track the bitcoin flow, thus better protects the privacy of the market and prevents the re-identification attack.

The Empire and Silk Road 3.1 Markets have similar transaction patterns as Dream Market for the deposit and withdrawal actions. We omit the tables for them. The Wall Street and Berlusconi Markets provide neither deposit nor withdrawal functions. They allow buyers directly pay from their own bitcoin addresses.

In the next, we study patterns in the resulting bitcoin transactions for the order and confirmation actions.

Table 5. Order and confirmation in the Point Tochka Market

Action	Observed bitcoin transaction		Balance
	Sender	Receiver	
Order ฿.0014	B1: ฿.0040 ⟶	C1: ฿.0014, B1: ฿.0026	฿.0026
Confirm	C1: ฿.0014 ⟶	D1: ฿.0014	฿.0026
Order ฿.0015	B1: ฿.0026 ⟶	C2: ฿.0015, B1: ฿.0011	฿.0011
Confirm	C2: ฿.0015 ⟶	D2: ฿.0015	฿.0011

Order and Confirmation in the Point Tochka Market: We purchase two orders and Table 5 shows the resulting bitcoin transactions. After we place the first order, the money is sent from the deposit bitcoin address B1 to an escrow account C1. The balance is sent back to B1. After the vendor fulfills the order, we confirm it. The money in the escrow C1 is then immediately transferred to a new bitcoin address D1, which is suspected of being the vendor's bitcoin address. In the second order, we pay ฿0.0015 to a different vendor. Similar to the transactions in the first order, the money moves to an escrow account C2 after the order and then moves from C2 to the destination bitcoin address after confirmation. The escrow address C2 is different than the old escrow address C1. From this experiment, we can see that the bitcoin transaction flows are transparent. For each new order, the market will generate a new escrow bitcoin address. We also observe that our deposit bitcoin address will not change. By tracking the money flowing out of the escrow accounts, we can potentially find the suspicious bitcoin addresses of vendors.

Order and Confirmation in the Dream Market: We also purchase two products in the Dream Market and Table 6 shows the resulting transactions. After we place the first order of ฿0.0014, we find that no transaction associated with the deposit bitcoin address B1 happen. After the vendor fulfills the order and we confirm it, still nothing happens. This means Dream Market uses a different escrow bitcoin address to pay the vendor and the money in the original deposit address B1 does not move. Since we know neither the

Table 6. Order and confirmation in the Dream Market

Action	Observed bitcoin transaction		Balance
	Sender	Receiver	
Order ฿.0014	B1: ฿.0040 does not change		฿.0026
Confirm	B1: ฿.0040 still no change. No transactions observed		฿.0026
Order ฿.0015	B1: ฿.0040 does not change		฿.0011
Confirm	B1: ฿.0040 still no change. No transactions observed		฿.0011

escrow address used to pay the vendor nor the vendor bitcoin address, there is no easy way for us to observe the relevant transactions. We suspect that the Dream Market has its own private ledger to record the balances of the deposit and escrow accounts for each user. After each order, the bitcoin in the deposit account will be transferred to the escrow account. After each confirmation, the bitcoin in the escrow account will be transferred out to vendor's accounts. The ledger of Dream Market might be a private and centralized ledger. This strategy makes the transactions within the Dream Market stealthy and cannot be seen from the public. This strategy well protects the privacy of the market and vendors.

Table 7. Order and confirmation in the Wall Street Market

Action	Observed bitcoin transaction	
	Sender	Receiver
Order ฿.0014	A1: ฿.0040 ⟶ C1: ฿.0014, A2: ฿.0026	
Confirm	C1: ฿.0014 is transferred to another address through mixing	
Order ฿.0015	A2: ฿.0026 ⟶ C2: ฿.0015, A3: ฿.0011	
Confirm	C2: ฿.0015 is transferred to another address through mixing	

Order and Confirmation in the Wall Street Market: The Wall Street Market does not have deposit function. It allows us to pay directly with our bitcoin address. When we purchase, we are required to send a specific amount of bitcoin to a newly generated escrow address and to provide a bitcoin address for receiving the refund if the order fails. Following this procedure, we purchase two products. Table 7 shows the resulting transactions. After we place the first order, we can see the escrow address C1. After we confirm the order, we can observe that the money in the escrow C1 is transferred to a new bitcoin address through a mixing service. Since there are multiple receivers, we do not know which one is the receiver corresponding to the escrow C1.

Order and Confirmation in the Berlusconi Market: The Berlusconi Market does not have deposit function neither. We directly pay with our bitcoin address and Table 8 shows the resulting transactions. After we place the first order, we can see the escrow address C1. But before we confirm the order, the money in the escrow C1 is already transferred to a new bitcoin address through the mixing service. This makes it hard for us to track the bitcoin flows. Similar pattern is observed for the second order. The

Table 8. Order and confirmation in the Berlusconi Market

Action	Observed bitcoin transaction	
	Sender	Receiver
Order ฿.0014	A1: ฿.0040 ⟶ C1: ฿.0014, A2: ฿.0026	
Confirm	C1: ฿.0014 is transferred to another address through mixing	
Order ฿.0015	A2: ฿.0026 ⟶ C2: ฿.0015, A3: ฿.0011	
Confirm	C2: ฿.0015 is transferred to another address through mixing	

Berlusconi Market applies mixing services on escrow addresses to further protect the privacy of the market and vendors.

Since the Wall Street and Point Tochka Markets provide more transparent bitcoin transaction patterns, the feedback reviews may help re-identify the bitcoin addresses of vendors. A feedback review is usually posted right after the buyer confirms the order. Each review represents an approximate bitcoin transaction including approximate date and money. We will see more details in the next sections.

6   Bitcoin Transaction Patterns in the Dream Market

In this section, we track back the bitcoin flows of the withdrawal operation in Dream Market with Algorithm 3. We find a bitcoin address containing more than 800 bitcoins which is worth over 3 million dollars at present, and it collects those bitcoins from multiple addresses in one transaction. Figure 7 shows part of the flow tree we observed. The red node represents our bitcoin address for receiving money in the withdrawal. We observe a bitcoin transaction pattern called "peeling chain" [14].

Peeling Chain: The head of a peeling chain is a bitcoin address with a lot of bitcoins. A small amount of bitcoin is peeled off from this address in a transaction and a "Shadow address" is generated to collect the remaining and still large amount of bitcoin. By repeating this process, the large amount of bitcoin can be peeled down. Peeling chain is popular for organizations dealing with a lot of clients. The bitcoin addresses in a peeling chain are not necessary the addresses of Dream escrow accounts. They might be exchange addresses [9].

The head of this peeling chain is a bitcoin address which receives more than 800 bitcoins. In each transaction, 10 bitcoins are transferred to a new address and the remaining amount is transferred to the shadow address. We call these blue addresses in the main chain the first level escrow addresses. Each of the addresses containing 10 Bitcoins becomes a head of a new smaller peeling chain. In this new chain, one transaction peels off even smaller amount of bitcoin to pay different users. We call the green addresses in the smaller peeling chains the second level escrow addresses. The bitcoins peeled off from the second order addresses are send to third level escrow address, which are white nodes in Fig. 7. The white nodes directly send bitcoins to users (red nodes) of dream market. The amount of bitcoin received by the third order escrow address is exactly the number of bitcoins required by users. No shadow addresses are generated.

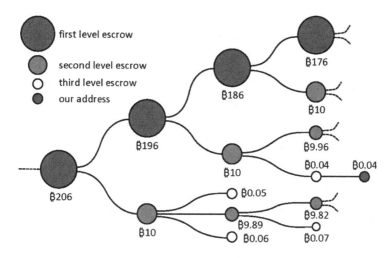

Fig. 7. Bitcoin "peeling chain" patterns in the Dream Market

In addition to this pattern, we also notice that the mixing pattern from the third order escrow addresses to users' addresses. The Dream market allows users to use mixing services. Users need to pay a certain percentage of fees to use mixing services when they withdraw bitcoins.

Clustering bitcoin addresses: The peeling chain patterns can potentially help cluster bitcoin addresses of users in the Dream Market. Since we can track the peeling chain easily, we may be able to identify other transactions happening in the Dream Market by comparing the white-red transactions with the feedback reviews.

7   Bitcoin Transaction Patterns in the Wall Street Market

In this section, we explore the possibility of linking Wall Street feedback reviews with bitcoin transactions. We order a product "Spotify Premium Lifetime Warranty" and pay $1.25 on about 4:40 pm, March 5, 2019, then we confirm the order and write a review by 01:36 am, March 8, 2019. Figure 8 shows some feedback reviews. In Fig. 8, the fourth review is written by us and "u***y" is our account ID. Since we know our bitcoin address "15v3...", we track the money flow. Table 9 shows the transaction relevant to the order action. The output address "33sY..." is the escrow account, and the other output address "14ZK..." is the shadow address containing our remaining money. Table 10 shows the transaction relevant to the confirmation action. It is a mixing transaction containing 24 inputs and 22 outputs. The escrow address "33sY..." is in the sender list. Table 10 shows top three output addresses whose receiving bitcoins are most close to the money we send. By comparing the bitcoins of the three outputs with our money $1.25, we can see that output address "3Jpp..." is most likely to be the vendor's address. We can also see that the transaction happens at 2019-03-08 02:06, which is 30 min later than our review time 01:36 am.

Fig. 8. Feedback ratings in the wall street market

Table 9. The bitcoin transaction relevant to the order action

Hash (txid)	25f33135c87b37205b49a9ade6faa1d6837a4fcb42340270753562b7e1802bee		
Time (UTC)	2019-03-05 16:49	Input count: 1; Output count: 2	
Input 0	15v3cQR4H9iz3nb1tXwNd33ETo7ZEX2wir	฿.03554909	$132.31
Output 0	33sYgQnBkBkm3mDbWJY6KMoT7no1eNd4j5	฿.00032256	$1.20
Output 1	14ZKcens6g6J58kBVGNk3Hs2a94NE3bnUT	฿.03517496	$130.92

We further explore the transactions related to "3Jpp...". Table 11 shows the list of transactions relevant to the reviews in Fig. 8. For example, the first transaction happens at 2019-03-08 23:07 and the amount of money is $1.12, which matches with the feedback review "H***e - 03/08 10:49 pm - 1.25 USD". The time of the transaction is 18-minute later than the time of review. Comparing the reviews in Fig. 8 with the transactions in Tables 10 and 11, we can see we successfully find the transactions of four reviews. For the first and sixth reviews in Fig. 8, we do not find them manually. This is because the vendor may have multiple bitcoin address for receiving money and "3Jpp..." might be just one of them.

We purchase the product again and find the same bitcoin address "3Jpp..." receiving the money. This further confirms that "3Jpp..." belongs to the vendor.

Table 10. The bitcoin transaction relevant to the confirmation action

Feedback	u***y - 03/08 01:36 am - 1.25 USD		
Hash (txid)	27c4946ad1e5e648e987d66a882d98f08ebcb3bae8d11aea70b9dac7219aa036		
Time (UTC)	2019-03-08 02:06	Input count: 24; Output count: 22	
Input 16	33sYgQnBkBkm3mDbWJY6KMoT7no1eNd4j5	฿.00032256	$1.20
Output 8	39o2XAjmFTkSGFrkUPsJRNrDUvUCYiXyP5	฿.00061720	$2.39
Output 10	336djQeGFA4etdRv3xRESoKVV3zHr8YvMv	฿.00020500	$0.79
Output 18	3JppEPMTeUXWY96g5D19k6hhK1QLATdwJV	฿.00029320	$1.14

Table 11. The bitcoin transactions relevant to the feedback reviews in Fig. 8

Feedback	H***e - 03/08 10:49 pm - 1.25 USD		
Hash (txid)	5542aaf1c045f951ba7623510237217d97009eb403778cec6ae101d4462583e1		
Time (UTC)	2019-03-08 23:07	Input count: 47; Output count: 42	
Output 40	3JppEPMTeUXWY96g5D19k6hhK1QLATdwJV	฿.00028800	$1.12
Feedback	h***5 - 03/08 06:33 am - 1.25 USD		
Hash (txid)	bb6a4c9d5c747d941eeb6fc5031973351382cb0550be35bfbefda0c07380b63d		
Time (UTC)	2019-03-08 08:26	Input count: 15; Output count: 20	
Output 19	3JppEPMTeUXWY96g5D19k6hhK1QLATdwJV	฿.00029290	$1.13
Feedback	a***k - 03/07 06:33 pm - 10 USD		
Hash (txid)	c022177c6bb26a2c3ad82b699bb9d3d950131a8b13dd54665e7f6e4f8d8263a3		
Time (UTC)	2019-03-07 19:21	Input count: 35; Output count: 38	
Output 26	3JppEPMTeUXWY96g5D19k6hhK1QLATdwJV	฿.00251950	$9.75

8 Conclusion

We find interesting Bitcoin transaction patterns associated with cryptomarkets. The results demonstrate that the privacy protection mechanism in Bitcoin is still vulnerable in terms of simple analysis. An adversary can easily gain valuable information for analyzing the activities happening in the markets. We discovered different mechanisms applied by different markets. In general, there are two main categories. The first mechanism applied by cryptomarkets like Dream Market, Empire and Silkroad 3.0 requires the users to deposit bitcoin to addresses managed by market owner. These markets has their own ledger to record the bitcoin balance of users. We couldn't observe corresponding bitcoin transactions of buyers' operations. For these market, we can trace the bitcoin flow from "Deposit" and "Withdraw" operations and analyze flow pattern. In second mechanism, buyers operation are directly related with bitcoin transaction, we can find seller's receiver address by matching the product review to the related transaction. WallStreet Market and Point Tochka apply this mechanism.

References

1. Bitcoin-blockchain-parser. https://github.com/alecalve/python-bitcoin-blockchain-parser. Accessed 10 Mar 2019
2. Bitcoin core. https://bitcoin.org/en/bitcoin-core/. Accessed 10 Mar 2019
3. Five surprising facts about bitcoin. https://www.washingtonpost.com/news/the-switch/wp/2013/08/21/five-surprising-facts-about-bitcoin. Accessed 10 Mar 2019
4. How bitcoin lets you spy on careless companies. http://www.https.com//web.archive.org/web/20140209202222/www.wired.co.uk/news/archive/2013-06/06/bitcoin-retail. Accessed 10 Mar 2019
5. How to parse the bitcoin blockchain. http://codesuppository.blogspot.com/2014/01/how-to-parse-bitcoin-blockchain.html. Accessed 10 Mar 2019
6. Mapping the bitcoin economy could reveal users' identities. https://www.technologyreview.com/s/518816. Accessed 10 Mar 2019

7. Running a full node. https://bitcoin.org/en/full-node#what-is-a-full-node. Accessed 10 Mar 2019

8. Androulaki, E., Karame, G.O., Roeschlin, M., Scherer, T., Capkun, S.: Evaluating user privacy in bitcoin. In: Sadeghi, A.-R. (ed.) FC 2013. LNCS, vol. 7859, pp. 34–51. Springer, Heidelberg (2013). https://doi.org/10.1007/978-3-642-39884-1_4

9. de Balthasar, T., Hernandez-Castro, J.: An analysis of bitcoin laundry services. In: Lipmaa, H., Mitrokotsa, A., Matulevičius, R. (eds.) NordSec 2017. LNCS, vol. 10674, pp. 297–312. Springer, Cham (2017). https://doi.org/10.1007/978-3-319-70290-2_18

10. Fleder, M., Kester, M.S., Pillai, S.: Bitcoin transaction graph analysis. arXiv preprint arXiv:1502.01657 (2015)

11. Genkin, D., Papadopoulos, D., Papamanthou, C.: Privacy in decentralized cryptocurrencies. Commun. ACM **61**(6), 78–88 (2018)

12. Gilbert, M., Dasgupta, N.: Silicon to syringe: cryptomarkets and disruptive innovation in opioid supply chains. Int. J. Drug Policy **46**, 160–167 (2017)

13. Harrigan, M., Fretter, C.: The unreasonable effectiveness of address clustering. In: 2016 International IEEE Conferences on Ubiquitous Intelligence & Computing, Advanced and Trusted Computing, Scalable Computing and Communications, Cloud and Big Data Computing, Internet of People, and Smart World Congress (UIC/ATC/ScalCom/CBDCom/IoP/SmartWorld), pp. 368–373. IEEE (2016)

14. Meiklejohn, S., et al.: A fistful of bitcoins: characterizing payments among men with no names. In: Proceedings of the 2013 Conference on Internet Measurement Conference, pp. 127–140. ACM (2013)

15. Nakamoto, S., et al.: Bitcoin: a peer-to-peer electronic cash system (2008)

16. Ron, D., Shamir, A.: Quantitative analysis of the full bitcoin transaction graph. In: Sadeghi, A.-R. (ed.) FC 2013. LNCS, vol. 7859, pp. 6–24. Springer, Heidelberg (2013). https://doi.org/10.1007/978-3-642-39884-1_2

17. Ruffing, T., Moreno-Sanchez, P., Kate, A.: CoinShuffle: practical decentralized coin mixing for bitcoin. In: Kutyłowski, M., Vaidya, J. (eds.) ESORICS 2014. LNCS, vol. 8713, pp. 345–364. Springer, Cham (2014). https://doi.org/10.1007/978-3-319-11212-1_20

18. Spagnuolo, M., Maggi, F., Zanero, S.: BitIodine: extracting intelligence from the bitcoin network. In: Christin, N., Safavi-Naini, R. (eds.) FC 2014. LNCS, vol. 8437, pp. 457–468. Springer, Heidelberg (2014). https://doi.org/10.1007/978-3-662-45472-5_29

19. Ziegeldorf, J.H., Grossmann, F., Henze, M., Inden, N., Wehrle, K.: CoinParty: secure multiparty mixing of bitcoins. In: Proceedings of the 5th ACM Conference on Data and Application Security and Privacy, pp. 75–86. ACM (2015)

Effectiveness of Machine Learning Based Intrusion Detection Systems

Mohammed Alrowaily[1(✉)], Freeh Alenezi[2], and Zhuo Lu[1]

[1] Department of Electrical Engineering, University of South Florida, Tampa,
FL 33620, USA
malrowaily@mail.usf.edu, zhuolu@usf.edu
[2] Department of Mathematics and Statistics, University of South Florida, Tampa,
FL 33620, USA
fnalenezi@usf.edu

Abstract. Security is the most significant issue in concerns of protecting information or data breaches. Furthermore, attackers present a new variety of cyber-attacks in the market, which prevent users from managing their network or computer system. For that reason, the growth of cybersecurity research studies, such as intrusion detection and prevention systems have great significance. The intrusion detection system (IDS) is an effective approach against malicious attacks. In this work, a range of experiments has been carried out on seven machine learning algorithms by using the CICIDS2017 intrusion detection dataset. It ensued to compute several performance metrics to examine the selected algorithms. The experimental results demonstrated that the K-Nearest Neighbors (KNN) classifier outperformed in terms of precision, recall, accuracy, and F1-score as compared to other machine learning classifiers. Nevertheless, All of the used machine learning classifiers except KNN trained their models in a reasonable time.

Keywords: Intrusion Detection System · Machine learning ·
IDS dataset · Cybersecurity · Classification algorithms

1 Introduction

Intrusion is an intense problem in security and a prime complication of data breaches, given that a single circumstance of intrusion may steal or even delete information coming from computer as well as network units in a few seconds. Intrusion can easily also destroy system equipment. Additionally, the intrusion may trigger significant reductions economically as well as weaken the IT crucial facilities, thereby causing info inferiority in cyber war. For that reason, intrusion detection is necessary, and also its prevention is required [1]. The appearance of cutting-edge attacks drives the commercial enterprise and academic community to look into for unique approaches, which manage to tightly keep track of this competition and fine-tune rapidly to the transformations in the field [11].

© Springer Nature Switzerland AG 2019
G. Wang et al. (Eds.): SpaCCS 2019, LNCS 11611, pp. 277–288, 2019.
https://doi.org/10.1007/978-3-030-24907-6_21

Network security can be attained by employing a software application called an Intrusion Detection Systems (IDS) that helps to withstand network breaches. The objective of these systems is to have shield wall which prevents such types of attacks. It identifies the illegal activities of a network or a computer system. Generally, there are two major categories of IDS, namely Anomaly detection and Misuse detection. The former learns from recorded normal behavior to identify new intrusion attacks. Any variance from existing baseline patterns is determined as attacks and alarms are triggered. Nevertheless, misuse detection detects the intrusion based on the repository of attacks signatures but has no false alarm.

Machine learning approaches has been extensively utilized in determining different sorts of attacks, which is a powerful tool to enhance network security. In addition, it can assist the network's monitoring team in taking the necessary countermeasures for protecting against intrusions.

In this paper, we utilize the public real-world intrusion dataset CICIDS2017 [13], which includes benign and the most sophisticated attacks and presenting results of seven machine learning classifiers, such as AdaBoost [8], Naive-Bayes (NB) [10], Random Forest (RF) [5], Decision Tree [12], Multi-layer perceptron (MLP) [14], K-Nearest Neighbors (KNN) [9], and Quadratic Discriminant Analysis (QDA) [6].

The main contributions of this paper at hand are as follows:

- First, the discussion of various existing literature studies for building an IDS using different machine learning classifiers is presented, emphasizing on the detection mechanism, applied feature selection, attacks detection efficiency.
- Second, we examine the CICIDS2017 dataset that includes benign and the most cutting-edge common attacks. Likewise, we carried out various machine learning algorithms to analyze the detection performance of IDS.
- Finally, we extensively evaluate our system over different performance metrics such as accuracy, precision, recall, and F1-score, training and prediction time.

The remaining parts of this paper are organized as follows. Section 2, presents a literature review of the related work that only uses the same CICIDS2017 dataset for intrusion detection. Section 3, introduces the implemented dataset in details with explanation of the attack scenarios. Section 4, gives a brief overview of machine learning classifiers. Section 5, discusses the performance results of the classifiers over different evaluation metrics. Finally, the conclusion to our work is given in Sect. 6.

2   Related Work to the CICIDS2017 Dataset

Over the last few years, attempts to attacks on determining sizable data have revved up. In this part, different research studies employing machine learning for intrusions detection have been analyzed. In each research study, the applied machine learning algorithms and system performance are provided. When selecting these research studies, the focus was on the ones that used different machine learning algorithms on the CICIDS2017 dataset.

Sharafaldin et al. [13] have proposed a new dataset named as the CICIDS2017. Their IDS experiments were performed over seven well-known machine learning classifiers, namely AdaBoost, Random Forest, Naive Bayes, ID3, MLP, KNN, and QDA. They claim that the highest accuracy was achieved by KNN, RF and ID3 algorithms, but this paper is lack of accuracy rate results.

Ustebay et al. [15] propose a hybrid IDS using the CICIDS2017 dataset, which combining classifier model based on tree-based algorithms namely REP Tree, JRip algorithm, and Random Forest. They claim that their proposed system experimental results prove superiority supremacy in terms of false alarm rate, detection rate, accuracy and time overhead as compared to state of the art existing schemes. Attacks are detected with 96.665% accuracy rate.

Boukhamla et al. [4] describe and optimize the CICIDS2017 dataset using Principal Component Analysis (PCA), which results in dimensionality reduction without losing specificity and sensitivity. Hence, decreasing the overall size and bring on faster IDS. This work has been employed on the recorded data of Friday and Thursday, which targeted various attacks (DDoS, Botnet, Port-scan, Web attacks and Infiltration). The dataset is examined employing three classifiers including KNN, C4.5 and Naive Bayes. The highest detection rate for DDoS was achieved by Naive Bayes, and KNN classifiers are 90.6% and 99% respectively. As a result, Naive Bayes has an elevated false alarm rate (59%) which in turn classify KNN (with 1.9% of false alarm rate) as a sufficient classifier for a DDoS attack. The number of attributes had notably been lowered, roughly by 75%, of the total attributes number.

Zegeye et al. [16] proposed a machine learning Multi-Layer Hidden Markov (HMM) model based intrusion detection. This multi-layer approach factors a substantial issue of large dimensionality to a discrete set of reliable and controllable elements. Moreover, it can be broadened further than two layers to capture multi-phase attacks over long periods of time. The portion of Thursday morning records in the CICIDS2017 dataset was used which comprises of Web Attack-Brute Force, SSH Patator, and Benign traffic. The proposed system reveals a good performance among all evaluation metrics as 98.98% accuracy, 97.93% precision, 100% recall, and 98.95% F_measure.

Aksu et al. [2] propose an IDS using supervised learning techniques and Fisher Score feature selection algorithm, on the CICIDS2017 dataset for benign and DDoS attacks. Their work was performed on Support Vector Machine, Decision Tree and K-Nearest Neighbours machine learning algorithms. The performance measurements show that the KNN performed much better outcomes with 30 features; the examination scores did not change for Decision Tree algorithm. Alternatively, SVM's outcomes did not fulfill with both 80 and 30 features. After using Fisher Score feature selection, the dataset was reduced by 60%. As an accuracy outcome of this study, 0.9997% KNN, 0.5776% SVM, 0.99% DT accomplished when selecting 30 features.

Hou et al. [7] presented a machine learning approach based DDoS attack detection via NetFlow analysis. Different machine learning classification algorithms were primarily evaluated namely C4.5 Decision Tree, Random Forest, AdaBoost, and Support Vector Machines against their NetFlow collected data. This DDoS detection approach was secondarily evaluated by using public dataset CICIDS2017 to prove its validity. The experiment consequences indicate that this approach obtains an average accuracy of 97.4% and a false positive 1.7%.

Bansal and Kaur [3] proposed an intrusion detection approach, named XGBoost. In the study, the relevant system created by employing the Wednesday recorded dataset that consists of various sort of DoS attacks from the CICIDS2017. The accuracy of 99.54% was obtained in the case of multi-classification of DoS attacks.

In the relevant works, it is witnessed that research studies employing the same dataset are presenting excellent results. However, when the research studies examined; it is observed that most of the authors partially used the CICIDS2017 dataset in their IDS implementation, which therefore indicates that their IDS are only exposed to some of the attacks in the subject dataset.

3   Data Pre-processing and Analysis

The process of analyzing any given dataset to develop an IDS should certainly involve understanding the dataset in hand, cleaning, then carrying out some powerful statistical methods, that assure achieving the study's goals, along with their predetermined performance metrics. This section shows the process of analyzing CICIDS2017 dataset.

3.1   Benchmark Dataset

CICIDS2017 Dataset [13] generated by the Canadian Institute for Cybersecurity at the University of New Brunswick. Benign and the most sophisticated widespread attacks, for instance, real-world data (PCAPs), are featured in CICIDS2017 dataset. This dataset includes five days records stream on a network generated by computer systems using updated operating systems (OS) which provides for Windows Vista/7/8.1/10, Mac, Ubuntu 12/16 and Kali. Monday records consist of benign traffic. The employed attacks are Brute Force SSH, Brute Force FTP, Infiltration, Heartbleed, Web Attack, DoS, Botnet, and DDoS. All attacks had been applied between Tuesday and Friday.

The formerly available network traffic datasets suffer from the absence of traffic diversity, volumes, anonymized packet information payload, constraints on the attacks range, the lack of the feature set and metadata. Therefore, the CICIDS2017 came to conquer these concerns like different protocols including HTTP, HTTPS, FTP, SSH and also e-mail protocols, which in turn were not offered in the dataset previously. The first two columns of Table 1 present the attack label and their corresponding counts. This number of attack labels is moderately large, where some labels are sufficiently smaller than others, this in fact what makes analyzing the CICIDS2017 dataset still an open issue and there is always a space for improvements in the existing or new machine learning algorithms.

Table 1. Attack distribution in CICIDS2017 dataset

Attack label	Flow count	Flow count (w/cleansing)	Difference	Proportion (%)
Benign	2273097	1893223	379874	0.167
DoS Hulk	231073	173791	57282	0.247
Port Scan	158930	1956	156974	0.012
DDoS	128027	128020	7	0.000
DoS GoldenEye	10293	10286	7	0.000
FTP-Patator	7938	6093	1845	0.232
SSH-Patator	5897	3360	2537	0.430
DoS Slowloris	5796	5385	411	0.070
DoS Slowhttptest	5499	5242	257	0.046
Botnet	1966	1437	10	0.269
Web: Brute Force	1507	37	0	0.024
Web: XSS	652	652	0	0.000
Infiltration	36	36	0	0.000
Web: SQL Injection	21	21	0	0.000
Heartbleed	11	11	0	0.000
Total	2830743	2230983	599760	2.477%

3.2   Description of Attack Scenarios

Here in this dataset, six attack profiles are covered based upon the most updated list of commonly used attack families, which can be explained as follows:

Web Attack: Three web attacks have been implemented in their dataset. First, SQL Injection is an application security vulnerability in which an attacker interferes with the queries that an application makes to its database, to let the unauthorized users view the data. Second, Cross-Site Scripting (XSS) which is happening when the attacker injects malicious code into the victim's web application. Last, Brute Force which tries a probabilistic entire possible passwords to decode the administrator's password.

Botnet Attack: A collection of internet-connected devices such as a home, office or public systems, contaminated by harmful malicious code called malware. It can enable the attacker access to the device and its connection for stealing, taking down a network and IT environment. Botnets attack are remotely controlled by cybercriminals and have turned into one of the most significant threats to security systems today.

Heartbleed Attack: is a severe bug in the implementation of OpenSSL, an open-source implementation of the Transport Layer Security (TLS) and Secure Sockets Layer (SSL) protocols. This vulnerability allows malicious hackers to read portions and steal data from the memory of the victim server.

Brute Force Attack: is a dictionary attack method that generates many successive estimates as to access encrypted data. This attack is commonly used for cracking passwords, locating the hidden web page or content, and decoding Data Encryption Standard (DES) keys.

DDoS Attack: is one of the most popular cyber weapons, in which attempt to exhaust the resources available to an online service and network by flooding it with traffic from several compromised systems, deny legitimate users access to the service.

DoS Attack: is a type of cyber attack on a network that is designed to prevent legitimate users temporarily from accessing computer systems, devices, or other network resources due to malicious cyber activities.

Infiltration Attack: is a piece of malicious that attempts to enter or damage the inside of the network which is generally manipulating a susceptible software like Adobe Acrobat/Reader.

3.3   Evaluation Metrics

Our work subject to different evaluation metrics, which are accuracy, precision, recall, F1-score, training time and prediction time. Since achieving the supreme accuracy does not essentially signify that the classifier properly predicts with high reliability. As a result, we utilize other strategies to examine the reliability of the proposed system results. Table 2 shows the description of confusion matrix.

Table 2. Confusion matrix

		Predicted class	
		Classified as normal	Classified as attack
Actual class	Normal	True Negative (TN)	False Positive (FP)
	Attack	False Negative (FN)	True Positive (TP)

The evaluation metrics are specified based on the following explanations:

- True Positive (TP): describes the number of attacks correctly detected.
- True Negative (TN): describes the number of normal correctly detected.
- False Positive (FP): describes the number of normal wrongly detected.
- False Negative (FN): describes the number of attacks wrongly detected.

Afterward, we calculate the evaluation metrics from the following formulas as shown in Table 3.

- Precision: the proportion of correctly predicted attack relative to all data classified as the attack
- Accuracy: the proportion of records are correctly determined as attack and normal

- F1-Score: a combination that measures the harmonic average of precision and recall.
- Recall: indicating the proportion of correctly predicted attack to all attack data.
- Training time: represents the time consumed for a particular algorithm to train the model for the entire dataset.
- Prediction time: represents the time consumed for a particular algorithm to predict the entire dataset as benign or attack.

Table 3. Evaluation metrics

Metric	Definition
Accuracy	$ACC = \frac{TP+TN}{TP+TN+FP+FN}$
Precision	$Pr = \frac{TP}{TP+FP}$
Recall	$Rc = \frac{TP}{TP+FN}$
F1-Score	$F1 = \frac{2 \times Precision \times Recall}{Precision + Recall}$

3.4 Data Cleansing

We observed that CICIDS2017 dataset include some significant pitfalls which cause the classifier to be biased, and the goal of this paper is to address those imperfections and apply machine learning classification properly to make more accurate results. It might be an essential step to make some modifications to the dataset employing it in practice, rendering it more reliable. For this purpose, in this part, some pitfalls of the CICIDS2017 dataset are remedied, and some data are modified. The dataset contains 2830743 records and 86 features. The updated distribution of this dataset can be shown in Table 1. When we examine these records, it can be noticed that 599760 are faulty records. The first step in the data pre-processing will be to remove these undesirable records.

An additional change that requires to be made in the dataset is that we remove all rows with features "Flow Bytes/s" and "Flow Packets/s" that have either "Infinity" or "NaN" values. Furthermore, we remarked that some features have zero values for all rows, namely Bwd PSH Flags, Fwd URG Flags, Bwd URG Flags, CWE Flag Count, Fwd Avg Bytes/Bulk, Fwd Avg Packets/Bulk, Fwd Avg Bulk Rate, Bwd Avg Bytes/Bulk, Bwd Avg Packets/Bulk, and Bwd Avg Bulk Rate, hence, they are also excluded.

We noticed that the attack label with small counts still maintains that count before and after cleaning the data. By looking at the proportion column, a tiny proportion of each attack type was deleted during the data cleaning process. Lastly, the first column "Destination Port" is also excluded, even though when it was included, we noticed an improvement in the performance of the classifiers. Therefore, the data size used for the analysis is 2230983 records by 69 features.

After the removal of these features, the dataset is randomly split into two parts, 70% was used for training, and 30% was used for testing the model, in order to evaluate their performance in the intrusion detection system.

3.5   Feature Selection

The Random Forest classifier was used to calculate the importance score for each feature. Then, along with the original dataset 69 features, we selected 10, 30 as the most efficient features that can distinguish the information in the most significant way.

4   Overview of Machine Learning Classifiers

This part presents a concise overview of the various machine learning supervised algorithms and demonstrates the needs to carry out machine learning algorithms in numerous areas just like IDS. The implication of ongoing development of modern technologies creates the demand for machine learning algorithms to emerge as more necessary for extracting and analyzing knowledge from a substantial number of created datasets. In this paper, our interest is employing the following machine learning algorithms; due to the fact that the intended CICIDS2017 dataset consists of the pre-defined classes.

Adaptive Boosting (AdaBoost): a boosting approach, is a machine learning algorithm designed to enhance classification efficiency. The fundamental working concept of boosting algorithms can be described as follows; the data are initially sorted into groups with rough draft rules. On any occasion the algorithm is run, new rules are contributed to this rough draft rules. In this manner, several feeble and low-performance rules called "basic rules" are acquired.

Multi-layer perceptron (MLP): is a category of artificial neural networks (ANN). ANN is a machine learning technique that **takes motivation from the method the human brain works.** The objective of this approach is to mimic the human brain properties, for instance, making decisions and obtaining new information. While the human brain is comprised of interconnected nerve cells, ANN is comprised of interconnected artificial cells.

Decision Tree (DT): is the most potent tool in classification and prediction. A Decision Tree is flow diagram such as tree structure, where each tree includes leaves, branches, and nodes. It divides a dataset into scaled-down subsets while simultaneously an associated decision tree is incrementally formed. The final outcome is a tree with leaf nodes and decision nodes.

Naive Bayes (NB): is a family of probabilistic classification technique that benefits from probability theory and the Bayes' Theorem for predictive modeling, which presumes that all attributes are statistically independent. It computes the probabilities for each factor in order to single out the result that has the highest probability.

K-Nearest Neighbors (KNN): is a versatile and sample-based method. It depends on in which the data points are separated into multiple classes, in other words, similar things are near to each other, in order to determine the K-nearest neighbors.

Quadratic Discriminant Analysis (QDA): is a discriminant analysis method that is utilized to identify which variables differentiate between two or more naturally taking place groups; it may have a predictive or a descriptive goal.

Random Forest (RF): is a machine learning approach that utilizes decision trees. Herein method, a "forest" is produced by putting together a substantial number of various decision tree structures which are created in various ways.

5   Test Results and Discussion

The results of using the aforementioned machine learning classifiers are given in Table 4. Based on the values of precision, recall, and F1-Score, the KNN has the best performance among other classifiers, followed by the MLP and Random Forest classifiers. Then, the performance of the Decision Tree, AdaBoost, and Naive Bayes are ranked as fourth, fifth and sixth, respectively. The QDA algorithm has the lowest performance results.

Table 4. Classifier performance results for all 15 attacks

Algorithm	Precision	Recall	F1-Score	Accuracy
Random Forest	0.9469	0.9571	0.9483	0.9571
KNN	0.9953	0.9955	0.9950	0.9955
Naive Bayes	0.7958	0.8487	0.7794	0.8488
Decision Tree	0.8821	0.9040	0.8920	0.9041
MLP	0.9641	0.9705	0.9662	0.9705
AdaBoost	0.8578	0.9173	0.8854	0.9173
QDA	0.7204	0.8488	0.7794	0.8488

The training and predicting times were also computed during the process, and given by Table 5. It can be noted that the KNN requires significantly more time during the training and testing process. This in fact could be a drawback of the classifier, as it memorizes all the training flows. Naive Bayes has the lowest training and predicting times among other classifiers, but, as mentioned earlier, it performed as a second worst classifier on the CICIDS2017 dataset. Thus, it is a trade-off between the performance and prediction time. On the other hand, the MLP classifier has a good balance between its performance and the prediction time.

Table 5. Classifier training and prediction time

Classifier	Training (sec.)	Prediction (sec.)
Random Forest	348.6	5.8
KNN	2590.6	1358.1
Naive Bayes	4.6	7.7
Decision Tree	19.9	0.2
MLP	103.7	1.1
AdaBoost	607.6	15.5
QDA	15.2	10

Since the total number of features after the data cleaning process is 68, the feature importance based on the Random Forest classifier was computed, which helped to rank the 10 and 30 most important features, respectively. The subject machine learning classifiers were carried out on the reduced CICIDS2017 dataset, and the results are given by Table 6. The results indicate similar performance consistency of the classifiers when using only 10 and 30 most important features, respectively. Nevertheless, the performance of the classifiers was higher when considering all the 68 features.

Table 6. Performance results of 10 and 30 features

Algorithm	No. of features	Precision	Recall	F1-Score	Accuracy
Random Forest	30	0.9395	0.9484	0.9382	0.9485
	10	0.9287	0.9401	0.9283	0.9401
KNN	30	0.9944	0.9945	0.9941	0.9946
	10	0.9690	0.9675	0.9675	0.9676
Naive Bayes	30	0.7958	0.8487	0.7794	0.8488
	10	0.7204	0.8488	0.7794	0.8488
Decision Tree	30	0.8816	0.9025	0.8907	0.9026
	10	0.9282	0.9417	0.9305	0.9418
MLP	30	0.9536	0.9625	0.9557	0.9626
	10	0.9347	0.9460	0.9356	0.9460
AdaBoost	30	0.8578	0.9173	0.8854	0.9173
	10	0.8692	0.8901	0.8576	0.8901
QDA	30	0.7204	0.8488	0.7794	0.8488
	10	0.7204	0.8488	0.7794	0.8488

The results can be wrapped up in the following points:

- Despite the training and predicting times, the best performer was found to be the K-Nearest Neighbors (KNN) classifier based on all four evaluation metrics.
- The MLP achieved the second highest performance, and it maintained reasonably small training and prediction times.
- The chosen machine learning classifiers excluding KNN trained their models in a reasonable time period.
- The feature selection based on the Random Forest classifier did not support the classifiers to perform better compared to the usage of all features after the data cleansing process.
- There is no significant difference in the performance of the Naive Bayes and QDA classifiers based on the evaluation metrics, where both have the worst overall performance, regardless of their small training and predicting times.

6 Conclusion

In this paper, several IDS experiments were carried out to examine the efficiency of seven machine learning classifiers, namely AdaBoost, Random Forest, Naive Bayes, Decision Tree, MLP, KNN, and finally QDA. We make use of public intrusion detection dataset (CICIDS2017), which includes benign and most sophisticated popular attacks. The experimental results attest the superiority of the K-Nearest Neighbors (KNN) classifier in terms of various performance metrics such as precision, recall, accuracy and F1-score among other machine learning algorithms. However, all of the selected machine learning classifiers excluding KNN trained their models in an acceptable time period.

Acknowledgments. Mohammed and Freeh would thank Aljouf and Majmaah Universities, respectively, for the scholarship funds.

References

1. Ahmad, I., Basheri, M., Iqbal, M.J., Rahim, A.: Performance comparison of support vector machine, random forest, and extreme learning machine for intrusion detection. IEEE Access **6**, 33789–33795 (2018)
2. Aksu, D., Üstebay, S., Aydin, M.A., Atmaca, T.: Intrusion detection with comparative analysis of supervised learning techniques and fisher score feature selection algorithm. In: Czachórski, T., Gelenbe, E., Grochla, K., Lent, R. (eds.) ISCIS 2018. CCIS, vol. 935, pp. 141–149. Springer, Cham (2018). https://doi.org/10.1007/978-3-030-00840-6_16
3. Bansal, A., Kaur, S.: Extreme gradient boosting based tuning for classification in intrusion detection systems. In: Singh, M., Gupta, P.K., Tyagi, V., Flusser, J., Ören, T. (eds.) ICACDS 2018. CCIS, vol. 905, pp. 372–380. Springer, Singapore (2018). https://doi.org/10.1007/978-981-13-1810-8_37
4. Boukhamla, A., Gaviro, J.C.: Cicids 2017 dataset: performance improvements and validation as a robust intrusion detection system testbed (2018)

5. Breiman, L.: Random forests. Mach. Learn. **45**(1), 5–32 (2001)
6. Hastie, T., Tibshirani, R., Friedman, J.: The elements of statistical learning, Chapter 6 (2001)
7. Hou, J., Fu, P., Cao, Z., Xu, A.: Machine learning based DDoS detection through netflow analysis. In: MILCOM 2018–2018 IEEE Military Communications Conference (MILCOM), pp. 1–6. IEEE (2018)
8. Hu, W., Hu, W., Maybank, S.: Adaboost-based algorithm for network intrusion detection. IEEE Trans. Syst. Man Cybern. Part B (Cybern.) **38**(2), 577–583 (2008)
9. Keller, J.M., Gray, M.R., Givens, J.A.: A fuzzy k-nearest neighbor algorithm. IEEE Trans. Syst. Man Cybern. **4**, 580–585 (1985)
10. Panda, M., Patra, M.R.: Network intrusion detection using Naive Bayes. Int. J. Comput. Sci. Netw. Secur. **7**(12), 258–263 (2007)
11. Papamartzivanos, D., Mármol, F.G., Kambourakis, G.: Introducing deep learning self-adaptive misuse network intrusion detection systems. IEEE Access **7**, 13546–13560 (2019)
12. Quinlan, J.R.: Induction of decision trees. Mach. Learn. **1**(1), 81–106 (1986)
13. Sharafaldin, I., Lashkari, A.H., Ghorbani, A.A.: Toward generating a new intrusion detection dataset and intrusion traffic characterization. In: ICISSP, pp. 108–116 (2018)
14. Tsai, C.F., Hsu, Y.F., Lin, C.Y., Lin, W.Y.: Intrusion detection by machine learning: a review. Expert Syst. Appl. **36**(10), 11994–12000 (2009)
15. Ustebay, S., Turgut, Z., Aydin, M.A.: Intrusion detection system with recursive feature elimination by using random forest and deep learning classifier. In: 2018 International Congress on Big Data, Deep Learning and Fighting Cyber Terrorism (IBIGDELFT), pp. 71–76. IEEE (2018)
16. Zegeye, W., Dean, R., Moazzami, F.: Multi-layer hidden markov model based intrusion detection system. Mach. Learn. Knowl. Extr. **1**(1), 265–286 (2019)

DNS Flood Attack Mitigation Utilizing Hot-Lists and Stale Content Updates

Tasnuva Mahjabin and Yang Xiao[✉]

The University of Alabama, Tuscaloosa, AL 35487, USA
tmahjabin@crimson.ua.edu, yangxiao@cs.ua.edu

Abstract. Domain Name System (DNS) has become a target of the Distributed Denial of Service (DDoS) attacks. When a DNS is under a DDoS flood attack, all the domain information under that DNS becomes unreachable, eventually causing unavailability of those particular domain names. In this paper, we propose a method which includes periodic stale content update and maintains a list of most frequently queried domain names of different DNS servers. Our simulation results show that the our method can serve more than 70% of the total cache responses during a massive DNS Flood attack.

Keywords: DNS Flood · DDoS · Hot-lists · DNS Cache · Stale update

1 Introduction

On Oct. 21, 2016, a huge distributed denial of service (DDoS) attack disabled tens of millions of Internet Protocol (IP) addresses via attacking domain name system (DNS) [1]. This attack proved that DDoS attacks are great danger to our cyberworld.

DNS Cache content and its time-to-live (TTL) have a significant impact on a DNS Flood attack. During a DNS Flood attack, the attacker targets name servers in the DNS hierarchy and floods their resources. Consequently, the name servers cannot continue its normal operations and deny services to the users. When the name servers become unreachable, all the domains under those servers also become unavailable as the servers cannot respond to the DNS-look-up operations. If the intermediate recursive servers maintain a larger cache or the records maintain a longer TTL threshold value – during a DNS flood attack, the resolver can respond to the DNS-look-up from its cache. Thus, the effects of the attack can be reduced by managing a larger cache with a longer TTL threshold value. According to [2], 2016s Dyn_DNS attack was influenced by the low TTL threshold value. But this also introduces some problems. A larger cache needs more memory space which is not always affordable for many organizations or systems. Moreover, during the attack, the victim servers used to move to new IP addresses. A longer TTL threshold value could force to access some invalid records or old addresses. This situation is called *Faulty DNS-Cache Lock* [3]. These invalid

© Springer Nature Switzerland AG 2019
G. Wang et al. (Eds.): SpaCCS 2019, LNCS 11611, pp. 289–296, 2019.
https://doi.org/10.1007/978-3-030-24907-6_22

records result in a large number of unsuccessful reload attempts and contribute to more bandwidth consumption. This makes the attacks severe. Indeed, DNS cache can act positively during an attack since it does not face the attack and it already contains the information needed to take part in address resolution process. But since the existing cache design still could not prevent or mitigate the attacks in 2016, it is time to rethink about improving its contents and functionality.

DNS has become a target of the DDoS attacks. When a DNS is under a DDoS flood attack, all the domain information under that DNS becomes unreachable, eventually causing unavailability of those particular domain names. Therefore, there is a need to mitigate the DDoS attacks to DNS [4]. In this paper, we focus on these cache contents of DNS servers and refresh these stale contents of DNS servers periodically. Moreover, we propose to utilize piggyback response [5] to create a hot list of domain names. This list constitutes the most frequently queried domain names in all queried servers from where a valid DNS response is received. The motivation behind this stale content update and hot list domain names is to keep the cache ready all the time for a prospective DNS flood attack. The refreshed stale content serve any past queries and the hot list domains serve the prospective future queries. Our simulation results show that for a complete outage of the upper level DNS servers for half (50%) of the simulation time due to a DNS flood attack, the resolver completely relies on its cache content.

Our contributions to this work is as follows:

- We propose a method to generate a *hot_list* using piggyback responses to mitigate the attacks.
- Through simulated DNS flood events, we analyze the impact of stale content update and *hot_Lists*.

We organize the rest of the paper as follows: in Sect. 2, we introduce our proposed method. We discuss performance metrics and simulated results in Sect. 3. Finally, we conclude this paper in Sect. 4.

2   Proposed Design

Caching is important and has many applications [6,7]. DNS cache is designed in a simple way to store the resource records for recently queried domains. Usually, these records mostly reflect the behaviors of the users of the system. The cache stores records based on its user's recent visits. Different researches on DNS cache propose to store these information for a longer period of time by either extending the TTL or keeping the TTL expired records in a separate cache [8,9]. These help to answer DNS queries from the cache during the DDoS attacks. But recent DDoS attacks on DNS are still successful, implying that existing cache cannot successfully prevent or mitigate the impact of the attacks. This is because the storage structure of the cache reflects only the recent visits of the users and does not consider any prospective past or future visit. In our work, we propose to upgrade this cache content in the following ways:

- DNS Cache stores not only recently visited records but records visited for a defined period of time. In our proposed design, the DNS cache will store resource records of the domains that have become TTL expired. We propose to update TTL expired records considering it a routine job.
- DNS Cache stores not only recently visited records but records that are mostly visited in upper level servers. We propose to design a cache that maintains a *hot_list*. The hot list contains most queried domains in all upper level servers where the resolver sends a DNS query and gets a valid response. That is when the resolver queries the upper level DNS servers for a particular domain name, in addition to the response to that query that server piggybacks some of its mostly queried domain records in response message.
- We propose to use piggyback response. In our method, we utilize the "Additional Record" section of a DNS response message to piggyback resource records (RRs) of the most frequently queried domain names of a server in the DNS hierarchy. Our system assumes that all the response messages are valid since we accept piggyback RRs from valid responses only. These additional records incur a trivial cost to the packet-switched Internet. A distinctive feature of this response is that it is applicable without any protocol level change. On top of that, it reduces the number of DNS traffic in both local and authoritative DNS servers. In our method, we assume that the DNS servers keep track of its most frequently queried domain names and piggyback RRs of a number of those domain names.

Table 1. Symbols and explanations

Symbol	Definition
S_c	Current cache size
S_e	Extended cache size
S	Proposed cache size after extension
T_c	Current time to update a stale content
T_e	Proposed time to update a stale content
C_c	Cost of current cache
C_e	Cost of proposed cache extension
C	Total cost of proposed cache
S_h	Hot list size
H_r	Cache hit ratio
H_{sr}	Stale content hit ratio
H_{hr}	Hot list content hit ratio
H_{nr}	Normal content hit ratio
ϵ	Optimal increase in size
γ	Optimal increase in cost

Assume that the current cache size in any system under the DNS hierarchy is S_c and the currently used time when a stale cache content is updated is T_c. S_e is the extended cache size in order to store the "Hotlist" and updated stale cache contents. In our system, $S_e \geqslant S_c$ and $S_c + S_e = S$, where S is the new cache size. We also consider, C_c – the current cost to maintain the cache and C_e – the new cost to extend and maintain the proposed cache where, $C_c + C_e = C$. We mainly consider the maintenance cost to handle the most updated cache contents since the storage is not size limited in DNS cache. The maintenance cost includes the overhead cost to keep the contents up-to-date as well as creating our proposed hot-lists. Moreover, we define the cache hit ratio H_r. We further subdivide this to Stale content hit rate H_{sr}, Hot list content hit ratio H_{hr}, and normal content hit rate H_{nr} to better understand the impact of stale update and the created hot list, where $H_{nr} + H_{sr} + H_{hr} = H_r$. We list all of these notations in Table 1. We find the best possible S_h and T_e such that the extended cache size S_e is the optimal size to ensure minimum increase in cost, C_e. We measure the best pair of $\alpha(S_h, T_e)$ to get the optimal value of S_e and as C_e which maximizes the cache hit ratio H_r. That is, to find $\alpha(S_h, T_e)$ such that $S_e \leqslant \epsilon$, $C_e \leqslant \gamma$, and $H_r \sim r_0\%$, where ϵ and γ are the optimal increase in size and cost and r_0 is the expected cache hit rate during a DNS Flood attack.

In our process, we assume that the cost of the storage of the extended cache is negligible. DNS records in the cache takes only 100 bytes storage which is insignificant to the available memory space of today's servers and computers [10]. In general caching in BIND, the very well known DNS software uses passive caching [11]. In other words, the resource records for any domain is obtained and stored in a cache only as a consequence of the client query. If the record is not in the cache, the resolver gets it from the cache or name servers of the upper level of the hierarchy. This information is kept in the cache until the TTL expires or if the name-server process dies. Thus, the cache records could be outdated or obsolete for some domains since during this time the IP address of the record could change. But, for a longer TTL or maybe an inappropriate TTL value, the cache stores these records until a DNS error occurs. This scenario is considered as a cache miss and a new DNS query is issued to get the authoritative records. In order to reduce this kind of cache miss, we consider proactive DNS caching policies or proactive cache renewal. This proactive renewal policies make *automatic-queries* in order to keep the cache contents fresh for the caching duration. In order to reduce the number of cache miss by one, on average, proactive caching performs more than one query. In our proposed method, for each DNS query made to the upper level, the piggyback response message contains fifteen more domain records other than the queried answers. These records also works to update the stale contents, already existing contents with a change in TTL as well as generates the contents of our hot list.

Considering all of these, the cost model of our process can be represented as follows: $Total\_cost = C_m + C_r + C_l$, where C_m represent the cost of cache miss for the first appearance of a host name, C_r is the cost to renew existing records, and C_l is the cost related to generate the hot-lists.

3   Simulations

In order to measure the performance of our system, we use cache hit rate as our metrics. The hit rate is the percentage of the requests served from the stored contents in the cache among all requests for the content [12]. Thus, $H_r = \frac{\sum_{i=1}^{n} h_i}{n}$, where h is the parameter that determines if the requested domain exists in the cache and n is the total number of requests for that particular domain. If the domain is in the cache, then h takes the value 1, otherwise 0. We also consider the relative change in cache miss and DNS queries. This is because our automatic-renewal and hot-list generation increases the number of DNS queries. But since the piggyback responses in our method could also update the stale contents and any current content with a TTL change, we expect to see a positive rate of change in cache hit and DNS requests. We measure how this change in the number of DNS queries contributes to the cache hit rate. Our goal is to increase the hit rate since it indicates improved performance of our process. We evaluate these metrics through a simulated DDoS scenario and analyze those for the performance measurement of our system.

We also consider to update the stale contents in every 10 s after making different trials with different possible update times. The result of these update times are shown that the maximum cache hit and minimum DNS requests are achieved with a 10 s duration of stale content updates. We also evaluate the cache hit rates for three different categories. This also indicates that 10 s period gives the most cache hit in all three categories.

We simulate the DNS address resolution process and the DNS flood attack as a discrete event simulation system. We considered a big range of domain names $(100,000)$ in order to increase the complexity of the method. In our DDoS implementation, we consider when an upper level DNS is under attack, all of the DNS requests are served from the cache. During this attack period, the resolver does not issue any query to the upper level servers for either cache miss or a stale content update. In our simulation, we consider 1 h (3600 s) of active simulation period and update the stale contents in every 10 s. This is because in the current internet structure and in the content centric networking or information centric networking, a very short TTL value is used for load distribution and to ensure mobility of the resources [13]. We also evaluate different stale update duration and based on the results, we see that 10 s provides the most satisfactory metric value. In our system, we consider extremely low (0 s) to moderate TTL (1800 s) value and analyze the impact. For this stale content update and short TTL value, we expect to see a relative increase in the number of DNS requests and a relative decrease in the total cache miss. But surprisingly in our simulation results, we observe a relative decrease in the number of DNS requests over the simulation time. This is because since in our method, we piggyback DNS records with a response message, it significantly improves the cache hit rate and reduces the total number of DNS requests required.

In Figs. 1 and 2, we see the results of our method during a DNS Flood attack. In Fig. 1 we consider an outage of the authoritative DNS servers for half (50%) of the total simulation time. That is half of the simulation time (1800 s) and the resolver could not make a DNS requests for any cache miss or stale update and solely depends on the cache contents. We consider here different DDoS start time from zero minute (at the very beginning of the simulation) to forty minute (more than halfway to the total simulation time) and evaluate how start time impacts the resolution process from the cache. We see that over the different start time, successful cache response increases and it reaches more than 90% even for the 50% downtime for the DDoS. This is because the cache becomes mature over the time with its stale content update and generated hot list contents. One significant result is the response rate from the hot list. It is always far more than the response rate from the normal cache content and updated stale content. It also serves more than 87% (on average) of the total cache hit during this simulation scenario. We also notice that the overall cache hit rate is more than 78% (on average) and it reaches more than 90% (for the 2400 s start time). This is because of the effect of the hot list. When the system recovers from the attack, it can enrich its cache again in a rapid way because of this piggybacked responses.

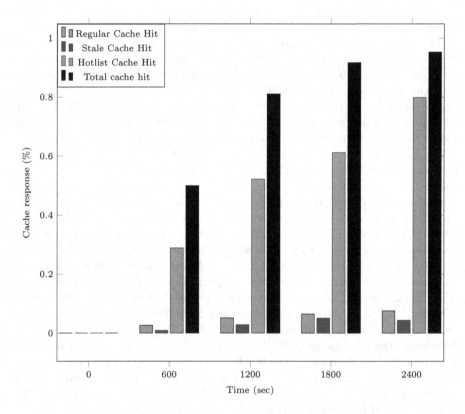

Fig. 1. Cache response (%) over different DDoS start time

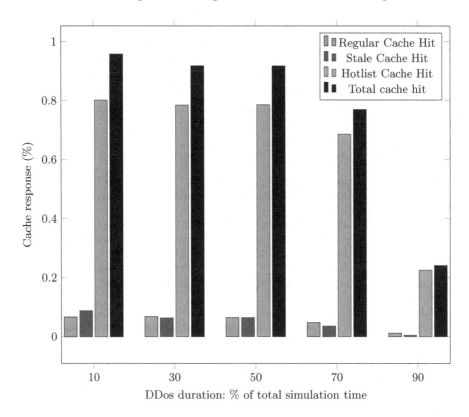

Fig. 2. Cache response (%) over different DDoS duration: 10% to 90% time of the total simulation time

Figure 2 represents the result of the Cache response over different DDoS attack durations. We consider 10% to 90% downtime for a DNS flood attack. During this time, all of the queries are served from the cache without any stale content update or addition of new entries to the hot lists. The resulting plot shows that the cache serves more than 25% of the queries even during 90% downtime. For an 80% downtime, the response is more than 50% and on average more than 78% responses are made from the cache during this simulation scenario. We also notice a very significant response from the hot list contents than from the other two types of the cache content. In this scenario, more than 68% (on average) of the total cache response is served from the hot list contents.

4   Conclusion

In this paper, we propose a robust system which can face DNS DDoS attacks successfully. DNS cache already contains information for address resolution process and never becomes a victim of flood attacks. It is possible to use DNS cache as an important part of the robust infrastructure. It is more like building infrastructure which stands in front of a catastrophic earthquake. In order to build a robust functioning cache, we propose to utilize stale content update and hot list generation using piggyback method. We simulate extreme DNS outage (90% of the total simulation time) and observe the impacts on DNS resolution. Our simulation results show a very promising impact of the proposed hot list.

References

1. Mahjabin, T., Xiao, Y., Sun, G., Jiang, W.: A survey of distributed denial-of-service attack, prevention, andmitigation techniques. Int. J. Distrib. Sens. Netw. **13**(12), 1–33 (2017)
2. Zeifman, I., Margolius, D.: The long and short of TTL – understanding DNS redundancy and the Dyn DDoS attack. https://www.incapsula.com/blog/the-long-and-short-of-ttl-the-ddos-perspective.html. Accessed 18 June 2018
3. Vlajic, N., Andrade, M., Nguyen, U.T.: The role of DNS TTL values in potential DDoS attacks: what do the major banks know about it? Procedia Comput. Sci. **10**, 466–473 (2012)
4. Mahjabin, T., Xiao, Y.: Mitigation process for DNS flood attacks. In: Proceeding of 2019 16th IEEE Annual Consumer Communications & Networking Conference (CCNC), Las Vegas (Short Paper), 11–14 January 2019
5. Shang, H., Wills, C.E.: Piggybacking related domain names to improve DNS performance. Comput. Netw. **50**(11), 1733–1748 (2006)
6. Chen, H., Xiao, Y.: Cache access and replacement for future wireless internet. IEEE Commun. Mag. **44**, 113–123 (2006)
7. Xiao, Y., Chen, H.: Optimal callback with two-level adaptation for wireless data access. IEEE Trans. Mob. Comput. **5**(8), 1087–1102 (2006)
8. Wei-min, L., Lu-ying, C., Zhen-ming, L.: Alleviating the impact of DNS DDoS attacks. In: Second International Conference on Networks Security, Wireless Communications and Trusted Computing, vol. 1, pp. 240–243. IEEE, April 2010
9. Ballani, H., Francis, P.: Mitigating DNS DoS attacks. In: Proceedings of the 15th ACM Conference on Computer and Communications Security, pp. 189–198. ACM, October 2008
10. Jung, J., Sit, E., Balakrishnan, H., Morris, R.: DNS performance and the effectiveness of caching. IEEE/ACM Trans. Networking **10**(5), 589–603 (2002)
11. Cohen, E., Kaplan, H.: Proactive caching of DNS records: addressing a performance bottleneck. Comput. Netw. **41**(6), 707–726 (2003)
12. Cao, P., Irani, S.: Cost-aware WWW proxy caching algorithms. In: USENIX Symposium on Internet Technologies and Systems, vol. 12, no. 97, pp. 193–206 (1997)
13. Jang, B., Lee, D., Chon, K., Kim, H.: DNS resolution with renewal using piggyback. J. Commun. Netw. **11**(4), 416–427 (2009)

Attack-Aware Recovery Controller-Switch-Link Cost Minimization Placement Algorithm in Software-Defined Networking

Cheng Chi Qin[1], Tan Saw Chin[1($\boxtimes$)], Lee Ching Kwang[2], Zulfadzli Yusoff[2], and Rizaluddin Kaspin[3]

[1] Faculty of Computing and Informatics, Multimedia University, Cyberjaya, Malaysia
sctan1@mmu.edu.my
[2] Faculty of Engineering, Multimedia University, Cyberjaya, Malaysia
[3] Telekom Malaysia Research & Development Sdn Bhd, Cyberjaya, Selangor, Malaysia

Abstract. An effective controller placement is vital in software-defined networking (SDN). The configuration of controller, switch, link and backup controller in a network will affect the cost of network planning. Hitherto, researchers in SDN have been addressing many issues related to SDN controller placement issues but only suggestion on the idea of deployment of backup controller (BC) placement due to network malfunction and attack. Here, we would like to propose an attack-aware recovery placement scheme with the main objective in reducing the network planning cost as well as providing uninterrupted service for SDN. Our approach is derived from a hybrid combination of heuristic and greedy strategy to generate array of combinations in a relative short time as compared to k-combination method that is highly complex and requires longer computation time. As a preventive technique, the generated BC will be connected to a fixed controller at a node to be readily used as a replacement in the event where controller malfunction occur due to attack and failure. The heuristic algorithm demonstrated a significant decrease in computation time required to produce distinct combination of controller by 99.25% compared to k-combination approach.

Keywords: Software-defined networking · Controller placement · Attack-aware algorithm

1 Introduction

Unlike legacy distributed network architecture, Software Defined Network (SDN) is a network architecture which separates the control plane from data plane as illustrated in Fig. 1. SDN yields more flexibility in terms of dynamic programmability whereby network components that operate in different software systems are interoperable and configurable under a centralized network operating system. This design is capable of reducing cost for the network planning and operation [6]. Despite of the benefits offered by SDN, this design has a fatal vulnerability that may incapacitate partial

© Springer Nature Switzerland AG 2019
G. Wang et al. (Eds.): SpaCCS 2019, LNCS 11611, pp. 297–308, 2019.
https://doi.org/10.1007/978-3-030-24907-6_23

network initially and may propagate the impact to the whole network subsequently due to attack or single point failure [14]. Should there be an attack or failure at the control layer, the network will lost its dynamic capability in adjusting the flow of the network forwarding. This dysfunction is also known as single point failure as discussed in [15]. Miu [13] reported that there are several methods in resolving this dysfunction by detection, mitigation, and prevention. Detection approach identifies a failure or attack before it causes any damage to the network. A mitigation method generally copes with active attack and reduces impact of the attack and mitigated the DDoS attacks towards SDN controller to some extent. However, it very much depends on the network traffic analysis and flow filtering design and easily presents high rates of false negatives and/or false positives if selecting improper filter parameters. Under this scenario, human intervention will be necessary to reinstall the network of the service. In generally, prevention technique is achieved by placing an additional backup controller for network recovery and ensuring uninterrupted network services in the event of attack or failure.

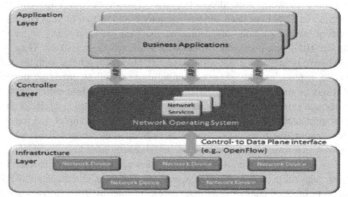

Fig. 1. SDN architecture

In network servicing, availability of the network is one of the key indicators for the design and planning purpose. The authors in [17] highlighted various requirements of availability based on priority of service demanded by the clients. Military defense system is one of the most stringent requirements among many network applications. It requires 99.9999% network availability or maximum of 31.5 s downtime per year. Second in priority list includes carrier grade telephony, health system and banking where requirement of 99.999% or maximum outage time of 5 min 15 s per year. Thirdly, more generally, data centre or the high end business system requires 99.99% uptime or 52 min and 33 s downtime per year. Thus, in this article, we focus on prevention approach with the objective to propose an attack-aware recovery controller-link-switch placement method (ARC) to provide controller, switch, and link placement based on the availability of the network requirement in various applications with the prime objective of reducing cost of network planning.

2 Related Work

In generally, prevention technique is achieved by placing an additional backup controller for network recovery and ensuring uninterrupted network services in the event of attack or failure. The single controller placement method introduced in [1, 2] is determined by measuring the degree of link and switch failure. A multiple controller placement method is proposed in [3] to overcome the limitation in previous work. The authors of [6, 9, 10] considered network flow and latency in their approaches in addressing traffic-oriented controller placement problem but [10] considered cost minimization in additional. Reference [5] suggests a dynamic flow management in SDN while reference [8] proposes a dynamic virtual machine controller addition and deletion. However, [5, 8] require additional equipment or software systems to perform dynamic control. In [4, 7], attack-aware model is introduced to provide defensive mechanism against attack neglecting the controller placement problem. However, the authors in [1–3, 6, 9, 10] did not address the issue of attack or failure in their model.

With the above shortcoming, it is our objective to introduce an attack-aware recovery controller-link-switch placement method (ARC) to provide controller, switch, and link placement with the prime objective of reducing cost of network planning. ARC uses a greedy algorithm to generate array of distinct and heuristic combination of controller. Network recovery is planned in advance in anticipating attack and failure at any node by additional backup controllers to replace the controller which is under attack. Section 2 illustrates the operation of ARC. Simulation and analysis conducted with five test cases are presented in Sect. 3. Summary is given in Sect. 4.

3 Attack-Aware Recovery Controller-Link-Switch Cost Minimization Placement Algorithm

3.1 Description

The proposed ARC scheme plans for prevention against attack on any node by the placement of additional backup controller to ensure uninterrupted network service under attack. Likewise any other common controller placement algorithm, ARC is capable of solving conventional controller placement problem. In addition, ARC performs switch and link placement as well. There are several inputs required to operate this method, such as:

- Controllers of different type with specification on number of port, processing power, quantity and cost.
- Switches of varying type with specification on number of packet and quantity.
- Backup controllers of different type with specification on number of port, processing power, quantity and cost.

- Individual network node with its ascending identification number start from one (1) and
- Frequency of attack at each node based on application type. The method will generates more backup controllers in the following scenario:

  (i) network operations which requires high availability such as military, health, banking and data center. or/and
  (ii) those nodes which experiencing higher frequency of attack.

- Link of various types with bandwidth and cost.

3.2 Notation

- Sets:

  1. $C = \{c1, c2, \ldots\}$, set of controllers of type $c \in C$ that is available to be selected.
     - j^c, number of port of a controller of type $c \in C$.
     - k^c, processing power of a controller of type $c \in C$.
     - v^c, cost of a controller of type $c \in C$.
     - t^c, controller quantity of type $c \in C$.
  2. $R = \{r1, r2, \ldots\}$, combination of controllers of type $r \in R$ that is selected from C to be installed in the SDN with the following property
     - j^r, number of port of a controller of type $r \in R$.
     - k^r, processing power of a controller of type $r \in R$.
     - v^r, cost of a controller of type $r \in R$.
     - t^r, controller quantity of type $r \in R$.
  3. $S = \{s1, s2, \ldots\}$, set of switches to be placed.
     - p^s, number of packet of a switch of type $s \in S$.
  4. $B = \{b1, b2, \ldots\}$, set of backup controllers that is available to be installed.
     - j^b, number of port of a controller of type $b \in B$.
     - k^b, processing power of a controller of type $b \in B$.
     - v^b, cost of a controller of type $b \in B$.
     - t^b, controller quantity of type $b \in B$.
  5. $L = \{l1, l2, \ldots\}$, set of link types that can be used to connect controller to controller, backup controller to controller, and switch to controller.
     - v^l / meter, cost of a link of type $l \in L$.
     - b^l / Mbps, bandwidth of a link of type $l \in L$.
  6. $N = \{1, 2, \ldots\}$, set of connector nodes that can be installed with a controller.
     - i, index of a node where $i \in N$.
     - f^i, frequency of attack or failure at node i where $i \in N$ according to application requirement. The defined frequency of DDoS attack is ranging from 0 to 3 where 0 represent no attack. 1, 2, 3 mean low, medium, high frequency of attack respectively. The model will generates more backup controllers in the following scenario: Network operations in which requires high availability such as military, health, banking and data center.
  7. M, set of end nodes that mirror the set of nodes N and can be connected to a connector node in N to form a matrix of connection.

- Constant:

  1. D_{ab} = Range between two points 'a' to 'b'. It's the distance between either two controllers D_NM, switch to controller D_SC or backup controller to controller D_BC.

- Decision variables:

  1. $T_{ci} = 1$, if a controller of type c ∈ C is installed to node i ∈ N, else 0.
  2. $T_{bi} = 1$, if a backup controller of type b ∈ B is installed to node i ∈ N, else 0.
  3. $Z_{si}^l = 1$, if a link of type l ∈ L is connected between switches of type s ∈ S and controller installed at node i ∈ N, else 0.
  4. $R_{bi}^l = 1$, if a link of type l ∈ L is connected between backup controller of type b ∈ B and controller installed at node i ∈ N, else 0.
  5. $R_{ih}^l = 1$, if a controller location i ∈ N is connected to controller location h ∈ M where h ≠ i with a link of type l ∈ L, else 0.

3.3 Formulation of ARC Scheme

Cost of network planning is defined as objective function f_v:

$$
\begin{aligned}
minimize\ f_v = &\left(\sum_{c=1}^{|C|} v^c \times T_{ci} \quad \forall i \in N \right) + \left(\sum_{b=1}^{|B|} v^b \times T_{bi} \quad \forall i \in N \right) \\
&+ \left(\sum_{l=1}^{|L|} v^l \times Z_{si}^l \times D_{SC} \quad \forall i \in N, \forall s \in S \right) \\
&+ \left(\sum_{l=1}^{|L|} v^l \times R_{bi}^l \times D_{BC} \quad \forall i \in N, \forall b \in B \right) \\
&+ \left(\sum_{l=1}^{|L|} v^l \times R_{ih}^l \times D_{NM} \quad \forall i \in N, \forall h \in M \right)
\end{aligned}
\tag{1}
$$

The objective function includes the cost of selected controller, backup controller, link for connection of controller to switch, link for connection of backup controller to controller, and link for connection of controller to controller at different nodes. The objective of ARC is to minimize the objective function value and subject to the following constraints:

- Ensure that the number of controller placed is n:

$$
\sum_{c=1}^{|C|} \sum_{i=1}^{|N|} T_{ci} = n
\tag{2}
$$

where $T_{ci} \in \{0, 1\}$, 1 when there is a controller placed in node i, and otherwise 0.

- Ensure that the total number of packet required by all switches is φ:

$$\varphi = \sum_{s=1}^{|S|} p^s \tag{3}$$

- Ensure that the total processing power of selected controller is larger or equal to total number of packet of all switches, φ:

$$\sum_{c=1}^{|C|} k^c \geq \varphi \tag{4}$$

- Ensure that each switch is only connected to one and only one controller:

$$\sum_{i=1}^{|N|} Z_{si}^l \leq 1 \quad \forall s \in S, \forall l \in L. \tag{5}$$

where $Z_{si}^l \in \{0, 1\}$, 1 if there is a switch connected to a controller in node i for switch s, and otherwise 0.

- Ensure that each switch is connected to a node that has a controller installed in it:

$$\sum_{i=1}^{|N|} Z_{si}^l \leq T_{ci} \quad \forall s \in S, \forall l \in L, \forall c \in C. \tag{6}$$

- Ensure each controller handles ε most switch such that the number of packets of switches is within the processing power of the specific controller:

$$\sum_{c=1}^{|C|} Z_{si}^l \cdot p^s \leq k^r \varepsilon \quad \forall r \in R, \forall l \in L, \forall s \in S, \forall i \in N. \tag{7}$$

- Ensure that for each node that has frequency of attack $f^i > 0$, the number of backup controller equals to f^i:

$$\sum_{b=1}^{|B|} T_{bi} = f^i \quad \forall i \in N \tag{8}$$

where $T_{bi} \in \{0, 1\}$, 1 when there is a backup controller placed in node i, and otherwise 0.

- Ensure only one link is used for each connection:

$$\sum_{l=1}^{|L|} \sum_{s=1}^{|S|} \sum_{i=1}^{|N|} Z_{si}^l = |S| \tag{9}$$

$$\sum_{l=1}^{|L|} \sum_{i=1}^{|N|} \sum_{b=1}^{|B|} R_{bi}^l = \sum_{i=1}^{|N|} \sum_{b=1}^{|B|} T_{bi} \tag{10}$$

$$\sum_{l=1}^{|L|} \sum_{i=1}^{|N|} \sum_{h=1}^{|N|} R_{ih}^l = \sum_{i=1}^{n} (n - i) \tag{11}$$

where $Z_{si}^l \in \{0, 1\}$, 1 if there is a switch connected to a controller in node i for switch s, and otherwise 0. $R_{bi}^l \in \{0, 1\}$, 1 if there is a backup controller connected to a node with controller in node i, and otherwise 0. $R_{ih}^l \in \{0, 1\}$, 1 if there is a node with controller connected to another node with controller in node i and j, and otherwise 0.

3.4 Flowchart of Algorithm

Processing power required by all switches and number of controller required are calculated in step 1 as shown in Fig. 2. Step 2 generates combination of controller based on the requirement from step 1. Next, controllers are installed to specific node in step 3. In step 4, switch placement is performed and a link is selected to connect each switch to

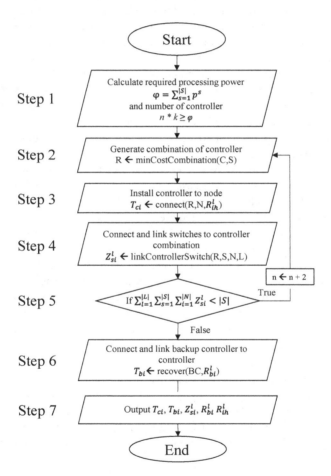

Fig. 2. Flowchart for ARC method

a controller. If the switch placement failed, ARC will start over the execution flow from step 2 again after incrementing the number of controller required. Through step 6, backup controller placement is performed and a link is selected to connect the each backup controller to a controller. Finally, the connection matrix is generated as output.

The proposed ARC scheme is using greedy method to obtain heuristic solution within a short time. The required processing power φ is the total summation of all switches where larger φ requires more controller to be placed and longer time to perform switch placement. Next, the minimum number of controller n required to form the combination of controller C is calculated by incrementing n until $n * k \geq \varphi$.

The core function is minCostCombination where greedy method and recursive programming is adopted to produce combination of controller C of size n and $n + 1$ with a sole objective to reduce cost of network planning. For each controller in C, a node i is denoted to install a primary controller based on possibility of attack and distance distribution factor. Link with sufficient bandwidth and lowest cost is selected to connect each controller in different nodes. The recursive sub-function of minCostCombination, getPossiblePair is the part that differentiate ARC from k-combination as it does not consider every possible combination for the given combination pair size. The function getPossiblePair select the controller with largest processing power for each iteration to generate a combination of controller that has sufficient processing power to possibly place with all switches.

Subsequently, linkControllerSwitch function is used to connect switches to primary controllers using links that selected based on bandwidth and cost whereby the total number of packet of switches does not exceed the processing power of the controller they are connected to and within the requirement of the number of controller port. If switch placement failed, n is incremented by two and minCostCombination is executed iteratively until all switches have been placed. Thereafter, recover function as shown will yields placement solution of backup controller with varying quantity to node that has high frequency of attack or failure. Link with sufficient bandwidth and cost is selected to connect the backup controller to controller at the affected node.

Finally, matrices of controller-to-node connection T_{ci}, backup controller-to-node connection T_{bi}, switch-to-node connection Z_{si}^l, link used for backup controller-to-node connection R_{bi}^l and link used for node-to-node connection R_{ih}^l are produced as an output from the algorithm. Active connection is indicated as positive (1) in the matrices, otherwise negative (0). The function minCostCombination consist of getPossiblePair recursive function that perform greedy selection on available controller to produce a combination of controllers. With every recurrence, the size of the sequence of controller C is reduced until the size of C is less than n which serve as the terminating condition. The function will also be terminated if there is no suitable controller to be chosen.

3.5   Complexity Analysis

Referring to the pseudocode provided in Fig. 2, ARC logically has the worst case of $O(n^3)$. The function minCostCombination solely has the worst case of $O(n^3)$ while the rest have the worst case of $O(n^2)$. The average performance of the ARC method can be observed through simulation result and analysis in the next section.

4   Experimental Classification Results and Analysis

Five test cases of different characteristics is selected to demonstrate the effectiveness of the proposed scheme on a computer with Intel Core i7-4720HQ CPU at 2.60 GHz and 16 GB RAM running Windows 10 operating system. Table 1 tabulated all the summarized information of test cases for a brief overview. Ratio of average processing power of controllers to average number of packet of switches is derived from input values to further differentiate the test cases. Comparison results and number of iteration for all test cases are given in Table 2 and Table 3 respectively. The results cover network grid size, computation time, objective function value of ARC simulation, and objective function value derived using Integer Linear Programming (ILP) as shown in Table 2. The objective function value derived using ILP is ideally the optimal solution of the placement problem.

Table 1. Difference among input

Difference	Test case				
	1	2	3	4	5
number of packet required by all switches, φ	49900	42200	28840	22000	159900
number of controllers, $|C|$	234	234	163	163	163
number of switches, $|S|$	13	13	9	9	20
number of backup controllers, $|B|$	75	75	190	190	280
Average processing power of controllers to average number of packet of switches ratio $\bar{K} = \frac{\overline{k^C}}{\overline{p^S}}$	1.40	2.39	2.20	2.88	0.88

Table 2. Arc simulation result

Test case	Network grid, $g = |N| \times |N|$	Time taken to produce combination of controller in second	Objective function value, f_v	Objective function value of ILP
1	9×9	1.53297	59251.75	59251.75
2	9×9	1.39368	43350.75	43350.75
3	15×15	0.572813	43952.75	43452.75
4	15×15	0.115084	18850.75	18850.75
5	100×100	2.21806	324507.75	324507.75

Table 3. Number of trial

Test case	1	2	3	4	5
Number of trial	1	1	1	1	2

Problem complexity increases as network grid size increases as the placement of controller at node requires more evaluation and iterations as shown in Table 2. Logically, test case 5 with 100 by 100 network grid size requires longest time to produce combination of controller. Both test case 1 and 2 have the same network grid size of 9 by 9 and same value of $|C|$ and $|S|$ except test case 1 requires more processing power as indicated by the total number of packet of all switches φ is totaled 49900 as compared to 42200 in test case 2 as shown in Table 1. Thus, the objective function value of test case 1 is higher than test case 2 as shown in Table 4. At the same time, the higher the $|C|$ and $|S|$ value, the more complex the problem will be. It can be observed that test case 1 and test case 2 has the largest $|C|$ value which resulting requires longer computation time than test case 1 as shown in Table 2 in producing combination of controller since there are more choices of controller to be evaluated and selected. It is also more likely to fail in K-combination simulation with large $|C|$ and $|S|$ value as it

Table 4. Results comparison against K-combination approach

Approach	Difference	Test case				
		1	2	3	4	5
ARC	Time taken to produce combination of controller in second	1.53297	1.39368	0.572813	0.115084	2.21806
	Objective function value, f_v	59251.75	43350.75	43452.75	18850.75	324507.75
	Number of selected controller, $|R|$	5	5	4	3	18
K-combination	Time taken to produce combination of controller in second	NA	NA	9.5626	0.734382	NA
	Objective function value, f_v	NA	NA	43452.75	18850.75	NA
	Number of selected controller, $|R|$	NA	NA	4	3	NA

requires enormous space for computation of possible pair of controllers as evidenced in Table 4 for test case 1 and test case 2. Test Case 3 and 4 have higher average controller processing power than test case 1 thus reducing the complexity of switch placement problem. Test Case 3 and 4 also has larger grid size compared to Test case 1.

Meanwhile, test case 5 has the highest $|S|$ value, thus requires time to produce combination of controller. The $|B|$ value generally contributes slight portion of complexity only in the problem space because it depends on the existing of the attack or failure at the nodes. Next, average processing power of controllers to average number of packet of switches ratio is the most important consideration of the proposed method. The higher the value of ratio indicates a higher possibility for all switches to fit into the combination of controller. It also indicates that the average number of switches a controller that can be supported in the method. Should the value of the ratio is lower than 1, the method has high possibility to fail at switch placement and it will undergo another sequence of generating combination of controller with larger size n until all switches are successfully placed. For all cases, the value of 1 in the number of trial as shown in Table 3 indicates a successful switch-to-controller placement for all switches in first run. The selected application lists for each class and the number of applications in each class are shown in Table 1.

ARC effectiveness is compared to k-combination method as shown in Table 4. Compared to k-combination method [16], ARC is approximately 133 times faster than k-combination when tested with test case 1. Due to limitation of hardware, the result of k-combination for test case 2 and 5 are not obtainable as the memory usage is overwhelmed the testing device. This shows that ARC consumes less memory than k-combination method.

5   Conclusion

In this article, an attack-aware recovery placement scheme with objective of minimizing cost named as ARC is introduced to tackles both controller-link-switch placement problem and (in conjunction with) attack prevention. The proposed scheme is tested in five different test cases ranging from simple to very complex network configurations. The results that obtained demonstrate that our proposed ARC scheme is capable of producing array of combination of controller within a short period of time as compare to k-combination. Our sub-optimal solution of ARC requires relatively shorter computation time as compare to k-combination in achieving the same objective function, which is the cost function. In conclusion, ARC is agile and generic as it is capable to solve problem of different sizes and inputs. As a result, it can be consider as a preventive approach for uninterrupted service as well as cost reduction in SDN.

Acknowledgments. This research work is fully supported by the research grant of TM R&D and Multimedia University, Cyberjaya, Malaysia. We are very thankful to the team of TM R&D and Multimedia University for providing the support to our research studies.

References

1. Tatipamula, M., Beheshti-Zavareh, N., Zhang, Y.: Controller placement for fast failover in the split architecture. EP Patent EP2552065A1, 30 January 2013
2. Beheshti-Zavareh, N., Zhang, Y., Halpern, J.: Controller placement for fast failover in the split architecture. U.S. Patent US 9225591 B2, 29 December 2015
3. Lin, S.C., Wang, P., Akyildiz, I., Luo, M.: Traffic-driven network controller placement in software-defined networks. U.S. Patent US20160323144A1, 3 November 2016
4. Collaborative theory-based DDoS (Distributed Denial of Service Attack) defence system and method. CN Patent CN106921666A, 4 July 2017

5. ul Huque, M.T.I., Si, W., Jourjon, G., Gramoli, V.: Large-scale dynamic controller placement. IEEE Trans. Netw. Serv. Manag. **14**(1), 63–76 (2017)
6. Guodong, W., Yanxiao, Z., Jun, H., Wei, W.: The controller placement problem in software defined networking: a survey. IEEE Netw. **31**(5), 21–27 (2017)
7. Dridi, L., Zhani, M.F.: A holistic approach to mitigating DoS attacks in SDN networks. Int. J. Netw. Manag. **28**(1), e1996 (2018)
8. Sood, K., Xiang, Y.: The controller placement problem or the controller selection problem? J. Commun. Inf. Netw. **2**(3), 1–9 (2017)
9. Killi, B.P., Rao, S.V.: Capacitated next controller placement in software defined networks. IEEE Trans. Netw. Serv. Manag. **14**(3), 514–527 (2017)
10. Sallahi, A., St-Hilaire, M.: Optimal model for the controller placement problem in software defined networks. IEEE Commun. Lett. **19**(1), 30–33 (2015)
11. Sallahi, A., St-Hilaire, M.: Expansion model for the controller placement problem in software defined networks. IEEE Commun. Lett. **21**(2), 274–277 (2017)
12. Hu, Y., Luo, T., Beaulieu, N.C., Deng, C.: The energy-aware controller placement problem in software defined networks. IEEE Commun. Lett. **21**(4), 741–744 (2017)
13. Miu, T.T., Hui, A.K., Lee, W.L., Luo, D.X., Chung, A.K.: Universal DDoS Mitigation Bypass. Black Hat USA (2013)
14. Scott-Hayward, S., O'Callaghan, G., Sezer, S.: SDN security: a survey. In: IEEE SDN for Future Networks and Services (SDN4FNS), pp. 1–7 (2013)
15. Qin, Q., Poularakis, K., Iosifidis, G., Tassiulas, L.: SDN controller placement at the edge: optimizing delay and overheads. In: Proceedings of IEEE INFOCOM, pp. 684–692 (2018)
16. Sufiev, H., Haddad, Y., Barenboim, L., Soler, J.: Dynamic SDN controller load balancing. Future Internet **11**, 75 (2019)
17. Fonseca, P., Bennesby, R., Mota, E., Passito, A.: A replication component for resilient OpenFlow-based networking. In: Network Operations and Management Symposium (NOMS), pp. 933–939. IEEE (2012)
18. Jalili, A., Ahmadi, V., Keshtgari, M., Kazemi, M.: Controller placement in software-defined wan using multi objective genetic algorithm. In: 2nd International Conference on Knowledge-Based Engineering and Innovation (KBEI), pp. 656–662. IEEE, 5 November 2015
19. Mitchell, B.: Availability concepts for networks and systems, lifewire (2017). https://www.lifewire.com/availabilityconcepts-for-networks-systems-817820

Challenges and Future Direction of Time-Sensitive Software-Defined Networking (TSSDN) in Automation Industry

Ng Kean Haur and Tan Saw Chin[(⊠)]

Faculty of Computing and Informatics, Multimedia University,
Persiaran Multimedia, 63100 Cyberjaya, Malaysia
sctan1@mmu.edu.my

Abstract. In Industry 4.0, Cyber physical system (CPS) is suffered from queuing delay during the process of data gathering and feedback generation by which affects the efficiency of providing hard real-time guarantees. Hard real-time cyber physical system requires software and hardware to operate strictly within the deadline. Time-Sensitive Software-Defined Networking (TSSDN) is an architecture which utilizes the centralized network controller in Software-Defined Networking (SDN) to facilitate the operation of software and hardware in CPS globally. Time-sensitive-aware scheduling traffic system in TSSDN is capable to minimize the queuing delay in the network which leads to hard real-time guarantees. Hence, the potential opportunities of TSSDN in automation industry has motivate the further investigate of its current states. This paper will discuss the challenges of TSSDN and suggest its future direction enhancement.

Keywords: Software-Defined Networking · Cyber physical system ·
Time-sensitive networking

1 Introduction

Industry 4.0 referred to the fourth industry evolution, is driven by a smart interconnected pervasive environment [1]. Industry 4.0 aims to provide information transparency, technical assistant, decentralized decision making and interoperability between human and machine. There are certain fields which related in the Industry 4.0 example cyber-physical systems, cloud computing and big data [2]. In Industry 4.0, Cyber physical system (CPS) [3] is a system which allows software component to interact with the physical component to provide intelligent feedbacks which can be referred to Fig. 1. It is controlled and monitored by the computer-based algorithms. There are lots of CPS from industrial automation nowadays example telerobotic, smart grid, and isochronous motion control systems. They are required to provide a high quality of performance and good decision making with real-time guarantee. In CPS, every element including sensors, actuators, and controllers are interconnected and wireless. Each device has its own IP address so that it can be addressed in the network. However, the qualities of control may be affected when packet lost or queuing delay occurs.

© Springer Nature Switzerland AG 2019
G. Wang et al. (Eds.): SpaCCS 2019, LNCS 11611, pp. 309–324, 2019.
https://doi.org/10.1007/978-3-030-24907-6_24

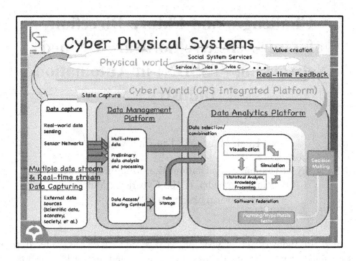

Fig. 1. Mechanism in cyber physical system [4]

Time-sensitive networking (TSN) is a standard of control system in Ethernet technology from IEEE TSN Task Group [5] which can be applied in the industrial and automation network. In this standard, there are three major components required in order to achieve real-time communication which are time synchronization (IEEE 802.1AS) [6], traffic scheduling (IEEE 802.1Qbv) [7], and network configuration (IEEE 802.1Qcc) [8]. The broadly used of Ethernet increase the adoption of TSN. The trend of standardization in TSN makes the cost of implementation reduced. TSN is now ready for application which requires time synchronization of machines in different locations. Besides, TSN reduce the complexity of network by providing multiple services in a same network. This allows TSN to increase the interoperability of the control system which leads to the high-speed of data transmission in network. Moreover, TSN is flexible on the system integration which the update of features and components will not affect the existing system. Last but not least, TSN provides built in security mechanism which do not provided in the historical control network.

TSN is suitable in industry field. The application which requires deterministic monitoring requires TSN. The reason is that TSN can provide time synchronization to measure and monitor the flows in the network. Besides, the application which requires machine control requires TSN. The reason is that TSN has control network to coordinate the actions of system in hard real time. Machine control requires hard real time to reduce the jitter and delay in the deterministic network. Moreover, TSN is required in the automation field. In the vehicle, TSN able to provide multiple services in a same network such as driving assistant, roadmap information, and temperature changed according climate. Furthermore, media networks require TSN to provide strict timing schedule since the transmission of audio and packets are not allowed to delay. Hence, Software-Defined networking (SDN) utilizes its architecture to assist TSN in facilitating the network.

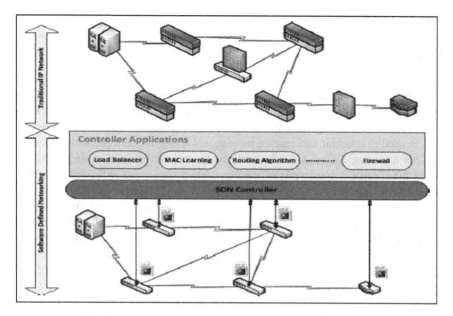

Fig. 2. Comparison between traditional IP network and SDN

Software-Defined networking (SDN) is an architecture of network which separated the switches into control plane and data plane. Figure 2 represents the comparison of SDN and traditional network. In traditional IP network, the configuration and reconfiguration of network is difficult since each switch has only its information. In SDN network, data plane has data forwarding function while the control plane has uplifted SDN controller to control the data plane according scheduling rules. This is known as centralization which the network controller is allowed to gather the information of network flows from the observation in global view. This allows the administrator to change the traffic network from centralization controller [10] with the implementation of monitoring, analysis, planning, execution (MAPE) loop.

In this section, the basic concept of Cyber physical system (CPS) in Industry 4.0 is briefly discussed. In Cyber physical system, Time-sensitive networking (TSN) is required to provide hard real-time guarantees. The centralized controller of Software-Defined networking (SDN) manages to assist TSN in facilitating and scheduling the network. In Sect. 2, motivation of SDN in TSN which is Time-Sensitive Software-Defined Networking (TSSDN) [17] will be discussed in details. In this paper, we aim to identify the gap of TSSN deployment in industry automation industry in literature and propose the possible future direction for works in this aspect. The rest of this paper is organized as follows. Section 2 discusses related works. Section 3 we discuss the challenges and problem of TSSDN. In Sect. 4, we identify future opportunities and research directions of TSSDN, and finally we conclude this paper on Sect. 5.

2 Related Work

2.1 Current State of TSN Networks

The advent of TSN is to handle the costly investment and the incompatible of fieldbus system in automation industry. The major network components are bridges, Central Network Controller (CNC) and Centralized User Configuration (CUC) which allows the TSN talker to transmit the data to TSN listener. Bridges is the Ethernet switches which is used to transmit and receive the data according the schedules of TSN flows. The TSN flows are routed and scheduled by Central Network Controller (CNC) according the specific requirements of the users which they were requested to the Centralized User Configuration before the communication [11]. However, TSN lack of the involvement of both static and dynamic configuration to achieve real time communication. Hence, IEEE protocols such as time synchronization, traffic scheduling and path selection are developed to handle the weakness of TSN which can be categorized into three main standards which are IEEE 802.1AS for time synchronization, IEEE 802.1Qca for path control and reservation and IEEE 802.1Qbv for traffic scheduling. IEEE 802.1AS which contains 1588 profile was first introduce to distribute time, measure link delay and select best master clock. According to [2], 1588 Precision Time Protocol (PTP) which known as the best master clock algorithm uses two-steps processing to synchronize the message with another follow up to ensure the precision of origin timestamp as well as the accurate time [6]. IEEE 802.1Qca is an extension of bridge networks control which aims to provide explicit path control for both shortest and non-shortest path, bandwidth and stream reservation and accurate data flow distribution [13]. IEEE 802.1Qbv is a time-aware queue standard which provide support on traffic scheduling to ensure no delay occurs during the data transmission process. The good quality of services (QoS) for traffic scheduling between the network components will ensure the stability of network and avoid the operational failure [7].

TSN successes to provide real-time communication for cyber physical system in IEEE 802 network example IEEE 802.3 Ethernet network. However, there is a lack of existing standard to generate the schedules in order to support the IEEE 802.1Qbv to handle the traffic scheduling problems. The reason is that IEEE 802.1Qbv is not able to preemptively transmit the high priority data over the low priority data once the opening of gate events. Therefore, guard bands are placed before and after the gate events to provide guarantees of the data transmission before its dateline [14]. There are two approaches which was developed to handle the scheduling problems those are No-wait Packet Scheduling [15] and Satisfiability Modulo Theories (SMT) [16]. No-wait Packet Scheduling is an approach which aim to reduce the flowspan with the method of no wait packet scheduling problem (NW-PSP). It started from the idea, Job Shop Scheduling (JSP) which aim to reduce the makespan between the job and resources (machines). NW-PSP maps the switches and end devices as machines while time-sensitive flows as jobs in order to eliminate the queueing delay. The minimizing of finishing time (flowspan) manages to compress the schedule cycle and reduce the number of gate events which leads to the saving of bandwidth. Satisfiability Modulo Theories (SMT) based schedule generation for time-triggered network is an approach which aims to determine the frame offsets and queue assignment. In the network, frame offsets refer as the time of the event while queue assignment refers as the location of the event. With the IEEE 802.1Qbv constraints, this approach manages to control the gate opening event precisely to ensure the transmission schedules are always working fine according the order of Central Network Controller (CNC).

However, NW-PSP is a method which is highly time complexity due to its optimization required and the implies of Shortest Path First (SPF) algorithms while SMT based schedule generation is not able to handle the scenarios with large number of flows [14]. Besides, both of these approaches start to have some critical issues when the demand of the network architecture become higher. One of the main reasons is the limitation of the flexibility since the program of these protocols is encoded into the switches and routers. Switches and routers are usually closed system. The modification of the program is not allowed to be done centrally once the product is deployed. Besides, the complexity of the switches and routers become higher due to the increasing number of the protocols. Moreover, the network applications are come in pack with the same brand which are costly and inflexible. In the traditional method, every switch and router can only visualize the information of its own connection. This is troublesome which all the configuration and update of the network has to be done for each switch separately. Therefore, Software-Defined networking (SDN) comes in the way.

2.2   Current State of TSSDN and Its Benefit

The implementation of Software-Defined Networking (SDN) in Time-sensitive networking (TSN) is known as Time-Sensitive Software-Defined Networking (TSSDN) [17]. The protocols involved are IEEE 802.1Qcc for network configuration, IEEE 802.1Qbv for traffic scheduling and IEEE 802.1AS for time synchronization. TSSDN is a model which contain three layers which are infrastructure layer, control layer and application layer. In north bound interface, application layer is used to design a user-friendly platform. It needs to provide an interactive design which fulfill the user requirements. In south bound interface, infrastructure layer which well-known as data plane is used to forward the packets according the scheduling rules in the flow table which is provided by the control layer. In TSSDN, control plane and data plane are separated which the data plane has only data forwarding function while control plane is uplifted to visualize the data plane globally. This approach successful to optimize the traffic scheduling system with a less complex and resource utilized method. The topology change, flow control, protocols deployment, applications modification and network visualization can now be done centrally by the administrator with the MAPE loop. For the southbound API, there are few choices of architectures such as ForCES [18] and Openflow [19]. ForCES has three major components which are Forwarding Element (FE), Control Element (CE) and Logical Function Block (LFB). In ForCES, Forwarding Element acts as a data plane to forward the data while Control Element acts as a control plane to control it. Meanwhile, ForCES has its own protocol for the architecture frameworks and modeling languages. Logical Function Block (LFB) which controlled by the Control Elements will act as a pre-defined functional block to perform the functions of the ForCES protocol. On the other hand, OpenFlow architecture is similar with the ForCES architecture which both of them separate the control plane and data plane for network centralization. However, OpenFlow used flow tables instead of

Logical Function Block (LFB) to determine the route of each time-sensitive flows. Flow tables consists flow entries such as rules, counters and instructions to handle the traffic scheduling. The flows in the table is programmable which has the associated potential to increase the revenue, precision and flexibility [20].

Time-Sensitive Software-Defined Networking (TSSDN) has few advantages. First of all, TSSDN is able to gain the information of the network globally due to the separation of data plane and control plane. In traditional TSN, multiple paths do not receive messages from each other. There will be no communication during the progression of the network flow since each of the routing flow can only update their current status to the connected switches separately. This global information not only can increase the bandwidth of the traffic scheduling, but can also form the statistics data for visualization. Nowadays, data collection is important since it can be used to assist for the diagnose of traffic performance and the error detection. Besides that, TSSDN provides centralize configuration and control which the administrator is able to change the flows, topology and requirements centrally without physical appearance. This is a great improvement which the Time-Sensitive Networking (TSN) in the industry is no longer static network. The administrator is able to deploy and modify both the protocols and applications dynamically such as adding or removing the nodes in real time network [21]. Furthermore, TSSDN provides alternative routes to handle the link or packet failures. This is to handle the exceptions immediately and to avoid the network congestion. Additionally, TSSDN can handle the network topology which exist the looping due to the global understanding of the whole topology. Moreover, TSSDN with OpenFlow provides software and protocols which are open source. The hardware and software are vendor-neutral which can be flexible and cost saving. Last but not least, TSSDN is efficient in multicasting which it will only send the frame to the intended receiver. This will not only save the routes but to secure the safety.

2.3   TSSDN in Industry 4.0 and Automation Applications

There are few industries start to implement Time-Sensitive Software-Defined Networking (TSSDN) as their network architecture. According to [22], devices in the industrial automation implements TSSDN via OpenFlow for the HMI interfaces due to the lack of real-time capabilities. The implementation of TSSDN manages to come out with some results and improvements. In the industrial automation network, the time-sensitive flows require network system to control and route the traffic in order to increase the accuracy of the scheduling. Centralize of the traffic configuration and control become critical since the minor changed of the traffic prioritize and requirements will affect the result of the network. Hence, there are a necessary to build certain parameters for decision making example the flow entries in OpenFlow such as counter, match fields and instructions. Counter in OpenFlow is normally used to collect the statistics of the flow while instructions is used to determine the methods to handle different packets which is based on the specific rules of the packets in match fields [22]. AVNU [23] is a community which create network system with diverse applications by providing time synchronization and configuration mechanisms to the industrial and automotive market. AVNU involves with IEEE 802.1 TSN mechanism which is used in the Time-Sensitive Software-Defined Networking (TSSDN) such as IEE802.1Qcc,

IEEE 802.1AS and IEEE 802.1Qbv. In AVNU industrial, IEEE 802.1Qcc is used to configure the network centrally. The global network knowledges are provided to the administrator for the assistance in configuration. The administrator can configure the traffic schedules and TSSDN network centrally via Centralized User Configuration (CUC) without physical appearance. Besides, AVNU will also select the suitable protocols such as NETCONF and RESTCONF to handle the network configuration in TSSDN. On the other side, AVNU industrial use IEEE802.1AS for traffic scheduling to utilize the bandwidth and to handle the delay. IEEE 802.1AS with 1588 profiles will be work on time synchronization to prevent the redundancy of the universal timestamps. The implementation of the TSSDN in AVNU industrial manages to improve the requirements such as time synchronization, guarantee of latency, reservation of bandwidth, topology flexibility, security and scalability [23]. Nowadays, hardware and software are started to enter virtualization environment. TSSDN with network virtualization is a novel idea which move the network from physical to cloud. In a virtual network, virtual switches are worked on the top of the servers instead of dedicated hardware to handle the complex problems.

3 Challenges in TSSN

Although Time-Sensitive Software-Defined Networking (TSSDN) brings a lot of benefits to the industry, there are some existing issues or challenges remained on the performance and implementation. In this section, we will discuss the challenges in five different quality attributes which are reliability, performance, scalability, security and interoperability.

3.1 Reliability

In Time-Sensitive Software-Defined Networking (TSSDN), the data plane and control plane are separated which the only centralized SDN controller will be given the instructions for switches and routers to route the transmission schedules. This is a good architecture in term of flexibility but may be a huge issue when come to the reliability. The reason is that centralized controller is the only controller to in charge of the whole network in TSSDN. If there is a failure for the centralized SDN controller, the whole network will be collapsed [25]. Hence, the administrator will not be able to configure the network centrally. Besides, there is another challenge which coming from the control plane. In TSSDN, control plane has its own in-band traffic which is able to transport when the critical information and data is transmitted in between the nodes. This will cause the overhead of the control plane. Although the control plane in-band traffic is rarely to run since it will only be trigger during the activities. However, in-band traffic will occur more frequent when come to the new TSSDN approach which require the frequent established of short lived TSN flows [26]. Moreover, the failure of the intermediate nodes such as switches and routers will be one of the challenges in TSSDN. In TSSDN, switches and routers will act as the data plane to forward the packets to the end users. When the switches or routers occur failure, SDN controller will reschedule the packet to the alternatives route. However, it may affect the schedules of other packets and their time accuracies.

3.2 Performance

In Time-Sensitive Software-Defined Networking (TSSDN), the traffic network tends to favor the high priority traffic rather than the low priority traffic. Hence, there will be a case where the low priority traffic needs to keep reschedules due to the preemption of high priority traffic when the schedules is pack. This will cause the endless loop which the low priority traffic has no chance to queue for the transmission. In TSSDN, there are many methods to improve the synchronization accuracy. IEEE 1588 profiles is the best master clock algorithm which is good in time synchronization. However, there is an insufficient knowledge for TSSDN to handle the synchronization inaccuracy. Synchronization inaccuracy may not be an issue for the big industries due to the high quality of time synchronization protocols, but it is significant when happen on the low-cost devices. Synchronization inaccuracy will delay the communication between each node and affect the results of traffic scheduling. In TSSDN, there is always a challenge between the choices of high performance and high flexibility. TSSDN is well-known due to its flexibility such as the configuration of network and the update of schedule which can be done centrally without physical appearance. However, TSSDN has suffer to achieve node bandwidth beyond 100 GB/s [20]. The choices of general-purpose processors (GPPs) over CPU manages to provide a high-level programming language but increase the usage of power. TSSDN tradeoff its performance to get a better flexibility.

3.3 Scalability

In Time-Sensitive Software-Defined Networking (TSSDN), there is a challenge for SDN controller to provide a global network view in term of scalability. SDN controller is an only centralized controller to communicate between the switches and routers. It is a heavy duty if the control plane has a lot of activities to be triggered. In order to increase the scalability of TSSDN, there is a require to extend SDN controller and share its knowledges to reduce the burden. However, this will be a back propagation to the traditional method which using more controllers to handle the data. Besides, there is an issue for the back-end operational database. In TSSDN, centralized SDN controller has its own database to store the operation which is used to forward the data plane. However, the size of the database will limit the scalability of the network. In this case, centralized SDN controller may not has the ability to fully control the network information once the database is full. Moreover, the communication between controllers, nodes and applications within southbound API and northbound API is important to provide a global network view. In TSSDN, southbound API which known as the interaction between controller and switches has well defined protocol such as OpenFlow and ForCES. However, there are not much explanation which focuses on northbound API which known as the interaction between the controller and applications. The undefined standard and details of the northbound API brings a lot of troubles for the application developer during the development process.

3.4   Security

In Time-Sensitive Software-Defined Networking (TSSDN), an application is able to access different network resources while different applications can be authorized to access the same network resource. There will be a possible the unauthorized user may access the resources which should be protected. Hence, TSSDN has to provide the protection of data from different applications and the network resources. Besides, open interface of SDN architecture and its well- known protocols will be one of the issues for attackers to attack TSSDN. The reason is that the attackers can easily learn the knowledges of SDN from different samples to master the access of networks and controllers. With the full understand of SDN architectures, the success rate for attacker to attack TSSDN will be higher. Moreover, centralized SDN controller is the spot which is full with protected information of the global network. Hence, it will always be the main target for attackers to conquer the networks. The insecure controller platform will easily masquerade by the attacker to carry out malicious activities. Furthermore, the way to transmit the packets can be one of the issues for TSSDN. In TSSDN, the validation of packets is based on the header information. This method of packet transmission can be easy for attacker to change the packets' memory and carry on DoS attack [20]. This will cause the collapse of the network. To solve this issue, the whole packet is required to transmit include the packet header and memory for a secure validation. However, this method will cause the overload of memory which affect the scalability.

3.5   Interoperability

In Time-Sensitive Software-Defined Networking (TSSDN), migration of the network is always a big issue to be considered. Before the migration, the administrator needs to research based on different aspects based on the requirements such as quality of the products, price values and network scalability. Simple swap out is not going to apply on the migration in network due to the heavy constraints. Although the existing solutions such as IETF path computation element (PCE) [27] can handle the partial migration, but the hybrid SDN infrastructure is still a challenge for TSSDN to handle.

Nowadays, network virtualization and cloud architectures grow rapidly due to the high demand. TSSDN with network virtualization manages to reduce the hardware cost, improve the network agility and increase the speeds of deployment. However, the security problem which often happen in network virtualization is always a concern. Although the centralized SDN controller is involved to solve the security problem, but it is always better to have a network services architecture to solve this problem. Besides, there is a challenge for TSSDN to step forward. TSSDN is always a closed environment without the involvement of outside network. However, the networks in industry and automation are often connected with the outside networks. Hence, the platform to interoperate TSSDN with outside network is required. Furthermore, there is another challenge for TSSDN to achieve. In TSSDN, IEEE 802.1 protocol is an IP-based Ethernet which is used to provide real-time communication which are time synchronization, traffic scheduling and network configuration. Since it is available to apply on micro-environments, it can also be applied on macroenvironments such as

Wide-Area Networks (WAN) [26]. In order to interoperate TSSDN and WAN network, WAN networks is required to has TSSDN characteristics while TSSDN need to be more scalable in order to handle the large number of flows from WAN.

4 Direction of TSSN

Time-Sensitive Software-Defined Networking (TSSDN) is an architecture with high potential extensibility due to its benefits. However, there are few issues and challenges which are mention in Sect. 3 are waiting to be solved. In this section, we will identify the future of Time-Sensitive Software-Defined Networking (TSSDN) on handling the existing issues and challenges. The discussion will be focused in five different quality attributes which are reliability, performance, scalability, security and interoperability.

4.1 Reliability

Centralized SDN controller in TSSDN is function to forward the data plane. It is a core application in the TSSDN architecture. Hence, there is a requirement to come out with a solution to solve the failure of the central controller in the network. SDN controller can provides a lot of functions such as traffic scheduling and multiple paths routing but not all the functions are required for the specific TSSDN. In order to prevent the failure of SDN controller, there is a necessary to utilize its functions carefully. Besides, there is a new architecture in [28] which involved the alternative controller to substitute the main SDN controller when there is a failure occurred. Frequency of in-band traffic in control plane is significant higher in the industry and automation. The reason is that TSSDN requires the established of short lived TSN flows. Hence there is a necessary to come out a design to reserve the resources accordingly based on the requirements of the control plane. The intermediate nodes in TSSDN is used to forward the packets from the sources to the destinations. The failure of the intermediate nodes may affect the schedules and the time delivery. Therefore, there is a requirement to come out with a mechanism to visualize the performance of each node. This mechanism needs to facilitate the behavior of the nodes during the transmission and generate their performance profile periodically. In this case, the administrator is able to consider the configuration based on the state and performance of the intermediate nodes.

4.2 Performance

In Time-Sensitive Software-Defined Networking (TSSDN), the traffic network tends to favor the high priority traffic rather than the low priority one. The low priority traffic has to reschedule when the schedule is pack before its turn. Hence, there is a requirement to come out with a mechanism which can provide the worst-case delay to the low priority traffic. In this case, low priority traffic will be able to get the chances to transmit the data without affecting the performance of the high priority traffic. TSSDN has suffered to achieve high node bandwidth due to its high flexibility such as network configuration and traffic scheduling. In TSSDN, there is always a challenge between the choices of high performance and high flexibility. Most of the cases, TSSDN tradeoff its performance to get a better flexibility. On the other hand, Application-specific standard products (ASSPs) is a high performance but less flexibility network which is able to handle large scalable of data. With the hybrid approach of TSSDN and ASSPs, satisfy balance between performance and flexibility will potential to be occurred. At the current stage, SDN specific ASSPs is able to support node bandwidth beyond 500 GB/s [20].

4.3 Scalability

In Time-Sensitive Software-Defined Networking (TSSDN), centralized SDN controller is required to provide a global view network. However, it is a challenge for TSSDN to maintain high scalability since the centralized SDN controller is not able to handle overload of knowledge. Hence, an extension application is potential to solve the controller overhead problem. For the extension of application layer traffic optimization (ALTO) data model [29], the data of the SDN controller will be stored in the ALTO server while SDN controller will only require to hold the represented links. In this case, ALTO server will send the desire data to the controller if needed to provide a global view network. In TSSDN, centralized SDN controller has its own database to store the operation which is used to forward the data plane. However, the size of the database will limit the scalability of the network. Hence, hybrid architecture is required to solve the volume of database, or else the communication between the controller and nodes have to be reduced. Southbound API and northbound API is important in the communication between controllers, nodes and applications. However, there are no policy which focuses on northbound API. Hence, network configuration language is required to come out with the standard of northbound API. Procera [30], Frenetic [31], FML [32] and Nettle [33] are the languages which allow the users to come out with their own policies. With these languages, the proposed policy of northbound API will act as the constraints for the controller while the user is allowed to apply different standard based on the network requirements.

4.4 Security

In Time-Sensitive Software-Defined Networking (TSSDN), there is always a challenge for unauthorized user to access others resources and privacy which should be protected. Hence, TSSDN has to ensure the applications which sharing the same resources from the same hosts are not allowed to view data and privacy of each other. FortNox [34] is a role-based authorization which can handle the conflicts of information from different sources. Hence, the interoperation of TSSDN and FortNox has the potential to provide good resource isolation between the users. Besides, open interface of SDN architecture and its well- known protocols provide an easy way for attackers to learn the knowledge of SDN. This has increased the success rate for attacker to attack TSSDN. Hence, TSSDN has to provide a high secure architecture to protect the network and system. In the current stage, SDN architecture can provide certain security supports such as firewall, intrusion detection system and network forensics. However, the security policy in TSSDN need to be strongly implemented in order to secure the network and system. Besides, the threat from the attackers are keep evolving. Hence, frequent update of the security mechanism is the only way to ensure the long term secure. Moreover, centralized SDN controller in TSSDN is always the main target for attackers to control the networks. In order to defend the network from being conquer, transport layer security (TLS) is required. TLS [35] is a security technology which provide mutual authentication in the network. TLS has the potential to handle the security threats if the standard of TLS is specified in TSSDN.

4.5 Interoperability

In Time-Sensitive Software-Defined Networking (TSSDN), migration of the network is always a big issue to be considered. Before the migration, the administrator needs to research based on different aspects based on the requirements such as quality of the products, price values and network scalability. However, compatibility is the main concern to be evaluated. In the current TSSDN, European Telecommunications Standards Institute (ETSI) Network Function Virtualization (NFV) Industry Specification Group [36], ForCES and OpenFlow are working on the standardization of their mechanisms, protocols and components. In the future, it will be great to see the cooperation of these big industry working groups to standardize most of their existing networks to provide a better environment on migration. Nowadays, TSSDN with network virtualization is growing rapidly. However, security is always a major concern in network virtualization. Hence, Network Function Virtualization (NFV) is introduced to solve the security problems. NFV is a network service architecture to provide routing and firewall in virtualization. With the interoperation of TSSDN and NFV, TSSDN is able to forward the data plane and schedule the traffic while NFV can provide a good virtualization and distribution of the resources in the network. Typical TSSDN is normally involved in the closed environment. However, the networks in industry and automation are often connected with the outside networks. Hence, centralized SDN controller is required to manage the difference between TSSDN network with outside networks. Time sensitive flows in TSSDN network is normally smoother compared with others network. TSSDN can reserved the delay characteristics of others network before entering TSSDN. Software-Defined Internet [37] is a novel idea for TSSDN to be applied on macro environments such as Wide-Area Networks (WAN). The idea is basically to separate the inter-domain components such as controller, switches and routers to involve in inter-domain task while the intra-domain components to involved in the software modification. Software-Defined Internet is potential to realize new Internet services in TSSDN. Table 1 suggests several future research directions in the realm of TSSN deployment.

Table 1. Future research directions of improvement for TSSN deployment

Quality attributes	Challenges & limitation	Future direction
Reliability	Failure of the only centralized controller will collapse the network	Involved alternative controller
	In-band traffic may cause the overhead in control plane	New Mechanism to handle in-band traffic
	Failure of intermediates nodes will affect the schedules of the other packets	Facilitate the behavior of the intermediate nodes and generate performance profile
Performance	Schedule of low priority traffic is preempted by the high priority traffic	Provide worst-case delay to low priority traffic which do not affect the performance of high priority traffic
	Time synchronization inaccuracy in the network especially for low-cost devices	Efficient Mechanism to handle synchronization inaccuracy
	Balance between the flexibility of network configuration and the bandwidth performance	Hybrid approach of TSSDN and ASSPs to balance the scalability and performance
Scalability	Balance between the flexibility and scalability	Extension application such as ALTO which provides the server to store the knowledge
	Size of database will limit the scalability	Hybrid architecture to handle the volume of database
	Lack of research and standard defined on northbound API	Proposed standard northbound API
Security	Unauthorized user accesses the network resources of authorized user through the same network	Role-based authorization to isolate different resources
	Protection from the attackers with full knowledges toward the open interface of SDN architectures and well-known protocols	Overhead-aware of the frequently update mechanism and evolve of security mechanism
	Protection of attractive centralized controller with full information	Transport layer security (TLS) to provide mutual authentication
	Protection of packets' information from Dos attack	Efficient Mechanism to recognize the packet's header
Interoperability	Migration of network	Big industry company cooperates to standardize their mechanisms, protocols and components
	TSSDN in network virtualization and cloud architectures	Cost-saving and hardware independent of using Network Function Virtualization (NFV) to provide firewall in virtualization
	Implementation of TSSDN in WAN network	Software-Defined Internet to separate the inter-domain components and intra-domain components

5   Conclusion

Time-Sensitive Software-Defined Networking (TSSDN) has a lot of potential in the future from the perspective of reliability, performance, scalability, performance and interoperability. Hence, different industries should start to involved themselves in TSSDN and overcome its challenges. In the end, the integration of TSSDN will leads to the hard real time guarantees in Cyber physical system (CPS) in automation industry in Industry 4.0.

References

1. Wang, S., Wan, J., Zhang, D., Li, D., Zhang, C.: Towards smart factory for Industry 4.0: a self-organized multi-agent system with big data based feedback and coordination. Comput. Netw. **101**, 158–168 (2016)
2. Sreedharan, V.R., Unnikrishnan, A.: Moving towards Industry 4.0: a systematic review. Int. J. Pure Appl. Math. **117**(2), 929–936 (2017)
3. Jazdi, N.: Cyber physical systems in the context of Industry 4.0. In: IEEE International Conference on Automation, Quality and Testing, Robotics, pp. 1–4 (2014)
4. Higashion Laboratory: Cyber Physical System (CPS) Research in Higashion Laboratory. http://www-higashi.ist.osaka-u.ac.jp/ ~ higashino/eng/research/cps-E.html. Accessed 18 Sept 2018
5. The Time-Sensitive Networking Task Group: IEEE 802.1 Time-Sensitive Networking Task Group. IEEE Working Group (2017). http://www.ieee802.org/1/pages/tsn.html. Accessed 18 Sept 2018
6. Teener, M.D.J., et al.: heterogeneous networks for audio and video: using IEEE 802.1 audio video bridging. Proc. IEEE **101**(11), 2339–2354 (2013)
7. Craciunas, S.S., Oliver, R.S., Chmelík, M., Steiner, W.: Scheduling real-time communication in IEEE 802.1 Qbv time sensitive networks. In: Proceedings of the 24th International Conference on Real-Time Networks and Systems, pp. 183–192 (2016)
8. P802.1Qcc – Stream Reservation Protocol (SRP) Enhancements and Performance Improvements. https://1.ieee802.org/tsn/802-1qcc/. Accessed 10 Oct 2018
9. Ahmed, K., Blech, J.O., Gregory, M.A., Schmidt, H.: Software defined networking for communication and control of cyber-physical systems. In: IEEE 21st International Conference on Parallel and Distributed Systems (ICPADS), pp. 803–808 (2015)
10. Nayak, N.G., Dürr, F., Rothermel, K.: Software-defined environment for reconfigurable manufacturing systems. In: 5th International Conference on the Internet of Things (IOT), pp. 122–129 (2015)
11. Cisco Public: Time-Sensitive Networking: A Technical Introduction White Paper Time-Sensitive Networking: A Technical Introduction (2017)
12. Böhm, M., Ohms, J., Gebauer, O., Wermser, D.: Architectural Design of a TSN to SDN Gateway in the Context of Industry 4.0
13. IEEE Standard for Local and metropolitan area networks — Bridges and Bridged Networks - Amendment 24: Path Control and Reservation. IEEE Std 802.1Qca-2015 (Amendment to IEEE Std 802.1Q-2014 as Amend. by IEEE Std 802.1Qcd-2015 IEEE Std 802.1Q-2014/Cor 1-2015), pp. 1–120, March 2016
14. Singh, S.: Routing algorithms for time sensitive networks (2017)

15. Dürr, F., Nayak, N.G.: No-wait packet scheduling for IEEE time-sensitive networks (TSN). In: Proceedings of the 24th International Conference on Real-Time Networks and Systems, pp. 203–212 (2016)
16. Craciunas, S.S., Oliver, R.S.: SMT-based task-and network-level static schedule generation for time-triggered networked systems. In: Proceedings of the 22nd International Conference on Real-Time Networks and Systems, p. 45 (2014)
17. Nayak, N.G., Dürr, F., Rothermel, K.: Time-Sensitive Software-Defined Networks for Real-Time Applications (2016)
18. Doria, A., et al.: Forwarding and control element separation (ForCES) protocol specification (2010)
19. McKeown, N., et al.: OpenFlow: enabling innovation in campus networks. ACM SIGCOMM Comput. Commun. Rev. **38**(2), 69–74 (2008)
20. Sezer, S., et al.: Are we ready for SDN? Implementation challenges for software-defined networks. IEEE Commun. Mag. **51**(7), 36–43 (2013)
21. Du, J.L., Herlich, M.: Software-defined networking for real-time ethernet. In: ICINCO, no. 2, pp. 584–589 (2016)
22. Gopalakrishnan, A.: Applications of software defined networks in industrial automation (2014)
23. Ditzel, G.A., Didier, P.: Time sensitive network (TSN) protocols and use in ethernet/ip systems. In: ODVA Industry Conference & 17th Annual Meeting (2015)
24. Quentin Monnet: An introduction to SDN (2016). https://qmonnet.github.io/whirl-offload/2016/07/08/introduction-to-sdn/. Accessed 23 Jan 2019
25. Shamugam, V., Murray, I., Leong, J.A., Sidhu, A.S.: Software defined networking challenges and future direction: a case study of implementing SDN features on OpenStack private cloud. IOP Conf. Ser. Mater. Sci. Eng. **121**(1), 12003 (2016)
26. Nasrallah, A., et al.: Ultra-low latency (ULL) networks: The IEEE TSN and IETF DetNet standards and related 5G ULL research. IEEE Commun. Surv. Tutor. **21**, 88–145 (2018)
27. King, D., Zhao, Q., Hardwick, J.: Path Computation Element Communication Protocol (PCEP) Management Information Base (MIB) Module (2014)
28. Lange, S., et al.: Heuristic approaches to the controller placement problem in large scale SDN networks. IEEE Trans. Netw. Serv. Manag. **12**(1), 4–17 (2015)
29. Tsou, T., Yin, H., Xie, H., Lopez, D.: Use Cases for ALTO with Software Defined Networks (2012)
30. Voellmy, A., Kim, H., Feamster, N.: Procera: a language for high-level reactive network control. In: Proceedings of the first workshop on Hot topics in software defined networks, pp. 43–48 (2012)
31. Foster, N., et al.: Frenetic: a network programming language. ACM Sigplan Not. **46**(9), 279–291 (2011)
32. Hinrichs, T.L., Gude, N.S., Casado, M., Mitchell, J.C., Shenker, S.: Practical declarative network management. In: Proceedings of the 1st ACM workshop on Research on enterprise networking, pp. 1–10 (2009)
33. Voellmy, A., Hudak, P.: Nettle: taking the sting out of programming network routers. In: Rocha, R., Launchbury, J. (eds.) PADL 2011. LNCS, vol. 6539, pp. 235–249. Springer, Heidelberg (2011). https://doi.org/10.1007/978-3-642-18378-2_19
34. Porras, P., Shin, S., Yegneswaran, V., Fong, M., Tyson, M., Gu, G.: A security enforcement kernel for OpenFlow networks. In: Proceedings of the First Workshop on Hot Topics in Software Defined Networks, pp. 121–126 (2012)
35. Software-Defined Networking: The New Norm for Networks ONF White Paper (2012)

36. Neghabi, A., Navimipour, N.J., Hosseinzadeh, M., Rezaee, A.: Load balancing mechanisms in the software defined networks: a systematic and comprehensive review of the literature. IEEE Access **6**, 14159–14178 (2018)

37. Ejaz, S., Iqbal, Z.: Network function virtualization: challenges and prospects for modernization. In: Proceedings of the International Conference on Engineering and Emerging Technologies (ICEET), pp. 1–5, February 2018

Method of Deep Web Collection for Mobile Application Store Based on Category Keyword Searching

Guosheng Xu[1] ![ORCID], Zhimin Wu[2], Chengze Li[2(✉)], Jinghua Yan[2(✉)],
Jing Yuan[2(✉)], Zhiyong Wang[2(✉)], and Lu Wang[1]

[1] School of Cyberspace Security, Beijing University of Posts
and Telecommunications, Beijing 100876, China
guoshengxu@bupt.edu.cn
[2] National Computer Network Emergency Response Technical
Team/Coordination Center of China (CNCERT), Beijing, China
{lichengze,yuanjing,yjh}@cert.org.cn,
w.zy@foxmail.com

Abstract. With the rapid development of mobile Internet, mobile Internet has come into the era of big data. The demand for data analysis of mobile applications has become more and more obvious, which puts forward higher requirements for the standard of mobile application information collection. Due to the large number of applications, almost all third-party app stores display only a small number of applications, and most of the information is hidden in the Deep Web database behind the query form. The existing crawler strategy cannot meet the demand. In order to solve the above problems, this paper proposes a collection method based on category keywords query to improve the crawl rate and integrity of the mobile app stores information collection. Firstly, get the information of application interfaces that include various kinds of applications by using the vertical crawler. Then extract the keywords that represent each category of applications by TF-IDF algorithm from the application name and description information. Finally, incremental crawling is performed by using keyword query-based acquisition method. Results show that this collection method effectively promoted information integrity and acquisition efficiency.

Keywords: Deep Web · TF-IDF algorithm · Incremental crawling

1 Introduction

With the rapid development of mobile Internet, more and more users choose mobile intelligent terminals to enjoy various services in the Internet era. According to iiMedia Research, the number of active users of third-party mobile application stores increased to 453 million in the third quarter of 2016, and nearly half of mobile Internet users chose mobile application stores as the channel to get application information [1]. Driven by the "Internet +" strategy, the mobile Internet is more closely integrated with more and more traditional industries. The requirements for application distribution,

G. Wang et al. (Eds.): SpaCCS 2019, LNCS 11611, pp. 325–335, 2019.
https://doi.org/10.1007/978-3-030-24907-6_25

security testing, user behavior analysis and other requirements expand significantly. The era of mobile Internet big data is facing greater opportunities and challenges.

At present, there are various methods of large data processing and analysis, but how to obtain more complete application sample data is the primary problem [3–6]. As an important entrance to the mobile Internet, the mobile application store market has steadily occupied the main entrance of application distribution since its birth, and there are more than 100 kinds of application stores in the market. According to statistics, as of December 2018, there were more than 2.68 million mobile apps on shelves in China's local third-party app stores, and more than 1.81 million apps on shelves in Apple stores (China). Therefore, the research objective of this paper is to obtain more complete application data from the mobile application store, so as to conduct more complete security detection and analysis of mass applications, otherwise, [7] implement a crawler that will help in getting more precise result for a focused crawler with ranking.

In China, the number of applications in the database of third-party application stores, such as Tencent App Store and Baidu Mobile Assistant, has reached hundreds of thousands or even millions. Since the majority of users only look at the first dozen pages, in order to save network resources, application stores only display some of the top-ranking applications in Surface Web, but hide most of them in Deep Web, which requires submitting forms to search and obtain. As a result, traditional crawlers gather application information that can only obtain surface web information. The completeness rate is low. To solve this problem, this paper studies and implements a data acquisition method for Deep Web, a mobile application store. By analyzing the matching mechanism and classification characteristics of mobile store application search, and combining with TF-IDF algorithm [10], an automatic keyword search method based on the application name and application description information is proposed. Incremental crawling is achieved by filling in search form automatically, which greatly improves the completeness and efficiency of application information collection.

2   Research Status of Mobile Application Data Acquisition

Traditional web crawlers aim to solve the problem of crawling efficiency and search results matching relevance, but ignore the information hidden in Deep Web. Deep Web contains more information than Surface Web. Brightplanet's White Paper on Deep Web pointed out that the amount of information on Deep Web is 400–500 times that of information on Surface Web, and that the growth rate of Deep Web is much faster than Surface Web. It can be seen that the study of Deep Web crawler is an effective way to further improve the collection rate of information [8].

Internet web pages can be divided into "Surface Web" and "Deep Web", also known as Hidden Web. Surface Web refers to the pages that can be indexed by traditional web search engines. It is mainly composed of static pages that can be accessed by hyperlinks. Deep Web refers to the collection of resources stored in the network database that cannot be accessed through hyperlinks but through dynamic page technology. It is proposed by Dr. Jill Ellsworth in 1994, and defined as web pages with information content that is difficult to find for ordinary search engines.

At present, there are some researches on Deep Web, most of which are based on the crawler technology of form filling. According to the method of filling in the form, there are two kinds: (1) filling in the form based on domain knowledge. (2) Form filling based on web page structure analysis. In domain-specific information search, relevant domain knowledge often helps to improve the search results. As the most powerful tool for describing the semantics of network information, Ontology is widely used in domain-oriented retrieval. The application of ontology in search technology is mainly divided into two aspects: one is to establish an ontology-based query model to specify user's search requests; the other is to set up the mapping between ontology and vocabulary set in web pages to identify network resources semantically.

In terms of search request specification, Navigli et al. [2] first proposed ontology-based query expansion, using the concepts of synonyms and specific subclass relationships in ontology to expand queries. In terms of information semantic identification, Baader [11] proposed an ontology-based information retrieval system FindUR, which uses description logic to represent synonyms, hypernyms and hyponyms in Wordnet. The resource is identified by reasoning to improve the accuracy of user response and recall rate.

Crawler technology based on Web page structure analysis generally needs structured analysis of the surface web pages to extract the information needed to fill in the form when there is no domain knowledge or only limited domain knowledge. Ntoulas [12] and others automatically generate new search keywords for the previous search results and prioritize them to obtain information hidden behind the form. The advantage of this method is that it can use the least number of submissions to get the data users want, but it cannot deal with forms with multiple forms. Zifei et al. [13] designed and implemented a web crawler system Spideep supporting Ajax, which can effectively capture Ajax dynamic script web pages to extract Deep Web resources. Aiming at the capture of Ajax pages, the system embedded an interface-free browser HtmlUnit. Firstly, the JavaScript script in the original web page source document is preliminarily parsed and the DOM tree is reconstructed. Then it simulates browser's various operational behaviors, and further reveals the hidden Deep Web information dynamically. Finally, the DOM tree is parsed by web page parsing tool to obtain valuable Deep Web information.

However, in mobile application information collection, there is no domain ontology library, and the use of generic ontology libraries such as ZhiWang (cnki.net) has little improvement on search results. Therefore, this paper considers the information structure features of mobile application store, uses Deep Web crawler technology based on Web page structure analysis, carries out statistical analysis of application information displayed on surface pages, and proposes a two-stage sampling strategy. The strategy is aimed to improve the crawl rate of application background application data acquisition.

At present, researchers have applied the general Deep Web acquisition technology to mobile application stores. Some scholar designed a Deep Web data acquisition system based on word frequency based on the acquisition strategy proposed by Ntoulas [12]. Firstly, the application names are extracted from the crawled Surface Web application information, and the high-frequency words are extracted as search keywords. Then, the search form is automatically filled to expose a large amount of application information hidden in Deep Web. Finally, the crawler system is used to collect information, so as to improve the acquisition integrity of the acquisition system.

However, the results of a single submission of a search form are limited. The main question at present is how to design a keyword extraction method to obtain more application information with fewer queries. Although the existing Deep Web acquisition strategy can improve the application store acquisition integrity rate, there are still some limitations such as low acquisition integrity rate and collection efficiency. Mobile App Store's surface information display has a clear hierarchical structure according to the application category, and is related to the background information storage, which is reflected in the application search matching mechanism. Therefore, this paper studies the design rules of mobile application stores, and proposes a Deep Web crawler strategy based on the application category keyword searching.

3   Research on the Law of Application Store Design

In order to mine the information in Deep Web of mobile application store, it is necessary to study the design rules of application store. By analyzing the surface structure information, the Surface Web crawling strategy is formulated to provide data support for keyword extraction. By analyzing the application of search matching mechanism, keyword extraction methods are designed for extracting more hidden application information.

3.1   Structural Characteristics of Application Stores

The overall structure of mobile application store website has its regularity. Macroscopically, it is composed of home page, classified page, next page and specific application page. For information collection, the structure of application store has become an advantage. Clear context can guide web crawlers to crawl Surface Web. However, different application stores have different web structure, so different crawling strategies and information extraction methods should be formulated according to the different application stores' web structures on the general method.

3.2   Analysis of Application Store Collection Entry Point

Through the analysis of dozens of mobile application stores, we find that although the name of the collection entry point is different, according to the actual function, it can be divided into: store home page, application links of various types, application search, popular software, download ranking, soaring ranking, and necessary installation. The crawler strategy for Mobile Application Store aims to crawl as complete application information as possible under the condition of ensuring the efficiency of crawling. The entry points of popular software, download ranking, soaring ranking, and necessities show only a small number of popular downloaded software or business cooperation software with application stores. Each entry point shows the application information overlapping, which cannot meet the requirements of the crawler system. For classified pages, the number of display applications is considerable, and there is no cross-display, which is suitable for Surface Web data acquisition entry point.

By submitting search forms with keywords, we can obtain application links displayed on the surface network, and expose applications hidden behind the forms. It is the best choice for application store Deep Web data crawling.

3.3 Search Matching Mechanism

By entering a large number of random keywords into the mainstream third-party mobile application stores, such as 360 Mobile Assistants, Tencent App Store, Baidu Mobile Assistants, and so on, and analyzing the corresponding search results, it is found that most of the search results of mobile application stores are related to the application name, application description information and application category.

Taking 360 mobile assistants as an example, according to the location of the search terms by typing "gold coin" keywords in the search bar, the search results can be divided into three categories: (i) in application name; (ii) in application description, and (iii) in application label.

According to the structural characteristics of mobile application stores, this paper proposes a method of crawling application information layer by layer, using XPath location to get the information of classified page nodes in the shop front page, and extracting application-related information layer by layer. In terms of search keyword extraction, this paper proposes a TF-IDF sorting algorithm based on application name and application description information according to the store search mechanism. The high-weight words of each application category are used as keywords submitted to the search form to obtain application information hidden in Deep Web. At the same time, the keywords proposed by us can better represent the application category information, and the cross-information of search results of different categories of words is less, which can greatly improve the efficiency of system completion.

4   Design and Implementation

4.1   Framework of the Acquisition Method

Based on the above research, this paper fully considers the characteristics of mobile application store, and designs and implements a Deep Web acquisition method for mobile application store. The framework of the acquisition method is shown in the following Fig. 1.

Application acquisition includes the following three steps: Surface Web crawling, search entry point analysis, and deep web crawling. Surface web crawling can obtain the application information in the application store and provide data basis for keyword extraction; entry point analysis uses string matching method to obtain the store search entrance, form submission form and content; Deep Web crawling can incrementally collect all kinds of application information, which can be divided into following three sub-steps.

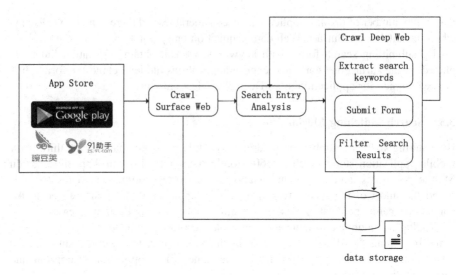

Fig. 1. Framework of the acquisition method

(i)   Keyword extraction. The latest application names of each application category are extracted from the database, and the corresponding descriptive information is taken as samples. Samples are segmented, weighted and ranked, and top-ranked words are selected as search keywords. The searching keywords of the same category in each application store need only be extracted once.

(ii) Form automatic submission. The extracted keywords are filled in the application store inquiry entry point, and the form is submitted.

(iii) Searching results filtering. Filter the links which is accessed and crawled; collect new application information and put it into the database.

4.2   Keyword Extraction

If a word or phrase appears frequently in one type of articles and rarely in other types of articles, it is considered that the word or phrase has superior ability to distinguish between categories. TF is a measure of the importance of a word in a class of articles, while IDF measures the universal importance of a word. The importance of each word is proportional to TF, but inversely proportional to IDF. By calculating and extracting the keywords with higher TF-IDF in each application category, we can search as many applications as possible with low cross-over rate in the whole process of information filling.

The extraction of keywords needs to extract the latest application information from database according to application categories, which includes the following four steps:

(i)   Pretreatment. The application name and description information are segmented and the stop words are removed. For the description information and the application name of an application A, the result of pretreatment can be expressed as $\{W_1, W_2, \ldots, W_n\}$. So for an application category C with m applications, it can be expressed as m-dimensional vectors $\{A_1, A_2, \ldots, A_m\}$.

(ii) For W_i, we define

$$TF(W_i, C) = \frac{f_{W_i}}{\sum_m A} \tag{1}$$

fW_i represents the frequency of W_i appears in Category C, and $\sum_m A$ represents the total number of words in Category C.

(iii) Similarly, we define

$$IDF(W_i) = \log\left(\frac{A}{\{j : W_i \in dA_j\}}\right) \tag{2}$$

A represents the total number of sampling applications, and $\{j : W_i \in A_j\}$ represents the number of applications that contain W_i.

(iv) Through formula

$$\text{TF–IDF(i)} = \text{TF}(W_i, C) * \text{IDF}(W_i) \tag{3}$$

The TF-IDF values of each word are calculated and sorted.

4.3 Crawler Implementation

Based on the Scrapy crawler framework of the Python language, this paper automatically submits the form to the target server by analyzing the protocol of the page containing the form. The process of web crawler page acquisition is as follows (Fig. 2):

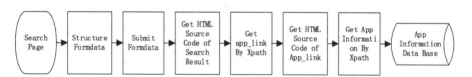

Fig. 2. Collection process

In the figure above, when the web crawler constructs the form, it extracts the query keywords extracted row by row and fills in the form as query words, and submits them to the target server. Then, according to the traditional crawler crawling mode, the search results crawl each application page through the URL association, and use Xpath location to obtain the matching information.

5   Experiment

5.1   Environment

This experiment tests the Deep Web acquisition system of the third-party mobile application store based on keyword search. In this experiment, a computer was used to build the environment. The configuration is as follows (Table 1):

Table 1. Computer configuration

Host computer	CPU	Operating system
Intel® Core™ i5-2430M CPU @ 3.30 GHz	Dual core	Windows 8

5.2   Query Keyword Extraction

In this experiment, traditional web crawler (Surface crawler), Deep Web crawler based on application name keyword searching [8] (Deep crawler by name), Deep Web crawler based on application category keyword searching (Deep crawler by category) were used to collect application information from Android official application store Google lay and nine mainstream third-party mobile application stores in China.

Because of the limited number of applications on the surface of a single application store, we cannot provide good data support for keyword extraction. First, we crawl nearly 50 mobile application stores to obtain app information in the surface web pages, and extract 100,000 application information from ten categories, respectively, as the basic data for keyword extraction. Because of the different classification mechanism of stores, we classify them by manual confirmation, such as "life" and "health" in Tencent app store [10], health care and "life rest" in 360 mobile assistant [11], and regard them as "life" category in the extraction process. The Deep crawler by category is computed by the steps mentioned in 3.1.1. Top 1000 words in each category are selected as keywords according to the weight.

5.3   Analysis of Completeness and Efficiency of Crawling

In this paper, we ranked 50 app stores according to the percentage of the total number of apps crawled from the store surface and the distribution of active users. As shown in Table 2, the top 10 mobile application stores are experimented. The application information is collected by three kinds of crawlers. It is found that the proposed method has better application crawling integrity and efficiency. Taking three third-party application stores and Android official stores as examples, the results of application quantity collection are shown in Table 3. Baidu Mobile Assistant, 360 Mobile Assistant and Tencent App Store are top three of the third-party mobile application stores in the active users ranking.

From the experimental results, we can see that the number of applications acquired by Deep crawler by category is far more than that of traditional Web crawler, and the application integrity rate of Deep crawler by name is a step forward. Due to the design

Table 2. Keywords extracted based on each category

Category	Keywords					
Travel	Map	Tourism	Hotel	Travel	Navigation	City
Shopping	goods	taobao	shopping	groupon	preferential	brand
Financial	finance	investment	earnings	fund	trading	loan
Life	service	provide	life	decorate	function	user
Communication	SMS	chat	call	voice	contact	social
System	phone	software	application	setting	program	function
Learning	learning	English	baby	vocabulary	test	kids
Video	music	video	ringtone	player	live	Movie
Reading	reading	novel	bookmark	download	cartoon	news

Table 3. Comprehensive ranking of third party app stores

Mobile app store	Active user distribution in third party app stores	Percentage of surface apps	Score
360	42.10%	65.60%	53.85
Tencent	34.70%	37.50%	36.15
Baidu	25.30%	72.40%	48.45
Wandoujia	11.10%	49.20%	30.15
PP Assistant	8.90%	56.40%	32.65
Android Store	7.90%	28.40%	18.15
Others	6.00%	66.68%	36.34

of anti-crawler and dynamic pages, the search results of a single search term are limited, which results in a large gap between the collection results of Deep crawler by name and other third-party stores. But it still far exceeds the number of traditional crawler collection results, greatly improving the application crawling integrity rate (Table 4).

Table 4. Mobile app store data collection contrast table

Mobile app store	Traditional web crawler	Deep web crawler based on applications' name	Deep web crawler based on category
Googleplay	22356	31568	45594
Baidu	13255	241205	416011
360	30786	264576	345763
Tencent	7356	85346	105464

Taking Baidu Mobile Assistant as an example, the crawling of application information on surface web pages takes 0.4 h, while Deep Web crawler finishes

10,000 keywords search after 28 h. Among them, the number of Deep Web crawler applications based on application category keyword searching declined rapidly, and the growth rate declined significantly after 8 h. After manual confirmation, it was found that because it did not consider the application store search mechanism, using the application category features, different searching keywords would produce a lot of duplicate information, which would cause a lower number of final applications, and a low efficiency. The number of applications crawled by Deep crawler by category has satisfied linear growth, which proves that the redundant application information collected is less and has higher efficiency of completion.

6 Conclusion

This paper analyses the structure characteristics, entry points and search matching mechanism of the application store, studies the keyword extraction method based on TF-IDF, and designs and implements a mobile application store Deep Web data acquisition system based on keyword search combined with traditional web crawlers. The system consists of keyword extraction module and web crawler module. The whole system is implemented in the Python language. Finally, the data acquisition results of the application store show that the system can effectively improve the efficiency and the integrity of the acquisition compared with the Deep Web data acquisition system based on the application name word frequency.

But there is still room for improvement. Although the system improves the efficiency and completeness of the collection, there are still many cross-applications in the search results, and it cannot guarantee that all the application information in the store background database is collected. How to further increase the coverage of search keywords for applications and reduce the number of cross-search applications, and improve the integrity and efficiency of collection, is the focus of follow-up research.

Acknowledgement. This research is supported by National Key R&D Program of China (No. 2018YFC0806900), Beijing Engineering Laboratory For security emulation & Hacking and Defense of IoV; This research is supported by National Secrecy Scientific Research Program of China (No. BMKY2018802-1) too.

References

1. iiMedia Research. http://www.iimedia.cn/c400/47250.html. Accessed 23 Dec 2016
2. Navigli, R., Velardi, P.: An analysis of ontology-based query expansion strategies. In: Proceedings of the 14th European Conference on Machine Learning, Croatia, pp. 42–49 (2003)
3. Hernández, I., Rivero, C.R., Ruiz, D.: World wide web (2018). https://doi.org/10.1007/s11280-018-0602-1
4. Olston, C., Najork, M.: Web crawling. Found. Trends Inf. Retriev. **4**(3), 175246 (2010)
5. Li, J.-R., Mao, Y.-F., Yang, K.: Improvement and application of TF * IDF algorithm. In: Liu, B., Chai, C. (eds.) ICICA 2011. LNCS, vol. 7030, pp. 121–127. Springer, Heidelberg (2011). https://doi.org/10.1007/978-3-642-25255-6_16

6. Li, W., Li, J., Zhang, B.: Saliency-GD: A TF-IDF analogy for landmark image mining. In: Zeng, B., Huang, Q., El Saddik, A., Li, H., Jiang, S., Fan, X. (eds.) PCM 2017. LNCS, vol. 10735, pp. 477–486. Springer, Cham (2018). https://doi.org/10.1007/978-3-319-77380-3_45
7. Mahale, V.V., Dhande, M.T., Pandit, A.V.: Advanced web crawler for deep web interface using binary vector & page rank. In: 2nd International Conference on I-SMAC (IoT in Social, Mobile, Analytics and Cloud) (I-SMAC)I-SMAC (IoT in Social, Mobile, Analytics and Cloud) (I-SMAC), 30–31 August 2018
8. Brightplanet. https://brightplanet.com/2013/03/whitepaper-understanding-the-deep-web-in-10-minutes. Accessed 12 Mar 2013
9. Zhang, L., et al.: Online modeling of esthetic communities using deep perception graph analytics. IEEE Trans. Multimedia **20**(6), 1462–1474 (2018)
10. Zhu, Z., Liang, J., Li, D., Yu, H., Liu, G.: Hot topic detection based on a refined TF-IDF algorithm. IEEE Access **7**, 26996–27007 (2019)
11. Baader, F.: The Description Logic Handbook: Theory, Implementation and Applications. Cambridge University Press, London (2003)
12. Ntoulas, A., Zerfos, P., Cho, J.: Downloading textual hidden web content through key-word queries. In: Proceedings of the 5th ACM/IEEE-CS Joint Conference on Digital Libraries, pp. 100–109. ACM (2005)
13. Zifei, D.: Design and Implementation of an Ajax Supported Deep Web Crawler Sys-tem. South China University of Technology, Guangdong (2015)

Using Machine Learning to Find Anomalies in Field Bus Network Traffic

Martin Peters[iD], Johannes Goltz[✉][iD], Simeon Wiedenmann[iD],
and Thomas Mundt[iD]

Institute of Computer Science, University of Rostock, 18051 Rostock, Germany
{johannes.goltz,simeon.wiedenmann,thomas.mundt}@uni-rostock.de

Abstract. Devices for building automation are often connected by field buses. Typically no encryption and authentication is available, hence the transmitted data can be read by anyone connected to the bus. This problem gave rise to the idea of developing an intrusion detection system. Due to the lack of information about previous attacks on building automation it is not possible to use a pattern-based IDS. Unsupervised machine learning algorithms should be able to find anomalies automatically and trigger an alarm in case of intrusion. A concept how to create such an IDS is hereby presented. For the analysis of the feature space local outlier factor, support vector machines and entropy analysis were used. The occurring addresses were also monitored.

Some of the tested attack scenarios could be detected. Attacks injecting traffic massively got found by nearly all four tested modules, while more cautious ones haven't been detected.

Keywords: Field bus · Machine learning · KNX · BAS · Anomaly detection

1 Introduction

For companies that use several large buildings, the automation of heating, ventilation, air conditioning and lighting is a good possibility to save energy and provide comfort benefits. The protocols for communication between devices doing this are often based on field buses. Looking at this problem from the security perspective, severe issues can be identified. There is neither authentication nor encryption in most of the standard KNX installations. This means anyone connected to the bus can listen to all data on it and can also inject traffic. Due to the nature of these system and the consequently implied ubiquitous presence of the network, the cables are often easily accessible and a small electromagnetic coil on the wall has shown to sometimes be sufficient to capture the traffic (see [9]). This leads to the problem, that the privacy sensitive information transmitted on the cable can easily be intercepted and thus even personal information can be extracted [8].

Since there are almost no commonly available security enhancing tools for field buses to find, an intrusion detection system (IDS) should be set up to

© Springer Nature Switzerland AG 2019
G. Wang et al. (Eds.): SpaCCS 2019, LNCS 11611, pp. 336–353, 2019.
https://doi.org/10.1007/978-3-030-24907-6_26

identify intrusive behaviour in the network and to increase its security. Due to the lack of recorded attack patterns it is not possible to set up a classic pattern-based IDS. Alternatively, unsupervised machine learning algorithms promise to counteract this fundamental disadvantage.

2   Background Knowledge

This section will provide a brief insight into the basics of field bus protocols, machine learning, and intrusion detection in general. As an example for field buses we chose KNX, since it is widely used in Europe and a reasonable sized sample of telegrams was obtained of the computer science building of the University Rostock. However, the proposed methods are not limited to the KNX technology, as the concepts are applicable to various other field bus systems.

2.1   KNX as Field Bus

This paper describes the implementation and design of an intrusion detection system using machine learning on the field bus level while evaluating the proposed IDS. It is therefore necessary to understand the content of telegrams on the bus and the main principle of operation.

The communication architecture of KNX can be described according to the OSI-layers (see Fig. 1). Depending on the observed features, the IDS will use information from different layers. Each device is configured with a physical address, unique to the network. Another bus node can send telegrams directly to this address (p2p). For normal operation, however, point-to-multipoint or - multicast communication is more commonly used. For point-to-multipoint communication all devices also listen to the address of their corresponding device group. One group address can be assigned to multiple devices, thus forming groups. In any given group only one device is allowed to be a sending device. The other devices just listen. The devices are organised in a hierarchical structure on the bus (see Fig. 2).

Physical addresses reflect this hierarchical order by distinguishing between area (4 Bit), line (4 Bit), and device part (8 Bit). In the string representation, these parts are separated by a dot, e.g. 1.1.1 (see Fig. 3). Group addresses, on the other hand, are divided by "/", e.g. 2/4/2. When planning a new building automation project it is possible to choose between 2- (5 Bits/11 Bits) or 3-layered (5 Bits/3 Bits/8 Bits) group addresses (see Fig. 3).

Within the scope of IDS the couplers could play a central role, since they are responsible for routing telegrams. Couplers exist in two variants: backbone- and line-couplers. While backbone-couplers connect different areas with each other, line-couplers connect different lines. Fundamentally, backbone- or line-couplers are the same type of device, the distinction is merely on the logical level. By assigning an address to the couplers, they recognise whether they operate as backbone- or line-coupler. Commonly couplers can also filter telegrams. If this feature is supported by the device, it has to be enabled in the Engineering Tool

Layer 5 - Application Layer	APCI	
	A_GroupValue_Read	A_GroupValue_Response
	A_GroupValue_Write	... (see DIN EN 50090-4-1)

Layer 4 - Network Layer	TPCI	
	connection-less	connection-oriented
	point-to-multipoint (multicast)	point-to-point (unicast)
	point-to-domain (broadcast)	
	point-to-all-points (system broadcast)	
	point-to-point (unicast)	

Layer 3 - Transport Layer	Addresses	
	Physical Address	Group-Address

Layer 2 - Data-link Layer	Network multiple access method	
	KNX-TP	CSMA/CA
	KNX-IP	
	KNX-RF	
	KNX-PL	CSMA (slotted access)

Layer 1 - Physical Layer	Communication media	
	Twisted Pair	Radio-Frequency
	IP	Power-Line

Fig. 1. KNX according to the OSI-layers; corresponding information given in each layer

Software (ETS). This program is used to plan and configure KNX-projects. ETS is also responsible for creating and loading a specific configuration onto each device. Frequently, the only available option for traffic filtering is to either turn it on or off. The filter rules are derived automatically by the ETS and configured along with the device configuration.

Filtering and routing of messages can be implemented in various ways, since KNX accounts for various physical transfer media. E.g. a line could be connected to the backbone with one or more IP gateways. Hence the concept presented here relies on telegrams captured from a KNX-IP gateway which are available in the cEMI format (see Table 1). This format is a generic data structure for exchanging KNX telegrams on different media types [3]. The information provided by cEMI telegrams are significant for the various communication aspects which can be monitored by the proposed system.

2.2 Machine Learning

Machine learning in the context of information processing, describes a set of algorithms used to extrapolate information from unknown data, using a prior known set of data, the so-called training set. In the specific context of IDS, machine learning can be used to differentiate abnormal and possibly malicious traffic from traffic caused by normal operation. This concept is based on the assumption that abnormal traffic appears as an outlier, which is a point in a vector space outside the main cluster of normal observations. According to [4] these algorithms can be put into one of three categories:

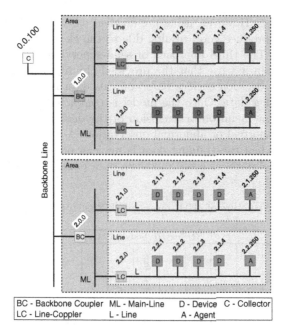

Fig. 2. Logical structure of a KNX network

Physical Address	4 Bit	.	4 Bit	.	8 Bit
Group Address (3-level)	5 Bit	/	3 Bit	/	8 Bit
Group Address (2-level)			5 Bit	/	11 Bit

Fig. 3. Address schema in KNX

1. **Unsupervised:** Detecting outliers without prior knowledge
2. **Supervised:** Modelling normal and abnormal data
3. **Semi-supervised:** Modelling only normal data

In approach 1 the data is treated as statically distributed. During the training phase a statistical curve reflecting the distribution of normal behaviour is established. Any outlier in the training data can be pruned using confidence intervals. Once the training is concluded, incoming data is compared to the derived distribution. If it lies outside a predefined confidence interval, it is considered to be an outlier. However, when too many outliers occur in the training data, they become part of the mean and the model gets distorted so it might accept actual malicious data as normal. Consequently, the quality of the model is directly proportional to the quality of the training data. Supervised models (2) work with pre-labeled training data, hence it is best suited to static data and stable systems. As the labelling process has to be repeated every time the base-line behaviour changes, this approach is less suited for continuously trained or dynamic systems. However, using pre-labelled data of normal and abnormal data promises to produce good results, due to the clear decision surface which can be modelled. The third approach of semi-supervised models also requires pre-labelled data, in a sense that the provided training data must be entirely free of outliers. A decision surface based on this data is derived, which tightly outlines the training data. Once the model is completed, every incoming data point is checked for inclusion or exclusion of the decision surface, resulting in a classification as normal or abnormal observation. A major concern using this technique arises when the training data is unclean or does not model the full spectrum of normal data, as every unknown data point is classified as outlier.

Table 1. Structure of cEMI-messages (KNXnet/IP-body) (c.f. [3]).

KNXnet/IP body (cEMI)																
cEMI-message-code	length of info	info	frame-type-flag	reserved ("0")	repeat-flag	system-broadcast-flag	priority	acknowledge-request-flag	confirm-flag	destination address type	hop count	extended frame format (eff)	source address	destination address	length	TPCI/APCI & data
1 byte	1 byte	variable	1 bit	1 bit	1 bit	1 bit	2 bit	1 bit	1 bit	1 bit	3 bit	4 bit	2 byte	2 byte	1 byte	variable

In this paper, the following classification algorithms were tested regarding their performance in detecting outliers in a dataset of KNX cEMI telegrams.

1. **k-Nearest neighbour (kNN):**
   This algorithm calculates the sum of the distances to the k nearest neighbours. Given the assumption that normal observations are more frequent than outliers, the calculated sum of distances is lower in clusters of normality. Consequently, outliers will have a higher summed distance and thus can be detected.

2. **Local Outlier Factor (LOF):**
   The main advantage of the LOF is the possibility to classify clusters with different densities by not relying on a global threshold. The LOF is based on the kNN, but is specially designed to distinguish outliers from clusters of varying density. It does so by enforcing locality and comparing the sum of distances for MINPTS nearest points. The MINPTS parameter specifies the number of nearest neighbours from which the distance is checked. If they are further away from the examined point than from each other, the point is considered to be an outlier.

3. **Support Vector Machines (SVM):**

SVMs are a classic technique for classification. A training algorithm defines decision surfaces within the vector space to separate different classes from each other. SVMs with one class can be used for outlier detection, whereby only the normality is modelled, resulting in the requirement that the full spectrum of normality needs to be modelled. This makes the sub-class of SVMs a representative of semi-supervised algorithms.

4. **Entropy:**

The entropy according to Shannon is a measurement of how much information a new data point provides compared to already found clusters [14]. There are multiple approaches known to use entropy in outlier detection. E.g. Toshniwal and Eshwar [16] separated the data in a fixed number of clusters and calculated the lowest entropy of a new data point when added to one of these clusters. The clusters consist of a running window and each data point is added to the cluster which produces the lowest entropy. This approach consequently promotes continuous training. Another approach is to model a probability mass function (PMF) out of a training set and use this to calculate the entropy for a new data point against it. Compared to the approach presented by Toshniwal and Eshwar it bears the benefit of separated training and operation phases. This separation eliminates the concern of an attacker slowly manipulating the baseline of network activity.

2.3   Intrusion Detection Systems

Intrusion Detection Systems monitor traffic in the network and attempt to find anomalies or special patterns, which can indicate possible intrusions. In a second step, the responsible administrators can be notified or the system itself can intercept. Systems that defend themselves against attacks are also called Intrusion Prevention Systems.

In generally IDSs can be roughly separated into anomaly-based and signature-based systems. Signature-based IDSs examine the bypassing traffic for anomalies. To distinguish normal traffic from possibly malicious activities they need to establish a baseline first, which is called a training phase. Bypassing data is then compared to this baseline in order to detect statistical deviations and possible intrusions. Signature-based systems are a more classic approach. They aim to detect intrusions by searching for known malicious patterns or packets that violate the underlying protocols. As a result, they are heavily dependent on the quality of their pattern library and the understanding of the used protocols [10].

2.4   Flow-Monitoring

A flow is a set of packets or telegrams that pass through an observation point with certain common properties in a certain time interval [15]. These properties have to be determined beforehand. At the end of a flow, it is forwarded to the collector. For the common properties in field buses like KNX, source and destination address as well as APCI could be used. Properties like hop count, payload length and TPCI can then be measured.

The final step is data analysis. This can be done either manually or automatically (as shown in Fig. 4). While a manual analysis would be feasible for research projects, this is not possible for larger industrial installations. Therefore an automated way has to be found.

KNX offers only 9600 Bits/s as data rate via twisted pair. To not be obligated to bring out an extra network for the network data to be analysed, it has to be transmitted in-band. Only flows are sent over the network to prevent excessive bus load. Otherwise the segment of the network would become useless. While this would indeed improve security by preventing any attacks on the bus, this is not the desired behaviour.

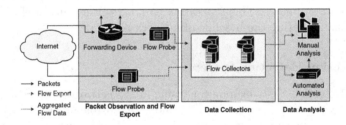

Fig. 4. Simple architecture of flow monitoring system [5]

3   Related Work

In [18] an IDS for SCADA (Supervisory Control and Data Acquisition) Systems is presented. These kind of systems are often used in industrial environments for some kind of automation or process control situations. Since such environments are well predictable, an IDS can show its full strengths there. The investigated building automation system is more difficult in that regard as a lot of actions are initiated by humans which are not easily predictable.

As stated in [12] BASs are more and more under attack. This is made worse since nowadays they are commonly connected to the internet. This means that the often referred air gap does not exist any more [1]. Adding gateways to such infrastructure eases maintenance work and increases flexibility but it also comes along with tremendous risks as shown in [2]. IP gateways open the door to the internal SCADA networks for attackers worldwide, even without direct physical access to the SCADA network. This becomes even more relevant when taking into consideration that critical infrastructure such as power plants and hospitals are also using such systems.

[11] presents a rule-based IDS. It is also based on BACnet and as an example scenario they use a system consisting of fire detection sensors acting in a deterministic way. In the past we saw attacks on such systems that could possibly have been detected by anomaly detection approaches like we suggest in this paper. One famous example is the Stuxnet attack that "replayed prerecorded input to the legitimate code during the attack" [6], which could possibly have been detected as abnormal behaviour.

4 Concept of the IDS

In this section, we describe the general conception and deduced architecture of the IDS architecture we introduced earlier. A more in-depth description of the underlying concepts ca be found in [7].

4.1 Architecture

Our proposed architecture of field bus IDSs is strongly inspired by [11]. However, some fundamental extensions with regard to scalability and continuous adaptation are made. Opposed to the inductive rule learning algorithm used in [11], we propose to employ an algorithm which can be trained on unlabelled data. This allows to fit the resulting models better to the heterogeneous nature of BASs. The otherwise necessary effort to train a model would suggest to provide a more general model. However, such a generally applicable model would be a rather broad definition of normality and consequently promises less precise results.

Further, to increase the scalability of the system, it was designed around a message passing pattern. It enables easy separation of application parts and recovery after crashes without any data loss. To keep the installation of such a system cost-effective and simple, no additional network and wiring besides the existing field bus is planned. Therefore the data is delivered from the agents to the collector in-band. To prevent increasing the traffic and load on the field bus network too much, we use flow-data instead of full traffic captures. Thus the transmitted data is aggregated and the additional load is minimised.

One problem with using flows in BASs is that there are mainly short commands or status messages transmitted from different sensors. These include light switches, PIR-sensors, temperature sensors and the like. These actions and the resulting telegrams are unpredictable and the brevity of the commands makes it very difficult to reach a good compression by aggregating it in flows. Therefore, the idea is to collect more statistical data about the traffic passing through a particular agent in a defined time frame and forwarding this kind of data.

To obtain a world view of the system for the analysis, an agent has to be installed in each line (see Agents in Fig. 2). The agents collect data and periodically send the collected information to the collector (see collector in Fig. 2).

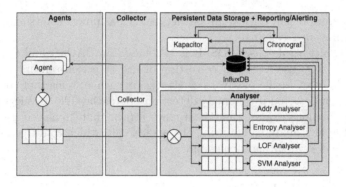

Fig. 5. Architecture of the presented IDS

Beside receiving data from agents, the collector is also responsible for time synchronisation of the agents. For this purpose the collector communicates regularly back to the agents to update the system clock and to adjust additional settings, like the window length in which data is aggregated. Synchronised clocks are of tremendous importance to evaluate the analysed data. Another important task of the collector is to align and match the windows of all agents before forwarding them to the analysers. To prevent possible deadlocks, a sensible timeout is set for the alignment process. When the timeout is exceeded, the current window is relayed even if there are still missing windows from some agents.

Figure 5 illustrates the fundamental system architecture. Incoming messages are buffered in message queues on their way to the next processing step. An InfluxDB instance is used for persistent storage. From there on the data can be pulled into Grafana, which is a tool for online data visualisation. Additionally, Grafana can be use to monitor thresholds and send alerts or warnings when those are exceeded.

The main idea of deploying the system is to operate in two phases: training and operation. In the training phase a baseline model is derived from the activities observed in the network. It is important to ensure that no malicious activities occur in the network during this period. Otherwise, those activities are incorporated into the baseline model and consequently would not be detected. During the operating phase the flow data of the network activities are compared to the trained model. Any deviation from this base model would then be considered an outlier. In order to adapt the model to changing user behaviour over time, a continuous adaptation training is possible. This can be achieved e.g. by training the model with a sliding window of past telegrams.

4.2   Feature Vector

To process the flow data received by the collector it first needs to be converted into a format suitable for analysing and training in machine learning models. This format is called a feature vector and is derived using the statistical distribution in the time window of all features recorded by the agents. To encode these features variations of One-Hot encoding and feature hashing are used. The individual features will get normalised against the maximum value within the time window in any case.

From analysing a log file, recorded in the computer science building of the University of Rostock, we deduct that only source and destination address has a significantly large variance. The other values are more or less stable. The features with lower variance (like APCI, hop count, payload length, TPCI, . . .) are not providing much information, so using them in a feature vector may appear less sensible. However, since the main objective is to detect anomalies, stable features might be considered useful anyway, since they provide a very narrow definition of normal activities.

The following features were selected in our proposed IDS to detect anomalies:

- seconds of the week
- source address
- destination address
- priority
- hop count
- payload length
- APCI

Using seconds of the week we are able to encode seasonal dependencies of events in the network, thus allowing models to incorporate seasonal sensitivity.

4.3   Test-Data

To verify our proposed concept and test its performance, we generated two test sets of KNX telegrams. Both sets were extracted from a log file of the KNX activity in the building for computer science of the University of Rostock. It is assumed, that this dataset is free of any intrusions.

The first set of test data was used as well in [7]. It was recorded from 21st of January in 2017 until 21st of February in 2017. The first two weeks are used as learning phase, while the third week serves as validation test set and in the fourth week injections have been made. They represent possible intrusions which shall be found:

- **First attack (starting 2017-02-12 03:00:00)**
  The traffic of three hours of the entire segment was replaced with traffic from 2017-02-06 10:00:00 until 2017-02-06 15:00:00
- **Second attack (starting 2017-02-13 09:00:00)**
  A DoS-attack was performed by flooding the system with A_RESTART telegrams on Line 3.4 with system priority (3 bursts of 15 min with 5 min of break time in between)

- **Third attack (starting 2017-02-13 21:00:00)**
  This attack simulates a device scan over the whole address space to determine which devices are present. This was performed by injecting A_DEVICE_DESCRIPTOR_READ telegrams with a maximised packet rate.
- **Fourth attack (2017-02-14)**
  As fourth attack two new devices are inserted. Because of the lack of other real KNX traffic the telegrams injected are derived from two devices (3.6.7 and 2.6.42) from 2017-02-08.

The second set of the test data was recorded from 11th of July in 2016 until 11th of September 2016. Under https://opsci.informatik.uni-rostock.de/ index.php/Fieldbus_traffic_simulation_logs this set can be found. The dataset was divided into three parts each one consisting of three weeks duration. The first weeks are used as learning phase. The last three weeks are used as validation test set and the three weeks in the middle include two attacks:

- **First attack (device**
  3.6.14) The hop_count value of this device was manipulated by setting it always to the value of 4.
- **Second attack (device**
  3.6.122) The communication of a new device was inserted. The new address is 3.6.122. Due to the lack of real KNX data the communication from device 3.6.12 (representing a motion sensor) was simply copied.

As it is easy to see, the two test sets are quite different according to the injected attacks. While the first set includes more "aggressive" or obvious patterns. The attacks in the second dataset do need a lot fewer telegrams which have to be sent out on the bus. Thus they might be harder to detect, but maybe more realistic.

4.4   Analyser Modules

The most simple analyser is observing the occurring **addresses**. This module collects all shown addresses during the learning phase and collects them in sets. During the operational phase addresses are compared to these sets. If an address has not appeared until now an alert shall be raised.

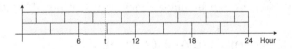

Fig. 6. Time shift of models for entropy analyser

The **Local Outlier Factor (LOF) analyser** is looking for neighbours of the currently reviewed window with similar distribution for the statistical values. For doing that the distances between the selected individual features are calculated. These values are compared with the world model and the agent specific model. If they are lying within certain limits, they are considered to be part of normality.

While **Support Vector Machines** (SVM) are normally used to cluster data the one-class SVM is well suited to detect anomalies. It is recommended to train several SVM models. One as world view model and one for each agent. The world view model will contain all appearing data and thus be quite general. To have a more specific and sensitive model one model per agent is a good plan. For deciding whether a time window is an in- or outlier the distances to the world and agent specific models are calculated. A positive distance means it is an inlier, while negative distances characterise outliers.

The **entropy analyser** is using the information theorem by Shannon to calculate how much information is gained by a new incoming window to the base model. The time dimension was excluded in this model as it is continuous. To map the seasonal sensitivity, slices of three hours were made. A second set of these slices was shifted half against the first set to prevent hard breaks at the borders. As shown in Fig. 6 for each window there will be two sets to compare the values against. Additionally, there are also a world- and an agent-specific model which are trained. While the world model is more general the agent specific models are trained to the single line they are operating in.

4.5 Monitoring and Alerting

A good monitoring and alerting solution is a main part of this concept for improving the security level of an application. A time series database and representation fits this concept quiet well. Presenting the measured information over the time gives the ability to quickly review the change of certain values. The ability to send alert-messages is very important too. Administrators needs to get informed if certain thresholds are exceeded to give them the chance to investigate as soon as possible. Therefore the use of the InfluxDB in addition with Grafana is well suited for this task, but nevertheless all other monitoring solutions can be used because of the modular system.

5 Prototype

The prototype is implemented in Python3 and can be found under [13]. As the experiments should be kept repeatable an agent simulator was developed. It takes a local log file and replays the telegrams as an active agent would do. In this way it is possible to repeat test cases and verify the recognition of the anomalies. The messages in our log are encoded in the cEMI-message format, because they were logged by a program taking them from an IP gateway and pushing them into a database. Before being able to analyse them they have to be decoded. For doing this a parser was developed in Python3 as well. The logs can be found under [17].

5.1   Analysers

It is to mention that a base module was developed for the agents to collect the features every agent needs. The individual analyser modules inherit this basic functionality and will additionally provide some more specific functions.

5.2   Feature Space

To reduce the number of dimensions for the addresses, which would be too extensive for each address (65535 addresses for source and destination), only the probability per address bit is monitored, resulting in 16 dimensions per address. Priority, hop count and APCI are directly mapped in the feature vector, since the cardinality of the respective value ranges is only four, seven and 44. For the APCI, the risk of over fitting is plausible, since 44 dimensions are already plenty. But as these are categorical values and since they are quite characteristic for the telegrams it was decided to not further compress them. There are 255 different possible payload lengths in KNX. As this could result in an over fitted model ten equally sized buckets were built for the 255 different payload-lengths.

6   Results

We investigated two different tests with varying data sets. The attacks in both data sets also differ from each other as described below.

6.1   Dataset I

As already mentioned, the attacks in the first record are somewhat more aggressive and send out much more telegrams. They should be easier to detect. In Fig. 7 two graphs can be seen. In both of the subordinated figures the attacks can be seen quite clearly. Table 2 shows a summary of the attacks or intrusions which could be detected. While the entropy analyser was not able to detect any of the attacks, the address analyser and the SVM-module performed both satisfactory.

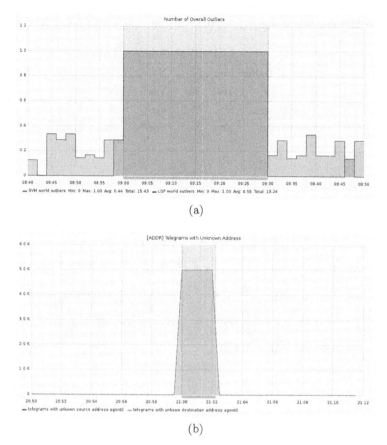

(a)

(b)

Fig. 7. Detection results of attacks 2 (see (a) - Number of detected outliers (SVM - red and LOF - blue)) and attack 3 (see (b) - Number of Telegrams with unknown addresses (source - green and destination - yellow)) of the first test dataset. The time while the attack was performed is highlighted in grey. (Color figure online)

6.2   Dataset II

The attacks in the second dataset consist of much fewer telegrams. Therefore they are more difficult to detect, but on the other hand they might be much more realistic because they are more specific and an intrusion detection system would have to detect such attacks as well. As it is fairly easy to see, the system performs very poorly in detecting the intrusions after the learning phase and it is not possible at all to tell when an intrusion took place. The time period of the attack injection is really hard to differentiate from the validation time. The unknown destination addresses in Fig. 8b are not even resulting out of the injections - they result from devices that were not present in the learning phase.

From these results it can be deduced that the system is able to detect some telegram intensive injections with the SVM or address analyser modules, but

Table 2. Summary of possibilities to detect intrusions with first test dataset

	LOF	SVM	Address	Entropy
Unusual traffic	No	No	No	No
DoS attack	Yes	Yes	Yes	No
Network scan	No	Yes	Yes	No
New device	No	No	Yes	No

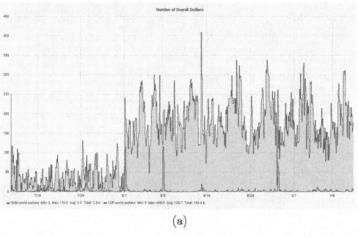

(a)

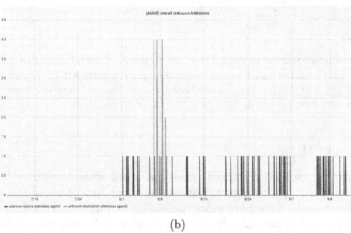

(b)

Fig. 8. Detection results of dataset 2. The whole period which got analysed is show. The first 3 weeks (first third) shows the learning phase. The second 3 weeks (second third) shows the time with injected intrusions while the third 3 weeks (last third) shows the validation period. (a) shows the number of detected outliers (SVM - red and LOF - blue), while (b) shows the number of Telegrams with unknown addresses (source - green and destination - yellow). (Color figure online)

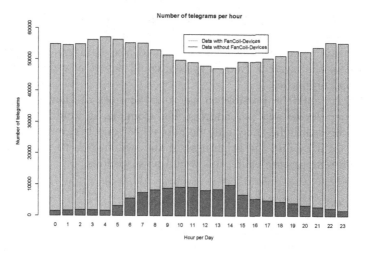

Fig. 9. Number of telegrams per weekday

more specific attacks cannot be found. One reason could be the loss of information during the aggregation of the telegrams in flows.

More of the figures can be found at https://opsci.informatik.uni-rostock.de/index.php/Using_machine_learning_to_find_anomalies_in_fieldbus_networks.

A further investigation of the second data set revealed that there were a total of 51 sending devices. Five of them are responsible for about 90% of the overall traffic. These devices are all FAN-COIL-devices. It is even necessary to filter them out in order to be able to determine the seasonality in the data set. As expected in Fig. 9 the traffic during working hours is significantly higher than at night. A look at the activity per weekday shows a similar behaviour. If the FAN-COIL-Devices are filtered out, the seasonality of the data can be seen directly.

7 Future Work

These results give some interesting hints for how to work with this topic in future. It seems that the loss of information due to aggregation in flows is a severe problem for the intrusion detection system. Specific intrusions which require only a few telegrams could not be detected.

Another approach for the problem could be to use an intrusion detection system with more logic on the agent. This enables the agents to decide for themselves whether a telegram on the wire is an intrusion or not, hence also decreasing the number of telegrams sent, as only anomalies could be reported. However, synchronisation between different agents would be desirable, so it is necessary to implement a language to describe abnormal traffic which has to be reported.

Furthermore, one could look closer on the physical layer. Monitoring the resistance, voltage and current on the wire as well as the amount of electricity consumed with precise timing know-how could also be a great benefit for an intrusion detection system. Such a system could detect new devices based on their physical properties.

Finally, it would be possible to use a set of rules of allowed or expected telegrams per device and per address. For example, it would be possible to define that light switches may only be allowed to send telegrams enabling and disabling a light or dim the brightness. If the switch were to send a telegram containing a temperature value, this would be suspicious.

References

1. Byres, E., Eng, P.: Unicorns and air gaps-do they really exist. Living with reality in critical infrastructures, Tofino (2012). https://www.tofinosecurity.com/blog/1-ics-and-scada-security-myth-protection-air-gap
2. CCC: SCADA - Gateway to (s)hell. https://media.ccc.de/v/34c3-8956-scada_-_gateway_to_s_hell
3. Deutsche Industrienorm: Offene Datenkommunikation für die Gebäudeautomation und Gebäudemanagement - Elektrische Systemtechnik für Heim und Gebäude: Teil 2: KNXnet/IP-Kommunikation (DIN EN 13321-2), March 2013
4. Hodge, V., Austin, J.: A survey of outlier detection methodologies. Artif. Intell. Rev. 22(2), 85–126 (2004). https://doi.org/10.1023/B:AIRE.0000045502.10941.a9
5. Hofstede, R., et al.: Flow monitoring explained: from packet capture to data analysis with NetFlow and IPFIX. IEEE Commun. Surv. Tutor. 16(4), 2037–2064 (2014). https://doi.org/10.1109/COMST.2014.2321898
6. Langner, R.: Stuxnet: dissecting a cyberwarfare weapon. IEEE Secur. Priv. 9(3), 49–51 (2011). https://doi.org/10.1109/MSP.2011.67
7. Peters, M.: Analysis of distributed in-band monitoring messages for field bus networks in building automation systems. Master thesis, Univerisät Rostock, Rostock (2018). https://github.com/FreakyBytes/master-thesis/releases/download/handing-in/master-thesis-peters.pdf
8. Mundt, T., Dähn, A., Sass, S.: An intrusion detection system with home installation networks. Int. J. Comput. 3, 13–20 (2014). https://platform.almanhal.com/Details/article/47923
9. Mundt, T., Wickboldt, P.: Security in building automation systems - a first analysis. In: International Conference on Cyber Security and Protection of Digital Services (Cyber Security), pp. 1–8. IEEE, Piscataway (2016). https://doi.org/10.1109/CyberSecPODS.2016.7502336
10. Northcutt, S.: Inside Network Perimeter Security, 2nd edn. Sams Pub, Indianapolis (2005). ISBN-13: 978-0672327377, ISBN-10: 9780672327377
11. Pan, Z., Hariri, S., Al-Nashif, Y.: Anomaly based intrusion detection for Building Automation and Control networks. In: IEEE/ACS 11th International Conference on Computer Systems and Applications (AICCSA), pp. 72–77. IEEE, Piscataway (2014). https://doi.org/10.1109/AICCSA.2014.7073181
12. Čeleda, P., Krejčí, R., Krmíček, V.: Flow-based security issue detection in building automation and control networks. In: Szabó, R., Vidács, A. (eds.) EUNICE 2012. LNCS, vol. 7479, pp. 64–75. Springer, Heidelberg (2012). https://doi.org/10.1007/978-3-642-32808-4_7

13. Peters, M.: BAS-observe (2018). https://github.com/FreakyBytes/bas-observe
14. Shannon, C.E.: A mathematical theory of communication. Bell Syst. Tech. J. **27**(3), 379–423 (1948). https://doi.org/10.1002/j.1538-7305.1948.tb01338.x
15. Sperotto, A., Schaffrath, G., Sadre, R., Morariu, C., Pras, A., Stiller, B.: An overview of ip flow-based intrusion detection. IEEE Commun. Surv. Tutor. **12**(3), 343–356 (2010). https://doi.org/10.1109/SURV.2010.032210.00054
16. Toshniwal, D., Eshwar, B.K.: Entropy based adaptive outlier detection technique for data streams. In: Proceedings of the International Conference on Data Mining (DMIN), p. 1. The Steering Committee of The World Congress in Computer Science, Computer Engineering and Applied Computing (WorldComp) (2014)
17. Wiedenmann, S.: Fieldbus traffic simulation logs (2018). https://opsci.informatik. uni-rostock.de/index.php/Fieldbus_traffic_simulation_logs
18. Yang, D., Usynin, A., Hines, J.W.: Anomaly-Based Intrusion Detection for SCADA Systems. In: 5th International Topical Meeting on Nuclear Plant Instrumentation, Control and Human Machine Interface Technologies (NPIC & HMIT 2005), pp. 12–16 (2006). 11.04.2019

Cyber Weapons Storage Mechanisms

Muhammd Mudassar Yamin[(✉)], Basel Katt, and Mazaher Kianpour

Norwegian University of Science and Technology,
Teknologivegen 22, 2815 Gjøvik, Norway
{muhammad.m.yamin,basel.katt,mazaher.kianpour}@ntnu.no

Abstract. In this paper, the current status of the art of cyber weapon storage methods and related processes are reviewed with particular reference to the safe guards present in storage of cyber weapons and contingency planning in case of losing controls of such weapons. Existing methods are summarized and new techniques which are currently under development are described. Some of the current limitations and challenges are also identified. To tackle these challenges, we propose a sociotechnical framework, in which Cyber Ranges can play a major role.

Keywords: Cyber · Weapon · Storage · Vulnerabilities · Exploits

1 Introduction

According to the NATO CCDCOE (Cooperative Cyber Defense Center of Excellence) [1], cyber weapons are *software, firmware or hardware designed or applied to cause damage through the cyber domain*. Cyber domain provides the means of electronic information exchange by utilizing multiple information exchange technologies. The purpose of cyber weapon is to steal, tamper or disrupt the information flow in the cyber domain. Due to the rapid growth of cyber domain, usage of cyber weapon is increasing both by nation states and cyber criminals. Due to recent CIA Vault7 leaks, requirements for secure storage of cyber weapons was raised. CIA malware and hacking tools target iPhone, Android and smart TVs, and are built by EDG (Engineering Development Group), a software development group within CCI (Center for Cyber Intelligence), a department belonging to the CIA's DDI (Directorate for Digital Innovation). The DDI is one of the five major directorates of the CIA. The EDG is responsible for the development, testing and operational support of all backdoors, exploits, malicious payloads, trojans, viruses and any other kind of malware used by the CIA in its covert operations world-wide. The CIA attacks systems by using undisclosed security vulnerabilities possessed by the CIA. But if the CIA can hack systems, then so can everyone else who has obtained or discovered the vulnerability. As long as the CIA keeps these vulnerabilities concealed from software vendors they will not be fixed, and the system will remain hackable.

These leaked exploit and vulnerability details are often used by cyber criminals for monetary gains. Two of the major ransomwares *WanaCray* and *Bad*

© Springer Nature Switzerland AG 2019
G. Wang et al. (Eds.): SpaCCS 2019, LNCS 11611, pp. 354–367, 2019.
https://doi.org/10.1007/978-3-030-24907-6_27

rabbit that affected global IT infrastructure used *EternalBlue* and *EternalRomance* exploits that were leaked from NSA Vault7 for the purpose of exploitation. Similarly, other Zero day vulnerabilities disclosure from security researcher and hacker groups affects the overall cyber security of governments and industries around the world. In this study we analyze the current state of the art of cyber vulnerabilities and exploit disclosure programs. The safe guards and contingency planning for storage of cyber vulnerabilities and exploit disclosure are examined. Usage of leaked cyber vulnerabilities and exploit in development of cyber weapons in cyber domain is highlighted, the limitation and problems present in secure cyber vulnerabilities and exploit storage are discussed, and finally the role of *Cyber Ranges* in assisting safe guards and contingency planning for leaked cyber weapons is presented.

2   Methodology

In order to understand the problem, we performed a literature review employing keyword-based research method. The researchers started with "Cyber" and "Weapon" with "Storage". They investigated the following keywords in academic databases like Google scholar, IEEE and ACM to acquire the better understanding of the given terms [2]. They also made themselves familiar with the related literature on the given topic. The researchers spotted a lot of related information but employed them in indexed research articles only.

Based upon the finding of literature review a comparative analysis [3] was performed on four key matrices (1) time to disclose the vulnerability, (2) payment for the vulnerability, (3) vulnerability information that is prone to leaking by human risk and (4) vulnerability information that is prone to technical risk of leaking. These matrices play an important role in cyber vulnerability disclosure for cyber weapon development.

Based upon the finding of the analysis, we propose a socio-technical approach to tackle these problems. As Fig. 1 illustrates, social component is composed of a *culture* and a *structure* elements describing a collection of values and the distribution of power in a given system, respectively. The technical component, on the other hand, is composed of methods and machines. Methods are the employed techniques, and machines are the technical artifacts that are used in different parts of a socio-technical system. These interconnecting components determine the overall security posture of the environment. A secure system maintains equilibrium among the four sub-components. Any change in one of these sub-components can change the state of the system into an insecure system [4].

3   State of Cyber Weapon Storage

The cyber weapons utilize vulnerabilities present in computer software and hardware [5]. These vulnerabilities, when weaponized, become exploits. These exploits can be used to achieve specific objectives. Tools are developed to use these exploits in an efficient manner and these tools becomes the cyber weapons.

Social   Technical

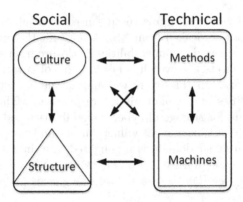

Fig. 1. The complex, dynamic socio-technical system. The interconnecting sub-components determine the overall security posture of the system [4].

Given below is the vulnerabilities equities process, unclassified vulnerability databases, exploit databases and tools repositories.

3.1 Vulnerability Equities Process VEP [6]

The United States government developed the VEP (Vulnerability Equities Process) between 2008 and 2009 and publicly disclosed its existence in 2016. The VEP deals with cyber security vulnerabilities identified by United States government agencies and contractors and a decision will be made whether to disclose the vulnerability for public safety or keep it as a secret for cyber weapon development. The details of VEP process were disclosed by *White House* in late 2017, in which the VEP work flow is presented. It is a six step work-flow that runs as fallows: (1) Submission, when a government agency or a private contractor working for government identifies a vulnerability that is considered to be new, the vulnerability information is submitted to VEP with minimum vulnerability information and recommendation whether to disclose the vulnerability or not. (2) Notification, VEP executives notifies the subject matter experts within one working day after acknowledging the submission. (3) Equity and Discussion, the subject matters experts from government agencies have 5 working days to discuss the vulnerability and its impact. (4) Determination, after the vulnerability discussion, a decision is to be made whether to disclose the vulnerability or not. The decision should be made by majority of subject matters experts by voting if consensus in not reached. (5) Contested Preliminary Determinations, if one of the experts is not satisfied with the decision, then the decision can be reviewed by VEP again within 5 working days. (6) Handling and Follow-on actions, if the decision is to releases the vulnerability then the vulnerability will be released within 5 working days, if the vulnerability is not released then the vulnerability will be reviewed by VEP annually for release.

Following United States government, United Kingdom GCHQ (Government Communications Headquarters) released their VEP details in November 2018.

The GCHQ VEP was developed in 2010 and was very similar to United States government VEP, compromising of six major steps i.e. (1) submission, a new vulnerability is submitted for review, (2) review, an expert meeting decide whether to retain the vulnerability or retain the vulnerability, (3) consensus, if consensus among the experts is not reached whether to retain or release the vulnerability, it is then escalated to a review board, (4) escalate, the review broad decide whether to retain the vulnerability or release the vulnerability, (5) review, after the review the review board forward its recommendation to NCSC (National Cyber Security Center) CEO to make final decision, (6) final decision, NCSC CEO decides whether to retain or release the vulnerability. In all cases where the vulnerability is retained, a review of vulnerability disclosure will be performed in twelve month. The GCHQ also have few exceptions to excludes vulnerabilities from their VEP which are:

- Vulnerabilities that are considered by similar VEP by one of the allies.
- Vulnerabilities that are identified in products that are not supported by their developers.
- Vulnerabilities that are present in products due to insecure design choice of developers which cannot be fixed.

Comparing to United States and United Kingdom, very little information is present about Chinese and Russian VEP, however, they have active vulnerability database details of which are given in Sect. 3.5

3.2   Responsible Disclosure Programs RDP

The disclosure of United States government global surveillance program by Edward Snowden in 2013 forced major information technology companies to asses their product security. The global surveillance program exploited undisclosed vulnerabilities in major operating system and software solutions to gather intelligence data. After realizing this situation multiple private organizations started their work on identification of Zero day vulnerabilities that are not discovered or disclosed by the government. These programs are started to enhance the overall security of software products offered by multiple organizations. Two of the major efforts led by private companies are Google Project Zero and Microsoft Offensive Security Research Team. Google Project Zero is a Google's counter-surveillance initiative to identify Zero day vulnerabilities in the software product not only developed by itself but the software products that are used by its users. It was conceptualized in 2010, however, major project efforts started in 2014 after the disclosure of United States government global surveillance program. Project Zero informs the software product developer about the discovered vulnerability and waits for 90 days to release the vulnerability. In the waiting period it expects the software product developer to release the patch for the discovered vulnerability. Google Project Zero identified multiple high risk vulnerabilities in Microsoft products and disclosed them after 90 days of reporting them to Microsoft. Microsoft argued that for complex product the 90 day disclosure window is not suitable and requested a coordinated vulnerability disclosure program. However Google insisted in quick patching of vulnerabilities. As a response, Microsoft established its Offensive Security Research Team to identify vulnerabilities in its rival products and responsibly disclose them. One of the high risk vulnerabilities that Microsoft Offensive Security Research Team discovered is a remote code execution in Google Chrome, which was responsibly disclosed to Google and patched in four days.

3.3   Exploit Acquisition Programs EAP

Private companies offer million of dollars to security researchers for selling working Zero day exploits in major IT products. The purpose of these programs are usually to develop new exploits and malware signatures of IDS/IPS, anti virus and anti malware programs. However, it can be argued that these programs can be run by government agencies to disguise their identity. Two of the major exploit acquisition programs are Trend Micro Zero Day Initiative and Zerodium Exploit Acquisition Program. Trend Micro Zero Day Initiative started in early 2005 for buying Zero day vulnerabilities discovered by independent security researchers. The purpose of this program was to gather vulnerability signatures for their intrusion detection and prevention system "Tipping Point". They offer lucrative payout to security researchers for the identification and exploitation of potential vulnerabilities present in mainstream software products. They held regular vulnerability discovery and exploitation competitions known as "Pwn2Own" in which they invite security researcher to demonstrate vulnerability discovery and exploitation. Zerodium was founded by the founder of Vupen a private company that used to independently identify Zero day vulnerabilities and sell then to private and government clients. Now, Zerodium invites independent researchers to sell their vulnerabilities exploits in major web browsers, smart phones and desktop operating systems, which it markets to private and government clients for research and development purposes.

3.4   Bug Bounties Programs BBP

Bug Bounties Programs are developed to crowd source security of a big IT infrastructure. Organizations conduct penetration tests in order to identify potential vulnerabilities in their infrastructure, however, these penetration tests are very costly and often don't cover the whole organizations infrastructure. Therefore these organizations invite independent researchers to identify vulnerability and responsibly report those vulnerabilities in order to receive a reward. This helps security researcher with extra income and organization with paying for only actual vulnerability. There are many platforms that are being used in management of these bug bounty program. Two of the major platforms that are being used actively by major organizations are given are Bugcrowd and Hackerone. Bugcrowd offers services to major information technology companies to manage their vulnerability reward programs. It connects security researchers with companies seeking to crowd source theirs information security program. It ranks the security researchers based upon number of valid submitted reports. Hackerone helps in vulnerability information coordination and disclosure between security researchers and information technologies companies. Its platform is quite similar to Bugcrowd, however, it offers rating system of vulnerability, exploits and researchers to better results in vulnerability disclosure and coordination. The vulnerabilities and exploits that are disclosed become available to relevant vulnerability databases, details of which are given below:

3.5   Vulnerability Databases [7]

Multiple vulnerability databases exists in literature, some are maintained by governments while majority is operated by private security companies and community driven efforts. These databases contain the details about the vulnerability, the affected system and the risk of exploitation it poses. Some of the well known vulnerability databases Vulnerability Database, Common Vulnerabilities and Exposure, National Vulnerability Database, China National Vulnerability Database and Russia National Vulnerability Database. VulnDB (Vulnerability Database) is one of the oldest vulnerability database, it is being operational since 1970. It is a crowd based vulnerability database which means it is operated by people and researchers in the security field. It uses OSVDB (Open Source Vulnerability Database) format, which includes a vulnerability id, vulnerability description, possible vulnerability solution and reference to further vulnerability details. CVE (Common Vulnerabilities and Exposure) was one of the very first vulnerability database that combine vulnerability information from different sources. It was launched by MITRE organization in 1999 to overcome the problem of multiple vulnerability nomenclature used by multiple organizations. The CVE includes a vulnerability id, a brief description of the vulnerability and any references related to that vulnerability. The NVD (National Vulnerability Database) was developed by NIST (National Institute of Standards and Technology) in 2005. It uses SCAP (Security Content Automation Protocol) to manage and present vulnerability information gathered from multiple sources including CVE. The NVD database consist of vulnerability impact matrices, security check lists, security misconfigurations details, affected product names and security related flaws in software and hardware. The CNNVD (China National Vulnerability Database), CNNVD is a national-level information security vulnerability data management platform for China's *information security assessment center* to effectively perform vulnerability analysis and risk assessment functions. CNNVD combines government departments, industry users, security vendors, universities, and scientific research institutions through independent vulnerability information submission, collaborative sharing of vulnerabilities information, network attacks information collection, and technical testing of vulnerable systems. One of its main function is to provide early warning against a suspected cyber security threat. vulnerabilities in CNNVD are disclosed often early compare to other vulnerabilities databases. Russia's NVD is run by the Federal Service for Technical and Export Control of Russia (FSTEC), a military organization with a closely defined mission to protect the state's critical infrastructure and to support counterintelligence efforts. It was established 15 years after the establishment of US NVD and roughly contains a record of 100000 vulnerabilities.

3.6 Exploit Databases

When the vulnerabilities are weaponized to compromise the security of the computer system then they become exploits. The exploits appeals nation states, cyber security companies and cyber criminals. Therefore their monetary value is quite high. Independent security researchers mostly publish these exploits free of charge, however, these exploits are also available for sale. Many of such platforms operate on TOR network, however, some of these platforms operates publicly like 0 day Today, Exploit Database, Rapid7 Vulnerability and Exploit Database. 0 day Today is one of the biggest crowd sourced exploit market place. Gray hat hackers can sell their exploit PoC (Proof of Concepts) in this marketplace. The platform was developed in 2008 due to increasing demand of cyber security exploits. It follows responsible disclosure guidelines and inform the software developer before releasing the exploits. It provide technical exploit information to peoples who are involved in ethical hacking activities and signature development activities for intrusion detection systems. Exploit DB (Exploit Data Base) was created by a private company "offensive security" in 2009. It also uses crowd sourcing, however, it doesn't sell exploits. All exploit available on Exploit DB are open source and free to use by anyone. The exploit database is CVE complaint and the information about the exploit is published with relevant vulnerability details. It includes remote, local, denial of service and web exploits, however, exploits targeting live websites are not published on exploit db. Rapid7, a private company, has been collecting vulnerability signatures since 2000 for the development of their vulnerability scanner. They integrated their vulnerability scanner with the metasploit exploitation framework and are now leading the metasploit exploit development. Until now they have the signature of nearly 70000 vulnerabilities and 3000 work exploits. Their vulnerability signature is CVE compliant and they follow open source exploit development techniques, however they also sell advance exploits to their customers.

3.7 Tools Repositories

Tools that automate the functionality of exploit and link multiple exploits to achieve specific objectives are considered as cyber weapons. Multiple platforms that distributes such tools are publicly available. These platforms mostly showcase tools that are publicly available and released by cyber security researchers. Some of the publicly available platforms are ToolsWatch, KitPloit, Black Arch Tools Repository. ToolsWatch is developed to distribute up to date penetration testing and security auditing tools between security professionals and researchers. It has a catalog of cyber security tools that are released by cyber security researchers in major security conferences like Blackhat and defcon. Security researchers can submit new tools to its submission portal, which is maintained by a group of volunteers. Most of the tools available at ToolsWatch are open source and free to use while some tools have their commercial versions as well. It also has a best tools of the year competition in which security researchers votes for the best tools that are released in a year. KitPloit was launched in 2012 in order to categorize and search the exploitation tools available for relevant platforms. It hosts exploitation tools related to major operating systems like Windows, Linux, MAC, Android and IOS. Additionally, it provides tools for performing OSINT, DDOS, Malwares attacks etc. Most of the tools available at KitPloit, similar to ToolsWatch, are open source and free to use while some tools have their commercial versions as well. It accepts tools submission from security researchers and the submissions are maintained by volunteers. It also hosts the installation and usage instruction of the submitted tools. Black Arch Linux is an Arch Linux-based penetration testing distribution for penetration testers and security researchers. The repository consists of 2082 tools. These tools could be installed individually or in groups. The tools present in the repositories are compatible with other Debian based penetration testing distribution like Kali Linux and Parrot OS.

4   Analysis

In this section we will discuss and analyze the various vulnerability disclosure programs and the risks associated with the cyber weapon storage mechanisms. Afterwards, we provide a general comparison.

4.1   Cost of Leaked Cyber Weapons

As explained above vulnerabilities and exploits are in high demand by governments, security researchers and cyber criminals. Securing this valuable piece of information should be of a high priority. However, in 2017 NSA vault7 leaks exposed CIA weapons arsenals to the cyber security community. Vault7 contains information about secret CIA cyber activities collected by Wikkileaks. Its 24 parts leaks released between 7 March 2017 to 7 September 2017. Among other tools, an exploit "EternalBlue" targeting Microsoft Windows was also released. This exploit was later weaponized in "Wannacry" ransomware malware attack which had nearly 200000 victims and 300000 affected systems in 150 countries [8]. The losses caused by this single cyber attack reached 4 billion USD. Similarly, the source code of "Mirai" Botnet was released on a hacker forum. Mirai botnet in 2016 exploited Linux based IoT device to launch a DDOS (Distributed Denial of Service) attack on United Stated domain name servers to hamper its internet communication service. During the "Wanacry" attack a kill switch was developed by identifying a hard coded domain in the malware code. The kill switch was activated when the domain is registered. However, the attacker used variant of "Mirai" botnet to launch a DDOS on the domain to disable the switch but luckily they were not successful. This indicated that new variants of cyber weapons can be used in combination of other cyber weapons to launch sophisticated cyber attacks. These cyber attacks affected health services as well, therefore, calculating the actual cost of such attacks is very difficult. Hundreds of million dollars losses in recent years are the consequence of increasing leaked cyber weapons in frequency and cost. These costs are variable across countries and industry sectors. Besides the cost of cyber incidents, understanding the different types of threats and challenges in securing cyber weapons can help to gain additional insight to counter or mitigate the impact of future incidents.

4.2   Threat Actors and Challenges in Securing Cyber Weapons

In the literature we identified multiple threat actors and challenges affecting the security of cyber weapons. These challenges are similar to challenges which are faced in securing any kind of sensitive information. Some of the major challenges, and associated threat actors, that are faced in securing cyber weapons are given below:

Human Negligence. Human error has been the most commonly reason of penetrated information systems. Attackers can boost their chance of success if they exploit knowledge about personal information and behavioral characteristics of targeted users. Upon the investigating of Vault7 leak's hacking tools, the United States investigation agencies are focusing on the possibility that NSA contractor or operative carelessly left the hacking tools and exploit on a remote target systems [9]. The remote target system was then exploited by "Shadow Brokers" from where they retrieved the hacking tools and exploits. There is also a possibility that the contractors or operative intentionally left the hacking tools an exploit for the "Shadow Broker" to retrieve. This leads us to next challenge in securing cyber weapons, which is Insider threat details of which are given below.

Insider Threat. The authorized users or employees have access to the confidential data and to the sensitive assets of an organization, so there is always a risk that employees may misuse this data access for any mischievous purpose [10]. An example of an insider case is Chelsea Manning, who was responsible for the leaking of more than 60000 U.S. department of defense documents on WikiLeaks and Edward Snowden, who exposed secret NSA documents in public. These two cases are important examples of Insider threat incidents. The insiders are either motivated by financial gains in leaking sensitive information to adversaries or they are motivated by moral principals. Both motivation scenarios are exploited by states sponsor agencies, details of which are given below.

Dissatisfied Gray Hat Hackers and Security Researchers. Security researchers and gray hat hackers often get dissatisfied by the treatment from the system vendors, or the vulnerability disclosure program, and releases the vulnerability information publicly. This give little time to vendors for development of security patch and provides an opportunity to cyber criminals to exploit unpatched systems.

Hacktivist Groups. Hacktivist groups are group of hackers that hack for social and moral reasons. Multiple hacktivist groups exist in cyber domain. The Vault7 leak was also credited to a hacktivist group "Shadow Broker". However, the United States government argued that they are sponsored by a country as they released the hacked tools without any financial incentives. This hacktivist group also uses multiple cyber misinformation techniques to affect the public opinion as per their requirements.

State Sponsored Attack. Intelligence operations in identifying your adversaries capabilities is a regular part of military operation. However, in cyber domain these operation further extends to obtain the information cyber weapon usage of their adversaries and identifying mitigation strategies to avoid malicious consequences of adversaries cyber weapons. This is achieved by performing offensive cyber security operation on the adversaries which include stealing of relevant information and launching misinformation campaign to demotivate the opponents work force.

4.3 Comparison

The VEP takes a minimum of 7 days to disclose a vulnerability, which it decides not to retain. The once they retain will be reviewed for release after 12 months of retention [6]. Compare to VEP, RDP release the vulnerability information after 90 days of informing the vulnerable product owner, regardless of the patch is released or not. In EAP and BBP vulnerability information disclosure solely depends upon the party which is paying for the vulnerability information therefore they have variable time for releasing the vulnerability information.

In term of monetary value of vulnerability information, no information of VEP programs is available due to their classified nature, RDP doesn't sell the vulnerability information rather than inform the affected product developers for a better secure environment for everybody. EAP business model is centered around selling the vulnerabilities to government and private clients. BBP offers security researchers payouts for identifying vulnerabilities. These programs and the associated cyber weapon storage system are also vulnerable to both technical and human risks as observed and discussed in Sect. 4.2. Table 1 compares the various vulnerability disclosure programs.

Table 1. Comparison of different vulnerability disclosure programs

Name	Time to Release	Payment	Technical risk	Human risk
VEP	>7 days	N/A	Yes	Yes
RDP	90 days	Yes	Yes	Yes
EAP	Variable	Yes	Yes	Yes
BBP	Variable	Yes	Yes	Yes

From Table 1, it can be concluded that this problem is not purely technical problem rather than a socio-technical problem [4]. RDP can be ideally used for vulnerability disclosure to avoid threat of leaked cyber weapons, however, it is not practical for governments and military purposes.

5   Socio-technical Framework

As we mentioned in Sect. 2, tackling the above described challenges in securing cyber weapons is a difficult task and requires considerations beyond software and hardware technologies. Accordingly, in this section, we present a socio-technical methodology to address the main sociological and technical components of these issues. Our proposed multidisciplinary solutions cover both components and their corresponding sub-components to protect cyber weapons from evolving cyber threats.

5.1   Culture

In a complex socio-technical system, culture is composed of beliefs, values, rules and identities of each stakeholder at different levels (e.g. individual, organization, national entities, etc.) of society. Below, we argue the role of human in cybersecurity and how it can influence the state of a secure system.

Human Moral Values. Basically, human factors are known as the weakest link in cybersecurity. Understanding human factors in cybersecurity can help us to design systems and security measures more efficiently. Ethics, the moral principles governing people's behavior, is a critical part of any cybersecurity defense strategy that is highly dependent upon each individual in the ecosystem. The moral of work force which deals with development and usage of cyber weapons should be kept higher. Considering Edward Snoden NSA leaks the work force is the biggest weakness is securing cyber weapons. Cyber Weapon information security can be achieved by setting high moral and ethical standards within the organization to reduce the affects of adversaries misinformation campaigns. However it should be noted that the adversaries are not bound by such high moral and ethical values in development and usage of such weapons. While ethics can be subjective and influenced by background, culture, education, etc., good financial incentives and important meaning to assigned missions can motivate the work force to perform their duties diligently.

5.2   Structure

Understanding the underlying work structure in a system help to identify conflicts, requirements and interdependencies among the stakeholders. Digital transformation has affected the relationships among the stakeholders, their business processes, and their performance. To maintain the system in the secure state, cooperation, as described below, and information sharing among the stakeholders is crucial.

Cooperation Among the Stakeholders. Interconnected digital ecosystem creates inter-dependencies among stakeholders and actors in cybersecurity. While this feature enables various the social and economic benefits to the stakeholders, it increases complexity, facilitates the propagation of threats and vulnerabilities, and increases the potential collective risk. This makes cooperation among stakeholders a necessity to encounter these risks. Cooperation is also a critical key to implement requires business and operational principles among the actors responsible for providing a secure environment. It is also essential for security and resilience measures respecting the non-technical aspects of cybersecurity, where humans have to modify their behavior and all management processes have to be adopted to support the changes due to the digital transformation in organizations.

5.3   Method

Understanding the methods and employing appropriate techniques is required not only for adopting new technologies, but also for controlling the dynamic behavior and unintended consequences of changes in other sub-components. Following, we discussed three methodological approach to secure cyber weapons against different threats.

Proactive Cyber Defense. In Proactive Cyber Defense an action is taken before the attack is even happened. There are two methods to deter the cyber incidents proactively; denial and cost imposition. Denial can be defensive and offensive. It is performed to deter a cyber attack in self defense. This can be achieved by first detecting potential adversaries attack plans and then neutralizing the attack with an active cyber operation. This is done in two phases, first a defensive cyber operation is performed to identify the threat, and secondly, an active cyber operation is performed to neutralize the threat. An example of such action can be seen in darkrode incident [11] in which a website which is involved in trading of hacking services, botnets and malware was taken down by United Sates FBI (Federal Bureau of Intelligence). In the other methods, imposing relatively large costs forces the attackers to change their strategic behavior. These two strategies can together make certain attack unappealing for the attackers. Denial can reduce the chance of success, and cost imposition can make them prohibitively expensive.

Cyber Threat Hunting. Cyber threat hunting is a form of active cyber defense in which it aims to proactively detect, identify and isolate threats that are not detected by security solutions. This approach is completely opposite to traditional signature and anomalies based detection mechanism in which investigation is performed after the incident. Cyber threat hunters detect and identify new attack signatures for the identification of new threat actors. This process is mostly done manually in which security analysts have to go through information from various data sources and utilizing their experience, knowledge and understanding of network environment isolate new threats.

Cyber Security Training and Awareness. Understanding the cybersecurity risks is vital when you are discussing the security of cyber weapons. Managing these risks requires appropriate skills to make responsible decisions. Training and education through practice and experience is one of the most efficient ways to acquire these skills. Therefore, the first stage of a cybersecurity risk management approach is raising awareness and acquisition of required skills to empower stakeholders. Cyber security exercises can play a key role in securing cyber weapons. Cyber security exercises are usually attack/defense exercise in which one team is involved in active attacking on a infrastructure while the other team is involved in active defenses of the infrastructure. New Cyber security exercise scenarios can be developed in which securing a hypothetical cyber security weapons can be set a task for the defenders. Similarly, an exercises scenario can be created in which the team of attackers have access to a hypothetical cyber weapons, its capabilities are public and defenders have the task to develop mitigation strategies against the known cyber weapon. This type of cyber security exercises will help in training of work force in securing cyber weapons and mitigating security issues in case of cyber weapon leakage.

5.4 Machine

The stakeholders have certain types of infrastructure and machines that they can use depending on their attitude or structure. These machines help them to achieve their desired performance and provide them with various opportunities to enhance their resources and skills. Below, we demonstrated that how cyber ranges can be employed as a platform to provide security in cyber weapons.

Cyber Range. A lot of new vulnerabilities are expected to be identified in cyber ranges, due to which their responsible disclosure is a need of the day. Cooperation among the stakeholders in sharing vulnerability information for responsible disclosure will ensure a secure cyber environment. Cyber ranges can also play a vital role in testing hypothetical scenarios of leaked cyber weapons and their effects on IT infrastructure to identify the effectiveness of different methods like proactive cyber defense and cyber threat hunting. Moreover, current way of conducting cyber security exercises is quite inefficient [12], cyber ranges can assist in security exercises, training and awareness campaign of ethical and moral reasoning for enabling organizations to tackle threat of leaked cyber weapons in a efficient manner.

6 Conclusion

In this paper we first presented the current state of art for cyber weapon storage mechanisms and vulnerability equities processes. This included (1) the details of available vulnerability databases, (2) information about different exploit databases that utilize those vulnerabilities, (3) tools repositories, in which weaponized versions of those exploits are present, and (4) the responsible disclosure programs, exploit acquisition programs and bug bounty programs that are currently running for the acquisition of new vulnerabilities and exploits. After that we analyzed the data we collected in the literature review, in which we discussed (1) the costs of leaked cyber weapons, (2) the threat actors and challenges in securing information related to vulnerabilities and exploit, and finally (3) provided a comparison for the various vulnerability disclosure programs. To tackle the challenges that we identified in our analysis, we propose in Sect. 5 a social technical framework for securing cyber weapon information.

References

1. Schmitt, M.N.: Tallinn Manual 2.0 on the International Law Applicable to Cyber Operations. Cambridge University Press, Cambridge (2017)
2. Jesson, J., Matheson, L., Lacey, F.M.: Doing Your Literature Review: Traditional and Systematic Techniques. Sage, London (2011)
3. Zschoch, M.A.: Configurational comparative methods: qualitative comparative analysis (QCA) and related techniques. Edited by Rihoux, B., Ragin, C., pp. xxv. Sage Publications, Thousand Oaks (2009). Canadian Journal of Political Science/Revue canadienne de science politique, 44(3), 743–746, 2011
4. Kowalski, S.: It insecurity: a multi-disciplinary inquiry (1996)
5. Peterson, D.: Offensive cyber weapons: construction, development, and employment. J. Strateg. Stud. **36**(1), 120–124 (2013)
6. Schwartz, A., Knake, R.: Belfer Center for Science, and International Affairs. Government's Role in Vulnerability Disclosure: Creating a Permanent and Accountable Vulnerability Equities Process. Harvard Kennedy School, Belfer Center for Science and International Affairs (2016)
7. Tripathi, A., Singh, U.K.: Taxonomic analysis of classification schemes in vulnerability databases. In: 6th International Conference on Computer Sciences and Convergence Information Technology (ICCIT), pp. 686–691. IEEE (2011)
8. Baram, G., Cohen, D., Shapira, Z., Wechsler, O., Hight, N., Ben-Israel, I.: 2017 strategic trends in the global cyber conflict (2018)
9. Shane, S., Perlroth, N., Sanger, D.E.: Security breach and spilled secrets have shaken the NSA to its core. New York Times, 12 November 2017
10. Nurse, J.R.C., et al: Understanding insider threat: A framework for characterising attacks. In: IEEE Security and Privacy Workshops, pp. 214–228. IEEE (2014)
11. Chaudhry, P.E.: The looming shadow of illicit trade on the internet. Bus. Horiz. **60**(1), 77–89 (2017)
12. Yamin, M.M., Katt, B.: Inefficiencies in cyber-security exercises life-cycle: a position paper. In: CEUR Workshop Proceedings, vol. 2269, pp. 41–43 (2018)

A New Intrusion Detection System
Based on Gated Recurrent Unit (GRU)
and Genetic Algorithm

Mahdi Manavi[1]([✉])[ID] and Yunpeng Zhang[2][ID]

[1] Mirdamad Institute of Higher Education of Gorgan,
0098171 Gorgan, Iran
`Mahdi.manavi24@gmail.com`
[2] Department of Information and Logistics Technology, University of Houston,
Houston 77004, USA

Abstract. Distributed systems are extensive nowadays. The challenge of preventing network penetration by malware and hackers in these systems has been extensively considered and many types of research have been carried out in this field. Due to the high volume of input and output data in distributed systems, definitive and static algorithms that are used for small environments are not appropriate. For this problem, one of the new techniques is the deep learning method, which allows one to find optimal answers. In this paper, deep learning is used to investigate the behavior patterns of requests that enter the distributed network and then attacks are detected based on these patterns, which send an alarm to administrators (Anomaly Detection). In the next step, the genetic algorithm is used with the rule-based database to examine misuse detection. In this paper, considering the results obtained, it can be seen that the proposed algorithm provides high accuracy in detecting attacks with a low false alarm rate.

Keywords: Intrusion detection · Recurrent neural network ·
Gated recurrent unit · Genetic algorithm · KDD ·
Hybrid detection method

1 Introduction

An intrusion detection system (IDS) is a system that monitors the network traffic for suspicious activity. In 1987, attack detection systems became a topic of discussion and many researchers have continued to focus on this issue. IDS are security tools that receive and monitor network traffic or scan logs of the system and inform about suspicious activity with alarms they send to the network administrator [1]. Misuse detection consists of rules in the database used for known attacks. These rules are either designed using knowledge-based systems that contain known types of attacks or based on machine training patterns based on the behavior of users on suspicious activities [2]. Machine training techniques

© Springer Nature Switzerland AG 2019
G. Wang et al. (Eds.): SpaCCS 2019, LNCS 11611, pp. 368–383, 2019.
https://doi.org/10.1007/978-3-030-24907-6_28

based on classifier algorithms with the supervisor may not respond properly to new attacks that are patterned much differently than that for which they were trained and they are not suitable for so-called zero day attacks. Anomaly detection is based on the expected behavior of the system, where any behavior that goes out of the model is considered abnormal, and it's suitable for zero day attacks. Hybrid detection is a combination of the above methods that can make the permeability more accurate. Usually, the combination of misuse detection and Anomaly detection methods is used to increase the effect of the permeability detection engines. However, the combination of these two methods is not suitable for detecting intrusion at the level of the hypervisor's IDS implementation methods [1]. The implementation of IDSs is also divided into two categories:

Distributed: In this model, intrusion detection systems are used to exchange data in the detection of an intrusion and to declare attacks in different parts of the network. This model of IDS systems can be effective in detecting attacks by attackers at a specific time.

Non-distributed: This model of intrusion detection systems is located in a network area, such as SNORT [3]. In Fig. 1 the architecture of GRU is shown. GRU is a variant of LSTM which was introduced by Cho [4]. LSTM, a variation of a recurrent network, was proposed as one of the machine learning techniques to solve a lot of sequential data problems. LSTM architecture consists of 4 main components:

1-Input gate 2-forget gate 3-output gate 4-memory cell.

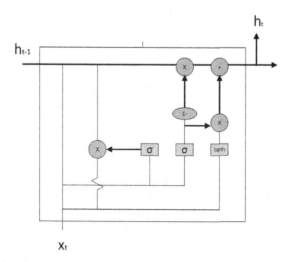

Fig. 1. Architecture of GRU

The cell makes decisions about what to store, read and write via gates that open or close and each memory cell corresponds to a time-step. Those gates pass the information based on set weights. Some of those weights like input and hidden states are adjusted during the learning process. GRU internal structure is simpler and therefore is faster to train since fewer computations are needed to make an update to its hidden state. GRU has two gates: Reset gate and update gate. The reset gate determines how to combine the new input with the previous memory cell and the update gate defines how much of the previous memory cell to keep around.

Genetic algorithm is one of the evolved computational subsets that have a direct relationship with the topic of artificial intelligence. It can be called a subset of artificial intelligence. Genetic algorithm is a search method that mimics the rules of natural biological evolution. Genetic algorithm applies the law of survival of the fittest to a series of problem solutions to obtain better answers. In each generation, better approximations of the final answers are obtained with the help of a selection process proportional to the value of the answers and reproduction and using operators that mimick natural genetics. This process adapts the new generations with the problem conditions.

In this paper, we propose a solution to detect attacks that go into the network with higher accuracy. Using each method like misuse detection and anomaly detection individually will enable the detection of the intrusions at a lower level. One of the challenges in misuse detection is the lack of recognition of zero-day attacks. Further, in anomaly detection, it can be noted that due to the low number of training data, a number of attacks are not given, so we use the hybrid algorithm for intrusion detection to minimize the challenges as far as possible. In the first section, we use the recurrent neural network in which we implement an anomaly method to detect new attacks by examining their behavior. Then, we use a genetic algorithm in which we detect the attacks using the knowledge base. We used the KDD cup 99 to implement the proposed solution and provide a comparison of our current work with other techniques as well.

The rest of the paper is organized as follows. Related works are introduced in Sect. 2. In Sect. 3, we present the proposed algorithm. The evaluation of the model is analyzed in Sect. 4. Finally, we draw conclusions in Sect. 5.

2   Related Work

Subba et al. [5] presented a simple Artificial Neural Network (ANN) based IDS model featuring feed forward and back propagation algorithms used by the presented Intrusion Detection System (IDS) with different optimization techniques. Xu et al. [6] presented a deep neural network in which the gated recurrent unit was used learn better network and multilayer perceptron network types examined on two KDD99 and NSL-KDD data types. Nguyen et al. [7] presented a convolutional neural network in which DoS attacks were detected and compared with other machine learning methods, such as KNN, Support Vector Machine (SVM) and nare bayes. The CNN introduced in this work was designed with two convolutional layers. Fu et al. [8] used the recurrent neural network and used LSTM-RNN to reach a high detection rate. Their experiment consisted of data preprocessing, feature abstraction, training and detection. LSTM were used during the training stage to classify whether the traffic was an attack or normal traffic. Balamurugan et al. [9] used a Markov model to predict cyber threat patterns based on the current known features and they used K-means clustering, a neural network, for an intrusion detection system. Kim et al. [10] proposed a deep neural network using 100 hidden units, combined with the ADAM optimizer and the ReLu activation function. Their approach was implemented on a GPU using TensorFlow and evaluated using the KDD data set. Maleh et al. [11] proposed a hybrid, lightweight intrusion detection system. Their intrusion detection model takes advantage of cluster-based architecture to reduce energy consumption. The model uses SVM for anomaly detection and a set of signature rules to detect malicious behaviors and provide global lightweight IDS. Kim et al. [12] constructed an IDS model with Long Short Term Memory (LSTM) architecture to a Recurrent Neural Network (RNN) and trained the IDS model on the KDD Cup 1999 dataset. Ishitaki et al. [13] presented the application of Deep Recurrent Neural Networks (DRNNs) for prediction of user behavior in Tor networks. They constructed a Tor server and a deep web browser (Tor client). Dong et al. [14] discussed different methods which were used to classify network traffic, and used different methods on the open data set. They further experimented with these methods to find out the best way of intrusion detection. Roy et al. [15] used deep neural network as a classifier for the different types of intrusion attacks and did a comparative study with SVM.

In most of the papers presented in this section, a method for detecting intrusions in the network was considered, which makes it possible to detect a shorter range of attacks. Our proposed approach is to study and implement a new model of intrusion detection that combines anomaly detection and misuse detection to cover the suffering of various types of attacks. In some related work, the hybrid methods for intrusion detection have been used, but the proposed approach has been better than others in terms of the accuracy parameter.

3   Proposed Algorithm

The proposed solution is a two-part process that combines the methods of misuse detection and anomaly detection to address the dangers of intruder behavior between vms. Considering the issues examined in the case of IDS and the high volume of input data to the network and the high number of vms, the use of machine training methods can be appropriate, but one of the most important problems in the neural network is the false positive problem. To decrease the rate of false positives, we use the recurrent neural network with GRU and genetic algorithm simultaneously. We use the recurrent neural network to divide the inputs into two categories: the first group, which performs as a normal task, and the second one, which includes the works that are considered an attack. We send normal tasks to the genetic algorithm so that the tasks that have the highest risk are found.

In Fig. 2 you see the flowchart for the proposed approach. First, we normalize the data that is used to train the network. Data normalization is one of the most important parts of the preprocessing of data so that the recurrent neural network can be properly trained. In the next step, we create the recurrent neural network and train it. After the network is trained, we test the network with new data. Tested data is entered into the network. This training and weighing of the parameters will continue as long as the accuracy of the validation is not improved in 3 epochs. After the network is trained, we test the network with new data. Test data is entered into the recurrent neural network, and After normalization, they are classified. In the genetic algorithm, using the training data, the initial population of chromosomes is constructed. Then the fitness function for each chromosome is calculated and new generations are created. These operations take place as long as the fitness function does not increase in 3 steps. During the generation, mutations in the chromosomes take place because the genetic algorithm can come to a better solution by using mutation. Eventually, a knowledge-base is constructed from rules. The knowledge base contains all known attacks. If a task is entered into the network and in terms of the values of the parameters (duration, src-bytes, wrong-fragment, dst-host-srv-error-rate and hot) is similar to the values in the knowledge-base rules, then it is detected as an attack, and the network administrator will be notified.

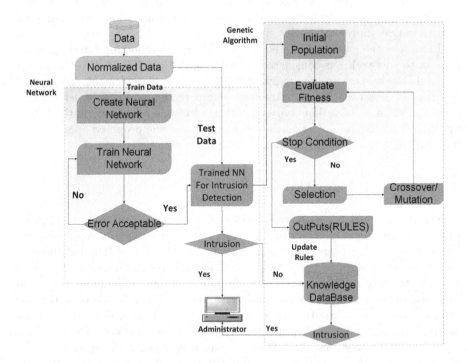

Fig. 2. WorkFlow of proposed IDS

In Fig. 3, we implemented this in the decision-makers (IDS) component. Decision makers (IDS) are deployed as a network-based IDS. The advantages of using this approach are: its deployment has little impact on the network. Since NIDS are usually passive devices that listen to the network wire without interfering with the normal operation of a network and a large network can be monitored by a few well-placed NIDS. The decision maker (IDS) is a module that the network tasks enter. Then each task is parameterized and, after normalizing the data, the operation of the two stages of intrusion detection is performed on it.

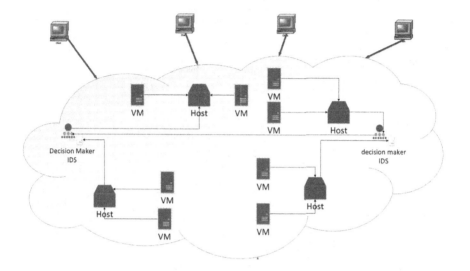

Fig. 3. Intrusion detection systems in network

A typical intrusion detection system consists of three functional components [20]:

Information source: It provides a stream of event records
Analysis engine: It finds signs of intrusions
Decision maker: It applies some rules on the outcomes of the analysis engine and decides what reactions should be done based on the outcomes of the analysis engine [21].

In this paper, we combine three components and call it Decision-maker (IDS). The decision-maker (IDS) is related to hosts for gathering information about vms and jobs that enter the network. First, anomalies are detected using the recurrent neural network. Then, we use the genetic algorithm to implement the misuse detection method. Decision makers inform the administrator to about attacks and update the knowledge database in incremental periods to increase accuracy. Decision makers are also associated with the general state of the network so that their knowledge databases are appropriate and up to date. Decision makers evaluate a task that enters into cloud computing, perform parallel processing and notify the network administrator. The lack of communication between decision makers and virtual machines makes them more secure and all the information required by decision makers (IDS) is collected through hosts.

3.1   Deep Neural Network

In the first step we normalized data and sent it to train the DNN model. The architecture of the GRU model is shown in Fig. 4. We create a four-layer GRU model and use drop out, which is a regularization technique introduced by Google for preventing of overfitting.

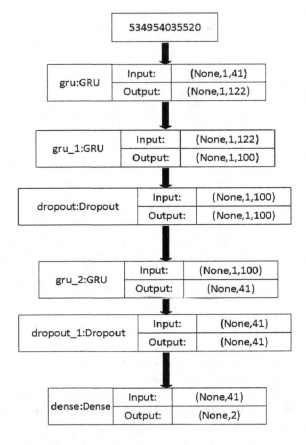

Fig. 4. Architecture of GRU (Proposed approach)

This model of DNN uses categorical-cross entropy for loss function and ADAM as an optimizer. ADAM is an algorithm for first-order gradient-based optimization of stochastic objective functions, based on adaptive estimates of lower-order moments [16]. We use the Softmax activation function in the last layer. Softmax is used to compute probability distribution from an array of real numbers. The softmax function produces an output which is a range of values between 0 and 1. We use parameters for stop training, i.e. the accuracy of validation data and the batch-size is 1000 and the max number of epochs is 100. The compilation time of creating this recurrent neural network is 0.118 s.

3.2   Genetic Algorithm

A genetic algorithm is used to detect attacks using misuse detection, which describes how to configure the genetic algorithm in this section. The number of generations to produce the optimal solution is 20.

Chromosome. In the genetic algorithms: each chromosome represents a possible solution to the problem that each chromosome consists of some constant genes. We use a decimal number to show each chromosome, which is the row of a rule in the training dataset. In Fig. 5 a representation of the chromosome can be observed. We describe five genes for each chromosome in our algorithm.

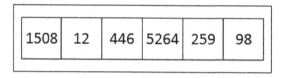

Fig. 5. Chromosome

Initial Population. The first stage of the genetic algorithm is the production of the initial population; to prevent early convergence, the initial population is randomly selected to cover a wide range of data. The fitness of the chromosomes is based on their gene fitness. The initial population size in our algorithm is 10000.

Selection Function. In this operator, from among the chromosomes in a population, some chromosomes are selected for reproduction. The elitism method is used to select the parent chromosomes to produce the children; we select 70% of the best chromosomes in terms of fitness to produce the next generation.

Crossver. As part of the integration process, parts of the chromosomes are replaced randomly. This makes the children have a combination of their parents' characteristics, so they do not exactly resemble their parents. In this solution, the multipoint crossover approach is used. In this method, various parts of the parent chromosomes are selected for the production of children.

Mutation. After completion of the crossover, the mutation operator is performed on the chromosomes. This operator randomly selects a gene from the chromosome and then changes the content of that gene. The mutation operator is used to avoid getting stuck in a local maximum or minimum. The probability of mutation in the solution presented in this solution is 0.1.

Fitness. To solve the problem using the genetic algorithm an appropriate fitness function must first be developed. The most important part of the genetic algorithm is a fitness function. As the function with higher is selected, more upper convergence is obtained, the algorithm runs faster, and the optimal answer is selected. Equation 1 shows the defined fitness function.

$$Fitness = \sum_{i=0}^{SC}(\frac{HTE(i) * CRL(i) * PR(i)}{HTR(i)}) \tag{1}$$

As seen in Eq. 1, SC is the size of a chromosome, HTE(i) is a count of rule i that is in the validation set of the genetic algorithm and it is known as an attack and HTR(i) is a count of rule i that is in the training set of the genetic algorithm and it is known as an attack. CRL(i) is considered as a conditional variable if the number of rule repetitions of i in the training data is lower than the threshold. This parameter is considered equal to the constant value of 4; otherwise, it is equal to 1 and PR(i) is the difference between the predictions of 2 classes of rule i in the recurrent neural network. If this difference is less than the threshold, then the parameter mentioned is equal to 1.3 and, if greater, it is equal to 1.

Considering the low amount of training data and the low difference between 2 class predictions in the recurrent neural network, the probability of error in the recurrent neural network test is increased. These last two parameters are used to find the optimal solution for the proper convergence of the genetic algorithm.

Early Stop Conditions. An early stop is determined so that the convergence of the algorithm does not go away and does not convert to divergence and it can be used to select more optimal solutions. Three conditions for early stopping of the genetic algorithm are considered:

1. The number of generations of offspring will exceed the threshold.
2. The mean of the fitness function in each generation is lower than the threshold.
3. The mean of the fitness function for the two consecutive generations is reduced.

4   Evaluation

The implementation of this paper has been done using the PYTHON programming language for the genetic algorithm, and it has been used by the TensorFlow library to implement the recurrent neural network. Table 1 shows the hardware system used to run the proposed approach.

In Table 2 the KDD Cup 99 dataset is shown. This dataset includes traffic with both normal and abnormal connections on the network and was used to evaluate the IDS performance objectively in the study. Each record has a field that shows 22 attack patterns or normal traffic and each row contains 41 features.

Table 1. Platform properties.

Properties	Values
Computer	Asus
CPU	Intel(R) Core(TM) i5-3230M CPU @ 2.60GHzCPU @ 2.60 GHz
RAM	6.00 GB (5.45 GB Usable)
Operating System	64-bit, Windows 8
IDE	Jupyter Notebook

Table 2. Data.

Type	Class	Number
ATTACK	DoS	391458
	Probe	391458
	R2L	4107
	U2R	1126
Normal	–	97278

Feature combinations of continuous and symbolic values and a data transformation were needed to convert them. Attacks can be categorized into exactly one of four types, as detailed below:

Denial of Service Attack (DoS): These types of attacks are usually related to busy resources and this high volume of requests sent to resources is related to the attackers to reject legitimate users' requests.

User to Root Attack (U2R): This is a type of security exploitation that allows an attacker to gain access to a normal user through conventional instruments, enabling the root to be accessed through the identification and exploitation of existing vulnerabilities.

Remote to Local Attack (R2L): This is when an attacker attempts access to a system over a network. The attacker can only transmit data packets over the network and the attacker tries to gain access to the machine by exploiting some vulnerability.

Probing Attack (Prob): This is when an attacker attempts to acquire information from a network to avoid the system's security protocols.

In this section, we use metrics for assessing the classification of the recurrent neural network that defines these metrics as follows:

True Positive (TP). Attack data that is correctly classified as an attack.

False Positive (FP). Normal data that is incorrectly classified as an attack.

True Negative (TN). Normal data that is correctly classified as normal.

False Negative (FN). Attack data that is incorrectly classified as normal.

We will be using the following measures to evaluate the performance of our proposed approach:

in Eq. 2 the accuracy measures the proportion of the total number of correct classifications.

$$Accuracy = (\frac{TP + TN}{TP + TN + FP + FN}) \tag{2}$$

in Eq. 3 the precision measures the number of correct classifications penalized by the number of incorrect classifications.

$$Percision = (\frac{TP}{TP + FP}) \tag{3}$$

in Eq. 4 The recall measures the number of correct classifications penalized by the number of missed entries.

$$Recall = (\frac{TP}{TP + FN}) \tag{4}$$

in Eq. 5 The false alarm measures the proportion of benign events incorrectly classified as malicious.

$$FalseAlarm = (\frac{FP}{FP + TN}) \tag{5}$$

in Eq. 6 The F1-score measures the harmonic mean of precision and recall, which serves as a derived effectiveness measurement.

$$F1\text{-}score = 2 * (\frac{Precision * Recall}{Precision + Recall}) \tag{6}$$

In this step, we show a graph of different parameters during training of DNN.

Figure 6 shows the degree of accuracy in the correct classification of the data. At the initial steps gradient of the graph, it is ascending and the validation accuracy rate and training accuracy rate are more than 99%.

The loss function is an important section in recurrent neural networks, which is used to measure the inconsistency between a predicted value and true value. It is a non-negative value. In Fig. 7 we show a graph of loss during the training. In each step, the level of the loss function is descending and lower than 0.02 in validation inputs.

In Fig. 8 the ROC graph is present. The receiver operating characteristic (ROC) curve it is a tool for visualization that can be utilized to determine whether a classifier is appropriate in terms of cost sensibility. It is the ratio of the false positive (FP) to true positive (TP) rate. This graph shows that fewer false positives than true positives have been created. The micro-average calculated the ROC curve between y-test and y-prediction and the macro-average calculated between all FPR (False Positive Rate) and mean TPR (True Positive Rate). In Table 3 the values of important parameters of two classes in the recurrent neural network are shown.

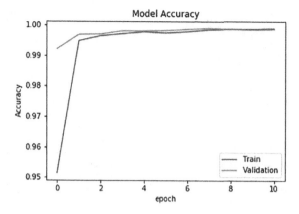

Fig. 6. Model accuracy

In Fig. 9, you can see the mean of the fitness function of the generation of chromosomes in each generation. As stated in the previous section, after sorting out chromosomes, 70% of the best are selected and some of them are used to produce children. In this graph, the improvement in the amount of fitness function is shown in general in each generation. At each stage, due to the reduction in the number of chromosomes and the selection of more relevant chromosomes, the total value of the fitness function is higher.

The condition intended to stop the genetic algorithm is that the algorithm stops if the algorithm does not provide an improvement in the two successive

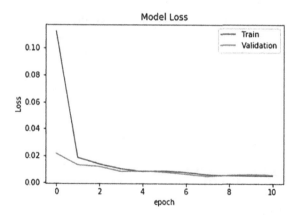

Fig. 7. Model loss

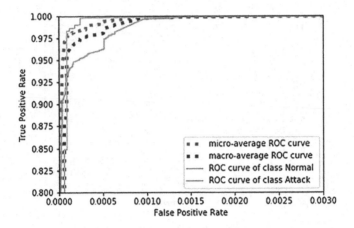

Fig. 8. ROC

Table 3. Results of recurrent neural network.

Type	F1-score	Recall-score	Precision-score
Normal	99.71	99.87	99.54
Attack	99.92	99.88	99.97

generations. This provides a good convergence representation of the genetic algorithm in obtaining the optimal set.

In Fig. 10, the fitness of each chromosome has shown in all generations. This graph shows the total number of chromosomes created in all generations and it shows that after an initial generation with a chromosome number of 10,000, there is an upward trend in the amount of fitness function. The most important challenge in heuristic algorithms is avoiding getting stuck in a local maximum

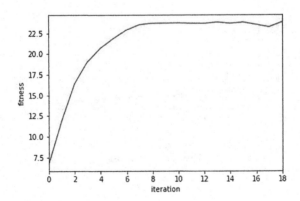

Fig. 9. Average of fitness in each generation

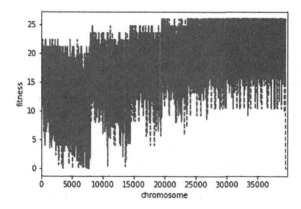

Fig. 10. Fitness function

or a local minimum. In the proposed algorithm we have tried to pass through this local maximum or local minimum with proper configuration, such as with proper use of the mutation operator. You can see the results of the mutation operator in this graph.

In this section, we compared our proposed approach with other papers in this field. In Table 4, the comparison between the proposed solution and the related work that has been carried out in recent years in this field suggests an improvement in the accuracy parameter in detecting attacks on the network.

Our proposed approach is highly efficient at decreasing the false positive rate, but it is challenging in terms of its running speed, which can be eliminated to a large extent by taking into account the strong hardware equipment. We have already seen good results and we are trying to increase the speed and accuracy with new technologies such as GRU in the recurrent neural network and the proper configuration of the genetic algorithm.

Table 4. Results of all competitive methods.

Techniques	Accuracy
CHI-SVM [17]	98
GA+FLN [18]	99.69
PSO+FLN [18]	99.68
LSTM [12]	96.93
GRU+SVM [19]	84.15
Proposed (GRU+GA)	99.91

5 Conclusion

Today, intrusion detection has become one of the most important challenges facing networks and this has led many researchers to focus on this field. In the proposed method, given that the existing networks are wide and the use of traditional methods is not responsive, machine learning methods and heuristic algorithms have been used. In our proposed approach, we have tried to consider the accuracy and speed of the network intrusion detection process by using new technologies such as GRU in the recurrent neural network, as well as the proper configuration of the genetic algorithm that can reduce the false positive rate. In this method, both anomaly detection and misuse detection methods are used simultaneously so that a wide range of attacks can be reported to administrators of the network. We have implemented our proposed model in TensorFlow and performed extensive evaluations on its capabilities. For our evaluations, we have utilized the benchmark KDD Cup '99 dataset and achieved desirable results. Our results have demonstrated that our approach offers high levels of accuracy with reduced training time because we have a suitable configuration in GRU and the genetic algorithm. In the last step, we compared the proposed algorithm with other related work over the last few years, which demonstrated the proposed solution's superiority to other solutions, given that the proposed solution has shown more than 99.91% accuracy.

References

1. Mishraa, P., Varadharajan, V., Pilli, E., Varadharajan, V., Tupakulab, U.: Intrusion detection techniques in cloud environment: a survey. J. Netw. Comput. Appl. **77**, 18–47 (2017)
2. Barbara, D., Jordia, S.: Applications of Data Mining in Computer Security, vol. 6. Springer, New York (2002). https://doi.org/10.1007/978-1-4615-0953-0
3. Milenkoski, A., Vieira, M., Kounev, S., Avritzer, A., Payne, B.D.: Evaluating computer intrusion detection systems: a survey of common practices. ACM Comput. Surv. (CSUR) **48**(1), 12 (2015)
4. Cho, K., et al.: Learning phrase representations using RNN encoder-decoder for statistical machine translation. In: EMNLP (2014)
5. Subba, B., Biswas, S., Karmakar, S.: A neural network based system for intrusion detection and attack classification. In: Twenty Second National Conference on Communication (NCC). IEEE, India (2016)
6. Xu, C., Shen, J., Du, X., Zhang, F.: An intrusion detection system using a deep neural network with gated recurrent units. IEEE Access **6**, 48697–48707 (2018)
7. Nguyen, S., Nguyen, V., Choi, J., Kim, K.: Design and implementation of intrusion detection system using convolutional neural network for DoS detection. In: Proceedings of the 2nd International Conference on Machine Learning and Soft Computing, ICMLSC 2018. ACM, Vietnam (2018)
8. Fu, Y., Lou, F., Meng, F., Tian, Z., Zhang, H., Jiang, F.: An intelligent network attack detection method based on RNN. In: Third International Conference on Data Science in Cyberspace (DSC). IEEE, China (2018)

9. Balamurugan, V., Saravanan, R.: Enhanced intrusion detection and prevention system on cloud environment using hybrid classification and OTS generation. Cluster Comput. 1–13 (2017)
10. Kim, J., Shin, N., Jo, S., Kim, S.: Method of intrusion detection using deep neural network. In: International Conference on Big Data and Smart Computing (Big-Comp). IEEE, South Korea (2017)
11. Maleh, Y., Ezzati, A., Qasmaoui, Y., Mbida, M.: A global hybrid intrusion detection system for wireless sensor networks. Procedia Comput. Sci. **52**, 1047–1052 (2015)
12. Kim, J., Kim, J, Thu, HLT., Kim, H.: Long short term memory recurrent neural network classifier for intrusion detection. In: International Conference on Platform Technology and Service. IEEE, South Korea (2016)
13. Ishitaki, R.T., Obukata, Y., Oda, T., Barolli, L.: Application of deep recurrent neural networks for prediction of user behavior in Tor networks. In: 31st International Conference on Advanced Information Networking and Applications Workshops. IEEE, Taiwan (2017)
14. Dong, B., Wang, X.: Comparison deep learning method to traditional methods using for network intrusion detection. In: 8th IEEE International Conference on Communication Software and Networks. IEEE, China (2016)
15. Roy, S.S., Mallik, A., Gulati, R., Obaidat, M.S., Krishna, P.V.: A deep learning based artificial neural network approach for intrusion detection. In: Giri, D., Mohapatra, R.N., Begehr, H., Obaidat, M.S. (eds.) ICMC 2017. CCIS, vol. 655, pp. 44–53. Springer, Singapore (2017). https://doi.org/10.1007/978-981-10-4642-1_5
16. Kingma, D., Ba, J.: Adam: a method for stochastic optimization. In: 3rd International Conference for Learning Representations. arXiv, USA (2015)
17. Thaseen, I.S., Kumar, C.A.: Intrusion detection model using fusion of chi-square feature selection and multi class SVM. J. King Saud Univ. Comput. Inf. Sci. **29**(4), 462–472 (2017)
18. Ali, M.H., Al Mohammed, B.A.D., Ismail, A., Zolkipli, M.F.: A new intrusion detection system based on fast learning network and particle swarm optimization. IEEE Access **6**, 20255–20261 (2018)
19. Agarap, A.F.M.: A neural network architecture combining Gated Recurrent Unit (GRU) and Support Vector Machine (SVM) for intrusion detection in network traffic data. In: Proceedings of the 2018 10th International Conference on Machine Learning and Computing, ICMLC 2018. ACM, China (2018)
20. Gurley Bace, R.: Intrusion Detection. Sams Publishing, USA (2000)
21. Yao, J., Zhao, S., V. Saxton, L.: A study on fuzzy intrusion detection. In: Proceedings Volume 5812, Data Mining, Intrusion Detection, Information Assurance, and Data Networks Security (2005)

Topic Model Based Android Malware Detection

Yucai Song[1], Yang Chen[2], Bo Lang[1(✉)], Hongyu Liu[1],
and Shaojie Chen[1]

[1] State Key Lab of Software Development Environment, School of Computer
Science and Engineering, Beihang University, Beijing 100191, China
{songyucai1206, langbo, liuhongyu,
chenshaojie}@buaa.edu.cn
[2] National Computer Network Emergency Response Technical
Team/Coordination Center of China, Beijing 100191, China
chenyang@cert.org.cn

Abstract. Nowadays, the security risks brought by Android malwares are increasing. Machine learning is considered as a potential solution for promoting the performance of malware detection. For machine learning based Android malware detection, feature extraction plays a key role. Thinking the source codes of applications are comparable with text documents, we propose a new Android malware detection method based on the topic model which is an effective technique in text feature extraction. Our method regards the decompiled codes of an application as a text document, and the topic model is used to mine the potential topics in the codes which can reflect the semantic feature of the application. The experimental results demonstrate that, our approach performs better than the state-of-the-art methods. Also, our method mines the features in the application files automatically without manually design, and therefore overcomes the limitation in present methods which relies on experts' prior knowledge.

Keywords: Android malware detection · Topic model · Machine learning

1 Introduction

Since the first Android smartphone HTC Dream was pushed in 2008, Android devices have grown exponentially. Meanwhile the number of Android applications has also increased rapidly, which has brought numerous security vulnerabilities and malicious attacks. According to the report of 360 Laboratory [1], there are 4.342 million new Android malware samples in 2018, with an average of 12,000 daily growth. Hence, it is important to find effective and efficient Android malware detection methods.

Current researches on Android malware detection can be classified into the static analysis methods and the dynamic analysis methods, depending on whether the codes are executed during the analysis. Without running the codes, static analysis methods obtain source codes by reverse engineering and extract different features of the source

G. Wang et al. (Eds.): SpaCCS 2019, LNCS 11611, pp. 384–396, 2019.
https://doi.org/10.1007/978-3-030-24907-6_29

codes; the ways to extract features include lexical analysis, syntax analysis, control flow analysis, data flow analysis and so on. Dynamic analysis methods run codes in a virtual environment such as a sandbox or a virtual machine, and records the behaviors of the application by triggers, and the behavior information is used to extract features for classification or detection.

At present, many studies employ static analysis to detect Android Malwares. Wang et al. [2] used the feature ranking approach to sort the risks of Android permissions, and used the machine learning model to detect malware. Aafer et al. [3] proposed the DroidAPIMiner to mine robust API features for Android Malware Detection. Ali Feizollah et al. [4] evaluated the effectiveness of Android Intent as a distinguishing feature. LeakMiner [5], TrustDroid [6], FlowDroid [7], DidFail [8] are methods of extracting features from data flow for detection. Yang et al. [9] proposed the Droid-miner which mined common structures and attributes in the control flow graphs of applications from the same malware families.

In dynamic analysis, Asaf et al. [10] proposed DroidHunter to detect the loading of malicious code by monitoring the key Android runtime APIs. Seo et al. [11] proposed the FLEXDROID which implemented an additional component in the Android application manifest. The component allowed developers to set permissions on local code. Afonso et al. [12] proposed the Going Native which generated strategy for local code to limit malicious behavior.

Since the applications are not executed, static analysis methods are more efficient and suitable for the massive Android malware detection tasks. This kind of analysis methods depend on different features, such as permissions, API, Intent, data flow analysis and control flow graph, which represent different analysis perspectives. Different features will lead to distinct attentions to Android code and different accuracy on distinguished types of datasets. Therefore, it is important to extract effective and comprehensive semantic features for improving the performance of detection.

Feature extraction methods, such as data flow analysis and control flow graph analysis, are based on experts' prior knowledge. This paper proposes a new feature extraction method for Android applications. We use the topic model to mine the potential topic information in the decompiled source codes of the Android applications. The topic model is a statistical model which is used to discover potential topics in a large number of documents, and the model can automatically analyze the document by counting the words. Based on the statistical data, the topic model judges the topics and the proportion of each topic in the document, so as to mine the deep implicit semantic information of the text. This paper regards the decompiled codes as a document and uses the topic model to mine potential topics. The topic model can reduce the loss of information in source code as much as possible. The method can overcome the limitations of manual design in the present methods and can automatically mine the information that best represent the characteristics of the application.

The main contribution of this paper is that, we propose a topic model based Android malware detection method and the method achieved a good detection effect. This method adopts a new perspective on feature extraction. The decompiled codes of an Android application are regarded as a text document, and the topic model is used to mine potential topic information for Android malware detection. This method was compared with state-of-the-art methods on two public datasets, Drebin [13], AMD [14] and a self-collected dataset. The sizes of the three datasets are 15121, 19561, and 14566, respectively. The accuracy was up to 99.9%, and our method performed better on the false negative rate and false positive rate, which demonstrates the effectiveness of the topic model based feature extraction method.

The rest of the paper is organized as follows. Section 2 highlights the related work. Section 3 introduces our topic model based method. Section 4 presents the experiment and analyzes the results. Section 5 summarizes the paper.

2 Related Work

Current researches on Android malware detection can be classified into static analysis methods and dynamic analysis methods.

Static analysis methods mainly extract static features by reverse engineering. Wang et al. [2] studied the risks of permissions in Android application. They used the feature ranking approach to sort the risks of Android permissions, and detect malwares using machine learning models, including SVM, logistic regression, decision tree, random forest, etc. The experimental results reached an accuracy of 94.62%. Aafer et al. [3] proposed the DroidAPIMiner, which extracted API sets with high risk and distinctiveness based on the probability distribution of API in the dataset. And they further extracted API-related package information and permission information to enrich the features. Cen et al. [15] extracted the API calls and permission information from the decompiled source codes as a combined feature, and used probability discriminant model to detect Android Malware. They improved the classification effect by applying feature selection. Ali Feizollah et al. [4] evaluated the effectiveness of Android Intent as a distinguishing feature for malware detection. The experimental results indicated that Intent has richened semantic information when describing the intention of malicious codes. However, the study also emphasized that the Intent feature is not the ultimate solution, but should be used in combination with other known valid features.

Data flow analysis, also known as taint analysis, traces data flow within the program to find potential and suspicious data leakage paths. Data flow analysis defines two concepts, i.e., the source and the sink. A source is the location where sensitive data is acquired, and a sink is the location where sensitive data is leaked. Through taint tracking, data flow analysis finds out if there is a path from a source to a sink. At present, the most popular data flow analysis tools include LeakMiner proposed by Yang et al. [5], TrustDroid proposed by Zhao et al. [6], FlowDroid proposed by Arzt et al. [7] and DidFail proposed by Burket et al. [8].

Yang et al. [9] proposed the Droidminer, which mined common structures and attributes in the control flow graphs of applications from the same malware families. Yao et al. [16] applied the community discovery algorithm to the function call graphs. For the function call graph of an Android application, risk weights were calculated for each function node, and is defined as the attributes of the nodes. Zhou et al. [17] extracted subgraphs for each API in the sensitive API list, and obtained the maximum isomorphic subgraph based on Malware family samples. Narayanan et al. [18] proposed an Android Malware Detection method based on the multi-view learning. They generated different types of subgraphs based on various features, including API subgraphs, data flow subgraphs, permission subgraphs, instruction sequence subgraphs, etc. Then they learned a Graph Kernel for each subgraph and used multiple kernel SVM as the classifier.

Static analysis methods can cover all possible paths of program execution. However, these kind of methods are vulnerable to code obfuscation. Dynamic analysis methods run codes in a virtual environment and observe the behaviors of the Android applications.

Asaf et al. [10] proposed DroidHunter to detect the loading of malicious codes by monitoring the key Android runtime APIs. Seo et al. [11] proposed the FLEXDROID which implemented an additional component in the Android application manifest. The component allowed developers to set permissions on local code. Afonso et al. [12] proposed the Going Native which generated strategy for local code to limit malicious behaviors. In addition, a variety of dynamic monitoring tools have been proposed for Android malware detection. Droidbox [19] and Droidmon [20] are both dynamic monitoring tools based on Android runtime instrument changes.

The shortcoming of dynamic analysis method lies in its limited code coverage, i.e., it cannot cover all the execution paths of an application. Besides, the time complexity of the dynamic analysis method is high and cannot meet the efficiency requirement of the large-scale Android malware detection.

3   Method

3.1   Overview

Existing static detection methods extract features from permissions, APIs, function call graphs, control flow graphs and data flow analysis. These observational perspectives are based on experts' prior knowledge, which is a rigorous requirement in some circumstances. This paper proposes an Android application feature extraction method based on the topic model, which mines potential thematic information in the decompiled codes for detection.

The topic model considers that a document selects one or more topics with a certain probability when it was generated, and each topic selects one or more words with a certain probability. Our method regards the decompiled codes of an Android application as a document. And the topic model is applied to mine the potential topic information in a large number of application samples. The topic vectors extracted by the topic model is used as the features of the applications to train the machine learning model for detection.

When decompiling the APK file to get the source codes, we choose to get the Java source codes instead of the smali source codes. The reason is that the amount of smali codes is much larger than that of the Java codes when they are expressing the same semantics. In addition, third-party libraries are widely used in Android applications. Those codes are generally not malicious and do not characterize the specific behavior of the application. Therefore, these codes should be removed before subsequent analysis.

Algorithm 1 Topic model Based Android Malware Detection

1: decompile the APK file to get the classes.dex and the AndroidManifest.xml
2: decomplie the classes.dex to obtain the Java source code files U
3: detect the third-party libraries and get the package path list L
4: $W = [\ ]$
5: **for** each file f in U
6:   **if** the path of f in the L
7:     **continue**
8:   **else**
9:     T = segmentation tokens of f
10:    $W = W \cup T$
11: use W to train the topic model and extract topic vector
12: extract the permission features from the AndroidManifest.xml file
13: combines the topic vectors and the permission features to train the classifier

---

As shown in Fig. 1, the steps contained in the method are described in Algorithm 1. Firstly, the Apktool [21] is used to decompile the APK file and obtain the classes.dex file and the AndroidManifest.xml file. The AndroidManifest.xml file is used to extract the permission feature. The JADX tool is used to decompile the classes.dex file to obtain the Java source codes. Then, the method use the LibRadar [22] tool to detect the third-party libraries that exists in the source codes and remove them. The lexical analysis is performed on the remaining Java source codes to obtain the word

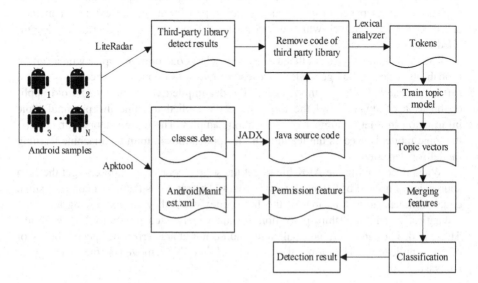

Fig. 1. Android malware detection process

segmentation result which is used to train the topic model. The topic vectors of each samples are extracted by the topic model. Finally, the method combines the topic vectors and the permission features to train the classification model.

3.2 Preprocessing

Firstly, the APK file is decompiled with the Apktool tool to get the AndroidManifest. xml file and the classes.dex file. Then the classes.dex file is decompiled by JADX tool to get the Java source codes.

We choose Java source codes instead of Smali code since Smali codes are much longer than Java codes when expressing the same semantics. Figure 2(a) shows a Java statement in the source code of an Android application, and Fig. 2(b) shows the smali codes that implements the same function. Comparing the two figures, it turns out that Java codes contains more semantic information than Smali codes.

After obtaining the Java source codes, the codes of third-party libraries need to be removed. During the development of Android applications, developers call a lot of third-party libraries to implement the functions of ad plug-in embedding and other extensions. Those codes should be filtered before subsequent processing.

```
boolean flag = "generic".equals(Build.BRAND.toLowerCase());
```

(a) Java statement

```
const/4 v0, 0x1
const-string v1, "generic"
sget-object v2, Landroid/os/Build;->BRAND:Ljava/lang/String;
invoke-virtual {v2}3, Ljava/lang/String;->toLowerCase()Ljava/lang/String;
move-result-object v2
invoke-virtual {v1, v2}, Ljava/lang/String;->equals(Ljava/lang/Object;)Z
move-result v1
```

(b) Smali statements

Fig. 2. Statements of Java and Smali

Existing Android third-party library detection method can be classified into two type. One is to build a white list of the third-party libraries, and extract the artificially designed features of the libraries in the white list. LibScout [23] is the research in this way. The other one is to extract static features based on the large amount of Android application samples, and use clustering method to mine potential third-party libraries. LibRadar [22] is the research of this kind. Compared these two kinds of method, the accuracy of the first one is limited to the size of the whitelist. While, the second one is based on big data, and therefore is more general and more suitable for large-scale scenarios. Hence, we choose the LibRadar tool to detect and remove the third-party libraries.

The Java lexical analyzer is used to segment the source codes. The word segmentation results contain identifier, keyword, number, string, separator, operator, bit operator, and logical operation. Since the number of words in the segmentation results may be too large which will exceed the range of storage and computing capability, we applied the following two measures to balance the contradiction between word quantity and the computing capability.

(1) Only identifiers, strings and numbers in the word segmentation results are retained. These retained words have more semantic than other types, and are more likely containing valid semantic information.
(2) 40,000 words are retained by random sampling if the number of filtered words still exceeds 40,000. For each Android application sample, up to 40,000 words are obtained, which will be regarded as a document.

3.3   Model

In our model, we use the Term Frequency-Inverse Document Frequency (TF-IDF) [24] to calculate the topic vector of each application sample.

In a document, Term Frequency (TF) refers to the frequency of a given word appearing in the file. For a word t_i in a document d_j, the TF of t_i is expressed as follows:

$$tf_{i,j} = \frac{n_{i,j}}{\sum_k n_{k,j}} \tag{1}$$

where $n_{i,j}$ represents the number of t_i in d_j, k represents the number of words in the dictionary, and the denominator represents the sum of the occurrences of all words in d_j.

Inverse Document Frequency (IDF) is a measure of the universal importance of a word. For a word t_i, the IDF of t_i is expressed as follows:

$$idf_i = \log \frac{|D|}{1 + |\{j : t_i \in d_i\}|} \tag{2}$$

where $|D|$ represents the total number of documents, $|\{j : t_i \in d_i\}|$ represents the number of documents containing the word $t_i(n_{i,j} \neq 0)$.

The TF-IDF of a word t_i is expressed as follows:

$$tfidf_{i,j} = tf_{i,j} \times idf_i \tag{3}$$

Therefore, when the frequency of a word is high in a particular document and the frequency is low in the entire sample set, the TF-IDF of the word has a high weight, and TF-IDF tends to highlight the significant words in a particular document and weaken the impact of the common words.

Our method then iterates through the segmentation results of the Android application samples to record all the words and count their occurrence numbers in all documents. We build the dictionary by taking the top 100,000 words with highest occurrences. Based on the established dictionary, TF-IDF model is used to calculate the TF-IDF vectors of each document.

After obtaining the TF-IDF vectors of each document, the topic vectors of each document are further obtained by the Latent Semantic Indexing (LSI) [25] model.

The LSI model is based on the Singular Value Decomposition (SVD). The SVD can be simply described as, a $m \times n$ matrix A can be decomposed into the following three matrices:

$$A_{m \times n} = U_{m \times m} \Sigma_{m \times n} V_{n \times n}^T \tag{4}$$

where the matrix U represents the correlation between the documents and the topics, the matrix Σ represents the correlation between the topics and the lexical meanings, and the matrix V represents the correlation between the words and the lexical meanings.

To reduce the dimension of the matrix to k, Eq. (4) can be approximated as:

$$A_{m \times n} \approx U_{m \times k} \Sigma_{k \times k} V_{k \times n}^T \tag{5}$$

where $k < m$. In the LSI model, the decomposition of the SVD can be described as following process. For the input m documents, construct a dictionary with n words and calculate the TF-IDF vectors of each document. A_{ij} corresponds to the TF-IDF of the dictionary's j_{th} word in the i_{th} document. k is the assumed number of topics that exist in the corpus. For the result of the decomposition, $U_{i,l}$ represents the correlation between the i_{th} document and the l_{th} topic, $\Sigma_{l,o}$ represents the correlation between the l_{th} topic and the o_{th} lexical meaning, and $V_{j,o}$ indicates the relevance of the j_{th} word and the o_{th} lexical meaning.

The extraction of the topic vectors is only based on the decompiled source codes. We also analyze other components of the APK file. We believe that the permission information is very important for the Android malware detection, and therefore refer to the list of risky permissions given by StormDroid [26], and extract 59-dimensional permission features from AndroidManifest.xml. Each dimension of the permission feature represents the existence or absence of a risky permission. The topic vector and the permission feature are joined together to form the final feature of each sample.

We select the XGBoost [27] model and the SVM [28] model as the classifiers to complete the detection task of Android Malware.

4 Experiments

4.1 Datasets

1. Drebin [13]. The Drebin datasets contains 5,560 Android malware samples from 179 different malware families. Samples were collected from August 2010 to October 2012.
2. AMD [14]. The AMD (Android Malware Dataset) contains 24,553 Android malware samples belonging to 135 varieties of 71 different malware families, collected between 2010 and 2016. This paper randomly extracted 10,000 samples for experiments.

3. Myblack. Myblack dataset was collected by us and contains 5005 Android malware samples.
4. AndroZoo [29]. The benign dataset was downloaded from the AndroZoo platform and detected as benign samples by VirusTotal [30]. The dataset contains 9561 benign samples.

4.2 Experiment Settings

- **Comparison Methods**

This paper selects the Drebin [13] method which is based on feature engineering and the CSBD [31] method which is based on control flow graph. Drebin performed a broad static analysis, gathering as many features of an application as possible. These features were embedded in a joint vector space which can be automatically identified and used for explaining the decisions. CSBD devised several machine learning classifiers that rely on a set of features built from applications' control flow graphs. These two methods are the state-of-the-art static analysis based methods. Since these two methods exposed their complete codes, they are often compared by other researches. Combining different features and models in our method, as well as the comparison methods, the experiments totally include six methods: LSI + XGBoost (ours), LSI + SVM (ours), LSI + Permission + XGBoost (ours), LSI + Permission + SVM (ours), Drebin and CSBD.

The benign dataset and the three malware datasets were used to construct three experimental datasets: AMD+AndroZoo, Drebin+AndroZoo and MyBlack+AndroZoo. The size of the three datasets are 19561, 15121 and 14566.

- **Indicators**

This paper analyzes the experimental results through the three indicators: the F-score, the False Negative (FN) rate and the False Positive (FP) rate.

The F-score comprehensively considers the accuracy rate and recall rate of the classification results, which is expressed as follows:

$$F - score = \frac{2 \times P \times R}{P + R} \tag{6}$$

where P represents the accuracy rate and R represents the recall rate. P and R are calculated as follows:

$$P = \frac{PP + NN}{PP + PN + NN + NP}, R = \frac{PP}{PP + PN} \tag{7}$$

where PP represents the number of malware samples which are classified correctly as malicious, PN represents the number of malware samples which are classified wrongly as benign, NN represents the number of benign samples which are classified correctly as benign, and NP represents the number of benign samples which are classified correctly as malicious.

The False Negative (FN) rate and the False Positive (FP) rate are also important indicators in the malware detection task. The FN rate represents the proportion of the positive samples which are classified wrongly as negative. The FP rate represents the proportion of the negative samples which are classified wrongly as positive. They are calculated as follows:

$$FN = \frac{PN}{PP + PN}, FP = \frac{NP}{NN + NP} \tag{8}$$

where the meanings of other symbols are the same as those in Formula (7).

4.3 Results

The performances of the six methods on the three datasets are compared and discussed in this section. Since the F-score integrates the accuracy and the recall rate, the two indicators of accuracy and recall are not separately discussed.

Table 1 shows the F-scores of the six methods on the three datasets, where the bold numbers are the best results and the blue numbers are the second best results. Firstly, we compare the four methods proposed in this paper. For classification models, the performances of XGBoost and SVM are equally well. XGBoost performed better on the AMD dataset and the Myblack dataset, while SVM performed better on the Drebin dataset. In terms of the features, the classification effects of the LSI topic vectors extracted from Java source codes are improved significantly by adding the permission feature extracted from the AndroidManifest.xml file.

Table 1. F-score results of the six methods on the three datasets

Methods	Drebin+AndroZoo	Myblack+AndroZoo	AMD+AndroZoo
LSI+XGBoost	98.09335722	**99.93120499**	96.00802065
LSI+SVM	98.61582131	99.79354502	95.97202646
LSI+Permission+XGBoost	98.30413772	**99.93120499**	98.07793736
LSI+Permission+SVM	**98.85196737**	99.86238668	97.59690895
Drebin	98.59478909	99.77529155	**98.31770479**
CSBD	96.66658106	98.72068462	97.43683561

Besides, the F-scores of our methods were compared with the two baseline methods. On the two datasets of Drebin and MyBlack, our methods obtained the best and second best F-scores. On the AMD dataset, the Drebin method achieved the best F-score, but the second best F-score achieved by our method was only 0.24 lower than the best one.

Tables 2 and 3 show the False Negative (FN) rates and the False Positive (FP) rates of the six methods on the three datasets respectively. In terms of the FN, Drebin method performed best on the Drebin dataset and the AMD dataset, and our method performed best on the Myblack dataset. For the FP, our method performed best on the three datasets. Drebin method brought high False Negative rates when showed low False Positive rates, while our method performed relatively well on the both two rates.

Table 2. False Negative (FN) rates of the six methods on the three datasets

Methods	Drebin+AndroZoo	Myblack+AndroZoo	AMD+AndroZoo
LSI+XGBoost	0.021838035	**0.001028807**	0.039798489
LSI+SVM	0.018198362	0.00308642	0.043828715
LSI+Permission+XGBoost	0.020928116	**0.001028807**	0.017128463
LSI+Permission+SVM	0.013648772	0.002057613	0.023677582
Drebin	**0.009099181**	0.002061856	**0.009202454**
CSBD	0.04599816	0.018575851	0.032307692

Considering the experimental results on the three datasets, our method obtained the best F-scores on the two datasets. And on another dataset, the performance of our method was close to the best one. Meanwhile, our method performed better on the False Negative rate and the False Positive rate. Based on the overall results, the effectiveness of the proposed method can be verified.

Table 3. False Positive (FP) rates of the six methods on the three datasets

Methods	Drebin+AndroZoo	Myblack+AndroZoo	AMD+AndroZoo
LSI+XGBoost	0.013082156	**0.000523286**	0.04029304
LSI+SVM	**0.005756149**	0.002093145	0.029304029
LSI+Permission+XGBoost	0.008372587	**0.000523286**	0.025641026
LSI+Permission+SVM	0.006802721	0.001046572	**0.025117739**
Drebin	0.024633124	0.002620545	0.039832285
CSBD	0.027450012	0.001746131	0.028620745

5   Conclusions

In this paper, we propose a new feature extraction method for malicious Android application detection, which introduces the topic model techniques from the text analysis area to mine potential semantic information in the decompiled source codes of Android applications. We use the extracted topic vectors and the permission information from AndroidManifest.xml as features to train the machine learning models for

Android malware classification. We compare the method with two state-of-the-art methods which are based on feature engineering on three datasets, and our method obtains the best overall result, which shows the effectiveness of the proposed method.

We will continue our work from the following two aspects. On the one hand, the LSI model are not interpretable enough. Therefore, other topic models can be considered to improve the interpretability of the topic vector. On the other hand, this method does not consider the code obfuscation in the source codes. The problem of code obfuscation can be addressed in the future.

References

1. Lab: 2018 Android malware special report (2019)
2. Wang, W., Wang, X., Feng, D., Liu, J., Han, Z., Zhang, X.: Exploring permission-induced risk in android applications for malicious application detection. IEEE Trans. Inf. Forensics Secur. **9**, 1869–1882 (2014)
3. Aafer, Y., Du, W., Yin, H.: DroidAPIMiner: mining API-level features for robust malware detection in android. In: Zia, T., Zomaya, A., Varadharajan, V., Mao, M. (eds.) SecureComm 2013. LNICST, vol. 127, pp. 86–103. Springer, Cham (2013). https://doi.org/10.1007/978-3-319-04283-1_6
4. Feizollah, A., Anuar, N.B., Salleh, R., Suarez-Tangil, G., Furnell, S.: AndroDialysis: analysis of android intent effectiveness in malware detection. Comput. Secur. **65**, 121–134 (2017)
5. Yang, Z., Yang, M.: Leakminer: detect information leakage on android with static taint analysis. In: 2012 Third World Congress on Software Engineering (WCSE), pp. 101–104. IEEE (2012)
6. Zhao, Z., Osono, F.C.C.: "TrustDroid™": preventing the use of SmartPhones for information leaking in corporate networks through the used of static analysis taint tracking. In: 2012 7th International Conference on Malicious and Unwanted Software (MALWARE), pp. 135–143. IEEE (2012)
7. Arzt, S., et al.: Flowdroid: precise context, flow, field, object-sensitive and lifecycle-aware taint analysis for android apps. ACM SIGPLAN Not. **49**, 259–269 (2014)
8. Burket, J., Flynn, L., Klieber, W., Lim, J., Snavely, W.: Making DidFail succeed: enhancing the CERT static taint analyzer for Android app sets (2015)
9. Yang, C., Xu, Z., Gu, G., Yegneswaran, V., Porras, P.: DroidMiner: automated mining and characterization of fine-grained malicious behaviors in android applications. In: Kutyłowski, M., Vaidya, J. (eds.) ESORICS 2014, Part I. LNCS, vol. 8712, pp. 163–182. Springer, Cham (2014). https://doi.org/10.1007/978-3-319-11203-9_10
10. Shabtai, A., Fledel, Y., Kanonov, U., Elovici, Y., Dolev, S., Glezer, C.: Google android: a comprehensive security assessment. IEEE Secur. Priv. **8**, 35–44 (2010)
11. Seo, J., Kim, D., Cho, D., Shin, I., Kim, T.: FLEXDROID: enforcing in-app privilege separation in android. In: NDSS (2016)
12. Afonso, V.M., et al.: Going native: using a large-scale analysis of android apps to create a practical native-code sandboxing policy. In: NDSS (2016)
13. Arp, D., Spreitzenbarth, M., Hubner, M., Gascon, H., Rieck, K., Siemens, C.: DREBIN: effective and explainable detection of android malware in your pocket. In: NDSS, pp. 23–26 (2014)

14. Wei, F., Li, Y., Roy, S., Ou, X., Zhou, W.: Deep ground truth analysis of current android malware. In: Polychronakis, M., Meier, M. (eds.) DIMVA 2017. LNCS, vol. 10327, pp. 252–276. Springer, Cham (2017). https://doi.org/10.1007/978-3-319-60876-1_12

15. Cen, L., Gates, C.S., Si, L., Li, N.: A probabilistic discriminative model for android malware detection with decompiled source code. IEEE Trans. Dependable Secur. Comput. **12**, 400–412 (2015)

16. Du, Y., Wang, J., Li, Q.: An android malware detection approach using community structures of weighted function call graphs. IEEE Access **5**, 17478–17486 (2017)

17. Zhou, H., Zhang, W., Wei, F., Chen, Y.: Analysis of Android malware family characteristic based on isomorphism of sensitive API call graph. In: 2017 IEEE Second International Conference on Data Science in Cyberspace (DSC), pp. 319–327. IEEE (2017)

18. Narayanan, A., Chandramohan, M., Chen, L., Liu, Y.: A Multi-view Context-aware approach to android malware detection and malicious code localization (2017). arXiv preprint: arXiv:1704.01759

19. Desnos, A., Lantz, P.: Droidbox: An android application sandbox for dynamic analysis (2011)

20. Droidmon. https://github.com/idanr1986/droidmon

21. Winsniewski, R.: Android–apktool: a tool for reverse engineering android APK files. Technical report (2012)

22. Ma, Z., Wang, H., Guo, Y., Chen, X.: LibRadar: fast and accurate detection of third-party libraries in Android apps. In: Proceedings of the 38th International Conference on Software Engineering Companion, pp. 653–656. ACM (2016)

23. Backes, M., Bugiel, S., Derr, E.: Reliable third-party library detection in Android and its security applications. In: Proceedings of the 2016 ACM SIGSAC Conference on Computer and Communications Security, pp. 356–367. ACM (2016)

24. Salton, G., Buckley, C.: Term-weighting approaches in automatic text retrieval. Inf. Process. Manag. **24**, 513–523 (1988)

25. Deerwester, S., Dumais, S.T., Furnas, G.W., Landauer, T.K., Harshman, R.: Indexing by latent semantic analysis. J. Am. Soc. Inf. Sci. **41**, 391–407 (1990)

26. Chen, S., Xue, M., Tang, Z., Xu, L., Zhu, H.: Stormdroid: a streaminglized machine learning-based system for detecting android malware. In: Proceedings of the 11th ACM on Asia Conference on Computer and Communications Security, pp. 377–388. ACM (2016)

27. Chen, T., Guestrin, C.: XGBoost: a scalable tree boosting system. In: Proceedings of the 22nd ACM SIGKDD International Conference on Knowledge Discovery and Data Mining, pp. 785–794. ACM (2016)

28. Fan, R.-E., Chang, K.-W., Hsieh, C.-J., Wang, X.-R., Lin, C.-J.: LIBLINEAR: a library for large linear classification. J. Mach. Learn. Res. **9**, 1871–1874 (2008)

29. Allix, K., Bissyandé, T.F., Klein, J., Le Traon, Y.: AndroZoo: collecting millions of android apps for the research community. In: 2016 IEEE/ACM 13th Working Conference on Mining Software Repositories (MSR), pp. 468–471. IEEE (2016)

30. Total, V.: VirusTotal-Free online virus, malware and URL scanner (2012). https://www.virustotal.com/en

31. Allix, K., Bissyandé, T.F., Jérome, Q., Klein, J., Le Traon, Y.: Empirical assessment of machine learning-based malware detectors for Android. Empir. Softw. Eng. **21**, 183–211 (2016)

A Verifiable Encryption Scheme Supporting Fuzzy Search

Ruwei Huang$^{(\boxtimes)}$, Zhikun Li, and Guang Wu

School of Computer and Electronic Information, Guangxi University,
Nanning 530004, China
ruweih@126.com

Abstract. Searchable encryption supports retrieval over encrypted data while protecting data privacy. How to prevent non-trusted cloud service providers from performing partial retrieval operations or tampering with or deleting some encrypted data in order to save computing resources and bandwidth, thereby returning partial or erroneous search results. Therefore, we proposed a verifiable encryption scheme supporting fuzzy Search (VESFS). Through principle of matrix operations, VESFS realizes the fuzzy retrieval over encrypted data, and enables the user to verify the correctness of the retrieval results efficiently by applying the RSA accumulator and the proposed challenge response-based search verification method. The security analysis proves that VESFS provides privacy security and verifiable security; the performance analysis and experimental results show that VESFS is effective and feasible.

Keywords: Searchable encryption · Matrix operations · Verifiable retrieval · RSA accumulator · Privacy security

1 Introduction

In recent years, with the rapid development of network technology, data has presented explosive increase, and more and more individuals and enterprises have outsourced data to cloud servers to reduce local computation overhead and storage costs. However, outsourcing causes users to lose direct control over the data, and the Cloud Service Provider (CSP), as an untrusted third party, may leak and abuse of user privacy data for some benefits or due to system failure. Although encryption can protect the privacy of data, the traditional encryption schemes does not support search operations on ciphertext. Therefore, the Searchable Encryption (SE) scheme which is supported to search on ciphertext has become a research hotspot.

The SE scheme [1] was first proposed by Song et al. in 2000. Subsequently, in order to meet different search requirements, a series of SE schemes [2–4] were proposed. Mei [2] proposed a scheme supporting fuzzy search, which allows users to perform search requests with misspellings and inconsistent formats; Cao [3] supported sorting of search results by similarity, which eliminates unnecessary download bandwidth; Zhang [4] allowed users to search multiple keywords at the same time on ciphertext, which improved the user's search experience. Those schemes are constructed on the assumption that the CSP is honest, but in fact the CSP is suspect, and it

© Springer Nature Switzerland AG 2019
G. Wang et al. (Eds.): SpaCCS 2019, LNCS 11611, pp. 397–411, 2019.
https://doi.org/10.1007/978-3-030-24907-6_30

may: (1) tamper or delete partial data that users store; (2) commit a malicious behavior with user's search e.g., in order to save computational resources and bandwidth, it only searches part of the data and returns part of the search results, or forges part of the search results; (3) attempt to analyze stored data, users' search patterns, search results, and related information flows in order to obtain private information. These malicious behaviors can lead to acquisition of incorrect search results for users. Therefore, there is a need for an SE scheme that supports verifying the correctness of search results. Based on "semi-honest and curious", Chai [5] first proposed the verifiable SE scheme, adopting tree-based index and hash chain technology. Wang [6] proposed a verifiable SE scheme supporting fuzzy search based on wildcard technology and Bloom Filter. Wang [7] proposed a fuzzy search scheme based on the locality-sensitive hashing technique, which does not require a predefined keyword set and improves efficiency. Yang [8] proposed a novel Chinese multi-keyword fuzzy rank searchable encryption scheme. Huang [12] proposed an encryption scheme supporting fuzzy search and sorting the results based on matrix operations. [7, 8, 12] did not implement the function of verifying search results. [6, 8] employed the Bloom Filter, but the Bloom Filter has higher computational complexity and suffers a false detection rate, and the computational complexity is inversely proportional to the false detection rate, making these methods subject to certain restrictions in applications. [5] applied the tree structure, which causes a larger computational overhead for updating data.

A verifiable encryption scheme VESFS that supports fuzzy search is proposed in this paper, which can sort on results by similarity degree. The verifiability here refers to the authenticity of the search results and the completeness of the search. Authenticity means that the search results have not been tampered, and are indeed derived from the data set originally uploaded by the data owner. Completeness of the search means that the CSP has honestly executed the user's search request and returned all results that match the search request. In this paper, the authenticity of the search results is verified by the RSA accumulator technology, and the verification of the completeness of the search is completed by a challenge response-based verification strategy.

1.1 Preliminaries

1.1.1 RSA Accumulator

The RSA accumulator [9] can accumulate all the elements in a set to a fixed-size value, and the value retains some original set information, which is often used to carry out verification of some set attributes. By calculating some proof of evidence, we can verify whether one or more elements belong to this set. Its security is derived from the strong RSA hypothesis.

First, two safe large prime numbers $u = 2u' + 1$ and $v = 2v' + 1$ are selected randomly, where u' and v' are both prime numbers. Then the modulus $N = uv$ is obtained and the cyclic group G_N is generated randomly. Therefore, for a set $S = \{e_1, e_2, ..., e_n\}$ with n elements, the accumulated value $acc(S) = g^{\prod_{i=1}^{n} P(e_i)} \mod N$ can be calculated. Here, $P(\cdot)$ is a prime number generating function, where, (u, v) is secretly held by the user, and (N, P, g) is publicly disclosed. Accordingly, for a sub-set S' of the set S, after calculation, we can obtain:

$$acc_{S'} = g^{\prod_{x \in S-S'} P(x)} \bmod N \tag{1}$$

Where $acc_{S'}$ represents the accumulated value of all elements in set S except S', and we refer to it as a verification evidence of set S'. Therefore, by examining whether the Eq. (2) is true to verify the correctness of $S' \subseteq S$ can be verified.

$$(acc_{S'})^{\prod_{x \in S'} P(x)} \bmod N = acc(S) \tag{2}$$

1.2 Search and Verification Strategy Based on Challenge Response

For the problem that the CSP may only perform search operations on some data in order to save computing resources and bandwidth, by reference to retrieval and verification method based on the cryptographic hash proposed by Sion [10], combined with the searchable encryption scheme constructed in this paper on the basis of matrix operations, we propose a challenge response-based search verification strategy, which enables the user to detect the malicious behavior of the CSP in the form of probability and verify the completeness of the search result. The specific idea is as follows:

VESFS implements fuzzy search on ciphertext, which supports sorting by computing scalar products between vectors. Therefore, for a certain search trapdoor q, data owner randomly selects the data c_i ($i \in [1, n]$) in the ciphertext set $C = \{c_1, c_2, ..., c_n\}$, and calculates a scalar product between both: $c_i \times q$, then constructs the Challenge Token (CT):

$$CT(C, p_i, \varepsilon) = \{H(\varepsilon \| c_i \times q), \varepsilon\} \tag{3}$$

Where, ε is a random number, '$\|$' means the connection symbol, and $H(\cdot)$ is a hash function.

When performing the search, User sends the CT along with the trapdoor q to the CSP and requests the CSP to return the ciphertext c_i corresponding to the CT. Because $H(\cdot)$ has a unidirectional nature, CSP only calculates the scalar product in q and the data in set C to complete the ciphertext search. The value obtained through re-calculation according to formula (1) during the search process is compared with CT to find the corresponding ciphertext c_i'. Therefore, the user can check whether the equation $c_i' = c_i$ is true to verify the completeness of the search results. However, this method only provides the guarantee with a certain probability, and there is the case where CSP finds *the* right c_i' through prediction or only searching partial data. Therefore, we improve the effectiveness of verification by introducing multiple CTs and forged CTs. Forged CT means that there is no corresponding ciphertext in set C. Therefore, for n ciphertexts, the probability that the CSP can pass the verification when only the $m(m \leqslant n)$ of them are correctly retrieved is:

$$P(m, r, f) = \sum_{i=0}^{r} \frac{\binom{i}{m}}{\binom{r}{n}} \times \frac{1}{\binom{f}{r+f-i}} \tag{4}$$

Where, r and f are the numbers of CT and forged CT, respectively. As shown in Fig. 1, $P(m, r, f)$ increases as m increases, which means that if the CSP wants to pass the verification with a higher probability, it needs to perform more search operations, and this probability is further reduced as the number of r and f increases. For example: in order to achieve a 50% probability, $m = 15$ when $r = 4$, and only $m = 9$ when $r = 1$. Therefore, by selecting the appropriate values of r and f, only a smaller overhead is required, and the completeness of the search results can be verified with a high probability.

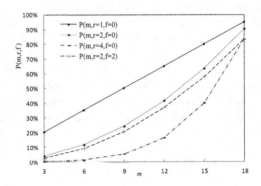

Fig. 1. Some values of $P(m, r, f)$ in the case of $n = 20$

2   System Model

There are three participants in the system model: data owner (Owner), cloud server provider (CSP) and User; the interaction process between them includes data encryption, ciphertext search and search result verification, with the specific model shown in Fig. 2. The detailed description is as follows:

(1) The Owner obtains the ciphertext $C = \{c_1, c_2, ..., c_n\}$ by using an encryption scheme to encrypt the plaintext data set $D = \{m_1, m_2, ..., m_n\}$ that needs to be outsourced to the CSP. The accumulated value $acc(C)$ of set C is then calculated and C is sent to the CSP for storage.

(2) After obtaining the authorization of the Owner, User encrypts the search keyword w to generate a search trapdoor T_w, and then Owner calculates the challenge *Token* and generates the relevant verification evidence $proof_{Token}$. Finally, T_w and *Token* are sent to the CSP.

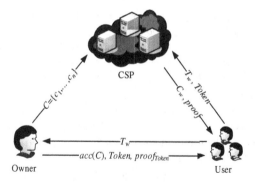

Fig. 2. System model

(3) Upon receipt of the trapdoor T_w and the *Token* sent by the User, the CSP performs the search operation on the ciphertext set C to obtain the search results and calculates the relevant verification *proof*. Finally, C_w and *proof* are returned to the User.

(4) Based on the obtained evidence *proof*, the User locally verifies the correctness of the search results C_w, and if the verification is passed, decrypts C_w to obtain the plaintext result; if the verification fails, User rejects the returned search result.

In our system model, from the user's point of view, they hope the outsourced data to be privacy-safe, correct and complete, and the results obtained through search are correct. However, since the CSP is untrusted, there may be malicious behaviors that threaten the outsourced data and the User' search operations, which make the user's privacy leaked and the incorrect retrieval results returned to User. Therefore, a searchable encryption scheme is needed, which supports fuzzy search, requires both protection of the privacy of the outsourced data and verification of the correctness of the search results to guarantee the interests of users.

Based on the above system model and design goals, the following formal definitions can be obtained.

Definition 1. A verifiable encryption scheme supporting fuzzy search VESFS = (*KeyGen, Enc, GenTrap, Search, Verify, Dec*) is consisted of the following six polynomial time algorithms:

- $(pk, sk) \leftarrow KeyGen(\sigma)$: a probabilistic algorithm, which is executed by Owner to initialize the system, input security parameter σ, and output public key pk and private key sk.
- $(C, acc) \leftarrow Enc(D, sk, pk)$: a probabilistic algorithm executed by the Owner to generate a ciphertext set and its accumulated value. To input plaintext data set D, private key sk, and public key pk, and output ciphertext set C and accumulated value $acc(C)$.
- $(T_w, Token, proof_{Token}) \leftarrow GenTrap(sk, w, C, pk)$, a probabilistic algorithm executed by the Owner to generate a search trap door, challenge token, and verify evidence. To input the search keyword w, the private key sk, the ciphertext set C,

and the public key pk, and output the search trapdoor T_w, the challenge *Token*, and the token verification evidence $proof_{Token}$.

- $(C_w, C_{Token}, proof_{acc}) \leftarrow Search(T_w, Token, K)$: a deterministic algorithm executed by CSP to generate search results and verify evidence. To input the search trapdoor T_w, *the* challenge token *Token* and the search demand K, and output the search result C_w, the verification evidence C_{Token} and the $proof_{acc}$.
- $(true, false) \leftarrow Verify(C_w, pk, proof)$: a deterministic algorithm executed by User to verify the correctness of the search results. To input the public key pk, the search result C_w and the verification evidence $proof = (C_{Token}, proof_{Token}, acc(C), proof_{acc})$, and output the verification result *true* or *false*.
- $(D_i) \leftarrow Dec(c_i, sk)$: a deterministic algorithm executed by User to decrypt the search result. To input ciphertext c_i ($c_i \in C_w$) and the private key sk, and output the plaintext data m_i.

3   A Verifiable Encryption Scheme Supporting Fuzzy Search —VESFS

3.1   Data Preprocessing

Before the formal construction scheme, the data preprocessing operations used in the scheme are first introduced. This process is performed by Owner to convert plaintext data and search keywords into vectors.

Given a plaintext data m and the dimension of the vector is $\check{n}$, let $len = (\check{n} - 1) \times 6$ be the maximum string length allowed by the scheme, that is, one element is composed of every 6 characters; the length of the data m is len', m can be divided into $\lceil len'/6 \rceil$ elements, and then the remaining $\check{n} - \lceil len'/6 \rceil$ elements are set to be 0; for the jth element, 23 is subtracted from the ASCII code corresponding to each character to get a two-digit number, then all the two-digit numbers are connected to form the figure v_j; based on the above calculation, m can be converted into a $(\check{n} - 1)$ dimensional vector $p' = (v'_1, v'_2, \cdots, v'_{\check{n}-1})$, where $v'_j = v_j \times 10^t$, $t = 12 \times (\check{n} - j - 1)$. In particular, when $len' > len$, m can be converted to $\lceil len'/len \rceil$ vectors, but since the subsequent operations of each vector are the same, this paper assumes that m *is* only converted into a $(\check{n} - 1)$ dimension vector. In addition, the same is for the conversion process of searching keyword.

3.2   Algorithms Construction

(1)   Key generation algorithm *KeyGen*

The scheme is executed by the Owner to initialize the system and input the security parameter σ, and the output public key $pk = (N, g)$ is used to calculate the RSA accumulated value and the verification evidence; the output private key $sk = (M, W, S)$ is used to encrypt and decrypt data. Where M is a $d \times d$ order invertible matrix, $W = \{w_1, w_2, \cdots, w_{k-2}\} (k \geq 4, w_i \in \mathrm{R}$ and $i \in [1, k - 2])$ is an array of random numbers, and $S \in \{0, 1\}^d$ is a d-ary split string.

(2) Encryption scheme *Enc*

The scheme is executed by the Owner to encrypt the plaintext data and calculate the accumulated value. After input of the plaintext data set $D = \{m_1, m_2, \ldots, m_n\}$, private key sk and public key pk, Owner carries out calculation as follows:

① To generate a vector set $P' = \{p'_1, p'_2, \ldots, p'_n\}$ corresponding to set D, where $(\check{n} - 1)$ dimension vector p'_i is converted and obtained by m_i through the above data preprocessing process.

② To generate d-dimensional vector $p_i = \{p'_i, -0.5 \times \|p'_i\|^2, r_1, w_2, \ldots,$ $r_{k-3}, w_{k-2}, -\left(\sum_{j=1}^{k/2-1} r_{2\times j-1} \times w_{2\times j-1}\right), 1\}^{\mathrm{T}}$, among which $p'_i \in P'$, $\|p'_i\|^2$ is scalar product of p'_i, r_i is a random number and $r_i \in R$. According to the split string S, p_i is divided into two d dimensional subvectors p_a and p_b, and the specific splitting rules are:

$$\begin{cases} p_a[z] = p_b[z] = p_i[z], & S[z] = 1 \\ p_a[z] + p_b[z] = p_i[z], & S[z] = 0 \end{cases}$$

Where $S[z]$ $(z \in [1, d])$ is the z-th position of the split string S.

③ To calculate $c_i = (M \times p_a, M \times p_b)$. Therefore, the ciphertext set $C = \{c_1, c_2, \ldots, c_n\}$ corresponding to the set D can be generated.

④ To calculate the accumulated value of set $C_{acc(C)} = g^{\prod_{i=1}^{n} P(c_i)} \bmod N$ by using the public key pk. Finally, set C is sent to the CSP.

(3) *Trapdoor* generation scheme *GenTrap*

The scheme is executed by the User to generate a search trapdoor, a challenge token, and verification evidence. To input the search key word w, ciphertext set C, private key sk and public key pk, and calculate as follows:

① First, according to the data preprocessing in Sect. 3.2, w is converted into a $(\check{n} - 1)$ vector q', and then on this basis, a d-dimension vector $q = x \times \left(q', 1, w_1, r_2, \ldots, w_{k-3}, r_{k-2}, 1, -\left(\sum_{j=1}^{k/2-1} r_{2\times j} \times w_{2\times j}\right)\right)$ is generated, where r_j and x are both random real numbers.

② According to the split string S, q is divided into two dimensional subvectors q_a and q_b, and the specific splitting rules are:

$$\begin{cases} q_a[z] = q_b[z] = q[z], & S[z] = 0 \\ q_a[z] + q_b[z] = q[z], & S[z] = 1 \end{cases}$$

Where $S[z]$ $(z \in [1, d])$ is the z-th position of the split string S Then trapdoor $T_w = (q_a \times M^{-1}, q_b \times M^{-1})$ is generated.

③ r data is randomly selected from the ciphertext set C without repetition to get the set $C_r = \{c'_1, c'_2, \ldots, c'_r\}$, where $c'_i \in C$. Then r scalar products $T_w \times c'_j (j \in [1, r])$

are calculated, f scalar products of the same format are forged, and then the $r + f$ scalar products are calculated according to formula (3) to get the challenge token set $Token = \{Token_1, Token_2, \ldots, Token_{r+f}\}$ and generate verification evidence $proof_{Token} = C_r$. Finally, User saves the $proof_{Token}$ and sends T_w and $Token$ to CSP.

(4) Search scheme *Search*

The scheme is executed by the CSP to obtain search results and verify evidence. The search trapdoor T_w, challenge token $Token$ and search request K are input. CSP will first perform the following calculations with T_w and ciphertext $c_i (c_i \in C, i \in [1, n])$:

$$T_w \times c_i = \left(q_a \times M^{-1}, q_b \times M^{-1}\right) \times (M \times p_a, M \times p_b) = q_a \times p_a + q_b \times p_b$$
$$= q \times p_i = x\left(p_i' \times q' - 0.5\|p_i'\|^2\right)$$

Moreover, during this process, according to $T_w \times c_i$, the challenge token is calculated again according to formula (3), and then the obtained result are compared with the elements in the $Token$ *in turn*, and the corresponding ciphertext set C_{Token} is found, where the elements in C_{Token} are all c_i corresponding to $Token$. Then CSP can get the first similar K search results C_w by ranking all scalar products $T_w \times c_i$ from large to small, and then, according to C_w and ciphertext set C, CSP calculates the corresponding verification evidence $proof_{acc} = g^{\prod_{x \in C - C_w} P(x)} \bmod N$. Finally, C_w, C_{Token} and $proof_{acc}$ are returned to User.

(5) Verification scheme *Verify*

The scheme is executed by User to verify the correctness of the search results. The public key pk, search result C_w and verification evidence $proof = (C_{Token}, proof_{Token}, acc(C), proof_{acc})$ are input. User first verifies whether the following equation is true, and if not, *false* is output.

$$proof_{Token} = C_{Token} \tag{5}$$

If the Eqs. (3–4) is true, User will continue to verify whether the following equation is true, and if it is true, *true is output*, otherwise *false* is output.

$$(proof_{acc})^{\prod_{x \in C_w} P(x)} \bmod N = acc(C) \tag{6}$$

(6) Decryption scheme *Dec*

The scheme is executed by User to decrypt the search results. If the output of the verification scheme *Verify* is *true*, the ciphertext $c_i (c_i \in C_w)$ and private key sk are input for decryption to get plaintext, where the specific decryption process is the reverse process of encryption scheme, we will not give a detailed introduction again here.

4   Analysis of Schemes

4.1   Security Analysis

Theorem 1. VESFS is private and safe, if it meets:

(1) data privacy: Outsourced data, search trapdoors, and search results are private and secure;
(2) Search mode: $[\forall w' = w, \exists \; GenTrap(w',sk) \neq GenTrap(w,sk)$.
(3) The challenge token is private and safe.

Prove:

(1) VESFS matrix vector operation principle encrypts outsourced data and generates search trapdoors. Their security is effectively protected by the private key sk = (M, W, S).

First, for the plaintext data m and the search keyword w, in the encryption process, they are first converted into d-dimensional vectors $p = \{p', -0.5 \times ||p'||^2, r_1, w_2, \ldots,$
$r_{k-3}, w_{k-2} - \left(\sum_{j=1}^{k/2-1} r_{2\times j-1} \times W_{2\times j-1}\right), 1\}$ and $q = x \times ((q', 1, w_1, r_2, \ldots, w_{k-3},$
$r_{k-2}, 1., -\left(\sum_{j=1}^{k/2-1} r_{2\times j} \times w_{2\times j}\right))$. Due to the existence of the random number r_i and the random number array W, CSP is unable to know the specific conversion process.

Secondly, VESFS first randomly splits vectors p and q into vector groups by a d-ary random split string $S(p_a, p_b)$ and (q_a, q_b), at this time there are 2^d kinds of splits. Then ciphertext $c = (M \times p_a, M \times p_b)$ and search trapdoor $T_w = (q_a \times M^{-1}, q_b \times M^{-1})$ are further generated, where M is the $d \times d$-order reversible matrix randomly generated by Owner. Since the result of the multiplication of the matrix and the vector is a vector, and the value of each element on it is the scalar product of the vector p and a row in the matrix. Therefore, due to the existence of random numbers, the probability that the CSP obtains private information from the ciphertext and the retrieval trapdoor is negligible under the circumstance of not knowing the private key. In addition, to derive the key M from the ciphertext, CSP needs to solve $2nd$ equations, where p_a and p_b contain $2nd$ unknowns, and M contains $d \times d$ unknowns when the split string S is unknown. At this time, the number of unknowns is much larger than the number of equations. Therefore, it can be concluded that the CSP cannot solve the matrix M, and its security is based on matrix multiplication [13], and the same is true for the search results. Therefore, outsourced data, search trapdoors, and search results are private and safe.

(2) Given the private key $sk = (M, W, S)$, the search trapdoor corresponding to the generated keyword w is $T_w = q \times M^{-1}$. Similarly, let the keyword $w' = w$, and its corresponding trapdoor is $T_{w'} = q' \times M^{-1}$, where there are a large number of

random numbers in the vectors q and q', the value of these numbers in each vector is random. Therefore, according to the multiplication rule between the matrix and the vector, as shown in Eq. (7):

$$M \times (v)^T = \begin{bmatrix} a_{11} & a_{12} \\ a_{21} & a_{22} \end{bmatrix} \times \begin{bmatrix} x \\ r \end{bmatrix} = \begin{bmatrix} xa_{11} + ra_{12} \\ xa_{21} + ra_{22} \end{bmatrix} \quad (7)$$

The values of each of the result vectors T_w and $T_{w'}$ are determined by the values of the multiple positions participating in the matrix and the vector and are affected by the random number x, which guarantees the trapping T_w and $T_{w'}$ are not equal and are not proportional. Therefore, under the same key, the search trapdoor generated by the same keyword in multiple retrieval processes is different. Therefore, VESFS satisfies $GenTrap(w',sk) \neq GenTrap(w,sk)$.

(3) According to the verification strategy of Sect. 1.2, for a given trapdoor T_w and ciphertext c, its challenge token $Token = \{H(\varepsilon \| T_w \times c), \varepsilon\}, \varepsilon\}$ is calculated, where $H(\cdot)$ is a hash function which is unidirectional. Therefore, it is computationally infeasible for the CSP to derive any information about the ciphertext c from the $Token$. Furthermore, due to the existence of the random number ε, the same trapdoor will generate random unequal challenge tokens, which can protect the User's search mode. Therefore, the challenge token is private and safe.

In summary, the proposed VESFS is private and safe.

Lemma 2. Given $x, y \in Z_N^*$ and $a, b \in Z$, $x^a = y^b$ is satisfied, $\gcd(a, b) = 1$. Then $\ddot{x} \in Z_N^*$ can be solved to lead that $\ddot{x}^a = y$.

Theorem 3. The RSA accumulator is safe. If for the adversary A of any polynomial time size, only the public key $pk = (N, g)$ is known, and a set $C' \neq C$ is found, the probability of satisfying the accumulated value $acc(C) = acc(C')$ is negligible.

Prove: Given the set $C = \{c_1, c_2, \ldots, c_n\}$, assuming that adversary A can find a set $C' = \{c'_1 c'_2, \ldots, c'_m\}$, satisfying $C' \neq C$ and $acc(C) = acc(C')$. Then there must be a set of S_C and $S_{C'}$, satisfying $S_C \subseteq C$, $S_{C'} \subseteq C'$, $S_C \not\subset C'$ and $S_{C'} \not\subset C$. Therefore, the verification evidence for calculating the set of S_C and $S_{C'}$ is respectively:

$$acc_{S_C} = g^{\prod_{x \in C - S_C} P(x)} \mod N, \quad acc_{S_{C'}} = g^{\prod_{x \in C' - S_{C'}} P(x)} \mod N$$

So there is:

$$acc(C) = (acc_{S_C})^{\prod_{x \in S_C} P(x)} = acc(C') = (acc_{S_{C'}})^{\prod_{x \in S_{C'}} P(x)}$$

Where, $P(\cdot)$ is a prime number generation function, satisfying: When $a_1 \neq a_2$, $P(a_1) \neq P(a_2)$. So there is $\gcd(\prod_{x \in S_C} P(x), \prod_{x \in S_{C'}} P(x)) = 1$.

Therefore, according to Lemma 2, we can know: It is easy to calculate the $\prod_{x \in S_C} P(x)$ power square of $acc_{S_{C'}}$, but this is contradictory to the strong RSA assumption. Therefore, the probability of $acc(C') = acc(C)$ is negligible, so the RSA accumulator is safe.

Theorem 4. The proposed VESFS is verifiable.

Prove: The following proves the verifiability of the scheme mainly from two aspects: correctness and security.

(1) Correctness

According to the verification scheme *Verify*, VESFS verifies the correctness of the search results by checking whether Eqs. (5) and (6) are true. In the execution of the scheme, the evidence calculated locally is $proof = (proof_{Token}, acc(C))$, and the CSP returns the search result C_w, evidence $proof_{acc}$ and C_{Token}. If the CSP is honest, according to the nature of the RSA accumulator, it will exist:

$$acc(C) = g^{\prod_{i=1}^{n} P(c_i)} \bmod N = \left(g^{\prod_{x \in C - C_w} P(x)}\right)^{\prod_{x \in C_w} P(x)} \bmod N$$

$$= (proof_{acc})^{\prod_{x \in C_w} P(x)} \bmod N$$

At this time, Eq. (6) is true. Since VESFS implements fuzzy search by calculating the scalar product between vectors, according to the verification strategy in Sect. 1.2, we pre-calculate a part of the scalar product to generate the challenge token *Token*, which is required to return the ciphertext set C_{Token} matching the *Token* during CSP execution. Due to the collision resistance of the hash function, if the CSP is honest, the returned C_{Token} must satisfy $C_{Token} = proof_{Token}$. At this time, Eq. (5) is true. Therefore, VESFS is correct.

(2) Security

For CSP, the purpose is to attempt to have the search results (whether correct or incorrect) to pass through the verification by User. So, for the wrong search results, CSP will forge verification evidence. Therefore, in order to prove that VESFS is verifiable and secure, we only need to prove that CSP cannot forge the search results and verification evidence that can be verified by User.

Assume that $(C_w, C_{Token}, proof_{acc})$ and $(C'_w, C'_{Token}, proof'_{acc})$ are correct and forged search results and verification evidence, respectively, where $C_w \neq C'_w$. According to the verification scheme *Verify*, User checks the correctness of the search results by checking whether Eqs. (5) and (6) are true. Therefore, for the wrong search result C'_w, assuming that the CSP can successfully falsify $proof'_{acc\,such}$ to make Eq. (6) true, then the CSP is able to find a set $C' \neq C$ to satisfy $acc(C') = acc(C)$. But this violates the security of the RSA accumulator as demonstrated in Theorem 3. Thus evidence $proof'_{acc}$ forged by CSP cannot be verified by the User; to satisfy Eq. (5), the CSP needs to forge evidence $C'_{Token} = C_{Token}$, but according to the authentication policy described in Sect. 1.2 and the privacy of the challenge token demonstrated in Theorem 1, the probability of successful forgery by CSP is very low. Therefore, the forged C'_{Token} cannot be verified by User.

In summary, the proposed VESFS is verifiable.

4.2   Capability Analysis

In this section, capability of VESFS was analyzed and compared with the existing schemes (Cao [3], Kurosawa [13]). For a better introduction, here we first set n to indicate the number of outsourced data, l indicates the number of keywords, t_{mul} indicates the multiplication time-consuming between two vectors, and t_g indicates the time-consuming of an exponential operation in the RSA accumulator, t_h indicates the time-consuming of one hash operation, and E indicates the time-consuming of one encryption.

In Table 1, we compare VESFS and Cao scheme [3] from four aspects: encryption, index generation, trapdoor generation and search. Both implement ciphertext retrieval based on matrix vector operations. Compared with the Cao scheme, VESFS does not need to construct an index. It can also be said that encryption and index are together. In addition, for massive data, l is usually greater than d, and the multiplication time-consuming of the Cao scheme is also relatively high. Therefore, the capability of VESFS is better than the Cao scheme.

Table 1.   Performance comparison

	Encryption	Index generation	Trapdoor generation	Search
Cao	nE	$2nlt_{mul}$	$2lt_{mul}$	$2nt_{mul}$
VESFS	$2ndt_{mul}$		$2dt_{mul}$	$2nt_{mul}$

In Table 2, we compare the overhead of search and verification between VESFS and Kurosawa scheme [13]. Both are single-keyword searches and the same RSA accumulator is used. By comparison, it can be found that in the verification aspect, for different participants, both schemes need to calculate the accumulated value. The Kurosawa scheme needs to calculate the accumulated value for the data set and the index separately, and VESFS only needs to calculate the accumulated value for the data set. Moreover, the overhead of exponential operations is much higher than that of hash operations. Therefore, VESFS outperforms the Kurosawa scheme.

Table 2.   Performance comparison

	Search overhead	Verification overhead		
		Owner	CSP	User
Kurosawa	$O(l)$	$n(l + 1)t_g$	$(nl - K)t_g$	$(n + K)t_g$
VESFS	$O(n)$	$nt_g + (r + f)t_h$	$(n - K)t_g + nt_h$	Kt_g

In addition, compared with the Cao and Kurosawa schemes, VESFS has the advantages of supporting fuzzy search, sorting of search results, hidden search mode and verifiability.

4.3   Experiment Analysis

In order to evaluate the time overhead of the scheme at each stage, the experimental simulation of the proposed VESFS is carried out in this section. The experiment is programmed in Java language, the program running environment is Windows 7 Operating System, the CPU is Inter Pentium G640 (2.80 GHz), and the memory is 4G. A 1024-bit RSA accumulator and a SHA-256 hash function were used in the experiment. At the same time, a comparison experiment with CESVMC [12] was added to analyze the performance impact of verifiability.

Figure 3 shows the actual performance comparison between VESFS and CESVMC in terms of data encryption, search trapdoor generation, ciphertext search and result verification. In Figs. 3(a) and (c), the encryption and search capability of VESFS is inferior to CESVMC. When the number of search results is set to $K = 10$, and as the number of data n increases, the encryption and search time overhead tends to increase linearly, and the time gap is also slowly increasing. This is because VESFS needs to calculate the RSA accumulated value for the data set in the encryption phase, and its time complexity is $O(n)$; in the search stage, relevant verification evidence needs to be calculated according to the search result, and the complexity at this time is $O(n - K)$ and $O(n)$ respectively. Furthermore, accumulation of accumulated value of RSA and generation of related keys are one-time consuming operations, and can effectively save the time overhead in subsequent stages. Example: The time difference between Fig. 3(c) and (a) is significantly reduced. In particular, due to the operational nature of the RSA accumulator, VESFS is efficient when updating data.

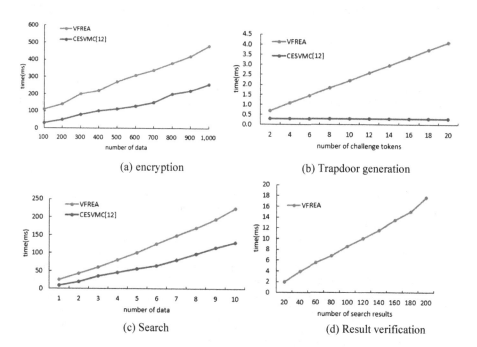

(a) encryption

(b) Trapdoor generation

(c) Search

(d) Result verification

Fig. 3. Overhead of time

In Fig. 3(b), trapdoor generation time of VESFS increases approximately linearly with the number of challenge tokens, while the time overhead of CESVMC is constant and {2} unchanged, this is because the two schemes are single-keyword search, CESVMC only needs to encrypt the keywords, and VESFS needs to generate additional challenge tokens to achieve the verifiable function of the results, with its time overhead related to the number of challenge tokens. The time complexity is $O(r + f)$. In Fig. 3(d), when $n = 1000$ is set, the verification time of VESFS increases approximately linearly with the number of search results, because in the verification process, it is necessary to calculate the verification evidence, with the time complexity of $O(K)$, and then determine whether the equations are equal according to the verification evidence, with the time complexity of $O(r + f + 1)$. In general, compared to CESVMC, although the additional time overhead is added after the introduction of verifiable function, time-consuming is within a reasonable range, and verifiability can cope with the threat of malicious CSP, verifying the correctness of search results, making these extra overheads is worthwhile and difficult to be avoided. Therefore, the VESFS in this paper is effective and feasible in practical applications.

5   Conclusion

In this paper, under the unreliable CSP model, a verifiable encryption scheme supporting fuzzy search is proposed. The scheme supports the fuzzy search of ciphertext, the ordering of search results and the correctness of user-verified search results. The security analysis proves that in the scheme is private and safe and search is verifiable. The experimental results show that the scheme is effective and feasible in practical applications. In the next step, we will continue to improve the scheme to enhance its efficiency.

Acknowledgments. This work was supported in part by the Guangxi Natural Fund Project under Grant No. 2016GXNSFAA380115, Guangxi Innovation-Driven Development Project under Grant No. AA17204058-17.

References

1. Song, D.X., Wagner, D., Perrig, A.: Practical techniques for searches on encrypted data. In: Proceedings of the 2000 IEEE Symposium on Security & Privacy (S&P), Piscataway, pp. 44–55 (2000)
2. Mei, Z.L., Wu, B., Tian, S.L., et al.: Fuzzy keyword search method over ciphertexts supporting access control. KSII Trans. Internet Inf. Syst. **11**(11), 5671–5693 (2017)
3. Cao, N., Wang, C., Li, M., et al.: Privacy-preserving multi-keyword ranked search over encrypted cloud data. IEEE Trans. Parallel Distrib. Syst. **25**(1), 222–233 (2014)
4. Zhang, W., Lin, Y., Xiao, S., et al.: Privacy preserving ranked multi-keyword search for multiple data owners in cloud computing. IEEE Trans. Comput. **65**(5), 1566–1577 (2016)
5. Chai, Q, Gong, G.: Verifiable symmetric searchable encryption for semi-honest-but-curious cloud servers. In: Proceedings of IEEE International Conference on Communications, Ottawa, pp. 917–922 (2012)

6. Wang, J., Ma, H., Tang, Q., et al.: A new efficient verifiable fuzzy keyword search scheme. J. Wirel. Mob. Netw. Ubiquitous Comput. Dependable Appl. **3**(4), 61–71 (2012)
7. Wang, K.X., Li, Y.X., Zhou, F.C., et al.: Multi-keyword fuzzy search over encrypted data. J. Comput. Res. Dev. **54**(2), 348–360 (2017)
8. Yang, Y., Zhang, Y.C., Liu, J.: Chinese multi-keyword fuzzy rank search over encrypted cloud data based on locality-sensitive hashing. J. Inf. Sci. Eng. **35**(1), 137–158 (2019)
9. Goodrich, M.T., Tamassia, R., Hasić, J.: An efficient dynamic and distributed cryptographic accumulator. In: Chan, A.H., Gligor, V. (eds.) ISC 2002. LNCS, vol. 2433, pp. 372–388. Springer, Heidelberg (2002). https://doi.org/10.1007/3-540-45811-5_29
10. Sion, R.: Query execution assurance for outsourced databases. In: Proceedings of the 31st International Conference on Very Large Data Bases, Trondheim, pp. 601–612 (2005)
11. Curtmola, R., Garay, J., Kamara, S., et al.: Searchable symmetric encryption: improved definitions and efficient constructions. J. Comput. Secur. **19**(5), 895–934 (2011)
12. Huang, R.W., Gui, X.L., Yu, S., et al.: A computable encryption method for privacy protection in cloud environments. J. Comput. **34**(12), 2391–2402 (2011)
13. Kurosawa, K., Ohtaki, Y.: How to update documents verifiably in searchable symmetric encryption. In: Abdalla, M., Nita-Rotaru, C., Dahab, R. (eds.) CANS 2013. LNCS, vol. 8257, pp. 309–328. Springer, Cham (2013). https://doi.org/10.1007/978-3-319-02937-5_17

A Verifiable Fully Homomorphic Encryption Scheme

Ruwei Huang[(✉)], Zhikun Li, and Jianan Zhao

School of Computer and Electronic Information, Guangxi University,
Nanning 530004, China
ruweih@126.com

Abstract. With development of cloud computing, how to keep privacy and compute outsourcing data effectively at the same time is highly significant in practice. Homomorphic encryption is a common method to support ciphertext calculation, but most schemes do not provide fully homomorphic properties. Some fully homomorphic encryption schemes feature complicated design, high computational complexity and no practicability. Some cloud service providers are not trustable and return incorrect computational results due to resource saving or other malicious behaviors. Therefore, this paper proposes a verifiable fully homomorphic encryption scheme VFHES. VFHES implements fully homomorphic encryption based on the principle of the matrix computing principle and matrix blinding technology and supports to verify correctness of the computational results. Security analysis proves that VFHES is privacy-safe and verifiable. The performance analysis and experimental results show that VFHES is practicable and effective.

Keywords: Cloud computing · Privacy security ·
Fully homomorphic encryption · Verifiable

Cloud computing is a new computing mode, which evolves from traditional computer and network technologies such as distributed computing, parallel computing, network storage and virtualization. The data or computing tasks are transferred to cloud server for storage or processing and a user can get the required storage or complete computing tasks by using the massive resources on the cloud via the network in a pay-on-demand manner. Especially for users with restricted resources, the cloud computing can make these users free of local resource restraints (e.g. memory, hard disk, CPU, etc.). Although cloud computing can facilitate users much, it also introduce new security issues and challenges due to features such as data outsourcing, service lease, virtualization, etc. Firstly, data outsourcing will make users fail to directly control data and computing tasks and the outsourcing data may include some sensitive user information. In addition, the operation details inside the cloud server are not transparent to users, Therefore, the cloud service provider (CSP) may conduct some dishonest behaviors due to some selfish motives. E.g. private user information is disclosed and misused for some interests; To save computing resources, the user computing tasks are not completed due to CSP "laziness" in execution of user's computing tasks and incorrect computing results are returned. In addition, the system failures or illegal external

G. Wang et al. (Eds.): SpaCCS 2019, LNCS 11611, pp. 412–426, 2019.
https://doi.org/10.1007/978-3-030-24907-6_31

attacks may affect user privacy security and correctness of computing results. Therefore, privacy security and computing reliability under the cloud computing environment is one of key issues in cloud computing research.

For privacy security issues, although some traditional encryption methods can protect privacy of user data, it cannot support effective ciphertext computing. The homomorphic encryption is different from the traditional data encryption algorithm and can support direct computing on ciphertext. After the obtained results are decrypted, the results are same as the computing results of the plaintexts. For this excellent property, users can trust the cloud servers to compute the homomorphic encrypted data without disclosure of private information, so it can take advantages of the cloud computing. Fully homomorphic encryption schemes can support any addition and multiplication operations. In 2009, Gentry [5] constructed the first truly fully homomorphic encryption scheme. However, the length of the ciphertext and computing complexity will grow quickly with growth of security strength. The expected security strength of this scheme is far from that required in practical applications. But it is no doubt that work of Gentry symbolizes a milestone. With years of efforts, now many achievements have been achieved in research on homomorphic encryption. The research process is roughly divided into three phases. The first phase is the fully homomorphic encryption scheme based on ideal lattice [1]. The second phase is the fully homomorphic encryption scheme based on integer [2]. The third phase is the fully homomorphic encryption schemes based on error learning [5] and loop error learning problem [3, 4]. Although the efficiency of homomorphic encryption schemes is continuously improved, now generally existing schemes feature complicated design, too large keys, low computing efficiency and high computing complexity and are far from practical applications.

For computing reliability, a mechanism is required to verify correctness of the computing results. Gennaro et al. [6] constructed a verifiable scheme with input/output privacy by using the Gentry [1] fully homomorphic scheme and Yao's Garbled Circuit. Jin et al. [7] designed a verifiable fully homomorphic encryption scheme, which is verifiable based on one-way function. Zhou et al. [8] combined the data aggregation scheme supporting addition and multiplication operation with Yao's Garbled Circuit to implement a verifiable fully homomorphic encryption scheme. Ahmed et al. [9] proposed noise-free verifiable fully homomorphic encryption scheme based on Lipschitz quaternion ring. Zhao et al. [10] proposed a verifiable computation scheme comes from the construction of re-randomizable garbled circuits in which the distribution of the original garbled circuit is computationally indistinguishable from the re-randomized garbled circuit. Xu et al. [11] presented a fully dynamic FHMT (Fully Homomorphic encryption-based Merkle Tree) construction, which was a construction that was able to authenticate an unbounded number of data elements and improved upon the state-of-the-art in terms of computational overhead. Although the above schemes can roughly implement the verifiable fully homomorphic encryption, [6, 10, 11] is not practicable; The feature extraction function and one-way function based on anti-collision hash function is used in the reference [7] and plentiful pre-processing operations are required; [8] is constructed based on Yao's Garbled Circuit, so it leads to low efficiency of the scheme. Therefore, how to design verifiable fully homomorphic encryption scheme is still a difficulty and hot spot.

This paper proposes a verifiable fully homomorphic encryption scheme (VFHES). The plaintext data is transformed to the triangular matrix and the matrix fuzzy technology is used to protect the privacy and security of the outsourcing data to implement the fully homomorphic encryption based on the matrix operation principle in this scheme. The verification proof is generated according to the special properties of the triangular matrix, so users can verify correctness of the computing results. Finally we strictly prove security of the scheme and completely evaluate effectiveness and feasibility of this scheme based on performance analysis and simulation tests.

1   Preliminaries

1.1   Homomorphic Encryption

If an encryption scheme can compute on the encrypted data directly to get the encrypted output results, and the decrypted results are equal to the computing results of the plaintext, this scheme is the homomorphic encryption scheme.

Definition 1 (homomorphic encryption scheme): One homomorphic encryption scheme HE $= (KeyGen, Enc, Dec, Eval)$ is composed for the following four algorithms:

(1) Key generation algorithm $KeyGen(\ )$: Input security parameter λ and output key K, $K \leftarrow KeyGen(\lambda)$.
(2) Encryption algorithm $Enc(\ )$: input the plaintext m and key K and output ciphertext c, $c \leftarrow Enc(K, m)$.
(3) Decryption algorithm $Dec(\ )$: Input the ciphertext c and key K and output the plaintext m, $m \leftarrow Dec(K, c)$.
(4) Ciphertext computing algorithm $Eval(\ )$: Input the key K, compute the function F and ciphertext set $C = \{c_1, c_2, \ldots, c_t\}$ and output computing results res, $res \leftarrow Eval(F, (c_1, c_2, \ldots, c_t))$.

Specifically, if the following Eq. (1) is satisfied, HE satisfies the addition homomorphic. If the Eq. (2) is satisfied, HE satisfies the multiplication homomorphic. If both the Eqs. (1) and (2) are satisfied and any number of homomorphic operations of addition and multiplication can be performed after addition and multiplication operation, HE will satisfy the full homomorphic.

$$c_1 + c_2 = Enc(K, m_1) + Enc(K, m_2) = Enc(K, m_1 + m_2) \tag{1}$$

$$c_1 \times c_2 = Enc(K, m_1) \times Enc(K, m_2) = Enc(K, m_1 \times m_2) \tag{2}$$

1.2   Matrix Blinding Technology

Our scheme is based on the matrix blinding technology. The invertible matrix is constructed for fuzzy processing of the plaintext matrix in order to protect privacy of the plaintext data. The invertible matrix is constructed based on the Kronecker function and random permutation. Next two methods are introduced as follows:

Kronecker function: It is a binary function and its independent variables (input values) include two integers. If two integers are equal, the output value is 1. Otherwise, the output value is 0. Therefore the function $\delta_{x,y}$ can be described as:

$$\delta_{x,y} = \begin{cases} 1 & x = y \\ 0 & x \neq y \end{cases}$$

Random permutation function: The permutation represents a mapping relation. Assuming that $S = \{1, 2, ..., n\}$, if σ represents a permutation on S, then σ is one-to-one mapping to S. Random permutation of the mapping relation is called as random permutation. Cauchy two-row representation method is used: the first row is the permutated primary image and the second row is the permutated images. So the random permutation function π and its inverse function on the set S are mathematically expressed as follows:

$$\pi = \begin{pmatrix} 1 & 2 & \cdots & n \\ p_1 & p_2 & \cdots & p_n \end{pmatrix}, \pi^{-1} = \begin{pmatrix} p_1 & p_2 & \cdots & p_n \\ 1 & 2 & \cdots & n \end{pmatrix} \quad (3)$$

And $\pi(i) = p_i(i = 1, 2, ..., n)$. The image of i in π is p_i. If $\pi(i) = i$, the permutation is called as identical permutation and is marked as I.

Then several construction algorithms used in the scheme are introduced as follows according to Kronecker function and random permutation function.

Algorithm 1: Construction algorithm for random permutation

    Input: order n

    Output: random permutation π

Step 1: set n-tuple identical permutation $\pi = I$.

Setp 2: for $i = 1:(n\text{-}1)$.

Setp 3: Select random number j $(i \leq j \leq n)$

Setp4: Exchange $\pi(i)$ and $\pi(j)$.

Setp5: End for.

Algorithm 2: Construction algorithm of invertible matrix

    Input: matrix order n

    Output: n-order invertible matrix M

Step 1: Construct the random permutation π which size is n *according to the algorithm* 1.

Step 2: Generate an n-order invertible matrix M, $M_{i,j} = \delta_{\pi(i),j}$

According to the above algorithm, the invertible M is constructed to easily compute its invertible M^{-1}, $M_{i,j}^{-1} = \delta_{\pi^{-1}(i),j}$, $M_{i,j}$ and $M_{i,j}^{-1}$ indicate the element of ith row and j^{th} column in the matrix M and M^{-1}.

2 System Model

The system model of the verifiable fully homomorphic encryption scheme proposed in this paper is shown as the Fig. 1. This model includes two entities: user and cloud service provider (CSP). The user is the consignor of the computing task and CSP is the actual executor of the computing task. Their interactions are shown as follows:

(1) The User encrypts the plaintext data $m_i (i \in [1,t], t \geq 1)$ by $Enc( )$ to get the ciphertext C_i and computes the related verification *proof* in this process. Next User saves *proof* and sends the computing function $F(\cdot)$ to the CSP server for computing.

(2) After CSP receives and identifies the outsourcing computing task of User, computes the ciphertext C_i according to the computing function $F(\cdot)$, and returns the computing results *Res to User.*

(3) User decrypts the received results *Res* by $Dec( )$ to generate the final result *res* and then verifies *res* correctness according to proof. If they are correct, the computing results of CSP will be accepted. Otherwise, the results will be rejected.

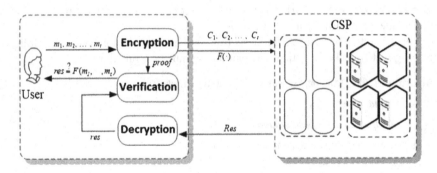

Fig. 1. System model

Security threats in the above models are from CSP, which is untrusted active attacker, may disclose and misuse private information of User, may dishonestly execute the computing task due to additional commerce interests (e.g. computing resource saving) or software and hardware bugs and return incorrect results to User. Therefore, the verifiable fully homomorphic encryption scheme based on this model shall satisfy the following targets:

(1) Correctness: If CSP honestly executes the computing task, the generated computing results shall be correct and can be correctly decrypted and accepted by users.

(2) Privacy: CSP cannot get any sensitive information on private user data from the input data and output computing results.

(3) Verifiability: User can verify correctness of computing results returned by the honest CSP at the extreme high probability and incorrectness of computing results returned by the dishonest CSP at the extreme high probability.

The following formal definitions can be obtained based on the above system model and design targets:

Definition 1 (A verifiable fully homomorphic encryption scheme): One verifiable fully homomorphic encryption scheme VFHES = (*VKeyGen, VEnc, VEval, VDec, VVerify*) is composed of 5 multinomial time algorithms, which are described as follows:

- $K \leftarrow$ *VKeyGen*(λ): Input the security parameter λ and output the key K.
- (*c, proof*) $\leftarrow$ *VEnc*(K, *m*): Input the key K and plaintext data set $D = \{m_1, m_2, \ldots, m_t\}$, output ciphertext set $C = \{C_1, C_2, \ldots, C_t\}$ and related verification proof *proof*.
- (*Res*) $\leftarrow$ *VEval* (*F*, *C*): Input the ciphertext set $C = \{C_1, C_2, \ldots, C_t\}$ and the computing function $F(\cdot)$ and output computing results *Res*, $Res = F(C)$ and $C_i = VEnc(K, m_i)$ ($i \in [1, t]$)
- *res* $\leftarrow$ *VDec* (*K, Res*): Input the key K and computing results *Res* and output the decrypted plaintext computing results *res*
- *res* $\cup \perp$ $\leftarrow$ *VVerify* (*res, proof*): Input the computing result *res* and verifiable proof *proof* to verify res correctness. If it is correct, output *res*. On the contrary, output $\perp$.

Definition 2 (security): The verifiable fully homomorphic encryption scheme VFHES = (*VKeyGen, VEnc, VEval, VDec, VVerify*) is secure, if it satisfied: for any probabilistic polynomial time opponent A, if the probability for challenge success in the probability test $\text{Expt}_A(\lambda)$ satisfies the following equation:

$$Adv_A(\lambda) = |\Pr[\text{Expt}_A(\lambda)] = 1| \leq \frac{1}{2} + negl(\lambda)$$

Wherein *negl*($\cdot$) is ignorable function and the experiment $\text{Expt}_{\hat{A}}(\lambda)$ is described as follows:

(a) Generate key $K \leftarrow$ *VKeyGen*(λ);
(b) The opponent A performs predictive access to *VEnc*
(c) The opponent A inputs data m_0 and $m_{1;}$
(d) Generate the ciphertext C_0 and C_1: $C_0 \leftarrow$ VEnc(K, m_0), $C_1 \leftarrow$ VEnc(K, m_1), randomly select $b \in \{0,1\}$, and send C_b to A;
(e) The opponent A accesses the encryption prediction machine again. After multiple polling, the guest b' of b is *outputted;*
(f) If $b' = b$, *1 is outputted. Otherwise, 0 is outputted.*

For the above test, if '1' is outputted, the opponent is challenged successfully.

3 A Verifiable Fully Homomorphic Encryption Scheme—VFHES

3.1 Data Pre-processing

Before the scheme is formally constructed, the used data pre-processing operations shall be introduced. This process is executed by Owner to transform the plaintext to the vector.

Given a plaintext data m_1, it is converted to a d-dimension vector P via the following steps:

Step (1): First randomly select a $(d_a - 1)$ numbers $\{ar_1, ar_2, \ldots, ar_{d_a-1}\}$ ($ar_i \in R$ and $i \in [1, d_a - 1]$), compute $ar_{d_a} = m_1 - \sum_{i=1}^{d_a-1} ar_i$ and generate a d_a-dimension vector $p = (ar_1, ar_2, \ldots, ar_{d_a-1}, ar_{d_a})$;

Step (2): Select d_a random numbers $\{cr_1, cr_2, \ldots, cr_{d_a}\}$ ($cr_i \in R$ and $i \in [1, d_a]$), convert the vector p to $p' = (ar_1 + cr_1, ar_2 + cr_2, \ldots, ar_{d_a} + cr_{d_a})$;

Step (3): Randomly select $(d_m - 1)$ numbers $\{mr_1, mr_2, \ldots, mr_{d_m-1}\}$ ($mr_i \in R$ and $1/mr_i$ is the finite small umber and $i \in [1, d_m - 1]$), and compute $mr_{d_m} = m_1 / \prod_{i=1}^{d_m-1} mr_i$. Therefore, p' can be converted to $(d_a + d_m)$-dimension vector $p'' = (ar_1 + cr_1, ar_2 + cr_2, \ldots, ar_{d_a} + cr_{d_a}, mr_1, mr_2, \ldots, mr_{d_m})$;

Step (4): Add random elements to expand p'' and generate a $d(d = d_a + d_m + k)$-dimension vector $P = (ar_1 + cr_1, ar_2 + cr_2, \ldots, ar_{d_a} + cr_{d_a}, mr_1, mr_2, \ldots, mr_{d_m}, r_1, r_2, \ldots, r_{k-1}, -\sum_{i=1}^{d_a} cr_i)$, wherein k is a positive integer and $k \geq 2$, r_j is a random number and $r_j \in R (1 \leq j \leq k - 1)$.

3.2 Scheme Construction

(1) Key generation algorithm VKeyGen( )

Tis algorithm is executed by User. Input the security parameter λ and compute as the following steps:

① Identify the key space α according to the security parameter λ and generate the non-zero random number set $\{x_1, x_2, \ldots, x_d\}$.

② Generate d-order invertible matrix M according to the invertible matrix construction algorithm 2.2 and compute the invertible matrix M^{-1}, $M_{i,j} = x_i \delta_{\pi(i),j}$ and $M_{i,j}^{-1} = x_j^{-1} \delta_{\pi(i),j}^{-1}$. Finally the key $K = (M, M^{-1})$ is sued for encryption and decryption.

(2) Encryption algorithm VEnc( )

This algorithm is executed by User. Input the key K and plaintext data set $D = \{m_1, m_2, \ldots, m_t\}$ in computing and compute it according to the following steps:

① According to the above data pre-processing process, the plaintext data m_1 is converted to corresponding d-dimension vector $P = (ar_1 + cr_1, ar_2 + cr_2, \ldots, ar_{d_a} + cr_{d_a}, mr_1, mr_2, \ldots, mr_{d_m}, r_1, r_2, \ldots, r_{k-1}, -\sum_{i=1}^{d_a} cr_i)$.

② Select d $(d-1)/2$ non-zero random real integer and construct a d-order lower triangular (or upper triangular) matrix S_1 with these random numbers and elements in the vector P. The elements in P will be set on the diagonal of the triangular matrix S_1 by the initial sequence and the generated random numbers are irregularly placed below (above) the diagonal of the matrix S_1, therefore, the corresponding triangular matrix set $S = \{S_1, S_2, \ldots, S_t\}$ of the set D can be generated.

③ The key $K = (M, M^{-1})$ is used for blinding of the triangular matrix S_1 in order to get the ciphertext matrix $C_1 = MS_1M^{-1}$, namely ciphertext encrypted with m_1, therefore, the corresponding ciphertext matrix set $C = \{C_1, C_2, \ldots, C_t\}$ of the set D can be generated.

④ Compute the corresponding verification data according to types of different outsourcing data functions. For addition operations, first select l random integers for $(u, v), u, v \in [0, d-1], l \geq 2$. Finally compute the corresponding verification value $V_{u,v} = \sum_{i=1}^{t} S_i[u][v]$ for each random integer and combine l different verification values as the verification proof. For multiplication operation, first select w random integer $r, r \in [0, d-1], w \geq 2$. Next compute the corresponding verification value $V_r = \prod_{i=1}^{t} S_i[r][r]$ for each random integer and combine w *different* verification values V_r as a set for verification proof *proof*.

E.g. The triangular matrix of the ciphertext matrix C_1 and C_2 are:

$$S_1 = \begin{bmatrix} ar_{p1} + cr_{p1} & 0 & \cdots & 0 \\ k_1 & ar_{p2} + cr_{p2} & \cdots & 0 \\ \vdots & \vdots & \ddots & \vdots \\ k_{d-1} & k_{2d-3} & \cdots & -\sum_{i=1}^{d_a} cr_{pi} \end{bmatrix}$$

$$S_2 = \begin{bmatrix} ar_{q1} + cr_{q1} & 0 & \cdots & 0 \\ k_1' & ar_{q2} + cr_{q2} & \cdots & 0 \\ \vdots & \vdots & \ddots & \vdots \\ k_{d-1}' & k_{2d-3}' & \cdots & -\sum_{i=1}^{d_a} cr_{qi} \end{bmatrix}$$

Finally User saves *proof* and send the ciphertext set C and computing function $F(\cdot)$ to CSP:

(3) Computing algorithm *Veval*( )

This algorithm is executed by CSP. Input the computing function $F(\cdot)$ and ciphertext set $C = \{C_1, C_2, \ldots, C_t\}$ and output corresponding computing results $Res = F(C)$. For addition operation, $F(C) = C_1 + C_2 + \ldots + C_t$. For the addition operation, $F(C) = C_1 \times C_2 \times \ldots \times C_t$. Finally CSP returns the result *Res* to User.

(4) Decryption algorithm *VDec*( )

This algorithm is executed by User. To input the key $K = (M, M^{-1})$ and computing result *Res*, User will first remove blindness of *Res* and compute to get the plaintext matrix $res = M^{-1}(Res)M$. *User gets the addition operation results according to the computing Eq. (4) for the addition operation according to different computing function types.*

$$\sum_{i=1}^{d_a} (res[i][i]) + res[d][d] \tag{4}$$

For the multiplication operation, User gets the multiplication operation results by computing the following Eq. (5).

$$\prod_{i=d_a+1}^{d_a+d_m} res[i][i] \tag{5}$$

(5) **Verification algorithm VVerify( )**

This algorithm is executed by User to verify correctness of the computing results. To input the computing result *res* and verification proof *proof*, for different computing function types, compare and check if the corresponding verification value $V_{u,v}$ is equal to $res[u][v]$ according to l random integer pair (u, v) pre-generated and saved by User in addition operation. compare and check if the corresponding verification value V_r is equal to $res[r][r]$ according to w random integer r pre-generated and saved by the algorithm in multiplication operation. If the above equation is satisfied, it indicates that the corresponding computing results are correct and res is outputted. On the contrary, it indicates that the computing results are incorrect and $\perp$ is outputted.

4 Algorithm Analysis

4.1 Homomorphism Analysis

The homomorphism of VFHES is proved in addition homomorphism, multiplication homomorphism and full homomorphism in this section.

Theorem 1: VFHES can satisfy the addition homomorphism and multiplication homomorphism.

Proof:

(1) To prove that VFHES satisfies the addition homomorphism, it is required to prove that the decrypted result of $C_1 + C_2$ is $m_1 + m_2$ according to the properties of the addition homomorphism. According to the decryption algorithm, we can get:

$$M^{-1}(C_1 + C_2)M = M^{-1}(M(S_1 + S_2)M^{-1})M = (M^{-1}M)(S_1 + S_2)(M^{-1}M)$$
$$= E(S_1 + S_2)E = S_1 + S_2$$

User can compute $m_1 + m_2$ via the elements on matrix $S_1 + S_2$ diagonal according to the data pre-processing process, so $VDec(K, C_1 + C_2) = m_1 + m_2$. Therefore, VFHES satisfies the addition homomorphism.

(2) To prove that this scheme satisfies the multiplication homomorphy, it is required to prove that the decrypted result of $C_1 \times C_2$ is $m_1 \times m_2$ according to the properties of the multiplication homomorphism. According to the decryption algorithm:

$$M^{-1}(C_1 \times C_2)M = M^{-1}(M S_1 S_2 M^{-1})M = (M^{-1}M)S_1 \times S_2 (M^{-1}M)$$
$$= ES_1 \times S_2E = S_1 \times S_2$$

User can compute $m_1 \times m_2$ value via the elements on matrix $S_1 \times S_2$ diagonal according to the data pre-processing process, so $VDec(K, C_1 \times C_2) = m_1 \times m_2$. Therefore, VFHES satisfies the multiplication homomorphism.

Theorem 2: VFHES satisfies full homomorphism.

Proof: To prove that this schemes satisfies full homomorphy, it is required to prove that this scheme can support time-unlimited homomorphic operations of the addition and multiplication.

From the Theorems 1 and 2, VFHES can satisfy the addition homomorphy and multiplication homomorphy. Give that $R_{add} = M(S_1 + S_2)M^{-1}$ is the result of one homomorphic additional operation and $R_{mul} = M S_1 S_2 M^{-1}$ is the result of one homomorphic multiplication operation, after computing, we can get:

$$R_{add} + C_1 = M(S_1 + S_2)M^{-1} + M S_1 M^{-1} = M(S_1 + S_2 + S_1)M^{-1}$$
$$R_{mul} \times C_1 = M S_1 S_2 M^{-1} \times M S_1 M^{-1} = M(S_1 S_2 S_1)M^{-1}$$

According to the description algorithm, $VDec(R_{add} + C_1) = S_1 + S_2 + S_1$ and $VDec(R_{mul} \times C_1) = S_1 S_2 S_1$. Similarly, based on the Theorem 1, the above computing can satisfy the addition homomorphy and multiplication homomorphy, namely after one homomorphic operation, the ciphertext can still satisfy the properties of the addition and multiplication homomorphy. Similarly, it is deduced that this conclusion is still applicable after any homomorphic cooperation, so the VFHES satisfies the full homomorphy.

In a word, the VEHES is a fully homomorphic encryption scheme in this paper.

4.2   Security Analysis

Theorem 3: The proposed VFHES is secure.

Proof: According to security test in the Definition 2, for the opponent A, two methods are provided for challenge. The first method is to directly distinguish the plaintext from the ciphertext. The second method is to export the key, pre-process and decrypt it to get the plaintext. Two methods are analyzed as follows:

For the first method, given that $K = (M, M^{-1})$, according to the encryption algorithm $VEnc(\ )$, the corresponding ciphertext matrix for the plaintext data m_1 is:

$$C_1 = M(S_1)M^{-1} = M \times \begin{bmatrix} ar_{p1} + cr_{p1} & 0 & \cdots & 0 \\ k_1 & ar_{p2} + cr_{p2} & \cdots & 0 \\ \vdots & \vdots & \ddots & \vdots \\ k_{d-1} & k_{2d-3} & \cdots & -\sum_{i=1}^{d_a} cr_{pi} \end{bmatrix} \times M^{-1}$$

Except ar_{d_a}, mr_{d_m} and $\sum_{i=1}^{d_a} cr_{pi}$, the elements in the matrix S_1 are random. The value of each element in the result matrix is determined by multiple elements in the computing matrix according to the multiplication operation rule between matrixes and is affected by random numbers. Therefore, the ciphertext matrix from multiple encryptions of one plaintext in the prerequisite of the given key is different and does not comply with certain law. Therefore, due to multiple random numbers, the probability for the opponent A to successfully distinguish the plaintext from the ciphertext is:

$$Adv_A(\lambda) = |\Pr[\text{Expt}_A(\lambda)] = 1| = |\Pr[b' = b]| \leq \frac{1}{2} + \frac{1}{|R|}$$

R is the number of the R elements n the real number field. It is obvious that this probability can be ignored.

For the second method, given that the ciphertext matrix is $C_1 = M(S_1)M^{-1}$, if the opponent A expects to get the contents in S_1, it shall also decrypt M or M^{-1} from C_1. The matrix M is constructed according to the Algorithm 2, this algorithm is implemented based on Kronecker function and random permutation, so the opponent A shall guest the random permutation π to use and find the random number set $\{x_1, x_2, \ldots, x_d\}$. According to the introduction in the Sect. 1.2, d-tuple permutation function includes $d!$ possibilities and the random number set includes $|\alpha|^d$ possibilities. Therefore, the probability for the opponent A to successfully decrypt M is $1/d! * |\alpha|^d$. When the matrix order d and the key space α are larger, this probability is ignored. According to the encryption algorithm, after the plaint text data m_1 is pre-processed, the matrix S_1 is further constructed. The massive random numbers are introduced in this process to effectively hide original plaintext information and further improve the scheme security. At this time, the success probability of the opponent A is ignorable.

In addition, according to the Theorem 2, VFHES satisfies the properties of the full homomorphy. Therefore, the whole structure of the ciphertext is not destructed in ciphertext computing. Security of the intermediate data and computing results does not change.

In a word, VFHES is secure.

Theorem 4: The proposed VFHES is verifiable.

Proof: The verifiability of the algorithm is proved in correctness and security.

(1) Correctness

According to the verification algorithm, the pre-calculated verification data is compared with the computing results from CSP to verify the result correctness in VFHES.

For addition operation, according to the encryption algorithm *VEnc*, the generated verification proof is $proof = \prod_{i=1}^{t} S_i[u][v]$. Therefore, if the computing result *Res* from CSP is computed and decrypted correctly, we can get:

$$Res = C_1 + \ldots + C_t = M S_1 M^{-1} + \ldots + M S_t M^{-1}$$
$$res = VDec(K, Res) = M^{-1} Res M = S_1 + \ldots + S_t$$

In addition, according to the operation rule of the matrix addition, the equation $proof = res[u][v]$ is satisfied.

For the multiplication operation, according to the encryption algorithm *VEnc*, the generated verification proof is $proof = \prod_{i=1}^{t} S_i[u][v]$, therefore, if the computing result *Res* from CSP is computed and decrypted correctly, we can get:

$$Res = C_1 \times \ldots \times C_t = M S_1 M^{-1} \times \ldots \times M S_t M^{-1}$$
$$res = VDec(K, Res) = M^{-1} Res M = S_1 \times \ldots \times S_t$$

According to the multiplication operation rule of the triangular matrix, the multiplication operation results of multiple lower triangular matrixes are still the lower triangular matrixes and the values of elements on the diagonal of the result matrix is equal to the product of elements at same position of the diagonal of all computing matrixes. Therefore, $proof = res[r][r]$ is satisfied and the VFHES is correct.

(2) Security

The CSP aims to verify the computing results (correct or incorrect) via User. Therefore, to prove that VHHES is verifiable and secure, we only prove that the probability of successful User verification of incorrect computing results is ignorable.

According to the encryption algorithm *VEnc*, the verification proof of the addition and multiplication operation is composed of l randomly selected and computed verification value $V_{u,v} = \prod_{i=1}^{t} S_i[u][v]$ and w randomly selected and computed verification value $V_r = \prod_{i=1}^{t} S_i[u][v]$. These verification data is locally computed by User and is secure. Therefore, to make an incorrect computing result pass User verification, CSP shall guest the values of l pairs of (u, v) or w *pairs of* (r,r). At this time, success probabilities are:

$$\prod_{i=0}^{l-1} \frac{l!}{(d-i)^2} \ 和 \ \prod_{i=0}^{w-1} \frac{w!}{(d-i)}$$

When the matrix order d is bigger, such probability is very small. Therefore, User can detect incorrect computing results at a higher probability. In addition, the computing results from CSP are a triangular matrix according to the decryption algorithm and can be verified based on this method to further improve successful verification probability.

In a word, VFHES satisfies verifiability.

4.3 Performance Analysis

The VFHES is compared with the existing scheme (GSW13 [9] and Gentry scheme [5]) in key size of ciphertext, algorithm computing complexity, noises and verifiability. The comparison results are shown as the Table 1.

Table 1. Scheme comparison

Property	Scheme		
	GSW13	Gentry	VFHES
Key size	$d^2 + d$	-	$2d^2$
Ciphertext size	d^2	-	d^2
Algorithm computing complexity	$O(d^3)$	$O(d^6)$	$O(d^2)$
Noises	Yes	Yes	No
Verifiable	No	No	Yes
Key selection	Matrix/vector	Multinomial	Matrix
Full homomorphy	Not satisfied with growth of depth	Satisfied	Satisfied

Comparison results show that VFHES and GSW13 ciphertexts are matrix and the addition and multiplication operation will not increase the dimension of the ciphertext, so there are simpler than Gentry's scheme. In addition, VFHES does not include noises in computing due to special properties of the triangular matrix used by VFHES. When the format of the new ciphertexts generated by addition or multiplication operation of the ciphertext matrix keeps unchanged, the decryption algorithm can precisely output the corresponding computing results. GSW13 noises will grow exponentially with growth of the computing depth. In addition, Some security issues of malicious cloud server model are considered in VFHES, so it can be verified.

4.4 Experimental Analysis

To evaluate actual performance consumption of the scheme, the proposed VFHES is simulated via experiments in this section. The experiment codes are programmed by using Java. The program runs on Windows 7 OS and Inter Pentium G640 (2.80 GHz) and 4G memory.

Shown as the Fig. 2, the key generation time t will grow with growth of the matrix dimension d because the key is generated by using the matrix fuzzy technology at time complexity $O(d^2)$. For the detailed construction process, refer to the Algorithm 2.

Shown as the Fig. 3, the encryption time consumption will grow with growth of the matrix dimension d. First the plaintext data is converted to the matrix and then is blinded in VFHES encryption. The consumption is caused by blinding on this phase and its time complexity is $O(d^2)$. Notice that here the encryption consumption only indicates consumption time for single plaintext encryption.

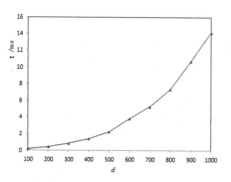

Fig. 2. Key generation consumption

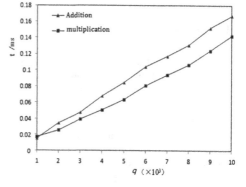

Fig. 3. Encryption consumption

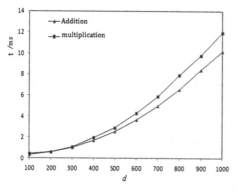

Fig. 4. Decryption consumption

Fig. 5. Proof generation consumption

Shown as the Fig. 4, the decryption time consumption of the addition and multiplication operation results will grow with growth of the dimension d of the matrix. The ciphertext matrix will be first de-blinded and then be further computed in VFHES decryption. The de-blinding time complexity is $O(d^2)$. In addition, decryption processes of the homomorphic addition and multiplication operations are different and their time complexities are related to d_a and d_m. We preset $d_a = d_m$ in this experiment. Shown as the Fig. 4, the time consumed by two decryption processes is similar.

Shown as the Fig. 5, given that $l = w = 3$, the proof generation time consumption of the addition and multiplication operation will linearly grow with growth of the outsourcing data quantity q because the proof generation of the scheme is independent of the matrix dimension d. For the addition and multiplication operation, the time complexity for proof generation is $O(l \times q)$ and $O(w \times q)$. Therefore, proper l and w can ensure security and efficient generation of verification proof.

5   Conclusions

This paper proposes a verifiable fully homomorphic encryption scheme VFHES for possible security issues in non-trustable cloud outsourcing computing model. This scheme supports fully homomorphic encryption and can verify correctness of the computing results. Security analysis proves that this scheme is secure and verifiable. The performance comparison and analysis shows that VFHES features higher performance and function strengths. The results of simulation experiments show that this scheme is efficient in key generation, decryption and verifiable phase, so this scheme is effective and practicable.

Acknowledgments. This work was supported in part by the Guangxi Natural Fund Project under Grant No. 2016GXNSFAA380115, Guangxi Innovation-Driven Development Project under Grant No. AA17204058-17.

References

1. Gentry, C.: Fully homomorphic encryption using ideal lattices. In: Proceedings of the Annual ACM Symposium on Theory of Computing, Bethesda, pp. 169–178. ACM (2009)
2. van Dijk, M., Gentry, C., Halevi, S., Vaikuntanathan, V.: Fully homomorphic encryption over the integers. In: Gilbert, H. (ed.) EUROCRYPT 2010. LNCS, vol. 6110, pp. 24–43. Springer, Heidelberg (2010). https://doi.org/10.1007/978-3-642-13190-5_2
3. Brakerski, Z., Vaikuntanathan, V.: Efficient fully homomorphic encryption from (standard) LWE. In: Foundations of Computer Science, CA, pp. 97–106. IEEE (2011)
4. Brakerski, Z., Gentry, C., Vaikuntanathan, V.: (Leveled)fully homomorphic encryption without bootstrapping. In: Proceedings of the 3rd Innovations in Theoretical Computer Science Conference, pp. 309–325. ACM Press, New York (2012)
5. Gentry, C., Sahai, A., Waters, B.: Homomorphic encryption from learning with errors: conceptually-simpler, asymptotically-faster, attribute-based. In: Canetti, R., Garay, Juan A. (eds.) CRYPTO 2013, Part I. LNCS, vol. 8042, pp. 75–92. Springer, Heidelberg (2013). https://doi.org/10.1007/978-3-642-40041-4_5
6. Gennaro, R., Gentry, C., Parno, B.: Non-interactive verifiable computing: outsourcing computation to untrusted workers. In: Rabin, T. (ed.) CRYPTO 2010. LNCS, vol. 6223, pp. 465–482. Springer, Heidelberg (2010). https://doi.org/10.1007/978-3-642-14623-7_25
7. Jin, F., Zhu, Y., Luo, X.: Verifiable fully homomorphic encryption scheme. In: International Conference on Consumer Electronics, Communications and Networks, Yichang, pp. 743–746. IEEE (2012)
8. Zhou, J., Cao, Z., Dong, X., et al.: EVOC: more efficient verifiable outsourced computation from any one-way trapdoor function. In: IEEE International Conference on Communications, pp. 7444–7449. IEEE (2015)
9. Ahmed, E.Y., El Kettani, M.D.E.C.: A verifiable fully homomorphic encryption scheme to secure big data in cloud computing. In: International Conference on Wireless Networks and Mobile Communications, Rabat, pp. 1–5. IEEE (2017)
10. Zhao, Q., Zeng, Q., Liu, X., Xu, H.: Verifiable computation using re-randomizable garbled circuits. J. Softw. **30**(2), 399–415 (2019)
11. Xu, J., Wei, L.W., Zhang, Y.: Dynamic fully homomorphic encryption-based Merkle tree for lightweight streaming authenticated data structures. J. Netw. Comput. Appl. **107**, 113–124 (2018)

Secure Communication in UAV Assisted HetNets: A Proposed Model

Aabid Rashid, Diwankshi Sharma, Tufail A. Lone, Sumeet Gupta,
and Sachin Kumar Gupta$^{(\boxtimes)}$

School of Electronics and Communication Engineering, Shri Mata Vaishno Devi
University, Kakryal, Katra 182320, Jammu & Kashmir, India
waniaabid1992@gmail.com, diwankshisharma96@gmail.com,
tufaillone1@gmail.com,
{sumeet.gupta, sachin.gupta}@smvdu.ac.in

Abstract. In the current scientific and technological world, every emerging/ advanced country employs Heterogeneous Networks (HetNets) assisted by Unmanned Ariel Vehicle (UAV) to serve its civilian, military and natural catastrophes, etc. The area of focusing in this work will be military zones for getting securely the reconnaissance information from enemy/hostile areas in their battlefields and nuclear war conditions. Though, once the network is created for such scenarios, the untypical nature of UAV assisted network demands protection evaluation. The UAV facilitated HetNets, therefore, demands trust worthy and secure communication among military users using the network. Authentication is one characteristic which enables to mitigate security issues. The prevalent identity and authentication scheme is thus intended to tackle the security threats in HetNets assisted by UAV. In this paper, a security model is proposed based on Identity Based (IB) authentication scheme for UAV-integrated HetNets. The absolutism of such a suggested scheme is screened using the AVISPA tool and some of its outcomes has shown that our scheme is resistant to the vulnerabilities of intruders like replay, impersonation etc.

Keywords: UAV · HetNet · IBE · Secure communication ·
Network performance

1 Introduction

The use of aerial pilotless vehicles has increased drastically in many applications for the last decade. The applications mostly include unforeseeable events which cannot be prevented for example natural disasters, country's safety, search, rescue and mostly military monitoring. For military applications UAVs find much importance and attention. As swarm of UAVs can go across the border/LOC and will perform some acknowledged task needed for the safety of country. All these applications of networked UAVs are possible because of autonomous navigation nature of UAVs. So, networked UAVs can be used for real-time applications with post-disaster recovery in case of emergency cases [1].

© Springer Nature Switzerland AG 2019
G. Wang et al. (Eds.): SpaCCS 2019, LNCS 11611, pp. 427–440, 2019.
https://doi.org/10.1007/978-3-030-24907-6_32

The HetNet comprises of low power additional network nodes in addition to Base Station (BS). The lower power nodes include small cells, picocells, femtocells that can support BS and provide wide variety of coverage zones. The coverage zones extend from an open outdoor surrounding to local offices, homes and sub-terrestrial regions. Because of heterogeneous nature, the HetNets overcome the major challenges of optimized homogeneous unrivalled traffic face and meet the demand for capacity and coverage efficiently. Also, the HetNets drift the services from voice to data-centric such as Long Term Evolution (LTE) of 5G and afar. So the HetNets exponentially increases the demanded capacity and coverage with minimizing the latency by optimizing the traffic allocation [2].

By collaborating UAVs with HetNet solved many research challenging problems that were not possible with UAVs and HetNets respectively. The UAV assisted HetNet not only satisfy the high demand capacity for proliferation of mobile users. But with proper optimization techniques in the network, the user's throughput increased drastically with reduced end to end delay and latency. Because of these incredible features, the UAV assisted HetNets increased the trustiness among users to use it for emergency cases such as natural disasters and also in collecting reconnaissance information from hostile areas (military surveillance), etc. But the information receiving with the help of this network particularly for surveillance cases should be free from intruder attacks. As the intruders can attack on the information confidentiality, message integrity, and can act as interceptors among the authorized users and even can make place as an authorized entity. To overcome these challenging issues, there is a trusty security system that make impossible for the intruders to access the network secret. This trusty security system will be based on the identity based parameters that have to authenticate by all authorized users in the network before secret exchanging. So there will be data encryption of authorized users with the server as well as with UAVs. In this way the UAV assisted HetNets will become trusty network. The conceptual overview of UAV integrated HetNet is shown in Fig. 1.

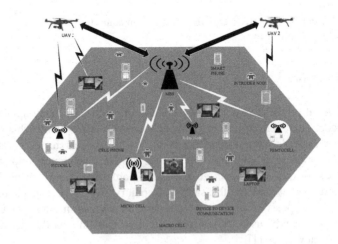

Fig. 1. Conceptual overview of UAV integrated HetNet

1.1 Motivation and Contribution

Due to proliferation of mobile users', the thirsty for the high demand capacity increased and hence became an open challenge for the researchers to fulfill users' demand satisfactorily. The solution of these challenges were made possible by extending the low capacity, high latency homogeneous cellular based network to high capacity, low latency UAV assisted HetNet. Due to which the information thirsty for authenticated escalated users' full filled to the satisfactorily level. But the proliferation of mobile users led to the evolution of large number of intruders and because of this the networks became prone to vulnerable attacks easily. Then obviously, there is need of a trusty security system for the network that preserves its data privacy and increase trustiness among the users. So that whatever the information going through the communication network must be free from adversary malicious attacks. Hence, to prevent drooping down of packets and easy stealing of the valid data of authorized users. Many traditional Public Key Cryptosystems were used. But these traditional types of Cryptosystems ran through many open challenges as Public Key Infrastructure (PKI) failed to take the burden of key management and storage. Also the Cryptographic Algorithms should be computationally lightweight as the entities in the communication network are always power constrained entities. Hence, the communication network should be implemented with such a cryptographic security system that removes the above challenges and makes the network smarter against the intruder attacks. The possible solution is in IDENTITY BASED authentication scheme. The identity based cryptosystem overcome these burdens by allowing the entities for authentication, sign, and transact encrypted information among them without involvement of PKI (central authority). This indicates that PKI is involving only at the time of registration (one time) and after that there is no role of it. In this way it will provide entity authentication within the UAV assisted HetNets. And in the process the whole communication system will become secure. The construction of this proposed literature work is assembled as follows: Sect. 2 presents related work that is carried out in this particular area. Section 3 discusses the proposed IBE security system scheme. Section 4 presents validating results and finally, Sect. 5 finally comes up with conclusion.

2 Related Work

There are numerous authors who introduced random key pre-distribution [3, 4]. However, those schemes were adopted for small size networks. Also, scaling was not to the good level as they require that each node is pre-installed with large number of keys. Almost, all the pre-installed key schemes were developed for homogeneous networks. So when these schemes were adopted in heterogeneous entities the challenges of high communication and storage overhead took a birth. Due et al. [5] overcomes these issues by proposing an asymmetric pre-installed key scheme by utilizing the features of hetero entities. Pietrowicz et al. [6] integrated public key cryptographic scheme known as Identity Based Encryption with Vehicular Data Transportation Layer Security (VDTLS) for secure User Datagram Protocol (UDP) based communication over the vehicle networks. Standing et al. [7] proposed Identity Based Encryption (IBE) scheme in a distributed network system for acquiring secure communication. As the IBE is an unsymmetrical cryptographic technique and hence overcome the problems of conventional symmetrical cryptographic scheme where each node's public key was signed by certificate authority (CA). Moreover. The IBE solved the problem of pre-installed knowledge of public keys that were incorporated with each significant node which leads to compromise for security and trust.

Liang et al. [8] proposed a peculiar identity authentication scheme integration of fingerprints code and identity based encryption that solved the problems of conventional cryptosystem, because absence of authentic link between cryptography keys with authorized user. Also, PKI lacks of improper mainframe of digital certificates in authentication networks. The traditional cryptographic techniques need identity keys for encryption and decryption due to varying of biometric signal on various site. Because of this reason the biometric and general cryptographic schemes are known by complementary trusty security schemes. The beauty of this work is using of fingerprint codes as identity for user authentication that improves the security strength of the network. Hence, biometric signal increased the power of confidentiality in security and privacy. The author proposed this scheme to meet the basic requirements of security, efficiency and privacy of real-time applications. Jia et al. [9] proposed a trusty IBE technique in Wireless Sensor Networks (WSNs) to decrease the necessity of resources that is power, computation and storage. Moreover, it overcomes the challenges of certificate management, session key distribution of symmetrical cryptosystem that were traditionally used in WSNs for secure communication. With IBE the resource identification, simple key management becomes very efficient. Therefore, provided a trusty communication in WSN applications with minimum need of resource consumption. Moreover, the comparative study of existing security approach of related surveys in the literature is illustrated in Table 1.

Table 1. Comparison of existing security approach of related surveys in the literature

N/W type	Attacks	Security approach	Validation	UAV +HetNet	Features
WSN, [10]	Listen to the traffic, mislead communication between nodes	Identity-Based Key Agreement and Encryption	_____	No + No	• Overcome the challenges of traditional public key and symmetric key distribution
5G Mobile, [11]	Active Attacks (impersonating), Passive Attacks (figure out the users' identity)	PEFMA in 5G network using IBE	AVISPA	No + No	• Securing long-term user's identity privacy • Identification and mutual authentication

(continued)

Table 1. (*continued*)

N/W type	Attacks	Security approach	Validation	UAV +HetNet	Features
UAV, [12]	Hardware attacks (Access of UAV autopilot components directly, wireless & sensor spoofing)	Selective Encryption Technique & Data Hiding Mechanism	NS3	Yes + No	• Reduce overheads • Increase confidentiality • Provides network flexibility by allowing nodes to serve as cluster heads periodically and dynamically
HetNets Sensor N/W [13]	Jamming, eavesdropping, spoofing, DoS, replication and Sybil attacks. Node capture, insider, and capture attacks involving cluster heads	TINY IBE	NS3	No + Yes	• Reduces key storage space & comm. overhead • Achieves high level security and storage resilience against node capture attack • Minimizes energy consumption to prolong the network lifetime
M2M comm.: IoT, [14]	Replay, man-in-the middle, impersonation, modification	IBE Using Elliptic Curve Cryptography	_____	No + Yes	• Solve privacy and security issues arise during M2M comm. in IoT applications
Internet & Smart Devices (IoT), [15]	Tempering of information Key distribution Issue	Authentication mechanism based-IBE	NS3	—	• Key-Escrow free feature • Look-up for IBE parameters in other domains & generate secret key for secure comm. between communicating entities

Note: M2M: Machine to Machine, IoT: Internet of Things, PEFMA: Privacy Enhanced Fast Mutual Authentication, HetNet: Heterogeneous Network, UAV: Unmanned Aerial Vehicle.

From the above related researches, it is clear and obvious that till now no such work has been done on security issues in UAV assisted HetNets that runs through many challenges of intruder vulnerabilities and malicious attacks. So there is necessity of such a cryptosystem that makes the given network for the particular application free from security threats.

3 IBE-Trust Security Scheme

The IBE is developed by Shamir in 1984. Later Boneh and Franklin successfully presented fully functional IBE scheme [16]. IBE overcomes the problem of requirement of certificate authority/third party authorization. Instead the IBE provides simplified certificate public key encryption scheme by utilizing generally known isolated attributes to extract public keys. The public key used in IBE is an unpredictable string estimated from any string like email, finger print, Aadhaar number, phone number, date of birth and other unique attributes. So, the public key in IBE will be calculated by any person who has important public with a secret writing scheme (Cryptographic Master Key) for calculating private key [17]. This is all possible only with the existence of trusted server that provides this confidentiality.

The cryptographic security scheme of IBE basically depends on the usage of bilinear map (pairing). In this mapping, the two groups are mapped with each other. Suppose G_1 be the additive cyclic group and G_2 be a multiplicative cyclic group contains all of large prime order q.

$$\hat{e} : G1 * G2 \rightarrow G2$$

Such that the following properties should be satisfied.

- Bilinearity: $\forall P, Q \in G_1$ and $\forall a, b \in z_q^* : \hat{e}(aP, bQ) = \hat{e}(P, Q)^{ab}$
- Non-degeneracy property: The map should not send all pairs in $G_1 * G_2$ to the identity in G2. Observe that G1, G2 are groups of prime order, this implies that if P is the generator of G1 then $\hat{e}(P, P)$ is a generator of G2.
- Computability: There exists an efficient algorithm to compute $\hat{e} : G_1 * G_2 \rightarrow G_2$ for any $P, Q \in G_1$.

For IBE implementation, two types of pairing are available that is Tate Pairing and Weil Pairing. But it has been estimated that Tate Pairing is more efficient than Weil Pairing when implemented for computation for constrained devices [18].

3.1 Algorithm IBE Cryptography

The original IBE of security scheme of Boneh Franklin consists of four randomized algorithms as shown in Fig. 2 namely Setup, Extract, Encrypt and Decrypt.

1. *Setup*: Given a security parameter 1^k, the parameter generator follows the steps:

   - Generate two cyclic groups G_1 and G_2 of prime order q and a bilinear pair map $\hat{e} : G_1 * G_2 \rightarrow G_2$. Pick a random generator $P \in G_1$.
   - Pick a random integer $s \in Z$; and compute $P_{pub} = sP$.
   - Pick four cryptographic hash functions $H_1 : \{0, 1\}^* \rightarrow G_1^*$, $H_2 : G_2 \rightarrow \{0, 1\}^n$, $H_3 : \{0, 1\}^n * \{0, 1\}^n \rightarrow Z^q *$ and $H_4 : \{0, 1\}^n \rightarrow \{0, 1\}^n$ for some integer n > 0.

   The space for message is $M = \{0, 1\}^n$. The cipher text space $c = G_1^* * \{0, 1\}^n *$ $\{0, 1\}^n$. The system parameters are *params* = $< q$, G_1, G_2, $\hat{e}$, n, P, P_{pub}, H_1, H_2, H_3,

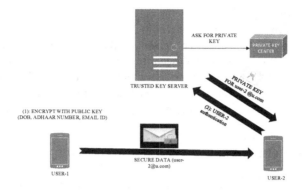

Fig. 2. The overview of IBE

$H_4 >$, whereas s is the master-key of the system. The most important thing to remember is that, *Setup* algorithm is performed by the Public Key Generator (PKG), instead, the security parameters provided by administrator, and *params* are publicly known attributes that have trust relationship with PKG, however master-key is kept by PKG.

2. *Extract:* Given a string Id ε $\{0,1\}^*$ (e.g. identity of the Communicating entity), *params* and the master-key s, the algorithm computes:

   - Public key as $U_{Id} = H_1$ (Id) ε G_1^*.
   - Private Key as $d_{Id} = sU_{Id}$.

   This is also performed by PKG. At the end of this algorithm, U_{Id} can be published whereas d_{Id} is stored secretly by the communicating entity.

3. *Publisher:* Given the *params*, a communicating entity selects a random number n_{Id} ε Z_q^* as sub-private key and computes $N_{Id} = nP$ as sub-private key.

   At the end of this algorithm the communicating entity can send N_{Id} to the directory station like *Base station,* for publishing and keeps n_{Id} as secret.

4. *Encrypt:* Given a message m ε M, the identity Id, system parameters *params* and sub-public key N_{Id}:

   - Pick a random α ε $\{0, 1\}^n$ and calculate i = H_3 (α,m).
   - Calculate $U_{Id} = H_1$ (Id) and t = $\hat{e}$ ($P_{pub} + N_{Id}$, U_{Id}).
   - Assign the cipher text C = < iP, α xor H_2 (t^i), m xor H_4 (α) >.

5. *Decrypt:* Now the Cipher text < x,v,w > ε C, d_{Id}, n and system parameters params, the algorithm calculates

   - $t' = \hat{e}$ (x, $d_{Id} + nU_{Id}$) and $\alpha' = v$ xor H_2 (t').
   - m' = w xor H_4 (α') and i' = H_3 (α', m').

   Provided the X should not be equal to i'P cancel the cipher text, otherwise return m' as the message. In this network, the trusty server will be the central base station and small cells for authorized users and UAVs. The placement of trusted entities must be a secure space and directly controlled by the network owner. In this way, it can provide better security and control environment within a network that is not possible with other PKC infrastructure. Another important feature of the identity based scheme that differentiates it from other server-based security algorithms that no communication is needed within the base server during encryption action. Also, for encrypting the restricted data, only the receiver's id is important for the transmitter. Moreover, the IBE implementation uses less recollection for storing public keys of authorized users.

4 Proposed Methodology

Most authentication schemes when comparing with this proposed methodology only recognize direct communication between things in a specific network type, such as WSN, in which power consumption was generally viewed. While this is a major issue in the sense of the WSN.

The probity of the base station and small cells platform is inspired and motivated with the measured platform above base functions [19]. By implementing the trusted platform equations in this proposed scheme, the base station and small cells depend on the information whatever comes from the users and UAVs. The proposed security scheme in our network will provide a secure communication among the users within the UAV assisted HetNet by authentication process with the base station and UAVs respectively. During authentication process the knowledge of intruders has been taken into consideration. The intruder can attack through many ways like eavesdrop, hijack, modify and can impregnate any data into the communication channel. These above authentication equation are developed into "HLPSL" language and will be verified with the "AVISPA TOOL".

- **CASE A:** Authentication between user and base station

Before establishing the network the base stations should have a set of user's id and their hm_U value (for authentication). Along with this, the authorized users should have public keys and common parameters. "Figure 3" Illustrates the IBE-prototype between user and base station. The HLPSL prototype for this case have been represented in an algorithm manner from Eq. 1 to 5.

$$U \to S : SND \left\{N'_u . \ hm\_U'\right\}\_K_s)$$ (1)

U: Requests S to verify on hm value.

$$S : Rcv\left(U.S.\left\{N'_u.hm\_U\right\}\_K_s\right) in \left(U.hm\_U, trust \ list\right)$$ (2)

S compares the recipient's hm_U with the value in the trust list.

$$S \to U : SND\left(\left\{N'_u.N'_v\right\}\_K_u\right)$$ (3)

S: Requests U to authenticate on N_v value.

$$U : Rcv \left(\{N_u.N'_v\}\_K_u\right) \tag{4}$$

$$U \rightarrow S : SND\left(\{N'_v\}\right)\_K_s \tag{5}$$

U: Requests base station to authenticate on Hm value.

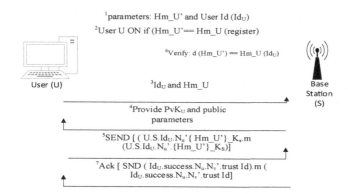

Fig. 3. Authentication between user (U) and base station (S)

In this way the server (S) authenticate on hm_U value only when the N_u and N_v are authenticated successfully. This authenticated syntax is free from adversary attacks. Due to successful authentication, the base station will create new list that contain the identity of trusted users. The size of the new list is smaller than the existed trust list which is publicized among the authorized users or can be stored in the server for the quicker authentication process. The users can share information with the users that have ID existed in this new list. The authorized users within the network remain trusted as long as it remains in ON condition. If shutdown occurs because of any reason, the users have to re-authenticate with the base station. The re-authentication failure process will remove the user's ID from the trusted list. So for new authentication the users have to go for the same process for becoming again part of network.

CASE B: Authentication between USER and UAV

In this case, the UAV will authenticate the users with the help of base station or by itself. Here, the user's packet will contain the transmitter and receiver address, its Id (Id_u, nonce number, and encrypted message (encrypted with general key)). The UAV will then verify the Id_u with the Id present in the trust list that is stored at the main server or in its own storage. If it exists the server will acknowledge the UAV and the communication will go ahead. The nonce plays an essential role to avert the repetition attacks of intruders in the network. "Figure 4" depicts the authentication process for this case.

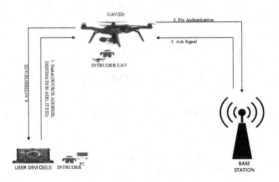

Fig. 4. Authentication between User (U) and UAV via Station(S)

The HLPSL codes for this case are listed out in terms of equation from 6 to 14.
First technique:

$$U : SND(U.D.IdU \{data.N'_u\}\_K_d \tag{6}$$

U: Send data with user identity(IdU) to UAV (D).

$$D : Rcv(U.D.IdU \{data.N'_u\}\_K_d \tag{7}$$

D: Receive the information from U.

$$SND (D.S.U.IdU) \tag{8}$$

Here the user's identity (IdU) by D is forwarded to station(S) for authentication.

$$S : Rcv (SND(D.S.U.IdU) / \backslash in (U.IdU, trustlist) =|> \tag{9}$$

S: Receive the user's information from D and mapped with the value stored in trustlist.

$$SND (S.D.Ok) \tag{10}$$

Station(S) sends an acknowledgement signal to D.

$$D : Rcv (S.D.Ok) =|> SND (D.U.Ok) \tag{11}$$

D: Receive the acknowledgement signal and authenticate the user.
U: proceed with next packet.
Second technique:

$$U : SND(U.D.IdU \{data.N'_u\}\_K_d \tag{12}$$

$$D : Rcv(U.D.IdU \{data.N_u'\}\_K_d / \backslash \ in \ (U.IdU, \ trustlist) \ =|> \qquad (13)$$

$$D : Snd(D.U.Ok) \qquad (14)$$

U: proceed with next packet.

The second scheme performs better by consuming less communication overhead. Both techniques achieve prevention of attacks on data confidentiality and authentication. In order to express clearly, symbols for subsequent use are listed in Table 2.

Table 2. Notations used in the proposed scheme

Symbol	Description
Hm_U	New trust value
N_u', N_v'	Nonce Random Numbers
K_U, K_S	User and Station Public Keys
SND	Send packet
$\_K_S$	Encrypted packet with KS public key
M	message
Id_U	User Node's identifier
PvK_U	User's private key
A.S	Sender ID. Receiver ID

5   Formal Validation of Proposed Protocol (Case A) Using Avispa Tool

The AVISPA is known as a push-button tool flourished for validating the large scale network security protocols and applications. The protocols are translated in a coded language called HLPSL (High Level Protocol Specification Language).

The basic process behind the HLPSL represents various participants and compositions of roles. There is independency among the roles, acquiring some initial information by parameters, communicating with the additional roles by channels [20]. The Format of output of AVISPA Tool is created using one of the four back-ends that is OFMC (on-the-fly model-checker), SATMC (SAT-based model-checker), Cl-Atse (Constraint logic based attack searcher) and TA4SP (Tree Automated based on Automatic Approximations for the Analysis of Security Protocols) [20].

For this case, the HLPSL proposed security protocol is simulated in presence of intrusion attacks who can attack on the information confidentiality, message integrity, and can act as interceptors among the authorized users and even can make place as an authorized entity (Dolev-Yao). The simulation output or execution of this security protocol under ATMC and OFMC back-end options provides the "SUMMARY" whether the protocol is SAFE or UNSAFE or if the analysis is inconclusive. From the output result it is clear that the proposed protocol for this case is SAFE. The (Fig. 5)

```
%%% BS-> U: {BS.U.Nv}_Ks
%%% U-> BS: {BS.U.Nv.s}_Ku

role role_BS(BS:agent,U:agent,Ks:public_key,Ku:public_key,SND,RCV:channel(dy))
played_by BS
def=
        local
                State:nat,Nv:text,S:text
        init
                State := 0
        transition
                1. State=0 /\ RCV(start) =|>
                   State':=1 /\ Nv':=new() /\ SND({BS.U.Nv'}_Ku)

                2. State=1 /\ RCV({BS.U.Nv.S'}_Ks) =|>
                   State':=2

                   %% BS checks that he receives the same nonce
                   %% that he sent at step 1.

                   /\ request(BS,U,auth_1,Nv)
end role
```

```
role role_U(U:agent,BS:agent,S:text,Ks:public_key,Ku:public_key,SND,RCV:channel(dy))
played_by U
def=
        local
                State:nat,Nv:text
        init
                State := 0
        transition
                1. State=0 /\ RCV({BS.U.Nv'}_Ku) =|>

                   State':=1 /\ SND({BS.U.Nv'.S}_Ks)

                   /\ secret(S,sec_1,{BS,U})
                   %% U hopes that Nv will permit to authenticate him
                   /\ witness(U,BS,auth_1,Nv')
end role
```

```
role session(BS:agent,U:agent,S:text,Ks:public_key,Ku:public_key)
def=
        local
                SND2,RCV2,SND1,RCV1:channel(dy)
        composition
                role_U(U,BS,S,Ks,Ku,SND2,RCV2) /\ role_BS(BS,U,Ks,Ku,SND1,RCV1)
end role

role environment()
def=
        const
                ks,ku:public_key,
                basestation,user:agent,
                s1:text,
                sec_1,auth_1:protocol_id
        intruder_knowledge = {basestation,user,ks,ku}
        composition
                session(basestation,user,s1,ks,ku) /\ session(basestation,user,s1,ks,ku)
end role

goal
        secrecy_of sec_1
        authentication_on auth_1
end goal
```

Fig. 5. Roles for session, goal and environment in HLPSL

and (Fig. 6) gives the pictorial view of simulated security protocol. Also the next option "DETAILS" provides the information under which conditions the security protocol is safe.

```
SUMMARY
  SAFE

DETAILS
  BOUNDED_NUMBER_OF_SESSIONS
  TYPED_MODEL

PROTOCOL
  /home/span/span/testsuite/results/finalresult.if

GOAL
  As Specified

BACKEND
  CL-AtSe

STATISTICS

  Analysed    : 30 states
  Reachable   : 24 states
  Translation : 0.01 seconds
  Computation : 0.00 seconds
```

Fig. 6. Result of analysis using ATMC of proposed scheme

6 Conclusion and Future Direction

The article proposed the security structure for UAV assisted HetNet for applications that require high security characters. The most important application include un-critical military communication, where the military users securely receive the reconnaissance information from enemy areas. Also it can be extended to improve the security issues in civilian surveillance, critical financial information and others. This security work presents an analysis of identity based trusty security techniques using AVISPA TOOL that validates data confidentiality and assure authentication within the communication network. The proposed trusty authentication process implemented will preserve the integrity of valid information going within the network. Future research on memory and energy are required to increase the lifetime of UAVs and minimize the communication overhead.

References

1. Tuna, G., Nefzi, B., Conte, G.: Unmanned aerial vehicles-aided communication system for disaster recovery. J. Netw. Comput. Appl. **41**, 27–36 (2014). https://doi.org/10.1016/j.jnca.2013.10.002
2. Yang, G., Xiao, M., Alam, M., Huang, Y.: Low-latency heterogeneous networks millimeter-wave communications. IEEE Commun. Mag. **56**, 124–129 (2018). https://doi.org/10.1109/MCOM.2018.1700874
3. Eschenauer, L., Gligor, V.D.: A key-management scheme for distributed sensor networks. In: CCS 2002. ACM, October 2002. https://doi.org/10.1145/586110.586117
4. Pietro, R.D., Mancini, L.V., Mei, A.: Random key-assignment for secure wireless sensor networks. In: Ist ACM Workshop on Security of Ad-Hoc and Sensor Networks, SASN 2003, Fairfax, Virginia, USA, pp. 62–71, January 2003. https://doi.org/10.1145/986858.986868
5. Du, X., Xiao, Y., Chen, H.: An effective key management scheme for heterogeneous sensor networks. Ad Hoc Netw. **5**, 24–34 (2007). https://doi.org/10.1016/j.adhoc.2006.05.012

6. Pietrowicz, S., Shim, H., Di Crescenzo, G., Zhang, T.: VDTLS - Providing secure communications in vehicle networks. In: INFOCOM Workshops 2008, Phoenix, AZ, USA. IEEE (2008). https://doi.org/10.1109/infocom.2008.4544651

7. Stading, T.: Secure Communication in a Distributed System Using Identity Based Encryption. In: CCGRID Third IEEE/ACM International Symposium on Cluster Computing and the Grid, Tokyo, Japan. IEEE (2003). https://doi.org/10.1109/ccgrid.2003.1199395

8. Li, L., et al.: A networking identity authentication scheme combining fingerprint coding and identity based encryption. In: Intelligence and Security Informatics, New Brunswick, USA, pp. 129–132. IEEE (2007). https://doi.org/10.1109/isi.2007.379545

9. Jia, C., Liao, Y., Chen, K.: Secure encryption in wireless sensor network. In: 4th International Conference on Wireless Communications, Networking and Mobile Computing, China, pp. 1–4. IEEE, October 2008. https://doi.org/10.1109/wicom.2008.870

10. Yang, G., Rong, C., Veigner, C., Wang, J., Cheng, H.: Identity-based key agreement and encryption for wireless sensor network. IJCSNS Int. J. Comput. Sci. Netw. Secur. **13**, 54–60 (2006). https://doi.org/10.1016/s1005-8885(07)60034-x

11. Khan, M., Niemi, V.: Privacy enhanced fast mutual authentication in 5G network using identity based encryption. J. ICT **5**, 69–90 (2017). https://doi.org/10.13052/jicts2245-800x.514

12. Haque, M.S., Chowdhury, M.U.: A new cyber security framework towards secure data communication for Unmanned Aerial Vehicle (UAV). In: Lin, X., Ghorbani, A., Ren, K., Zhu, S., Zhang, A. (eds.) SecureComm 2017. LNICST, vol. 239, pp. 113–122. Springer, Cham (2018). https://doi.org/10.1007/978-3-319-78816-6_9

13. Szczechowiak, P., Collier, M.: Tiny IBE: identity-based encryption for heterogeneous sensor networks. In: International Conference on Intelligent Sensors, Sensor Networks and Information Processing (ISSNIP), Melbourne, VIC, Australia, pp. 349–354, 7–10 December 2009. https://doi.org/10.1109/issnip.2009.5416743

14. Adiga, B.S., Balamuralidhar, P., Rajan, M.A., Shastry, R., Shivraj, V.L.: An identity based encryption using elliptic curve cryptography for secure M2M communication. In: SecurIT 12 Proceedings of the First International Conference on Security of Internet of Things, Kollam, India, pp. 68–74, August 2012. https://doi.org/10.1145/2490428.2490438

15. Anggorojati, B., Prasad, R.: Securing communication in inter domains Internet of Things using identity-based cryptography. In: 2017 International Workshop on Big Data and Information Security (IWBIS), Jakarta, Indonesia, pp. 137–142. IEEE, September 2017. https://doi.org/10.1109/iwbis.2017.8275115

16. Boneh, D., Franklin, M.: Identity-based encryption from the weil pairing. In: Kilian, J. (ed.) CRYPTO 2001. LNCS, vol. 2139, pp. 213–229. Springer, Heidelberg (2001). https://doi.org/10.1007/3-540-44647-8_13

17. Martin, L., Appenzeller, G., Schertler, M.: RFC5408 - Identity-Based Encryption Architecture and Supporting, Network Working Group (2009)

18. Galbraith, S.D., Harrison, K., Soldera, D.: Implementing the Tate pairing. In: Fieker, C., Kohel, D.R. (eds.) ANTS 2002. LNCS, vol. 2369, pp. 324–337. Springer, Heidelberg (2002). https://doi.org/10.1007/3-540-45455-1_26

19. Challener, D., Yoder, K., Catherman, R., et al.: A practical Guide to Trusted Computing. IBM Press (2008)

20. AVISPA. Automated validation of internet security protocols and applications. http://www.avispa-project.org/. Accessed Nov 2015

Detection of Application-Layer Tunnels with Rules and Machine Learning

Huaqing Lin[1], Gao Liu[1], and Zheng Yan[1,2(✉)] (iD)

[1] State Key Lab of ISN, School of Cyber Engineering,
Xidian University, Xi'an 710071, China
answer3lin@qq.com, 986976804@qq.com zyan@xidian.edu.cn
[2] Department of Communications and Networking,
Aalto University, 02150 Espoo, Finland

Abstract. Application-layer tunnels are often used to construct covert channels in order to transmit secret data, which is often applied to raise network threats in recent years. Detection of application-layer tunnels can assist identifying a variety of network threats, thus has high research significance. In this paper, we explore application-layer tunnel detection and propose a generic detection method by applying both rules and machine learning. Our detection method mainly consists of two parts: rule-based domain name filtering for Domain Generation Algorithm (DGA) based on a trigram model and a machine learning model based on our proposed generic feature extraction framework for tunnel detection. The rule-based DGA domain name filtering can eliminate some obvious tunnels in order to reduce the amount of data processed by machine learning-based detection, thereby, the detection efficiency can be improved. The generic feature extraction framework comprehensively integrates previous research results by combining multiple detection methods, supporting multiple layers and performing multiple feature extraction. We take the three most common application-layer tunnels, i.e., DNS tunnel, HTTP tunnel and HTTPS tunnel as examples to analyze and test our detection method. The experimental results show that the proposed method is generic and efficient, compared with other existing approaches.

Keywords: Application-layer tunnels detection · Machine learning ·
DGA domain name · Feature extraction

1 Introduction

1.1 Background

Current networks are becoming more and more complex and easy to suffer from various network attacks. Many typical attacks, such as Trojan, Botnet, and Advanced Persistent Threat (APT) need to establish Command & Control (C&C) communication channels in order to hack a target network system. Therefore, it is possible to analyze and detect these threats during network communication phase for the purpose of blocking the communication process of network threats in real time and protecting the network system. In order to avoid being identified, attackers usually build a covert

© Springer Nature Switzerland AG 2019
G. Wang et al. (Eds.): SpaCCS 2019, LNCS 11611, pp. 441–455, 2019.
https://doi.org/10.1007/978-3-030-24907-6_33

channel in the form of an application-layer tunnel to implement C&C communications. Therefore, many kinds of network threats can be detected by identifying application-layer tunnels [1].

The application-layer tunnel refers to encapsulating data packets of a protocol into the payload of the data packets of an application layer protocol and is in a form of "Protocol over Protocol" [2–4]. We refer to the outer protocol data packet carrying the data as delivery packet and the protocol data packet carried in the inner layer of the delivery packet as payload packet. Due to the superiority of tunneling technology in secure transmission, protocol compatibility, firewall penetration, etc., the application-layer tunnel is often used to construct covert channels to transmit secret data. As shown in Fig. 1, a threat disguises as a normal application layer protocol to bypass security control policies of a firewall or an Intrusion Detection System (IDS) in order to carry arbitrary data in and out of an internal network. A malicious application-layer tunnel is a kind of network covert channels that assist attackers to communicate with intruded hosts in the Intranet [3–5], realize malicious remote access [3, 4, 6]; and steal traffic [5]. In recent years, more and more network threats used the application-layer tunnels to construct covert channels for covert communications, including C&C, desktop control, stealing private data and transmitting secret files.

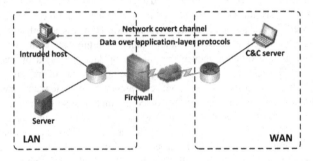

Fig. 1. The threat model of application-layer tunnels.

1.2   Three Methods of Tunnel Detection

The high communication traffic volume of application layer protocol and complicated business and services cause challenges to application layer tunnel detection. There are three detection methods in the current literature: feature signature-based detection [9], protocol anomaly-based detection [2, 6, 7, 9] and behavior statistics-based detection [2–6, 8–15]. The feature signature-based detection method is to detect tunnels by building a signature library and matching signatures in protocol data. This method suffers from a high false positive rate and low efficiency. In addition, this method cannot work on encrypted tunnels. The protocol anomaly-based detection method detects the tunnels by analyzing whether the communication data conform to the standard of normal network protocol. However, with the development of protocol camouflage technology, the identification rate of protocol anomaly-based detection becomes low. The behavior statistics-based detection method is widely studied, which detects tunnels by analyzing the behavior of network communication data. However, this method has some disadvantages caused by behavior analysis difficulty, complex modeling and poor real-time performance. With the continuous enrichment of network services and the increasing complexity of network protocols, it is difficult for a single detection method to achieve high accuracy and low false positive rate. Therefore, we propose to integrate the advantages of these three kinds of detection methods to efficiently and comprehensively detect application-layer tunnels.

1.3   Rules and Machine Learning

Early intrusion detection methods employ anomaly detection or misuse detection for extracting rules to detect threats, intrusions and attacks. The rule-based detection method is simple to implement and is very useful for identifying obvious anomalies. However, it is difficult to describe complex attack modes. When the rules are complex, rule conflict issues might appear. In recent years, with the development of artificial intelligence, the application of machine learning and deep learning to network security has become a hot topic [16, 17]. Machine learning based detection can learn the features of normal and malicious samples [22]. It can combine the advantages of detection and misuse detection to achieve high detection accuracy. The simple modeling of machine learning saves a lot of time and manpower. Moreover, it can describe high-dimensional features and mine potential association rules. However, its disadvantage is that modeling requires a large-scale labeled dataset, otherwise over-fitting often occurs. Usually, rules and machine learning were used separately, but we try to make use of the advantages of these two methods for detecting application-layer tunnels efficiently and accurately. Concretely, simple rules are used to filter obvious tunnels, thus improving the detection efficiency and real-time performance. The machine learning model can be applied to detect complex tunnels, thus ensuring high detection accuracy. Therefore, an efficient and accurate tunnels detection method can be proposed based on the above idea.

1.4   Contributions

In order to overcome the shortcomings of existing work, we propose a method to efficiently, comprehensively, and accurately detect application layer tunnels by applying both rules and machine learning. It consists of two parts, namely rule-based DGA domain name filtering and machine learning based on our proposed feature extraction framework for tunnel detection. When the domain name adopted by the communication data does not satisfy the DGA domain name filtering rule, these data are blocked directly. Otherwise, a machine learning model will be used to further analyze them. Specifically, the contributions of this paper can be summarized as follows:

- We propose an application-layer tunnel detection method by applying rules and machine learning. We employ a trigram model to design rule-based DGA domain name filtering, which can identify tunnels with obvious features for reducing the amount of data for machine learning-based detection. We further propose a generic feature extraction framework by combining multiple machine learning detection methods, supporting network layer, transport layer and application layer and performing multiple statistical and security-related features extraction for tunnel detection.

- We test the effectiveness of the proposed method by conducting experiments on common Domain Name System (DNS), Hyper Text Transfer Protocol (HTTP) and Hypertext Transfer Protocol Secure (HTTPS) tunnels. Experimental results show that our proposed method is more generic and efficient compared with other existing works.

The rest of the paper is organized as follows. Section 2 gives a brief review of related work on application-layer tunnel detection. We provide detailed design of our detection method in Sect. 3. In Sect. 4, we evaluate and analyze the proposed method. Conclusions and future work are presented in the last section.

2 Related Work

Many related works only extract the statistical features of data packets behavior in network and transport layers [3, 4, 8, 10–15, 23]. The advantages of this kind of methods are easy to implement, high efficiency and can be applied into various tunnel detection. However, due to the lack of application layer features, their detection accuracy is low. On the contrary, the accuracy of feature extraction in application layer is high, but it also suffers from some other problems [2, 5–7, 9]. For example, Borders et al. [2] proposed an HTTP tunnel detection method named Web Tap to detect HTTP tunnels by analyzing application layer data content features and behavioral features. Its accuracy is high, but its real-time performance is poor and this method is not generic. Qi et al. [7] analyzed domain names in DNS packets based on a bigram model to detect DNS tunnels in real time. This method has low computational complexity and does not need flow recombination, so that it has high real-time performance. But when the character frequency of some normal domain names does not follow the Zipf's law, it easily produces false positive rate. Liu et al. [9] extracted four kinds of 18 features from the content and behavior of DNS tunnel traffic by considering network, transport and application layers in order to achieve a high detection accuracy. However, this method uses n query/response pairs to form a window as an analysis unit, which results in a large detection delay.

3 Proposed Detection Method

We combine the feature signature-based detection method, the protocol anomaly-based detection method and the behavior statistics-based detection method and use machine learning and rules to analyze the collected data to identify the application-layer tunnels for preventing unauthorized data transmission. As shown in Fig. 2, the proposed application-layer tunnel detection method includes five modules: (1) data collection module. This module is responsible for collecting communication data for subsequent

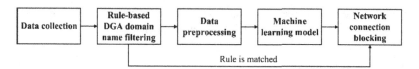

Fig. 2. Application-layer tunnel detection method.

analysis; (2) rule-based DGA domain name filtering module. This module first extracts the domain name from the communication data and then matches the domain name with the proposed filtering rule. If the matching is successful, a network connection blocking module will be notified to block the connection. Otherwise, the data will be transmitted to a data preprocessing module for further analysis; (3) data preprocessing module. This module is responsible for performing feature construction and feature extraction in order to process communication data to transfer them into the data format required by a machine learning model; (4) machine learning module. This module can classify the communication data to detect whether there is an application layer tunnel. When a tunnel is identified, the network connection blocking module is notified to block the network connection; (5) network connection blocking module. This module can cut off the network connection and block data transmission.

3.1   Data Collection

The first step in the proposed detection method is to collect data. After obtaining normal data and malicious data, we can further analyze the data and detect threats, intrusions, or attacks. In our study, normal network traffic data are collected through port mirroring in our university campus network. Because we mainly focus on DNS, HTTP and HTTPS tunnels as detection examples, we only need to collect their corresponding data. DNS, HTTP and HTTPS tunnel data are all collected in the university campus network and VPS (Virtual Private Server). Malicious tunnel communication data were simulated by applying some tunnel tools as listed in Table 1. As shown in Table 1, we collected 727052 DNS tunnel sessions by three DNS tunneling tools, 43442 HTTP tunnel sessions by five HTTP tunneling tools and 16129 HTTPS tunnel sessions by three HTTPS tunneling tools. The payload protocols over application-layer

Table 1. Application-layer tunnel data collection.

Delivery protocol	Tunnel tool	Payload protocol	Dataset size (sessions)
DNS	dns2tcp, dnscat2, iodine	Shell (SSH), Data (SSH), Chat (Ncat), Shell (Ncat), Reverse shell (Ncat), Data (Ncat), RDP	727,052
HTTP	ABPTTS, Httptunnel, reDuh, reGeorg, Tunna		43,442
HTTPS	Stunnel, Ghostunnel, Meterpreter		16,129

tunnels include remote access protocol, reverse remote access protocol, data transfer protocol, chat protocol and Remote Desktop Protocol (RDP).

3.2   Rule-Based Detection

We design a rule to efficiently and accurately detect some application-layer tunnels with obvious features for reducing the amount of data needed for machine learning based detection. This filtering rule can be applied to most application-layer tunnels, thus having generality. DGA is a technical mean of generating C&C server domain names by creating random characters. It can bypass the detection of domain name blacklists by generating a large number of random domain names [18, 19]. DGA based communication connection is flexible because attackers can change the domain name of C&C server through DGA to effectively avoid the detection based on domain name blacklist. This attack technology is applied to a variety of network threats, such as XShellGhost and CryptoLocker. DGA is also paired with application-layer tunnels to achieve higher concealment. DNS, HTTP and HTTPS tunnels often generate C&C server domain names through DGA to implement C&C communications. Therefore, we can identify DGA domain names to filter application-layer tunnels with obvious domain name characteristics.

In order to design an efficient DGA filtering rule, we do not consider deep learning models such as CNN and LSTM [19], but test the classification performance of DGA domain names by means of information entropy, bigram model and trigram model. The test dataset is comprised of Alexa global traffic top 1 million website [20] and 1164838 DGA domain names from 360 Netlab [21]. The experimental results show that the trigram model has the best classification performance for DGA domain names, as shown in Fig. 3. Generally speaking, if the accuracy of classification can reach 99.9% in a production environment, it can meet demands. Therefore, in order to meet the accuracy requirement, we choose −3 as the average logarithmic probability threshold of trigram model. In this case, the precision, recall and false positive rate are 0.99903, 0.33973 and 0.000383, respectively. That is to say, by adopting this rule, we can directly filter 33.973% of the application-layer tunnels, which greatly reduces the data preprocessing and prediction time of machine learning-based detection and saves computing resources. At the same time, the proposed rule can directly analyze and

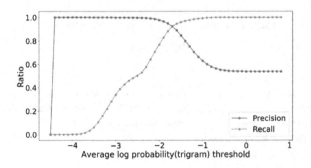

Fig. 3. Classification result of DGA domain names with trigram model.

detect tunnels without reassembling packets and constructing analysis units (flows), thus improving the real-time performance of detection.

3.3 Machine Learning Model Construction

Generic Feature Extraction Framework. In order to construct a machine learning model that can detect multiple application-level tunnels, we first propose a generic feature extraction framework. Through the analysis of Sect. 1.2, we found that the existing three tunnel detection methods have their own problems. Moreover, many related works mainly extract some statistical features from the network and transport layers and rarely extract security-related features from the application layer. In fact, these are the most discriminative features that affect the accuracy of tunnel detection. Therefore, we combine feature signature-based detection, protocol anomaly-based detection and behavior statistical-based detection to design a generic feature extraction framework that can extract security-related features and statistical features from the network, transport and application layers. As shown in Table 2, we introduce the proposed framework in detail according to different detection methods.

Table 2. A generic feature extraction framework for application-layer tunnel detection.

Detection method			Protocol layer	Direction	Export value
Behavior statistics	Length	Absolute length	Network layer	Upstream	Max
		Relative length			Min
	Time	Relative time	Transport layer		Mean
	Count	Absolute count	Application layer	Downstream	Variance
		Relative count			Sum
Feature signature	Key fields of request data header				
	Key fields of response data header				
Protocol anomaly	Protocol request data anomaly				
	Protocol response data anomaly				
	Protocol interaction anomaly				

Feature Signature Based Detection Method. Different from traditional feature signature-based detection methods, we do not consider payload data here and do not need to build a signature library. The advantage of this modification is to solve the issue of payload data encryption and preserve user privacy, and to especially improve the detection efficiency. That is, in this method, we only record the key fields of application layer protocol header, including request and response (e.g., flag and TTL in DNS packets).

Protocol Anomaly Based Detection Method. In this method, we take the request, response and interaction anomalies of the request and response as features. The request anomaly mainly refers to whether the fields of protocol request data have a match error. The response anomaly mainly refers to whether the fields of protocol response data have a match error. The protocol interaction anomaly refers to whether the response data satisfy the request made in the request data. For example, when the record of DNS response packet is A, the resource data should be IPv4. Otherwise, an anomaly is triggered.

Behavior Statistics Based Detection Method. Behavior statistics-based detection method is studied widely and many related works only extract the features related to the behavior of data packets. Behavior statistics related features include packet size (length), arrival time and number (count). The size and number include absolute value and relative value. However, the absolute value of time is meaningless for detection, and thus only the relative value of time is considered. Absolute value refers to the value of the data itself while the relative value refers to the correlation among these values. Additionally, the features are extracted from an application layer in addition to network and transport layers. Moreover, the data packets are upstream and downstream. Basically, each feature can derive five values: maximum, minimum, mean, variance and sum.

Application-Layer Tunnel Detection Model Construction

DNS Tunnel Detection Model. First, we reassemble DNS packets into sessions. We define a DNS session as a query with a corresponding response. Based on the proposed generic feature extraction framework, we then extract 36 features for the DNS tunnel. Finally, a tree model based feature selection method is used to select 25 feature subsets to construct a DNS tunnel detection model.

HTTP Tunnel Detection Model. First, we reassemble HTTP packets into sessions. We define an HTTP session as a TCP stream that is divided by a 5-tuple (source IP, destination IP, source port, destination port and protocol type). Based on the proposed generic feature extraction framework, we then extract 79 features for the HTTP tunnel. Finally, a tree model based feature selection method is used to select 32 feature subsets for constructing the HTTP tunnel detection model.

HTTPS Tunnel Detection Model. First, we reassemble HTTPS packets into sessions. The definition of an HTTPS session is the same as the HTTP session that consists of a TCP stream. Based on the proposed generic feature extraction framework, we then extract 72 features for the HTTPS tunnel. Finally, a tree model based feature selection method is used to select 30 feature subsets for constructing the HTTPS tunnel detection model.

4 Experimental Results and Analysis

4.1 Machine Learning Model Evaluation

DNS Tunnel Detection Model Evaluation

Comparison of Different Classification Algorithms. First, we used six common machine learning algorithms to test DNS tunnel classification performance, including Gaussian Bayesian, Gaussian kernel SVM, C4.5 decision tree, random forest, GBDT and XGboost. As shown in Table 3, we can find that the classification results of the five machine learning algorithms except Gauss Bayes are very good.

Table 3. Performance comparison of different classification algorithms for DNS tunnel detection.

Classification algorithms	Precision	Recall	Accuracy	F1 score	Training time/s	Testing time/s
Gaussian Bayes	0.73423	1.0	1.0	0.84513	1.6674	1.1981
SVM	0.99999	0.99836	0.99836	0.99917	194.5913	43.7776
C4.5	0.99999	0.9992	0.9992	0.9996	10.3534	0.5064
Random forest	1.0	0.99966	0.99966	0.99983	8.4319	0.9932
GBDT	0.99999	0.999	0.999	0.99949	487.3548	1.4265
XGboost	1.0	0.99981	0.99981	0.9999	50.3657	0.7284

Comparison of Our DNS Tunnel Detection with Related Work. Due to the different test datasets used in different papers, the experimental results in multiple papers are not comparable. Therefore, in order to further test the performance of our proposed method, we implemented three existing detection methods and compared them with our proposed method based on the collected datasets. The comparison results of our DNS tunnel detection model based on random forest and behavior-based detection model in [9] are shown in Fig. 4. The behavior-based DNS tunnel detection model extracts 18 features. In the experiment, the window size is set to 5 and SVM with the best performance was selected as the modeling algorithm. As depicted in Fig. 4, we can see that our feature extraction framework based DNS tunnel detection model offers higher detection accuracy, consumes less time and has better real-time performance compared with the model in [9]. The window size of behavior-based DNS tunnel detection model in [9] is set to 5, which suggests its detection delay is 5 times of that of our proposed detection model because our proposed model only processes a DNS session but the model in [9] needs to process 5 sessions in a window. Based on the same dataset, our model needs to process five times as much data as the model in [9] does and the feature

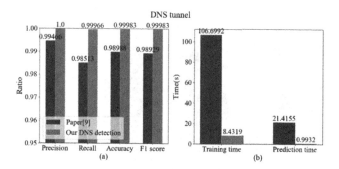

Fig. 4. Comparison of our DNS tunnel detection with the detection in [9].

dimension of our model is higher. However, the processing performance of random forest is better than SVM, so that the computation time of our model is shorter than [9].

HTTP Tunnel Detection Evaluation

Comparison of Different Classification Algorithms. As shown in Table 4, we can find that the classification results of the five machine learning algorithms except Gauss Bayes are very good.

Table 4. Performance comparison of different classification algorithms for HTTP tunnel detection.

Classification algorithms	Precision	Recall	Accuracy	F1 score	Training time/s	Testing time/s
Gaussian Bayes	0.5404	0.99414	0.5743	0.70018	0.7186	0.4912
SVM	0.97279	0.98712	0.97976	0.9799	11130.3015	396.2684
C4.5	0.99884	0.99894	0.99889	0.99889	8.733	0.1173
Random forest	0.99939	0.9985	0.99895	0.99895	3.9287	0.7579
GBDT	0.99615	0.99331	0.99474	0.99473	251.1598	0.5194
XGboost	0.9931	0.99471	0.99389	0.9939	18.7661	0.2602

Comparison of Our HTTP Tunnel Detection with Related Work. In order to further test the performance of our proposed method, we implemented HTTP tunnel detection model based on statistical features in [10] and compared it with our proposed random forest based HTTP tunnel detection model based on the collected datasets. The comparison results of these two HTTP tunnel detection models are shown in Fig. 5. The statistical features based detection model selects 21 features and uses C4.5 decision tree as the modeling algorithm. As described in Fig. 5, we can see that our proposed HTTP tunnel detection model has higher detection accuracy compared with the model in [10]. This is because we extract security-related features from the application layer while the model in [10] only consider the features from the network and transport layers.

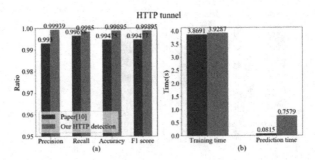

Fig. 5. Comparison of our HTTP tunnel detection with the detection in [10].

However, the prediction time of our detection model is a bit longer, since C4.5 decision tree is faster than random forest.

HTTPS Tunnel Detection Model Evaluation

Comparison of Different Classification Algorithms. As shown in Table 5, we can find that the classification results of the five machine learning algorithms except Gauss Bayes are very good.

Table 5. Performance comparison of different classification algorithms for HTTPS tunnel detection.

Classification algorithms	Precision	Recall	Accuracy	F1 score	Training time/s	Testing time/s
Gaussian Bayes	0.89127	0.73891	0.77196	0.77078	0.0607	0.0741
SVM	0.99377	0.99729	0.99551	0.99552	11.2404	3.2969
C4.5	0.99879	0.99912	0.99895	0.99895	0.9605	0.0152
Random forest	0.99938	0.99949	0.99943	0.99943	0.8882	0.6313
GBDT	0.99831	0.99904	0.99867	0.99867	23.588	0.0687
XGboost	0.99873	0.99932	0.99902	0.99903	3.1652	0.0595

Comparison of Our HTTPS Tunnel Detection with Related Work. In order to further test the performance of our proposed method, we implemented HTTPS tunnel detection model in [15] and compared them with our random forest based HTTPS tunnel detection model based on the collected datasets. The model in [15] selects 10 features and also use random forest as the modeling algorithm. As shown in Fig. 6, we can see that our HTTPS tunnel detection model has higher detection accuracy compared with the model in [15]. This is because we extract security-related features from the application layer while the model in [15] only considers the features from the network and transport layers. Since this method also uses random forest as the modeling algorithm, the training and prediction time of the two models is similar.

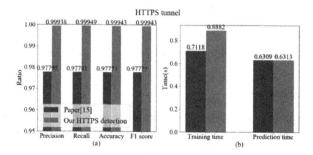

Fig. 6. Comparison of our HTTPS tunnel detection with the detection in [15].

4.2 Evaluation on DGA Filtering Rule

In addition to the above test metrics related to the machine learning model, we should also test whether the detection efficiency of the proposed detection method is improved after adding the DGA filtering rule. We only analyzed the effectiveness of the proposed DGA filtering rule by comparing the time taken before and after applying the DGA filtering rule.

Recall that applying the DGA filtering rule can detect 0.33973 black samples when the precision and false positive rate are 0.99903 and 0.000383 respectively. In other words, while meeting the requirements of high precision and low false positive rate, we can directly eliminate 0.33973 application-layer tunnels after adding the DGA filtering rule. The preprocessing time and prediction time of each session of DNS, HTTP and HTTPS tunnel detection models is shown in Table 6 and the DGA filtering rule takes 0.04853 ms (millisecond) to compute each domain name. The time consumption taken before and after applying the DGA filtering rule is shown in Fig. 7. We can see that the efficiency with regard to detection time of the proposed method for detecting DNS, HTTP and HTTPS tunnels is improved by applying the DGA filtering rule.

Table 6. Preprocessing and prediction time of three tunnel detection models.

Detection model	Single sample preprocessing time (ms)	Single sample prediction time (ms)
DNS tunnel	10.154624649468178	0.00125437832283
HTTP tunnel	3.007999029759786	0.00162138299147
HTTPS tunnel	44.167038655595921	0.00107835463776

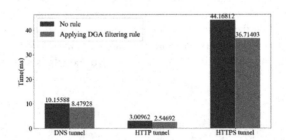

Fig. 7. Time taken before and after applying the DGA filtering rule.

4.3 Further Discussion

In summary, the proposed method has the following advantages. **High efficiency.** The designed DGA domain name filtering rule can effectively identify some tunnels with obvious domain name features, thereby reducing the amount of data used for machine learning and improving detection efficiency. In addition, by optimizing the feature signature-based detection method, we do not process and analyze the protocol payload data for further improving detection efficiency. **Generality.** Our method can be applied to detect most tunnels based on application layer protocols. **Real-time.** In this paper, a DGA filtering rule is designed to avoid the recombination of some network sessions, thus improve the response speed of tunnel detection. Of course, in order to achieve high detection accuracy, it is necessary to reassemble a network session in the step of machine learning-based detection. **High accuracy and low false positive rate.** Compared with the existing work, the proposed generic feature extraction framework achieves high accuracy and low false positive rate. **Resistance against bypassing attack.** The feature extraction of detection method is based on the generic feature extraction framework and extracts features from multiple perspectives. Thus, it is difficult for an attacker to spoof the detection. **Resistance against encryption issue.** In the proposed method, we do not analyze protocol payload data, but only analyze the protocol header and communication behaviors. Therefore, we can deal with the network data whose payload is encrypted. **Privacy preservation.** Without analyzing and processing the protocol payload data, the privacy leakage of protocol payload is avoided and the availability of this method is improved.

The shortcoming of this work is that the experimental data is collected in the campus network, i.e., the proposed method is not tested in the actual production environment.

5 Conclusion

The application-layer tunnel is one of the main means of communications for network threats in recent years. In order to detect network threats and block their communication connections, we studied the application-layer tunnel detection methods and proposed a comprehensive detection method based on rules and machine learning. We first applied the DGA domain name filtering rule to eliminate the application layer tunnels with obvious domain name features for reducing the amount of data needed by the subsequent machine learning-based detection in order to improve detection efficiency and support real-time detection. For ensuring detection accuracy, machine learning-based detection is further applied with the support of a feature extraction framework. Concretely, we constructed DNS, HTTP and HTTPS tunnel detection models as examples to evaluate our method. Experiments showed that it is a generic framework with high accuracy and low false positive rate. In the future, we plan to extend the proposed method to other types of application-layer tunnels and deploy it in practice.

Acknowledgements. This work is sponsored by the National Key Research and Development Program of China (Grant 2016YFB0800700), the National Natural Science Foundation of China (Grants 61672410 and U1536202), the Academy of Finland (Grants 308087 and 314203), the open grant of the Tactical Data Link Lab of the 20th Research Institute of China Electronics Technology Group Corporation (grant No. CLDL-20182119), the Key Lab of Information Network Security, Ministry of Public Security (Grant C18614).

References

1. Nuojua, V., David, G., Hämäläinen, T.: DNS tunneling detection techniques – classification, and theoretical comparison in case of a real APT campaign. In: Galinina, O., Andreev, S., Balandin, S., Koucheryavy, Y. (eds.) NEW2AN/ruSMART/NsCC 2017. LNCS, vol. 10531, pp. 280–291. Springer, Cham (2017). https://doi.org/10.1007/978-3-319-67380-6_26

2. Borders, K., Prakash, A.: Web tap: detecting covert web traffic. In: Proceedings of the 11th ACM Conference on Computer and Communications Security, pp. 110–120. ACM, New York (2004)

3. Crotti, M., Dusi, M., Gringoli, F., Salgarelli, L.: Detecting http tunnels with statistical mechanisms. In: 2007 IEEE International Conference on Communications, Glasgow, pp. 6162–6168. IEEE (2007)

4. Dusi, M., Crotti, M., Gringoli, F., Salgarelli, L.: Tunnel hunter: detecting application-layer tunnels with statistical fingerprinting. Comput. Netw. 53(1), 81–97 (2009)

5. Do, V.T., Engelstad, P., Feng, B., van Do, T.: Detection of DNS tunneling in mobile networks using machine learning. In: Kim, K., Joukov, N. (eds.) ICISA 2017. LNEE, vol. 424, pp. 221–230. Springer, Singapore (2017). https://doi.org/10.1007/978-981-10-4154-9_26

6. Almusawi, A., Amintoosi, H.: DNS Tunneling detection method based on multilabel support vector machine. In: Security and Communication Networks 2018 (2018)

7. Qi, C., Chen, X., Xu, C., Shi, J., Liu, P.: A bigram based real time DNS tunnel detection approach. Procedia Comput. Sci. 17, 852–860 (2013)

8. Aiello, M., Mongelli, M., Papaleo, G.: DNS tunneling detection through statistical fingerprints of protocol messages and machine learning. Int. J. Commun. Syst. 28(14), 1987–2002 (2015)

9. Liu, J., Li, S., Zhang, Y., Xiao, J., Chang, P., Peng, C.: Detecting DNS tunnel through binary-classification based on behavior features. In: IEEE Trustcom/BigDataSE/ICESS, Sydney, pp. 339–346. IEEE (2017)

10. Ding, Y.J., Cai, W.D.: A method for HTTP-tunnel detection based on statistical features of traffic. In: 2011 IEEE 3rd International Conference on Communication Software and Networks, Xi'an, pp. 247–250. IEEE (2011)

11. Piraisoody, G., Huang, C., Nandy, B., Seddigh, N.: Classification of applications in HTTP tunnels. In: 2013 IEEE 2nd International Conference on Cloud Networking (CloudNet), San Francisco, pp. 67–74. IEEE (2013)

12. Li, S., Yun, X., Zhang, Y.: Anomaly-based model for detecting HTTP-tunnel traffic using network behavior analysis. High Technol. Lett. 20(1), 63–69 (2014)

13. Mujtaba, G., Parish, D.J.: Detection of applications within encrypted tunnels using packet size distributions. In: 2009 International Conference for Internet Technology and Secured Transactions (ICITST), London, pp. 1–6. IEEE (2009)

14. Wang, F., Huang, L., Chen, Z., Miao, H., Yang, W.: A novel web tunnel detection method based on protocol behaviors. In: Zia, T., Zomaya, A., Varadharajan, V., Mao, M. (eds.) SecureComm 2013. LNICST, vol. 127, pp. 234–251. Springer, Cham (2013). https://doi.org/10.1007/978-3-319-04283-1_15

15. Allard, F., Dubois, R., Gompel, P., Morel, M.: Tunneling activities detection using machine learning techniques. J. Telecommun. Inf. Technol. 2011(1), 37–42 (2011)

16. Buczak, A.L., Guven, E.: A survey of data mining and machine learning methods for cyber security intrusion detection. IEEE Commun. Surv. Tutor. 18(2), 1153–1176 (2016)

17. Mishra, P., Varadharajan, V., Tupakula, U., Pilli, E.S.: A detailed investigation and analysis of using machine learning techniques for intrusion detection. IEEE Commun. Surv. Tutor. **21**(1), 686–728 (2018)
18. Wang, T.S., Lin, H.T., Cheng, W.T., Chen, C.Y.: DBod: Clustering and detecting DGA-based botnets using DNS traffic analysis. Comput. Secur. **64**, 1–15 (2017)
19. Khehra, G., Sofat, S.: BotScoop: scalable detection of DGA based botnets using DNS traffic. In: 2018 9th International Conference on Computing, Communication and Networking Technologies (ICCCNT), Bangalore, pp. 1–6. IEEE (2018)
20. Alexa Top 1 Million Sites. http://www.alexa.com/topsites. Accessed 20 Jan 2019
21. 360 Netlab Open Data DGA. https://data.netlab.360.com/dga/. Accessed 20 Jan 2019
22. Jing, X., Yan, Z., Pedrycz, W.: Security data collection and data analytics in the Internet: a survey. IEEE Commun. Surv. Tutor. **21**(1), 586–618 (2019)
23. Lin, H., Yan, Z., Fu, Y.: Adaptive security-related data collection with context awareness. J. Netw. Comput. Appl. **126**, 88–103 (2019)

An Anonymous Protocol for Member Privacy in a Consortium Blockchain

Gyeong-Jin Ra[1], Daehee Seo[2], Md Zakirul Alam Bhuiyan[3],
and Im-Yeong Lee[1($\boxtimes$)]

[1] Department of Computer Science and Engineering,
Soonchunhyang University, Asan-si 31538, Republic of Korea
{rababi, imylee}@sch.ac.kr
[2] Department of Computer Science, Kennesaw State University,
Marietta, GA, USA
dseol@kennesaw.edu
[3] Department of Computer Science and Information Sciences,
Fordham University, Bronx, NY 10458, USA
m.bhuiyan.dr@ieee.org

Abstract. A consortium blockchain is that multiple groups of authorized members that share one ledger. Transaction validation and membership authentication are executed by trusted nodes which create and store full block (a.k.a full node). Other lightweight nodes which stored only header block request validating transaction to full node. Therefore, because the lightweight node requesting of validation transaction and sharing ledger of members between groups in consortium blockchain creates a privacy problem. In this paper, we propose an anonymous protocol based on a credential system for privacy in a consortium blockchain. This solves the problem of computation overhead and privacy in the consortium blockchain.

Keywords: Consortium blockchain · Anonymous credential system ·
Blind signature · Multi-Bloom filter · Anonymous identity

1 Introduction

Recently, with the emergence of bitcoin, the blockchain only is appended transaction and is shared by all participants as a distributed ledger [1]. Therefore, it provides strong integrity and reliability from forgery and tampering without central organization so it has been attracting attention. The blockchain consists of a public blockchain, which can be joined by anyone and permission blockchain in which only authorized members can participate. The permission blockchain is divided into 2 types, one a private blockchain is trusted one node joined multiple users and the other consortium blockchain is unioned multiple private blockchain like a group. Among them, a consortium blockchain that multiple groups of authorized members share one ledger. Transaction validation and membership authentication are executed by trusted some nodes which create and store full block (a.k.a full node). Other lightweight nodes which stored only header block request validating transaction to full nodes. Therefore, because of the lightweight

G. Wang et al. (Eds.): SpaCCS 2019, LNCS 11611, pp. 456–464, 2019.
https://doi.org/10.1007/978-3-030-24907-6_34

node requesting of validation transaction and sharing ledger of members between groups in consortium blockchain creates a privacy problem.

2 Related Work

The blockchain is a one ledger system with all the same records based on a distributed network. It solves the single point of failure of the existing database system, minimizes the middle man, and provides transparency and reliability. However, the availability of the blockchain has a tradeoff between privacy. Privacy means the ability of an individual or a group to selectively express information hiding about himself or herself. However, anonymity is derived from Greek and means "no name" or "no related name" [2]. Thus, anonymity is a part of privacy meaning that even if a message (transaction) is disclosed in the blockchain, the public key is not associated with the person's off chain (not digital, related real world) ID [3] or it through a message (or collecting) cannot identify and infer personal identity. For this, unlinkability and untraceability must be satisfied. The former means "No idea where the transactions are going" and the latter means "No idea which funds are spent in Tx1". For this, a common method is "encryption". That is Homomorphic Encryption or Confidential Transaction. Recently, for Anonymity and privacy, the scheme is "Hidden in a crowd" [4]. That is Group Signature and Mixing Service. It mixes the transaction of the member by a trusted server like an anonymous credential system or a combination of multi-signature or blind signature [5]. However, this again causes spoof and privacy problems on the mixing server. Therefore, it can hide through Ring Signature without proxy of the same server as group manager [6]. If we can prove ownership of the secret through a dialog without a key, it can provide anonymity. Zero-Knowledge Proof (ZKP) is applied to Zero coin etc. [7]. Since ZKP was very slow because of interactive Z-Cash is proposed as a non-interactive ZKP [8]. Also, in order to increase the efficiency, off chain storage and on chain can be separated. Here, separated on-off chain storage is the separating roles of data storage (off chain) and data integrity verification (on chain).

3 The Privacy Problem

In this paper, there are two privacy problems that occur in consortium blockchain. First, the server with the SPV and trusted power generates a block and propagates it to the confirmed member [9]. A member has only a block header with a lightweight node. The server has a full node with the header and body of the block. Therefore, the transaction of the member requests verification from the server or the surrounding Full Node. It is often an SPV (Simplified Payment Verification) in a public blockchain [10]. At this time, the disclosure of the transaction creates privacy problems for members. The second is the privacy issue of members when sharing one ledger between groups.

Transaction Validation. We perform validation of the transaction of the member through Multi Bloom Filter. The member receives a transaction pattern from the Full Node through the transaction pattern value of the Bloom Filter, and returns a set of whether or not the transaction includes a merge tree. However, since the overhead is increased by increasing the positive error rate of the Bloom Filter, a hash function and a Multi Bloom Filter using various Bloom Filters are used.

User and Message Authentication. We use anonymous protocols based on Blind Signature and anonymous credentials. The ID of a member can have multiple ID according to the anonymous credit system, and the other groups recognize the user as an ID. The server issues a letter of credit to the user, and the user proves ownership of the letter of credit to the other authority without revealing the identity, indicating that he has successfully authenticated for the first time. Signature of the trusted server guarantees authentication of the members and messages belonging to other groups in the consortium blockchain without disclosing the user's message.

4   Proposed Scheme

We created four phase (see Fig. 1). Client A (signer) generates a signature; a block-chain server generates and issues a certificate from Client A; and a blockchain network (including the blockchain server) transmits that certificate to Client B (verifier), who in turn verifies the signature. The blockchain network creates a global timestamp. At this point, Clients A and B are lightweight nodes possessing only the block header. The block-chain server and blockchain network are full nodes with their own headers and bodies; they engage in mutual verification. Therefore, Clients A and B must verify transactions by secure and efficient recourse to the full nodes.

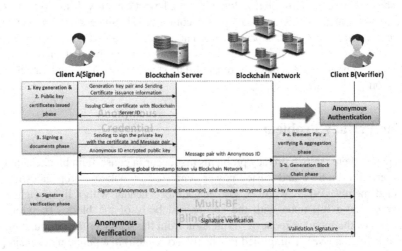

Fig. 1. Our proposed anonymous protocol in a consortium blockchain scenario

4.1   System Parameters

The system parameters of our proposed scheme are shown in Table 1. It includes user, verifier, and server key pair definition and timestamp, operations too.

Table 1. Our proposed system parameters

Parameter	Meaning
H	One-way hash function
E	Elliptic curve on point group
r	Random value $r \in [1.n - 1]$
R	Public random value, $R = r * G$
ID_{SA}	Client A identification private value, $ID_{SA} \in E$
ID_{PA}	Client A identification ID, $ID_{PA} \in E$, $ID_{PA} = ID_{SA} * G$
ID_{SB}	Blockchain server identification private value, $ID_{SB} \in E$
ID_{PB}	Blockchain server identification ID, $ID_{PB} \in E$, $ID_{PB} = ID_{SB} * G$
ID_{SV}	Client B identification private value, $ID_{SV} \in E$
ID_{PV}	Client B identification ID, $ID_{PV} \in E$, $ID_{PV} = ID_{SV} * G$
PK_{Ai}	Client A onetime public key $(1 \leq i \leq n)$, $PK_{Ai} = g_2^{SK_{Ai}}$
SK_{Ai}	Client A onetime private key $(1 \leq i \leq n)$, $SK_{Ai} \leftarrow Z_p$
PK_{Bi}	Blockchain server one time public key $(1 \leq i \leq n)$, $PK_{Bi} = g_2^{SK_{Bi}}$
SK_{Bi}	Blockchain server one time private key $(1 \leq i \leq n)$, $SK_{Bi} \leftarrow Z_p$
M	Client's electronic message
σ_A	Root signature via one time public key
σ_B	Root signature via client certificate information
S_t	Global timestamp token generated by blockchain network's hash tree and block chain
t_0	Client global timestamp creation time
t_n	Client electronic message time value with authentication session key, $t_n = t_0 + i$, $(1 \leq i \leq n)$
MBF	Multi bloom filter operation

4.2   Key Generation and Request Public Key Certificate Phase

In this phase, Client A generates a public/private key via the hash chain and the hash tree issues a public key certificate.

Step 1. Client A generates public key ID_{PA}, private key ID_{SA}, public key for authentication PK_{Ai}, and private key SK_{Ai}.

Step 2. Next, a σ value allowing for public key verification is computed as $P_i = H(r * ID_{PB}) * G + ID_{PA}$, $\sigma_A = \sum_1^n P_i^{SK_{Ai}}$

Step 3. Client A sends certificate information $(ID_{PA}, \sigma, t_0, PK_{Ai})$ to the blockchain server and requests a certificate.

4.3 Public Key Certificate Issuing Phase

Step 1. The blockchain server verifies R using the disposable public key PK_{Ai} of the certificate information sent by client A. Verification is successful if

$$P'_i = H(R * ID_{SB}) * G + ID_{PA}, \ (\sigma, g_2) = \prod_{i=i}^{K} e(P_i, PK_{Ai})$$

$$ID_{SB} * R = ID_{SB} * r * G = ID_{SB} * r \tag{1}$$

$$E(\sigma, g_2) = e\left(P^i, g_2^{SK_{Ai}}\right) = \left(P'_i, PK_{Ai}\right) = OK \tag{2}$$

Step 2. If client A is verified, the blockchain server signs using its own SK_{Bi}.

$$H(r * ID_{PA}) * G + ID_{PB} \tag{3}$$

Step 3. The blockchain server generates certificate signature information on multiple clients using the single signature σ_B.

$$P_i = H(r * ID_{PB}) * G + ID_{PA}, \ \sigma_B = \sum_{1}^{n} P^{iSK_{Bi}} \tag{4}$$

Step 4. The blockchain network and server verify the signature of the server.

$$ID_{SA} * R = ID_{SA} * r * G = ID_{SA} * r \tag{5}$$

$$E(\sigma, g_2) = e\left(P^i, g_2^{SK_{Bi}}\right) = \left(P'_i, PK_{Bi}\right) = OK \tag{6}$$

Step 5. After verification, the blockchain network collects a signature from the blockchain server and manages the certificate as a leaf node of a hash tree.

Step 6. The blockchain server returns certificates $(ID_{PA}, \sigma_A, t_0, PK_{Ai}, ID_{PB}, \sigma_B)$ containing ID and verification (σ_B) data to client A.

Step 7. Client A and the blockchain server verify the certificate including the ID and verification σ_B.

$$ID_{SA} * R = ID_{SA} * r * G = ID_{SA} * r \tag{7}$$

$$E(\sigma, g_2) = e\left(P^i, g_2^{SK_{Bi}}\right) = \left(P'_i, PK_{Bi}\right) = OK \tag{8}$$

4.4 Signing of Documents Phase

In this phase, the public key certificate and the message of Client A are used to sign the blockchain server. The server generates client A' anonymous ID and sends blockchain network include global timestamp is committed blockchain.

Step 1. Client A sends a disposable private key $(ID_{PA}, \sigma_A, t_0, PK_{Ai}, ID_{PB}, \sigma_B)$, SK_{Ai} and SK_{Ai}, along with certificate information, to the blockchain server for authentication and simultaneously creates the pair $x = H(m, SK_{Ai})$ to request a signature.

Step 2. The blockchain server verifies the validity of the public key certificate using the hash tree of the blockchain network after confirming the authenticity of client A with the aid of the disposable private key SK_{Ai} and public key PK_{Ai} $(PK_{Ai} = g_2^{SK_{Ai}})$.

Step 3. The blockchain network generates a global hash tree using the relationship $x = H(m, SK_{Ai})$, and then a global timestamp value S_t, by linking the global coordinated time to the root value.

Step 4. The blockchain network broadcasts client A' anonymous ID to the blockchain server after generating $\text{Token}(S_t, SK_{Bi})$ via internal consensus and returns it to client A.

4.5 Signature Verification Phase

In this phase, after Client A sends a message to Client B, Client B requests the blockchain server to verify the message and authenticate Client A. The clients are lightweight nodes; they do not know the entire content of the transaction. Therefore, the client receives a verification value from a full node (the blockchain server). Privacy is assured via blind signature and use of a multi-Bloom filter.

Step 1. Client A sends his/her public key certificate $(ID_{PA}, \sigma_A, t_0, PK_{Ai}, ID_{PB}, \sigma_B)$, the private key SK_{Ai}, the token (S_t, SK_{Bi}) for the message, and $E(ID_{PV}(M))$ (encrypted using the public key) to the verifier.

Step 2. Client B creates ID_B, S_I, p, PK_B. This is a hash fragment of the client A certificate information and message. S_I consists of the signature, the private key and the public value of client B.

$$S_I = h(S_t, x_i)(h(p) + S_k) \tag{1}$$

Step 3. Client B combines the authentication elements by hashing the values of the user and public key.

$$h_1, \ldots, h_n = h(S_I \| ID_A \| PK_A) \tag{2}$$

Step 4. The separated hash fragments are assigned to filter. Here, rather than using the hash function of the Bloom filter, an arbitrary number of pieces is inserted into the array.

Step 5. Client B sends a multi-Bloom filter value to the blockchain server, requesting verification.

Step 6. The blockchain server sends a signature profile for a blind signature request.

$$U = rh_0(b_r \| p) \tag{3}$$

Step 7. Client B generates Blind Signature.

$$V = (h(p) + S_k)^{-1} U \qquad (4)$$

Step 8. The blockchain server checks the blind signature and returns a transaction path to the multi-Bloom filter.

$$S_R = r^{-1} V$$
$$MBF[h(S_R)...] \qquad (5)$$

5 Analysis of Proposed Scheme

The security analysis of our scheme are summarized in Tables 2. Our scheme is compared other scheme.

Table 2. Comparison of other scheme and proposed scheme

	[11]	[12]	[13]	[14]	Proposed scheme
Authentication/Integrity	Offer	Offer	Offer	Offer	**Offer**
Non-repudiation	Offer	Offer	Offer	Offer	**Offer**
Replay attack	Weakness	Medium	Weakness	Weakness	**Strength**
MITM attack	Weakness	Medium	Weakness	Weakness	**Strength**
Verification privacy	Not offer	Not offer	Offer	Offer	**Offer**

- **MITM Attack**: The blockchain network using blockchain distributes attack to a single point to prevent MITM attack.
- **Replay Attack**: The blockchain network using blockchain distributes attacks against a single point to prevent replay attacks.
- **Single point of failure**: The blockchain network using blockchain distributes attacks against a single point and blocks potential internal attackers through the internal process of blockchain.
- **Authentication:** A legitimate user ensures that a new user is valid by issuing a public key certificate containing a public/private key pair and a global timestamp generated by a hash chain and a hash tree.
- **Reliability:** Network participants form a mutually trusting group, no member of which "strays" or seeks to illegitimately modulate activity; fault tolerance is limited by employing a consortium blockchain.
- **Efficiency:** The user and the authentication network operate efficiently and securely using the single hash function of a multi-Bloom filter rather than the many hash functions of a single Bloom filter.
- **Privacy:** Transaction authentication by group members of the blockchain enables validation without exposing the requestor. The multi-Bloom filter structures data stochastically.

6   Conclusion

This paper, we used a multi-Bloom filter, blind signature-based authentication, and a digital signature system to ensure privacy within a consortium blockchain. Efficiency was improved, security requirements satisfied, and privacy guaranteed by exploiting the features of the bloom filter while avoiding multi-hash operations. We used a blind signature to ensure mutual authentication without message disclosure.

In the future, we will test our protocol in a real-world environment implementation.

Acknowledgements. This research was supported by the MSIT (Ministry of Science and ICT), Korea, under the ITRC (Information Technology Research Center) support program (IITP-2019-0-00403) supervised by the IITP (Institute for Information & communications Technology Planning & Evaluation).

References

1. Ra, G.J., Lee, I.Y.: A study on KSI-based authentication management and communication for secure smart home environments. KSII Trans. Internet Inf. Syst. **12**(2), 892–904 (2018)
2. Pfitzmann, A., Köhntopp, M.: Anonymity, unobservability, and pseudonymity — a proposal for terminology. In: Federrath, H. (ed.) Designing Privacy Enhancing Technologies. LNCS, vol. 2009, pp. 1–9. Springer, Heidelberg (2001). https://doi.org/10.1007/3-540-44702-4_1
3. Mercer, R.: Privacy on the blockchain: unique ring signatures. arXiv preprint arXiv:1612.01188 (2016)
4. Maksutov, A.A., Alexeev, M.S., Fedorova, N.O., Andreev, D.A.: Detection of blockchain transactions used in blockchain mixer of coin join type. In: IEEE Conference of Russian Young Researchers in Electrical and Electronic Engineering (EIConRus), pp. 274–277. IEEE (2019)
5. Zhu, H., Tan, Y.A., Zhu, L., Wang, X., Zhang, Q., Li, Y.: An identity-based anti-quantum privacy-preserving blind authentication in wireless sensor networks. Sensors **18**(5), 1663 (2018)
6. Au, M.H., Chow, S.S.M., Susilo, W., Tsang, P.P.: Short linkable ring signatures revisited. In: Atzeni, A.S., Lioy, A. (eds.) EuroPKI 2006. LNCS, vol. 4043, pp. 101–115. Springer, Heidelberg (2006). https://doi.org/10.1007/11774716_9
7. Paul, J., Xu, Q., Fei, S., Veeravalli, B., Aung, K.M.M.: Practically realisable anonymisation of bitcoin transactions with improved efficiency of the zerocoin protocol. In: Arai, K., Kapoor, S., Bhatia, R. (eds.) FICC 2018. AISC, vol. 887, pp. 108–130. Springer, Cham (2019). https://doi.org/10.1007/978-3-030-03405-4_8
8. Groth, J., Kohlweiss, M., Maller, M., Meiklejohn, S., Miers, I.: Updatable and universal common reference strings with applications to zk-SNARKs. In: Shacham, H., Boldyreva, A. (eds.) CRYPTO 2018. LNCS, vol. 10993, pp. 698–728. Springer, Cham (2018). https://doi.org/10.1007/978-3-319-96878-0_24
9. Feng, Q., He, D., Zeadally, S., Khan, M.K., Kumar, N.: A survey on privacy protection in blockchain system. J. Netw. Comput. Appl. (2018)
10. Morishima, S., Matsutani, H.: Accelerating blockchain search of full nodes using GPUs. In: 26th Euromicro International Conference on Parallel, Distributed and Network-Based Processing (PDP), pp. 244–248. IEEE (2018)

11. Schukat, M., Cortijo, P.: Public key infrastructures and digital certificates for the Internet of Things. In: Signals and Systems Conference (ISSC), pp. 1–5 (2015)
12. Gu, K., Wu, N., Liu, Y., Yu, F., Yin, B.: WPKI certificate verification scheme based on certificate digest signature-online certificate status protocol. Math. Prob. Eng. (2018)
13. Zhu, X., Su, Y., Gao, M., Huang, Y.: Privacy-preserving friendship establishment based on blind signature and bloom filter in mobile social networks. In: IEEE/CIC International Conference on Communications in China (ICCC), pp. 1–6. IEEE (2015)
14. Haghighat, M.H., Tavakoli, M., Kharrazi, M.: Payload attribution via character dependent multi-bloom filters. IEEE Trans. Inf. Forensics Secur. **8**(5), 705–716 (2013)

Automated Construction
of Malware Families

Krishnendu Ghosh[1]($\boxtimes$) and Jeffery Mills[2]

[1] Department of Computer Science, College of Charleston,
Charleston, SC 29424, USA
ghoshk@cofc.edu
[2] Department of Computer Science, Northern Kentucky University,
Highland Heights, KY 41099, USA
millsj12@mymail.nku.edu

Abstract. Discovery of malware families from behavioral characteristics of a set of malware traces is an important step in the detection of malware. Malware in the wild often occur as variants of each other. In this work, a data dependent formalism is described for the construction of malware families from trace data. The malware families are represented in an edge labeled graph where the nodes represent a malware trace and edges describe relationship between the malware traces. The edge labels contain a numerical value representing similarity between the malware traces. Network theoretical concepts such as hubs are evaluated on the edge labeled graph. The formalism has been elucidated by the experiments performed on multiple data sets of malware traces.

Keywords: Malware Families · Malware Traces ·
Kullback-Leibler divergence · Discrete-Time Markov Chain ·
Algorithm · Network theory

1 Introduction

Malware attacks on IT infrastructure are increasing exponentially every day. Advanced persistent threats (APT) exploit the vulnerabilities in the IT infrastructure and evolves to attack on new vulnerabilities. The threat of APT malware is dynamic and hence, traditional approaches to mitigate evolving attacks are not effective. Malware creators (writers) often use a foundational code base to create variants of malware by modifying the code for obfuscation. There is a large body of published literature that has addressed malware detection techniques [5,13,15,26,36]. Reverse engineering from byte signature of code is not effective in detection [3] but malware detection based on behavioral features seems promising [5]. Study of malware behavioral features using machine learning has been studied in detail and there is a large body of literature using machine learning applications in malware detection [33,34]. The outcome of using machine learning methods in malware detection have been shown inconclusive [28] because of non-availability of *ground* truth data. Studies have shown the

© Springer Nature Switzerland AG 2019
G. Wang et al. (Eds.): SpaCCS 2019, LNCS 11611, pp. 465–474, 2019.
https://doi.org/10.1007/978-3-030-24907-6_35

malware datasets should be carefully selected [18, 35, 38] for reproducible results. The data often does not contain details such as inaccurate assumptions on the data set, the experimental set up for the data collection and presence or absence of security precaution [35]. Therefore, it is important to address the problem of malware detection by creating a method that has minimal assumptions and is exclusively dependent on imprecise malware trace data. The malware trace data is imprecise because the experimental conditions for data generation is not known. There are published works that have been motivated by computational biology approaches given, morphing of malware variants is analogous to morphing of human virus [16, 19].

Behavioral features of a malware execution are represented in a sequence of actions. Therefore, it is natural to motivate the analysis of malware execution data using formalisms used in biological sequence analysis. The data available for analysis is trace data. A sequence of system calls is a *trace*. Biological sequence analysis leads to deeper understanding of genomic code and similarly, the analysis of malware traces containing the behavioral characteristics could potentially lead to understanding of malware variants represented in the form of malware families. A preliminary version of comparing trace sequences with minimal assumptions using Kullback-Leibler divergence was reported [10]. In this work, we describe (i) a formalism to compare trace sequence with minimal assumptions, (ii) automate the construction of malware families using network theory.

2   Background and Related Work

The work described in the paper is based on different theories malware lineage construction, alignment-free biological sequence analysis and network theory. We combine these theories to create our formalism for construction and validation of malware families.

2.1   Malware Lineage

Malware lineage has been studied for more than two decades [4, 12, 19, 37]. The premise in the construction of malware families (groups) based on the behavioral characteristics did not reflect the notion of ordering as in a lineage tree. A malware variant is represented as an offspring to an ancestor (original malware), represented by a root in the lineage tree. The lineage concepts from biology are limiting in the study of malware due to code fragment inheritance from different malware instances [30] and lack of temporal information. The automated lineage algorithm, *iLine* had been constructed [17] and it requires the additional information such as the development methodology of malware. Therefore, it has been a challenge to create malware families from set of malware. Recently, malware lineage was studied with the assumption that there is a set of malware executable from the same family and construction of *lineage* graph constructed where nodes are members of a malware family and edges represent relation between members of a family.

2.2   Phylogeny Inspired Analysis of Malware

Recently, there has been a focus to study malware construction inspired by phylogenetic approaches. The premise of this line of research is that there are parent-offspring relationships between the variants of malware that are similar in behavior. A malware family [2] is defined as consisting of malware instances, having a common codebase and similar behaviors during execution. An automated construction of malware families and variations [14] on phylogenetic models were reported. Recent work addressing malware families have been reported using phylogenetic-inspired methods [4,20,23]. Alignment of gene (biological) sequences in phylogenetic analysis of malware was reported [20]. There is no direct mapping with biological sequences with that of sequences of system calls as in malware trace. It is not known if malware A is constructed before malware B or otherwise. Recently, identification of malware families using discrete time Markov chain (DTMC) representing each trace was proposed [10] and computations of similarity on DTMCs using KLD and Janson-Shanon- divergence were described.

2.3   Network Theory

Community detection in graphs has been used to identify [9,31] network-based properties of graphs such as hubs and authority [24]. The aim of application of network theoretic properties in community detection is to find the set of nodes in a network that share common properties. Algorithms for community detection [27] have been reported. Community detection have primarily applied in the problems of social and biological network analysis [11]. Network theoretic concepts, in particular community detection was used to cluster the malware into malware families [22]. The similarity was computed as the weighted sum of features of trace sequences. In our work, the formalism is created and the score is based on the (dis)similarity of the DTMCs representing the trace sequences.

3   Preliminaries

In this section, we review the definitions that are used in our formalism.

Definition 1. *Discrete-Time Markov Chains (DTMC): a discrete-time Markov chains is a tuple:* $\mathcal{M}\langle S, S_0, \iota_{init}, \mathcal{P}, L \rangle$ *where:*

- *S is a finite set of states.*
- *S_0 is the set of initial states.*
- *$\mathcal{P} : S \times S \rightarrow [0,1]$, where $\mathcal{P}$ represents the probability matrix and $\sum_{s,s' \in S} \mathcal{P}(s, s') = 1$.*
- *$\iota_{init} : S \rightarrow [0,1]$ where $\sum_{s \in S} \iota_{init}(s) = 1$ is the initial distribution.*
- *$L : S \rightarrow 2^{AP}$. where AP the set of atomic propositions.*

The definition of dtmc is stated in terms of state-based. The comparison of two discrete time markov chains (dtmc) have been studied [8,32]. One of the measures that has been used in the analysis of (dis)-similarity of stochastic models is Kullback-Leibler Divergence (KLD). KLD [25] or relative entropy is a non-symmetric measure between two probability distributions. Formally,

Given P and Q be two probability distributions over the random variable X, the KLD is denoted by $H(P,Q)$ of P with respect to Q is, $H(P,Q) =$

$$\sum_{x \in X} P(x) log \frac{P(x)}{Q(x)}$$

$H(P,Q)$ is not a metric because $H(P,Q) \neq H(Q,P)$. Jensen-Shannon divergence (JSD) is a distance metric [29] that is constructed from KLD. Also, KLD is computed on DTMCs over identical state space.

We define malware execution trace on a set of finite alphabets, Σ.

Definition 2. *A trace, $T = \alpha_0, \alpha_1, \alpha_2, \ldots \alpha_n$ where $n \in \mathbb{N}$ and $\alpha_n \in \Sigma$.*

A *trace* is a sequence of system calls. In a graph, traces are represented by a set of states (nodes). The traces provide a snapshot of the behavior of the program with respect to the request to the operating system serviced. The transition matrix of the dtmc $\mathcal{M}_1$, $\mathcal{P}_1$ is compared with transition matrix of another DTMC $\mathcal{M}_2$, $\mathcal{P}_2$, using KLD. A lower value of $H(\mathcal{P}_2, \mathcal{P}_1)$ implies the malware trace represented by $\mathcal{M}_2$ is proximal $\mathcal{M}_1$.

4   Model

In this section, we describe our model for construction of malware families and feature extraction from the constructed malware families. The formalism involves a three-step process.

- Construction of a discrete time Markov chain from trace data.
- Construction of edge labeled (malware-trace) graph where nodes are malware traces, edges depict the relationships between the nodes and the edge labels store numerical value of (dis)similarity.
- Construction of malware families based on the values of the edge labels on the malware-trace graph.
- Validation of malware families.

4.1   Computation of Similarities Between Traces

Given a set of traces, $\mathcal{T}$, we construct discrete time Markov chain for each pair of traces, $T_1, T_2 \in \mathcal{T}$. For a pair of traces, a set of distinct systems calls, Σ is constructed where $\Sigma = \Sigma_1 \cup \Sigma_2$, Σ_1 and Σ_2 are set of system calls of T_1 and T_2, respectively. We construct an edge-labeled graph, $\mathcal{G}(\mathcal{V}, \mathcal{E}, \mathcal{L})$ where V is the set of nodes representing a system call from the set, Σ and there is an edge connecting each node to every other node and no self-edges are allowed. The edge labeling function, $L : E \rightarrow \mathcal{E}$ labels each edge to a set of labels, $\mathcal{E}$. The edge label on each edge is initialized to 1. The DTMC, representing T_1 is constructed by updating the edge labels of $\mathcal{G}$ with the number of occurrences of each pair of system calls in T and weighting each value with the sum of all edge labels from a node. The creation of G with a set of unique system call is motivated to ensure identical state space for KLD computation for two DTMCs.

Example 1. (Construction of DTMCs for pairwise comparison of traces) If there are three nodes, s_1, s_2 and s_3 in $\mathcal{G}$, then there are six edges, $s_1 \rightarrow s_2, s_1 \rightarrow s_3, s_2 \rightarrow s_1, s_2 \rightarrow s_3, s_3 \rightarrow s_1$ and $s_3 \rightarrow s_2$. Initially, all the edge labels are assigned a value of 1. If $s_1 \rightarrow s_2$ and $s_1 \rightarrow s_3$ in a trace T occurs 5 and 11 times, respectively. The edge labels from $s_1 \rightarrow s_2$ and $s_1 \rightarrow s_3$ are updated to 6 and 12, respectively. After updating the edge labels, each value in the edge label from a node is divided by the sum of edge labels from the node. Therefore, the values on the edges, $s_1 \rightarrow s_2$ and $s_1 \rightarrow s_3$ are $\frac{6}{18}$ and $\frac{12}{18}$, respectively. Similarly, computation on the edge labels of s_2 and s_3 is performed. Hence, a DTMC is created.

For a given set of traces, $T_1, T_2 \in \mathcal{T}$, pairwise dtmcs, $\mathcal{M}_1$ and $\mathcal{M}_2$, respectively are constructed. For each pair of traces, $T_1, T_2 \in \mathcal{T}$, a (dis)similarity numerical value is computed. The measures that were computed are Jenson-Shannon Divergence(JSD) and Kullback-Leibler divergence (KLD) for each pair of traces. The pairwise computation of JSD and KLD is performed throughout the dataset. An edge labeled graph, $\mathcal{G}_t(V, E, L_t)$ is constructed where V, the set of nodes represents traces $T \in \mathcal{T}$, E, the set of edges and L_t is the edge labeling function on each edge. Formally, $L_t : E \rightarrow \mathcal{E}_t$ where $\mathcal{E}_t$ is the set of JSD values. There are edges from every node to every other node with edge labels storing the JSD values. Call $\mathcal{G}_t(V, E)$ as malware trace(MT)-graph. Given KLD is not a metric and therefore, JSD was selected for further analysis. Also, in our experiments, the graph constructed using the KLD values and JSD values were correlated. A minimum spanning tree(MST) was constructed from an MT-graph. The weights, JSD values on the edges were minimized in the construction of MST. A greedy algorithm to compute the MST used the minimum weight on the edges which were the JSD values on edges.

Roadmap (i) The steps that were performed to construct an MST from a set of trace data are:

1. Construct discrete time Markov chains representing a pair of traces.
2. Compute Jenson-Shannon Divergence for the pair of DTMCs
3. Create a MT-graph, $\mathcal{G}_t$ for the data set.
4. Construct minimum spanning tree, $\mathcal{K}$ from the MT-graph.

4.2   Community Detection on Minimum Spanning Tree

The construction of malware families from MST, $\mathcal{K}$ is posed as a community detection problem. A malware family are denoted as a community. Prior work

[10] demonstrated the malware families are constructed with the decreasing of the KLD values. Only the nodes that were connected with less than a specific threshold of KLD were assumed to be a part of the family. We hypothesized that there are few nodes, *hubs* representing traces in $\mathcal{K}$ that have higher degree and centrality. The assumption is that the traces that are in the family are potentially created from the trace that is a *hub* in $\mathcal{K}$. The hub is computed based on the number of edges from a node in $\mathcal{K}$. The more the number of edges from the node the more likely it is a hub. The centrality on the edges were computed to check the position of hubs. The construction of communities is shown in Fig. 1 and the node in red is hub between two distinct malware families, colored with green and blue. In the example shown in Fig. 1, the values of α_1, α_2 and α_3 are comparable to each other ($\alpha_1 \approx \alpha_2 \approx \alpha_3$) and $\rho_1 > \alpha_1$. Therefore, the node with color red becomes green or the hub is part of the family with nodes in green. If $\rho_1 < \alpha_1$, then the hub would be colored blue. The application of community detection on minimum spanning tree on $\mathcal{K}$ is a way to separate the malware families that have contain overlapping nodes.

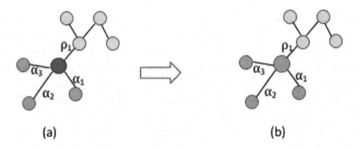

(a)   (b)

Fig. 1. Construction of Communities of Malware (a) Red node representing hub (b) Red node changes its color to blue to be part of blue colored nodes representing a malware family. (Color figure online)

Roadmap (ii) The steps that were performed to validate

1. Construct malware families by posing it as a community detection problem in the MST.
2. Evaluate network theoretic concepts such as hubs and centrality on the MST.

5   Results

The formalism was validated on datasets from csmining.org [1] and ADFA. The csmining data set (DataSet1) has 378 traces. The dataset from ADFA- Linux data set [6,7] consisted of two sets of data, Linux-training(DataSet2) set and Linux-attack(Dataset3) set, containing 833 and 747 traces, respectively. Figure 2 shows the minimum spanning tree using JSD values for each of the data sets in the experiments. The proximity of the nodes representing is dependent on the JSD. Nodes that are closer to each other means the edges connecting the nodes have lower JSD values. The size of the nodes is dependent on the number of edges connected to the nodes.

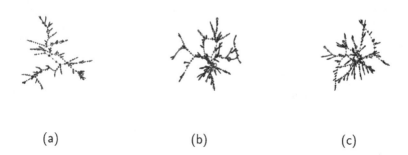

(a)   (b)   (c)

Fig. 2. Minimum spanning tree with hubs (a) Dataset1 (b) Dataset2 and (3) Dataset3

Figure 3 demonstrates histograms based on the degrees and centrality from the minimum spanning trees from the datasets. The histograms demonstrate that there are few nodes that have high degrees. The number of nodes in the datasets that are hubs are very few which validates the hypothesis that there are few nodes that are hubs and several hubs representing traces are connected to other traces forming a malware family.

Figure 4 shows the hubs constructed on the MST, $\mathcal{K}$ using the proximity of the edges that are similar based on the JSD values. The edges in the figure are in three dimensions and hence, there are blobs showing the hubs in Fig. 4(a)–(c).

Figure 5 demonstrates construction of malware families using the edge betweenness to construct a community. The hubs are clustered in community and hence, the malware family are extracted are shown in colored circle.

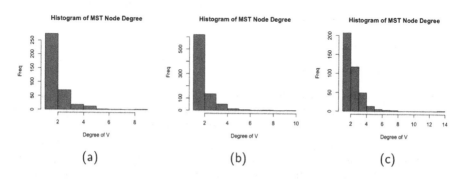

(a)   (b)   (c)

Fig. 3. Malware families detected from MST (a) Dataset1 (b) Dataset2 and (3) Dataset3

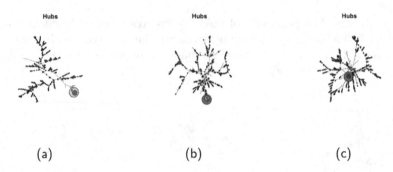

(a)   (b)   (c)

Fig. 4. Hubs in the minimum spanning tree (a) Dataset1 (b) Dataset2 and (c) Dataset3

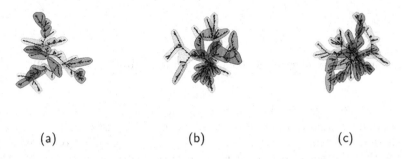

(a)   (b)   (c)

Fig. 5. Malware families detected from MST (a) Dataset1 (b) Dataset2 and (3) Dataset3

The formalism is computationally intensive for the constructions of the JSD values which are computed pairwise with the DTMCs. The limitation of this formalism was magnified during experiments on datasets. The longer the trace, the longer time it would take to construct the DTMC and then compute the JSD values. The experiments often took several days in the order of weeks for a dataset to compute the JSD values. The computer on which experiments were performed on architecture with dual cores with i7 Intel processors.

6   Conclusion

In this paper, we described a formalism that is able to construct malware families from a set of trace data. The malware families were constructed using network theoretic concepts such as hubs and centrality. The goal of the formalism was to formulate an automated approach to construct malware families from data with minimal assumptions while addressing the imprecision in data. The approach described in this work is computationally intensive because of pairwise computation of KLD and JSD from traces. Large sizes of the traces and the number of traces in the order of thousands was not computationally feasible. A hardware with parallel architecture can potentially lead to an efficient computation Future work includes the use of machine learning on large data sets [21] based on the features of each malware family.

References

1. Csmining group. http://csmining.org/index.php/malicious-software-datasets-. html. Accessed 5 May 2017
2. Anderson, B., Lane, T., Hash, C.: Malware phylogenetics based on the multiview graphical lasso. In: Blockeel, H., van Leeuwen, M., Vinciotti, V. (eds.) IDA 2014. LNCS, vol. 8819, pp. 1–12. Springer, Cham (2014). https://doi.org/10.1007/978-3-319-12571-8_1
3. Canali, D., Lanzi, A., Balzarotti, D., Kruegel, C., Christodorescu, M., Kirda, E.: A quantitative study of accuracy in system call-based malware detection. In: Proceedings of the 2012 International Symposium on Software Testing and Analysis, pp. 122–132. ACM (2012)
4. Carrera, E., Erdélyi, G.: Digital genome mapping-advanced binary malware analysis. In: Virus Bulletin Conference, vol. 11 (2004)
5. Christodorescu, M., Jha, S., Seshia, S.A., Song, D., Bryant, R.E.: Semantics-aware malware detection. In: 2005 IEEE Symposium on Security and Privacy, pp. 32–46. IEEE (2005)
6. Creech, G., Hu, J.: Generation of a new IDS test dataset: time to retire the KDD collection. In: Wireless Communications and Networking Conference (WCNC), 2013 IEEE, pp. 4487–4492. IEEE (2013)
7. Creech, G., Hu, J.: A semantic approach to host-based intrusion detection systems using contiguous and discontiguous system call patterns. IEEE Trans. Comput. **63**(4), 807–819 (2014)
8. Deng, K., Sun, Y., Mehta, P.G., Meyn, S.P.: An information-theoretic framework to aggregate a Markov chain. In: American Control Conference, 2009. ACC 2009, pp. 731–736. IEEE (2009)
9. Fortunato, S.: Community detection in graphs. Phys. Rep. **486**(3–5), 75–174 (2010)
10. Ghosh, K., Mills, J., Dorr, J.: Phylogenetic-inspired probabilistic model abstraction in detection of malware families. In: 2017 AAAI Fall Symposium Series (2017)
11. Girvan, M., Newman, M.E.: Community structure in social and biological networks. Proc. Natl. Acad. Sci. **99**(12), 7821–7826 (2002)
12. Goldberg, L.A., Goldberg, P.W., Phillips, C.A., Sorkin, G.B.: Constructing computer virus phylogenies. J. Algorithms **26**(1), 188–208 (1998)
13. Haq, I., Chica, S., Caballero, J., Jha, S.: Malware lineage in the wild. Comput. Secur. **78**, 347–363 (2018)
14. Hayes, M., Walenstein, A., Lakhotia, A.: Evaluation of malware phylogeny modelling systems using automated variant generation. J. Comput. Virol. **5**(4), 335–343 (2009)
15. Idika, N., Mathur, A.P.: A Survey of Malware Detection Techniques, vol. 48. Purdue University (2007)
16. Jang, J., Brumley, D., Venkataraman, S.: Bitshred: Fast, scalable malware triage. Cylab, Carnegie Mellon University, Pittsburgh, PA, Technical report CMU-Cylab-10, vol. 22 (2010)
17. Jang, J., Woo, M., Brumley, D.: Towards automatic software lineage inference. In: Presented as Part of the 22nd USENIX Security Symposium (USENIX Security 13), pp. 81–96 (2013)
18. Jordaney, R., Wang, Z., Papini, D., Nouretdinov, I., Cavallaro, L.: Misleading metrics: on evaluating machine learning for malware with confidence. Technical report (2016)

19. Karim, M.E., Walenstein, A., Lakhotia, A., Parida, L.: Malware phylogeny generation using permutations of code. J. Comput. Virol. **1**(1–2), 13–23 (2005)
20. Khoo, W.M., Lió, P.: Unity in diversity: phylogenetic-inspired techniques for reverse engineering and detection of malware families. In: SysSec Workshop (SysSec), 2011 First, pp. 3–10. IEEE (2011)
21. Ki, Y., Kim, E., Kim, H.K.: A novel approach to detect malware based on API call sequence analysis. Int. J. Distrib. Sens. Netw. **11**(6), 659101 (2015)
22. Kim, H.M., Song, H.M., Seo, J.W., Kim, H.K.: Andro-simnet: android malware family classification using social network analysis. In: 2018 16th Annual Conference on Privacy, Security and Trust (PST), pp. 1–8. IEEE (2018)
23. Kim, H., Khoo, W.M., Liò, P.: Polymorphic attacks against sequence-based software birthmarks. In: 2nd ACM SIGPLAN Workshop on Software Security and Protection (2012)
24. Kleinberg, J.M.: Hubs, authorities, and communities. ACM Comput, Surv. (CSUR) **31**(4es), 5 (1999)
25. Kullback, S., Leibler, R.A.: On information and sufficiency. Ann. Math. Stat. **22**(1), 79–86 (1951)
26. Lakhotia, A., Notani, V., LeDoux, C.: Malware economics and its implication to anti-malware situational awareness. In: 2018 International Conference On Cyber Situational Awareness, Data Analytics And Assessment (Cyber SA), pp. 1–8. IEEE (2018)
27. Lancichinetti, A., Fortunato, S.: Community detection algorithms: a comparative analysis. Phys. Rev. E **80**(5), 056117 (2009)
28. Li, P., Liu, L., Gao, D., Reiter, M.K.: On challenges in evaluating malware clustering. In: Jha, S., Sommer, R., Kreibich, C. (eds.) RAID 2010. LNCS, vol. 6307, pp. 238–255. Springer, Heidelberg (2010). https://doi.org/10.1007/978-3-642-15512-3_13
29. Lin, J.: Divergence measures based on the shannon entropy. IEEE Trans. Inf. Theor. **37**(1), 145–151 (1991)
30. Liu, J., Wang, Y., Wang, Y.: Inferring phylogenetic networks of malware families from API sequences. In: 2016 International Conference on Cyber-Enabled Distributed Computing and Knowledge Discovery (CyberC), pp. 14–17 (2016)
31. Pattanayak, H.S., Verma, H.K., Sangal, A.: Community detection metrics and algorithms in social networks. In: 2018 First International Conference on Secure Cyber Computing and Communication (ICSCCC), pp. 483–489. IEEE (2019)
32. Rached, Z., Alajaji, F., Campbell, L.L.: The Kullback-leibler divergence rate between Markov sources. IEEE Trans. Inf. Theor. **50**(5), 917–921 (2004)
33. Rieck, K., Holz, T., Willems, C., Düssel, P., Laskov, P.: Learning and classification of malware behavior. In: Zamboni, D. (ed.) DIMVA 2008. LNCS, vol. 5137, pp. 108–125. Springer, Heidelberg (2008). https://doi.org/10.1007/978-3-540-70542-0_6
34. Rieck, K., Trinius, P., Willems, C., Holz, T.: Automatic analysis of malware behavior using machine learning. J. Comput. Secur. **19**(4), 639–668 (2011)
35. Rossow, C., et al.: Prudent practices for designing malware experiments: status quo and outlook. In: 2012 IEEE Symposium on Security and Privacy (SP), pp. 65–79. IEEE (2012)
36. Singh, J., Nene, M.J.: A survey on machine learning techniques for intrusion detection systems. Int. J. Adv. Res. Comput. Commun. Eng. **2**(11), 4349–4355 (2013)
37. Sorkin, G.: Grouping related computer viruses into families. In: Proceedings of the IBM Security ITS (1994)
38. Ugarte-Pedrero, X., Graziano, M., Balzarotti, D.: A close look at a daily dataset of malware samples. ACM Trans. Priv. Secur. (TOPS) **22**(1), 6 (2019)

A Closer Look at Anonymous Proxy Re-Encryption Schemes

S. Sharmila Deva Selvi[1](✉), S. Harish[2](✉), Swethashree Dhanabal[2],
and C. Pandu Rangan[1]

[1] Theoretical Computer Science Lab, Department of Computer Science
and Engineering, Indian Institute of Technology Madras, Chennai 600036, India
sharmioshin@gmail.com, prangan55@gmail.com
[2] PSG College of Technology, Coimbatore 641004, India
harish.slal@gmail.com, swethashree.dhanabal@gmail.com

Abstract. Anonymity is one of the most desired properties of a Proxy
Re-encryption scheme. Any user communicating over the public channel, availing cloud for proxy re-encryption services requires that any
entity (an attacker or cloud administrator) must not infer either the
contents of the ciphertexts (confidentiality) or the identities of the participants (anonymity). It is clear that a proxy re-encryption scheme must
be collusion-resistant to satisfy the anonymity notion. There are no CCA-
secure collusion-resistant proxy re-encryption schemes in the literature
which satisfy the anonymity property. In ASIA CCS '14, an anonymous
proxy re-encryption scheme was presented [14] and we present a weakness
in the CCA-security proof of their scheme. We present the first proxy
re-encryption scheme which is anonymous, collusion-resistant and prove
its CCA-security in the random oracle model. We also design a simple, efficient, collusion-resistant CCA-secure proxy re-encryption scheme
which is interesting in its own right. In fact, our anonymous scheme is
an extension of our novel collusion-resistant scheme.

Keywords: Proxy re-encryption · Anonymity · Collusion resistance ·
Random oracle model · CCA Security

1 Introduction

With rapid developments in communications and technology, the need to store
data securely and even more importantly, share data over public channels without compromising confidentiality has emerged has as an important goal of cryp-
tographers. In real life, frequently there arises a need to share some encrypted
data with a third party and to satisfy this need, proxy re-encryption was developed. Blaze, Bleumer and Strauss introduced a powerful primitive called proxy
re-encryption. In proxy re-encryption, a ciphertext encrypted under public key
of Alice is converted by a proxy server to a ciphertext for the same message
such that it is now decipherable by Bob using his secret key. The proxy server

© Springer Nature Switzerland AG 2019
G. Wang et al. (Eds.): SpaCCS 2019, LNCS 11611, pp. 475–489, 2019.
https://doi.org/10.1007/978-3-030-24907-6_36

is given a re-encryption key by Alice to facilitate the conversion of ciphertexts. We place very little trust on the proxy server and therefore, we ensure that the proxy server cannot obtain the secret keys of the involved users or the actual message from the ciphertext which it re-encrypts.

A proxy re-encryption scheme is said to be anonymous if the proxy server colluding with a set of users, can identify neither the public keys related to a re-encryption key (anonymity of re-encryption key) nor the public key related to a ciphertext (anonymity of ciphertext). We highlight the importance of the anonymity property using the following example. A company has a mail server handling the e-mails of its employees. It has availed a third-party cloud computing service to handle expensive computations. Any employee, say Alice, may delegate her decryption rights to another employee, say Bob, by providing the mail server with a re-encryption key. When the mail server receives an e-mail for Alice, it sends the re-encryption key and the encrypted mail to the cloud proxy server, which performs the heavy computations involved in re-encryption and sends back the re-encrypted mail. Here, the company places very little trust on the third-party cloud proxy server and requires that the proxy server be unable to infer which employees have been communicating with whom. Proxy re-encryption has many applications such as encrypted email forwarding, secure distributed file system, digital rights management (DRM), all of which can benefit greatly from the anonymity property.

In 2001, Bellare et al. [3] proposed key-privacy(anonymity) for an encryption scheme which intuitively implies that a set of colluding users cannot determine the public key under which a given ciphertext has been encrypted. Many public-key encryption schemes have been shown to satisfy their key-privacy security notion. Atienese et al. [1] introduced the concept of anonymity of re-encryption keys as a useful property of proxy re-encryption scheme. Following their work, Shao et al. [12], Shao et al. [13] and Zheng et al. [14] presented anonymous proxy re-encryption schemes. In the next section, we discuss each of the above-mentioned schemes and conclude that there are no existing CCA-secure anonymous proxy re-encryption schemes in the literature, to the best of our knowledge.

Atienese et al. [1] have provided two necessary conditions for the construction of anonymous proxy re-encryption scheme: the underlying encryption scheme must be anonymous and the re-encryption algorithm must be probabilistic. Additionally, we state and prove that the proxy re-encryption scheme must be collusion-resistant to satisfy the anonymity notion. Intuitively, a proxy server colluding with a set of malicious users can use the knowledge of secret keys, to identify the delegator of a re-encryption key. There are few collusion-resistant proxy re-encryption schemes in the literature by sharmila et al. [11] in public key setting and Paul et al. [10] in the identity-based setting; surprisingly, none of these schemes satisfy the anonymity property.

1.1   Review of Previous Schemes

In the section, we review the existing anonymous proxy re-encryption schemes and highlight the specific properties of their schemes. For a detailed analysis of prominent proxy re-encryption schemes in the literature, we refer the reader to Nunez et al.'s paper [9]. We also explain why their anonymity notions are insufficient for practical applications.

ABH09. Key-privacy for proxy re-encryption introduced by Atienese et al. [1] prevents a malicious adversary colluding with the proxy server and corrupt users from learning the contents of ciphertexts and the identities of involved participants from a re-encryption key. They showed that proxy re-encryption schemes already present in literature such as [2,4,5,8] are not key-private and provided important impossibility results for key-privacy. Throughout their work, they assumed that there is at most one re-encryption key between a pair of users. Also, they defined CPA-security notion for key-privacy and provided a single-hop unidirectional scheme satisfying their security notion in the random oracle model (Table 1).

Table 1. Comparison of existing Anonymous PRE schemes

Scheme	Security	Proof model	Underlying assumptions	Remarks
Ateniese et al. [1]	CPA	RO	DBDH, EDBDH	Provides CPA security
Shao et al. [12]	CCA	RO	DDH	Weak anonymity notion as pointed out by Zheng et al. [14]
Shao et al. [13]	CCA	SM	5-EDBDH, DDH	The scheme is not CCA secure, attack shown in [7]
Zheng et al. [14]	CCA	RO	DBDH	The scheme is not CCA secure, attack shown in this paper

SLWL12. Shao et al. [12] presented a CCA-secure collusion-resistant scheme under the DDH assumption in the random oracle model. They presented a single-hop unidirectional proxy re-encryption scheme without pairings and allowed multiple re-encryption keys between a pair of users. As explained in [14], in the security proof of anonymity notion for re-encryption keys of Shao et al.'s scheme, the adversary cannot obtain first level ciphertexts generated using the challenge re-encryption key, which greatly weakens the adversary's capability of distinguishing a real or random re-key.

SLZ12. Shao *et al.* [13] addressed the open problem left by Atienese *et al.* [1], to design a CCA-secure key-private scheme and prove its security in standard model. Isshiki *et al.* [7] have demonstrated an attack on the IE-CCA security of this scheme.

ZZZZ14. Zheng *et al.* [14] propose an unidirectional proxy re-encryption scheme which satisfies both security and anonymity against chosen-ciphertext attack. However, in a later section, we briefly describe their scheme and show that it does not satisfy CCA-security.

The existing proxy re-encryption schemes does not satisfy all three properties: CCA-security, collusion resistance and CCA-anonymity. The scheme presented here is the first to satisfy all the three properties.

Our Contribution: In this work, we concentrate on the anonymity property for proxy re-encryption schemes. We provide a detailed analysis of existing anonymous proxy re-encryption scheme and infer the necessary conditions for a proxy re-encryption scheme to satisfy the anonymity notion. We expose a weakness in the security proof of the anonymous proxy re-encryption scheme presented by Zheng *et al.* [14]. We then formulate the anonymity notion through adversarial game in the random oracle model. We present the first proxy re-encryption scheme which is anonymous, CCA-secure and collusion-resistant.

2   Preliminaries

2.1   Hardness Assumption

In this section, we review the computational assumptions that are relevant to our scheme. Let $\mathbb{G}_1, \mathbb{G}_T$ be groups with prime order p having an admissible bilinear mapping $e : \mathbb{G}_1 \times \mathbb{G}_1 \to \mathbb{G}_T$.

1-weak Bilinear Diffie-Hellman Inversion(1-wBDHI) Assumption: The l-weak Bilinear Diffie-Hellman Inversion (1-wBDHI) assumption is said to hold if, given the elements $(P, aP, bP) \in \mathbb{G}_1$, no probabilistic polynomial adversary can compute $e(P, P)^{a^2 b}$ with a non-negligible advantage, where P is a generator of $\mathbb{G}_1$ and $a, b \xleftarrow{\$} \mathbb{Z}_q^*$.

Modified Bilinear Diffie Hellman (mBDH) Assumption: The modified Bilinear Diffie-Hellman (mBDH) assumption is said to hold if, given the elements $(P, aP, bP, cP, a^2 P) \in \mathbb{G}_1$, no probabilistic polynomial adversary can compute $e(P, P)^{abc}$ with a non-negligible advantage, where P is a generator of $\mathbb{G}_1$ and $a, b, c \xleftarrow{\$} \mathbb{Z}_p^*$.

Modified Decisional Bilinear Diffie Hellman (mDBDH) Assumption: The modified Decisional Bilinear Diffie-Hellman (mDBDH) assumption is said to hold if, given the elements $(P, aP, bP, cP, a^2 P) \in \mathbb{G}_1$ and $T \in \mathbb{G}_T$, no probabilistic polynomial adversary can distinguish whether $T \stackrel{?}{=} e(P, P)^{abc}$ or a random element of $\mathbb{G}_T$ with non-negligible advantage, where P is a generator of $\mathbb{G}_1$ and $a, b, c \xleftarrow{\$} \mathbb{Z}_p^*$.

Modified Discrete Logarithm (mDL) Assumption: The modified Discrete Logarithm (mDL) assumption is said to hold if, given the elements $\langle P, aP, a^2P \rangle \in \mathbb{G}_1$, no probabilistic polynomial adversary can compute a with a non-negligible advantage, where P is a generator of $\mathbb{G}_1$ and $a \xleftarrow{\$} \mathbb{Z}_p^*$

3 General and Security Model of Anonymous Proxy Re-Encryption Scheme

In this section, we provide the security model for the original and transformed ciphertext security, and anonymity property of anonymous PRE scheme.

3.1 Security Model of Anonymous Proxy Re-Encryption Scheme

In this section, we define the security notions for our PRE scheme. In our scheme there are two types of ciphertext, original ciphertext and transformed ciphertext. It is essential to prove the security of both original and transformed ciphertexts. Our model is based on the Knowledge of Secret Key (KOSK) model. The challenger computes and provides the public key of Honest users (HU) and public/private key pairs of the Corrupt users (CU) beforehand and the adversary cannot determine which users are to be compromised adaptively. Adversary $\mathcal{A}$ can adaptively query the following oracles and the challenger $\mathcal{C}$ responds to queries and simulates an environment running the PRE scheme for $\mathcal{A}$.

- **Re-Key Generation Oracle** $\mathcal{O}_{RK}(pk_i, pk_j)$: Given as input two public keys pk_i, pk_j, $i \neq j$, $\mathcal{C}$ runs the algorithm $ReKeyGen(sk_i, pk_i, pk_j, params)$ and returns the re-encryption key $RK_{i \to j}$.
- **ReEncryption Oracle** $\mathcal{O}_{re-enc}(\mathbb{C}_i, pk_i, pk_j)$: Given as input two public keys pk_i, pk_j and original ciphertext $\mathbb{C}_i$, challenger $\mathcal{C}$ runs the algorithm $ReEncrypt(\mathbb{C}_i, ReKeyGen(sk_i, pk_i, pk_j, params))$ and returns re-encrypted ciphertext $\mathbb{D}_j$.
- **Decryption Oracle** $\mathcal{O}_{dec}(\mathbb{C}_i, pk_i)$: Given as input an original ciphertext $\mathbb{C}_i$ and a public key pk_i, $\mathcal{C}$ runs the algorithm $Decrypt(\mathbb{C}_i, sk_i)$ and returns the result.
- **Re-decryption Oracle** $\mathcal{O}_{re-dec}(\mathbb{D}_j, pk_j)$: Given as input a transformed ciphertext $\mathbb{D}_j$ and a public key pk_j, $\mathcal{C}$ runs the algorithm $ReDecrypt(\mathbb{D}_i, sk_i)$ and returns the result.

Indistinguishability of Encryptions against Chosen Ciphertext Attack for Original Ciphertext (IE-CCA-OC): In original ciphertext security game, the adversary $\mathcal{A}$ is challenged with an original ciphertext $\mathbb{C}_T$ encrypted under the target public key pk_T. We describe below the IE-CCA-OC adversarial game. In this game, the Re-Key Generation oracle cannot be queried for the re-encryption key between a honest and corrupt user, otherwise the adversary $\mathcal{A}$ can trivially win the security game.

- **Setup:** The challenger $\mathcal{C}$ takes the security parameter λ, runs the algorithm $Setup(\lambda)$ and returns the public parameters $params$.
- **Key Generation:** The challenger $\mathcal{C}$ runs the KeyGen algorithm and returns the public keys of the honest users(HU) and the public/private key pair of the corrupt users(CU) to $\mathcal{A}$.
- **Phase 1:** $\mathcal{A}$ adaptively queries the Re-Key Generation oracle, Re-encryption oracle, Decryption oracle and Re-Decryption oracle and $\mathcal{C}$ responds to the queries.
- **Challenge:** $\mathcal{A}$ outputs two message $m_0, m_1 \in \mathcal{M}$ and a target public key $pk_i^* \in HU$, when it decides that phase 1 is over. $\mathcal{C}$ picks a random bit $\psi \in \{0,1\}$ and computes challenge ciphertext $\mathbb{C}^* = Encrypt(m_\psi, pk_i^*, params)$ and returns $\mathbb{C}^*$ to $\mathcal{A}$.
- **Phase 2:** $\mathcal{A}$ interacts with the challenger $\mathcal{C}$ as in phase 1, with the following constraints,
  - $\mathcal{A}$ cannot issue a re-encryption query $\mathcal{O}_{re-enc}(\mathbb{C}^*, pk_i^*, pk_j)$ where $pk_j \in CU$.
  - $\mathcal{A}$ cannot issue a decryption query $\mathcal{O}_{dec}(\mathbb{C}_i, pk_i)$ if $(\mathbb{C}_i, pk_i)$ is a challenge derivative of $(\mathbb{C}^*, pk_i^*)$.
  - $\mathcal{A}$ cannot issue decryption query on $\mathbb{C}^*$ under pk_i^*.
- **Guess:** Finally, $\mathcal{A}$ outputs a guess ψ' and wins the game if $\psi = \psi'$.

Definition 1 (*Challenge Derivative*). *The definition of a challenge derivative presented here is adopted from [5].*

- *Reflexitivity:* $(\mathbb{C}_i, pk_i)$ *is a challenge derivative of its own.*
- *Derivative by re-encryption:* $(\mathbb{D}_j, pk_j)$ *is a challenge derivative of* $(\mathbb{C}_i, pk_i)$ *if* $\mathbb{D}_j = \mathcal{O}_{re-enc}(\mathbb{C}_i, pk_i, pk_j)$.
- *Derivative by re-key:* $(\mathbb{D}_j, pk_j)$ *is a challenge derivative of* $(\mathbb{C}_i, pk_i)$ *if* $RK_{i \to j} = \mathcal{O}_{RK}(pk_i, pk_j)$ *and* $\mathbb{D}_j = ReEncrypt(\mathbb{C}_i, RK_{i \to j})$.

Indistinguishability of Encryptions Against Chosen Ciphertext Attack for Transformed Ciphertext(IE-CCA-TC): In transformed ciphertext security game, the adversary $\mathcal{A}$ is challenged with a transformed ciphertext $\mathbb{D}^*$ encrypted under the target public key pk_j^*, where $\mathbb{D}^*$ is the re-encryption of original ciphertext $\mathbb{C}_i$ encrypted under the public key pk_i. $\mathcal{A}$ does not have access to underlying original ciphertext $\mathbb{C}_i$. The security for the transformed ciphertext remains unaffected by the fact whether pk_i is a corrupt user or not. We describe below the game template for CCA-security of transformed ciphertext. In this game, there are no restrictions on re-key generation queries, therefore we need not provide a Re-encryption oracle explicitly.

- **Setup** and **Key Generation:** Same as in IE-CCA-OC game.
- **Phase 1:** $\mathcal{A}$ adaptively queries the Re-Key Generation oracle, Decryption oracle and Re-decryption oracle and $\mathcal{C}$ responds to the queries.
- **Challenge:** When $\mathcal{A}$ decides phase 1 is over, it outputs two messages $m_0, m_1 \in \mathcal{M}$, a target public key $pk_j^* \in HU$. $\mathcal{C}$ picks a random bit $\psi \in \{0,1\}$ and a public key pk_i. $\mathcal{C}$ computes the challenge ciphertext $\mathbb{D}^* = ReEncrypt(Encrypt(m_\psi, pk_i), RK_{i \to j^*})$ and returns to $\mathcal{A}$.

- **Phase 2:** $\mathcal{A}$ interacts with the challenger $\mathcal{C}$ as in phase 1, with the constraint that $\mathcal{A}$ cannot query $\mathcal{O}_{re-dec}(\mathbb{D}^*, pk_j^*)$.
- **Guess:** Finally, $\mathcal{A}$ outputs a guess ψ' and wins the game if $\psi = \psi'$.

Collision Resistance: Collusion resistance or Delegator Secret Key(DSK) security ensures that even if the proxy server colludes with a delegatee, it cannot recover the delegator's private key i.e, any entity with the knowledge of $RK_{i \to j}$ and sk_j, cannot recover sk_i. This property allows a user to delegate decryption rights, without affecting his/her own signing rights [2]. In our collusion-resistance proof, we follow the adversarial game defined in [6].

- **Setup:** Same as in IE-CCA-OC game.
- **Queries:** $\mathcal{A}$ adaptively queries the following oracles and $\mathcal{C}$ responds as follows.
  - Honest Key Generation: $\mathcal{C}$ runs the KeyGen($U_i, params$) algorithm to generate the Public/Secret Key pair (pk_i, sk_i) of user U_i and returns pk_i to $\mathcal{A}$.
  - Corrupt Key Generation: $\mathcal{C}$ runs the KeyGen($U_i, params$) algorithm to generate the Public/Secret Key pair (pk_i, sk_i) of user U_i and returns (pk_i, sk_i) to $\mathcal{A}$.
  - Re-Key Generation Oracle $\mathcal{O}_{RK}(pk_i, pk_j)$: Given as input two public keys $pk_i, pk_j, i \neq j$, $\mathcal{C}$ runs the algorithm $ReKeyGen(sk_i, pk_i, pk_j, params)$ and returns the re-encryption key $RK_{i \to j}$.
- **Output:** $\mathcal{A}$ returns sk_i^* as the private key of the public key pk_i^*. $\mathcal{A}$ wins the game if sk_i^* is a valid private key of an uncorrupted user with public key pk_i^*.

Next we provide the adversarial games for anonymity of original ciphertext and anonymity of re-encryption keys against chosen ciphertext attack. A proxy re-encryption scheme satisfies anonymity of ciphertext property when an attacker cannot recognize the public key of recipient from the ciphertext. The anonymity of the transformed ciphertext is implied by the anonymity of original ciphertext, which is explained in [12]. We therefore, provide security proofs for the anonymity of original ciphertext and anonymity of re-encryption key.

Indistinguishability of Keys Against Chosen Ciphertext Attack for Original Ciphertext(IK-CCA-OC): We define below the adversarial game for Indistinguishability of Keys against Chosen Ciphertext Attack for Original Ciphertext in the random oracle model. In this game, the Re-Key Generation oracle cannot be queried for the re-encryption key between a honest and corrupt user, otherwise the adversary $\mathcal{A}$ can trivially win the security game.

- **Setup** and **Key Generation:** Same as in IE-CCA-OC game.
- **Phase 1:** $\mathcal{A}$ adaptively queries the Re-Key Generation oracle, Re-encryption oracle, Decryption oracle and Re-decryption oracle and $\mathcal{C}$ responds to the queries.
- **Challenge:** When $\mathcal{A}$ decides phase 1 is over, it outputs a message $m \in \mathcal{M}$ and two public keys pk_0^*, pk_1^*, where pk_0^* and pk_1^* are both both honest users. $\mathcal{C}$ picks a random bit $\psi \in \{0, 1\}$ and computes the challenge ciphertext $\mathbb{C}^* = Encrypt(m, pk_\psi^*, params)$ and returns $\mathbb{C}^*$ to $\mathcal{A}$.

– **Phase 2:** $\mathcal{A}$ interacts with the challenger $\mathcal{C}$ as in phase 1, with the additional constraints.
  - $\mathcal{A}$ cannot issue a re-key query $\mathcal{O}_{re-key}(pk_i, pk_j)$ where $pk_i = pk_0^*$ or pk_1^* and pk_j is a honest user.
  - $\mathcal{A}$ cannot issue a re-encryption query $\mathcal{O}_{re-enc}(\mathbb{C}, pk_i, pk_j)$ where $\mathbb{C} = \mathbb{C}^*$ and $pk_i = pk_0^*$ or pk_1^*.
  - $\mathcal{A}$ cannot issue a decryption query $\mathcal{O}_{dec}(\mathbb{C}, pk)$ where $\mathbb{C} = \mathbb{C}^*$ and $pk = pk_0^*$ or pk_1^*.
– **Guess:** Finally, $\mathcal{A}$ outputs a guess ψ' and wins the game if $\psi = \psi'$.

Indistinguishability of Keys Against Chosen Ciphertext Attack for Re-encryption Keys(IK-CCA-RK): We present below the game template for Indistinguishability of Keys against Chosen Ciphertext Attack for Re-encryption Keys in the random oracle model.

– **Setup** and **Key Generation:** Same as in IE-CCA-OC game.
– **Phase 1:** $\mathcal{A}$ adaptively queries the Re-Key Generation oracle, Re-encryption oracle, Decryption oracle and Re-decryption oracle and $\mathcal{C}$ responds to the queries.
– **Challenge:** When $\mathcal{A}$ decides phase 1 is over. It outputs a message $m \in \mathcal{M}$ and two public keys pk_i^*, pk_j^*, where pk_i^* and pk_j^* are both honest users. $\mathcal{C}$ picks a random bit $\psi \in \{0, 1\}$ and computes the challenge re-encryption $RK_{i^* \to j^*} = ReKeyGen(sk_{i^*}, pk_{i^*}, pk_{j^*}, params)$ if $\psi = 1$. If $\psi = 0$, then $\mathcal{C}$ picks a random key from the re-encryption key space and returns $RK_{i^* \to j^*}$ to $\mathcal{A}$.
– **Phase 2:** $\mathcal{A}$ interacts with the challenger $\mathcal{C}$ as in phase 1, with the following constraints that $\mathcal{A}$ cannot query $\mathcal{O}_{re-dec}(\mathbb{D}_j, pk_j)$ when $pk_j = pk_j^*$. This restriction is necessary because it is hard for the challenger to determine whether the transformed ciphertext $\mathbb{D}_j$ was computed using the challenge rekey or not.
– **Guess:** Finally, $\mathcal{A}$ outputs a guess ψ' and wins the game if $\psi = \psi'$.

4   Analysis of Zheng *et al.* Scheme [14]

We first present the scheme of Zheng *et al.* [14] and then provide the attack on their security proof.

4.1   Weakness in the Security Proof of Zheng *et al.*

In [14], Zheng *et al.* had proposed an anonymous proxy re-encryption scheme in the random oracle model. They claimed that the scheme is CCA secure. In this section, we show that the scheme is not CCA secure and is malleable. According to their model a user is considered corrupt if the private key of the user is known to the adversary $\mathcal{A}$. Also the adversary, $\mathcal{A}$ is allowed to query the KeyGen, ReKeyGen, ReEnc and Dec oracles in phase 1, with the restriction that $\mathcal{A}$ cannot query for an re-encryption key or a re-encryption from a honest to corrupt user. Now let us consider that $\mathcal{A}$ issues a public key pk^* of a honest user and two messages m_0, m_1 to the challenger $\mathcal{C}$. In the challenge phase, the challenger picks a message m_ψ where $\psi \in \{0, 1\}$ and encrypts under pk^* and returns the challenge ciphertext C^* to $\mathcal{A}$. After the challenge phase, $\mathcal{A}$ continues to query the oracles with the additional restrictions provided in the security model, $\mathcal{A}$ is not allowed to query the Dec oracle with a ciphertext C computed with a re-encryption key from pk^* to pk_j. Now we show that an adversary $\mathcal{A}$ can trivially win the game without the knowledge of the private key by performing the following.

- The challenge ciphertext $C^* = \langle C_1^*, C_2^*, C_3^*, C_4^*, C_5^* \rangle = \langle g^r, R \cdot e(pk^*, H_0(pk^*))^r, m_\psi \oplus F_1(R), g_1^r, H_2(C_1^*, C_2^*, C_3^*, C_4^*)^r \rangle$ where $R \xleftarrow{\$} \mathbb{G}_T$, $r = H_1(m_\psi, R)$ and m_ψ is either m_0 or m_1.
- $\mathcal{A}$ queries the ReEnc oracle $\mathcal{O}_{re-enc}(pk^*, pk_j, C^*)$ where pk_j is honest. This query is legal according to the model.
- The re-encrypted ciphertext $C' = \langle C_1', C_2', C_3' \rangle$ where, $C_1' = rk_6^{r'} = e(pk_j, g)^{twr'}$, $C_2' = R'rk_5^{r'} = R'e(pk_j, pk_j)^{twr'}$, $C_3' = \Gamma \oplus F_2(R')$
- $\mathcal{A}$ modifies the re-encrypted ciphertext C' to ciphertext C'' under the same public key pk_j, as follows.

  • Pick $t^*, w^* \xleftarrow{\$} \mathbb{Z}_q^*$ and then computes the values $T_1 = e(pk_j, g)^{t^*w^*}$ and $T_2 = e(pk_j, pk_j)^{t^*w^*}$.
  • Compute $C_1'' = C_1'T_1 = e(pk_j, g)^{twr'}e(pk_j, g)^{t^*w^*} = e(pk_j, g)^{r'tw+t^*w^*}$.
  • Compute $C_2'' = C_2'T_1 = R'rk_5^{r'}T_1 = R'e(pk_j, pk_j)^{twr'}e(pk_j, pk_j)^{t^*w^*} = R'e(pk_j, pk_j)^{r'tw+t^*w^*}$.
  • Set $C_3'' = C_3'$ and returns $C'' = (C_1'', C_2'', C_3'')$.
- $\mathcal{A}$ can query the decryption oracle $\mathcal{O}_{dec}(C'', pk_j)$ to obtain the plaintext. This is allowed as (C'', pk_j) is not a challenge derivative of C^*, pk^*, though (C', pk_j) is a challenge derivative. Thus the decryption of C'' will output the message m_ψ. Hence the adversary can easily find out m_ψ without the knowledge of sk^*.

Thus, in the scheme presented by Zheng et al. the second level ciphertexts are not secured against chosen ciphertext attack. As Zheng et al. was the only reported scheme in the literature satisfying CCA-security and anonymity, we conclude that none of the existent proxy re-encryption schemes satisfy both CCA-security and anonymity.

5 A Collision-Resistant Unidirectional Proxy Re-Encryption Scheme

We had shown earlier that a proxy re-encryption scheme can achieve anonymity of ciphertexts and re-encryption key, only if it is collusion-resistant. We therefore first attempt to design a collusion-resistant proxy re-encryption scheme, bearing in mind our ultimate objective to design an anonymous proxy re-encryption scheme as.

Notice that in the re-encryption algorithm of our scheme, the only inputs are an original ciphertext, a re-encryption key and the public parameters. In some proxy re-encryption schemes, the public key of the delegator is additionally given as input to the re-encryption algorithm, to help verify the validity of the ciphertext, which trivially causes the scheme to fail the anonymity property.

5.1 Proposed Scheme

- **Setup(λ):** Let $\mathbb{G}_1$, $\mathbb{G}_T$ be groups of prime order p and $e : \mathbb{G}_1 \times \mathbb{G}_1 \to \mathbb{G}_T$ is bilinear map. Let P and Q be generators of the group $\mathbb{G}_1$ and set $\alpha = e(P,Q)$. The hash functions are defined as, $H_1 : \{0,1\}^{l_0} \times \{0,1\}^{l_1} \times \mathbb{G}_1 \to \mathbb{Z}_p^*$; $H_2 : \mathbb{G}_T \to \{0,1\}^{(l_0+l_1+|\mathbb{G}_i|)}$; $H_3 : \{0,1\}^* \to \mathbb{G}_1$. l_1 is a positive integer chosen as length of the random salt used internally in the scheme, l_0 is the length of a message and the message space $\mathcal{M}$ is $\{0,1\}^{l_0}$. The public parameters are, $params = \langle p, \mathbb{G}_1, \mathbb{G}_T, P, Q, \alpha, H_1, H_2, H_3 \rangle$
- **KeyGen($U_i, params$):** Pick $x_i \xleftarrow{\$} \mathbb{Z}_p^*$ and set the private key $sk_i = x_i$, public key $pk_i = \langle X_i, Y_i, Z_i \rangle = \langle x_i P, \frac{1}{x_i} Q, e(x_i P, Q) \rangle$.
- **ReKeyGen($sk_i, pk_i, pk_j, params$):** Given the public key $pk_i = \langle X_i, Y_i, Z_i \rangle$ and private key $sk_i = x_i$ of user i, the public key $pk_j = \langle X_j, Y_j, Z_j \rangle$, of user j. Compute the re-encryption key $RK_{i \to j} = sk_i \cdot Y_j = \frac{x_i}{x_j} Q$ and return it.
- **Encrypt($m, pk_i, params$):** To encrypt a given message $m \in \mathcal{M}$ under a public key $pk_i = \langle X_i, Y_i, Z_i \rangle$.
  - Choose $w \xleftarrow{\$} \{0,1\}^{l_1}$ and compute $r = H_1(m, w, X_i)$ and $C_1 = rP$.
  - Compute $C_2 = H_2(Z_i^r) \oplus (m\|w\|X_i) = H_2(e(P,Q)^{x_i r}) \oplus (m\|w\|X_i)$.
  - Compute $C_3 = rH_3(C_1\|C_2)$ and return the ciphertext $\mathbb{C}_i = \langle C_1, C_2, C_3 \rangle$.
- **ReEncrypt($\mathbb{C}_i, RK_{i \to j}, params$):** Given an original ciphertext $\mathbb{C}_i$ and a re-encryption key $RK_{i \to j}$, the re-encrypted ciphertext is computed as shown,
  - Check if the following condition holds, $e(C_1, H_3(C_1\|C_2)) \stackrel{?}{=} e(P, C_3)$ If the check fails return $\perp$. Else,
  - Compute $D_1 = e(C_1, RK_{i \to j}) = e(P,Q)^{r\frac{x_i}{x_j}}$ and set $D_2 = C_2$.
  Return the transformed ciphertext $\mathbb{D}_j = \langle D_1, D_2 \rangle$.
- **Decrypt($\mathbb{C}_i, sk_i, params$):** On input of an original ciphertext $\mathbb{C}_i$ and private key $sk_i = x_i$, the decryption is performed as follows.
  - Extract the message $(m\|w\|X_i) = C_2 \oplus H_2(e(C_1, Q)^{x_i})$
  - Return m if the following conditions hold, $C_1 \stackrel{?}{=} H_2(m, w, X_i)P$, $C_3 \stackrel{?}{=} H_1(m, w, X_i)H_3(C_1\|C_2)$. Else return $\perp$.
- **ReDecrypt($\mathbb{D}_j, sk_j, params$):** On input of a transformed Ciphertext of the form $\mathbb{D}_j = \langle D_1, D_2 \rangle$ and a private key $sk_j = x_j$, the re-decryption is performed as follows.
  - Extract the message $(m\|w\|X_i) = D_2 \oplus H_2(D_1^{x_j})$
  - Return m if the following condition holds, $D_1 \stackrel{?}{=} e(X_i, Y_j)^{H_1(m,w,X_i)}$. Else return $\perp$.

5.2   Security Proof

For the scheme presented in the previous section, we provide the security proofs below. We prove the security of original ciphertexts and transformed ciphertexts, against chosen ciphertext attack in the random oracle model. Also, we prove that our scheme collision-resistant. Throughout our security proofs, we consider a user as corrupt if the private key of the user is known to the adversary $\mathcal{A}$. Otherwise, the user is considered to be honest.

Indistinguishability of Encryptions Against Chosen Ciphertext Attack for Original Ciphertext (IE-CCA-OC):

Theorem 1. *Our proposed scheme is CCA-secure for the original ciphertext under the 1-wBDHI assumption. If an adversary $\mathcal{A}$ breaks the IE-CCA-OC security of the scheme, then the challenger $\mathcal{C}$ can solve the 1-wBDHI problem.*

Due to page limitation the proof is given in the full version of the paper.

Indistinguishability of Encryptions Against Chosen Ciphertext Attack for Transformed Ciphertext (IE-CCA-TC):

Theorem 2. *Our proposed scheme is CCA-secure for the transformed ciphertext under the mBDH assumption. If an adversary $\mathcal{A}$ breaks the IE-CCA-TC security of the scheme, then the challenger $\mathcal{C}$ can solve the mBDH problem.*

Due to page limitation the proof is given in the full version of the paper.

Collision Resistance:

Theorem 3. *Our Proposed scheme is DSK-secure under the mDL assumption. If an adversary $\mathcal{A}$ breaks the DSK security of the scheme, then the challenger $\mathcal{C}$ can solve the mDL problem.*

Due to page limitation the proof is given in the full version of the paper.

6   An Anonymous Unidirectional Proxy Re-Encryption Scheme

In this section, we present our anonymous proxy re-encryption scheme satisfying CCA-security and CCA-anonymity notions. We have carefully designed our scheme, in accordance to the observations made from flaws in previous schemes and our CCA-anonymity notion. Therefore, in our scheme the *ReKeyGen* and *ReEncrypt* algorithms are probabilistic. The components of the re-encryption key are not relatable using public values, hence the adversary cannot trivially distinguish between a real or random re-encryption key.

6.1 Proposed Scheme

- **Setup**(λ): Let $\mathbb{G}_1$, $\mathbb{G}_T$ be groups of prime order p and $e : \mathbb{G}_1 \times \mathbb{G}_1 \rightarrow \mathbb{G}_T$ is bilinear map. Let P and Q be generators of the group $\mathbb{G}_1$. Set $\alpha = e(P, Q)$. The hash functions are defined as follows.

$$H_1 : \{0,1\}^{l_0} \times \{0,1\}^{l_1} \times \mathbb{G}_1 \rightarrow \mathbb{Z}_p^*$$

$$H_2 : \mathbb{G}_T \rightarrow \{0,1\}^{(l_0+l_1+|\mathbb{G}_1|)}$$

$$H_3 : \{0,1\}^* \rightarrow \mathbb{G}_1$$

$$H_4 : \mathbb{G}_1 \rightarrow \mathbb{G}_1$$

$$H_5 : \mathbb{G}_T \rightarrow \{0,1\}^{(l_0+l_1+2|\mathbb{G}_1|+|\mathbb{G}_T|)}$$

$$H_6 : \mathbb{G}_T \rightarrow \mathbb{Z}_p^*$$

$$H_7 : \mathbb{G}_1 \times \mathbb{G}_1 \rightarrow \mathbb{G}_1$$

  The hash functions are modelled as random oracles in the security proof. l_1 is a positive integer chosen as length of the random salt used internally in the scheme, l_0 is the length of a message and the message space $\mathcal{M}$ is $\{0,1\}^{l_0}$. The public parameters, $params = \langle p, \mathbb{G}_1, \mathbb{G}_T, P, Q, \alpha, H_1, H_2, H_3, H_4, H_5, H_6, H_7 \rangle$

- **KeyGen**$(U_i, params)$: Pick $x_i \xleftarrow{\$} \mathbb{Z}_p^*$. Set the private key $sk_i = x_i$ and public key $pk_i = \langle X_i, Y_i, Z_i \rangle = \langle x_i P, \frac{1}{x_i} Q, e(x_i P, Q) \rangle$.

- **ReKeyGen**$(sk_i, pk_i, pk_j, params)$: Given the public key $pk_i = \langle X_i, Y_i, Z_i \rangle$ and private key $sk_i = x_i$ of user i, the public key $pk_j = \langle X_j, Y_j, Z_j \rangle$ of user j and the public parameter $params$, compute the re-encryption key $RK_{i \rightarrow j}$ as follows.
  - Pick $s \xleftarrow{\$} \mathbb{Z}_p^*$.
  - Compute $\beta = H_6(e(X_j, H_4(Y_j))^s)$ and $RK_{i \rightarrow j}^{(1)} = \beta \cdot sk_i \cdot Y_j = \beta \cdot \frac{x_i}{x_j} Q$.
  - Compute $RK_{i \rightarrow j}^{(2)} = sP$ and $RK_{i \rightarrow j}^{(3)} = sH_7(RK_{i \rightarrow j}^{(2)}, sX_j)$.
  - Compute $RK_{i \rightarrow j}^{(4)} = \beta P$ and $RK_{i \rightarrow j}^{(5)} = e(X_j, H_4(Y_j))^\beta$.

  $RK_{i \rightarrow j} = \langle RK_{i \rightarrow j}^{(1)}, RK_{i \rightarrow j}^{(2)}, RK_{i \rightarrow j}^{(3)}, RK_{i \rightarrow j}^{(4)}, RK_{i \rightarrow j}^{(5)} \rangle$ is returned.

- **Encrypt**$(m, pk_i, params)$: To encrypt a given message $m \in \mathcal{M}$ under a public key $pk_i = \langle X_i, Y_i, Z_i \rangle$,
  - Choose $w \xleftarrow{\$} \{0,1\}^{l_1}$ and compute $r = H_1(m, w, X_i)$ and $C_1 = rP$.
  - Compute $C_2 = H_2(Z_i^r) \oplus (m \| w \| X_i)$ and $C_3 = rH_3(C_1 \| C_2)$.

  Return the ciphertext $\mathbb{C}_i = \langle C_1, C_2, C_3 \rangle$.

- **ReEncrypt**$(\mathbb{C}_i, RK_{i \rightarrow j}, params)$: Given an original ciphertext $\mathbb{C}_i$ and a re-encryption Key $RK_{i \rightarrow j}$, the re-encrypted ciphertext is computed as shown,
  - Check if the following condition holds, $e(C_1, H_3(C_1 \| C_2)) \overset{?}{=} e(P, C_3)$. If the check fails, return $\perp$.
  - Pick $t \xleftarrow{\$} \mathbb{Z}_p^*$, compute $D_1 = e(C_1, RK_{i \rightarrow j}^{(1)})$ and set $D_2 = C_2$.
  - Compute $D_3 = tRK_{i \rightarrow j}^{(4)}$ and $D_4 = tH_4(tP)$.
  - Compute $D_5 = (D_1 \| D_2 \| RK_{i \rightarrow j}^{(2)} \| RK_{i \rightarrow j}^{(3)}) \oplus H_5((RK_{i \rightarrow j}^{(5)})^t)$.

  Return the transformed ciphertext $\mathbb{D}_j = \langle D_3, D_4, D_5 \rangle$.

- **Decrypt**$(\mathbb{C}_i, sk_i, params)$: On input an original ciphertext $\mathbb{C}_i$ and private key $sk_i = x_i$,
  - Extract the message $(m \| w \| X_i) = C_2 \oplus H_2(e(C_1, Q)^{x_i})$.

- Return m if the following conditions hold, $C_1 \overset{?}{=} H(m, w, X_i)P, C_3 \overset{?}{=} H(m, w, X_i)H(C_1 \| C_2)$. Else return $\perp$.
- **ReDecrypt**($\mathbb{D}_j, sk_j, params$): On input the private key $sk_j = x_j$, corresponding to the transformed ciphertext $\mathbb{D}_j = \langle D_3, D_4, D_5 \rangle$,
  - Compute $(D_1 \| D_2 \| RK_{i \to j}^{(2)} \| RK_{i \to j}^{(3)}) = D_5 \oplus H_5(e(D_3, H_4(Y_j))^{x_j})$
  - Check if the following condition holds. $e(RK_{i \to j}^{(2)}, H_7(RK_{i \to j}^{(2)}, x_j \cdot RK_{i \to j}^{(2)})) \overset{?}{=} e(P, RK_{i \to j}^{(3)})$.
  - Compute $\beta = H_6(e(RK_{i \to j}^{(2)}, H_4(Y_j))^{x_j})$
  - Check if the following condition holds $e(\beta^{-1}D_3, H_4(\beta^{-1}D_3)) \overset{?}{=} e(P, D_4)$. If the condition fails return $\perp$.
  - Extract the message $(m \| w \| X_i) = D_2 \oplus H_2(D_1^{x_j \beta^{-1}})$.
  - Return m if the following condition holds $D_1 \overset{?}{=} e(X_i, Y_j)^{H_1(m,w,X_i)\beta}$, Else return $\perp$.

6.2   Security Proofs

We now prove that our proposed scheme satisfies the security notions of CCA-security, collusion-resistance and CCA-anonymity.

Indistinguishability of Encryptions Against Chosen Ciphertext Attack for Original Ciphertext(IE-CCA-OC):

Theorem 4. *Our proposed scheme is CCA-secure for the original ciphertext under the 1-wBDHI assumption. If an adversary $\mathcal{A}$ breaks the IE-CCA-OC security of the scheme, then the challenger $\mathcal{C}$ can solve the 1-wBDHI problem.*

Due to page limitation the proof is given in the full version of the paper.

Indistinguishability of Encryptions Against Chosen Ciphertext Attack for Transformed Ciphertext(IE-CCA-TC):

Theorem 5. *Our proposed scheme is CCA-secure for the transformed ciphertext under the mBDH assumption. If an adversary $\mathcal{A}$ breaks the IE-CCA-TC security of the scheme, then the challenger $\mathcal{C}$ can solve the mBDH problem.*

Due to page limitation the proof is given in the full version of the paper.

Indistinguishability of Keys Against Chosen Ciphertext Attack for Original Ciphertext(IK-CCA-OC):

Theorem 6. *Our proposed scheme is IK-CCA-OC secure for the original ciphertext under the 1-wBDH assumption. If an adversary $\mathcal{A}$ breaks the IK-CCA-OC security of the scheme, then the challenger $\mathcal{C}$ can solve the 1-wBDH problem.*

Due to page limitation the proof is given in the full version of the paper.

Indistinguishability of Keys Against Chosen Ciphertext Attack for Re-Encryption Keys(IK-CCA-RK):

Theorem 7. *Our proposed scheme is IK-CCA-RK secure for the reencryption keys under the mDBDH assumption. If an adversary $\mathcal{A}$ breaks the IK-CCA-RK security of the scheme, then the challenger $\mathcal{C}$ can solve the mDBDH problem.*

Due to page limitation the proof is given in the full version of the paper.

Collision Resistance:

Theorem 8. *Our Proposed scheme is DSK-secure under the mDL assumption. If an adversary $\mathcal{A}$ breaks the DSK security of the scheme, then the challenger $\mathcal{C}$ can solve the mDL problem.*

Due to page limitation the proof is given in the full version of the paper.

7   Conclusion

We consider the anonymity property for proxy re-encryption schemes, which is useful in many applications of encrypted communications and places the least amount of trust on the proxy server. We have discussed why prior anonymous proxy re-encryption schemes are not CCA-secure and have presented an attack on the only existing scheme of [14] that has reported collusion resistance and anonymity. We then presented the first CCA-secure single-hop unidirectional proxy re-encryption scheme which is both collusion-resistant and anonymous. We have presented the security and anonymity proofs for our scheme in the random oracle model. Our scheme uses bilinear pairings. An interesting open problem would be to design a CCA-secure anonymous proxy re-encryption scheme without bilinear pairings. Also, there are no anonymous proxy re-encryption schemes which are secure in the standard model.

Acknowledgments. This work is supported by Ministry of Electronics & Information Technology, Government of India under Project No. CCE/CEP/22/VK& CP/CSE/ 14-15 on ISEA-phase II.

References

1. Ateniese, G., Benson, K., Hohenberger, S.: Key-private proxy re-encryption. In: Fischlin, M. (ed.) CT-RSA 2009. LNCS, vol. 5473, pp. 279–294. Springer, Heidelberg (2009). https://doi.org/10.1007/978-3-642-00862-7_19
2. Ateniese, G., Fu, K., Green, M., Hohenberger, S.: Improved proxy re-encryption schemes with applications to secure distributed storage. ACM Trans. Inf. Syst. Secur. **9**, 1–30 (2006)
3. Bellare, M., Boldyreva, A., Desai, A., Pointcheval, D.: Key-privacy in public-key encryption. In: Boyd, C. (ed.) ASIACRYPT 2001. LNCS, vol. 2248, pp. 566–582. Springer, Heidelberg (2001). https://doi.org/10.1007/3-540-45682-1_33

4. Blaze, M., Bleumer, G., Strauss, M.: Divertible protocols and atomic proxy cryptography. In: Nyberg, K. (ed.) EUROCRYPT 1998. LNCS, vol. 1403, pp. 127–144. Springer, Heidelberg (1998). https://doi.org/10.1007/BFb0054122
5. Canetti, R., Hohenberger, S.: Chosen-ciphertext secure proxy re-encryption. In: ACM Conference on Computer and Communications Security, pp. 185–194. ACM (2007)
6. Chow, S.S.M., Weng, J., Yang, Y., Deng, R.H.: Efficient unidirectional proxy re-encryption. In: Bernstein, D.J., Lange, T. (eds.) AFRICACRYPT 2010. LNCS, vol. 6055, pp. 316–332. Springer, Heidelberg (2010). https://doi.org/10.1007/978-3-642-12678-9_19
7. Isshiki, T., Nguyen, M.H., Tanaka, K.: Proxy re-encryption in a stronger security model extended from CT-RSA2012. In: Dawson, E. (ed.) CT-RSA 2013. LNCS, vol. 7779, pp. 277–292. Springer, Heidelberg (2013). https://doi.org/10.1007/978-3-642-36095-4_18
8. Libert, B., Vergnaud, D.: Unidirectional chosen-ciphertext secure proxy re-encryption. In: Cramer, R. (ed.) PKC 2008. LNCS, vol. 4939, pp. 360–379. Springer, Heidelberg (2008). https://doi.org/10.1007/978-3-540-78440-1_21
9. Nuñez, D., Agudo, I., López, J.: Proxy re-encryption: analysis of constructions and its application to secure access delegation. J. Netw. Comput. Appl. **87**, 193–209 (2017)
10. Paul, A., Srinivasavaradhan, V., Sharmila Deva Selvi, S., Pandu Rangan, C.: A CCA-secure collusion-resistant identity-based proxy re-encryption scheme. In: Baek, J., Susilo, W., Kim, J. (eds.) ProvSec 2018. LNCS, vol. 11192, pp. 111–128. Springer, Cham (2018). https://doi.org/10.1007/978-3-030-01446-9_7
11. Sharmila Deva Selvi, S., Paul, A., Pandurangan, C.: A provably-secure unidirectional proxy re-encryption scheme without pairing in the random oracle model. In: Capkun, S., Chow, S.S.M. (eds.) CANS 2017. LNCS, vol. 11261, pp. 459–469. Springer, Cham (2018). https://doi.org/10.1007/978-3-030-02641-7_21
12. Shao, J., Liu, P., Wei, G., Ling, Y.: Anonymous proxy re-encryption. Secur. Commun. Netw. **5**(5), 439–449 (2012)
13. Shao, J., Liu, P., Zhou, Y.: Achieving key privacy without losing CCA security in proxy re-encryption. J. Syst. Softw. **85**(3), 655–665 (2012)
14. Zheng, Q., Zhu, W., Zhu, J., Zhang, X.: Improved anonymous proxy re-encryption with CCA security. In: ACM ASIACCS, Kyoto, Japan - 03–06 June 2014, pp. 249–258 (2014)

Approximate String Matching for DNS Anomaly Detection

Roni Mateless[1] and Michael Segal[2(✉)]

[1] Department of Software and Information Systems Engineering,
Ben-Gurion University of the Negev, 84105 Beer-Sheva, Israel
mateless@post.bgu.ac.il
[2] School of Electrical and Computer Engineering,
Department of Communication Systems Engineering,
Ben-Gurion University of the Negev, 84105 Beer-Sheva, Israel
segal@bgu.ac.il

Abstract. In this paper we propose a novel approach to identify anomalies in DNS traffic. The traffic time-points data is transformed to a string, which is used by new fast approximate string matching algorithm to detect anomalies. Our approach is generic in its nature and allows fast adaptation to different types of traffic. We evaluate the approach on a large public dataset of DNS traffic based on 10 days, discovering more than order of magnitude DNS attacks in comparison to auto-regression as a baseline. Moreover, the additional comparison has been made including other common regressors such as Linear Regression, Lasso, Random Forest and KNN, all of them showing the superiority of our approach.

Keywords: Anomaly detection · Approximate string matching · Similarity measures

1 Introduction

Domain Name System (DNS) is the white pages of the Internet allowing to map hostnames/domains to IP addresses and it facilitates the communication of devices over the Internet. DNS is based on Standards (RFCs 1034, 1035-> STD13, Updated by a number of RFCs). It's a distributed and hierarchical database. Since DNS is an open ASCII protocol with no encryption, it is quite vulnerable for many known security holes. It uses a very rudimentary authentication mechanism which is based only on the SIP, port and transaction ID and, therefore, naively trusts source of information. Caching allows to bypass authoritative records and to store unreliable information in many locations in the internet.

Recently, it was reported that FireEye's Mandiant Incident Response and Intelligence teams have identified a wave of DNS hijacking that has affected dozens of domains belonging to government, telecommunications and internet infrastructure entities across the Middle East, North Africa, Europe and North America [33]. Additionally, the Internet Corporation for Assigned Names and Numbers (ICANN), which supervises the DNS reported on February 2019 that the DNS servers for a variety of

© Springer Nature Switzerland AG 2019
G. Wang et al. (Eds.): SpaCCS 2019, LNCS 11611, pp. 490–504, 2019.
https://doi.org/10.1007/978-3-030-24907-6_37

prominent targets across the world have been subject to a rush of attacks known as DNS hijacking attacks [34].

Several known malicious actions detectable by analyzing DNS data are known to the community: (D)DoS, Cache poisoning, Tunneling, Fast flux, Zone transfer hijacking, Dynamic update corruption and few others. To address the serious concerns related to the DNS attacks, we introduce unsupervised learning method based on string matching algorithm. We chose to deal with the unsupervised method due to the existence of large amount of unlabeled traffic data. Our approach is general and fast (it runs in linear time), easy to extend to other protocols and easy to maintain because there is no model to train.

In the past, to identify and prevent above-mentioned attacks, a number of statistical indicators for DNS traffic were considered: increase in number of DNS packets, decrease in cache hit ratio, increase in average DNS queries of individual source IP addresses, increase in number of recursive queries, increase in number of source IP addresses within a limited time slot and decrease in ratio of resolved queries. We went one step further by considering several statistical indicators in relation with potentially periodic data traffic. Our method is quite generic and can be applied to other types of traffic. In particular, our scheme performs well in identifying the events related to DDoS and compromising servers attacks. The contributions of this work are:

1. A new fast, generic approximate string matching algorithm for anomaly detection.
2. Simulative comparison between our technique and auto-regressive unsupervised scheme and other common regressors such as Linear Regression, Lasso, Random Forest and KNN, using DARPA 2009 dataset from IMPACT Cyber database.
3. Simultaneous use of scale dependent and invariant similarity measures (mean squared error and cosine similarity) to predict anomaly in the DNS data traffic.

The general idea of our solution is to identify similar periodic instances of investigated statistical indicators on the fly and to make a predictive suggestion based on historical data. The prediction is made by our extended approximate string matching algorithm based on KMP algorithm [32]. We can also control the length of historical data that we use during the algorithm. As said above, our solution is very fast in terms of time and memory complexity, and can be applied to different types of traffic. Moreover, as it is shown by experimental results (Sect. 5), it greatly outperforms (in terms of precision) auto-regression model with many variables, Linear Regression, Lasso, Random Forest, KNN and quite speedy.

This paper is organized as follows. We start with related work on DNS anomalies, then we present our approach and the solution with explanations. Next, we evaluate the proposed solution analytically (Sect. 4) and experimentally (Sect. 5) comparing it with auto-regression approach and other common regressors such as Linear Regression, Lasso, Random Forest and KNN. Finally, we conclude the paper.

2 Related Work

A number of research works have been dealing with identifying of DNS anomalies. As mentioned above, popular technique used by cyber-criminals to hide their critical systems is fast-flux. The ICANN Security and Stability Advisory Committee [1] released a paper giving a clear explanation of the technique. Jose Nazario and Thorsten Holz [2] did some interesting measurements on known fast-flux domains. Villamarn-Salomn and Brustoloni [3] focused their detection on abnormally high or temporally concentrated query rates of dynamic DNS queries. The research by Choi et al. [4] created an algorithm that checks multiple botnet characteristics. Born and Gustafson [5] researched a method for detecting covert channels in DNS using character frequency analysis. Karasaridis [6] used the approach of histograms' calculations of request/response packet sizes using the fact that tracking and detecting the changes in the frequencies of non-conforming packets sizes lead to possible identification of DNS anomaly. Yuchi et al. [7] investigated DNS anomalies in the context of Heap's law stating that a corpus of text containing N words typically contains on the order of cN^{β} distinct words, for constant c and $0 < \beta < 1$. Cermák et al. [8] identified that only four DNS packet fields are useful for most of the DNS traffic analyzing methods: queried domain name, queried record type, response code and IP address returned. Yarochkin et al. [9] presented an open source DNSPACKETLIZER tool to analyze DNS traffic in-real time. The analyzer calculates a Statistical Feature String for every event and stores it along with the query domain name and IP addresses (if such are known). The papers [12, 13] investigated some statistical features of the domain name in the context of DNS traffic. The research described in [10] aimed detect the botnet traffic by inspecting the following parameters: Time-Based Features (Access ratio), DNS Answer-Based Features (Number of distinct IP addresses), TTL Value-Based Features, Domain Name-Based Features (% of numerical in domain name). Satam et al. [11] used a dnsgram which is a data structure the captures important properties of consecutive DNS queries and replies. In [14] the authors presented an approach in which the flow of DNS traffic between the source and the destination DNS server is used to detect attacks. For taking care of Feature-Based Detection, variations of entropy based learning mechanisms were developed [15–18]. Based on the definition of context, there is a cause-effect relation among the features that characterize the context C and the corresponding consequences.

We note that some past attempts were made in order to bring unsupervised machine learning mechanisms to find DNS related anomalies. Raghuram et al. [19] proposed a method for detecting anomalous domain names, with focus on algorithmically generated domain names which are frequently associated with malicious activities. They [19] used the well-known maximum likelihood estimation (MLE) framework wherein the parameters of a probability model are found by maximizing the likelihood of a training data set under that model. Kirchler et al. [20] presented modified k-means algorithm and evaluated it on a realistic dataset that contains the DNS queries. Chatzis and Popescu-Zeletin [22] study the effect email worms have on the flow-level characteristics of DNS query streams a user machine generates using similarity search over time series analysis. The authors in [21] show that they can correctly classify DNS traffic using clustering (k-means) analysis.

3   Our Approach

Our unsupervised approach is based on approximate string matching strategy as explained in the following subsections.

3.1   General Approach

We consider the historical traffic feature (for example, the total number of DNS packets measured per each minute) as the text T, the last load traffic measurements as the pattern P and the currently measured load as E. The idea is to find a set S of the starting indices of non-overlapping approximate appearances of P in T where the absolute difference between any two elements in S as at least $|P|$. Then we make a prediction $Pred$ based on S and compare it to E. We use the "approximate appearance" of P in T to identify a possible periodicity in the history. In particular, we set up different values, α and β to control the approximate appearance of P in T. The parameter α controls the possible difference between each measurement in P versus corresponding measurement in T, while the parameter β gives an upper bound on the total difference between all the measurements in P versus corresponding measurements in T. After the sequence S is found, we make a prediction $Pred$ based on the average value of the measurements that are located immediately after the indices in S. (We also consider the boundary cases as well, for example the cold-start when the sequence S could be empty). Visually, our solution works as shown in Fig. 1.

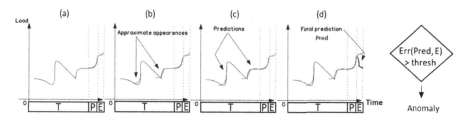

Fig. 1. (a) shows the traffic load as the function of time, where the red part is the last load pattern P and the orange part is currently measured load E; (b) the algorithm looks for the approximate appearances of P in T; (c) the predictions (in green) are made based on appearances we found in (b) stage; (d) the prediction $Pred$ (in blue) for the currently measured traffic load E is made; if no correlation between $Pred$ and E exists, the anomaly is reported. (Color figure online)

In order to understand whether the anomaly happens in the current time, we compare the current measurements E with $Pred$ as explained in the above paragraph. The comparison is made using the cosine similarity measure and the mean squared error.

3.2   The Approximate KMP Algorithm

Below we present our matching algorithm and elaborate on the details of proposed solution. We must point out that approximate string matching strategy is based on

Knuth-Morris-Pratt fast string matching algorithm [32], but can work, in fact, with any standard string pattern matching solution. We will also show how to use the algorithm in an incremental fashion in order to speed up the running time.

The modified function π is defined as follows:

```
π(P, α):
    ret = [0]
    for i in range(1, len(P)):
        j = ret[i - 1]
        while j > 0 and abs(P[j] - P[i]) > α:
            j = ret[j - 1]
        ret.append(j + 1 if abs(P[j] - P[i]) <= α else j)
    return ret
```

The **total_error** function computes the total difference between the pattern P and text T at given offset:

```
total_error(P, T, offs):
    total = 0
    for i in range(len(P)):
        total += abs(P[i] - T[offs + i])
    return total
```

Finally, the approximate searching solution based on Knuth-Morris-Pratt algorithm and modified π function was designed. The returned array "ret" of indices contains the starting indices in text T where the approximate matches of P are found. The presented algorithm has, obviously, linear (in terms of T and P sizes) running time.

```
search(T, P, α, β):
    π, ret, j = π(P, α), [], 0
    for i in range(len(T)):
        while j > 0 and abs(T[i] - P[j]) > α:
            j = π[j - 1]
        if abs(T[i] - P[j]) <= α: j += 1
        if j == len(P):
            temp_j = j
            j = π[j - 1]
            if total_error(P, T, i-len(P)+1) <= β:
                ret.append(i - (temp_j - 1))
                j=0
    return ret
```

3.3   Identifying Anomaly

We have used mean squared error and cosine similarity measures (plus additional parameters) in order to make the decision about a possible anomaly in the current data traffic. Assuming *Pred* is a vector of *k* predicted values and *E* is a vector of *k* observed values, the mean squared error is defined as:

$$MSE = \frac{1}{k}\sum\nolimits_{i=1}^{k}(Pred_i - E_i)^2 \tag{1}$$

Mean squared error represents the difference between the actual measurements and the measurement values predicted by the model. The choice of cosine similarity measure has been done due to the fact that cosine similarity is a scale invariant similarity measure. It is defined as:

$$Cos(Pred,\ E) = \frac{\sum (Pred_i, E_i)}{\sqrt{Pred_i^2} \cdot \sqrt{E_i^2}} \tag{2}$$

However, the cosine similarity measure assumes that both vectors *Pred* and *E* are non-zero vectors which can be problematic in the context of measuring traffic, since it is possible sometimes to obtain zero values. In order to overcome this difficulty, we consider only the case when the vector *Pred* is non-zero vector. This is because no anomaly is expected in data when vector *E* contains only zero values. Also, for the case when the *Pred* vector does not exist (e.g. a cold-start case when no approximate matching has been found), we compare the currently observed measurements vector *E* with the pattern *P*. We note that these measurements of vector *E* come exactly after the occurrence of pattern *P* at the end of data *T*. In case, where vector *E* values are significantly (order of magnitude) larger than vector *P* values, it may indicate a possible anomaly in data.

4   Analysis

First, we show the evaluation of our proposed technique to ensure that it does not suffer from cold-start problem. Next, we explain how to make our algorithm incrementally faster without the need of actual recomputing the data.

4.1   Cold-Start Evaluation

We are interested to analyze whether we can experience the problem of cold-start when applying our approximate matching solution. We have an alphabet of 10^d letters (every value in pattern *P* is considered to be a letter), and since the length of *P* is *k*, the number of possible matching patterns of *P* in *T* without any error is 10^{dk}. If we ignore the parameter β, the number of choices without β is $(2\alpha+1)^k$ and the total number of choices with parameter β is:

$$\beta \geq \binom{k}{\lfloor\frac{\beta}{\alpha}\rfloor} \cdot (2\alpha+1)^{\lfloor\frac{\beta}{\alpha}\rfloor} \cdot \max(1, \beta \bmod \alpha) \tag{3}$$

In fact, if we assume that $d = 3$, $k = 5$, the number of possible patterns will be 10^{15}. When we take α and β to characterize 10% and 25% of shift, respectively, of the maximum measurement value that can be obtained (in other words $\alpha = 100$, $\beta = 250$), the number of choices for the particular approximate search of pattern P inside of historical data T is equal to at least $\binom{5}{2} \cdot (201)^2 \cdot 50 \approx 10 \cdot 4 \cdot 10^4 \cdot 50 = 2 \cdot 10^7$. In order to evaluate the number of times P may appear in T we proceed as follows. Let P be i.i.d. $\{x_1, \ldots, x_k\}$, and the history T be i.i.d. $\{y_1, \ldots, y_l\}$. Let R be defined as:

$$R = (l - k + 1)\binom{k}{\lfloor\frac{\beta}{\alpha}\rfloor}(2\alpha+1)^{\lfloor\frac{\beta}{\alpha}\rfloor}\max(1, \beta \bmod \alpha) \tag{4}$$

The expectation of the number of times that the pattern P is included in the history is given by the following expression:

$$E(\text{number of times that } x_1, \ldots, x_k \text{ appears in } y_1, \ldots, y_l)$$
$$= E\left(\sum_{i=1}^{l-k+1} [y_i, \ldots, y_{i+k-1} = x_1, \ldots, x_k]\right) = \sum_{i=1}^{l-k+1} P(y_i, \ldots, y_{i+k-1} = x_1, \ldots, x_k) \tag{5}$$

We can simplify this expression, by noticing the following:

$$\sum_{i=1}^{l-k+1} P(y_i, \ldots, y_{i+k-1} = x_1, \ldots, x_k)$$
$$= (l - k + 1)\binom{k}{\lfloor\frac{\beta}{\alpha}\rfloor}(2\alpha+1)^{\lfloor\frac{\beta}{\alpha}\rfloor}(\max(1, \beta \bmod \alpha)) \cdot P(y_1, \ldots y_k = x_1, \ldots x_k) \tag{6}$$
$$= R \cdot \prod_{i=1}^{k} P(y_i, \ldots x_i) = R \cdot (P(y_1, \ldots x_1))^k$$

On the other side, we have

$$R \cdot (P(y_1 = x_1))^k = R \cdot \left(\sum_{i=1}^{10^d} P\left(\{y_1 = \text{some letter}\} \cap \{x_1 = \text{the same letter}\}\right)\right)^k \tag{7}$$

Consequently, we can write that it equals the following:

$$R \cdot \left(\sum_{i=1}^{10^d} P(y_1 = \text{some letter}) \cdot P(x_1 = \text{the same letter})\right)^k = R \cdot \left(\sum_{i=1}^{10^d} \frac{1}{10^{2d}}\right)^k \tag{8}$$

In our case of above-mentioned example for length $l = 1440$ (minutes in one day), we obtain that the expectation is $1436 \cdot 2 \cdot 10^7/10^{10} \approx 3$. We can even obtain a better bound for this expectation if we use inclusion-exclusion principle. In this case the number of choices with β

$$\beta \geq \sum_{i=0}^{\beta/\alpha} (-1)^i \cdot \binom{k}{i} \cdot \binom{\beta - i\alpha - 1}{k - 1} \tag{9}$$

and therefore

$$R = (l - k + 1) \cdot \sum_{i=0}^{\beta/\alpha} (-1)^i \cdot \binom{k}{i} \cdot \binom{\beta - i\alpha - 1}{k - 1} \tag{10}$$

For the given specific parameters provided above, we obtain that the expectation is at least 9. We should note that this evaluation takes into account only the case when the parameter α controls the possible difference between each measurement in P versus corresponding measurement in T by original value (and not by absolute value, which is in fact done in practice). This analysis shows that our algorithm will not suffer from cold-start problem in general setting.

4.2 Incremental Evaluation of the Algorithm

One of the interesting properties of our solution is that it allows to perform the incremental evaluations of the results avoiding recomputing the entire process over and over. For example, when we iterate from the current pattern P to the next pattern P', we know that the first element of new pattern should be deleted, and the new element (the last one) should be inserted. It means that by brute-force approach, we again need to recompute the function π for the new pattern P' from the beginning. Fortunately, we can do it much faster as follows. We do not delete the first element from the new pattern, but only insert the last element (in other words, the pattern grows up by one measurement). In this case, the function π should be updated only once – for the newly inserted last element. Moreover, in the process of the search itself, during the comparison between the measurements in T with those that are located in new pattern P', we will make sure that the first element of the new pattern P' can match any element of T, thus, in fact, ignoring the first element of P'. We can continue with this approach over and over, generating new patterns, and ignoring each time the next element in the prefix of the current pattern. Eventually, when the size of current pattern P' grows up to twice size (or some constant times) of initial pattern, we can restart the next pattern having the initial size length and to compute the original function π. This allows us to significantly speed up the entire process.

5 Evaluation

We have evaluated our technique on DARPA 2009 dataset from IMPACT Cyber database. The DARPA 2009 dataset is created with synthesized traffic to emulate traffic between a /16 subnet (172.28.0.0/16) and the Internet. This dataset has been captured in 10 days between the 3rd and the 12th of November of the year 2009. It contains, in particular, synthetic DNS background data traffic. The dataset is large (over 6 Tb) and has a variety of security events and attack types that describes the modern style of attacks. In particular it contains the events related to the DDoS and compromising DNS servers attacks. This dataset has been already evaluated using the supervised learning techniques; see [23]. The features we have looked at are:

- **Feature A**: The total number of DNS packets per minute in the traffic.
- **Feature B**: The number of malformed received DNS packets per minute, per each IP.
- **Feature C**: The number of transmitted DNS packets per minute, per each IP.

In order to evaluate the efficiency and the accuracy of our approach, we have compared it with auto-regression model (also, unsupervised method) and with other common regressors such as Linear Regression [28], Lasso [29], Random Forest Regressor [30] and KNN Regressor [31]. The common regressors have trained with the predicted window lag. We note here that the use of auto-regression as a baseline is not new, see for example [24–27]. The validation of our results has been done using standard PC server with 12 cores, 32G RAM. The entire traffic has been normalized for our string matching strategy. The normalization process has been performed according to the current logarithmic value of the average number of seen (per feature) packets. Consequently, the current error threshold $error_{threshold}$ that we have used for error evaluation was computed as a squared value of $\log_{10-\varepsilon} maxvalue$, where $maxvalue$ is the current maximal number of seen (per feature) packets. Finally, parameters α and β were defined as:

$$\alpha = error_{threshold} \cdot (1+\varepsilon) \cdot \frac{mean(P)}{|P|}, \beta = error_{threshold} \cdot mean(P) \qquad (11)$$

where the value of mean (P) denotes the average number of packets in pattern P.

In order to evaluate the influence of each feature on the analyzed data traffic, we have associated an unique numerical value for each of the features. Feature A has a score of 1, Feature B has a score of 2 and Feature C has a score of 4. In this way, we can control the relevance of specific feature for the seek anomalies. For example, if we require the total score of currently evaluated traffic be larger than, e.g. 4, it means that we require that mean squared error and the cosine similarity will go over the thresholds for Feature C, and at least either Feature A or Feature B. The evaluated dataset has been provided with the ground truth events according to the intervals of time for their appearances. If the anomaly has been detected by our method within time interval that overlaps with the corresponding time interval in ground truth events file, we report this as true positive. If there is no such overlapping interval in ground truth events file, we report this as a false positive event. If there is any interval in ground truth events file which was not hit by any of our identified intervals of anomalies, it is considered as false negative event. All other cases are treated as true negatives.

We have also investigated how the consideration of the length of lookback history correlates with the running time of the evaluated solutions and the precision of our obtained results.

(a)

(b)

(c)

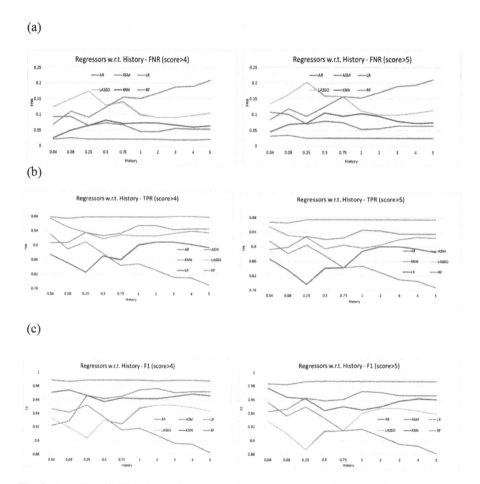

Fig. 2. (a) FNR (b) TPR (c) F1 for score 4,5 for all methods. ASM outperformed the other methods for all measures.

Figure 2 contains True Positive Rate (TPR), False Negative Rate (FNR), F1 (harmonic mean of precision and sensitivity) measures for all methods: Approximate String Matching, Auto-Regression, Linear Regression, Lasso, Random Forest and KNN with lookback history length (in days) from set of {0.04, 0.08, 0.25, 0.5, 0.75, 1, 2, 3, 4, 5} days and scores larger than {4,5}. ASM abbreviation stands for Approximate String Matching solution, AR stands for Auto-Regression solution, LR for Linear

Regression, RF for Random Forest and KNN for K-Nearest Neighbors. The graphs for FNR, TPR and F1 score (Fig. 2) clearly support that our ASM method is quite stable in regard with the lookback history length, opposite to the others. In the Auto-Regression model, Linear Regression and Lasso the longer history mean better results which are still worse when comparing with ASM, while the random forest behave in the opposite trend. The second stable method was the AR, although it performed similar to the KNN method. F1 score shows almost perfect precision and recall for ASM.

Table 1 below shows the absolute values for the mean FN, FP errors over all history for all methods. From Table 1 we can learn that in general, over all considered lookback history lengths, our method is much better than the others. The linear regression methods (LR and Lasso) performed the best false-positive (0), while their false negative were almost the worst. The AR performed worse FN but good (29.9 – 34.3) FP, while the ASM significantly reduces the number of FP and FN decisions (from up to 12 times for FP to 3 times for FN).

Table 1. Mean False Positive and False Negative decisions for all methods

	Mean FP		Mean FN	
Scores >	4	5	4	5
AR	5.1	0	29.9	34.3
ASM	0.4	0	**10**	**12.7**
LR	**0**	0	55.7	62.5
LASSO	**0**	0	55.5	62.4
KNN	1.5	0	29.3	37.8
RF	1.6	0	67.4	69.5

For the Auto-regression method we evaluated the calculated lags by the AR. The results are shown in Fig. 3. The lags are identical for all IPs, while the lags are larger for longer history.

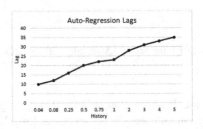

Fig. 3. Auto-Regression lags w.r.t history length

Additionally, we have evaluated the raw traffic for a few IPs to see the anomalies. Figure 4 shows the sum of packets for IP 172.28.10.6 which serves as the Firewall. The traffic trend is periodical, where from 14:00 PM to 12:00 AM there are ~200 K packets per hour and from 12:00 AM to 14:00 PM there are ~75 K packets per hour. At the 3-Nov and at the 12-Nov there are two peaks in traffic, which are reported as DNS attacks and are shown in Fig. 4.

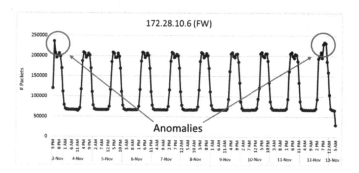

Fig. 4. Traffic of specific IP with 2 anomalies

Figure 5 below shows the relation between the anomaly events found by our method (ASM) and the actual anomaly events in the system (GT) for the case of lookback history of length 1. In the upper, attacks related to IP 172.28.108.88 and in the bottom DOS attacks. As we can see, there is a difference of some single events per each day.

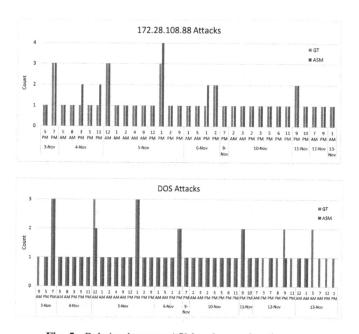

Fig. 5. Relation between ASM and ground truth events

We also have evaluated the processing time for all the evaluation methods. First, we calculated the processing time for the entire dataset running, as shown in Fig. 6(a) below; this is useful for offline scenario, when an organization wants to find anomalies on all historical data it has. In this scenario we train a model (when it is required by the evaluation method) every 1 min for the updated data (shift in 1 min), and predict the future values using this model. Obviously, if a method has an incremental mode like our solution, it is much faster than the others. In Fig. 6, the results without incremental mode are presented. Alternatively, we show in Fig. 6(b), the 1-time query processing time which is useful for online scenario.

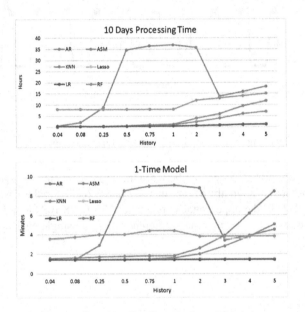

Fig. 6. (a) Entire dataset processing time for all methods and (b) 1-time query processing time

In the 10 days processing time, the auto-regression technique performed worst in terms of running time, and it is very inefficient in comparison to the others including our solution. For example, for half-day lookback history, auto-regression evaluation takes more than one day of run for the offline scenario, while the approximate string matching is near order of magnitude faster, taking only a few minutes. In the 1-time query processing time the results are similar, while our solution runs quite fast and can be deployed as the online solution due to its incremental mode option.

6   Conclusions

In this paper we have introduced and analyzed the performance of approximate string matching as one of the unsupervised machine learning techniques applied to the problem of detecting anomalies in DNS traffic. Our method is quite generic and can be applied to other types of traffic as well. Our analysis has shown a superiority of our method (both in terms of anomaly detection precision and running time) over the standard unsupervised auto-regression model as well as against other common regressors such as Linear Regression, Lasso, Random Forest and KNN. One of possible extensions could be generating the combined features normalized data (instead of looking at them separately and applying a total score mechanism). Another possibility is to consider the traffic offline data in reverse order.

References

1. Security and Stability Advisory Committee (SSAC). SSAC advisory on fast flux hosting and DNS (2008)
2. Nazario, J., Holz, T.: As the net churns: fast-flux botnet observations. In: International Conference on in Malicious and Unwanted Software, pp. 24–31 (2008)
3. Villamarn-Salomn, R., Brustoloni, J.C.: Identifying botnets using anomaly detection techniques applied to DNS traffic. In: Consumer Communications and Networking Conference, pp. 476–481 (2008)
4. Choi, H., Lee, H., Lee, H., Kim, H.: Botnet detection by monitoring group activities in DNS traffic. In: IEEE International Conference on Computer and Information Technology, pp. 715–720 (2007)
5. Born, K., Gustafson, D.: Detecting DNS tunnels using character frequency analysis, CoRR, abs/1004.4358 (2010)
6. Karasaridis, A.: Detection of DNS Traffic Anomalies, AT&T report (2012)
7. Yuchi, X., Wang, X., Lee, X., Yan, B.: A new statistical approach to DNS traffic anomaly detection. In: Cao, L., Zhong, J., Feng, Y. (eds.) ADMA 2010. LNCS (LNAI), vol. 6441, pp. 302–313. Springer, Heidelberg (2010). https://doi.org/10.1007/978-3-642-17313-4_30
8. Čermák, M., Čeleda, P., Vykopal, J.: Detection of DNS traffic anomalies in large networks. In: Kermarrec, Y. (ed.) EUNICE 2014. LNCS, vol. 8846, pp. 215–226. Springer, Cham (2014). https://doi.org/10.1007/978-3-319-13488-8_20
9. Yarochkin, F., Kropotov, V., Huang, Y., Ni, G.-K., Kuo, S.-Y., Chen, I.-Y.: Investigating DNS traffic anomalies for malicious activities. In: DSN Workshops, pp. 1–7 (2013)
10. Krmcek, V.: Inspecting DNS Flow Traffic for Purposes of Botnet Detection, manuscript (2011)
11. Satam, P., Alipour, H., Al-Nashif, Y., Hariri, S.: Anomaly behavior analysis of DNS protocol. J. Internet Serv. Inf. Secur. 5(4), 85–97 (2015)
12. Yamada, A., Miyake, Y., Terabe, M., Hashimoto, K., Kato, N.: Anomaly detection for DNS servers using frequent host selection. In: AINA, pp. 853–860 (2009)
13. Wang, Y., Hu, M.-z., Li, B., Yan, B.-r.: Tracking anomalous behaviors of name servers by mining DNS traffic. In: Min, G., Di Martino, B., Yang, Laurence T., Guo, M., Rünger, G. (eds.) ISPA 2006. LNCS, vol. 4331, pp. 351–357. Springer, Heidelberg (2006). https://doi.org/10.1007/11942634_37
14. Karasaridis, A., Meier-Hellstern, K., Hoeflin, D.: Nis04-2: detection of DNS anomalies using flow data analysis. In: GLOBECOM, pp. 1–6 (2006)
15. Gu, Y., McCallum, A., Towsley, D.: Detecting anomalies in network traffic using maximum entropy estimation. In: Proceedings of the 5th ACM SIGCOMM Conference on Internet Measurement (2005)
16. Berezinski, P., Jasiul, B., Szpyrka, M.: An entropy-based network anomaly detection method. Entropy 17, 2367–2408 (2015)

17. AlEroud, A., Karabatis, G.: Queryable semantics to detect cyber-attacks:a flow-based detection approach. IEEE Trans. Syst. Man Cybern. Syst. **48**, 207–223 (2017)
18. Lakhina, A., Crovella, M., Diot, C.: Mining anomalies using traffic feature distributions. SIGCOMM Comput. Commun. Rev. **35**(4), 217–228 (2005)
19. Raghuram, J., Miller, D.J., Kesidis, G.: Unsupervised, low latency anomaly detection of algorithmically generated domain names by generative probabilistic modeling. J. Adv. Res. **5**, 423–433 (2014)
20. Kirchler, M., Herrmann, D., Lindemann, J., Kloft, M.: Tracked without a trace: linking sessions of users by unsupervised learning of patterns in their DNS traffic. In: AISec@CCS, pp. 23–34 (2016)
21. Erman, J., Arlitt, M., Mahanti, A.: Traffic classification using clustering algorithms. In: MineNet 2006, pp. 281–286 (2006)
22. Chatzis, N., Popescu-Zeletin, R.: Flow level data mining of DNS query streams for email worm detection. In: Corchado, E., Zunino, R., Gastaldo, P., Herrero, Á. (eds.) Proceedings of the International Workshop on Computational Intelligence in Security for Information Systems CISIS 2008. Advances in Soft Computing, vol. 53, pp. 186–194. Springer, Heidelberg (2009). https://doi.org/10.1007/978-3-540-88181-0_24
23. Moustafa, N., Slay, J.: Creating novel features to anomaly network detection using DARPA-2009 data set. In: Proceedings of the 14th European Conference on Cyber Warfare and Security 2015: ECCWS (2015)
24. Münz, G.: Traffic anomaly detection and cause identification using flow-level measurements. Technical University Munich 2010, pp. 1–228 (2010). ISBN 3-937201-12-2
25. Hong, L.V.: DNS Traffic Analysis for Network-based Malware Detection. Technical University of Denmark, Informatics and Mathematical Modelling (2012)
26. Nikolaev, I.: Network Service Anomaly Detection. Czech Technical University, Prague (2014)
27. Greis, R., Reis, T., Nguyen, C.: Comparing prediction methods in anomaly detection: an industrial evaluation. In: MILETS (2018)
28. Freedman, D.A.: Statistical Models: Theory and Practice. Cambridge University Press, Cambridge (2009)
29. Tibshirani, R.: Regression shrinkage and selection via the lasso. J. Roy. Stat. Soc.: Ser. B (Methodol.) **58**(1), 267–288 (1996)
30. Ho, T.K.: Random decision forests. In: Proceedings of the 3rd International Conference on Document Analysis and Recognition, pp. 278–282 (1995)
31. Altman, N.S.: An introduction to kernel and nearest-neighbor nonparametric regression. Am. Statist. **46**(3), 175–185 (1992)
32. Knuth, D.E., Morris Jr., J.H., Pratt, V.R.: Fast pattern matching in strings. SIAM J. Comput. **6**(2), 323–350 (1977)
33. Hirani, M., Jones, S., Read, B.: Global DNS Hijacking Campaign: DNS Record Manipulation at Scale. https://www.fireeye.com/blog/threat-research/2019/01/global-dns-hijacking-campaign-dns-record-manipulation-at-scale.html. Accessed 9 Jan 2019
34. https://www.icann.org/news/announcement-2019-02-22-en

Author Index

Printed in the United States
By Bookmasters